The Boundaries of 'the Japanese'

Volume 1
Okinawa 1818–1972
Inclusion and Exclusion

JAPANESE SOCIETY SERIES
General Editor: Yoshio Sugimoto

Lives of Young Koreans in Japan
Yasunori Fukuoka

Globalization and Social Change in Contemporary Japan
J.S. Eades, Tom Gill and Harumi Befu

Coming Out in Japan: The Story of Satoru and Ryuta
Satoru Ito and Ryuta Yanase

Japan and Its Others:
Globalization, Difference and the Critique of Modernity
John Clammer

Hegemony of Homogeneity: An Anthropological Analysis of Nihonjinron
Harumi Befu

Foreign Migrants in Contemporary Japan
Hiroshi Komai

A Social History of Science and Technology in Contemporary Japan, Volume 1
Shigeru Nakayama

Farewell to Nippon: Japanese Lifestyle Migrants in Australia
Machiko Sato

The Peripheral Centre:
Essays on Japanese History and Civilization
Johann P. Arnason

A Genealogy of 'Japanese' Self-images
Eiji Oguma

Class Structure in Contemporary Japan
Kenji Hashimoto

An Ecological View of History
Tadao Umesao

Nationalism and Gender
Chizuko Ueno

Native Anthropology: The Japanese Challenge to Western Academic Hegemony
Takami Kuwayama

Youth Deviance in Japan: Class Reproduction of Non-Conformity
Robert Stuart Yoder

Japanese Companies: Theories and Realities
Masami Nomura and Yoshihiko Kamii

From Salvation to Spirituality: Popular Religious Movements in Modern Japan
Susumu Shimazono

The 'Big Bang' in Japanese Higher Education:
The 2004 Reforms and the Dynamics of Change
J.S. Eades, Roger Goodman and Yumiko Hada

Japanese Politics: An Introduction
Takashi Inoguchi

A Social History of Science and Technology in Contemporary Japan, Volume 2
Shigeru Nakayama

Gender and Japanese Management
Kimiko Kimoto

Philosophy of Agricultural Science: A Japanese Perspective
Osamu Soda

A Social History of Science and Technology in Contempory Japan, Volume 3
Shigeru Nakayama and Kunio Goto

Japan's Underclass: Day Laborers and the Homeless
Hideo Aoki

A Social History of Science and Technology in Contemporary Japan, Volume 4
Shigeru Nakayama and Hitoshi Yoshioka

Scams and Sweeteners: A Sociology of Fraud
Masahiro Ogino

Toyota's Assembly Line: A View from the Factory Floor
Ryoji Ihara

Village Life in Modern Japan: An Environmental Perspective
Akira Furukawa

Social Welfare in Japan: Principles and Applications
Kojun Furukawa

Escape from Work: Freelancing Youth and the Challenge to Corporate Japan
Reiko Kosugi

Japan's Whaling: The Politics of Culture in Historical Perspective
Hiroyuki Watanabe

Gender Gymnastics: Performing and Consuming Japan's Takarazuka Revue
Leonie R. Stickland

Poverty and Social Welfare in Japan
Masami Iwata and Akihiko Nishizawa

The Modern Japanese Family: Its Rise and Fall
Chizuko Ueno

Widows of Japan: An Anthropological Perspective
Deborah McDowell Aoki

In Pursuit of the Seikatsusha:
A Genealogy of the Autonomous Citizen in Japan
Masako Amano

Demographic Change and Inequality in Japan
Sawako Shirahase

The Origins of Japanese Credentialism
Ikuo Amano

Pop Culture and the Everyday in Japan: Sociological Perspectives
Katsuya Minamida and Izumi Tsuji

Japanese Perceptions of Foreigners
Shunsuke Tanabe

Migrant Workers in Contemporary Japan:
An Institutional Perspective on Transnational Employment
Kiyoto Tanno

The Boundaries of 'the Japanese', Volume 1:
Okinawa 1818–1972 – Inclusion and Exclusion
Eiji Oguma

Social Stratification and Inequality Series

Inequality amid Affluence: Social Stratification in Japan
Junsuke Hara and Kazuo Seiyama

Intentional Social Change: A Rational Choice Theory
Yoshimichi Sato

Constructing Civil Society in Japan: Voices of Environmental Movements
Koichi Hasegawa

Deciphering Stratification and Inequality: Japan and beyond
Yoshimichi Sato

Social Justice in Japan: Concepts, Theories and Paradigms
Ken-ichi Ohbuchi

Gender and Career in Japan
Atsuko Suzuki

Status and Stratification: Cultural Forms in East and Southeast Asia
Mutsuhiko Shima

Globalization, Minorities and Civil Society:
Perspectives from Asian and Western Cities
Koichi Hasegawa and Naoki Yoshihara

Fluidity of Place: Globalization and the Transformation of Urban Space
Naoki Yoshihara

Japan's New Inequality:
Intersection of Employment Reforms and Welfare Arrangements
Yoshimichi Sato and Jun Imai

Minorities and Diversity
Kunihiro Kimura

Inequality, Discrimination and Conflict in Japan:
Ways to Social Justice and Cooperation
Ken-ichi Ohbuchi and Junko Asai

Social Exclusion: Perspectives from France and Japan
Marc Humbert and Yoshimichi Sato

Global Migration and Ethnic Communities:
Studies of Asia and South America
Naoki Yoshihara

Stratification in Cultural Contexts: Cases from East and Southeast Asia
Toshiaki Kimura

Advanced Social Research Series

A Sociology of Happiness
Kenji Kosaka

Frontiers of Social Research: Japan and beyond
Akira Furukawa

A Quest for Alternative Sociology
Kenji Kosaka and Masahiro Ogino

MODERNITY AND IDENTITY IN ASIA SERIES

Globalization, Culture and Inequality in Asia
Timothy S. Scrase, Todd Miles, Joseph Holden and Scott Baum

Looking for Money:
Capitalism and Modernity in an Orang Asli Village
Alberto Gomes

Governance and Democracy in Asia
Takashi Inoguchi and Matthew Carlson

Liberalism: Its Achievements and Failures
Kazuo Seiyama

Health Inequalities in Japan: An Empirical Study of Older People
Katsunori Kondo

The Boundaries of 'the Japanese'

Volume 1
Okinawa 1818–1972
Inclusion and Exclusion

By

Eiji Oguma

Translated by
Leonie R. Stickland

Trans Pacific Press
Melbourne

First published in Japanese in 1998 by Shin'yōsha as *'Nihonjin' no kyōkai*.
This English edition first published in 2014 by:
Trans Pacific Press, PO Box 164, Balwyn North, Victoria 3104, Australia
Telephone: +61 (0)3 9859 1112 Fax: +61 (0)3 8611 7989
Email: tpp.mail@gmail.com
Web: http://www.transpacificpress.com
Copyright © Eiji Oguma 2014
Designed and set by Digital Environs, Melbourne, Australia. www.digitalenvirons.com

Distributors

Australia and New Zealand
James Bennett Pty Ltd
Locked Bag 537
Frenchs Forest NSW 2086
Australia
Telephone: +61-(0)2-8988-5000
Fax: +61-(0)2-8988-5031
Email: info@bennett.com.au
Web: www.bennett.com.au

USA and Canada
International Specialized Book
Services (ISBS)
920 NE 58th Avenue, Suite 300
Portland, Oregon 97213-3786
USA
Telephone: 1-800-944-6190
Fax: 1-503-280-8832
Email: orders@isbs.com
Web: http://www.isbs.com

Asia and the Pacific
Kinokuniya Company Ltd.
Head office:
3-7-10 Shimomeguro
Meguro-ku
Tokyo 153-8504
Japan
Telephone: +81-(0)3-6910-0531
Fax: +81-(0)3-6420-1362
Email: bkimp@kinokuniya.co.jp
Web: www.kinokuniya.co.jp
Asia-Pacific office:
Kinokuniya Book Stores of Singapore Pte., Ltd.
391B Orchard Road #13-06/07/08
Ngee Ann City Tower B
Singapore 238874
Telephone: +65-6276-5558
Fax: +65-6276-5570
Email: SSO@kinokuniya.co.jp

All rights reserved. No reproduction of any part of this book may take place without the written permission of Trans Pacific Press.

ISSN   1443–9670 (Japanese Society Series)
ISBN   978-1-920901-48-6 (Hardcover)
        978-1-920901-42-4 (Softcover)

Cover photo: Confrontation between demonstrators and U.S. soldiers. Courtesy of *The Okinawa Times*. Published on 5 June 1969.

Contents

Chronological Table xi
Acknowledgements xiii
Map of the main island of Okinawa xiv

   Introduction 1
1 The Ryukyu Disposition (*Ryūkyū shobun*) 15
2 Okinawan Education and 'Japanisation' 36
3 The Creation of Okinawan Nationalism 54
4 The Distortion of Orientalism 108
5 Islands on the Boundary 137
6 From Pro-Independence to Pro-Reversion Discources 164
7 The Significance of 'Japan, the Ancestral Land' 188
8 The Idea of Progressive Nationalism 213
9 The Dialect Placards of the 1960s 255
10 Anti-Reversion 306

Conclusion 339
Notes 359
Bibliography 380
Name Index 405
Subject Index 408

Chronological Table

1609 Satsuma invasion of the Ryukyu Kingdom
1868 Meiji Restoration
1879 Ryukyu Disposition (Ryukyu Kingdom dismantled, and Okinawa Prefecture established)
1894 Sino-Japanese War
1898 Conscription Law imposed in Okinawa; in Tokyo, Jahana Noboru appeals for the dismissal of the prefectural governor
1903 The 'Hall of Mankind (Jinruikan)' incident (the 'exhibition' of Okinawans, Ainu and Taiwanese aborigines in a project by anthropologists in conjunction with the Fifth Industrial Exhibition held in Osaka)
1911 Ifa Fuyū publishes *Ko-ryūkyū* (Old-Ryukyu).
1912 The Lower House Members' Electoral Law implemented on the main island of Okinawa
1919 The Lower House Members' Electoral Law implemented throughout Okinawa Prefecture
1920 Post-World War I recession develops; and Okinawa, also, experiences the 'sago-palm hell.'
1922 Yanagi Sōetsu (Muneyoshi) argues against the demolition of Seoul's Gwanghwamun (Gwanghwa Gate).
1925 Ifa Fuyū leaves Okinawa for Tokyo.
1931 Start of the 'Manchurian Incident'
1937 Sino-Japanese War begins.
1940 Yanagi Sōetsu visits Okinawa; Okinawan language debate erupts.
1941 Pacific War begins.
1944 Large-scale air-raids on Naha by U.S. bombers in October
1945 In the Battle of Okinawa from March to June (mopping-up operations until August), one third of residents of the main island of Okinawa perish. Military government by the U.S. military begins in Okinawa. Japan surrenders in August.
1946 The Japanese Communist Party issues a 'Message celebrating the independence of the Okinawan people (*minzoku*).'

1950 Pro-U.S. candidate defeated in election for governor in the Okinawan island-group government (*guntō seifu*); U.S. military abolishes public election of the Chief Executive and switches to a system of appointment by the U.S. military.
1951 Treaty of San Francisco concluded in September; a provisional central government set up by the U.S. military, replacing the island group governments
1952 Treaty of San Francisco comes into force in April; Government of the Ryukyu Islands (GRI) established; U.S. military occupation of Japan ends, but U.S. military continues interim control of Okinawa.
1956 'Island-wide struggle [for land]' erupts over the issue of land used for U.S. military bases; from the late 1950s, in concert with heightening of the anti-U.S.-base movement in mainland Japan, a tendency arises towards a reduction of U.S. bases in mainland Japan and an increase in bases in Okinawa.
1957 Naha's Mayor, Senaga Kamejirō, purged by order of the USCAR High Commissioner and banned from re-election
1960 In mainland Japan, anti-AMPO (Japan–U.S. Security Treaty) conflict heightens; Okinawa-ken Sokoku Fukki Kyōgikai (Council for the Reversion of Okinawa Prefecture to the Ancestral Land) formed with Yara Chōbyō from the Okinawa Teachers' Association assuming the post of president.
1964 U.S. military begins full-scale military intervention in Vietnam; use of bases in Okinawa intensifies.
1965 Prime Minister Satō Eisaku visits Okinawa.
1968 B52 bomber crashes at Kadena in Okinawa; anti-U.S.-base movement intensifies; U.S. military recognises a system of public election of Chief Executive, and Yara Chōbyō is elected, defeating pro-U.S. conservative candidate.
1969 Agreement reached at the November talks between Prime Minister Satō and President Nixon that administrative rights over Okinawa would be restored in 1972; criticism intensifies over the policy of retention of U.S. military bases in Okinawa, and the 'anti-reversion debate' erupts.
1970 Implementation in Okinawa of Japanese Diet Lower House elections
1972 In May, Okinawa 'reverts' by means of restoration of administrative rights to Japan.

Acknowledgements

I express my deep gratitude to Dr Leonie Stickland, who tackled this challenging translation, and Emeritus Professor Yoshio Sugimoto whose sterling efforts culminated in its publication. Without the work of such individuals, this book would not have been introduced to the Anglophone world.

I would also like to acknowledge a Grant-in-Aid for Publication of Scientific Research Results bestowed by the Japan Society for the Promotion of Science (JSPS) in support of the translation and publication of this volume.

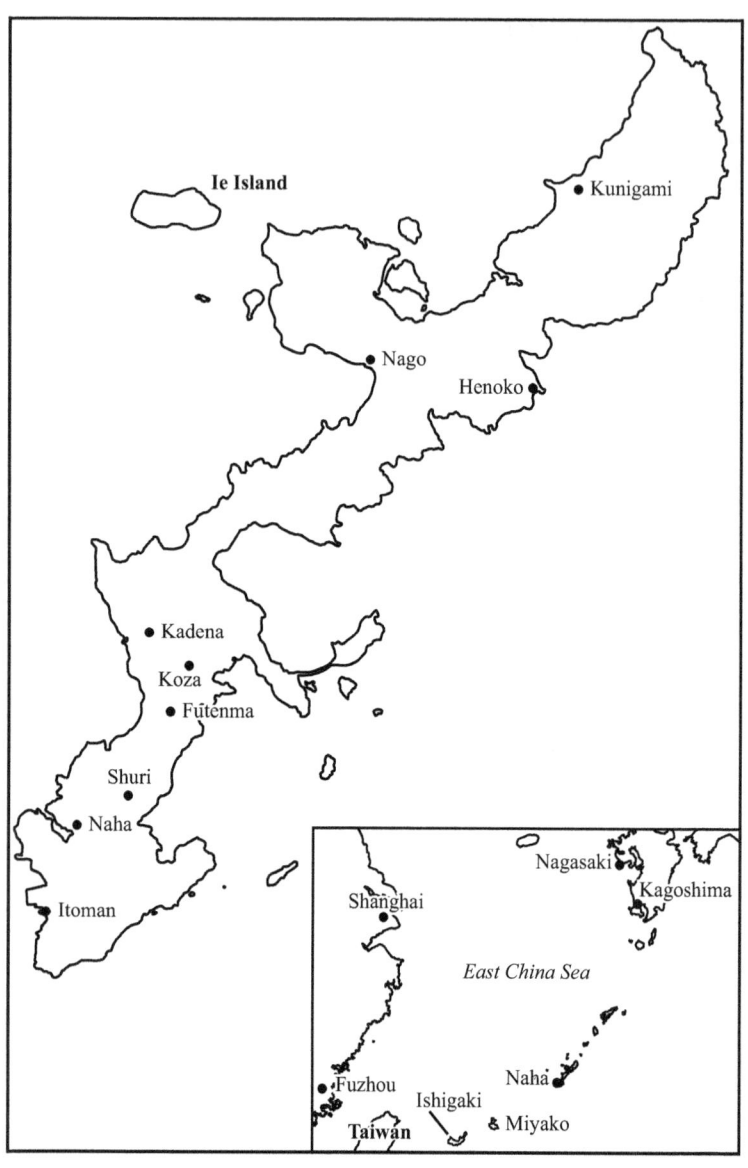

Map of the main island of Okinawa

Introduction

Okinawa is the southernmost prefecture in Japan, and is located at the southern extremity of the Japanese archipelago. Even seen from an anthropological perspective, the inhabitants of that land are 'Japanese.' At least, this is the Japanese government's view. Japanese nationals who have been educated through textbooks approved by Japan's Ministry of Education, Culture, Sports, Science and Technology, as well as the people of the world that believe the Japanese government's official view, think thus.

On 9 March 2012, however, the United Nations Committee on the Elimination of Racial Discrimination decided to question the Japanese government as to whether plans to relocate a U.S. military base on Okinawa possibly constituted discrimination against the 'Ryukyuan indigenous inhabitants.'

Ryukyu is the name of a dynasty which survived until the nineteenth century. In 1879, the Ryukyu Dynasty was abolished by the Japanese government which invaded Okinawa Island, where the dynastic capital was situated, and 'Okinawa Prefecture' was established. Okinawan residents even now continue to have a collective awareness that differs from the Japanese 'mainland.'

If one banishes one's preconceived notions and looks at a map, Okinawa is one part of a long, arc-like archipelago lying to the east of the Eurasian continent. This archipelago stretches from the Kamchatka Peninsula to the Chinese mainland, branching as far as Taiwan and The Philippines, and segmented by several national boundaries. At present, the northern portion of the archipelago belongs to Russia, the central zone to Japan, and the south to Taiwan and The Philippines. The Okinawan islands are included in the part belonging to Japan.

It was in the late nineteenth century that clear-cut national boundaries were drawn in this region. Before that, though each area had its own dynasty, precise national boundaries did not exist. It was merely that there were relationships of belonging, in that tax was paid to the dynasties from the inhabitants. None of the dynasties showed any interest in uninhabited islands from which no tax could be exacted, such as Takeshima (called Dokdo in Korean) and the Senkaku Islands (Diaoyutai in Chinese) whose ownership is currently being disputed between Japan and Korea, and Japan and China, respectively, and accordingly, neither their possession nor national boundaries were clear-cut.

In the mid-nineteenth century, the European powers showed interest in these islands, and steam-driven warships arrived. In Japan, which feared colonisation, the Meiji Restoration took place, and the newly-formed Meiji government boosted Japan's military and economic strength through a modernisation policy on the one hand, and learned European international law on the other. Moreover, the Meiji government endeavoured to cement its sphere of influence in this region, based on the concept of a modern state delimited by precise national boundaries. In this manner, many conflicts arose over the way to divide this archipelago. Their scars still smart even today, and sometimes radiate heat.

Okinawa is also a place shaken about by the development of such national boundaries and fluctuations. Okinawa, which was an independent kingdom, became the site of boundary conflict between Japan and Qing (China), and was incorporated into Japan. After the Pacific War, it was severed from Japanese administrative rights, and for the twenty-seven years until 1972, martial rule was implemented by the United States military. Following that, it again became part of Japan, but seventy-four percent of U.S. military bases in Japan are concentrated in Okinawa, and there is no end of problems over bases.

Fluctuations in national boundaries exert huge impact on the inhabitants of those places. In particular, because the notion of the modern nation-state was brought into East Asia, the people of the area integrated into Japan due to changes in national boundaries were subsequently forced to 'become Japanese.' As I will describe in this book, theories from anthropology and history were advocated with the aim of justifying their 'becoming Japanese.'

This book has 'becoming Japanese' as its subject. Why, and in what manner, were the people of Okinawa incorporated into 'the Japanese?' In that process, what kind of discord existed? This volume probes these questions.

Here, 'Japanese' is a constructed concept. The boundary between 'Japanese' and 'those who are not Japanese' is something that moves.

Introduction

It is for such reasons that I consistently place inverted commas around 'Japanese' in this book.

The analytical perspective

Present-day Okinawa has a population of 1.33 million. The majority lives on the main island of Okinawa, approximately 100 kilometres long and twenty-two kilometres wide (approximately the same area as Hong Kong SAR), and whose centre is Naha, a city with 300 thousand people.

Furthermore, Okinawa is the place with the world's highest density of U.S. military bases. These bases occupy nineteen percent of the total area of the main island of Okinawa, and about seventy-four percent of U.S. military bases in Japan are concentrated in Okinawa. U.S. military personnel stationed in Okinawa number approximately 24,000, this corresponding to about sixty percent of U.S. military personnel in Japan, and about one-tenth of the U.S. military's permanent overseas presence anywhere on the globe.

This state of affairs is one that became established through U.S. martial rule that endured for twenty-seven years following the Pacific War.

In the Battle of Okinawa waged over three months from March 1945, some 12,000 U.S. troops lost their lives. There is no other place so small in area that yielded so many U.S. combat casualties. The enormity of that number can be appreciated when compared to the 55,000 dead from the decade-long Vietnam War. By contrast, Japanese military casualties totalled 94,000, and the same number of Okinawan inhabitants also perished.

The number of dead among Okinawan inhabitants is said to be as many as 150,000, including those temporarily mobilised by the Japanese military and counted as Japanese military war dead, as well as those who perished in submarine attacks on evacuation vessels, and those who died from illness outside the combat zone. This corresponds to a quarter of the population of Okinawans at the time, and a third of the population of the main island of Okinawa. This was not only due to the fighting having taken place on a small island with a concentrated population: there were also many people whose death was due to having been mobilised as rear-guard support for the Japanese military, or having been massacred by the Japanese or U.S. forces. This memory remains vivid even now among Okinawan residents, and has become the basis of antipathy towards Japan and the United States.

After the cessation of hostilities, the U.S. military laid down martial rule in Okinawa. Following the conclusion of the war, the Japanese mainland also fell under U.S. military control, but Okinawa came under separate rule from mainland Japan. That rule continued even after the San Francisco Peace Treaty was concluded in 1951, and after the occupation of Japan proper had ceased. Ultimately, U.S. military rule ended up continuing until 1972.

As I describe in my main discourse, the true state of this U.S. martial rule was something that could appropriately be called a military colony. There was formal autonomy by the residents, but the U.S. military had free hand in confiscation of land for its bases, and the rental for that land was also cheap. In this way, Okinawa became a base for U.S. military missions in the Korean and Vietnam Wars, as an island of bases under U.S. martial control.

Though there are many regions which were occupied by the U.S. military due to the Pacific War and came under its martial rule, there is no other area in which that continued for a whole twenty-seven years. The U.S. military bases which were constructed in this period of no rights remain even now. I have already mentioned that the United Nations Committee on the Elimination of Racial Discrimination took issue with these circumstances.

Moreover, when one looks back at the history of Okinawa, what is consistent is that in geographical terms, it has been a place which has been unable to sever connection with military affairs.

The main island of Okinawa is exactly halfway between the Japanese archipelago and Taiwan, which are about 1,300 kilometres apart. Okinawa Island is the only island in these 1,300 kilometres where large-scale ports and airfields can be constructed. Establishing a military base here means being able to place Tokyo, Seoul, Beijing and Hanoi within the range of strategic bombers.

As I will state in my main discourse, a certain post-war Japanese politician described Okinawa as 'islands which produce nothing except sweet potatoes and brown sugar.' Seen from an economic perspective, Okinawa was a place not worth occupying for the Japanese government. The Ryukyu kingdom had flourished due to intermediary trade, but since modern times that function had disappeared. Even now, Okinawa's largest industry is tourism, as a resort destination in the South Seas, and all of its economic indices are low.

In military terms, however, the value of Okinawa rose from the late nineteenth century onwards. The Meiji government's occupation of Okinawa was in order to forestall the establishment of military bases there by Western powers, and to build a southern bastion. The U.S. military's having occupied Okinawa in the last stages of the Pacific War at great cost, and not having relinquished Okinawa from martial rule in the later Korean War and Vietnam War periods, also, were due to those islands' military value. Okinawa was dubbed 'the keystone of the Pacific' by the U.S. military, and even today it houses the largest U.S. bases in the Far East.

In other words, Okinawa's military worth was extremely high, yet its economic value was low by comparison. It was a desirable possession in military terms, but economically, it lacked such merit. These constitute the two vectors that determine Okinawa's historical trends.

As I discuss in Chapter One, when the Japanese government overthrew the Ryukyu Dynasty in 1879 and incorporated the islands into its own territory, its French consultant expressed objection. If Japan were formally to take possession of Okinawa, it would have to make its inhabitants 'Japanese.' The expenses of governance would cost more than the tax revenue it could gain by possession. The gist of it was that if that was the idea, then it would be better to retain the Ryukyu Dynasty and control Okinawa as an autonomous colony.

In other words, military value functions as a vector to subsume Okinawa into 'Japan.' By contrast, economic cost works as a vector to exclude it. This conflict between inclusion and exclusion forms one of the themes of this book.

In regard to this matter, the Japanese government chose the path of possession, even if it meant ignoring the economic cost. The securing of a base of forward deployment was prioritised in order for Japan, which was inferior in terms of military strength, to rival the West. Furthermore, thorough 'Japanisation' was carried out through education, and it was hoped that the military mobilisation of the local inhabitants would become possible. Its success was exhibited by the cooperation of the local residents with the Japanese military and their massive fatalities in the 1945 Battle of Okinawa.

On the other hand, in order to keep economic and political costs down, the improvement of such infrastructure as railways and ports was not carried out, and the granting of suffrage was delayed until more than twenty years after other prefectures. It became the Japanese government's official view that if the local inhabitants showed a spirit of loyalty towards the Japanese government, and it were recognised that they had completely assimilated culturally, also, then political and economic equality would be given them, as well.

Conversely, the samurai class from the Ryukyu Dynasty directed their hopes to Qing (China), which had initially been the Ryukyu Dynasty's protector. However, when Qing was defeated in the 1894 Sino-Japanese War, those hopes also vanished. In addition, though ordinary Okinawan residents had no feelings of allegiance towards the Japanese government, either, they had scant affection for the Ryukyu Dynasty's samurai class that had dominated them.

Later, some of the Okinawan intellectuals set their sights upon the elevation of Okinawa's status through modernisation. The sole actual means to achieve that was to climb on the basis of the rules which the Japanese government had established. This became an orientation towards 'assimilation' which included such things as assimilating to the Japanese standard language (*hyōjungo*) and standard Japanese culture, and allegiance to the Japanese government and the emperor.

However, as previously mentioned, the Japanese government side took the position that unless Okinawans first displayed cultural assimilation and a sense of loyalty, then there could be no granting of rights. In this way, the Okinawan side became mired in a dilemma between a desire for 'assimilation' and a desire for 'uniqueness.'

Moreover, the U.S. military which governed Okinawa from 1945 onwards tried to emphasise Okinawa's uniqueness in order to pull Okinawa away from Japan. For that reason, the dilemma grew even more complicated, because if Okinawan inhabitants stressed their uniqueness, then this would have meant they were capable of justifying U.S. military control.

Consequently, Okinawan residents carried on with a movement for 'reversion' to Japan while emphasising their cultural commonality with Japan, in order to escape from U.S. military domination. However, this, too, was something that involved many dilemmas. Such dilemmas, also, are matters to be given weight in this book.

Introduction 7

The original Japanese-language version of this volume dealt with the process of incorporation and integration into 'Japan' not only of Okinawa, but also of Korea and Taiwan. In the publication of the English version, I have left the chapters on Taiwan and Korea to Volume 2. In Taiwan and Korea, a policy of 'Japanisation' similar to that implemented in Okinawa was carried out. In those places, too, there existed the abovementioned dilemmas of 'inclusion' and 'exclusion,' and 'assimilation' and 'individuality.' Amid those circumstances, there emerged diverse endeavours – not only secession [and] independence movements, but also suffrage movements, movements for establishment of an autonomous parliament, and the like.

Unlike in Okinawa, however, in the case of Taiwanese and Koreans, who to the bitter end were never granted legal equality as 'Japanese,' this issue was resolved by separation from Japan. In Okinawa's case, after it was severed from Japan in 1945, at the same time as Taiwan and Korea, a movement for 'reversion' away from the harshness of U.S. military rule arose, and it was again subsumed into Japan. Even after reversion, though, U.S. bases in Okinawa did not reduce in number, and even now it is the poorest prefecture in Japan. In recent years, there has been no dearth of voices calling for 'Okinawan independence.'

In this book, I depict the dynamism of Okinawa's inclusion into and exclusion from Japan, from Okinawa's history. There are two things which I wish to draw from that historical description. The first is the universal regularity of such dynamics. The dynamics of inclusion and exclusion are things that can emerge in a common manner in any society, and the primary objective of this book is to sketch socio-scientifically how they have operated in the real history that comprises the century-long relationship between Japan and Okinawa. To that end, I have conducted a macroscopic historical treatment spanning a hundred years.

Another thing which this book examines is the reactions occurring when people are caught up in such dynamics. Regardless of the kind of social-scientific regularity, people who live in reality become concretely involved in it. For those persons, such things as regularity are invisible. Even while unconsciously moving in accordance with that regularity, those people often endeavour to escape from the inevitability of regularity. Their struggles on those occasions only appear in minute historical facts and subtle use of language in texts. The reason why this volume, even while on the one hand conducting a macro description, has cited a huge amount of source material and attempted the description of minute historical facts stems from such an aim.

I hope that people all over the world who read this book will direct their imagination towards the inhabitants of Japan and Okinawa, and will at the same time empathise with the human struggles that are likely to be shared by the societies in which readers live their lives.

Discourse politics

This book is also one which depicts the history of discourse politics. In this volume, I appraise the relationship between discourse politics and real politics in the following ways.

Exclusion from and inclusion into 'the Japanese' is carried out by means of dynamics such as those already mentioned. In other words, the Japanese government and U.S. military include the people of Okinawa in 'the Japanese' or exclude them as being 'Okinawans' due to military and economic factors. On the other hand, with the goal of obtaining political and economic rights, the people of Okinawa aim for inclusion into 'the Japanese' or try to stand on their own feet as 'Okinawans.'

Such real politics produces linguistic discourses, historical discourses, and the like. In claiming possession of Ryukyu, the Japanese government asserted that the residents of Okinawa were linguistically, racially and historically 'Japanese.' In its education policies in Okinawa, as well, something similar was advocated by the Japanese government as a justification for education to instil patriotism towards Japan.

Meanwhile, the assertion of rights on the Okinawan side was also carried out in line with this discourse. In other words, it was claimed that as long as Okinawans were linguistically and historically 'Japanese,' they ought to be granted rights as 'Japanese.' The post-Pacific War struggle in opposition to U.S. bases and the reversion movement, also, were conducted in line with such a discourse. This type of phenomenon can be called discourse politics which has taken the form of linguistics or history.

Real politics and discourse politics are in a recursive relationship. It was in order to justify its territorial claims in the eyes of Qing China that the Japanese government claimed that Okinawan residents were 'Japanese.' In other words, the initial formation of the discourse was in response to the needs of real politics. When campaigns for the obtaining of rights and reversion movements are conducted by means of a narrative aligned with such a discourse, however, it has an impact upon real politics.

The political actors in such discourse politics were not only the Japanese government and Okinawan residents. The U.S. military, which took control of Okinawa after the war, and progressive forces such as the Japanese mainland's Communist Party and Socialist Party, which were in an adversarial relationship with the Japanese government, were also powerful players. Within Okinawa, too, there emerged some people who agreed with the Japanese government or U.S. military, some who agreed with mainland Japanese progressive forces, and some who rejected both and tried to shape their own unique narrative.

These diverse actors unfurled a politics of discourse under conditions of a complex competitive relationship. Amid the discourse politics, matters such as the definition of 'Japanese' and 'Okinawans,' and the historical view of Okinawa were disputed. As previously mentioned, 'the Japanese' and 'the Okinawans' here are constructed concepts, and arenas for contention in discourse politics. This volume describes, among other things, the way in which such discourse politics related to real politics.

The word '*minzoku*'

In the descriptions of discourse politics in this volume, there is a term which has become an important point of contention, this being the Japanese word '*minzoku*.'[1]

When this word is translated into English, it is usually rendered differently according to the context in which it is used, as 'ethnic group,' 'nation,' 'people,' and the like. Let me explain by tracing the term back to its roots.

The Chinese ideograph '民' is pronounced *min* in Japanese. Formerly, in the Edo period, this referred to common people, such as peasants or merchants. The ruling class, consisting of people such as the nobility and samurai, are not included in this '*min*.' Samurai were subservient to *daimyō* (feudal lords), and *daimyō* in turn were subservient to the *shōgun* (generalissimo), each pair being in a master–subordinate relationship, and those in the lower position in that relationship being called '*shin*' or '*shi*,' meaning 'subject.'

'*Zoku*,' the latter half of *minzoku*, on the other hand, means 'tribe.' It was originally a referent for a kinship group. It appears in words such as '*kazoku* (family)' in which it is combined with '*ka*,' meaning 'house,' and '*banzoku* (barbarian),' in which it is joined with '*ban*,' meaning 'brute.' For this reason, '*zoku*' sometimes incorporates the sense of 'ethnic' and 'race.'

Japan's traditional class system (*mibun seido*) was abolished by the 1868 Meiji Restoration. In the early years of the Meiji era, men who had been samurai during the Edo period (1603–1868), along with their family members, were called the '*shizoku* (samurai class),' a term consisting of '*shi*,' meaning 'samurai' and the aforementioned '*zoku*.' There was, however, no custom of using '*minzoku*' as a referent for people whose former class status was that of peasants, artisans or merchants.

In this period, '*min*' came to be used politically in a different sense. In the 1880s, there arose a democratisation movement by the name of '*Jiyū-minken* (Freedom and Popular Rights)' which was against the Meiji government. '*Jiyū*' means 'freedom,' and '*ken*' means 'right(s).' Many of the movement's leaders were samurai who opposed the Meiji government, but many common people also took part. In parallel with this movement, many translations of Western political thought were accomplished. In these, 'democracy' was translated as '*minshu*,' combining the aforementioned '*min*' with '*shu*,' meaning 'master' or 'main.'

In 1898, Japan adopted the format of a constitutional monarchy through the Constitution of the Empire of Japan, established by the Meiji government. In this constitution all ordinary nationals are defined as '*shinmin* (subjects).' In this way, the '*shin*' (samurai) and '*min*' (peasants, artisans and merchants) together came to be subordinate to the emperor, who was the sovereign.

The coining of the Japanese word '*minzoku*' is taken to have occurred in about that same period. The word itself also exists in sixth-century Chinese documents, but was a term referring to barbarians from the outlands. The Japanese word '*minzoku*' had little connection with this root, and is assumed to have been spawned from the aforementioned political background.

The word included diverse meanings from the beginning. The Japanese government and intellectuals who supported that government used the expression in the sense of a 'group of people equally subordinate to the emperor, though the class system was abolished,' or a 'culturally and racially uniform group which swears allegiance to the emperor.'

There were also some members of the anti-government intelligentsia from the Meiji era until after the Pacific War who invested the word with a different meaning. They emphasised the sense of the 'common people' contained in '*min*,' and the sense of a group of equals now that the class system had been abolished.

In such a context, '*min*' was an expression belonging to the democratisation movement. Terms such as '*shimin* (citizen),' formed by adding '*shi*' (meaning 'city'); '*jinmin* (the people),' formed by adding '*jin*' ('person' or 'human'); and '*minshū* (the common people),' formed by adding '*shū* (mass),' were employed as denominations by leaders of the modern Japanese democratisation movement.

As I will discuss in Chapter Eight of this book, for a time after the Pacific War, '*minzoku*' also was used in such a sense. It could be suggested that this stemmed from Asian and African anti-colonial movements and independence movements having been translated into Japanese as '*minzoku* independence movements.' The Japanese Communist Party, in particular, argued that Japan was currently in the situation of a semi-colony of the United States, and that it was U.S. military power and a comprador force subservient to U.S. capital that was dominating Japan. The Japanese Communist Party thus claimed that the direction in which the '*min*,' made up of peasants, workers and the like, should head was that of a '*minzoku* independence movement' fighting against the U.S. occupation forces and the forces controlling Japan.

Due to such circumstance, the Japanese word '*minzoku*' came to have diverse meanings, including 'ethnic group; nation; race; people,' and so on. This does not suggest, however, that English (American English) is universal, while Japanese is unique. American English, in turn, has a special character shaped by American history.

The birth of the term 'ethnic group' in the U.S., for example, is taken to have occurred in the early twentieth century. The first usage of the term dates back to 1935, and it entered the Oxford English Dictionary in 1972 (Huxley and Haddon 1935, pp. 108, 164, 268). From the fourteenth through the middle of the nineteenth century, the term 'ethnic' and related forms were used in English in the meaning of 'pagan,' or 'heathen.' The modern usage of 'ethnic group' came to reflect the different kinds of encounters which industrialised states have had with external groups such as immigrants and indigenous peoples. 'Ethnic' thus came to stand in opposition to 'national,' to refer to people with distinct cultural identities who, through migration or conquest, had become subject to a state or 'nation' with a different cultural mainstream. Moreover, the term 'nationality' in a political context may be used synonymously with citizenship in a sovereign state.

The word 'ethnic group' refers to a group which has a cultural identity. Unlike 'nation,' it does not assume the formation of an independent state. Nor, unlike 'people,' does it imply an assembly seeking political rights, led by the common people. It is a descriptor for a group which does not gain independence, nor has separate political rights, but simply has cultural uniqueness within a particular state. To use 'ethnic group' to refer to a group which, like Okinawa, was formerly a kingdom and where there is even now a discourse of independence from Japan, would in itself have a specific significance in discourse politics.

In German, there is the word *'Volk.'* Until 1871, speakers of German were divided among numerous 'Territoriums' such as Prussia and Bavaria. German speakers also inhabited what is now Czech or Polish territory. Moreover, the nobility in each 'Territorium' were influenced by the French language and French culture, they having been occupied as a result of Napoleonic invasion in the nineteenth century. Against such a background, it was *'Volk'* – a word which, though analogous to the English 'folk,' had a political meaning all of its own – that emerged when ideas calling for German unification came to prominence. This word has the implication that the bearers of German culture are the common people who have not been eroded by French culture, and that a unified nation extending as far as they extend should be created. This was the background against which the Brothers Grimm compiled a German dictionary and collected the common people's folk-tales.

It is for this reason that *'Volk'* is also difficult to translate into English, as it incorporates multiple aspects such as the common people; an ethnic group which shares folkways, the German language and German culture; and a nation which fights against its occupiers and tries to achieve national unification and independence. Even in Nazi times, *'Volk'* had an aspect of a race which attempted to exterminate the Jews, and an aspect of the common people which valued workers and peasants.

In Japan, also, by collecting folk-tales of the common people from the 1920s, Yanagita Kunio (about whom I wrote in my 2002 book, *A Genealogy of 'Japanese' Self-images*) endeavoured to foster a consciousness of being 'Japanese' in people divided by region and class. The 1930s feminist, Takamure Itsue, asserted that the nobility and samurai class, influenced by Confucian culture from China, had shaped a climate of misogyny, and that the ancient culture of Japan, based on the native religion of Shinto, did not contain discrimination against women. While this does not mean that these individuals and their ilk were influenced by German thought, there were also others such as Uehara Senroku (to be discussed in Chapter Eight of this book) who, based on knowledge gained by researching German history, championed the forming of a *minzoku* that would subjectively fight against U.S. occupation forces.

The term 'ethnic group' in English is one that emerged as an expression by which a domestic majority group indicated a minority group. By contrast, the Japanese word '*minzoku*' and the German '*Volk*' were used by domestic majorities to refer to themselves. '*Minzoku*' and '*Volk*' are connected with such political meanings as citizenship, democratisation and independence, and the relative lack of such a tendency in English is probably due to the differing sequence of events through which the terms arose.

In Japan, however, there were also people who used the word '*minzoku*' in emulation of the French '*nation*' from the eighteenth century onwards. The '*nation*' in France had something of the aspect of an ethnic group, but strongly implied one in which modern '*citoyens* (citizens)' were politically unified. When the French Communist Party waged a war of resistance against Nazi occupation, they argued for the transcending of political positioning and cooperation with the Free French forces of de Gaulle and others in order to combat the invaders; and the formation of a *Front National* was advocated. As I will discuss in Chapter Eight, after Japan's defeat in the Pacific War, the Japanese Communist Party drew on this, calling for a democratic *minzoku* front (*minshu minzoku sensen*) to fight the U.S. occupation forces.

Of course, in today's France, *Front National* is the name of an ultra-rightist group which advocates the exclusion of immigrants. In a similar manner, the Japanese word '*minzoku,*' also, includes the aspect of ethnic group and race, and the aspect of nation and people. South Korea and China, which conveyed the culture of Chinese ideographs to Japan, reverse-imported the word '*minzoku*' invented in Japan along with modernization, though the Korean '*minjok*' seems to be being used in a sense closer to '*Volk*' than the Japanese term. This is due to a political environment akin to that in nineteenth-century Germany, in which Korean-speaking groups inhabit a zone spanning multiple states, including South Korea, North Korea and Manchuria.

In present-day China, as well, for the political reason that there are multiple ethnic groups within its borders whose independence the state does not acknowledge, the word '*mínzú*' (written with the same characters as the Japanese '*minzoku*') appears to be being employed in two different senses, one used when calling each distinct ethnic group a '*mínzú*,' and another which transcends the first, using '*mínzú*' to refer to nations formed as the result of political unification and wars of independence.

According to the context of each country and era, such words become an arena for battle in the discourse politics of various political forces. In South Korea, for example, the term '*minjok*' was employed in a manner that transcended ideology amid the North–South unification movement, and in the democratisation movement which fought the military dictatorship tied to the U.S. At the same time, however, the military dictatorship has a history of having attempted national unification with the word '*minjok*' as its catch-cry. Discourse politics around the term '*minjok*' are conducted in that situation. A similar phenomenon probably exists in China, as well.

This applies equally in Japan. The question of whether to call the people of Okinawa a '*minzoku*' becomes a point of contention in discourse politics. In like manner, in this book I will examine the sequence of events in which terms such as '*kokumin* (nationals),' '*kokugo* (national language),' '*futsūgo* (standard language)' and '*hyōjungo* (standard language)' similarly became points at issue. I would like readers to understand the conflicting feelings that reside in each of these expressions which have appeared in such discourses.

1 The Ryukyu Disposition (*Ryūkyū shobun*)

In 1872, the Meiji government, which had only just seized power four years previously, absorbed a kingdom to its south-west. This land, called the Ryukyu Kingdom, was renamed Okinawa Prefecture seven years later, becoming a prefecture of the Empire of Japan. Here, I will examine how Ryukyuan people were positioned as 'Japanese' in the process of this Ryukyu Disposition. That sequence of events is something that shows part of the prototype for the later expansion of 'the Japanese' towards Taiwan, Korea, and elsewhere, as I argued in Japanese edition.

Assimilation into and exclusion from 'internal humanity'

The Ryukyu Kingdom was incorporated into Japan in the early Meiji era, but that kingdom was not an independent state in the modern sense. In East Asia up to the nineteenth century there existed an international principle called a vassal relationship, which differed from that of modern sovereign nations. All over the region, there were kings acknowledged by the emperor of China – the Ryukyuan king also numbering among them, along with the kings of Korea and Vietnam – but they were obliged to manifest their intention of political and cultural submission by such means as regular tributes to the emperor, and use of the Chinese calendar. Their 'kingdoms' were ones that maintained a certain degree of limited autonomy, while submitting to the 'empire' over which the Chinese emperor reigned.

In 1609, Satsuma, a Japanese regional *daimyō* (feudal lord), invaded the Ryukyu Kingdom and placed it under his material control. Satsuma did not abolish the Ryukyu Kingdom, though, having it still use the Chinese calendar and continue its tributes to China, as before. In a tributary/vassal relationship, as large quantities of return gifts are bestowed upon the tributary countries in order to show the authority of the emperor, a type of trading relationship is established. At that time, Japan had entered into a trade control structure called *sakoku* (national isolation) imposed by the Tokugawa regime; and Satsuma was able to operate a brokerage trade by obtaining valuable Chinese products via Ryukyu. Satsuma enriched its economy through this brokerage trade and by exploitation of Ryukyuan products, including sugar, and became an entity able to constitute the driving force for the Meiji Restoration. As such, while being materially dominated by Satsuma, yet still existing as a kingdom and showing submission to China, Ryukyu was in a 'condition of dual subordination to Japan and China,' so to speak. Moreover, in order to maintain the kingdom and to make the distinction clear-cut, Satsuma forbade Ryukyuan assimilation to Japanese customs. 'Dual subordination,' which could even be called bizarre when seen from the concept of the modern international order, was also something that was possible prior to the introduction of the system of modern states in East Asia. In the mid-nineteenth century, however, Western countries advanced into this East Asian region, as well. When the Meiji government, in response, was about to begin its metamorphosis into a modern nation-state, the Ryukyu Kingdom's dual subjection situation, which was a legacy of the old order, came to be forcibly reorganised under new principles. In short, this was nothing other than a process by which Ryukyuans became subsumed into 'the Japanese.'

This course of unification did not necessarily follow a straight line, but rather was one that included many twists and turns. In 1868 (the first year of Meiji), the newly-inaugurated Meiji government conveyed a Grand Council of State Order to the Ryukyuan royal administration regarding the change of era to Meiji, and effected a manifestation of intention of Ryukyu unification. For Satsuma, though, the Ryukyu Kingdom was a precious source of funds, and at the time of the abolition of feudal domains and establishment of prefectures in 1871, the Kagoshima *Han* (domain) (the successor to the Satsuma Domain) insisted upon the retention of Ryukyu in its traditional situation of dual subjection, and decided that Ryukyu, remaining a kingdom, would become an area under the jurisdiction of Kagoshima Prefecture for the time being. After this condition of subordination to Satsuma, the Domain of Ryukyu was set up in 1872, still maintaining its royal administration; and the Ryukyuan king, Shō Tai, while on the one hand being king of the domain, was ranked with the Japanese nobility along with the former feudal lords of mainland Japan. Moreover, as I stated at the beginning, it was only after another seven years, in 1879, that the Ryukyu Kingdom was abolished and was completely incorporated into the Empire of Japan as Okinawa Prefecture.[1]

In this way, Ryukyu was incorporated into the Empire of Japan after an interim period of more than a decade, but during that time, there were arguments against unification from the Japanese side, also, and yet these islands were too small to be perceived as attractive in terms of territory. Satsuma utilised the situation of dual subjection and garnered huge profits, but if the Ryukyu Kingdom were abolished, that advantage would be lost. The early Meiji government had only just reached the beginning of its policy of modernisation in military, educational, economic, and other terms; it had no fiscal leeway whatsoever, and was faced with widespread revolt by peasants and samurai. In such circumstances, it was doubtful in terms of cost theory whether there was sufficient merit to send troops and police – of which there tended to be a shortage – as well as bureaucrats, teachers and so forth to Ryukyu, which was nothing more than a remote group of small islands, and to take decisive action on possession, even with the expectation of international friction from Qing, for a start.

In 1875, for example, three years after the establishment of the Ryukyu Domain, a debate over the abandonment of Ryukyu was waged in the world of criticism. This article, published in the *Yūbin hōchi shinbun*, was one asserting that 'to expend labour and capital uselessly in trying to subordinate Ryukyu' was nothing other than an act of 'the government's penchant for empty titles,' and that the government 'should repress its childlike mentality which likes empty [titles], discard Ryuku (*sic*), too, and sell off Yezo (= Hokkaido) also,' in order to pour all of its efforts into its 'domestic' administration (Shibahara, Ikai and Ikeda 1988, p. 420).

Such a tone of argument also existed within government departments. In 1875, an opinion was submitted from Kawarada Morizane, a government official dispatched from the Ministry of the Interior to the branch office of the Ryukyu Domain, describing the abolition of the Ryukyu Kingdom as 'a stupid policy whose advantages and disadvantages in a state of emergency are unknown.' The stated reason was that considerable difficulty and cost was anticipated for modernising Ryukyu as a part of Japan, and 'by what means would solitary islands in a distant sea compensate for the government's unprofitable expenditure?' and 'its being uneconomical would be unavoidable because it would multiply and divide the advantages and disadvantages' (Kawarada 1965–1977, p. 204).

In the arguments against the abolition of the Ryukyu Kingdom, there was also another motivation apart from such a cost aspect. This was a discriminatory consciousness towards Ryukyu. Abolishing the Ryukyu Kingdom and making it into a prefecture meant incorporating Ryukyuans into the state as 'Japanese.' That being the case, conversely speaking, it would be better to preserve the Ryukyu Kingdom in order to exclude them from 'the Japanese.'

One example of an opposing argument arising from such a motivation was the reply which the legislative body of the time, the Chamber of the Left (*Sain*), submitted to the government in June 1872, immediately prior to the Ryukyu Domain being newly established. As previously mentioned, the Japanese government – and especially the Foreign Ministry – hammered out a plan to incorporate Ryukyu into the empire as a domain, and to rank the Ryukyuan king with the nobility in the same manner as the former feudal lords, but the Chamber of the Left responded to this, saying: 'The Ryukyuan king, being, that is, a member of the Ryukyuan race, must not be confused as being the same as the domestic race.' In this way, the Chamber of the Left asserted that if the Japanese government both excluded the Ryukyuan king from 'the Japanese,' and, without abolishing the Ryukyu Kingdom, included it in Japan as a 'vassal state' while preserving its existing dual subordination system, then friction with Qing could also be avoided (Shimomura 1972, p. 9).

Such a realisation could not necessarily be said to represent a minority faction within the government. As I will later elaborate, even Matsuda Michiyuki, the Disposition Officer who ultimately enforced the Ryukyu Disposition, had declared that even if Japan were to abolish the Ryukyu Kingdom, making a loss was inevitable in economic terms, and Ōkuma Shigenobu and Kido Takayoshi, also, were claiming that Ryukyuans were not 'Japanese,' to the extent that Itō Hirobumi, the Secretary of the Interior at the time of the abolition of the feudal domains, having taken such opinions into account, also was saying that if possible, it would be better to make Ryukyu subordinate to Japan while it stayed a kingdom. Why, then, in spite of this, did the Meiji government carry out the Ryukyu Disposition?

While arguments against the Ryukyu Disposition were voiced from the perspective of the relationship between Japan and Ryukyu only, so to speak, including the economic cost and discriminatory consciousness, the argument in favour of the disposition was made from a position that considered a different relationship, that being national defence against the West.

Amid the threat of Asian colonisation by European major powers, Japan at the time was compelled by the need for definition of its national borders and fortification of its perimeters. For Japan, which was overwhelmingly inferior in military strength in comparison with the major powers, it was desirable to draw its national borders as far as possible from the country proper, and to secure points of national defence. Already, in the north, the securing of Hokkaido as a point of national defence against Russia had been advanced from the end of the Edo era, but preparations in the south were only launched at last with the Ryukyu Disposition.

In May 1872, the Deputy Minister for Finance, Inoue Kaoru, implemented a proposal advocating possession of Ryukyu, but the reasons advanced in it were to 'sweep away the evil mistake of the previous ambiguity,' fix the national boundary, and secure Ryukyu as a 'key point' in Japanese defence, or, in other words, as a 'protective wall for the Japanese Empire' (Shimomura 1972, p. 8).[2] The Foreign Ministry's call for the incorporation of Ryukyu also arose from the diplomatic relations triggered by the Taiwan incident to be discussed below. Moreover, it is known that the Deputy Minister for the Army, Yamagata Aritomo, also made a proposal relating to a Ryukyu disposition. As land, Ryukyu was nothing more than narrow islands, but topographically it was situated midway between mainland Japan, Taiwan and the Chinese mainland, and was a presence that could not be overlooked as a base for maritime traffic. Though it was some years later, an article by Briton Frederick Henry Balfour was submitted to the Minister of the Right, Iwakura Tomomi, in 1877, two years before the abolition of the Ryukyu Kingdom, in an abridged translation by Mori Arinori, Senior Vice Minister for Foreign Affairs (*Okinawa kenshi* 1965–1977, p. 235). It more lucidly tells of the military value of Ryukyu:

> There is no doubt that the possession of a group of islands, situated as Liuchiu (*sic*) is, may be of immense advantage to a great country in time of war. Had we only such a group, where we could station a regiment and which we could use as an independent house of call in the Pacific Ocean, our position in the East would be materially improved. But as regards Japan, the public feeling appears to be against it; that is,

if we can form any idea of that feeling from the native newspapers. The *Hochi Shimbun* devoted a very ably written and somewhat amusing article to the consideration of the matter, deprecating in the strongest terms the unprofitable expenditure now incurred. The arguments of the writer are tersely put. He asks what benefit to Japan will ever accrue from the possession of these islands; what diminution of taxes it is likely to bring about; what the Japanese will gain by garrisoning the islands for their protection against invaders; and whether they, the Japanese, will be more feared by England, Russia, France or Prussia in consequence? To this last question we think we may safely hazard a negative reply (Balfour 1876, pp. 60–61.)

If Western great powers, starting with Britain, were to occupy Ryukyu, then it would mean giving them a potent military base. For that reason, Japan had to amend the situation of dual subordination and secure Ryukyu, even if it meant overlooking some cost. The claims made in this argument in opposition to the Ryukyu abandonment discourse in the newspapers were clear.

The aforementioned anti-Ryukyu-disposition argument from the Chamber of the Left and the like took a contrasting view of Europe and America from that of the pro-disposition discourse, which was conscious of such a threat from the West. There, it was acknowledged that even if Japan left Ryukyu in its situation of dual subordination, 'if we associated openly with all countries, both East and West, in good faith on our part, then they, too, likewise, would have no way of breaking that good faith and invading land that belongs to us.' Moreover, this reply from the Chamber of the Left stated at the same time that 'the Japanese empire is an empire generally known in the East and West,' and so 'it is natural for there to be kingdoms or principalities under its jurisdiction.' In other words, it seems that the Chamber of the Left apprehended the Ryukyu issue as an extension of the pre-modern tributary/vassal relationship in which 'kingdoms' in each area existed under an 'empire' ruled by an emperor; and, if so, then it could be argued that this was premised on the supposition that the major Western powers would not destroy the international order in East Asia, centring upon China. Both its advocating of the preservation of the dual subordination system, and its calling for avoidance of friction with Qing, became one with such a view of the West.

In the end, as of 1872, it evolved into a form in which a policy that was an eclectic mix of pro- and anti-disposition discourses was adopted. In the aforementioned proposal, Inoue Kaoru advocated a change to 'a single domestic system of taxation, tributes and the like, instituted in all prefectures,' in order to 'return [Ryukyu] clearly to our jurisdiction.' In other words, he advocated remodelling into an identical legal system to '*naichi*' for the securing of Ryukyu. Afterwards in Okinawa, and in Korea and Taiwan, as well, this issue of legislative standardisation came to be an extremely important criterion in determining whether those places were 'Japan' or not, but at that time, the Ryukyu Kingdom was maintained, with just the domain being established. Soejima Taneomi, the then Foreign Minister, promising not to alter the kingdom's regime for the time being, quelled the fears of the Ryukyu side. On the other hand, overcoming opposition from the Chamber of the Left, the ranking of the Ryukyuan king with the Japanese nobility was implemented. Moreover, though the Ryukyu Domain did detach from the jurisdiction of Kagoshima, it fell under the jurisdiction of the Foreign Ministry, unlike other domains which were controlled by the Finance Ministry (the Ministry of the Interior being set up the following year, in 1873). These were also things that went along with the Foreign Ministry's proposals, but it can be seen that they largely settled midway between the two policies.

The subsequent state of affairs took a sudden turn, however. The international order in East Asia, centred upon China, easily crumbled in the face of Western intrusions. In the midst of those circumstances, a policy such as the Chamber of the Left advocated, namely of keeping the Ryukyu Kingdom as a 'vassal state' with the cooperation of the West and Qing while continuing to exclude Ryukyuans from 'the Japanese,' was losing its viability. Another policy line – in other words, a policy of subsuming Ryukyu and its residents as 'Japanese' in order to secure it as a stronghold – gradually gained prevalence.

The recommendations of foreign consultants

The first step towards the incorporation of Ryukyuans into 'the Japanese' consisted of negotiations between Japan and the Qing government over an incident in 1871, in which islanders from Miyako (a group of islands south of the Okinawan archipelago), having drifted ashore on Taiwan, were killed by Taiwanese aborigines, who at the time were disparagingly called 'wild tribespeople (*seiban*).' In the spring of 1874, two and a half years after the occurrence of this incident, the Japanese government, with the added domestic objective of deflecting the brunt of discontent over its policy of conquering Korea by military force, dispatched troops to Taiwan on the pretext of a retaliatory measure for the protection of 'Japanese.' One of the focal points of negotiations conducted between Japan and Qing in regard to this incident was whether Ryukyuans were 'Japanese,' the reason being that if they were not 'Japanese,' then the pretext of dispatching troops for the purpose of protecting 'Japanese' would no longer hold water.

In 1873, the year before the dispatch of troops, the Qing side commented at the negotiating table: 'We still do not hear that the Ryukyuans whom the wild tribespeople violently killed the year before last are people of your esteemed country.' According to the Qing side, because 'Ryukyuans are our vassal state,' their protection was the jurisdiction of Qing, and there was no reason for Japan to interfere. In reply to this, the Japanese side asserted that the people of the Domain of Ryukyu were to the bitter end 'our nationals,' and that 'killing Ryukyuans and injuring Satsuma people is the same as obstructing the right of our government's protection' (Shimomura 1972, p. 28).[3] Furthermore, two months after the dispatch of troops, it shifted jurisdiction over the Ryukyu Domain from the Foreign Ministry to the Interior Ministry, and indicated its positioning of Ryukyu as being within the home country of 'Japan.'

In actuality, however, as in the Chamber of the Left's assertion that the King of Ryukyu was not a member of the 'domestic race,' the recognition that Ryukyuans were 'Japanese' had not taken hold in Japanese government departments of the day. Ōkuma Shigenobu, who opposed the dispatch of troops to Taiwan, mentioned Ryukyuans in a written opinion, saying: 'only the people of the so-called outer domain, surprisingly, are not the same as our people,' and Kido Takayoshi, who was similarly of the opposing faction, insisted that: 'there should be a difference in the degree of intimacy between the domestic populace and themselves.' Ultimately, however, the assertion that Ryukyuans were 'Japanese,' and that making reprisals for their killing was the natural duty of the Japanese government was approved, and the dispatch of troops was carried out (Cited in Yasuoka 1992, pp. 11, 12). Here, it was clear that the question of whether Ryukyuans were 'Japanese' or not was merely something subordinate to the arguments for and against the dispatch of troops.

The Ryukyu Disposition

Negotiations between Japan and Qing over the dispatch of troops to Taiwan failed to reach agreement, but the British Minister, who feared that economic interests would be threatened by the breakout of war between Japan and China, intervened, and Qing, which had border disputes with Russia in its north, had Japan withdraw its troops from Taiwan by paying a small sum in indemnities. The indemnities acquired by the Japanese side did not even amount to one tenth of the expense of the expedition, but on the other hand, it succeeded in having wording that deemed Ryukyuans to be 'subjects of Japan' inserted into this treaty. This was interpreted as having secured a pledge that Qing acknowledged that Ryukyuans were 'Japanese' – in other words, that the Ryukyus were Japanese territory.

The individual who gave advice to the Japanese government on this point was Gustave-Emil Boissonard, a French consultant in the Ministry of Justice. After peace negotiations over the Taiwan expedition had concluded, Boissonard stated in a written opinion he submitted to the Meiji government in March 1875 that in the treaty provisions, having made Qing 'name the [Ryukyu] people as Japanese subjects' was 'the most fortunate result of the treaty,' and that this meant the same thing as having made Qing recognise that sovereignty over the Ryukyus was held by Japan (dated 17 March 1875; cited in Hiratsuka 1982, p. 32).[4] Furthermore, Boissonard asserted that from then on, 'the Ryukyus should be regarded as one region of Japan,' and that 'it should be mandatory for the Ryukyu Islands to be included within the borders of maps of Japan.' He also advised that, as policy vis-à-vis the Ryukyus, Japan force the abolition of diplomatic relations between the Ryukyus and Qing, and the closure of the Ryukyu Kingdom's diplomatic mission in Fujian.

In Boissonard's written opinion, however, a different point of view from the Meiji government's later policy vis-à-vis Ryukyu was expressed. In a sense, this meant advocating allowing the King of the Ryukyu Domain to exercise autonomy for the time being, in a similar manner to the Chamber of the Left.

Boissonard's advice was far more specific than that of the Chamber of the Left, however. In other words, according to his proposal, in diplomacy, the Japanese government should seize Ryukyuan sovereignty and abolish the dual subordination situation, and force the abrogation of the Ryukyu Kingdom's existing diplomatic relationships; in regard to internal administration, it should limit itself to dispatching a Resident Extraordinary from the centre, basically leaving government ordinances and justice within Ryukyu to the Royal Government, and it 'should permit some measure of independence.' Moreover, in order to prevent confusion among the residents, as regards 'civil trading, business taxation and military affairs,' it should maintain traditional customs for the time being; and, as to criminal law, it should go no further than to amend only the parts that were harsher than Japanese criminal law.

In one sense, it could be said that Boissonard's view that the Japanese government should seize sovereignty and diplomatic rights, but that in the near term it should leave internal affairs to the traditional dynasty and preserve the old customs, was one which proposed making Ryukyu an autonomous region within the Empire of Japan: one country, two systems. It is thought, however, that this probably would be more appropriately interpreted as something advocating the kind of indirect rule employed in colonial control by European countries of that time, especially Britain, namely, utilising an existing local dynasty. In indirect rule, local internal affairs are entrusted to the existing dynasty, and the suzerain state exclusively holds diplomatic rights. In this manner, by having the local populace take charge of the terminus of control, the suzerain state can reduce the number of government officials it sends to the locality and cut costs while at the same time keeping contact and friction with local residents at a minimum, and carry out efficient control. As I will discuss in Volume 2, such a policy of indirect rule happened to be proposed to the Japanese government by a foreign consultant at the time when it took possession of Taiwan, as well.

A proposal like this was one that also oddly concurred with the aforementioned argument against disposition that stemmed from cost theory. Certainly, if one considers it from the relationship solely between Japan and Ryukyu, then this might have been a rational method of governance. However, the Japanese government did not adopt such a proposal, but went on to abolish the Ryukyu Dynasty and incorporate Ryukyu as one prefecture of Japan.

The reason which could be cited as the Meiji government's rejection of Boissonard's proposal was its foreign relations, after all. In this case, though, it was its diplomatic relations with Qing, rather than with Europe and America. About a week after Boissonard's written opinion had been submitted, the Qing government side submitted two questions to the Japanese side, which designated Ryukyu as a 'vassal domain' on the occasion of negotiations. One of

The Ryukyu Disposition

these was: 'Is your noble country's [position] in the Ryukyus just like Britain's in India?' and another was: 'Have you already attributed the Ryukyu Islands to your noble country, or, is it in the name of a feudal prince belonging to a vassal domain?' (negotiations of 24 March 1875, cited in Gaimushō 1950, p. 300).

These questions were ones that attacked the ambiguity of the relationship between Japan and the Ryukyus. If the Japanese government acknowledged that the Ryukyus were, to Japan, a similar presence to that of India to Britain, then it was clear that this would give rise to a contradiction with the claims made hitherto by the Japanese government which dispatched troops to Taiwan on the pretext that Ryukyuans were 'Japanese.' This was because though India was a British colony, Indians were not British nationals. Moreover, if it were claimed that Ryukyuans were 'Japanese' and the Ryukyus were one region of Japan, then the Ryukyus ought to have been a 'province or county' or else a prefecture, but in reality they were a feudal domain in which a Ryukyuan king existed. If Japan recognised that the Ryukyus were a 'vassal domain' which the king of the domain ruled, then it should have been permissible, by the wishes of the Ryukyuan king, to choose not Japan but Qing as the other party under whose jurisdiction they fell.

What is more, because British rule of India was not something that treated India as a 'province or county,' but one that combined indirect rule, which took the form of local clan kings being under British jurisdiction, these two questions almost amounted to the same thing. If the Japanese government had taken an indirect rule line which left internal affairs to the Ryukyu Domain's king, as Boissonard had advised, then one would expect the relationship between Japan and the Ryukyus to have become something close to that between Britain and India, and the Ryukyus to become not a 'prefecture' of Japan, but a 'dependent vassal domain.'

It was obvious that if, in response to such questions, Japan had declared that it would implement indirect rule in the Ryukyus, then this would have given Qing an opportunity to take advantage in negotiations. Of course, the Japanese side also saw through this aim on the part of Qing, and retorted that the Ryukyus had been a part of Japan since ancient times, and 'How is it comparable to India?' To the second question, also, Japan replied that it intended to 'soon make Ryukyu a prefecture, because our state wanted to abolish the feudal system.' By means of these answers, Japan evaded a diplomatic offensive from Qing for the time being, but this naturally meant the rejection of the indirect rule line which Boissonard had advised.

At this time, Japan had confidence in its military strength vis-à-vis Qing, and if it had been thinking that it was possible to secure the Ryukyus even by means of indirect rule, then there might not have been the necessity to make such a reply. However, confrontation between Japan and Qing had currently arisen over Korea, as well, and military preparations for war against Qing were still insufficient. If Japan had had confidence in its military might from the beginning, then there should not have been the actual need to acquire the Ryukyus, which had been regarded as inevitably meaning a financial deficit even if Japan did take possession. In the situation, the most effective means for Japan to justify and ensure its possession of the Ryukyus was the policy of subsuming them into 'the Japanese.'

Ryukyuans as 'Japanese'

After the policy of subsumption into Japan had been declared at the negotiations between Japan and Qing, the Secretary of Home Affairs, Matsuda Michiyuki, was appointed Disposition Officer for the Ryukyu issue, and began negotiations to press the Ryukyuan Royal Government for a change of regime.

The terms which Matsuda presented to the Royal Government side spanned several areas. Firstly, in terms of foreign affairs, it was demanded that the Ryukyus cease paying tribute to Qing and withdraw their Ryukyuan Mission to Qing, as Boissonard had advised; change their use of the Chinese calendar to the Meiji era name; and simultaneously approve the stationing of Japanese troops. In terms of domestic affairs, a political merger with Japan was raised, consisting of such things as abolishing Ryukyuan conventional criminal law and implementing that of the Japanese government; embarking on reform of the domain administration; and sending students to Tokyo to have them learn 'educational affairs about civilisation.' Finally, the domain king's leaving Ryukyu and going to Tokyo in order to 'express gratitude' to the emperor was added. For the Ryukyuan side, this was equivalent to being forced to abandon the whole of their existing system.

In these negotiations, there were two points which Matsuda made the reasons for his demands. One was that, as for 'the land of Ryukyu,' 'because there are often also countries which hope to make a ship repair dock with this land for the convenience of Asian voyages, and because it is not made clear that Ryukyu constitutes our Japanese government's territory, it is impossible not to fear that these will link with the future survival of the domain in question.' This means that as long as Ryukyu – a key zone in both transport and strategic terms – did not make it clear that it was a territory of the Japanese government, there was a high risk that that it would be seized by a foreign country. In negotiations with Qing in later years, too, the Japanese government side stated: 'Though [Ryukyu] is an impoverished archipelago, if we leave it be as before, then it is unclear how it will relate to the defence of *naichi* if by some chance it is occupied by another country. That is the reason why our government will now not begrudge the expense, and, even in peacetime, it will station police just like common soldiers,' and it can be seen what kind of a presence Ryukyu was to Japan.[5]

The second part of this explanation of reasons was that 'it goes without saying that Ryukyu has been our Japan's territory all along, as illustrated in its topography, race, manners, language and various histories from time immemorial.' It says that from every aspect, including race, geography, language, history and the like, Ryukyu is a part of Japan, and Ryukyuan residents are 'Japanese,' and there is not 'a single connection' with the 'geography, race, manners, language, et cetera, of Qing.' Moreover, in Inoue Kaoru's written opinion of three years previously, the incorporation of Ryukyu into Japan was deemed as being after the invasion by Satsuma in the seventeenth century; but, according to Matsuda, Ryukyu had submitted to the imperial house since ancient times, and it was merely because 'since the middle ages' there had not been the leeway to extend the emperor's authority to Ryukyu in the midst of the 'commotion of battle' that the 'truly absurd' relationship, namely dual subordination with China, had come about (Shimomura 1972, pp. 94, 121, 105). In other words, it said that Ryukyu was not being newly absorbed into the Empire of Japan, but was merely reverting to its ancient condition.

The Ryukyuan Royal Government side was not convinced by such rationales. The Royal Government side counter-argued that even if they allowed the stationing of military forces in a small country like Ryukyu, it would have the opposite effect of stirring international friction; it stated that reform of its internal affairs and changes to criminal law would involve much confusion to do with customs; and it replied that the domain king could not go to Tokyo 'for health reasons.' Furthermore, in counter to the claim that Ryukyuans were 'Japanese,' it argued: 'this domain is situated halfway between the Japanese empire and China; its geographical connections are contiguous with both countries; and in race and custom, also, it resembles both countries,' so dual subordination was a natural condition (Shimomura 1972, p. 127. Punctuation added).

In response to this, Matsuda once again quoted the document, and conducted an even more detailed rebuttal.

> The Ryukyu race is of our Satsuma race in skeletal structure and body. Its appearance in greatest part [reflects] the manners of our country, especially having the elegance of our ancient times ... [They use] many obsolete words, Kamakura [period] words, Satsuma dialect, and so on, and mix in a little Chinese ... Upon hearing Ryukyuan people's tone of voice, it is purely our country's tone of voice, [while] the speech sounds are those of Satsuma. In regard to sentence structure, such employment of nouns above and verbs below is the most marked proof of [it being] our country's language (Shimomura 1972, pp. 137–138. Punctuation added).

This says that Ryukyuans are not only racially 'Japanese,' but that they have preserved much in terms of language and customs from Japan's ancient and medieval times. Matsuda cites as his grounds for argument the example of the word order of nouns and verbs, and it can be seen that the Japanese government dealt with the negotiations after having prepared their Ryukyu argument based to a certain degree on modern linguistics.

The Ryukyuan Royal Government side doggedly resisted this kind of treatment. While aiming to prolong the situation on the one hand, they made repeated petitions to the Meiji government via the Ryukyu Office in Tokyo. During that period, while requesting aid from Qing, they also sent secret messages to the ministers of each European country in Tokyo, engaging in motions seeking aid. Qing submitted an objection through its minister to Japan, but the Japanese government effectively ignored it, and the situation descended into a stalemate.

On the other hand, in terms of diplomacy, the incorporation of Ryukyu into the Japanese empire progressed steadily. In January 1876, Mori Arinori, the then Minister to Qing, reported to the

Minister for Foreign Affairs that Qing still regarded Ryukyu as a vassal state of its own country; and he advised [the Minister] 'to acknowledge members of the Domain of Ryukyu themselves to be Japanese,' and extend protection to them overseas, as well. The technique of extending diplomatic protection to them as 'Japanese' as part of compiling established facts in order to make Ryukyu into Japanese territory came to be employed also on the occasion of the annexation of Korea, as I will discuss in Volume 2 of this book. Furthermore, we could also note that two months after this, Mori recommended the abolition of the Ryukyu nomenclature, and its 'renaming as the Domain of Naha' (Yokoyama 1980c, pp. 132, 139). Naha was the name of the city that later became the capital and prefectural seat of Okinawa Prefecture.

A struggle over history

In November 1878, in the midst of stalled negotiations with the Royal Government, Matsuda petitioned the Minister of the Interior, Itō Hirobumi, with the idea for Ryukyu disposition, which deemed that even if forcible measures were taken, there was no alternative but to abolish the domain. What is very interesting is that by Matsuda's having pointed out here that 'in comparing the revenue within the domain up till now with the expenditure of a new administration in the future, the [latter's] income will not be sufficient to support its expenses,' the incorporation of Ryukyu into Japan was a policy made with the resignation that costs would outweigh returns. In response to this idea for disposition, Ito replied that if Ryukyu obeyed orders, it would be permissible for it to remain as a domain, but abolition of the domain was already inevitable (Shimomura 1972, pp. 203, 214).[6] In March 1879, the following year, Matsuda forced through this disposition, accompanied by a garrison and police, and at this point, the Ryukyu Kingdom was annihilated and was renamed Okinawa Prefecture.

However, Qing naturally protested to the Japanese government. Just as the British minister had done on the occasion of the dispatch of troops to Taiwan, this time it was decided that the former American president, Ulysses S. Grant, would serve as mediator in negotiations between Japan and China. Though Qing told Grant: 'Even if it means giving said islands to Japan, we definitely do not desire a war,' Qing stated: 'Nevertheless, now, if the Chinese government does not easily hand this [Ryukyu] to Japan, then [Japan] will also invariably make an advance on Korea.' Furthermore, Qing expressed a sense of impending crisis, saying: 'This, of course, will be the first step to letting Japan invade the Asian [main]land, ultimately leading to attacks even on Peking' (Yokoyama 1980c, p. 328). At the time, such misgivings must have appeared to be excessive paranoia, but subsequent history showed that these were not mere groundless fears.

Grant, who arrived in Japan in July 1879, held talks with the Minister of the Interior, Itō Hirobumi, and others. On that occasion, the Japanese side prepared a document that was a 'Memorandum in reply to the Chinese government's objections: that Japan has the sovereign right exclusively to control the Ryukyu Islands.' This was something which, enumerating Ryukyu history, language, race, religion, and so on, in addition to the particulars of traditional negotiations with Qing and the Ryukyu Royal Government, asserted that Ryukyuan people had been 'Japanese' since time immemorial (Yokoyama 1980c; subsequent citations from pp. 330, 333–335).

According to that document, the Ryukyuan script was the same as the Japanese *i-ro-ha kana* syllabaries, 'its language has the same roots as the dialects spoken in every part of Japan,' and, moreover, 'obviously, in racial terms, there is close mutual resemblance.' It claims, furthermore, that 'the religion in which Ryukyuans believe is Shinto,' and 'the protocols they employ when [conducting] rituals are overall in the so-called Ogasawara style, from Japan,' while meal customs and the like, also, were 'entirely homologous with Japanese ordinary customs.' In addition, the nomenclature of Okinawa, which was newly made the prefectural name, was one which the local residents had traditionally used as a name for the main island, but this, too, was argued to be 'pure Japanese.'

Moreover, it was asserted that, historically, the Ryukyus had belonged to Japan since the eighth century, this relationship being far older than its tributary one towards China. It is further said that the first Ryukyuan king, Shunten, was a child fathered locally by Minamoto-no-Tametomo who had journeyed there in the twelfth century; and that *i-ro-ha* script, also, had been 'imparted by Tametomo.' As the Minamotos were deemed to share the same bloodline as the Imperial House, Tametomo's son being the first Ryukyuan king was immediately tied to the assertion that 'the Ryukyu islands = descendents = of our emperor.'

In Onoue Kaoru's proposal seven years prior to this, after deciding that 'for some time it had ceased to be said that the founder, Shunten, was a successor of Minamoto-no-Tametomo,' recognition was being shown that Ryukyu had belonged to Japan following its invasion by Satsuma in the seventeenth century. But now, Ryukyu's belonging to Japan came to extend back to ancient times, and, simultaneously, focus came to be directed closely upon the legend of Tametomo's visit. In addition, the Ryukyuan king, whom the Chamber of the Left had once described as not being of the 'domestic race,' went on to be deemed a relative of the Japanese emperor. Moreover, as I discussed in my previous book, *A Genealogy of Japanese Self-images* (Oguma 2002), after the annexation of Korea, the claim began to be made from the Japanese side that Dangun, the first king of Korea, was a descendant spawned by Susano-o, from *Kojiki* and *Nihonshoki* mythology, when he crossed to Korea.

In spite of this, as previously mentioned, the Ryukyuan Royal Government did not share this kind of view of Ryukyu. Qing, too, asserted that the 'two species, Outlander Japanese and Native Ryukyuans,' were different races (Yokoyama 1980a, Vol. 1, p. 171). Similar opinions were also shared by the prevailing views of Westerners of the day: Perry, whose ship called at Okinawa in 1850, for example, also regarded Okinawan residents as different from 'the Japanese.' As I mentioned in Volume 2 of this book, such a view of Okinawa continued to be handed down even as far as to the American Occupation Forces after the Pacific War. In the late nineteenth century, though, it was only the Japanese government that was strongly asserting that Ryukyuans were 'Japanese.'

In fact, the Japanese government of the time also struggled to find a foundation for such claims. This fact can been seen in the report which the Ministry of Internal Affairs prepared in the Ryukyu Disposition process.[7] This report is thought to be what constituted the underpinning for the 'memorandum' submitted at the negotiations, and advisors contributed answers from an academic standpoint on each of the items published in the 'memorandum,' including race, language, customs and religion. Interestingly, however, though questions were posed in order to back up the similarities between Japan and Ryukyu, the answers to almost all of them were negative.

According to the answers in the report, though written symbols similar to the Japanese *hiragana* syllabary were indeed being used in some parts in Ryukyu, these were only being utilised in documents meant for Japan, and, moreover, obviously some symbols that differed from 'Japanese writing' were included. Furthermore, phonemes in the Ryukyuan language were completely dissimilar to the Satsuma dialect of Japanese, and the religion, also, differed from Japanese Shinto in all too many ways. Even in terms of customs, though Ryukyuans did employ Ogasawara-type rituals when associating with Japan, the report stated it was clear that 'popular customs greatly differ from the Japanese.' Racially, too, Ryukyuans were deemed to have 'features which express a specific character.'

As for the advisors who responded at the government's request, it seems they were reluctant to issue such conclusions, as such awkward wording as the following can be seen at every turn in the report: 'Discussion on the debate in question (the ethnological discussion) has no benefit for the rights of Japan, yet it perchance may become an instrument for confuting them,' or 'As to how it has been argued, from the points about belief in Ryukyu religion and its folk customs, that Japan has the sovereignty to possess Ryukyu exclusively, we are unable to make further prudent judgement about this,' and so on. This meant that only disappointing answers were obtained as far as the Japanese government was concerned, but the 'memorandum' tabled in negotiations was described in a form that ignored these responses.

On the occasion of talks with Grant, the Japanese government side, in accordance with the contents of the 'memorandum,' strongly asserted that Ryukyu had been a uniquely Japanese territory since ancient times. Moreover, it said that the '*Kyūjin* (Ryukyuans)' had from the start been people who, craving the profits from trade, liked to tell lies for the sake of achieving that objective,' and that Qing's claim that Ryukyu had been submitting to China had arisen merely because the Ryukyuan Royal Government, which had gained advantages from trade with Qing on the pretence that it was not Japanese territory, had 'fallen into the error of swindling' (citations of the conference with Grant in Yokoyama 1980a, pp. 242–243, 252, 254, 257). Setting aside the veracity of the theory that Ryukyuans were 'Japanese' and that the King of Ryukyu was a relative of the Japanese emperor, 'the Japanese' having asserted that those 'Japanese' were people who nonchalantly deceived others for their own benefit could called quite paradoxical.

Apparently being perplexed at the difference between the claims of Qing and the Ryukyu side, and those of the Japanese government,

Grant avoided drawing conclusions, saying: 'Because much of what both sides argue relates to historical material, it will be difficult to make a decision until after examining it minutely.' The Japanese government side, in turn, stating that: 'China is a neighbouring country to Japan,' and that it was a brother country in Asia with a 'homologous civilisation, religion, writing system, laws, customs, and so on,' ended the negotiations with the expressed wish of solving the Ryukyu issue peacefully. Even though the Japanese government desired dominion over Ryukyu, wishing to avoid war with Qing while balance was still not achieved was probably its true feeling. However, when Matsuda, the Disposition Officer, asserted the commonality between Ryukyu and Japan, the differences between Qing and Japan's 'civilisation, religion, writing system, laws, customs, and so on' received greater emphasis.

The Japanese side later proposed a draft amended treaty for division of the Ryukyu archipelago in negotiations with Qing. This was a proposal saying that if Qing amended the 1871 Sino-Japanese Amity Treaty, and recognised Japanese trading rights within Qing, then Japan would cede the Miyako and Yaeyama island groups to Qing in return. There, the people who, as 'Japanese,' were made the pretext for dispatching troops to Taiwan, were taken as being bargaining tools in diplomacy.

These negotiations met with a deferral of signing on the part of Qing and collapsed, and in negotiations in 1885, six years after the establishment of prefectures, the Japanese government responded to the Qing side having asked about the current situation of Ryukyu by saying: 'Since the abolition of the domains, it has been no different from *naichi* in everything, such as situating courthouses, establishing schools and stationing barracks in that place' (Gaimushō 1950, p. 288).[8] Unification was complete in such major aspects of the state as law, education and military affairs, and the assertion was that Ryukyu was a part of Japan which was 'no different from *naichi*.'

The view of Ryukyu and historical perspective which the Japanese government took on the occasion of the Ryukyu Disposition also went on to circulate without modification in Japanese publications of the time. In 1880, the year after abolition of the domains, several introductory volumes on Ryukyu were published, including Matsui Junji's *Ryūkyū jiken* (The Ryukyu incident) (1880), and Nakanishi Saiichirō's *Nihon Shina Ryūkyū kibun: shohen* (Annals of Japan, China [and] Ryukyu: first edition) (1880), but each of them expounded the legend of Tametomo's visit and the usage of the *i-ro-ha* syllabaries, saying that 'all of the customs, language, script and so forth are no different from that of *naichi*,' and 'much [of the language] is a corrupted version of our country's classical language' (both in Yokoyama 1980b, pp. 254, 172). These treatises were not yet ones that assumed the guise of modern social sciences such as anthropology, linguistics or history, but they were things that went on to comprise the models for theory in these academic fields in later years.

In spite of such official opinions, it did not mean that the policy of attempting to differentiate Ryukyuans from the 'domestic race' vanished along with the Ryukyuan Disposition, however. In June 1879, Matsuda, who presided over the disposition, stated as follows in a proclamation entitled: 'Official notice to the samurai class in general in Okinawa Prefecture.'

> Unless you [Ryukyuans] see the light and amend the old state of affairs, in the new prefecture, you will be deemed to be of no possible use, the people of *naichi* will take all of the myriad occupations, and, finally, there being not one of you native people able to engage in an occupation, you will end up in a condition just like that of the natives of America, or the Aino (*sic*) of Hokkaido, courting the contempt of your own society, and mostly being differentiated from the general population. And this will be something that you bring upon yourselves ... (Shimomura 1972, p. 269. Punctuation added)

Matsuda says that as long as they do not amend their 'old state of affairs' as Ryukyuans, and devote their allegiance to the Empire of Japan as 'Japanese,' they will be 'differentiated from the general population' like 'the natives of America.' Even if they are incorporated into Japan for the reason that they are racially identical, that would not be the goal of having been recognised as 'Japanese,' but would be no more than the starting line of a long process of assimilation. If they shirk efforts for allegiance and assimilation, then the fate of being 'differentiated from the general population' would automatically await them. Moreover, he claims that this would not be the fault of the side seeking to discriminate, but something which the side that shirked the effort would bring upon itself.

Through this Ryukyu Disposition, the indigenous inhabitants of the Ryukyus were incorporated into 'the Japanese.' In that process, there was conflict between two policies, namely, an indirect rule line which rejected their integration into 'the Japanese' from the standpoint of cost theory and discrimination, and an integration and assimilation line which, placing emphasis upon national defence and external affairs, subsumed them into 'the Japanese.' From then on, these two changed their form in various ways, and, while casting their shadow across policy debates and historical perspectives, went on to influence the confrontation over whether to subsume those people into 'the Japanese,' not only in Okinawa but also in places like Korea and Taiwan.

2 Okinawan Education and 'Japanisation'

In Okinawa, which had been incorporated into part of the Empire of Japan in the form of 'Okinawa Prefecture' through the Ryukyu Disposition, 'education for becoming nationals (*kokumin kyōiku*)' was undertaken by Japan. That was surely nothing other than an operation to remould Okinawa residents into 'Japanese.'

The preservation of old customs and the cultivation of loyalty

Though it could be said that Japan's policy vis-à-vis Okinawa was, in principle, to subsume it into Japan, there are seemingly contradictory aspects to this.

Firstly, the Meiji government adopted a so-called policy of preservation of old customs. In criminal law and the like, practices from Japan proper (*naichi*) were implemented, but the first Prefectural Governor, Nabeshima Naotsugu, issued an administrative order saying that, out of the various *hatto* (laws) from the days of the Ryukyu Kingdom, 'those portions to which an official announcement of revision does not extend are all to be as before,' and the taxation system and suchlike remained as they had been in the time of the Ryukyu Kingdom. Furthermore, government officials dispatched from the central government occupied the nucleus of the prefectural administration, but government officials from the former royal dynasty continued to work under them. The taxation system from the age of the Ryukyu Kingdom was a huge burden for peasants, and the second Prefectural Governor, Uesugi Mochinori, who saw how excessively poverty-stricken they were, submitted a petition to his superiors for reform, arguing that Okinawans, who ought similarly to have been 'subjects of the Emperor,' were being made to suffer by the 'old laws,' but this was not accepted.[1] As we saw in the previous chapter, the conservation of old customs was something approaching Boissonard's assertion advocating the preservation of the Ryukyu

Kingdom, and could be supposed to run counter to the direction of subsuming Okinawa into Japan.

On the other hand, thoroughgoing 'Japanisation' was made an objective in education, and measures were worked out in rapid succession. In the year following the abolition of domains and establishment of prefectures, a facility for learning spoken Japanese was established in the prefectural office, and four months later, teacher training was begun with this as a 'normal school' (teacher's training school); and around then, secondary schools (*chūgakkō*) were also established. At the same time, in a mere three years, fifty-one elementary schools were also set up. Moreover, in spite of the fact that school fees were levied even in primary education in other prefectures at the time, in Okinawa it was quite the opposite, with subsidies, stationery, and so on being provided to attendees.

Such apparently contradictory policies were, however, ones that had been considered from the time of the Ryukyu Disposition as a means to implement governance. In his 'Ryukyu Disposition Proposal' submitted to Itō Hirobumi, the Minister of the Interior, immediately prior to the abolition of domains and establishment of prefectures, the Disposition Officer, Matsuda Michiyuki, had pointed out that though abolition of the kingdom *per se* was possible, difficulties were anticipated in later governance (Shimomura 1972, pp. 202, 204).[2] What he meant by those difficulties was not only that literate 'natives' were few in number, but that in order to facilitate linguistic communication, the Japanese government would have to utilise all of the Ryukyuan samurai class and above, and make them the catalyst for laying down laws and carrying out government, but he surmised that 'because [the kingdom's] samurai class would become a party of malcontents, they would falsely convey the will of their superiors and lie about the condition of the common people, becoming a fine means for obstructing government.' In actuality, during the initial period of rule, the Ryukyuan samurai class cohort did not cooperate with the prefectural office's policy, there was a series of sabotage incidents, and there were even moves among the pro-Qing samurai class, who were nicknamed a 'stubborn bunch,' to smuggle themselves onto the continent and ask the Qing court for help against the Japanese conquering army.

The solution to this issue that Matsuda presented was something like the following: namely, 'principally, to strive as much as possible not to destroy the land system, manners, business operations and things that generally comprise the traditional customs of the samurai class and commoners of the location in question,' and, above all, to avoid disaffection by conserving old customs such as the measure of hereditary stipends, which comprised the income basis for the samurai class; and concurrently to 'reform old regulations' selectively in relation to policing, education, religious doctrines, and the like. In other words, he advocated trying to placate the samurai class by temporarily conserving old customs, while teaching the Japanese language to commoners and advancing the 'Japanisation' of the next generation though education.

It was Yamagata Aritomo that indicated an almost identical governing policy from a different angle. Being Minister of the Interior, he inspected Okinawa Prefecture and islands such as Itsushima and Tsushima in 1886, but his discourse on Okinawan governance stated in a later report was one that consistently hammered the point of view of national defence (Yamagata 1886). According to Yamagata, 'Okinawa is our southern gateway,' and a bastion of national defence which was 'at a time of crisis for the East, quite risky in the case where an enemy nation's warships held its ports and, by those means, tried to make it into a place to quarter troops.' Yamagata further asserted that the best way of securing this bastion was to foster loyalty to Japan in Okinawans, and ultimately to foist responsibility for the defence of Okinawa onto them.

In Yamagata's view, from the cost aspect, as well, it was 'the principle of troops to employ natives for protecting' that land. At that point in time, however, Okinawans' loyalty towards Japan was doubtful, and it was solely a condition of it 'being by no means possible at the present time to endeavour to make such people defend the southern gateway, a strategic location for us.' Accordingly, 'stirring up a patriotic temperament and smashing the obstinate notion of pseudo dual subordination, and advancing them unwittingly along the path of enlightenment' was 'the most necessary for political manoeuvres,' and education became vital for that purpose. This was because 'the only thing that would bring Okinawans' patriotism along with it was education.' Moreover, he suggested that if [the government] implemented conscription while making loyalty permeate by means of education, and 'acted with the aim of gradually making those islanders form a body of regular troops ... then it might be possible to reduce the expense (of dispatching military force) greatly.' Further, he stated: 'The administration should make efforts preferably to conserve old customs and manners and to pacify public sentiment' until such cultivation of loyalty were advanced.

It can be appreciated that it was from pragmatism to do with governance in Matsuda's case, and from reasons involving national defence in the case of Yamagata, that they each hammered out a policy of prioritising education, and postponing unification in the institutional aspect. In this manner, the parallel existence of the preservation of old customs and education for 'Japanisation' – which at a glance appear to be contradictory – were advocated.

Yamagata's inspection was also a manifestation of the Japanese government's having reaffirmed Okinawa's value in terms of national defence. At the time, amid intensifying friction between Qing and Japan over the Korean peninsula, Okinawa drew renewed attention as a frontline base against China, and it is said that Britain's having applied to lease Okinawa as a military base further provoked the government. The next year after Yamagata's inspection, in February 1887, the Minister for Education, Mori Arinori visited Okinawa, followed in November by the Prime Minister, Itō Hirobumi, and the Ministers for the Army and Navy, in turn. As previously mentioned in Chapter One, Mori was the man who had pointed out Okinawa's military value to the Japanese government, and Itō, too, on the occasion of his Okinawa inspection, composed a poem saying: 'Who knows the plans for a militant nation's frontier defences? Hardships [and] management occupy one's mind' (Yoshihara 1970, p. 187). The month after Prime Minister Itō's inspection, an imperial portrait (*go-shin'e*) was bestowed upon the normal school ahead of the rest of Japan, and Mori, in turn, lectured all over Okinawa on the need for education, and especially emphasised the importance of education for females, who would become the mothers that would raise the next generation. This encouragement of female education later came to exert a subtle influence upon the anti-Japanese attitude of intellectuals on the Okinawa side, but I will elaborate on this point in a later chapter.

In this manner, education became a major policy item in Okinawa, but this naturally was not a colourless and transparent general education, but one in which the cultivation of being 'Japanese' was given emphasis. In 1890, a 'frontier defences' special educational discourse targeting the strategic areas in terms of national borders, including Oki, Tsushima, Okinawa, Ogasawara and Hokkaido, which were home to people who, 'not understanding their own part as worthy members of the nation, often harboured the will for dual subordination' was published in the mainland Japan journal, *Kyōiku jiron* (Contemporary comment on education). In it, the 'language of nationals' was taken as 'being greatly related to the maintenance of a country's security,' and it was asserted that because residents of borderlands 'often harboured the will for dual subordination due to differences in customs,' 'sentiments of reverence for the emperor and patriotism' should be fostered through language unification, reform of customs, cultivation of morality, and the like. Originally, in December 1879, also, immediately after the abolition of domains, the Okinawa Prefectural Office had spelt out the aims of upgrading schools in a petition to the Ministry of Finance, saying: 'Making language and customs the same as mainland Japan is the most urgent task in administering this prefecture, and of course there is no other means but education' (Tsuji 1890).[3]

This does not mean, however, that education in Okinawa progressed easily. As previously mentioned, though the government had opened a facility for learning spoken Japanese immediately after the establishment of prefectures and expanded it into a normal school, there were not many applicants, and so naturally school fees were not charged, and students were even provided with lunch money and subsidies. As Okinawa was territory which Japan had seized in full anticipation of incurring an economic deficit, it arguably did not refuse to carry out such an education policy as this, either, for the sake of procuring it as a stronghold for national defence. Yet even so, the school enrolment rate was exceptionally low, and throughout the early 1880s, when the average elementary school enrolment rate in other prefectures was in the fortieth percentile, that in Okinawa was around three percent. Even though Japan's standard language was taught at schools from the beginning, it was not something of any use in everyday life in Okinawan society. Schools were nicknamed '*Yamato-ya*' (Yamato being a traditional name for mainland Japan (*naichi*), and '*-ya*' commonly signifying a business establishment), and a rumour apparently arose that if children were allowed access to 'Yamato learning,' they would abandon their homes and be spirited away by the *naichi* (Ōzato 1969, p. 49).

Such a reality was known to the government, also. Even as late as 1894, fifteen years after the abolition of domains and establishment of prefectures, Ichiki Kitokurō, Secretary in the Ministry of the Interior, reported on the condition of the Japanese language which they had taken the trouble to teach at schools, saying: 'Once they quit school, [Okinawans] will end up forgetting the greater part of the scant Yamato (= Japanese) language that they have memorised, as well, because those who mix with them are all people who do not understand the Yamato language.' While stating: 'There is no other way to break down Okinawans' obstinate thinking and make them assimilate to the civilisation of *naichi* except to rely on education,' Ichiki was pessimistic, saying: 'The goal of assimilating Okinawans by means of education will be impossible to achieve unless at least one generation has passed' (Ryūkyū Seifu 1965d, p. 508).

What greatly altered such circumstances, however, was the Sino-Japanese War which erupted in that year of 1894. Not only for the pro-Qing samurai class, but also for ordinary Okinawa residents, the defeat of Qing brought about a huge psychological transformation, to the extent that even among children, playing Japanese soldiers and singing Japanese military songs reportedly made a clean sweep of all other games. Amid such a situation, the school enrolment rate leapt to forty-five percent for boys and seventeen percent for girls, and by 1907, even overall, it had climbed to ninety-three percent (Naha Shiyakusho 1978, p. 249, 146; Asato 1983, p. 160).

Furthermore, the shape of education unfolded there in Okinawa came to form the model for the kind of education that the Empire of Japan would implement in areas newly incorporated under its domination, such as Korea and Taiwan.

'Civilisation' and 'Japanisation'

In 1896, the Okinawa Prefecture Private Education Society listed items such as the following as points for educational reform.
1. To incite loyal determination and national ideology
2. Strictly [to enforce] the manner of bowing in order to make [people] respect order.
3. To impose oral examinations and to set up conversation clubs at higher elementary schools with the objective of popularising the standard language (*Ryūkyū kyōiku* 1896)[4]

Ryukyu education, the journal in which these resolutions were published, was launched immediately after victory in the Sino-Japanese War, and became a pivotal journal for educators in

Okinawa at that time. Let us take a look at their thoughts from the teachers' contributions below.

As can be seen in the above items, it goes without saying that importance was placed at that point upon cultivation of loyalty towards and assimilation into Japan. This was not a task of fostering loyalty in people who were already 'Japanese,' though, but of taking people who had no self-consciousness of being 'Japanese' and remoulding them into 'Japanese.' An 1896 contribution from a certain teacher, for example, argued as follows.

> The children of this prefecture ... not knowing of Tokyo Prefecture in the Japanese Empire, Aomori Prefecture in the Japanese Empire, Kumamoto Prefecture in the Japanese Empire, and Okinawa Prefecture in the Japanese Empire, ... make a distinction between mainland Japan and Okinawa as separate things by using the terms 'mainland Japan (*naichi*)' and 'Okinawa,' and, imagining Okinawa to be one great world [in itself], they have a tendency to view mainland Japan as a foreign country.

According to this teacher, not only children, but their parents and guardians, too, 'at the sight of people who arrive from the various prefectures in mainland Japan, deem the latter to be Japanese, deem themselves to be Okinawans, and, in the upper samurai class, they particularly call themselves Ryukyuans,' and lack an awareness of being 'Japanese' (Kawakami 1896 [1970], pp. 35, 34).

The need to eliminate this condition was advocated for reasons of national defence, as might be expected. According to this teacher, the reason why Okinawa residents' lack of self-awareness of being 'Japanese' was problematic was that 'people who ally themselves with the various prefectures in mainland Japan and understand that they generally have a duty to be useful in defending the country in times of emergency are quite rare' (Kawakami 1896 [1970], p. 33).

All educational subjects could even be said to have had the aim of cultivating 'Japanese' equipped to be state resources for such national defence. This naturally applied in the case of the Standard Japanese 'conversation' course and moral education (*shūshin*) classes which cultivated loyalty to the emperor, and, as I will later elaborate, history education comprised content which emphasised that Okinawans had been part of 'the Japanese' since ancient times, and in geography education, making children conscious that 'this prefecture (= Okinawa) is the strategic fortress for our southern gateway' was made the objective (Ōshiro 1896 [1978], p. 25). The descriptor *sayaku*, meaning 'locking the door' came to be applied not only in respect to Okinawa, but to Hokkaido and Taiwan, as well. Even songs taught at schools pointed out the parameters of the Empire of Japan and duty in regard to national defence, such as the fourth verse of *Hotaru no hikari*, set to the tune of 'Auld Lang Syne,' whose Japanese lyrics were composed in 1885.

> The far reaches of Chishima, and Okinawa, too,
> Will be the home guard for Japan;
> Do your duty, valiantly, in the provinces where ye will go,
> My dears, fare ye well.

After the Sino-Japanese and Russo-Japanese Wars, 'Taiwan' and 'Karafuto (Sakhalin)' were reportedly sung instead of 'Chishima' and 'Okinawa' in this song. Even now, the song is still sung at Japanese schools, and all Japanese know it, but this fourth verse has stopped being sung since the end of the Pacific War.

Such emphasis upon national defence obligations was something that reflected a sense of danger on the Japanese side towards the partitioning of Asia by the West. A 1900 discussion published in *Ryukyu education* states as follows:

> The implantation of a national consciousness into prefectural residents is a major issue for education in the prefecture ... Without a concept of what one calls our nation, the rise and fall of the nation will be nothing more than somebody else's problem ... It being an occasion when other states are surely vying to divide up our neighbouring countries, and the nation will surely be very busy from here onwards, without the thoughts of prefectural residents being thus, this very thing should even be called the nation's great problem. I believe that in education in the prefecture, that thing for which we should expend the most efforts is the enforcement of spiritual Japanisation upon the more than 400 thousand inhabitants of this prefecture, that is, not only in outer appearance, but also in their innermost thoughts (Ōshiro 1900 [1978], p. 88).

It goes without saying that the 'spiritual Japanisation' mentioned here means the cultivation of loyalty. According to an 1898 contribution in *Ryukyu education*, 'Our Okinawa, which from time immemorial was viewed as a foreign land and regarded as useless, [has become] a vital location worthy of being the empire's southern gateway,' and though it could not 'possibly become a source of wealth for the empire, it being poor in products,' the value of 'Okinawa in national terms' far exceeded that of such an 'Okinawa in material terms.' For that reason, 'Okinawan people were obliged to consider themselves as equipped to be the advance guard for defence of open seas,' and 'to sacrifice their very life for the sake of the Emperor' as 'a member of the Japanese nation' (Honda 1898 [1978], p. 57).

Concurrently with such cultivation of loyalty, the 'civilising' of [backward] Okinawa was also emphasised. Among the existing customs of Okinawa, those that were regarded as particularly barbaric were the men's hairstyles and the women's tattoos, and many cases are recorded of students at the teacher's training school and so on having been forced to cut their hair. Moreover, guidance in such hygienic aspects as improving physique, bathing in bathtubs of disinfectant, and clothes washing, as well as the injection of a modern work ethic such as 'the idea of diligence,' 'a mind for savings' or 'an enterprising temperament' were also added to the list of important points.[5] These were things that were necessary for remoulding Okinawans into modern nationals.

However, more than such emphasis on 'civilising,' priority was persistently given to 'Japanisation.' A certain teacher stressed that while the civilising type of 'knowledge and skills' education was also necessary, 'in the education of this prefecture's children, the thing which should be deemed most important is national education – in other words, making them exhibit a spirit befitting Japanese nationals.' The reason was that unless this were accomplished after having injected 'a spirit befitting Japanese nationals' into them, 'even if they were endowed with a multitude of knowledge and skills, this would be no different from lending troops to the enemy, and providing food to a thief' (Kawakami 1896 [1978], p. 33).[6] If loyalty could not be expected of them, then teaching modern knowledge would conversely only be an obstacle to governance.

Moreover, overemphasising 'civilisation' was accompanied by a certain kind of risk. In European countries' colonial education, the touting of 'civilisation' was able unproblematically to become the justification of domination by suzerain states. For Japan, however, civilisation meant something belonging to the West. If they only touted 'civilisation,' then the residents' admiration and loyalty possibly would turn not towards Japan, but towards Europe and America, which were Japan's enemies. For that reason, teachers had to insist that 'our country's education is Japanism, not Westernism' (Andō 1897b, p. 42).

This issue also surfaced in the reform of customs. As part of the reformation of Okinawa's [barbarous] customs, making people swap Okinawan dress for Japanese-style clothing was encouraged. However, the question could naturally have arisen as to why they had people change to Japanese-style rather than Western-style clothing in Okinawa's case, though a changeover to Western dress was currently being advocated in mainland Japan. A 1901 editorial in *Ryukyu education* addressed this issue thus:

> Just as the reform of female clothing in *naichi* (mainland Japan) and the reform of female clothing in this prefecture have mutual resemblance, there is a huge difference in their meaning. What these days is often being advocated in *naichi* is something akin to changing *naichi* women's clothing into something different, and making it imitate Western-style clothing a little. Nonetheless, the reform of female dress in this prefecture, needless to say, consists of discarding the traditional costume of this prefecture and approximating the clothing of the women of *naichi* ...
>
> Furthermore, the principal reason as to why a discourse on the reform of female dress has arisen in mainland Japan is that with the current clothing, the *obi* sash is ridiculously large, the sleeves are long, and, in that condition, it is inconvenient in actual practice, but in our prefecture it is not so. Our prefecture's clothing is behind the times; it looks bad, and it is not proper for people to use an exotic clothing system while being in the one Japan; just as we make the standard language (*futsūgo*) our tongue, this means we have to make regular dress (*futsū-fuku*) our clothing ... Speaking from a practical point of view, because the present clothing of this prefecture is more convenient, there is no necessity to don such inconvenient dress from *naichi*, but still, it is clear that the drive to make Okinawan dress into *naichi* wear is namely not for practicality, but for the unification of customs (Andō 1897a [1970], p. 96).

However, utmost efforts were made to prevent such a contradiction between 'civilisation' and 'Japanisation' from being realised.

While '*naichi*' and 'other prefectures' claimed distinctiveness vis-à-vis the West, they conversely brandished universality vis-à-vis Okinawa.

The word which expressed that subtlety was the adjective '*futsū* (regular/standard).' As can also be seen in the above quote, the terms 'Japanese-style clothing (*Wasō*)' and 'Japanese language (*Nippongo*)' were avoided, 'regular dress (*futsū-fuku*)' and 'standard language (*futsūgo*)' or else 'national language (*kokugo*)' being used instead. These were not unconscious nicknames: this was clearly conscious use, as in: 'Ordinary people's naming female students' clothing *Wasō* (Japanese costume) must be called a slip of the tongue' (*Ryūkyū kyōiku* 1899d [1970], p. 83). As Okinawa was part of Japan, the usage of differentiating terms such as 'Japanese language' or 'Japanese dress' was not allowed. For the Okinawans, moreover, 'Japanese dress' and 'Japanese language' were merely foreign culture that was unrelated to themselves, but they were taught that 'regular dress' and 'the standard language' were a norm to which they had to assimilate. These were not the 'civilised clothing' or 'civilised language' which were universal all over the world, but they were a presence that compelled assimilation within the national borders.

This was striking in the case of language, for example. An argument for survival of the fittest, as in: 'The Ryukyuan language is a dialect that must without fail be eradicated at a certain time for the sake of a superior language, the so-called standard language,' a general-purpose argument, as in: 'We must make efforts to spread a national language understandable to the general population, and replace a dialect that cannot have currency,' and a civilisation argument that said, by making Okinawans learn Japanese, 'we must facilitate the gaining of contemporary civilised knowledge by the people of this prefecture, and increase their happiness' were cited in *Ryukyu education* (Hoashi 1903 [1970], p. 125; Shimaoka 1897, p. 4). However, the language which was the strongest in the world, was understandable to 'the general population,' and which made it easy to learn civilisation, ought to have been English or French, not Japanese.

For that reason, while Japanese was emphasised as being a universal language, in regard to 'the West,' it was applauded as being a special regional language: 'Travelling around in the West, when I encountered a perfect stranger, if I met someone with whom I could converse by means of our country's language, even someone I did not know, I would feel somewhat nostalgic, just as if I had met my own parents. This is because we use the same national language.'

There were limits to the grounds for Japanese language education if the logic of 'civilisation' alone was employed. In the end, the fostering of loyalty and national integration were given more weight as the mission of Japanese language education, with such arguments as that 'the national language,' rather than 'civilisation' was 'the lifeline that maintains sentiments befitting members of the nation, or in other words, national ideology,' or 'If we liken the state to the human body, language is what perhaps should be called the blood, and the non-unification of its language may be called an illness of the state' (Shimaoka 1897, p. 4; Hoashi 1903 [1970], p. 124).

Remodelling of the historical perspective

What was even more emphasised in regard to education in Okinawa was the restructuring of the historical perspective. This meant, in other words, the injection of the recognition that Okinawans historically and racially were 'Japanese,' which the Japanese government had advocated from the time of the Ryukyu Disposition.

In 1897, after the Sino-Japanese War, six years before it had been decided that elementary school textbooks would be published by the government nation-wide, the Ministry of Education had already been compiling an ordinary elementary school reader for use in Hokkaido and Okinawa. The following year, the Conscription Law was brought into force in Okinawa. (Its application to Miyako and Yaeyama was four years later.) And in this reader, in line with the government's official view, it was written that Minamoto-no-Tametomo had crossed to Okinawa, his son had become the first lord of the islands, had propagated the *kana* syllabaries and 'rectified customs,' and had enriched the livelihood (*Okinawa-ken yō jinjō shōgakkō dokuhon* 1897–99 [1982].[7]

Furthermore, in the same way as the Japanese government, those educators whose activities centred upon contributing to the journal *Ryukyu education* also were adopting the view that despite Okinawans having been 'Japanese' from ancient times, they had simply 'forgotten that they deserved to be Japanese' because communication with mainland Japan had been interrupted since the

Middle Ages. For that reason, their education was deemed not to be one that newly implanted national consciousness, but one that 'made them revert to the Japanese of ancient times by departing from the evil customs from the Middle Ages' (Kawakami 1896 [1970], p. 34; Ōshiro 1900 [197], p. 88).

A 1901 contribution to *Ryukyu education*, purporting to 'hear that there are some' among the young people of Okinawa 'who claim that Okinawa is not in the empire, and who are regarded as barbaric by people of other prefectures,' asserted:

> One should of course not entertain doubts about Okinawa being of the Japanese race. The lineage and type of its language has already proved this, the greater part of its customs have already proved this, the greater part of its literature has already proved this, and the residents' facial features and skeletal structure also prove this. Even so, people mistakenly judge themselves to be a different race, and conversely suspect their qualifications for being Japanese. Okinawan education can correct this bad habit. One only wishes that the government will encourage Okinawan education by funding it from the national treasury, principally rectify this bad habit, and make Okinawa [a place] befitting a true Okinawa (Okinawa 1901 [1970], p. 98).

To 'make Okinawa [a place] befitting a true Okinawa' meant, of course, restoring it to the condition of 'the Japanese' of ancient times. Here, it was considered that the existing culture and customs of Okinawa were nothing other than things which had been implanted by 'China,' and the more that Okinawans discarded these, the more they would return to their original shape.

Such a historical perspective also performed the function of covering up the contradiction between civilisation and 'Japanisation.' Together with the saga of the Tametomo crossing, it had become accepted opinion among educators that Okinawan customs and language were 'relics from the age of battles between the two clans of Genji and Heike, 700 years before.' As for the disparity between mainland Japan and Okinawa, it was believed that 'it is certainly not that there is a disparity, but merely the difference between other prefectures in mainland Japan which have progressed, and this prefecture, which has not progressed.' As long as the 'progressed' form of Okinawa was 'mainland Japan (*naichi*),' assimilating to '*naichi*' would, in short, equate to 'progress' for Okinawa (*Ryūkyū kyōiku* 1899a [1970], pp. 77, 35).

In 1899, *Ryukyu education* carried a statement of intent saying that the then prefectural governor, Narahara Shigeru, had awarded an Okinawan-born female teacher who took the initiative in wearing *naichi*-style 'regular dress.'

> Even though we no longer harbour doubts about [Okinawan residents] comprising the same race (*minzoku*) [as *naichi* people], nevertheless, among the three urban prefectures and forty-three other prefectures, there are still people living with the old attitudes of the Genji and Heike, and cannot help but say that their own prefecture alone exists; others change day by day and renew month by month, and, moreover, their progress, too, makes them each gallop around almost to the same extent, and, finally, they end up either erroneously deeming other prefectures to be different races from the nation's, or recognise them as some unusual tribe. If that be the case, in other words, nowadays it is the role of enlightened persons to plan for unification through rectifying this, and do away with errors such as letting people mistake other prefectures as being different races from the nation's; and, moreover, to be the ones to stop our three urban prefectures and forty-three other prefectures from regarding [Okinawans] as a strange race. Additionally, as for the appearance of parents of the prefecture's children and so on being dissimilar to that of other prefectures, their mentally regarding other prefectures as foreign countries, and being unable to be candid while at the same time not being able to generate the concept of the nation, themselves thinking that Okinawa is a large country ... for that reason, revolutionising customs and attempting to unify the state by those means is the most important task for educators (*Ryūkyū kyōiku* 1899c [1970], p. 79).

Here, it is pointed out that the remoulding of customs is not simply assimilation, but part of the cultivation of 'Japanese' who have loyalty towards the Empire of Japan. Moreover, Okinawa seeming as if it were a different race, and its having insufficient consciousness of being 'Japanese' were, after all, merely the result of its 'progress' lagging behind. As such, here, too, escaping from the gaze by which it was seen as 'a different race,' and becoming 'Japanese,' were deemed to be 'progress' for Okinawa.

A similar line of reasoning was applied to language, as well. The Okinawan language was not an independent language, they merely having 'created a sort of dialect like Ryukyuan due to natural topography and artificial divisions.' In addition, while 'language in other prefectures of *naichi* [was] now advancing and changing by leaps and bounds,' Okinawa Prefecture was thought to be in a state where 'language was not evolving, and the language of ancient times was extant.' Further, as long as Okinawan was nothing more than a dialect of Japanese, it was not worth being preserved, the reason being that, if we defer to the words of the Secretary of the Prefectural Office: 'There might be some people with the biased opinion that the Okinawan language is also a characteristic of Okinawa and that there is a need for its preservation, but in my mind, as much of it is a corruption of the standard language, it is natural to suggest it be amended to Standard Japanese' (Hoashi 1903 [1970], p. 125; Shimaoka 1897, p. 35; *Ryūkyū kyōiku* 1904 [1970], p. 133).

Moreover, as an essential element constituting such a worldview, the discovery was carried out of 'people regarded as a more exotic race' and people more backward than Okinawa. A study serialised in *Ryukyu education* from 1895 by Nitta Yoshitaka, a teacher at the Okinawa Prefectural Ordinary Teacher's Training School, could be called a typical example.

Nitta's point of view may be called a compilation of the aforementioned worldviews of teachers in Okinawa. In other words, Okinawans were 'racially Japanese, being our fellow countrymen,' and the objective of education was 'to create a splendid army of nationals' (Nitta 1895, pp. 48–50).[8] His characteristic, however, was to have collectively described the image of Okinawa he needed to repudiate with the word 'Ryukyu.'

According to Nitta, it was a mistake to suggest that the name 'Okinawa' was one dating from after annexation and that 'Ryukyu' was the original nomenclature. 'Okinawa' had been its very name since ancient times, and 'Ryukyu' was nothing more than a 'Chinese name' that had been attached for the several hundred years hitherto, and the change of name to Okinawa was 'mainly intended not to replace it with something new, but to return to the old days of its original nomenclature.' Furthermore, 'Ryukyu' was the name of 'the unchaste woman called dual subordination,' who 'lowered her head to China and bowed to China, taking no account of our national polity,' and where there 'existed an ingrained, corrupt morality, stubbornly sticking to old ways,' while 'Okinawa' was the name 'restored to the chaste woman who would give birth to the sons of Japan' (Nitta 1895, pp. 48, 49). The question was of identifying what area should be regarded as a more different race than Okinawa.

The place that Nitta targeted was Taiwan, which Japan had only recently seized due to the Sino-Japanese War. According to Nitta, 'Okinawa had since our ancient times been our fellow countryman, of the same tribe, and not an outsider,' but '[places] like Taiwan' merely 'depend on a different race and separate tribe having newly become an adopted child in our family.' Moreover, he said that the motivation for his advocating the abolition of the 'Ryukyu' denomination also stemmed from 'being unable to bear to call [Okinawa] by a name that makes it similar to a different race and separate tribe, in the same way as Taiwan and the like' (Nitta 1895, pp. 50, 52).

Furthermore, as the series progressed, Nitta began to advance the idea that 'Okinawa being in all respects the Okinawa Islands of our Japan, ... the country of Ryukyu has its own separate land.' According to him, in old documents from China's Sui Dynasty (581--619 CE), the inhabitants of 'Ryukyu' were believed to have the custom of eating human flesh, and 'those called Ryukyuans' were nothing but 'a barbaric race for whom Sui and Tang people and the like had absolute contempt.' By contrast, Okinawa was 'obviously ethnically Japanese (*Nihon minzoku*), racially Japanese, Japanese compatriots, with common ancestry with Japan,' and he 'guaranteed that they were not the descendants of a barbarous race such as would eat human flesh.' In addition, based on a newspaper article at the time from the Japanese side which said that the 'wild tribespeople (*seiban*)' of Taiwan were practising cannibalism, he claimed that 'the country of Ryukyu which appeared in the Sui Dynasty's *Historical Record* and *History of Northern Dynasties*' referred to Taiwan (Nitta 1896, pp. 411, 413, 414; 1897, pp. 103, 107).

According to Nitta, the name Ryukyu having been attached to Okinawa meant that 'those crafty Chinese ... had appropriated the name Ryukyu from elsewhere, and sullied the honour of Okinawa.' He further stated:

> In order not to allow this prefecture to be seen in the same light as Taiwan in terms of our national polity, I have no choice but to try also to inquire into this, with the aim of elucidating the racial properties

of the samurai class and commoners in the archipelago, washing away the shame of their having previously been treated in the same way as foreigners, and completely actualising their status and rights as befitting Japanese ... This prefecture is of course Okinawa; and as for its qualifications for being Japanese, unlike the Ryukyu of old, which equates to present-day Taiwan, it is naturally endowed with elements that ought to make its status and rights complete in terms of the national polity (Nitta 1897a, pp. 104, 108).

This says that 'Ryukyu' means Taiwan, which is the home of a 'barbaric race,' and the purpose of historically substantiating that Okinawa is not 'Ryukyu' is to prove that Okinawans are 'Japanese,' and to save them from discrimination. As I noted in the Japanese edition of this book, at that time, there was a proposal to incorporate Okinawa, along with Taiwan, under the jurisdiction of the Ministry of Colonial Affairs, but having heard that rumour, Nitta protested, saying that this was 'utterly deplorable,' as it would be treating Okinawa, which was 'authentic Japan,' as a colony. Nitta himself hailed from Japan proper, but he dubbed himself 'Nitta the resident of Okinawa,' and in his personal opinion, that assertion probably was for the purpose of having Okinawa acquire 'status and rights befitting Japanese,' and represented good intentions 'for the people of Okinawa' (Nitta 1897b, pp. 198, 200, 201). Moreover, the theory that the 'Ryukyu' mentioned in Chinese archives referred to Taiwan later became fixed, and has been handed down to the present day.

The tendency to keep on highlighting the idea that Okinawa is 'Japanese' by pointing out an opposite number deserving of exclusion was not Nitta's alone. In an editorial in *Ryukyu education*, it was emphasised that as a contrast to Japan, of which Okinawa had become a member, there was 'a lack of people's public loyalty' in 'China, Korea, and so forth.' In addition, in relation to education about Korean history, it stressed that Koreans lacked loyalty to the state, and Okinawans therefore must not emulate them (speech by Tsubaki Taiichirō in *Ryūkyū kyōiku* 1899 [1970], p. 78; Kawakami 1896 [1970], p. 36). The insertion of such a worldview, as I shall discuss in the next chapter, went on to give rise to a later tendency for Okinawans themselves to exclude Taiwanese and Koreans in order to become 'Japanese.'

Little by little, such education for 'Japanisation' started to show results. In *Ryukyu education* in 1904, as 'the situation of standard language (*futsūgo*) in school districts,' it was reported that children 'had come to be extremely ashamed when they used the local tongue by mistake.' The popularisation of *futsūgo* in itself was by no means easy, however, and in this report, also, there was a series of accounts such as: 'There appear to be a few females aged around twenty and the like – non-attendees at school – who playfully use the standard language,' or 'One hears that there are times when, being drunk on alcohol, parents and older brothers use the standard language,' so the level of acceptance can be understood to have been not at all extraordinary; but even then, the fact that consciousness of being ashamed of the 'local tongue' was permeating among children was a huge change (Shinohara 1904 [1970], 140, 141).

For national defence purposes, the necessity arose to implement education for fostering loyalty, even if it meant wasting the national budget; and language and history as 'Japanese' was implanted. As I elaborate in Volume 2 of this book, the 'Japanisation' of Okinawa was begun in this manner, and the success of this educational policy went on to exert an influence upon latter-day Taiwan and Korea, as well.

3 The Creation of Okinawan Nationalism

'Even the Okinawans themselves of those days did not really know whether they were Japanese or Chinese. As such, situating them as an ambiguous populace was convenient for [Satsuma's] smuggling operations' (Hattori et al. 1974b, p. 417).

This is how Ifa Fuyū,[1] called the Father of Okinawan Studies, described Ryukyu under Satsuma rule.[2] Born in 1867, Ifa was the first native of Okinawa to have studied at Tokyo Imperial University, the Japanese government's highest institution of learning. He was engaged in the identification of the position of Okinawans in linguistic terms, and the writing of its history. For this, Ifa is known as the founder of Okinawan Studies, and he himself became an important figure in the history of Okinawa.

Residents of that area which had been newly incorporated into the Empire of Japan continued to be placed in a position of being 'Japanese' and not 'Japanese' as suited the 'convenience' of the ruling side. In contrast to Korea and Taiwan, where legal demarcation from *naichi* (Japan proper) never disappeared, general discrimination tenaciously remained in Okinawa's case even though unification had been completed by 1920.[3] Throughout this, residents of Okinawa came to grope for identity amid their relationship with 'the Japanese.'

In this chapter, I focus upon Ifa Fuyū as a person who endeavoured to create Okinawan 'national' identity. There have been many studies on Ifa, but my rationale for taking him up here is to verify the response of the minority side that had been placed in the kind of ambiguous situation mentioned above. There, one can see a vacillating form commonly visible in Okinawan people, which I discuss in Volume 2 of this book.

The model for incorporation into 'the Japanese'

In Chapter Two, I mentioned how Okinawans were made the target of national education as 'Japanese,' and the Conscription Law enforced. Here, I will make a quick investigation into transitions in its institutional aspect, including suffrage.

The rise of a resident-led movement for the acquisition of franchise in Okinawa can be traced back to 1898, the same year as the enforcement of the Conscription Law. At the time, Okinawa was under the dictatorship of a prefectural governor who belonged to the Satsuma Clan, Narahara Shigeru; and in economic aspects, as well, Okinawa was monopolised by Satsuma and Osaka merchants. Governor Narahara declared: 'I think that in places corresponding to colonies which have differing histories and popular sentiment, such as Taiwan or Okinawa, we must carry out government gradually, awaiting the development of civic wisdom' (Narahara 1902 [1995], p. 148). Unlike Taiwan or Korea, however, Okinawa was an area where the Japanese constitution was in force, and had no legislative power or the like. It was not impossible for people to relocate their registered domicile, either, but under circumstances where, '[among bureaucrats,] Party A would plan abrupt reform without considering the particular popular sentiment, and, without thorough investigation of the pros and cons of regional customs, determinedly carry out bizarre policy based on *naichi* ... [while] Party B, holding completely opposite political views to the former, would wholly overturn what Party A had implemented without examining its merits and demerits, and intently resurrect the former customs,' the situation was similar to that of Korea and Taiwan, where '[they] enforced a police state, and subjugated the people' (Takahashi 1915, p. 39).[4]

In Okinawa at that time, a special system was laid down in the taxation and local government systems under a policy for the conservation of old customs; neither a prefectural assembly nor village councils existed; and even after the Diet was established in mainland Japan, no elections for Lower House members were carried out. In those circumstances, the one who mounted a campaign for acquisition of suffrage was a man called Jahana Noboru, a commoner back home from studying in Tokyo who was Okinawa's first graduate with a Bachelor's degree from an imperial university.

What one needs to bear in mind is the social position of this Jahana. In Okinawa in the early days of Meiji (from 1868), when the children of the samurai class were disinclined even to share the same classroom as commoners, schools were called '*Yamato-ya*' and shunned by the offspring of the samurai class, but Jahana, of commoner origin, reportedly was a child who enthusiastically attended school. In the period when Korea was a protectorate, as well, school fees were waived and meals provided at schools run by the Japanese side, as in Okinawa, but these likewise did not attract children from the upper stratum, and were disparagingly dubbed '*hinmin gakkō* (schools for the poor).' Jahana went to Tokyo to study, having been a top student at a 'school for the poor,' and was admired by commoners in Okinawa as a 'symbol of the smashing of the class barrier,' but he is said to have been 'treated as a rebel' by members of the samurai class who yearned for the Ryukyu Dynasty.

The form of the movement which this Jahana launched was also one that differed from that of the traditional samurai class. Jahana chose the direction of gaining suffrage as 'Japanese,' not the revival of the Ryukyu Dynasty or the like. For him, who had originally been in a position to be discriminated against by the samurai class under the Ryukyu Dynasty, this was probably a natural choice.

The thing which became the most problematic in granting suffrage to Okinawa was that the taxation system remained as it had been in Ryukyu Dynasty days, and land consolidation had not been carried out, so the private ownership of land was not determined. As suffrage in the Empire of Japan at that time was a limited suffrage in which eligibility for political participation arose according to the amount of tax paid, Okinawa was deemed to be an area excluded from the the Lower House Members' Electoral Law for the reason that the amount of individual tax could not be determined as long as private property remained unclear.

After his return home from studying in Tokyo, Jahana worked at the prefectural office, but he was forced to resign for having opposed Narahara. While carrying on his campaign locally on the one hand, he went to Tokyo in 1898 and made a direct appeal for the dismissal of Governor Narahara to the Home Minister, Itagaki Taisuke. He took the course of requesting the help of the *naichi* Popular Rights forces against the oppressive rule of a dicator who could not be countered within Okinawa.

Itagaki showed sympathy, and privately consented to Narahara's dismissal, but the Cabinet collapsed and the plan came to nothing. Jahana, accompanied by kindred spirits, travelled again to Tokyo, and engaged in lobbying activities seeking the Okinawan implementation of the Lower House Members' Electoral Law. Though this gained the favour of such Popular Rights politicians as Hoshi Tōru, Shimada Saburō and Takagi Masatoshi, in the Diet arena, it was blocked by the government's stance that until land consolidation had been established, enforcement would be impossible. Though the intent to implement the Electoral Law in Okinawa was written into the law to a slight extent through the efforts of friendly Diet members, only a nominal amendment, namely that the effective date was 'to be instituted by Imperial ordinance' was achieved in 1899. Moreover, the quota set at this time for Okinawan Diet members was a mere two persons, and Miyako and Yaeyama were excluded.

After this, the movement met a tragic end, Jahana becoming mentally ill due to excessive despair, but while admittedly only a formality, the accomplishment of having had Okinawa written into the Lower House Members' Electoral Law was not trifling. In 1907, a group from Miyako and Yaeyama petitioning for the implementation of suffrage went to Tokyo to the Imperial Diet, and Okinawan newspapers also advocated the granting of suffrage. Behind this lay not only the fact that land consolidation had been completed and the taxation system put in order, but also that for the government, the administration of Okinawa was in the black, some three million yen annually being paid into the state coffers from Okinawa, and more than 2,000 Okinawan-born soldiers had participated in the 1904 Russo-Japanese War. In other words, the awareness had burgeoned that Okinawa had made a contribution to Japan both economically and militarily, and that the granting of rights was a matter of course. In addition, the fact that Okinawans killed in action in the Russo-Japanese War amounted to a tenth of their troops also resulted in promoting the establishment in Okinawan residents of a consciousness of being 'Japanese.'

This was clear in the petition which the delegation from Miyako and Yaeyama submitted, as well. This petition emphasised that 'amid the joy of bathing in the Emperor's benevolence ... education, also, having spread to the general population, human knowledge has greatly advanced; the Conscription Law, also, has long since been allowed to be implemented, and [we] have also devoted [ourselves] well to the duty of military service.' Moreover, continuing on from there, the petition begged for grant of the right to participate in 'nonpartisan constitutional government' as 'Japanese,' stressing that they had 'discharged their responsibility as befitting Japanese nationals, and that there was nothing lacking in the least in their qualifications or competency' (*Ryūkyū shinpō* 1907 [1995], p. 411).

Local Okinawan newspapers of the day, also, in championing suffrage, emphasised that Okinawa was a 'pure part of the ancestral land,' asking: 'Are not the [Okinawan] people (*minzoku*) the same as the pure [members] of the ancestral land? This is so in language, and in lifestyle.' As the Lower House Members' Electoral Law had already been implemented in Hokkaido, and suffrage had been tentatively granted to Ainu, as well, the local Okinawan newspapers laid emphasis on the fact that Okinawa was the sole region in '*naichi*' not to have suffrage. The positioning of Okinawans as 'Japanese,' which the Japanese government had promoted when it seized Ryukyu and which it had instilled by means of national education, was thrown back unchanged as a claim by the movement seeking rights as 'Japanese,' though it was something which showed blatant discrimination towards people other than 'the Japanese,' saying such things as: 'Okinawa [was] not a ceded territory like Taiwan in the first place, [but] one which had belonged to Japan since olden times,' and 'The people are not of the Ainu type.'

At the culmination of such moves, in 1912, an Imperial ordinance for enforcement of the Lower House Members' Electoral Law in Okinawa was finally issued. It goes without saying that local newspapers welcomed this, expressing the gratitude of 'Okinawan prefectural residents for the favour of His Sacred Majesty' (*Ryūkyū shinpō* (1911 [1965f]; *Okinawa mainichi shinbun* 1911 [1995], p. 469). What must be noted here, however, is that it was the Home Minister, Hara Takashi, who made a request to the then prime minister, Saionji Kinmochi, for a Cabinet meeting on this issue where he presented a draft ordinance.

In the prior stage to this grant of suffrage, along with preparations being made towards a local government system identical to *naichi* – a municipal system having been implemented through an Imperial ordinance promulgated in 1907, and a prefectural system in 1909 – elections for prefectural assembly members began to be held, albeit in the anomalous form of indirect election by local municipal council members. In the document which Hara presented to Saionji, the reason given for the implementation of the Electoral Law was that already in Okinawa 'a municipal system, of course, and something akin to a prefectural system, also, has already been implemented several years ago, and now civilisation has greatly progressed,' which implies that he regarded the maintenance of a local government system as a preparatory stage for the right to vote in the Imperial Diet. Moreover, in a document entitled 'Private views on the rule of Korea,' which Hara handed to the Governor-

General of Korea, Saitō Makoto, in advocating that the Korean local government system be changed to one similar to that of *naichi*, he stated: 'It should be appropriate to carry out measures like those in Okinawa Prefecture, which began from an irregular system' (Ryūkyū Seifu 1965d, p. 948).[5]

It is very interesting to superimpose the process of the legal incorporation of Okinawa into 'Japan' upon the attempted institutional reforms in Korea and Taiwan in which Hara was involved. 1907, the year when the implementation of the municipal system was promulgated vis-à-vis Okinawa, was one in which a reform plan for the Taiwan Government-General drawn up by a Kyoto Imperial University professor of law, Okamatsu Santarō, was stymied due to Hara's opposition; and also a year after Gotō Shinpei, considered to be the father of Taiwan's modernisation, left for Manchuria. It was also the year in which Hara, overcoming the resistance of the Army, laid to rest a plan to grant legislative power to the Administrator of Karafuto Prefecture (southern Sakhalin).

In addition, while stating in his diary in April 1911 that '[We] should not regard Korea as a regular colony, and should finally have it assimilate into Japan,' Hara wrote: 'In the future, [it] will probably want something like a prefectural assembly, and will wish to produce Diet members, too, but I would not mind in the least, it being just like Ryukyu or Hokkaido in *naichi*.' Immediately following this, he set out on an inspection of Korea, and wrote: 'It is more and more certain that it would be easy to implement the same kind of education for Koreans as for Japanese, and have them assimilate to Japan' (Hara 1911, pp. 114, 131).[6] What is important here is that at this point in time, no Lower House members having yet been elected from Okinawa, if he were going to make Okinawa a precedent for the granting of suffrage, in line with these words, then it was necessary to enforce the Lower House Members' Electoral Law. Eleven months after this diary entry, Hara put this into practice.

As we have already seen, it was not at all unusual to cite Okinawa as a precedent for the assimilation of Korea and Taiwan. However, if we exclude exceptions such as the legal scholar Ume Kenjirō, this was in the form of a precedent for the cultivation of loyalty, not a precedent for institutional equality. If we consider the role which Hara played in the enforcement of the Electoral Law in Okinawa, then it was not mere lip-service for him to have mentioned Okinawa in 1911 in discussing the grant of suffrage to Korea. In his document requesting a Cabinet meeting relating to the enforcement of the Electoral Law in Okinawa, as well, what Hara raised as the reasons for granting suffrage was that the local government system had been developed and 'civilisation' had 'greatly progressed.' He did not touch upon cultural assimilation, loyalty or suchlike, and here, too, one can glimpse his direction.

Such a policy towards Okinawa did not necessarily represent an existing line for the Japanese side. In 1908, the year prior to the implementation of the prefectural system, a plan emerged to incorporate Okinawa under the direct control of the Taiwan Government-General, and newly establish a 'Nan'yōdō (South Seas Road, analogous to Hokkaidō=North Sea Road), and Narahara expressed his agreement. Such a plan had apparently existed informally before that, as well, and according to reports in Okinawan local newspapers, when the amalgamation of Okinawa and Taiwan was suggested, Gotō Shinpei, who had the mistaken idea that Okinawa was still being run at a loss, vetoed the plan, and it fizzled out – such was the sequence of events. I will discuss the plan to include Okinawa under the jurisdiction of the Ministry of Colonial Affairs at the time of Taiwanese possession in Volume 2 of this book. Colonial policy scholar Yamamoto Miono penned an essay entitled: 'Ryukyu: the malformed child of mistaken colonial policy,' discussing Okinawa from the perspective of colonial policy.[7] This plan to newly establish Nan'yōdō was not realised in the end, but at the stage of the first decade of the 1900s, the question of whether Okinawa would be subsumed into 'Japan' was still fluid.

For Hara, the series of preparations for the local government system and the granting of suffrage as their culmination can be seen as being perceived as a model when incorporating Korea and Taiwan into 'Japan.' The 1912 enforcement of the Electoral Law was one which allowed only two Diet members, with Miyako and Yaeyama excluded, but in May 1919 the Electoral Law was amended once more, the quota was lifted to five, and suffrage was granted to Miyako and Yaeyama, also. In succession, all special systems were scrapped in the local government system, as well, and in this aspect, too, it became identical to *naichi*.

In Okinawan history, it is appraised as being 'the time when the true abolition of feudal domains and establishment of prefectures occurred,' and it is deemed to be the moment when Okinawa became 'Japan' in both name and substance, as it were (Higa 1970, p. 458). That May in 1919 was two months after the March First Independence Movement in Korea, and was the time when Hara, as Prime Minister, was engaged in reform of Korean rule, as I discuss in Volume 2 of this book. Of course, even after this, discrimination against Okinawans in general continued, and though not once prior to the end of the Pacific War was anyone Okinawan-born appointed as prefectural governor (each prewar governor being appointed by the central government, rather than chosen by public election), it could be said that a tentative institutional equality was achieved.

After Taiwan became a Japanese possession, Okinawa's significance as a bastion of national defence halved, and it ceased to be a presence with utility value for the Empire of Japan. As previously mentioned, a petition for grant of suffrage was made from Okinawa to the Imperial Diet, but it was ignored, which suggests that it was of no concern whatsoever to the Japanese government. If Okinawa had not been positioned by Hara as a model for administrative reform in Korea and Taiwan, it is not impossible to imagine that either suffrage would not have been granted, or it would have been substantially delayed. After the local government system was put into shape, thirty years on from the abolition of feudal domains and establishment of prefectures, in three years the right of political participation in the Imperial Diet was tentatively granted, but Korea and Taiwan were left as they were for the entire period, without having been granted suffrage even after land surveys and the organisation of the local government system.

Assimilation in Okinawan eyes

Before launching into an investigation of Ifa, it is necessary first to offer a rough explanation of the circumstances of the Okinawan press from the period in which he shaped his ideology.

Ever since the defeat of Qing in the First Sino-Japanese War, Okinawa's pro-Qing faction had almost ceased to exist, and the discourse of assimilation into Japan had thrived in the critical arena centred upon *Ryūkyū shinpō*, which had been Okinawa's main newspaper from mid-Meiji. It is well known that Ōta Chōfu, editor-in-chief of this *Ryūkyū shinpō*, stated in a 1900 talk: 'If one were to enumerate the urgent tasks of Okinawa nowadays, from first to last they would be to emulate other prefectures. To go to extremes, this means emulating other prefectures even as far as their manner of sneezing' (Hiyane and Isa 1993, pp. 277–278).

However, the discourse of assimilation from the Okinawan side differed somewhat from that of the ruling side. For example, in a 1903 editorial, Ōta wrote as follows:

> In my consideration, there is no question apart from: 'How can we make Okinawa Prefecture as strong as other prefectures?' If, by retaining our hair in a (conventional Ryukyuan) *katakashira* topknot and tying on an *orari* sash, we can compare favourably with the people of the whole nation, I will be compelled not to recommend cutting our hair. If we can compare favourably with the people of the whole nation through knowledge of the Four Books and Five Classics [of Confucianism], then I will not go so far as to encourage new education, either (Hiyane and Isa 1993, pp. 289, 285).

Ōta says that the aim is to 'enhance the power of Okinawan prefectural residents,' and 'the premier means to accomplish this aim is, namely, assimilation.' Here, assimilation is a means to an end, not an end in itself.

Though Ōta was advocating assimilation on the one hand, his sense of rivalry and hatred towards the 'Yamato people' was fierce. He describes 'Yamato people (Japanese mainlanders)' as 'ones who view the people of Okinawa as slaves, in the same manner as European races regard American or those primitive African natives, [and] who harbour the notion of a colony vis-à-vis this prefecture.'

While holding such consciousness, the reason for Ōta's having advocated assimilation was his awareness of Okinawa's predicament, that is: 'it being a region that comprises no more than one percent of the whole country, it cannot possibly preserve its traditional customs with only such a degree of strength.' In other words, 'if preservation is impossible, then the paths we should follow are these two [alternatives]: either to assimilate of our own volition, or to let things follow their natural course – in other words, the two [alternatives] of acting proactively, or acting passively.' However, passive assimilation would have meant leaving the then current ruling situation as it was, and 'being governed by the principle of survival of the fittest, one would have to feel some measure of disadvantage.' Moreover, even while proposing 'harmony' between the 'Yamato people' and the Okinawans, at the same time what he asserted was thus: 'The harmony which I advocate is harmony in equality, not one in which I call for prefectural residents to submit meekly to [the Yamato people] and avoid a clash of sentiments' (Hiyane and Isa 1995, pp. 58, 59; 1993, p. 270).

Behind such acknowledgment by Ōta was the failure of the Kōdōkai (Society for Public Unity) incident that took place in 1896, and in which he also participated. This incident involved the collection of more than 70,000 signatures by the Ryukyuan former samurai class in a petition to the central government to deploy a special system differing from that of mainland Japan, installing as prefectural governor the former Ryukyuan king, who had been escorted away to Tokyo at the time of the Ryukyu Disposition, and establishing a prefectural assembly. In its prospectus, this petition prescribed becoming 'pure imperial subjects' with the Ryukyuan king in the lead, but in material terms, it was none other than something that demanded Okinawan autonomy with the Ryukyuan king as its chief – to borrow a phrase from Ifa Fuyū, 'a kind of special system, like Ireland.'[8] While Northern Ireland remained British territory, Free Ireland came to have its own Executive Council and legislature in 1922, and Ifa's comment is based upon this.

1896 was a time when Qing was defeated in the first Sino-Japanese War, and hopes for the resurrection of the Ryukyu Kingdom through the power of Qing had already petered out. Furthermore, the 70,000 signatures arguably brought together the greater part of Okinawa's adult males at the time, and could be said to have been the final wager for members of the former samurai class. However, this movement met with rejection from the Japanese government, and ended in failure. Moreover, one of the factors in its failure was its leaking in a scoop by a newspaper reporter while in progress, and there was criticism that rather than autonomy, it should promote reform of the system in similar regions in *naichi*. A letter of thanks was sent to the reporter by the aforementioned Hara Takashi (Hattori et al 1976a, p. 394), who is thought to have wanted Okinawa to be granted suffrage as 'Japanese' rather than being given autonomy.

It was after the end of such a movement to gain autonomy by the former samurai class that a suffrage request was made by the commoner Jahana Noboru. Given that prospects for the realisation of resurrection of the Ryukyu Kingdom and special autonomy had already been dashed, it was unthinkable for the Okinawan side, including Ōta, for there to be any way forward except to acquire equality as 'Japanese' through assimilation.

However, apart from the demands for acquisition of equality, there was yet another causal factor in the heightening of the assimilation discourse. This was the viewing of assimilation as an opportunity for 'civilisation.'

Ōta's example does show, however, that he found much to criticise in conventional Okinawan customs. Unnecessarily ostentatious feast days and funeral rites, and 'class-related evil practices' which separated the former samurai class from commoners were among the things he raised as a target of criticism.

Above all, what he deemed 'the first thing that must be rectified in this prefecture' was the lowness of the traditional status of women. As targets of reform, he listed such things as the abolition of the custom of concubinage and red-light districts, and the diffusion of female education, and lamented that many of the formerly class-bound ways of dressing and speaking, also, survived among women (Hiyane and Isa 1993, pp. 255–261).

The expounding of assimilation into Japan as the encouragement of 'civilisation' was something that was also being carried out in the pages of the journal *Ryūkyū kyōiku* (Ryukyu education) mentioned in Chapter Two. When 'civilisation' and 'Japanisation' came into conflict in *Ryukyu education*, though, arguments which clearly prioritised the latter were expressed. However, Ōta stated that because there were 'many quite unsightly things among the customs of other prefectures,' he did not 'suggest combining both good and bad,' and he asserted that in some cases, it was 'definitely necessary to make reforms in a Western manner, in one bound.' His discourse of assimilation was also one that called for reforming 'uninteresting things, appealing to humanity and appealing to the sensibilities of Western civilisation,' from Okinawan customs to social-status discrimination, the status of women, and so on (*Ryūkyū shinpō* 1898b [1965f], p. 15; Bōkan 1899 [1965f], pp. 31, 33).

In the pages of *Ryūkyū shinpō*, which had Ōta as its editor-in-chief, there can be found articles which, while superficially extolling assimilation, actually argue for the acquisition of equality as 'Japanese' and the promotion of civilisation. In 1898, for instance, the paper criticised the payment of special allowances only to those employees of Naha Post and Telegraph Office who were 'people from other prefectures,' calling for the abolition of discrimination with the rationale that 'both people from other prefectures and from this prefecture alike are subjects of the Japanese Empire.' The next year, moreover, when criticising the tyranny of police officers who had arrived from the mainland, it proposed that the 'right of bodily safety' was 'something that the constitution guaranteed,' and that this kind of 'barbaric vice' which went against an 'atmosphere of civilisation and freedom' was 'something unlikely to exist in other prefectures.'[9] These could have been said to have stemmed from the discourse of assimilation having functioned as a means of obtaining equality.

However, the aspect of the Okinawans' discourse of assimilation which they had had as a means to an end was gradually lost. In time, the tension of staking their own identity as a way of realising political objectives vanished, and assimilation itself turned into their own goal.

There were several determining factors present. Firstly, in late-nineteenth-century Okinawa, the dividing line between 'civilisation' and 'Japanisation' tended to be lost. As I elaborate in Volume 2 of this book, in 1920s Korea and Taiwan, due to the development of means of communication, a tendency for 'civilising' elements to be directly imported from the West appeared, even if these were not learned from Japan; but in Okinawa at that time, the route for importation of 'civilisation' was limited to via *naichi*.

Even Ōta, who was sensitive to the demarcation between 'Japanisation' and 'civilisation,' said: 'By calculation from the state of affairs in the world, something such as trying to reform this prefecture is an outrageous hope. What I urge of prefectural residents these days is to have them go abreast of each of the regions in *naichi*, and to have them cast off the status of the subjugated,' and he regarded the seeking of 'civilisation' outside of the boundaries of 'Japanisation' to be impossible in the near term. He cited the 'two conditions of "non-deviation from the spirit of the national polity" and "having to go along with the general trends of the world" as the 'major principles for construction of the new Okinawa,' but there was a great possibility that the balance between the two would crumble, and incline towards 'Japanisation' (Hiyane and Isa 1993, pp. 271–272, 262).

Furthermore, this setting of 'civilisation' as a goal naturally led to many conventional Okinawan customs being regarded as 'barbaric.' Ōta criticised Okinawa's *moashibi* (outdoor social gatherings of men and women) as being 'abominable barbarism,' and, having proposed the 'establishment of civilised clubs,' later ended up advocating that 'it is the natural course of events that the more refined [Okinawa] becomes, the more mainland-style it will be, and will end up conforming to the whole country.' Articles in the *Ryūkyū shinpō*, also, came to carry such descriptions as: 'Very few of our old or ancient rites are ones that we developed uniquely to these islands, most being ones that were inherited, having come from the mainland or else from China,' and claimed that they 'wished the prefectural authorities would exercise strict control in regard to travel [outside the islands] by tattooed women,' for the reason that they would be 'regarded with a scornful eye by people of other prefectures' (Hiyane and Isa 1993, pp. 256, 257, 259; *Ryūkyū shinpō* 1916 [1965f], p. 57; *Ryūkyū shinpō* 1900 [1965f], p. 696).[10]

In fact, it was in a talk proposing the promotion of female education as part of 'civilisation' that Ōta articulated his call for assimilation even to the extent of 'sneezing.' The extreme discourse of assimilation which he expounded on that occasion was probably also one in which, being irritated at Okinawa's backwardness, he urged residents to 'awaken and arise.' At the same time, though, in this talk Ōta especially emphasised that women's 'external appearance' differed from that of Yamato, saying: 'In order to make this prefecture similar to other prefectures, firstly we must of course remove the idea of *naichi* from the heads of the people of this prefecture, and also remove the notion of Ryukyu from the heads of people from other prefectures; yet the way things are, the imposition of a kind of special view of Ryukyu will be unavoidable' (Hiyane and Isa 1995, p. 59). As a result of the standard of civilisation being set at 'other prefectures,' its being differentiated from 'other prefectures' was immediately perceived as meaning that Okinawa was regarded as 'barbaric.'

Ōta stated that there was conflict between 'conservatism and progressivism' in Okinawan society, saying: 'I always stood in the progressive camp and fought hard' (Hiyane and Isa 1993, pp. 276, 277). Personally, he probably thought he was not hoping for servile submission to Yamato, but simply for Okinawa's 'progress.' But even Ōta was slave to the sphere comprising the binary opposition schema which the ruling side had established, namely the choice between 'assimilation = civilisation' and 'anti-assimilation = barbarism.'

Yet another causal factor in his making assimilation his own objective was that the discourse of assimilation which ought to have been advocated as a positive act for improvement of the situation by personal effort underwent an about-turn at some point, and transformed into a logic that regarded insufficient effort towards assimilation to be to blame for the circumstances. The article below, which was carried in the *Ryūkyū shinpō* sometime later, in 1916, tells of the distance from Ōta's earlier discourse of assimilation.

> One sees that there are prefectural residents who take the holding of a kind of discriminatory view towards the people of this prefecture by those from other prefectures to be unjust, and generally resent this. While we also tentatively take this to be not unreasonable, upon dispassionate consideration, we think that the residents of this prefecture ought to shoulder the majority of the blame. Even though the customs and language of prefectural residents have gradually been improved, when we compare this to other prefectures, however much we might regard things with a biased eye, we cannot match the others. Even though there might be something within their spirit that provokes an overflow of national sentiment, women's clothing and ordinary prefectural residents' language, in particular, cannot possibly arouse the same kind of feeling in well-bred people from outside the prefecture. These are grounds for us to assume that prefectural residents should carry the greater part of the responsibility for making people of other prefectures harbour discriminatory feelings (*Ryūkyū shinpō* (1916 [1965f], p. 697).

The practice of calling Okinawans 'people of this prefecture,' as used here, was one that had become fixed due to the word 'Ryukyuans' having come to be recognised as discriminatory. The expression 'other prefectures,' also, was one that had spread because of the demand for adopting nomenclature indicating that Okinawa was one prefecture of 'Japan,' and not a name intimating, in other words, that it was a country called 'Ryukyu' in opposition to 'Japan proper (*naichi*),' in order – to borrow a phrase from Ōta – to 'remove the idea of *naichi* from the heads of the people of this prefecture.' Moreover, the logic that attributed discrimination to insufficient efforts towards assimilation steadily encroached upon the interior of Okinawa.

In such circumstances, Okinawans' discourse of assimilation also changed to a discourse on discrimination towards Korea, Taiwan, the Ainu, and so on, in like manner to that of the teachers in *Ryukyu education*. As I discuss in Volume 2 of this book, in a similar situation to that of colonists from mainland Japan in Korea, a craving for rights as 'Japanese' had given rise to claims emphasising their difference from non-'Japanese.' Ōta stated: 'Okinawa is by no means a new territory of Japan.' He emphasised that Okinawa was 'Japan,' not a 'colony,' and vehemently opposed the regarding of Okinawans by the Yamato side as an 'inferior breed with a rebellious air,' 'the same as the Ainu of Hokkaido.' Articles in the *Ryūkyū shinpō*, too, described the people of agrarian villages who amused themselves with *moashibi* and Okinawan music as 'barbaric in the extreme,' saying that they 'made one think of the wild tribespeople (*seiban*) of Taiwan' (Hiyane and Isa 1993, pp. 266, 337; *Ryūkyū shinpō* 1898a [1965f], pp. 16, 17). The writers themselves had probably never seen any Ainu or 'wild tribespeople,' but these expressions continued to be employed as descriptors for things which they regarded as 'barbaric.'

This set the scene for the so-called 'Jinruikan (Hall of Mankind) Incident' of 1903. This referred to the 'exhibition' of live Koreans, 'wild tribespeople,' Ainu, Okinawans and the like in a project by anthropologists from the Anthropological Society of Tokyo in conjunction with the Fifth Industrial Exhibition held in Osaka. At this time, Ōta expressed fierce opposition, writing in a *Ryūkyū shinpō* article: 'This is tantamount to regarding me as a *seiban* [or] an Ainu,' and he emphasised the progress of assimilation, saying: 'The civilisation of this prefecture is advancing in great strides now, and in such things as clothing, also, eight or nine out of every ten males have already made amendments, while as for females, the number changing their way of dressing is tending to increase year by year' (Hiyane and Isa 1995, p. 213).[11]

What is noteworthy in Ōta's argument against this incident is his insistence that in racial terms, Okinawans were 'Japanese,' with the words: 'Though there are some among the people of other prefectures who generally point at people of this prefecture and deem them to be a special race within Japan, we do not acknowledge there to be any difference at all in their innate qualities.' Moreover, the year after the Hall of Mankind Incident, while newspapers posed the question: 'Has it been forgotten that our ancestor is none other than Chinzei Hachirō Tametomo (= Minamoto-no-Tametomo), the august descendent of Qing and the Japanese emperor whose name is celebrated?,' articles that welcomed the territorial expansion of the Empire of Japan appeared (Higa 1904 [1965f], p. 223). These both meant that the assertion circulated at the time of the Ryukyu Disposition from the Japanese side that Okinawans were 'Japanese' permeated into the heart of Okinawa.

Before the advent of Ifa Fuyū, self-definition had been brewed in this manner on the Okinawan side, and Ifa took on the expectations of academically supporting such vague public opinion, and went on to develop Okinawan Studies.

A dual minority

Ifa Fuyū was born into a Naha samurai-class family in 1876. While Shuri, the seat of the Ryukyuan Royal Government, was the political centre, the port city of Naha was the trading and economic centre. Along with the abolition of the Ryukyuan Royal Government, the Japanese government set up an Okinawa Prefectural Office in Naha, and in the present day, Naha has become Okinawa's political and economic centre. When Ifa was young, however, the Shuri samurai class used to look down upon Naha.

Ifa's family apparently was so antagonistic to Yamato that they would never rent a room to a Yamato person, but his mother reportedly submitted an application for admission to the primary school attached to the teacher's training school on her own initiative, and had her son enrol.

There is one thing about Ifa's early childhood that cannot be overlooked in relation to his historical perspective on Okinawa in later years, namely that, along with his changing schools, he alone left his family and was sent to board in Shuri. According to his memoirs, at this time Ifa was astonished that 'the pupils' language and customs were different from Naha.' Moreover, 'at that time, the lingering remnants of the class system remained, and children of the former samurai class scorned the commoners' children,' and the pupils from Shuri jeered at Ifa the 'outsider,' always calling him 'Naha-*jin* (Naha-ite), Naha-*jin.*' Having been a cry-baby and a spoilt child from the start, Ifa grew homesick, and said that at night he usually 'dreamt of nothing but home,' and returning to Naha on weekends was what he 'looked forward to more than anything' (Hattori et al. 1976, Vol. 10, p. 93).

We of the present day have our attention drawn by the conflict between Yamato (the nomenclature employed by the Okinawan side when referring to Japan as a separate country) and Okinawa, and tend to overlook disparities within Okinawa at the time. The language difference was not insignificant, to the extent that though Ifa eventually coped with school life by assimilating to the Shuri dialect, when he returned to Naha his family and others heard his Shuri accent and laughed to hear the 'weird tone' that his speech had assumed. As for the vestiges of the class system, even in the case of people like Higaonna Kanjun, for instance, six years Ifa's junior, and second only to Ifa as a renowned Okinawan scholar of Okinawan history (Hattori et al. 1976, Vol. 10, p. 93), it was said that even after he had reached adulthood, 'whenever his name came up in private conversation, people would question his origins, and would only feel relieved once they had confirmed his class, as in "Ah, he's from the former samurai class," or "Hmm? He's a peasant," and so on' (Arazato and Ōshiro 1969, p. 106). Ifa and Higaonna both ended up conducting academic debate as scholars of Okinawan history in later years, but while Higaonna, who was descended from the Shuri samurai class, had an extremely positive attitude towards the Ryukyu Dynasty, Ifa came to assume a somewhat complex position.

Whatever the case, it is worth noting that Ifa was ostracised as an 'outsider,' and his first counterpart to have overcome this through assimilation was someone hailing not from Yamato, but from the Shuri samurai class. Assimilation does not stop with language – in Naha, for example, there was a custom of holding a ceremony of attainment of manhood at the age of thirteen, but in order to align with the pupils from Shuri, Ifa ended up having his manhood ceremony and tying his hair into a topknot at eleven. It is hard to imagine that such an experience would have stimulated his attachment to the hairdo. Later, at the middle school which Ifa attended, there was an incident in which the Yamato-born deputy principal pressed all to cut their hair, declaring: 'I saw a photograph of American Indians where the pupils all had short hair and were wearing Western clothes, yet it is really deplorable that there are places among middle schools in the Japanese Empire where [pupils] still have the [traditional] hairdo and have an unkempt air,' at which he forced the pupils to cut off their topknots, but Ifa describes in an extremely matter-of-fact manner the way pupils from the samurai class refused to cut their hair short and ran around trying to escape (Hattori et al. 1976a, p. 97).

In ethnic studies in sociology, it is known that among minority groups, it is minorities within those minorities that readily respond to pressure from the majority to assimilate. This is because the experience of oppression within minority society leads to the fostering of a comparative stance in relation to culture.

Even though such discord existed, it appears that the reason for education by the Japanese government having permeated into the pupils in its own way was, after all, that assimilation was accepted as 'civilisation.' It is hard to tell whether hair-cutting constituted 'Japanisation' or 'civilisation,' but after the hair-cutting incident, this deputy principal made the middle-school students give examples of things in Okinawa that should be reformed. The examples consequently raised included hairdos, the tattooing of females, early marriage, female education, language, and the policy of preserving old customs. Language and the like could be said to represent assimilation, but it can be appreciated that overall, the middle-school students were thinking to amend those things among Okinawa's existing customs which they considered were opposed to 'civilisation,' such as the status of women. A school trip to the Kyoto–Osaka area was held in the period when Ifa was a fourth-year student, and the students said that, having been 'shown so many [examples of] material civilisation that they felt giddy,' they had hatched a desire to continue on to an even higher level of schooling; and *naichi* was, more than anything else, perceived as 'civilisation' (Hattori et al. 1975b, pp. 363, 365).

For that reason, the pupils rebelled against anything which they regarded as the enforcement of assimilation that ran counter to 'civilisation.' A well-known example is the middle-school strike incident which occurred immediately after the First Sino-Japanese War. During the Sino-Japanese War, such was the tension in the air in Okinawa – a front-line base – that denizens from Yamato organised volunteer militia groups in preparation for attack by Qing naval fleets, and middle-school pupils, including Ifa, were made to do firing practice. Moreover, in the summer of 1895, the Okinawa Prefectural Ordinary Middle School Regulations were amended, and it was decided to demote English to the status of an optional subject. The pupils vehemently objected to this decision, and it escalated into an incident led by Ifa and his fellows in which applications to quit school were submitted by all of them.

Kodama Kihachi, who originally was a principal at the time and also headed the School Affairs Section at the Okinawa Prefectural Office, had already in the previous year excited the animosity of pupils by advocating the abolition of the English course, saying: 'You all are in pitiful circumstances, having to go so far as to learn English in spite of not having a perfect command even of the standard language (*futsūgo*).' The *de facto* decision to abolish the English course which was implemented via such a train of events was perceived as follows, as expressed in the words of Ōta Chōfu: 'If it merely inspires national spirit, then it is obvious that one can deem the work of education to have ended,' and it being taken as something that 'treats Okinawa as a colony,' support for the strike in Okinawan society and public opinion censuring Kodama increased.[12]

Thanks to victory in the Sino-Japanese War, demonstrations of patriotic sentiment towards Japan and enthusiasm for the standard language had already grown, and there had been applicants to join the military emerging from among the pupils, also. Having judged from such circumstances on the Okinawan side, even if English were abolished and the switch made to education in which even more emphasis were placed on '*futsūgo* (standard language)' and 'boosting national spirit,' Kodama may not have thought that these would invite a backlash. However, though the Okinawan side was advocating assimilation of language and customs on the one hand, they regarded the omission of English – the symbol of 'civilisation' – and the placing of emphasis on '*kokugo* ([Japanese] national language)' and the cultivation of loyalty to be 'treating [Okinawa] as a colony.'

As a result of the strike, which lasted six months, Kodama was appointed to a different position in the Government-General of Taiwan, but Ifa and the others who had played leading roles were also expelled, and Ifa ended up heading for Tokyo in pursuit of educational opportunities. Timid from the start, Ifa apparently participated in the strike at the invitation of kindred spirits after much anguish, and describes his experience at that time as follows: 'I was an exceptionally hesitant youth at that time, but even so, I resolved to become a politician some day and make strenuous efforts for the sake of my compatriots who had been insulted' (Hattori et al. 1974a, p.12). It could be argued that through this incident, he gained a perspective that transcended regional consciousness such as Naha or Shuri, and regarded the whole of Okinawa as his 'compatriots' – coming to a deeper realisation of Okinawan nationalism, so to speak.

Ifa's career after arriving in Tokyo could not be described as smooth, however. While he did graduate from middle school, having transferred in midway, he failed the high school entrance examination a whole three times, and was already thirty when he graduated from Tokyo Imperial University. As his family back home was economically stable, he apparently had no hardship on that front, but during his setbacks he judged his 'own disposition and circumstances' to be unsuited to a politician and changed his ambitions, majoring in linguistics at Tokyo Imperial University (Hattori et al. 1974a, p. 12). In short, his wishes changed from the improvement of politics in Okinawa to the establishment of its collective identity.

There is doubt, however, whether this about-face of Ifa's was necessarily due solely to the reason of his disposition. In a talk on 17 May 1910, he stated that for Okinawa's promising youth, 'however impatient they are today, and however much they campaign, a kind of unwritten rule is that Okinawans will not be granted power in politics or business. Unavoidably, there is no alternative but to extend their capabilities by turning towards unrestrained scholarship,' and he was taken to have 'substantiated that animosity towards Japanese mainlanders stretched as far as scholarship, and though Okinawans, they would be worthy to rival *naichi*, depending on the extent of their studies' (Hekigotō 1910, p. 56). Ifa certainly was the possessor of a disposition that was hardly suited to a politician, but the fact of his social position as a member of such a minority probably cannot be ignored.

Having aspired to seek Okinawan identity in this way, Ifa started to publish essays from before his entrance to high school, and as early as when at university, he came to propose his 'Japan–Ryukyu common-ancestry theory' as a theory of the racial origins of Okinawa. Before inspecting it, however, let us take a look at his respective views on Okinawa and Japan prior to university entrance.

First, he writes as follows about the relationship between Japan and Okinawa in a 1900 contribution immediately before his entry to school (Hattori et al. 1976a, p. 3).

> As Ryukyu is an archipelago interposing between Japan and China, from ages past it always paid fearful attention to the snorts of both countries. It made tributary offerings of its local products to China and received its imperial edicts, in order firstly to gain trading advantages, and secondly to gain its protection, while its demonstrating vassalage

to Japan by means of tributary missions was none other than for the same reason.

From the historical perspective seen here, there can no longer be inferred any necessity for Okinawa to become one with Japan. At the same time, Ifa assessed an article in *Ryukyu education* touting patriotic education towards Japan, as aforementioned in Chapter Two, as being 'gibberish' (Hattori et al. 1976a, p. 5).

It can be inferred from this that Ifa harboured resistance towards Japan, yet he was not of the pro-Qing faction. According to the Ifa of those days, Okinawan history had its basis in the 'mutual rise and fall of Japanese and Chinese thought,' but he himself described Sai On, an eighteenth-century thinker from the Ryukyu Kingdom whom he esteemed as a great man in Okinawan history, as 'a harmoniser of both schools of thought' (Hattori et al. 1976b, p. 229). This implies that his aim was not confrontation between Japan and Qing (China), but unbiased harmony.

I further wish to draw your attention to the fact that not only harmony between Japan and China, but also harmony within Okinawa was being intended. According to this first letter of Ifa's, an 'archipelago ... has to be peaceful, like a family, but sadly this definition does not apply to this place (= Okinawa),' and inside Okinawa, '[they] do nothing but quarrel over petty advantages and disadvantages, and petty interests.' Moreover, if we go along with his theory, then this conflict is a historical one, and while prior to its unification by the Ryukyu Dynasty in the fifteenth century, Okinawa was split into 'the three kingdoms called Chūzan (Mid-mountain), Nanzan (South-mountain) and Hokuzan (North-mountain)' and became war-torn, Ifa claims that 'even nowadays, the walls from the Sanzan ("Three-mountains") era [1322–1429] are thought seemingly to stand in people's hearts still' (Hattori et al. 1976a, p. 6).

From this, one can glimpse the problem-consciousness that became his subsequent basic theme, namely how to guide the conflict between Japan and Okinawa, and that inside Okinawa, to harmony. It goes without saying this reflects Ifa's experience of being a minority in a dual minority sense, so to speak – having fretted over confrontation with Shuri as a Naha-ite, and having been troubled over conflict with Japan as an Okinawan. In regard to the relationship with Japan, in this first letter of his he already had touched upon Basil Hall Chamberlain's Ryukyuan linguistic studies, and later came to present the prototype of his 'Japan–Ryukyu common-ancestry theory' based on this doctrine, but let us look a little further at his opinion vis-à-vis internal conflict in Okinawa.

While at high school, Ifa penned a unique discourse on Okinawans entitled 'The three peoples in Ryukyu.' According to this, Okinawa had had 'at least three waves of racial migration,' and historically 'things like the Sanzan unrest originated from this racial competition.' This means that Ifa at this point was regarding the historical conflict within Okinawa as 'racial competition' (Hattori et al. 1976a, p. 13).

Moreover, according to Ifa at that time, Okinawans in this Sanzan era were 'an uncivilised people fond of brutality, who devoted themselves to strife,' and sustained a bloody state of war (Hattori et al. 1976a, p. 7). Furthermore, it was the Shō family, originating from Chūzan and founders of the Kingdom of Ryukyu, who arbitrated in this conflict. According to Ifa, unification by the Shō Dynasty underwent three stages. Firstly, 'the military power of Shō Hashi simply smashed the divisions between the three "mountains," [then] the foreign expeditions of Shō Toku inspired the spirit of Ryukyu in general,' and finally unification was completed by means of 'Shō Shin's centralised authoritarian rule,' and 'the three peoples were amalgamated for the first time' (Hattori et al. 1976a, p. 13). In other words, 'racial' strife was led to harmony by following a course that consisted firstly of the forced destruction of mutual boundaries by military power, next, the heightening of nationalism through the joint waging of war against external enemies, and ultimately, centralised authoritarian rule and institutional unification.

It goes without saying that these three stages were ones that directly applied to the relationship between Japan and Okinawa. In other words, the stages in which the boundary between Japan and Okinawa was destroyed by the militarily-enforced Ryukyu Disposition, and the spirit of 'Japan in general' was inspired by fighting the Sino-Japanese War together were already complete. Moreover, according to a different article Ita contributed in the same year, it was now time for Okinawans to 'demand their rights as pure Japanese nationals' (Hattori et al. 1976a, p. 9). As we will see later, his concern in Okinawan history always had emphasis placed upon the unification of Okinawa by the Ryukyu Dynasty, and the relationship between Japan and Okinawa, but the unification process in Okinawan history was always taken to the model for unification with the Empire of Japan. For Ifa, researching Okinawan history constituted an act of seeking the key to simultaneous resolution of the two issues of 'internal Okinawan harmony' and 'harmony between Japan and Okinawa.'

This does not mean, however, that Ifa was unconditionally applauding such unification. While on the one hand saying that in the unification of Okinawa by the Ryukyu Dynasty, the populace 'sang the praises of *Sjuitin ganasi* (His Majesty the King of Shuri),' he has handed down a stern judgement upon the Shuri-ites, who were the rulers. It was his theory that in the Okinawa of his day, antagonism among 'the three peoples' had been resurrected, but this was antagonism among the 'Shuri-ites, Naha-ites, and country folk.' Originally, Shuri had been the centre of Chūzan, conquering both Nanzan, to which Naha belonged, and Hokuzan, a mountainous region, and it became the capital of the unified Ryukyu Kingdom. Further, according to Ifa, the Shuri-ites who were the main players in the Ryukyu Dynasty were 'a people crafty in terms of political wisdom and abounding in *esprit de corps*,' who excluded 'Naha-ites' and 'country folk' from politics, and who 'intimidated the Sanzan survivors at will' (Hattori et al. 1976a, p. 14). Naturally, from the seventeenth century onwards, the Ryukyu Dynasty's Shuri samurai class was also placed under the control of Satsuma, one of the Yamato clans, but, according to Ifa, the word '*yukatchu*,' which had referred to the samurai class in the days of the dynasty, originally was one that indicated 'a bunch that became the stooges of the conquerors, and engaged in activity to enslave their compatriots' (Hattori et al. 1975b, p. 280).

Moreover, under such rule by the Ryukyu Dynasty, when circumstances developed in which 'complaints welled from every class in society,' from whence did 'the great strength that could break down the distinctions between the three classes and amalgamate their people' spring? According to Ifa, it was not from within Okinawa, but from this: 'that is, the incorporation of Ryukyu which came from central Japan' (Hattori et al. 1976a, p. 14). In other words, the Ryukyu Dynasty had been abolished by Japan, and conventional regional divisions and class discrimination were on the way to being eliminated. Yet, as we have already seen, Ifa was not lauding the Japan that had carried out such 'amalgamation,' either. In a contribution in the same period, he described Okinawa after 'Ryukyuan incorporation' as a 'colonial age' (Hattori et al. 1974a, p. 229).

Let us sort out Ifa's basic worldview from the above study. In short, within Ifa there coexisted an admiration for and rejection of political power. In his opinion, conflict between 'races (*minzoku*)' would only be resolved by forced unification by martial means, the shaping of a sense of unity through nationalism, and unification in institutional aspects. Even if conflict were once guided to harmony in this manner, though, under the rulers' authority discrimination and control would become fixed. Any power which overthrew that authority would also repeat new domination and discrimination. For Ifa, politics was a Janus-like presence that on the one hand brought about stability and unification, while giving rise to discrimination and domination on the other.

It is conceivable that this kind of worldview might have arisen from Ifa's experiences in childhood. When he was ostracised by pupils from the Shuri samurai class, it was probably a Yamato-born teacher who mediated in that situation, using political power that was greater than theirs. It was at the home of a teacher at the primary school attached to the teachers' college that the young Ifa had originally boarded in Shuri. However, at the same time, Ifa had had to fight against discrimination from those Yamato teachers at a strike at his middle school. And Ifa himself was a person who, even while yearning to become a politician, abandoned the idea because of his own disposition and circumstances. After that, also, he continued to adopt an ambivalent stance towards the Ryukyu Dynasty and Japan, but it is thought that in the background there lay a double-bind of admiration for and rejection of politics.

The intervention of authority becomes necessary in order to mediate in conflict. However, authority breeds domination and discrimination. Ifa was at that time standing amid such a political ideological aporeia. This was something which reflected his position as a twofold minority, unable completely to assimilate either to 'Japan' or to 'Ryukyu,' and he started to engage in the situating of Okinawa in order to resolve that.

The common-ancestry theory as a bulwark

It was from his 1901 letter while at high school that Ifa published the prototype for his 'Japan–Ryukyu common-ancestry theory.' Here, based on the linguistic research of the aforementioned Chamberlain, he asserted that 'the great majority of today's Ryukyu inhabitants' were 'probably descendants who survived after having cut their ties during the great translocation of divine imperial descendants (*Tenson*)' (Hattori et al. 1974a, p. 526).

The essentials of Chamberlain's theory are basically summarised into two points. The first is that the connection between the Ryukyuan language and Japanese is a close one, akin to that between 'Spanish and Italian,' or 'Spanish and French,' and both are assumed to have a common 'parent language.' The other is that based on Japan's ancient *Kojiki* and *Nihonshoki* myths, groups that had this shared parent language are likely first to have landed in Kyushu from the Korean peninsula, and the greater part of them, while conquering the indigenous tribes, carried out an eastern advance known as the eastern expedition of Emperor Jimmu, but some of them moved south and ended up in Okinawa (Hattori et al. 1975c, p. 515). Ifa's describing Okinawans as 'descendants who survived after having cut their ties during the great translocation of divine imperial descendants' was along the lines of this theory.

Again according to Chamberlain, it was Ryukyuan rather than Japanese that more strongly preserved the characteristics of the common ancestral language (Hattori et al. 1975c, p. 515). On this basis, Ifa claimed that Okinawa had a good command of language similar to that in the *Kojiki*, had myths that bore a close resemblance to the myths in the *Kojiki*, and, moreover, preserved many things that seemed to be hereditary customs from Japan's ancient times (Hattori et al. 1974a, p. 525). This was also something that matched the theory circulated at the time of the Ryukyu Disposition and the Japanese annexation of Korea, saying that ancient Japanese customs remained in the territorial areas. Ifa's subsequent theory came to be developed basically along this line.

After this, Ifa entered the Philology Department in the Faculty of Letters at Tokyo Imperial University, which had been established with Chamberlain as a hired foreign instructor, and studied the lectures of Kanazawa Shōzaburō and Ueda Kazutoshi. Furthermore, he became friends also with the anthropologist Torii Ryūzō, and when Torii conducted a survey in Okinawa in 1904, Ifa accompanied him as his guide. Moreover, the study relating to Okinawan history which he had released while a student was also carried in the *Ryūkyū shinpō*, and amid heightened demands for assimilation, expectations began to gather towards Ifa as a personage who would academically substantiate that Okinawans were 'Japanese.'

In 1906, what Ifa published after graduating from Tokyo Imperial University and returning to his hometown was a series in the *Ryūkyū shinpō* entitled 'About the ancestors of Okinawans.' This was reprinted upon the revision of *Old-Ryukyu*, published in 1911, the year after the Japanese annexation of Korea, and became a standard text in prewar Okinawan history.

The theory which Ifa unfolded here could be said to be a fleshing-out of the aforementioned Chamberlain's theory with Torii Ryūzō's research in anthropology and Kanazawa Shōzaburō's research in linguistics. Firstly, speaking from a philological perspective, he cited examples of similarities between the ancient Japanese seen in the *Kojiki* and *Nihonshoki* myths and *Man'yōshū* poetry, and modern Okinawan, offering them as proof of common ancestry. As well, from Kanazawa's research, he advocated that the ancestors of the Okinawans had come south from Kyushu, giving the examples that the original meaning of the word for 'west' in standard Japanese, '*nishi*,' was '*inishi*' (the past), educing the theory that it indicated 'the place that we ourselves have passed through' via the Eastern Expedition of Emperor Jimmu; while in Ryukyuan, by contrast, north is called '*nishi*' (Ifa 1906 [1965f], p. 306; Hattori et al. 1974, p. 44).[13] This of course was nothing more than a reinforced version of Chamberlain's theory that a group which had landed in Kyushu from the Korean peninsula had split into two groups, one proceeding east, and another going south.

Moreover, Torii's survey which Ifa referenced was something like the following.

Torii excavated historic sites on the main island of Okinawa and in the Yaeyama Islands, proposing that Okinawa had once been home to Ainu, and that Yaeyama, in turn, had until about the fifteenth century been inhabited by a Malay race of the same type as the 'wild tribespeople' of Taiwan. According to Torii, the reason why there were so many hirsute Okinawans was that their blood was mixed with Ainu bloodlines. Ifa supported this theory of Torii's, and argued that Okinawa had a scattering of Ainu-like place-names, and he used the idea that 'there are occasionally some among the residents of the Ryukyu Islands who have "Malay" eyes' as proof that they had some Malay blood (Ifa 1906 [1965f], p. 309; Hattori et al. 1974, p. 43).

If we consider that Okinawan public opinion at the time adopted the assertion that Okinawans were 'Japanese,' different from Ainu and 'wild tribespeople,' then Ifa's theory that Ainu and Malay bloodlines were mixed in even looks like a contradictory view. Nevertheless, such a claim of mixed blood was an indispensable element for Ifa's 'Japan–Ryukyu common-ancestry theory,' because in anthropology at that time, starting with Torii, it was decided that there were Ainu and Malay indigenous people in the archipelago in ancient times; a continental race came over from the Korean peninsula and subjugated them, and the Japanese race was formed by a mingling of the three bloodlines (Oguma 1995a). In other words, the theory that Okinawans had mixed bloodlines with Ainu and Malays was nothing bar an assertion that in terms of pedigree, they were of the same composition as the Japanese race.

Moreover, according to Ifa it was precisely the Okinawans that most strongly preserved the characteristics of the common ancestors who had crossed over from continental Asia, and he said that Okinawa was 'a place that supplied those who would study Japan's ancient history or pursue historical research into the Japanese lexicon with unique material.' In this way, he concluded that due to the Ryukyu Disposition, 'now, having had a chance meeting with brothers from whom we cut all ties two thousand years ago, we have come to live our lives under the same government' (Hattori et al. 1974, p. 525; Ifa 1906 [1965f], p. 310).

It is unclear as to what extent Ifa was aware of it, but, as I discussed in *A Genealogy of 'Japanese' Self-images* (2002), Kanazawa and Torii were thinkers who used the 'Japan–Korea common-ancestry theory' to justify the control and assimilation of Korea. On dialects, they extended Chamberlain's theory, saying that the connection between the Japanese and Korean languages was equivalent to that between 'Spanish and French,' and asserted that Korean was 'nothing more than a branch of our own national language, having a similar relationship [to Japanese] as that between the Ryukyu dialect and our national language.' Based on such a theory, the Korean Government-General and the Japanese critical arena advocated that the annexation of Korea was not an invasion, but a restoration. It was also deemed that though Korea had the same ancestors, as a disparity in 'cultural standard' had arisen between it and Japan during several thousand years of living separate lives, the existence of discrimination was unavoidable until it recovered from that backwardness through an assimilation policy. The popular belief that customs from Japan's ancient times were being preserved in Korea was also nothing less than material to verify Korea's stagnation and backwardness.

Seen in this light, Ifa's 'Japan–Ryukyu common-ancestry theory' could be said to have been born inseparably from the 'Japan–Korea common-ancestry theory,' and also appears simply to follow the discourse created by the ruling side. However, his common-ancestry theory included elements that went further than that. In 1905, he made the following claims, based on the premise that Okinawa's myths and tales preserved things from Japan's ancient past.

- We have the need and duty to preserve these spiritual products in every respect
- Still, there are some primary school teachers who, determining from a kind of patriotism, attempt systematically to destroy these precious tales. One must say that this is something which will eventually sever the connection between the Yamato race and the Amamikiyo faction [who are the ancestors of the Okinawans]. This, in other words, is a crime of not knowing that a similarity in myths and legends, along with a similarity in physical constitution, language, and so forth, is something that indicates a close relationship between the two races (Hattori et al. 1976, pp. 33–34. Punctuation added).

Ifa says that the myths and language of Okinawa are 'Japanese' as they stand, and to destroy them would be to destroy 'Japan.' In other words, for Ifa, having 'common ancestry' did not constitute a rationale for enforcing assimilation, but, conversely, could become a bulwark to protect the uniqueness of Okinawa.

Describing post-Ryukyu-Disposition Okinawa in a 1907 talk, Ifa stated: 'Nobody can defy the general trend. People who do not desire self-destruction must comply with it. Japanisation [proceeded] in ones and twos, and, finally, about the time when the Sino-Japanese War was finishing, one began to hear cries of "Long live the Empire!" from the mouths of people who had once abused the Meiji government' (Hattori et al. 1975b, p. 8). In such circumstances, ways of defending the uniqueness of Okinawa were limited, yet in cases where the minority side was robbed of any means of resistance by armed force, naturally, but also by thought, and only had ways of expressing their own standpoint through the language of their rulers, one method they could take was to appropriate the ruling side's discourse in a form advantageous to themselves. Just as the early Black Liberation Movement in America complained of the unfairness of discrimination by using the words of the Bible, appropriating and throwing back the discourse of the ruling side can at times become an effective weapon. Originally, 'common ancestry' was a description used by the Japanese side which continued to position the people of Okinawa, Korea and the like as ones who were 'Japanese' and not 'Japanese,' in order to discriminate against them while assimilating them. Ifa utilised it as an expression indicating a condition of having a different individuality from 'the Japanese' while becoming equal to 'the Japanese.'

In the 1907 talk, he talked about his own image of 'the Japanese,' while deeming the most recent history of Okinawa to be 'a case in point of so-called socialisation in sociology.' According to this, 'Okinawans are a people that were a branch family of the Japanese, who diverged and came to the southern islands prior to the founding of the Japanese nation, but who naturally mutated during two thousand years' – in other words, as a people who are 'Japanese' and not 'Japanese,' they have an 'individuality' that is 'inherent.' Thus far, it is the same as the ruling side's common-ancestry theory, but what Ifa next proposed was that 'members of the nation with composure who embrace people who have all kinds of differing individuality are, in effect, the people of the empire,' and 'if there are any Okinawans who can obliterate their individuality, this in other words would be to have committed spiritual suicide. There is perhaps no greater loss for the nation than this.' These very 'people of the great empire (*Daikokumin*),' who encompass the 'differing individuality' described here, are none other than the image of 'the Japanese' that Ifa asserted (Hattori et al. 1975b, pp. 7, 10, 11).

Such an image of 'the Japanese' was not advanced as a rebellion against the Japanese Empire, but rather as a higher-dimension 'unification.' In a talk in 1909, Ifa stated: 'Nationalists often talk of unification, but what constitutes that so-called unification preserves only the special qualities possessed by a certain section of the populace, and systematically eliminates anything differing from these,' and asserted: 'Action where all people exhibit their respective special qualities and which has some flexibility, including the aforementioned, is what one calls true unification' (Hattori et al. 1976a, pp. 336, 337). According to Ifa, 'respecting other people's individuality will eventually become grounds for being loyal to that nation,' and preferring diverse 'people of the great Empire' rather than a narrow-minded discourse of assimilation was 'loyalty to the nation' (Hattori et al. 1975b, p. 11).

Such an image of a pluralistic 'Japanese' does not lead in the direction of Okinawan independence, just as the Japanese right-wing activist Nakano Seigō's pluralism around 1920 had been a negation of the Korean independence movement (Oguma 2005). For Ifa, all-out confrontation with Japan was not only circumstantially impossible, but also was something that should be avoided from the perspective of his own preferences, he disliking conflict between 'races.' In 1909, he remarked: 'From a young age I felt as if there were a great trench between the people of other prefectures and Okinawans, and I wanted in one way or another to try to fill in that great trench,' which implies that he preferred harmony over confrontation to the bitter end (Hattori et al. 1976a, p. 336). Furthermore, in 1910, he spoke as follows:

> It is questionable whether we – being aware that we are Okinawans – should finish up merely continuing to imitate Japanese mainlanders (*naichi-jin*) ... Though they would do nothing as stupid as bidding farewell and plotting to overthrow the Okinawa Prefectural Office or suchlike, those secret dissatisfactions did make them run in a curious direction at some times, there has been an increase in young men who read socialist books, heart-rending Russian novels, and the like. If this ethos gradually grows, terrifying racial conflict may well arise (Hekigotō 1910, pp. 56–57).[14]

Ifa was apprehensive that if the then-current state of discrimination were allowed to continue, this could later bring on 'terrifying racial conflict.' This was not only something he had feared for some time, but something only expected to turn into an explosive situation which would be disadvantageous to Okinawa from the aspect of political power relations, as well. In his talk, Ifa further stated: 'What until ten years ago was a simple society that merely destroyed its ancient things and imitated Japan has nowadays sent forth shoots and begun to keep its ancient things and cast out imitation.' However, Ifa's ideological task arguably was to make the emergence of 'self-awareness as Okinawans' and the avoidance of 'terrifying racial conflict' coexist. The pluralistic image of 'the Japanese' which he created by rereading the common-ancestry theory was something in order to respond to that task.

Okinawan nationalism and 'common ancestry'

Having thus secured harmony between Okinawa and Japan through the common-ancestry theory, Ifa went on further to advocate Okinawan 'individuality.' In short, he proposed that Okinawans were a unique nation called the 'Ryukyuan race (*minzoku*).'

Ifa's early historical perspective on Okinawa, represented by *Old-Ryukyu*, was one that had a dual structure, so to speak. In other words, while 'common ancestry' with Japan was emphasised on the one hand, the history of the glory of the 'Ryukyuan race (*minzoku*)' was also explained.

According to Ifa, the 'Amamikiyo tribe' established the Ryukyu Kingdom and achieved the 'unification of the Ryukyuan race,' which included Miyako, Yaeyama and so on. Moreover, this 'Ryukyuan race,' as 'stalwart youth of the waves' who ventured out onto the ocean, 'absorbed Japanese and Chinese civilisation and produced their own unique culture,' sending ships as far as Sumatra in South Sea trade (Hattori et al. 1974a, pp. 46, 47). He said that though Okinawans were later placed in a 'slave-like' situation due to invasion by Satsuma in the sixteenth century, and lost their former political triumphs and memories of their overseas advances, turning into something akin to an acorn barnacle that had forgotten how to swim, this was not Okinawa's original form (Hattori et al. 1976a, p. 19).

Ifa remarked as follows on the 'Ryukyuan race':

> The Ryukyu Disposition was truly something akin to having brought lost children back into the care of their fathers and mothers. However, though they were wandering the islands in the China seas for two thousand years, these lost children called the Ryukyuan race ... carried on political life, centred upon Shuri. They left behind the [compilation of songs and poems called] *Omoro sōshi*, which is comparable to the *Man'yōshū*. They went out as far as the vicinity of the Malacca Straits. And they even accomplished the writing of epigraphs on stone monuments in their own language, which was something that their northern compatriots had previously not done. They indeed possessed the capacity to form a national society, materially and spiritually (Hattori et al. 1974a, p. 61).

In this way, Ifa sang of the pride of the 'Ryukyuan race' which displayed greater political ability than 'the Japanese' who were their 'northern compatriots.' He further carried out the work of depicting great men in Ryukyuan history such as Sai On and Shō Shōken, and his series of historical studies indicating the origins of the 'race,' showing proof of its politico-cultural capability, and describing its exemplary great men is indispensable. Ifa's historical studies could be said to be acts that sang of the memory of the lost glory of the 'Ryukyuan race' and created Okinawan nationalism, so to speak. It was the mightiest work that he could accomplish in order to give pride to his 'insulted compatriots.'

However, what differentiated Ifa's work somewhat from the regular process of creating nationalism was that, speaking from the then-current circumstances in Okinawa, it could not be something that extolled confrontation with Japan. Ifa had to fight a battle on two fronts, as it were: harmony with Japan, and the creation of Okinawan nationalism.

In these difficult circumstances, the historical perspective which Ifa took had two components. One was a positive appraisal of the Ryukyu Disposition, such as seen above. For someone who had described post-Disposition Okinawa as a 'colonial age,' this could be perceived even as slightly odd. However, if he were to extol Okinawan nationalism in the form of situating the Ryukyu Disposition as an invasion, that could only have turned into something that advocated all-out confrontation with Japan. In a situation where confrontation with Japan was impossible, describing the Ryukyu Disposition as an invasion ought to have resulted merely in giving Okinawan people an even greater sense of humiliation. Rather than that, it was more effective for restoring pride to his 'insulted compatriots' to express the Ryukyu Disposition as certainly not having been a humiliation.

The other component was that though Okinawans were 'Japanese,' they differed from 'the Japanese.' In other words, while emphasising their 'common ancestry,' Ifa proposed that they were the 'Ryukyuan race.' Only by guaranteeing harmony with Japan by first establishing the frame of 'common ancestry' did it become possible to encourage Ryukyuan nationalism within that frame. Here, too, 'common ancestry' functioned as a bulwark that assured Okinawan individuality.

It should be noted that the expression 'Ryukyuan race (*minzoku*)' apparently had not been in general use in Okinawa until Ifa began to employ it. Prior to modern times, the expression '*minzoku* (race/nation/ethnic group)' was also unlikely to have been used in the sense it is today. For Okinawan public opinion in this period, which had ended up in a situation of extreme fear of being regarded by Japan as a 'special race within the Japanese nation,' an expression such as the 'Ryukyuan race' ought to have been more of a target for evasion. However, after Ifa gave a lecture on Okinawan history in 1906 upon his return home, the expression 'Ryukyuan race' appeared in the *Ryūkyū shinpō* in a form that said: 'It has almost been decided that the Ryukyuan race is of the same root as the Yamato race.' Moreover, this article said that 'because the people of this prefecture are unaware of their own racial worth, they mistakenly think that people born in these little islands and those born in a large country differ in terms of the value of their innate talents,' and 'it is for this reason that they become servile.' It expressed the wish that 'Mr Ifa's project would expand even more in future, and stimulate prefectural residents' sense of self-satisfaction,' and called for the insertion of 'Ryukyuan history' into the primary-school curriculum (*Ryūkyū shinpō* 1906 [1965f], p. 302). In other words, at that time, it was only after Ifa had emphasised the assurance that constituted 'common ancestry' that Okinawan public opinion was able to reclaim enough confidence to take pride in its own 'individuality.'

Ifa also stressed that the 'Japan–Ryukyu common-ancestry theory' was not something that had been imposed by foreigners such as Chamberlain, or the Japanese government, but something that had been proposed by such personages as Shō Shōken and Giwan Chōho, whom he took to be great men in Okinawan history (Hattori et al. 1974a, p. 54). It would not be possible to create Okinawan nationalism if the recognition remained that the historical perspective needed for them to reclaim their pride was one given to them by foreigners or invaders. For that purpose, rightly or wrongly, the logic had to be a restoration of something that had been advanced from the Okinawan side. In a 1911 talk, Ifa stated: 'After all, research on the Ryukyuans will be incomplete and not thorough unless we Ryukyuans carry out research ourselves' (Hattori et al. 1974a, p. 243).

An excerpt dated 29 April 1911 from the diary of Higa Shunchō (1833–1977), a scholar of Okinawan history, tells of how this assertion of Ifa's was received by the younger generation in Okinawa at the time.

> I have read the Ryukyuan race theory. Its conclusion is that [Ryukyuans] are of the Japanese race. This is Mr Ifa's cherished opinion.

However, there is a reason as to why Mr Ifa has made such a theory public. In his mind, for the Ryukyans of today, assimilating quickly to the Japanese is the path to obtaining happiness, and because of that, he argues as follows: men called Shō Shōken, Sai On and Giwan Chōho were by no means pro-Japan. Rather, their thought was to worship China. However, they extolled 'common-race, common-ethnicity' for the sake of the happiness of all. Mr Ifa is of course no China-worshipper, but he has Ryukyuan racial self-esteem, Ryukyans, as civilised people, being a race of which he is not ashamed; nay, a race that has been able to build a special kind of civilisation, or is capable of building one. This is where we defer to our Teacher [=Ifa], and so even we ourselves sometimes say that Ryukyans are not in a position to insist [they have] a just cause. Now, they are saying [Ryukyuans] are of the same race as the Japanese, but praise for the theory of being racially the same as China might [in future] be sung from the mouths of people who appoint the leaders of Okinawa due to some kind of change in the times (Higa 1973, p. 295).[30]

Higa's acknowledgement that Ifa's claim inspired 'racial self-esteem,' even while superficially citing 'common ancestry,' roughly hit the mark.

The connection between exclusion and assimilation

In such a way, Ifa created Okinawan nationalism in difficult circumstances, though two problems accompanied this.

One was his contempt for Ainu and 'the wild tribespeople of Taiwan,' such as in his remark: 'The results of my research tell that Okinawans' eligibility to be Japanese is in itself something different from the eligibility of Ainu and wild tribespeople (*seiban*) to be Japanese.' While this matched the general trend of Okinawan public opinion at the time, at the same time it also had roots in his mistrust of politics. In other words, he claimed that 'if there had not been such [cultural] similarities' between Japan and Okinawa, 'Okinawans' eligibility to be Japanese would be merely political, [just] having a similar connection to the worthiness of Taiwan's *seiban* and Hokkaido's Ainu to be Japanese' (Ifa 1906 [1965f], p. 310; Hattori et al. 1976, p. 34). As long as he recognised that even if unification by means of political power were temporarily achieved, it would later breed discrimination, Okinawans being 'Japanese' had to be something more than merely 'political.'

On the other hand, Ifa's admiration for politics made him situate Ainu and 'wild tribespeople' as objects of comparison when applauding the political capability of the 'Ryukyuan race.' In sketching the history of the 'Ryukyuan race,' he has made such comments as: 'As we have seen, the Ainu and *seiban* did not exist as a people, but coexisted as a nation' (here, Ifa uses the English pronunciation of the terms 'people' and 'nation'), and 'Look at the Ainu. They joined the ranks of Japanese nationals much earlier than we Okinawans. And yet ... aren't they wrestling with bears as always?' (Hattori et al. 1974a, pp. 61, 63).

The word 'people' here indicates a race or ethnic group that lacks political capability, and 'nation' one which has sufficient ability to form a nation. In the then-current racial ideology of thinkers including Gustave Le Bon, the political capability collectively to form a nation, rather than individual ability, was taken to be the criterion for determining racial superiority or inferiority. As I will later elaborate, as Ifa had read the racial theories of the day, starting with Le Bon, it is plausible that he was influenced by these, as well.

The assertion that Okinawan ancestors had subjugated the Ainu and Malay aboriginal tribes and mixed their bloodlines was also proof of the political capability of the 'Ryukyuan race' for Ifa at the time. He said: 'All over Okinawa Island and Ōshima there are legends about the extermination of the demons (hairy people), but these are probably things that allude to word of contact between the two parties [= the ancestors of Okinawans and Ainu].' Furthermore, using Torii's theory as his grounds for argument, having deemed Yonaguni Island to be the place where the Malay residents were, and taking the position that 'such oral traditions as that heroes crossed to Yonaguni and conquered the flesh-eating race ... makes one imagine contact between the [continental] Mongol tribes and Malay tribes,' and he claimed that 'it was the Malay race that had a hearty appetite for human flesh.' This, of course, was something that aligned with the general tone of argument of the day that the 'wild tribespeople' of the 'Malay race' had an 'appetite for human flesh.' Ifa expressed the opinion that 'Okinawans were the offspring of people that had colonised the southern isles from part of Kyushu before the Common Era,' and were 'colonists of ancient times,' but this naturally implied that the Okinawan ancestors were great colonists who had subjugated the Ainu and 'wild tribespeople' (Ifa 1906 [1965f], pp. 310, 309).

Further, in a newspaper series in 1906, Ifa criticised Japanese historian Kume Kunitake's theory that a southern race had travelled north via Okinawa to the Japanese archipelago, even though it was similarly a common-ancestry theory (Ifa 1906 [1965f], p. 305). If this theory were adopted, it would mean that it would be the Okinawans who indeed strongly retained the qualities of a southerly race with a 'hearty appetite for human flesh.' This is why Ifa had consistently advocated the theory that a northern race had moved south via Kyushu and subjugated the Ainu and *'seiban.'*

From a contemporary perspective, it is easy to criticise Ifa's assertion, yet this was constrained by the situation at that time, rather than reflecting Ifa's personal limitations. For Okinawan public opinion of the day, unless there was emphasis not only upon their having common ancestry with 'the Japanese,' but also upon their disparity with Ainu and 'wild tribespeople,' it probably would have been difficult to accept an expression like 'Ryukyuan race.' Moreover, one probably cannot overlook the fact that when they appropriated the common-ancestry theory which was the discourse employed by the rulers, they also allowed the influx of the discrimination incorporated within it.

In addition, this was also a limitation of nationalism itself. In order to form an identity for its own group, not only does nationalism create a history that extols racial superiority creation, but it makes some kind of object of comparison and exclusion necessary. Much minority nationalism satisfies that condition by criticising rulers and making them the target of exclusion, but in Ifa's case, it would not have done to emphasise any difference from Japan. As far as this went, he could only seek his target of exclusion in Ainu and 'wild tribespeople.'

There was yet another problem in Ifa's Okinawan nationalism, this being the issue of assimilation within Okinawa. Originally, he had said that there had been multiple 'races' in Okinawa even apart from indigenous tribes, including Ainu; and these had been unified by the Ryukyu Dynasty, and a consciousness of 'Ryukyu in general' had become established. Ifa described the process of the 'unification of the Ryukyuan race' as follows:

> Formerly, when the Ryukyu government assimilated Miyako and
> Yaeyama, at the same time as sending forth politicians, it designated

women from powerful families in those localities as priestesses and took pains to propagate the ethnic (*minzoku*) religion. The fact that Okinawans led the people of the so-called 'thirty-six islands' and built a kingdom while battling steep, ferocious waves is more than sufficient to prove that they are worthy of being a political populace. On this point, too, they closely resemble their northern compatriots (Hattori et al. 1974a, p. 34).

Ifa says that unification of the 'Ryukyuan race' was completed by dispatching politicians and by means of an 'assimilation policy' which implemented 'propagation of the ethnic religion' (Hattori et al. 1974a, p. 46). According to his 1913 study, the Sanzan ('Three mountains') era in Okinawan history was one of struggle among 'groups which thought they had different blood and different gods,' but 'Shuri-isation' was carried out through rule by the Ryukyu Dynasty, and it is deemed that 'the three tribes merged and formed a nation (*minzoku*),' and 'the gods of the Shō Dynasty ... [became] the gods of the entire nation (*minzoku*)' (Hattori et al. 1975d, pp. 343, 344). This process was something that 'closely resembled' the assimilation policy of the Japanese who were their 'northern compatriots' and substantiated the Okinawans' political capability.

Ifa speaks of this 'Shuri Royal Government's assimilation policy' as follows. Firstly, the Shuri Royal Government proactively intermarried with the various surrounding tribes, introduced new civilisation from Japan and China, and 'at the same time as absorbing much blood and creating a superior species, these conquerors approached those they had conquered, incorporating new thinking of the times.' However, because King Shō Shin, who was its institutional consummator, treated the conquered as 'people of his own country,' and 'used the same laws in order to do this, making efforts to treat his existing people and newcomers the same so that there would be no discrimination between them, they were able easily to enter into one community' (Hattori et al. 1974a, p. 439). Ifa also displayed the recognition that 'according to sociologists' theories, two different races may come into close contact through conquest, but they cannot possibly assimilate. The conquerors always regard the conquered with contempt, and enslave them by every means. The conquered, even while having no choice but to obey, acknowledge not a single thing other than the military force of the conquerors,' and without the institutional equalisation of King Shō Shin, assimilation of the conquered would not have been possible (Hattori et al. 1976a, p. 73).

It goes without saying that this, in Ifa's own way, was probably something that showed a model for an assimilation policy to his 'northern compatriots' who were conquerors. Criticising the Satsuma clan which had governed the Ryukyu Kingdom, he said that 'as the people of Satsuma Province who were the conquerors did not view Okinawans, who were the conquered, as compatriots, but as slaves,' and denied them assimilation to Japanese ways, 'Okinawans of the day began not to know really whether they were Japanese, themselves' (Hattori et al. 1974a, p. 50; 1974b, pp. 4–7). Moreover, in a 1912 study, he described 'the present circumstances of Japan,' which encompassed Korea, Taiwan, the Ainu, Okinawa and the like, as 'having aspects that bear a close resemblance to those in the times of King Shō Shin,' and advocated that 'the Japanese should spiritually unify and amalgamate the surrounding races (*minzoku*),' and, using the reign of King Shō Shin as a reference, become 'even greater members of the nation (*kokumin*)' (Hattori et al. 1976a, pp. 57, 60). Nonetheless, this means that Ifa did take the historical perspective that the 'Ryukyuan race,' which was a minority, was itself formed by means of an 'assimilation policy' pursued by Shuri-ites.

Predictably, two causal factors can be considered in such a view of Ifa's on the 'Ryukyuan race.' One is that there was a tendency for the political capacity of the 'Ryukyuan race (*minzoku*)' also to be measured always by the criterion of their 'northern compatriots,' as Ifa had endeavoured to create Okinawan nationalism within the bounds of the ruling side's discourse. In concrete terms, even speaking from the environment in which Okinawan intellectuals had been educated, there was perhaps no model to be seen in building Okinawan nationalism other than Japanese nationalism. Whenever Ifa lauded the 'Ryukyuan race,' too, he often employed such a description as: 'It displayed capabilities that would not be shameful for the heroic Yamato race,' and Ifa's Okinawan nationalism was shaped as a small-scale version, so to speak, of Japanese nationalism, which progressively subjugated and assimilated the surrounding areas (Hattori et al. 1974a, p. 50). He probably imported into Okinawa the knowledge he gained in Tokyo of the forms of modern nationalism and its means.

As expected, the other causal factor related to the essence of what is called nationalism. In other words, despite being a minority group, it was unlikely to have been homogeneous from the start, and in order for nationalism to be formed as one entity, there ought to have been the necessity to assimilate minorities within Okinawa along with such targets of exclusion as Ainu and 'wild tribespeople.' It is considered that for Ifa, a Naha native, it was unthinkable for a consciousness of 'Ryukyu in general' to be formed naturally without any kind of friction or policy.

That said, at this point in time, Ifa was giving a positive appraisal to this kind of Ryukyu Dynasty 'assimilation policy' as something that demonstrated Okinawans' political capability, as their subjugation of Ainu and 'wild tribespeople' had done. Though the Okinawan nationalism thus created incorporated the tacit assertion that it showed a model for Japan's assimilation policy, it was indeed a martial nationalism in which assessment of military strength and political capability took central place. It was one which reduced and repeated, in chain-fashion, similar exclusion and assimilation to that which Japan had carried out in surrounding areas, including Okinawa.

However, such glorification of nationalism was actually not his true nature. In later years, he came to speak as follows about the Ryukyu Dynasty:

> The Shuri-ites, conquerors who carried out not only economic exploitation, but even the exploitation of blood, reached the first year of Meiji having ingeniously made practical use of the various institutions; and for these three or four hundred years, made slaves out of those they conquered, who outnumbered them more than tenfold (Hattori et al. 1975b, p. 279).

It goes without saying that what is meant here by 'the exploitation of blood' is the promotion of an assimilation policy though marriage.

It is widely known that Ifa said that the Ryukyu Disposition was a 'type of slave liberation.' This expression has been said to be one that criticised rule by Satsuma and justified Japan's Ryukyu Disposition. For Ifa, though, not only was the Ryukyu Disposition something that had to be affirmatively described in order to encourage Okinawan nationalism, as previously mentioned, but one which, even in terms of his own feeling, was also the end of 'enslavement' by the Shuri-ites. In a roundtable discussion in a later year, he went so far as to say: 'It is thought that in the case of ordinary peasants, it was simply that forced labour was abolished and they were grateful for the *Yamato-yū* (= Japanese age). Before the abolition of the clan system, when they were commandeered into forced labour, and made to carry palanquins, and so on, they used to be whipped on the accusation that their way of carrying was bad,' and so the Ryukyu Dynasty was by no means an object deserving unconditional praise (Hattori et al. 1976a, p. 384).

Moreover, in later years, Ifa said that it was in the reign of King Shō Shin that the 'establishment of the class system' took place in Ryukyuan Dynastic times, something that he really regarded as the institutional culmination of the forming of the 'Ryukyuan nation (*minzoku*),' and advocated as the ideal model for government in Korea and Taiwan (Hattori et al. 1975b, p. 279). He extolled the Okinawan nationalist historical perspective which argued that Okinawan ancestors had demonstrated the political capacity to carry out an assimilation policy and national unification on the same level as their 'northern compatriots,' but, on the other hand, this sustained his political view that the completion of unification was also the beginning of discrimination.

Ifa did not publish such a negative Okinawan historical perspective while he was residing in Okinawa, however. The aforementioned written contributions from his high school days were from the time of his studies in mainland Japan, and the above text was published in 1926, after he had left Okinawa and returned once more to Tokyo. In an article he had published in 1908 in an Okinawan newspaper, while assessing Shuri-ites as a 'political populace' that had the power to unify, and Naha-ites as a 'non-political populace' whose members were individually without cohesion, he proposed that Okinawa had to overcome its internal strife and head towards unification (Hattori et al. 1974a, p. 147). Though he personally was a member of the 'non-political populace,' this was a claim that positioned unification as an extension of Ifa's having grieved for some time over the conflict within Okinawa and called for unification.

Seen in this light, Ifa's views on Japan and the Ryukyu Dynasty could be said to have been more correlative than confrontational. To him, both Japan and the Ryukyu Dynasty (Shuri-ites) were entities that possessed political capability superior in such terms as national unification and assimilation policy. He was one of the strong who had had assimilation forced upon them. Examination of his historical perspective will show that a positive appraisal of Japan and a positive appraisal of the Ryukyu Dynasty prior to the Satsuma invasion had fused together into one.

In this manner, Ifa's assessment of Japan and the Ryukyu Dynasty (Shuri-ites) was vacillating between affirmation and negation, but it is difficult to argue that one was his true feeling and the other a polite fiction. He was not a person well-endowed with the sort of political acumen to use different assertions according to the circumstances, and he heaped great censure upon the 'double-dealing principle' which changed the target of its allegiance in all situations and times as being 'Okinawans' worst fault' (Hattori et al. 1974a, p. 64). In spite of this, the wavering of his words and deeds is thought to have been a reflection of his admiration for and rejection of 'the Japanese' and Shuri-ites, who were the strong. Something which gives an insight into such feelings of Ifa's is a passage from his 1915 talk, entitled: 'The mentality of the weak.'[15]

> Okinawans are weaklings when they are coping with the outside or face-to-face with the strong, but when they are facing inwards or face-to-face with the strong (*sic*) *they* are the strong. At those times, they expend all their strength in jostling and devouring and killing each other ... I would like to eradicate their bad ethnicity (*minzoku-sei*). And I want to become a true member of the strong. I confess that I myself am one of the weak. For that reason, I will never stop wishing to become one of the strong (Hattori et al. 1976a, p. 353).

Because they are the weak, internally they are divided and fight each other, discriminate against those who are even weaker, and opportunistically toady to the strong. Did Ifa's feelings of self-hatred for the ugliness of such 'weaklings' and his desire to 'become a true member of the strong' perhaps compel him to compose a martial discourse of Okinawan nationalism which probably did not suit him, and to applaud the Ryukyu Dynasty and Japan, which comprised a 'political populace' and 'the strong.' Though in the beginning he had been a student weak in both mind and body, he was fond of reading books on international relations in the age of imperialism, such as Inagaki Manjirō's *Tōhōsaku* (Eastern policy), and he spent a boyhood in awe of such heroes as Napoleon and Toyotomi Hideyoshi. Moreover, as previously observed, he was someone who had abandoned the path to becoming a politician and switched to the study of culture.

Though harbouring self-hatred towards the ugliness of the weak and thirsting to become one of the strong, on the other hand he was acquainted with the pain of rule and discrimination by the strong. While appreciating the importance of politics and admiring politicians, he still could not erase a sense of discomfort and repugnance towards politics. Though mired in such a dilemma, Ifa in the years from late Meiji till early Taishō had an aim to hone Okinawans into 'the strong.' Moreover, in order to achieve that goal, he came to advocate harmony with Japan and Okinawan nationalism on the one hand, while at the same time engaging in awareness campaigns to work on Okinawan society.

Being an enlightened intellectual

In his book *Old-Ryukyu*, Ifa commended Shō Shōken who had advanced the 'Japan–Ryukyu common-ancestry theory,' writing: 'in all things pertaining to society, it is difficult to establish objectives; once objectives are established, unless one does something especially wrong, then the spirit of the age will itself lead the way' (Hattori et al. 1974a, p. 55). Being subsumed into 'the Japanese' while escaping from the 'ambiguous situation' that symbolised Satsuma times and preserving uniqueness became Ifa's assertion in the 1910s.

For Ifa, in 1912, the year after the publication of *Old-Ryukyu*, the execution of the Lower House Members' Electoral Law in Okinawa was truly something that gave him a real sense of the rightness of that direction. On the occasion of that election, he remarked: 'This marks a great period in the history of our Okinawa, and we have come to be able once again to taste the true flavour of politics which we had been unable to taste for such a long time since [the Satsuma invasion] in the Keichō era [1596–1615]' (Hattori et al. 1976a, p. 62). Amid such expectations of acquiring rights as 'Japanese,' Ifa in 1918 went so far as to record the words: 'The most urgent task above all in Okinawa is to Japanise the language, customs and manners' (Hattori et al. 1974a, p. 57).

Such a call for 'Japanisation' naturally did not emerge without any reason. Not only was there hope for the securing of institutional equality by way of the granting of suffrage – Ifa at the time was also enthusing over an awareness campaign for 'civilising' Okinawan society.

In fact, the abovementioned expression: 'to Japanise the language, customs and manners' was one that Ifa had used when he published a series of newspaper articles on the status of women in Okinawa. As previously stated, Ōta Chōfu's exhortation to assimilate even to the point of 'sneezing' was also one which had leapt out in a talk on female education. Both Ōta and Ifa were Okinawan nationalists, but in regard to such matters as the status of women and the class system, they were painfully aware of the necessity to amend Okinawa's conventional customs. Moreover, as mentioned in Chapter Two, Education Minister Mori Arinori had expounded the importance of female education on a visit to Okinawa in 1887. While that of course sprang from intention to acquire women's offspring for the state by creating good mothers who would offer allegiance to that state, it still appeared to be an opportunity to improve the existing status of women in Okinawa.

From the start, Ifa had had reasons for having to become sensitive to women's status. One was his relationship with his wife. As he has not left any written accounts about his relationship with her, it is not definite, but in accordance with what was customary in Okinawan society at the time, he apparently had his wife chosen for him by his family at an extremely young age, without regard for his own intentions. From 1909, he was part-time Head of the Okinawa Prefectural Library, but despite having graduated from Tokyo Imperial University, which ought to have set him on a central career track, he returned to his native home and started such a job for reasons he describes as follows:

> Frankly speaking, as female education in Okinawa was not as prolific in our young days as it is now, our friends all made unhappy – or, rather, mismatched – marriages. For that reason, certain of them, out of need for success in life, ended up having to part from the wives who had stood by them through thick and thin – though I myself could not do that – while certain others took their wives and set out for other prefectures. But as living life in refined society was like being in prison, they not long afterwards returned to their native place [as I chose to do] ... It is said that husband and wife are like the two wheels of a cart, but we, in an age of transition, have conducted our activities in the narrow sphere that was our native place, centred

around our unmoving wives, as if spinning round and round on the same spot, pivoting on one cartwheel which did not turn (Hattori et al. 1975b, p. 56).

This passage is followed by the aforementioned words: 'The most urgent task above all in Okinawa is to Japanise the language, customs and manners,' and further continues: 'No – it is to make female education more robust, and attempt to reform the home' (Hattori et al. 1975b, p. 58). The vacillation in his state of mind probably can be read from his declaration of resolve to 'Japanise' and the subsequent 'No.'

The presence of Ifa's mother, Matsuru, could be cited as the second reason for Ifa's focus of concern on the status of women. Ifa's natal home was that of a wealthy family in Naha which had amassed its family fortune through trade and the like under the supremacy of the Shuri samurai class. Since the Ryukyu Disposition, however, merchants from Kagoshima had monopolised economic activity, and Ifa's father had lost hope and begun to spend all his time drinking and frequenting a red-light district, while his mother had supported the family business.

As previously mentioned, it was also she who had overcome the family's opposition with its hatred of Yamato, and enrolled Ifa in primary school. In his memoir of his early childhood, Ifa stated that thanks to his father's debauchery, 'the peace of the home was destroyed, and I felt sorrow in my childish heart' (Hattori et al. 1976a, p. 91); and furthermore, in a study discussing the status of women, he wrote: 'It should be written large that while the men were drowning their sorrows with drink, unlettered Naha women had for a long time intuitively perceived the advent of a new age, sent their children to school, and had them receive the new education' (Hattori et al. 1975b, p. 48). As previously mentioned, it was Ifa's mother who overcame his father's opposition and enrolled Ifa in a primary school established by the Japanese government. In the case of the aforementioned Okinawan rights activist Jahana Noboru, also, it was his mother that had him enter a school run by the Yamato side.

According to Ifa, such men's dissipation and women's hardship was intimately connected with the issue of female education. In his words, this was because for members of the Ryukyu samurai class who 'debated politics' all day long, ignorant 'wives could hardly serve as their husbands' conversation partners,' and so courtesans, who comprised a 'class sufficient to seduce human hearts, while being superior in both ability and appearance,' and red-light districts developed 'in order to make up for that deficiency.' Ifa at the time said: 'The flourishing of red-light districts in Okinawa, where women's status is low, is a matter that should not be avoided,' and 'as long as the economic unit called the household (*ie*) does not reduce further in size and allow even individuals to progress, and as long as female education is not more actively pursued and women gain influence in the home,' he asserted, Okinawa would not be able to attain a state like that of 'Western countries where the status of women is high at present' (Hattori et al. 1974a, p. 52, 53).

In an ethnic group (*minzoku*) implanted in a state of subordination, in an environment where the existing social order and values are crumbling, the tendency can be seen for men of the upper echelon who especially harbour affection for the traditional order to sink into such deviant behaviour as drinking and debauchery, and for the burden to fall upon the women. The situation which Ifa confronted was a phenomenon which had arisen all over the world, such as in Native American society and in Ainu society in Japan, though Ifa at the time found the reason for the tragedy in the insufficient modernisation of Okinawan society rather than in such dismantling of a society. For that reason, Ifa gave weight generally to Okinawa's 'individuality,' but when it came to the issue of women, in particular, a strong tendency emerged for him to preach 'civilisation.'

A symbolic example of this was his stance vis-à-vis the Okinawan belief in shamans (*yuta*), a caste of female mediums. These *yuta* were a presence whose eradication was advocated in the *Ryūkyū shinpō* newspaper as being a 'barbaric' custom in Okinawa, and Ifa, too, was in favour of this. According to Ifa's discussion on *yuta* serialised in *Ryūkyū shinpō* in 1913, Okinawan women in ancient times rode on horseback and acted in a way equal to men; and when the Ryukyu Dynasty assimilated Sanzan and Miyako-Yaeyama, as mediums they fulfilled the role of spreading the 'national (*minzoku*) religion' which worshipped the gods of the Shō Dynasty. However, he claimed that after the 'unification of the Ryukyuan race (*minzoku*)' was completed and these women had finished their mission, this belief in female shamans degenerated as a useless white elephant, but after that, 'because only boys, and not girls, were allowed to be educated,' belief in the shamans survived among women in the form of a superstition. In Ifa's words, 'old-fashioned Okinawan women whose activities centre around shamanism are a whole two thousand years behind the new women who are active in women's issues' (Hattori et al. 1975d, pp. 355, 342).

As could be expected, underpinning Ifa's fixation on shamans there was the existence of his mother. She reportedly had become seriously ill when Ifa was still in his infancy, and had leant towards shaman worship ever since, experiencing 'supernatural possession two or three times in a year.' Ifa said: 'In Okinawa, when a husband goes crazy over women, his wife starts to have a connection with religious rituals. My mother was probably like that, too.' For Ifa, his mother's shamanistic belief was not a matter of some abstract cultural theory such as the defence of Okinawan tradition, but none other than a tragedy originating in family breakdown and an insufficiency in female education (Hattori et al. 1974a, p. 389).

Ifa assessed his mother as being a 'wise person, a tolerant person, one who could have been a politician if she were a man,' and considering that he himself had aimed to become a 'politician' but had been thwarted, this was the highest form of praise.[16] Alternatively, his image of the ideal politician might have been the very image of his mother. The circumstances in which his mother turned to belief in shamans amid hardship and ignorance are thought to have been enough to cause him pain. In 1913, Ifa remarked: 'I consider that to educate the descendants of those Ryukyuan women once active on horseback and to let them engage in modern activities are most pleasant enterprises.' He wrote that Okinawan women who had received a modern education 'might someday conduct such activities as will make those topknotted samurai who drag down women's issues pale in the face,' these being words triggered by the kind of circumstances described above (Hattori et al. 1975d, p. 365).

Having become the Head of Okinawa Prefectural Library, Ifa collected materials on local history in the library while also holding a study circle bringing together young men and women at his own house, and giving lectures all over the place, making efforts to popularise the 'new thought' of the time. He could be said to have been taking the kind of action typical of intellectuals in developing areas, strengthening the historical identity of the race on the one hand, while carrying out awareness campaigns aimed at promoting modernisation on the other, as it were.

As in the case of intellectuals from areas with a sparse population of educated elites, Ifa conducted all kinds of enlightenment lectures whose content fell into four broad categories. The first was content relating to Okinawan history, followed by that connected with Christianity, criticism of Okinawan society, and that relating to 'racial hygiene.' Of these, I have already made mention of Ifa's talks on Okinawan history, but how were the other fields chosen?

Firstly, as for Christianity, though it is not known whether Ifa was baptised, it is certain that he had been inclined towards Christianity from his youth, and in 1907, he was recommended for the position of President of the Okinawa Young Men's Christian Association. For Ifa, this, too, was not unconnected with the reform of Okinawan society, however. In his opinion 'advocating scientific thought was the most urgent task in eliminating superstitions' such as shaman-worship, but 'at the same time as this, the propagation of religious ideology' was also an 'urgent task.' In Ifa's cognisance, 'women who do not have a child sometimes play with dolls, but while the spirit of love for a child is a belief, for example, the spirit of love for a doll is a superstition,' but he said that because 'it is cruel simply to shout: "Throw away the dolls! Abandon superstition!" ... we have to give them a child and a faith to replace dolls and superstitions' (Hattori et al. 1975d, pp. 364, 365). Herein probably lay the reason for his having given talks relating to Christianity. Moreover, the abovementioned metaphor of 'women who do not have a child' was one penned six years after the stillbirth of Ifa and his wife's first child.

In his lectures critiquing Okinawan society, Ifa in this period frequently called for Okinawans to make self-help efforts. In 1914, having declared that the 'Ryukyu Disposition was a kind of slave liberation,' he urged Okinawans with the words: 'Having been gradually habituated to a slave-like life for 300 years, the spirit of independence and self-employment, meaning keeping on improving oneself by one's own efforts, is becoming almost non-existent.' According to him, 'Herein also lies the reason why Ryukyuans meekly comply with the duties they are ordered to do, and hesitate to acquire the rights they have been given. Accordingly, here also lies the reason for the non-development of their politics, industry and education' (Hattori et al. 1974a, pp. 493, 494). One of his aims in daring to call the Ryukyu Disposition 'slave liberation' could be said to be encouragement to Okinawan society to depart from their slavish spirit.

As a prior example of 'slave liberation,' Ifa also often mentioned the American Black activist, Booker T. Washington (Hattori et al. 1974a, p. 493). Among Black activists of that era, Washington is known for having advocated conciliation, unlike ones such as W. E. B. Du Bois, who expanded a radical struggle for abolition of discrimination, and Marcus Garvey, who proposed separation from white society. What Washington basically advocated was for Black people not to criticise whites or to wait for supporters while lamenting their own lot, but to cultivate their capacity by their own self-help efforts, and this was welcomed by contemporary influential whites. Washington's famous saying was: 'Cast down your bucket where you are,' something that advocated self-help efforts at people's own feet, but, Ifa employed Nietzsche's words: 'Where you're standing, dig, dig out; Down below's the well' for the epigram in *Old-Ryukyu*.

'Racial hygiene,' the final element in Ifa's campaign of enlightenment lectures, was one relating to eugenics. Nowadays, eugenics is known wholly as a racist form of scholarship, but in Ifa's time, it circulated as public-health knowledge aimed at social reform for the purpose of passing down superior offspring. In the 1920s in Japan, as well, the magazine *Yūseigaku* (Eugenics) was published, but its principal content dealt with the reform of lifestyle customs which were taken to be the cause of genetic disorders, with specific emphasis on the necessity for hygiene management, the harmful results of drinking alcohol, and so on. The very idea of 'the Japanese,' a yellow race, having adopted eugenics to begin with surely must have seemed odd to Western racial ideologists, but in Japan, which at the time was a developing country, eugenics was accepted as the branch of scholarship of the lifestyle-improvement movement. Such eugenics was something that Ifa, tackling the reform of Okinawan society, was also able to accept, and it can be inferred from citations in his writings that he read racial ideologists such as Davenport, Lombroso and Le Bon.[17]

From around 1919, Ifa gave lectures all over Okinawa on 'racial hygiene,' entitled 'The negative legacy of blood and culture,' but his talks on those occasions seem entirely to have been ones that drew attention to such things as the harmful effects of drinking and intermarriage. Even here, he advocated to women that they make their husbands stop drinking and dissipation, on the basis of the content of his talks. In addition, from about 1909, Ifa had already said that Okinawans were shorter in stature than people of other prefectures because 'for a long time they have inhabited isolated islands in the distant seas, and they did not mix their blood much with that of others, and even within the islands, consanguineous marriage was frequently carried out' (Hattori et al. 1974, p. 66) and he encouraged Okinawans to abandon their class system and ethnic antagonism, and to marry mainlanders and people from other regions (see Kano 1993, p. 143). Here can be seen a comparatively rare pattern comprising a combination of eugenics ideology and assimilation discourse. As I discussed in my 2002 English publication, *A Genealogy of 'Japanese' Self-images*, Japanese eugenicists disliked mixed blood, and for that reason, they were opposed to assimilation policies directed at Korea and the like. Le Bon, who was a racialist thinker and an Orientalist, asserted that the nature of race could not be altered, and was opposed to a policy of assimilation in French colonies.

Ifa also afforded the highest praise to Le Bon's *Lois psychologiques de l'évolution des peuples* (1895), calling it a masterpiece (Hattori et al. 1974a, p. 484), but what resonated with him seems to have been its claim that a radical assimilation policy would bring about the ruin of that race. In a 1909 talk, while expounding that 'when one thinks of the laws of heredity, uniqueness is something that simply cannot be annihilated,' he asserted the individuality of 'Okinawans' (Hattori et al. 1975b, p. 10). Just as in the case of the 'Japan–Ryukyu common-ancestry theory,' Ifa transformed racial ideology, also, into a discourse of respect for Okinawan 'individuality.'

In the way discussed above, Ifa's thought in the 1910s could be said to be something which promoted 'civilisation' while giving consideration to respect for 'uniqueness,' and which modernised Okinawan society and made it stand on its own feet. Accordingly, modernising the 'Ryukyuan race' and raising it into prosperity was most vital, and seeking to cling to Okinawan culture was not always possible.

This is well-expressed in Ifa's stance towards the Okinawan language. There was criticism of his having given enlightenment lectures in Okinawan, saying that it would have an adverse effect upon the encouragement of *futsūgo* (Standard Japanese), but even while saying: 'I could not bring myself to hate the language I was taught by my mother,' Ifa replied that promotion of Okinawan was 'disadvantageous for Okinawa.' According to him, his use of Okinawan in his talks was nothing more than a kind of expedience, because he thought the diffusion of eugenics ideology relating to the 'life of the race' even as far as regions where use of the standard language was not sufficiently universal was an 'urgent task.' Moreover, he said that once language had 'accomplished its mission, it would be natural for it to disappear,' and that he 'did not think it regrettable' for the Okinawan language to perish along with generational change (Hattori et al. 1974a, pp. 277, 280, 287). As I will elaborate in Chapter Four, at the time of the Okinawan language debate in later years, also, he asserted that suppressing Okinawan and 'causing the loss of ethnic pride' should be avoided, but that 'allowing it to become extinct naturally' was 'the wisest measure.' From this, the idea can be read that the important thing was the 'life of the altogether,' and that the disappearance of language amid modernisation and unification could not be helped.

For Ifa at this time, now that there was hope that a tentative institutional equality as 'Japanese' would be achieved by the acquisition of suffrage, the revival of Okinawa through modernisation and self-help efforts probably appeared most realistic. Just as Washington's had been, this was also considered by the Japanese government to be a moderate ideology. In 1915, the conferral of posthumous rank upon Shō Shōken (Shō Shōchin), Sai On and Giwan Chōho, whom Ifa had ranked as the three great men of Ryukyu, on the occasion of the coronation of the Taishō emperor also speaks of the moderate nature of Ifa's ideology (Kano 1993, p. 123). Once the 1920s had dawned, however, change began to descend upon his perspectives on Okinawa and Japan.

Thwarted Okinawan nationalism

The event which crushed Ifa's conception of Okinawan modernisation through self-help efforts was the great recession which hit Okinawa after the First World War. This recession, dubbed the 'sago palm hell' because it was said that people even ate poisonous sago palm fruit, as there was no food, was one in which a recession in mainland Japan spread to Okinawa. Unification with Japan proper brought even the mainland's recession to Okinawa, prostrating those islands, which were the weakest part of Japan.

Originally, from 1915, Ifa had been alarmed at the state of affairs in which Okinawa was having its taxes seized by the national treasury due to an excessive burden of taxation, and he had already declared his anxiety that 'while the slavery that restrained Okinawan politics somehow seemed to have been abolished, a slave-like environment was beginning to dawn under the new format, namely, the economic format' (Hattori et al. 1976a, p. 77). Furthermore, in 1919, when suffrage was granted even to Miyako and Yaeyama, in complete contrast to his expression of passionate expectations towards the granting of suffrage to Okinawa's main island seven years previously, he now asked whether 'political parties which claim they did us the favour of demolishing a clannish cabinet and liberating Japanese nationals from slavery' were not also 'in the process of creating a new prison' (Hattori et al. 1974a, p. 270). Ifa was consistently unable to eliminate the long-held anxiety that even if slave liberation had been implemented by political power, it would perhaps again turn into 'a new prison,' and the advent of the 'sago-palm hell' became the form in which that anxiety hit the mark.

In the very midst of this recession, Ifa began to say that Okinawan prefectural residents had 'long since passed the juncture when they could save themselves by their own hand' (Hattori et al. 1974b, p. 264), and he reached the point of totally negating the days of his own awareness campaigns. He already had said: 'Now, the racial hygiene movement is lax, the enlightenment movement is lukewarm, and economic salvation is the sole means left to us,' and he criticised Buddhism and Christianity, which preached nothing but spiritual salvation, going so far as to say that they had become 'sorcerers who hypnotise people and enslave them' (Hattori et al. 1974a, p. 299, 301). Once, he had criticised the conventional system of co-ownership of land as pre-modern, and had welcomed the abolition of co-ownership through land rezoning, and the determination of the amount of tax payable as a prerequisite for suffrage, but Ifa started to reveal that in this case, too, 'rather than gaining the good name of suffrage and falling into the sago-palm hell, would it not have been more sensible to have preserved this unique land system, and slowly await the next age?' (Hattori et al. 1974b, pp. 451, 452). Self-help efforts, civilisation, eugenics and Christianity were all completely powerless in the face of economic recession.

More than anything, the bitter acknowledgement that he 'had once extolled the "Japan–Ryukyu common-ancestry theory," and had succeeded in gaining the understanding of scholars and educators, but had been unable to gain the sympathy of politicians and business people' enveloped Ifa after the sago-palm hell. This recognition was expressed simultaneously with a pessimism which said that 'having a special history and language in spite of being a small race' had to be 'at least one of their misfortunes in the present day.' He argued that even this alone could be said to equip Okinawans with 'ample qualifications for being made into slaves' (Hattori et al. 1976a, p. 314).

Thereafter, in the epigrams of his writings, Gourmont's words: 'We are being crushed by history,' came to be cited in place of Nietzsche's exhortations for self-help efforts. This was an expression whose substance said: 'We should completely abandon history. In other words, in every age, we should resolve to erase altogether the useless traces of the past' (Hattori et al. 1964a, p. 315). This was close to a *de facto* declaration of defeat by Ifa, who formerly had proposed that crushing Okinawans' individuality meant to 'ignore history' (Hattori et al. 1976b, p. 10).

Due to the recession, the members of Ifa's study circle also reached a situation in which they had no jobs and had to cross to mainland Japan. The impasse in the awareness campaigns gradually made him turn in the direction of purely academic research, and this was accelerated by the 1921 visit to Okinawa by Yanagita Kunio, the pioneer of Japanese folkloristics introduced in the previous chapter, and his encouragement of Ifa's research. The problem was not only an ideological deadlock, however. In his private life, too, Ifa's relationship with his wife collapsed, and he fell in love with a female member of his study circle. The scandal involving Ifa, who had garnered such popularity and respect with his enlightenment lectures, drove him into a painful position, and finally, in 1925, at the age of forty-nine, he had no choice but to leave Okinawa with his new lover and go to Tokyo.

It was also after he had moved to the capital that he penned his words questioning King Shō Shin's institutional reforms, which he once had idealised as having treated conquered subjects equally. According to Ifa, 'the Second Shō king presented the mechanism of exploitation which he had taken such pains to construct to the Shimazu clan, as is,' and 'around the time when nothing remained in the pockets [of ordinary Okinawans] out of all the things that could be squeezed out of them, they were liberated for a short while thanks to the Ryukyu Disposition, then were absorbed into the new system, but forty years on, before they have been able to restore the things they have lost, they are on the brink of falling into poverty again' (Hattori et al. 1975b, p. 283).

After this, as well, Ifa did not quit his research into Okinawan history, though it could not be the same thing as before. After going to Tokyo, his contemptuous view of the Ainu also vanished, and he began to describe Amami-Ōshima, which he had cited as being a place within Okinawa where Ainu lineage was particularly prolific, as being 'a people that had been more persecuted than the Okinawans' (Hattori et al. 1976a, p. 322). In regard to the issue of Korea, which he had once proposed be modelled on the reign of King Shō Shin, also, he indicated in 1921 that he had 'heard that [Woodrow] Wilson's declaration on ethnic self-determination moved Koreans' hearts more intensely than a university professor's Japan–Korea common-ancestry theory, or Christian missionaries' sermons on compatriotism' (Hattori et al. 1974a, p. 489).

However, what changed more than anything was that he gradually stopped advocating Okinawan nationalism in the way he had done before. When the relationship with Japan spawned an economic tragedy, and it came to his also ceasing to deride the Ainu, it was a matter of course that Ifa would later distance himself from once-martial Okinawan nationalism.

I will not make much further mention of Ifa's later Okinawan studies in this book.[18] Basically he placed more emphasis on Okinawa's commonality with Japan rather than its uniqueness, and took a direction that concentrated more on culture studies, focused upon the collection of poems and songs entitled *Omoro sōshi*, rather than on political history. This was a step forward from the 'common ancestry' idea, positioning Okinawa as a collateral line of the Japanese race and Japanese culture. From the 1920s, Yanagita Kunio, who at that time was Ifa's supporter, became negative about the theory of the existence of indigenous tribes, and, in concert with the gradual rejection in 1930s Japanese anthropology of the theory that Ainu and Malays had been the indigenous tribes, too, the necessity to emphasise the subjugation of the Ainu and Malays in order to stress the homogeneity of the Japanese race also disappeared. In 1925, Ifa sent a reply to Matsuoka Shizuo repudiating his own conventional theory that there were Ainu place-names in Okinawa (Hattori et al. 1976, p. 100), and the following year, while emphasising the disparity between the Japanese race and Koreans, from Shiratori Kurakichi's numerical study, stated that 'conversely, the age when the ancestors of the Ryukyuans migrated to the southern isles, though seemingly far, is unexpectedly near,' coming to sever the 'Japan–Korea common-ancestry theory' from the 'Japan–Ryukyu common-ancestry theory' (Hattori et al. 1975, p. 356). Ifa died in

The Creation of Okinawan Nationalism

1947, after Japan's defeat, but in his *Okinawan historical narrative*, which became his posthumous work, it appears that the expression 'Ryukyuan race' had completely withdrawn into the background.

The path that Ifa followed, which we have examined here, shows many patterns of exploration that minority-group intellectuals placed in difficult circumstances experience, from aspiring to be a politician to historical studies for the sake of forming nationalism, and awareness campaigns. Speaking in terms of the context of this book, Ifa's characteristic was not to wage all-out confrontation with Japan, but, by means of re-reading the discourse created by the ruling side, to endeavour to defend Okinawa. Though Ifa's strategy – which involved making Okinawans' positioning as 'Japanese' and not 'Japanese' function conversely as a bulwark for their individuality, and conceiving a pluralistic image of 'the Japanese' by means of the expression '*Daikokumin* (people of the great Empire)' – included many limitations and ultimately ended in failure, it was arguably one which held potential. Moreover, it also functioned as a kind of precursor for the tactics employed by other minorities in Taiwan and Korea in the Empire of Japan, which I investigated in Volume 2 of this book.

4 The Distortion of Orientalism

In 1940, a fierce debate involving central intellectuals, the Okinawa Prefectural Office and Okinawan local newspapers erupted. Now, this debate is called by such names as the 'Okinawa dialect debate' or 'Okinawa language debate.'

In Okinawa, the dissemination of Standard Japanese (*hyōjungo*) had been continued since Japan took possession of the islands, but in this period, an even stricter enforcement movement was implemented under the guidance of the prefectural office. Coincidentally, the Sino-Japanese War was intensifying, and Korea and Taiwan, also, were in the midst of calls for the strict enforcement of '*kokugo* (national language=Japanese)' as part of the movement to turn the populace into imperial subjects. Every corner of Okinawa was plastered with posters saying 'Standard Japanese [for] the whole family!' and at schools, students who spoke Okinawan were forced to wear a 'dialect placard (*hōgen fuda*)' by way of punishment. A group visiting that Okinawa from the Mingei Kyōkai (Folk Art Association), led by Yanagi Muneyoshi (also known as Yanagi Sōetsu), confronted the prefectural office with an appeal for the preservation of Okinawan language and Okinawan culture.

This debate is often depicted as being a conflict between the prefectural office, which was endeavouring to suppress the Okinawan language, and the conscientious intelligentsia. As we shall see below, however, this debate encompassed other elements, also, namely discussions around how to situate Okinawa within the boundaries of 'the Japanese.' Moreover, that issue developed into a debate between advocates in Japan's centre, and Okinawans who were being thus situated.

'Folk craft' as Orientalism

In order to investigate the Okinawan language debate, it is first necessary to look at the relationship between Yanagi Sōetsu and Korea.

Yanagi, known for the Folk Craft Movement which discovered Japanese popular arts, was born in 1889; despite having a father who was a rear admiral in the navy, he consistently disliked politics, and loved religion and beauty; and at Gakushūin (Peer's School) high school, he took part in the *Shirakaba* (White birch) magazine, renowned as the coterie magazine of such writers as Mushakōji Saneatsu and Shiga Naoya. At Tokyo Imperial University, he majored in psychology; while still a student, he published his first book, and he later came to be known for his studies on religion, philosophy and fine arts, as well as on the poets Walt Whitman and William Blake. In art, his principal objects of interest seem to have been Rodin, Matisse, the later Impressionists, and the like.

It was probably an interest in Korean art that constituted the relay point, so to speak, for Yanagi – with such stylish Western tastes – to take an interest in earthy 'folk craft.' Through his travels in Korea in 1916 and 1920, Yanagi became infatuated with Joseon Dynasty art and architecture, and came to pen a series of articles on Korea.

The best-known of Yanagi's Korean articles is 'For a Korean building about to be lost,' which he published in 1922 at the age of thirty-three, when echoes from the 1 March Independence Movement were still resounding. It was one protesting against moves due to a construction plan by the Government-General to demolish Seoul's Gwanghwamun (Gwanghwa Gate), which had been erected in the Joseon Dynasty. This plan was part of a governing policy ready to flaunt its prestige and power to civilise by erecting a pompous Western-style government office building amid the shaky rule that followed the 1 March Independence Movement; and the 1995 demolition by the South Korean government of this office building, symbolising colonial control, happened just as was reported even in Japan. When this article of Yanagi's was published in a Japanese magazine, it was filled with blanked-out censored words, but it was translated into Korean and English and circulated, so in the end the Government-General cancelled the demolition, and was pressed into a compromise consisting of relocating the gate with conservation of its architecture.

Yanagi's objection is taken to have illustrated the conscience of the Japanese intelligentsia, while conversely he was even tailed at one time by police detectives sent by the government, but Yanagi himself consistently assumed an apolitical position. On the occasion of his discussion of Korea after the 1 March Independence Movement, also, he stated: 'I have not the slightest faith in military force or politics. You [Koreans], too, must not place any trust in your own military force or politics.' His protest was one persistently made from the standpoint of artistic preservation, and in 1923 he wrote: 'The people of the Government-General do not make tyranny their policy. I know that there are numerous cultured people there, and that they have enthusiastic intent, wishing to carry out good government to the best of their ability' (Yanagi 1981a, pp. 39, 228).[1]

Why, then, did Yanagi love Korean art so much? In a lecture he gave upon going over to Korea in 1920, he spoke as follows as to 'why [he] especially emphasise[d] Korean art.'

> Western material culture surged in like the tide in Japan in early-modern times, and the native beauty of the latter gradually disappeared, but fortunately Korea has not yet reached the point of civilisation jeopardising its native beauty (Yanagi 1981, p. 660).

Korean art as Eastern beauty, preserved in the face of waves of 'civilisation' from the West – such a world-view of Yanagi's also ran through 'For a Korean building about to be lost.' He called Gwanghwamun 'purely Eastern art,' described the Government-General's buildings as 'Western-style, devoid of any creative beauty whatsoever,' and called for 'ardent love for purely Eastern things, for the sake of our honour.' In order to appeal to his Japanese readers' sentiments, he asked how they would feel if Korea were to annex Japan and wanted to destroy Edo Castle, but what he hypothesised the Korean side would build at that eventuality was not a Korean-style building, but an 'Occidental-style Japanese Government-General' (Yanagi 1981a, pp. 150, 149, 145).

For Yanagi, Japan had already been situated as a presence that had transformed into part of the West. When Yanagi was shown model embroidery that Korean students had to make as part of their vocational education in Korea, he described it as 'contemporary Japanese-style work in which one could not recognise native Korean beauty – in other words, semi-Westernised work with neither taste nor elegance, of foolish design and pale colouration – and he lamented the 'loss for Korea which has such education forced upon it, and will lose its traditional beauty' (Yanagi 1981a, p. 29). For Yanagi, the Japanese assimilation policy vis-à-vis Korea constituted destruction of the 'purely Eastern' by the 'semi-Western.'

It seems slightly odd for Yanagi, whom one would expect to have been a stylish youth who loved Western art, to be showing opposition to the destruction of the East by Western civilisation to such an extent. In fact, though, behind the formation of Yanagi's orientation in art and literature lay his companionship with the British ceramic artist, Bernard Leach, who was connected with the White Birch (*shirakaba*) faction. According to Yanagi's recollections, along with being taught much from Leach about Impressionist painting and Blake's poetry, topics on such Western art finally developed into talk about Japanese art, which Leach loved. Yanagi especially cites Leach and Lafcadio Hearn as Westerners who understood Japan, but both were people who loved the Japanese traditional arts which were being lost, and abhorred shallow Westernisation. Moreover, in his own discussions on Korea, Yanagi stated that even though colonists from Japan proper had migrated to Korea in large numbers, 'there [was] still not a single figure like Hearn among those living in Korea and talking about Korea' (Yanagi 1981a, p. 24). Leach, on his own part, had already shown strong interest in the Joseon Dynasty pottery he saw at a colonisation exhibition held in Ueno in 1912, and it is also said that this was inherited by Yanagi. In other words, Yanagi's anti-Western-civilisation orientation and his adoration for Eastern arts was something cultivated by his contact with Europeans, and while this is somewhat paradoxical, that itself may be said to have been an extension of a Western orientation.[2]

Yanagi endeavoured to take a similar stance towards Korean art as Leach and Hearn's towards Japanese art. According to Yanagi, Korean art embodied the 'beauty of sorrow.' In other words, Korea was always troubled by invasion from external enemies and civil war, and the 'history of Korea, which for a long time had been tragic and heart-rending, secretly incorporated desolation and sadness in its arts.' It was 'tired of waiting for a warm heart,' and 'there [was] no art that waited so long for love to arrive than had Korean art.' Yanagi's criticism of Korean rule included such words as: 'Japan might have sent large amounts of money, and troops, and politicians to that land (= Korea), but then one wonders when it has ever sent love from its heart,' 'all Koreans are more starved simply of a scrap of human kindness than of money, or politics, or troops.' It was Yanagi himself who understood that the issue was not politics or economics, but love and beauty, and that such 'beauty of sorrow,' 'a symbol of their hearts which hungered for beauty,' was the meaning of Korean art; and to extol its value and love it (Yanagi 1981a, pp. 42, 43, 24, 27).

Later, in 1924, Yanagi set up a Korean folk art gallery in Seoul (called Keijō or Gyeongseong 1910–1945), but, motivated by being moved by the plain and simple Buddhist statues he happened to encounter in mainland Japan that same year, he immersed himself henceforth in travelling in search of regional art in Japan proper. Then, in 1926, he made plans to establish a museum to house a collection of domestic *'mingei'* – a term of his own coinage meaning 'folk craft,' derived from *'minshū no kōgei* (crafts of the common people)'* – with which he had become acquainted during his travels. In regional areas and among the common people, he had discovered a 'purely Eastern' beauty which had already been lost in Japan in the face of civilisation, and which was thought to exist only in Korea.

In the sense that it sought the lingering fragrance of tradition in the regions and among the ordinary populace within a Japan that was gradually being Westernised, starting from the cities and the upper classes, Yanagi's Folk Craft Movement could be said also to have shared elements with the ethnology of Yanagita Kunio, which had come to prominence in about the same period; and the late 1920s, when they launched their movements, was a time that saw the end of the age of 'Taisho democracy,' in which discourses on enlightened civilisation in fashionably Western-influenced taste had been popular, and the gradual heightening of an extremely patriotic tone that extolled Japanese tradition. It was in 1927 that the collected works of Lafcadio Hearn, who had been regarded as nothing but an eccentric hired foreign advisor in the Meiji era, were also published for the first time in Japanese translation, and it was after this that he started to gain attention as a supporter of Japanese culture. Yanagi himself consistently shunned any connection with politics, but, as can also be seen in that a display by the 'Folk Craft Museum' at an exhibition promoting domestic products, held in 1928 to commemorate Emperor Hirohito's accession to the imperial throne, was what constituted the take-off point for the Folk Craft Movement, he was not indifferent to the tide of ultranationalism's revival, whether he liked it or not.

In one aspect, however, Yanagi did differ considerably from Yanagita. Though Yanagita hardly mentioned the folkways of anyone but the ethnically Japanese from the late 1920s onwards, styling them as *'ikkoku minzokugaku* (one-nation folklore studies),'

Yanagi showed interest not only in Korean folk craft objects, but in Ainu, Taiwanese and Chinese ones, as well. In Yanagita's case, there was a tendency to look for remaining national customs that were uniquely Japanese, in order to secure a Japanese national identity, and for that purpose, the folkways of other peoples were outside his interest, but Yanagi, with his aversion for politics, seems to have set out for any place that would enable him to find folk craft which he deemed to be 'pure.'

Yanagi had high admiration not only for Korean art, but also for Ainu and Taiwanese folk craft, but his method of appraisal was basically similar in all cases. Seeing Ainu artefacts, he would be amazed, saying: 'Their beauty has no falseness. It has no dishonesty. Could we discover such an astonishing phenomenon in the works of present-day culturati?' and, in regard to garments from the South Sea Islands, said: 'Indeed, those from a people who are despised as savages were overwhelmingly beautiful. As for those of so-called civilised countries ... there was no way that one could hide the insincerity of their production.' Moreover, he appraised woven cloth from aboriginal inhabitants of the Taiwan mountains with the words: 'In the history of textiles, too, the beauty is truer the further one goes back, and savage cloth that is not washed away by time naturally will acquire beauty.' According to Yanagi, things less tainted by civilisation were of purer beauty, and even among Ainu artworks, he said, 'those in which tradition accurately survived were ones from the Ainu of Karafuto (Sakhalin), while those from Hokkaido, due to quite frequent connection with people from *naichi*, had inevitably been forced gradually to change,' and he revealed that even in the Han Chinese craft workshops in Taiwan, 'the hand of mainland Japanese was unmistakeably involved' (Yanagi 1981b, pp. 501, 503, 564, 525, 606). It goes without saying that such insight on Yanagi's part approaches that which is currently being criticised as Orientalism.

Alternatively, it may be that only one aspect of Yanagi is being overemphasised here. He criticised Japanese scholars of Korean art, saying: 'Their studies are efforts made wholly for the satisfaction of their own knowledge, and not out of a desire to safeguard and elucidate Korea's worth; not to mention that they have not the slightest concern as to the fate of that people Though their knowledge might be accurate, their sentiments are extremely cold' (Yanagi 1981a, p. 17). Moreover, in his Ainu discourse, also, he asserts: 'Compassion towards the Ainu cannot be a greater power than respect towards the Ainu', 'One forever hopes that you will not be pessimistic over your destiny, but will discover some pride in having been born as Ainu people,' and writes: 'Our ancestors, too, had the same capacity. Now, however, [they] are in a state of inability to keep up with you at all' (Yanagi 1981b, pp. 508, 536). As such, it is certain that Yanagi did not stop at mere adoration of objects of art, but also paid respect to the people who had created them.

Meanwhile, though, Yanagi had a perception that 'it is probably the Japanese rather than the Chinese that can best appreciate the value of Chinese folk craft. By contrast, it is precisely the Chinese that have abundant capability to make and produce things. For that reason, if the Japanese who view and the Chinese who produce work collaboratively, then great results will be obtained.' His having called for the Ainu and Taiwanese to have pride was at one with the logic that reasoned: 'They might not know the difference between the good and the bad. In the long run, it is the Japanese that discover beauty. That is why the Japanese ... have to elevate the others' aesthetic consciousness ... To do that, they need first to acknowledge the magnificent things that their opposite number possesses, and respect those things' (Yanagi 1981b, pp. 574, 602). He respected the aesthetic creativity of 'primitive peoples,' but presumed that the ones to assign it value and to teach and guide them would be he himself and 'the Japanese,' who were on the civilised side.

Here, what is important is those on the receiving end of Yanagi's logic. Though he expressed the idea that Korean art was starved of love, when this was translated in Korea in the postwar, there was a string of criticism such as: 'In all respects, Yanagi's position was nothing more than something akin to a master having sympathy for a subordinate,' or 'Yanagi's moral objection to Japanese imperialism was no more than self-consolation. To regard Korean beauty as the beauty of pity or the beauty of lamentation was the angle taken in Japanese imperialist days' (Yanagi 1981a, pp. 690, 691). Yanagi had not received such criticism in his own times, and even if he had received any, he probably would have been nonplussed. However, just as Hearn, whom Yanagi had described as someone who understood Japan well, had declared in private correspondence to Westerners that '[the Japanese], naturally are children,' and as the anthropologist Gustave Le Bon had also been a passionate scholar of Oriental art, the line between respect for traditional beauty and

Orientalism was an extremely subtle one (Ōta 1994, p. 55). This means that in debates over Okinawa, Yanagi's thinking came to sustain a lot of direct criticism from Okinawa itself.

Ferocious opposition from the Okinawan side

The beginning of the Okinawa language debate was a visit to Okinawa from late 1939 until January of the following year by a party led by staff from the Folk Art Association and International Tourism Association. When the party held roundtable discussions involving Okinawan business people, culturati, officials from the prefectural office and the like, a debate erupted.

According to newspaper reports and Folk Art Association records, the opinions of Yanagi and the others were as follows. Firstly, Yanagi stated such things as: 'I am not opposed to the use of Standard Japanese, but it would not do to neglect the language of the Ryukyus for that reason,' 'I would like you actively to equip Shuri and Naha as tourism cities,' and 'it is regrettable there are no souvenirs with a richly Okinawan air.' Furthermore, staff from the Tourism Association forwarded such opinions as: 'We want to preserve the traditional beauty and characteristics which look beautiful from tourists' point of view,' 'It seems that you are promoting Standard Japanese, but frankly speaking, aren't you going a bit too far?' 'In order to give full play to regional characteristics, in terms of taste, for example, what we want you to prohibit is the [concrete] fence below Shuri Castle,' and 'The lack of hotels is also inconvenient.' From Folk Art Association members, moreover, the following views were voiced: 'The ugly power poles in front of the Sōgenji Stone Gate, which we had wished to be relocated when we came last time, are still there,' and 'How injurious to elegance are the modern motor-vehicle garages!' All in all, while the provision of such facilities as hotels was being carried out, from the perspective of 'conservation of natural features unique to the prefecture, and its scenic and historic sites,' what the visitors asserted was the 'desire to preserve the Ryukyuan language and tombs as they were' (*Okinawa nippō* 1940b [1970], p. 355; *Gekkan mingei* 1940d, p. 374).

In response to this, the local electricity company said that the removal of power poles would be difficult. The Chief of Police at the prefectural office said that the strict enforcement of Standard Japanese and the modernisation of gravesites were 'the prefecture's major policies,' and that he wanted people 'not merely to come by chance from outside the prefecture and lavish praise in a touristy manner, but to think deeply,' and the discussion in that forum ended with things remaining as far apart as ever (*Okinawa nippō* 1940b [1970], p. 355; *Gekkan mingei* 1940d, p. 374). Nonetheless, the incident grew larger, as the Okinawa Prefecture School Affairs Division had published a statement in the three Okinawan newspapers, entitled: 'Do not be led astray by the Folk Craft movement which dares to appeal to prefectural residents.'

Along with emphasising that the popularisation of Standard Japanese was a movement for assisting the 'historically sacred work' of the '2,600 years of the Imperial era' the statement was something that demanded the thorough implementation of that movement without being led astray by the opinions of 'outsiders.' It cited such examples as the existence of a 'recent flock of migrant workers who contributed news of their gratitude at having avoided contempt and discriminatory treatment, thanks to the promotion of Standard Japanese,' and 'findings by the military that [Okinawa] prefecture-born soldiers' shared deficiency in expressing their intentions is suddenly turning to the better' (Okinawa-ken Gakumu Bu 1940 [1970], p. 356). Okinawa had been a prolific source of temporary migrant workers and emigrants since earlier times due to economic suffering, but after the serious depression in the Taisho era called the 'Sago-palm hell,' there had been increasing labour migration to the main islands of Japan and emigration to the South Sea Islands, in particular. Migrants were the object of intense discrimination because of their language and customs, and in the South Sea Islands, they were called such names as 'Japan Kanakas,' a twist on the derogatory term 'Kanaka' applied to indigenous inhabitants. It is true that such 'temporary migrant workers' were discriminated against because they could not speak Standard Japanese, but the claims from the prefectural office end arguably repeated logic that had been unchanged since Meiji times, namely that the diffusion of Standard Japanese was indispensable for integration into 'the Japanese,' including in military affairs. After this, the prefectural office took the action of arresting Yanagi and his companions on the charge of having photographed a defence facility without authorisation, and the Folk Art Association party had no choice but to leave Okinawa.

The Yanagi side also mounted a counter-argument against the prefectural office's stance. According to Yanagi, compared to the language of Tokyo, which had brought about the 'unnecessary admixture of Western languages,' Okinawan had maintained a pure form. In addition, 'Eastern virtue always collects around the worship of ancestors,' and 'Okinawans should be proud that they are enshrining their ancestors and their compatriots in the finest tombs in the world.' He further applauded Okinawa, where the inhabitants 'live amid folk songs,' in contrast to the modern cities of mainland Japan, where lifestyles had become detached from the arts. Moreover, as for folk craft, his speciality, he commended Okinawa, saying that its crafts which preserved traditional forms were 'pure,' and 'display[ed] a wonderful Oriental form' (Yanagi 1981b, pp. 150, 161, 164, 166).

Such claims by Yanagi were basically the same as his artistic theories vis-à-vis Korea, Taiwan and the Ainu which we have already seen. However, they invited a huge backlash from the Okinawan side.

First of all, Yoshida Shien, a government official in the Okinawan Prefectural Office, published a critique entitled 'My pet prefecture.' Criticising the mainland's central intelligentsia, he stated:

> What they say is always this: 'As we have taken the trouble to come all this way, it would be embarrassing not to have you preserve strange and interesting things.'
>
> They make the prefecture too much an object of their own curiosity. Yet it would still be better for them to make it the target of curiosity – in an even worse case, there are even some who think of it only as an ornamental plant or pet animal. These, of all people, are always indiscriminately broadcasting praise of Okinawa, making one think: 'Not again?' (Yoshida 1940a [1970], p. 375, double-quoted from *Gekkan mingei* 1940d, p. 375).

This Yoshida was to become the representative of the Southern Compatriots' Assistance Association (Nanpō dōhō engokai), a postwar conservative Okinawan reversion movement group, and in his memoirs, he has recorded his feelings when having debated with Yanagita.

Yoshida was born in Shuri as the eldest son among eleven siblings. His family's business declined because of the 'sago-palm hell' recession, and he lost his mother. Though he had set out for Japan proper to study, with his family's assistance, on the mainland Yoshida apparently had a 'dreadful complex over fluent Standard Japanese.' At Tokyo Imperial University, which he had entered after painful study, he majored in sociology and made the issue of poverty his subject, but the atmosphere at the university, where Hani Gorō, Shimizu Ikutarō and their ilk were working as research assistants, had a 'bourgeois air, with talk of nothing but how the coffee in such-and-such a place tasted so bad as to be undrinkable. I rebelled against them, thinking them "repulsive guys" with their hair all shiny with pomade. My complex also got worse at their refined demeanour and witty banter.' After Yoshida had been arrested for participating in a Nationalist Socialist group in the Showa Depression period at the beginning of the 1930s, when he was still at university, he gave up on his activities out of consideration for his family situation, and apparently cried as he burned documents relating to the organisation (Tsuitō Bunshū Kankō Iinkai 1990, pp. 327, 328,329).[3]

Yoshida's encounter with this language debate came after he had written a poverty studies dissertation and graduated from university, and was engaged in a movement for improvement of living conditions as a supervisor of community services which had been newly established in the Okinawa prefectural office back home. Of course, this 'improvement of living conditions' encompassed not only the dissemination of knowledge about hygiene and nutrition, for example, but in addition, also included the transformation of customs and language. For Yoshida, who had the awareness that he was engaged in a movement to save his birthplace from poverty, the 'homespun-clad aristocratic tastes and bourgeois-like words and deeds of the Folk Art Association's party were insufferable.' As such, he emphasised the existence of discrimination symbolised by the term 'Japan Kanakas,' and criticised Yanagi with the words: 'One of my friends outside the prefecture is raising a heartbreaking cry, saying: "Outside the prefecture, Standard Japanese is next in importance to life itself," and "What tangible and intangible losses prefectural residents are incurring because they cannot speak Standard Japanese well enough!"' (Tsuitō Bunshū Kankō Iinkai 1990, p. 331; Yoshida 1940b [1970], p. 361).

Such criticism did not only come from Yoshida. A large number of readers' letters were sent to local newspapers in regard to this debate, but most of them were ones vehemently criticising Yanagi. One contributor, who had had the experience of being a migrant worker in the Osaka–Kobe area, wrote: 'Poets and artists see Okinawans' plain and simple customs, and say that they are very "tropical" or "passionate." But people who have this view are one in ten, at most.' 'Old things should be left to those few people who study old things. We should work toward building the Okinawa of tomorrow.' A different reader asserted: 'We oppose foolish affection and needless caresses; we wish both to be loved and despised with the same eye that regards Satsuma people or Edoites' (Tana 1940 [1970], p. 368; Shiroma 1940b [1970], p. 362).

A local newspaper reporter further criticised Yanagi and the others, saying:

> When power poles become a nuisance in the eyes of these people of refined tastes, stopping them from photographing Old-Ryukyu-style scenery, they impudently demand the removal of the poles. In their hearts, they want us to get by without using electric light and electric power in Okinawa. Because [the poles] get in the way of their making sport with Okinawa, they care nothing about benefit to the citizens or prosperity for the nation. One cannot help admiring their thoroughly selfish hearts (Higa 1940 [1970], double-quoted from *Gekkan mingei* 1940d, p. 376).

Criticism from the Okinawa side was also directed at the thinking of Yanagi's Folk Craft Movement. One contributor turned a suspicious eye towards Yanagi's sensitivity, he having claimed that he had discovered the beauty of Okinawa by intuition; and described it as 'not having been by intuition, but being something nurtured as a backlash against the machine-made craftwork of capitalist culture, which Mr Yanagi abhorred in the extreme.' A different letter to the editor said: 'Much of the ancient lacquer-ware [that Yanagi admired] was work from the Kaizuri Bugyōsho (a production facility under the royal administration), and was nothing more than official craftwork made without heed to time or expense (and not folk craft),' and claimed that Yanagi had not seen the class relationships and exploitation of labour inside Okinawa, which formed the backdrop of the works of art (Shiroma 1940a [1970], p. 363; Yamada 1940 [1970], p. 450).

Furthermore, a letter was received from a teacher from the Kunigami district, saying: 'Though glib reference is made to the

Okinawan dialect, the reality is that it comprises ten or twenty layers,' and 'the residents of the main island do not understand the Miyako dialect, nor do they understand the Yaeyama dialect. Based on such a reality, it is both efficient and effective [to proceed] by the single line of promoting Standard Japanese, in order also to aim for the unity of prefectural residents.' According this man, until learning Standard Japanese, he had been unable to speak anything but a 'weird dialect that was not intelligible to other villages,' but he claimed 'now to be able to converse freely with the elegant and well-bred people of Shuri' (Kaneshiro 1940 [1970], p. 365). As homogenisation by means of Standard Japanese destroyed the social order from the days of the Ryukyu Kingdom, where language had been differentiated by region and class, it was perceived by this contributor to be a kind of liberation. The 'Okinawa' which Yanagi understood as if it were a single presence was also something that involved complex struggle for the people who lived in it.

Actually, opinions such as those seen in these letters to the editor were nothing new to the Okinawans. Already in 1901, Ōta Chōfu, Editor-in-Chief of the *Ryūkyū shinpō* newspaper, was able to declare that 'though there are artists from the mainland who come and hear the clothing of our prefecture's women praised and foolishly proclaim arguments for its preservation, they are people who have an eye for art, but no eye for society.' Moreover, in 1926, immediately following the 'sago-palm hell' period, Ifa Fuyū also stated that it was Okinawa's 'bourgeoisie that claimed that Okinawan art was superior,' and he 'felt as if this [did] not apply in the case of ordinary Ryukyuans down in the countryside, especially the Old-Ryukyans.' It was in a contribution to a special issue on Okinawan culture compiled by a Tokyo magazine that Ifa published these words, but, surrounded by ranks of sentences extolling the spirit of Okinawa and its scenic beauty, Ifa wrote: 'Contrary to what people in the centre are thinking, land in the Ryukyus is not fertile, nor are its coastal waters teeming with fish,' in a tone as if to say: 'Do they imagine that Okinawans can live by scenery and spirit alone?' (Hiyane and Isa 1993, p. 261; Hattori et al. 1974, pp. 270, 265). There was also a tendency among letters from the Okinawan side to argue back, having regarded all utterances from members of the Tourism Association, Folk Art Association and suchlike to have been Yanagi's, as well, but there was no small number that cut to the quick of Yanagi's thought, either.

However, as was also seen in Yoshida's case, the backlash from the Okinawan side in this debate was something mixed with a warped sense of inferiority vis-à-vis Yanagi and his ilk, who were Tokyo intellectuals. A letter entitled 'To the big shots,' published in a local newspaper, said:

> ... Present-day Okinawa is making utmost efforts to keep pace with rapidly-advancing Japan. You criticise that with a mistaken, strange sense of superiority ... You probably have a really light-hearted feeling – it might be something akin to pacifying a baby by calling its red clothing the best thing in the world, and saying it was a really lovely kimono ... Okinawa is really a nice place – it is our native home, after all – but if I said to you: 'If it is such a nice place, how about living here permanently?' I think that you would run away, saying: 'Children are too much trouble. We cannot handle them.' ... We know better than you of the wretchedness of Okinawa, and for that very reason, we are trying our hardest (Ōgimi 1940 [1970], p. 357)

This contributor poses the question: 'Take, for example, the clothing of us women, which you praise as being lovely garments – would you have the courage to send us to an exhibition in America, saying that Japanese women are like this?' This would not have been a mere metaphorical issue for the Okinawan side, which still remembered the discriminatory 1903 'Jinruikan (Hall of Mankind) Incident' at the Osaka Industrial Exhibition, where Okinawan prostitutes were exhibited as 'Ryukyuan noble-women.' If it had been Yanagi, he would have boldly displayed his Ryukyuan costume at the American exhibition, but the writer did not have such confidence.

This debate is nowadays called the 'Okinawan language debate,' but actually linguistic issues were but one part of it; many statements from the Okinawan side, in particular, mention problems of modernisation and development. A significant characteristic of such counterarguments, however, was that there were none which discussed the issues of development and Standard Japanese separately. In other words, none of the discussants sympathised with criticism of the strict enforcement of Standard Japanese while criticising the perspective on development held by Yanagi and others. For those Okinawans, the development of Okinawa and the strict enforcement of Standard Japanese had already become inseparable. For that very reason, the aforementioned Yoshida and those like him, also, argued without making a distinction between solving the problem of poverty and promoting Standard Japanese, and the writers of letters to the editor, even while criticising Yanagi, asserted: 'how much better it might be for prefectural residents as a whole to do as they pleased and then die amid the red earth of their native home, if the alternative meant indicating their intentions [outside the prefecture] with a stammer, and in broken Japanese, moreover, and thus continuing to injure the prefecture's honour' (Tana 1940, p. 368).

This reflected the situation in Okinawa where, unlike in the case of Korea or Taiwan, assimilation was the very thing that had been viewed as the only method of development and of reducing discrimination, without any distinction having been made between 'civilising' and 'Japanising.' Yanagi was not necessarily opposed to the promotion of Standard Japanese or of development *per se*, but in the minds of Okinawan contributors there were only two alternatives left, namely, assimilating and gaining a reduction in discrimination, or remaining in a state of backwardness and discrimination; and the leeway to ask what had brought about the discourse structure of such alternatives had been lost. In such an environment, not only were Yanagi's words accepted as a kind of Orientalism that attempted to keep Okinawa in a situation of being discriminated against, but the Okinawan side's feeling of antagonism towards Orientalism turned in the direction of intensifying efforts for assimilation.

Dialect advocacy as 'Westerners'

Meanwhile, in Tokyo, too, this debate drew attention, and many intellectuals made statements about it, but in contrast to the Okinawan side, most of these were in support of Yanagi.

Their focus, however, was not so much upon Okinawan residents' circumstances, but upon the abstract proposition of whether or not to respect regional culture. Moreover, what the central intelligentsia had in common was an eye that regarded the relationship between Okinawa and Japan as being a miniature copy of that between Japan and the West. The poet Hagiwara Sakutarō, for example, when asked for a comment by *Gekkan mingei* (Folk craft monthly) magazine, said:

> Foreign travellers touring Japan, while admiring Japan's unique architecture and the beauty of its natural features, lament that the

Japanese unsparingly destroy these things and intently engage in vulgar imitation of the West, and they often give kindly advice for Japan's sake. Yet not only are the Japanese by no means willing to heed that advice, but they conversely become angry and hurl back the accusation that it constitutes needless interference which inhibits the development of emergent Japan, or else is a remark stemming from the tourists' exoticism, aimed at making Japan a land of spectacle for themselves. The incident in Ryukyu, also, could be considered to have exact resemblance to this.

... The attitude of contempt which the people of Ryukyu have towards the products of their folk culture and their worshipful attitude to central culture are thought to be probably the same as that which ordinary Japanese people have towards Western civilisation (Hagiwara 1940 [1970], p. 387).

There were many other examples. The critic Satō Nobue, for one, commented: 'I think it is interesting that these days, people from *naichi* have an attitude to the Ryukyus just like that which Westerners formerly took towards Japan during its *"bunmei kaika"* Westernisation movement days. It seems that today's Ryukyuans are the Japanese of those former times' (double-quoted from *Gekkan mingei* 1940c [1970], p. 403). Shimizu Ikutarō, in turn, remarked: 'It is a well-known fact that foreigners visiting Japan turn their eyes away from the cities, and prize this fragment [=the traditional culture of agrarian villages], instead. When people who are starting to have regrets over things that might be called the forefront of present-day Japanese culture come into contact with Ryukyuan culture, it is probably natural that their hearts are captivated by it' (Shimizu 1940 [1970], p. 370). Yanagita Kunio, too, said at a roundtable discussion published in *Gekkan mingei* (Folk craft monthly): 'Essentially, Naha people are frivolous and opportunistic, and have an attitude just like that of the Japanese in early Meiji towards foreign cultural products' (Yanagita et al. 1940 [1970], p. 398).

In response, a special feature article in *Gekkan mingei* commented:

When we asked ordinary culturati from the centre about the current problem, the opinion of the majority was expressed as: 'Ryukyu now is just like the Japanese of the previous age, with their civilisation and enlightenment [ideas] à propos Western culture.' Having found out, through the reform of manners in present-day Okinawa, how people who fancy themselves as moving at the so-called cutting edge of culture are regarded by intellectuals in the centre, I would wish for deep reflection [on their part] (*Gekkan mingei* 1940c, p. 403).[4]

Such remarks indicate the kind of concerns and attitudes with which central intellectuals were dealing with this Okinawan language debate. In the long run, the majority of them were discussing Okinawa as material for talking about Japanese cultural identity, and it is doubtful whether they really had an interest in Okinawa *per se*, which they hardly even knew.

Moreover, at that point they were able to take the position not of the weak who were troubled by a sense of cultural inferiority, but of the strong who advised the preservation of regional culture. In other words, it was something that allowed them to experience a feeling 'just like that Westerners formerly desired of Japan in "civilisation and enlightenment" days.' In the abovementioned *Gekken mingei* article, also, there flickered a sense of superiority, demanding of the Okinawan side that they be conscious of 'how they were viewed by the central intelligentsia,' and that they 'reflect deeply.'

What deserves notice, moreover, is that the schema of 'The West versus Japan = Japan versus Okinawa,' which enjoyed so much agreement in the centre, was not being accepted by the Okinawan side. Yanagi, also, in response to Yoshida's counterargument to himself, said: 'People like Mr Yoshida are exactly the same type as that portion of the Japanese who were seduced by Western culture in the transition period between Meiji and Taisho [in the early 1910s], and displayed an insulting attitude towards Westerners,' but Yoshida, who was named, responded by saying: 'This is unexpected. In his trying to apply the relationship between Japan and the West in those days to that of Okinawa, as is, one is made to perceive a touch of anxiety in Yanagi's cognition towards the prefecture' (Yanagi 1981b, p. 152; Yoshida 1940b [1970]). Such a statement from Yanagi probably had no effect except to anger Yoshida even more.

It was not only Yoshida who thought thus. There was nobody to be seen on the Okinawan side that sympathised with this schema. If one considers that this schema was a projection inseparable from the narcissism of the central intelligentsia, it was also a matter of course. From the start, the concern of the Okinawan side had been the improvement of their own lifestyles and the reduction of discrimination, and they would not have cared regardless of whether this issue bore any resemblance to the relationship between Japan and the West. Furthermore, in the remarks from the majority of central intellectuals, in contrast to the passion with which they expounded this subject as a cultural issue, there was hardly any concern given to the Okinawan lifestyle or discrimination problem.

Speaking somewhat paradoxically, the central intelligentsia were at one with the nation called Japan to the extent that they regarded the relationship between Japan and the West automatically to be an issue of their own cultural identity. By contrast, even while touting the strict enforcement of Japanese out front, the Okinawan side actually was giving greatest priority to local interests. Though it appears that the former extols respect for regional culture and the latter is taking a stance of placing emphasis on the nation if one looks only at their superficial claims, it is difficult to judge which of them really deserved to be called nationalist. A local newspaper's commentary on current events stated that while Mr Yanagi was dealing with this debate 'from a national (*kokka-teki*) point of view,' advocates from the Okinawan side were speaking 'from the interests of the prefecture' (*Ryūkyū shinpō* 1940c [1970], pp. 403, 363). Yanagi might have been surprised to be associated with the term 'national,' but this could not necessarily be said to have missed the mark.

Of course, even among central intellectuals, there were counterarguments to Yanagi. As in the case of linguist Hoshina Kōichi and others, there did exist the opinion that dialects were not desirable from the perspective of unification of the state, but there were also some thinkers who made opposing arguments from the perspective of Okinawan development.

One of these, literary critic Sugiyama Heisuke, speaking from his own experience of visiting Okinawa, stated: 'If their horrific, poverty-stricken lives are not confronted, nothing but their past folk craft objects are praised, and [Okinawa] is bandied about as being islands where [the inhabitants] live happy, correct lives, and suchlike, then residents of Okinawa prefecture will have no chance to get on in the world,' and attacked Yanagi, saying: 'You must not impose a role like that of a museum guard onto all Okinawan prefectural residents. Okinawan prefectural residents must not be people living in the past, but ones living in the future' (Sugiyama 1940a [1970], p. 421; 1940a [1970], p. 419).

Sugiyama's counterargument was not one that doubted the either-or discourse structure such as previously mentioned, but rather one that declared: 'The policy of the authorities who are thoroughly popularising Standard Japanese and suppressing regional languages is wholly correct,' and 'As Japanese, to live on in future using that sort of language will be a fearsome handicap.' The Okinawan side's having spoken in that way was due to their having been forced by circumstances, but even if superficially he had uttered the same words, for Sugiyama to say that – being on the side facing Okinawa and enforcing Standard Japanese – was an act that ignored his own advantageous position. To make matters worse, Sugiyama said things like: 'Having stayed in Naha for twenty-three days, my mind was made up,' and 'I simply came here because of a vague admiration for the Ryukyuan spirit, akin to Westerners coming to Japan to see Fujiyama (*sic*) and cherry blossoms' (Sugiyama 1940c [1970], p. 371; 1940b [1970] p. 416). In Sugiyama's case, he probably merely brought out the issue of Okinawan development as material for refuting Yanagi, whom he regarded as hypocritical; his principal motivation was his sense of competitiveness within the central world of criticism, and the fate of Okinawa was unlikely to have been his true concern, after all.

Ultimately, in Tokyo's critical arena, most of the advocates were more engrossed in their own cultural discourses than in the conditions in Okinawa, and it is hard to suggest that much fruitful discussion was carried on. That paralleled the way the discourse on governing Korea and Taiwan by politicians in Japan proper was made political capital, ignoring the local circumstances.

Emphasising 'the Japanese'

Amid such debates, unlike many thinkers, Yanagi published a series of discussions in which he was strongly aware of the various predicaments in Okinawa. In these, he made appeals, saying that even in terms of economic development and the lessening of discrimination, 'Okinawa should not open its way by emulating other prefectures, but must pioneer its future by its own inner resources, which will not allow the emulation of other prefectures.' 'Prefectural residents, have confidence! Reflect on the cultural value that you yourselves possess, and feel pride in being Okinawans!' 'Though there are some who preach that changing to Standard Japanese as soon as possible is what prefectural residents themselves desire, if prefectural residents developed confidence, then they would probably not say such a thing.' While these words express Yanagi's sympathy for Okinawa, at the same time there was a recognition that 'the best gift is prefectural residents' "spiritual confidence" rather than material property,' just as there once had been in relation to Korea, also (Yanagi 1981b, pp. 182, 177, 595).

However, in Yanagi's discourses on Okinawa, there were included the following assertions which had not been mentioned in relation to Korea, Taiwan, the Ainu, and so on.

> Unhappily, notions relating to Ryukyu held by the people of *naichi* are generally slipshod in the extreme ... Ryukyu is near Taiwan, and one thinks of it rather as being like a continuation of savage lands. Otherwise, one imagines it to be close to Hokkien [=Fujian], its natural features all perhaps being Chinese-like ... The very saving of prefectural dwellers from self-abasement is probably more vital than saving them from poverty. For that, [we] must turn outwards and promote how obvious a presence Okinawa is within the Japanese cultural sphere, and turn inwards and make ourselves aware of it. Ryukyu is different from a colony. It differs in type and quality from a history like Taiwan's. It is one of the precious Japanese cultural regions. Moreover, it is one region which even now carries on numerous traditions important for Japan (Yanagi 1981b, pp. 184, 185).

Enlighten the people outside the prefecture that Okinawa is part of 'Japan,' is 'near Taiwan,' and 'different from a colony,' and make Okinawa residents 'aware' of these things – these were the means which Yanagi chose in order to make the people of Okinawa have pride.

Such ideas actually were ones that had been embraced by Yanagi from the early period of the language debate. From the time of Yanagi's discussions with the Chief of Police when he visited Okinawa, he had stated as the rationale for the conservation of Okinawan language that 'when it comes to determining the Japanese language in future, there is no guarantee that Ryukyuan will not give vital suggestions.' That, in other words, was something that sprang from his recognition that 'as linguists agree, out of the various kinds of regional languages that currently survive in Japan, those which most prolifically include traditional, pure Japanese (*Wago*) are the local dialects of Tohoku and Okinawan. Especially in the latter case, on that point they rather have value even akin to a national treasure,' and in the text of the first counterargument, also, he stated: 'When the compilation of a great dictionary of the Japanese [Empire]'s national language can be accomplished at an early date, in the article on the purest *Wago*, they will probably discover that they need to cite numerous examples from Okinawan' (Yanagi 1981b, pp. 355, 149, 150).

Behind Yanagi's making such assertions lay the temporal circumstance of 1940, when this debate was carried on. This was because, in contrast to the intensification of imposition of Japanese as the 'national language (*kokugo*)' in Korea, Taiwan, Okinawa and the like, a revival of regional agricultural village culture on Japan's main islands was being declared amid a heightening of ultra-nationalism. This was influenced by the rise of anti-capitalist, anti-liberal and anti-Western civilisation assertions, and by Nazi Germany, with its touting of 'blood and soil,' having commended [wholesome] regional agricultural village culture. Yanagi, too, in his rebuttal to the prefectural office, asked: 'How will [we] venture to criticise the way measures for the stimulation of regional languages, customs, literature, handicrafts, architecture and so on are being discussed on a large scale recently, in Germany [and] in Italy?' and asserted: 'When the central language is disordered by motley tones, and is on the way to losing its purity as the Japanese language through adulteration by foreign loanwords, in particular, the Okinawan language appears before us just as if in close-up' (Yanagi 1981b, pp. 153, 159).

Such a tenor of argument was not confined to Yanagi. A member of the Folk Art Association, Shikiba Ryūzaburō, for one, presuming that 'Germany's recent growing emphasis upon cultural regionality is due to its realisation that national characteristics remain there markedly,' has stated that 'the fact that wholesome folk craft has vanished from the centre, and remains in parts of Tohoku and Kyushu, Ryukyu, and so on, is what gives the movement for affirmation of the Japanese spirit the finest material.' In addition, the likes of Hasegawa Nyozekan and Ishiguro Osamu, also, referring to the Nazi regional language revival movement, explained the significance of preserving Okinawan language; while the English literature scholar, Jugaku Bunshō, opposed the enforcement of Standard Japanese, saying: 'If the hideous vocabulary and grammar that young women and the like in Tokyo today are using is the model for living Standard Japanese, then to hell with Standard Japanese!' (Shikiba 1940 [1970], p. 371;

Hasegawa 1940 [1970], p. 390; Ishiguro 1940 [1970], p. 406; Jugaku 1940 [1970], p. 390).

It is not impossible to regard the claims of Yanagi and others as a camouflage tactic in this age of vehement suppression of free speech. As previously mentioned, however, the Folk Craft Movement, which adopted the principles of opposing Western civilisation and protecting traditional culture, had had elements that were easily tied to nationalism from the start. Moreover, nationalism had two contradictory faces – one aspect that homogenised regional languages and culture under the banner of modernisation and universality, and another that championed anti-modernisation and racial distinctiveness while resisting homogeneity. While the prefectural office side, following the logic of the former, carried out the strict enforcement of Standard Japanese, Yanagi and his ilk tried to resist, going by the logic of the latter.

Amid such logic, Yanagi leaned towards such assertions as 'coming to Okinawa, which is imagined to be different from Japan, one can encounter unspoilt Japan for the first time,' and 'when the recent styles have sunk into a shallow form and quality, and vulgar designs and tones, Okinawa alone has retained the style of Yamato, and is maintaining superior quality and beauty.' Naturally, the 'unspoilt Japan' which nobody had ever seen was a product of his imagination, and it goes without saying that this claim became linked to the Japan–Ryukyu common-ancestry theory which said that Okinawan language and culture were not peculiar to Okinawa, but merely appeared to be singular because those of ancient Japan were being preserved there. In the debate, Yanagi asserted that '[in Okinawa] the language which our Japanese ancestors were using from the Kamakura through to the Muromachi periods is being used, as is,' and 'Ryukyuan traditional clothing is more or less that of the Muromachi period,' and he remarked: 'The old Tenpyō capitals must have been so beautiful. People who dream of those old capitals should visit Okinawa' (Yanagi 1981b, pp. 159, 162, 579, 580, 161).

In other words, Yanagi's claim was that in its present form, Okinawa was 'more Japan than Japan,' and did not need to be encroached upon by semi-Westernised Tokyo language and Tokyo culture which had become a 'Japan that was not Japan.' The logic that Japan's ancient culture was being preserved was the same in the Japan-Korea common-ancestry theory, but in this language debate, though Yanagi has written: 'I recalled having once composed a public text for a Korean building,' he insisted on declaring that 'Okinawa is not the same as Korea or Taiwan, much less China and the like' (Yanagi 1981b, p. 594; 1940 [1970], p. 372).

The deployment of such logic was also shared by the Okinawan historian Higaonna Kanjun, for example, who was one of the few Yanagi supporters from the Okinawan side. According to Higaonna, the prohibition of Okinawan language had the potential to yield the 'outrageous, mistaken notion that the Okinawan language is not Japanese,' and it constituted 'the presumption of an uncomprehending bureaucrat who saw Okinawa in the same light as Korea and Taiwan ... [and] insulted the prefectural residents.' For Higaonna, it was Okinawa's – which was supposed to be 'Japan' – having been treated along the same lines as Korea or Taiwan, rather than the promotion of Standard Japanese itself, that was an 'insult,' and he emphasised that 'there is nothing more important than to make [people] realise that all of Okinawan culture occupies a significant position, from the perspective of Japanese culture as a whole' (Ryūkyū Shinpōsha 1980, pp. 174, 176).

The logic that declared Okinawa to be 'Japan' and emphasised its difference from Korea and Taiwan looked to be easily acceptable to the Okinawan side, as well. Sugiyama Heisuke, criticising Yanagi, commented:

> Certainly, these days, Ryukyuans who use the *sōrōbun* [epistolary writing style] can be perceived to be far more 'Japanese-like' than we ourselves who indiscriminately use questionable language sprinkled with translations.
>
> For a new traveller, this is a 'discovery,' because it is the blunt truth that ordinarily irresponsible people from the mainland normally have no deep thoughts whatsoever about Ryukyuans, and vaguely imagine them to be something akin to a mixed race of Japanese, Chinese and Koreans ...
>
> Mr Yanagi is proclaiming: 'Ryukyu is different from Taiwan and Korea.' It made me laugh to read it, because Mr Yanagi is echoing the very cry of some conscientious Ryukyuan people.
>
> They are constantly nervous lest Ryukyu be thought to be something other than Japanese.

> For example, they would probably become angry if [someone] were to use the word *naichi* (mainland Japan, or Japan proper) in their presence. This is because if from Kyushu northwards is *naichi*, then this will mean that Ryukyu is *gaichi* (outlying or foreign parts), and is treated as a colony. That is why I was promptly warned after my arrival that if I did not use the expression '*tafuken* (other prefectures)' instead of the term '*naichi*,' I would upset the locals. (Nonetheless, the Ryukyuan general populace who are not intellectuals do call the area from Kyushu northwards '*naichi*.')
>
> They do not even like to have the word Ryukyu used, for the reason that it is a name bestowed by the emperor of China (Sugiyama 1940b [1970], p. 418).

Certainly, whether or not the 'general populace' did so, the contributors of letters on the Okinawan side feared being excluded from 'the Japanese.' In letters supporting the encouragement of Standard Japanese, taking the movement in Taiwan for turning the people into imperial subjects as an example, they voiced such opinions as: 'Okinawa is far inferior to Taiwan, for in Taiwan, no matter where anyone goes, one does not hear dialect [=the local language],' or 'Prefectural residents! Do not lose out to Taiwan!' (*Okinawa nippō* 1940a [1970], p. 367; 1940c [1970], p. 364).

Unlike the speculations of the central intelligentsia, letters from the Okinawan side were also opposed to this theory that 'Okinawan culture = pure Japan.' A certain contribution said: 'Okinawan language is unmistakeably something that is precious as material for studies of old language, but however precious something may be, unless it has currency elsewhere it has no *raison d'être* as a language,' and counter-argued that 'though the opinion has also emerged that Okinawan may be of use in determining Standard Japanese, when on earth will that future be?' According to them, 'Ryukyuan was not something born in order to take part in 'the compilation of a great dictionary of the Japanese [Empire]'s national language ... [to be] accomplished at an early date,' but something over which the people of Ryukyu had mutually exchanged thought and sentiment, and which manifested its true function for the pursuit of cultural life,' and because from the start; 'in our life experience nowadays, we cannot express our intentions at all in the language of Old-Ryukyu ... and, needless to say, the Ryukyuan language that we are using at present is not a pure one.' The Okinawan language which Yanagi tried to honour by means of the expression 'national treasure' was a tool for everyday life for its users, and 'Ryukyu's being prized because it provides excellent material for studies of Yamato language due to its hoary old dialect is equivalent to the configuration of the American Indian family being prized for being ideal material for studies of ancient societies ... it is certainly no honourable suggestion' (Yamada 1940 [1970], p. 450; Shiroma 1940a [1970], p. 363; Sugiyama 1940a [1970], p. 418).

Ifa himself, too, having originally championed the Japan–Ryukyu common-ancestry theory, had already said in 1926 that 'as Ryukyu is said to have preserved many forms of lifestyle from ancient times, in the same sense that the Ainu, who are dying out, are being valued as national treasures, it is deplorable that apart from attracting the attention of scholars, it does not draw the notice of the world's intelligentsia, and especially of politicians.' The brief comment which Ifa made on the occasion of this language debate was one saying: 'I think that Mr Yanagi's attitude is earnest and sincere, but the one thing I think is wrong is that he is confusing language with folk craft.' He means that unlike folk craft objects which can be displayed anywhere, language is a living tool of human beings, and people's happiness must be prioritised over conservation. Ifa's assertion vis-à-vis Okinawan language was one that said the suppression of regional languages was not desirable because it 'caused loss of national pride,' but the 'languages of small racial groups, not becoming generalised, would naturally disappear, and so artificial interdiction or the like would be futile.' Ifa's twisted irony can be sensed in his description of Yanagi as 'sincere' (Nihon Mingei Kyōkai 1940 [1970], pp. 414, 425, 427).

However, the major reason for newspaper readers on the Okinawan side having been unable to accept Yanagi's assertions was, just as one letter said: 'Our promotion of Standard Japanese is an enlightenment movement to make every last prefectural resident into the Japanese they should be,' they themselves were thinking that their assimilation into 'the Japanese' was still insufficient (Kaneshiro 1940 [1970], p. 364). To these people, who were seized with the fear that as long as there was a disparity, they would not be acknowledged as 'Japanese,' and if they were not recognised as 'Japanese,' then they would be exposed to discrimination, the description 'more Japan than Japan,' too, was taken only to be an expression that was trying to exclude Okinawa from 'the ordinary Japanese.'

The final stage of Okinawan assimilation

In response to this, Yanagi – in order to give Okinawans confidence – demanded: 'Why don't you say "See Japan here," and call yourselves Okinawans?' and inclined further and further towards calling for Okinawa residents to 'have the awareness that more than anything, it is Okinawa that possesses the uniqueness of Yamato culture in the greatest quantity' (Yanagi 1981b, pp. 159, 167). Now, the more concerned he was for the feelings of the Okinawan side, the more effort he came to pour into incorporating Okinawa within the boundaries of 'the Japanese.'

The prefectural office end, however, was moving by means of a logic that was completely unrelated to such a debate. In response to Yanagi, who advocated conservation with the words: 'Isn't Okinawan language purely a dialect of Japanese lineage?' Fuchigami Fusatarō, the prefectural governor who met Yanagi in the midst of the debate in August 1940, said: 'There will be no development of this prefecture unless it switches to Standard Japanese. Actually, on such occasions as their physical examination there are some [conscripts] that still cannot use the language correctly – it is risible.' 'It would not do to regard this prefecture's circumstances in the same light as other prefectures, for there were even some people in this prefecture who wanted to side with China in the days of the Sino-Japanese War' (Yanagi 1981b, pp. 599, 600).

This reply indicated that the governor's recognition had not changed whatsoever from the assimilation discourse of mid-Meiji times, which aimed at securing Okinawa as a bastion of national defence. It had been so already from the statement that marked the beginning of this debate, but the example which the prefectural office produced as a merit of the popularisation of Standard Japanese was that of the physical examination for conscripts, and what was important was the self-commitment of residents' spirit of allegiance in wartime.

On the other hand, in an interview with Yanagi, the governor mentioned nothing about the reduction of discrimination by means of assimilation into 'the Japanese' for which the Okinawan writers of letters to the editor desperately longed. What was important for the governor was not whether Okinawan culture was 'undamaged Japan,' but whether they showed a spirit of allegiance to the Japanese government and to himself in the form of using Standard Japanese.

Without opposing the encouragement of Standard Japanese, Yanagi advocated that it should be used in tandem with regional languages, but the governor rejected this, also. If it were mere languages in question, there would probably have been the potential for dual use, but there could only be one single target of loyalty. For this governor, also, to be 'Japanese' was an expression that meant not rights and equality, but allegiance and submission, and the greater the pain suffered by residents in abandoning Okinawan language, the deeper the sense of loyalty that was demonstrated by it would grow.

In response to such a stance by the governor, Yanagi and his supporters were driven into a position where they had no choice but to resist by emphasising all the more that Okinawa was 'Japan.' In November 1940, three months after the interview with the governor, the Folk Art Association published its 'Argument vis-à-vis the Okinawan language problem' as a final opinion on this debate in *Gekkan mingei* ((Nihon Mingei Kyōkai 1940 [1970], pp. 414, 425, 427). This argument divides the history of Okinawa's policy on Standard Japanese policy into three periods.

The 'first period' identified by the Folk Art Association ranged from the Ryukyu Disposition until after the Sino-Japanese War, and 'what constituted the fundamental spirit of this first period was something with an extremely strongly political nature which strove to turn Okinawa Japanese by the diffusion of Standard Japanese.' Its grounds reportedly were that 'quite a serious idea of China-worship was mixed ... in with public sentiment in Okinawa at the time,' and 'in Okinawa under such conditions, popularising this Standard Japanese had the same significance as Japan's present exporting of the Japanese language to China and Manchuria, or its disseminating the national language (*kokugo* = Japanese) to Korea and Taiwan.' It was, 'in short, a semi-colonial policy towards Okinawa.'

The second period which followed it was 'an age when Okinawan prefectural residents left their native place, or migrated to the South Sea Islands, or went to Osaka and suchlike as temporary migrant labour, or had new connections with the outside through occasional trips, and so on.' Furthermore, 'in these times, because inhabitants of Okinawa Prefecture had so-called Okinawan rustic elements, they were misunderstood as being racially different from residents of other prefectures,' and 'the prompt eradication of this rustic cultural odour was thought by people to be the only path to devising the advancement of Okinawa.'

In other words, in the first period it was the 'Japanisation' of Okinawa for political and military reasons, while in the second it was avoidance of 'mistakenly being understood to be racially different' by other prefectures, and breaking away from discrimination, that respectively comprised the motivation for the promotion of Standard Japanese. One could say that the former was Governor Fuchigami's logic, and the latter the logic employed by an advocate on the Okinawan side who argued against Yanagi.

As such, this written opinion stated that 'we must pay deep respect from the bottom of our hearts to the people who, in the difficult times of this first and second period, expended all their efforts for this encouragement of Standard Japanese,' and 'for Okinawa in that transition period, to do so was a compelling historical path,' but having said that, it asserted that now, such periods had passed. Furthermore, it explained that 'even among the whole of Japan, the culture of Okinawa is an especially pure form,' and, saying that 'recently, in the *Shina jihen* (Second Sino-Japanese War), the scene of the send-off at that thriving Naha port for the brave troops setting out for the battlefield was nothing if not the picture of an overflow of Japan's most enthusiastic patriotic sincerity,' it emphasised that Okinawans had completely become splendid 'Japanese.' Moreover, while commending the Nazis' protection of regional culture, it speaks as follows.

> We declare again that Okinawan folk culture is a purely Japanese cultural entity. Today, when such a fact has become almost too clear, in order to bestow national spirit upon the prefectural residents, there is absolutely no necessity to bring in the whole of that Japanese spirit from outside, as with other colonies. It must be that we revive a brilliant Japanese spirit from amid their boundless self-confidence and affection for their native place, and, in this way, additionally convey the urgent central will under wartime circumstances, in the same way as other prefectures.

The written opinion finally ends by emphasising that 'our future job' is to convey 'to people outside Okinawa that Okinawan culture is a culture with a Japanese lineage.

In this manner, the Okinawa language debate, which had been waged for about a year, came to an end. This debate was not simply one between the side that suppressed local culture and a side that respected it. As the Folk Art Association positioned it, it was a debate between the side that thought Okinawa had not yet become completely 'Japanese,' and that which deemed Okinawa to be sufficiently 'Japanese.'

As for Yanagi the individual, his perspective on art was exposed to a great crisis in this incident. While preventing his own assertions from falling into the logic of Orientalism and exclusion, he once endeavoured to give pride and confidence to Okinawa's uniqueness. However, in the then-current patterns of discourse, this emerged solely in a form that incorporated Okinawa within the boundaries of 'the Japanese' and stressed its difference from Korea and Taiwan. Moreover, in this debate, the recognition and awareness that Okinawa was 'Japanese' became firmly established in both the Okinawan and central camps. Just as the Folk Art Association had positioned it, this, after all, was what could be called the final stage of Okinawan assimilation which had continued since mid-Meiji.

When exposed to much counterargument in the process of debate, Yanagi wrote: 'I am now quietly remorseful that the work which we did in Okinawa hitherto was probably bad for Okinawa.' Continuing on from this, he noted: 'When I think thus, all right, even if there were parts where our efforts were insufficient, fortunately we can have the unshakeable belief that we were far from corrupting Okinawa.' 'I do not mind even if this is called mere hubris on our part. We are fully convinced of its truth' (Yanagi 1981b, p. 175). He being in the midst of the central intelligentsia who participated in this debate, there is no doubt that Yanagi was the individual that showed the most respect and affection towards Okinawa. However, it is unlikely to be easy even today to judge how to appraise the role he fulfilled in the debate.

Later, the Okinawan streetscape which Yanagi had loved was reduced to ashes in the war, and its previous form came to be remembered only through the photographs and films which the Folk Art Association had recorded. The GwanghwamunGate in Korea which he had saved was destroyed in the Korean War, leaving only its cornerstone. After the Pacific War, and until his death in 1961, Yanagi never again visited Korea or Okinawa. His heart may have been too delicate to bear confrontation with the raw reality of the things that he had loved.

5 Islands on the Boundary

In the Battle of Okinawa which lasted from March to June 1945, there were such fierce naval bombardment, air strikes and shelling from U.S. forces that the islands' very topography was altered, and in Okinawa tales of this have been handed down as the so-called 'typhoon of steel.' Approximately 12,000 U.S. troops, 94,000 Japanese troops, and 150,000 Okinawan residents (including some 28,000 temporarily mobilised by the Japanese military) died in the battle. The number of casualties among residents was equivalent to a quarter of the then population of Okinawa Prefecture, and a third of that of the main island of Okinawa. Moreover, no small number of residents was massacred by Japanese or U.S. troops. Many young people of Okinawa who had received patriotic education as 'Japanese,' believing that the Japanese forces which purported to defend Okinawa against invaders would be victorious, eagerly responded to mobilisation as soldiers or nurses, but they ended up being betrayed by the outcome of the battle and the true state of the Japanese military.

Then, in August 1945, following the atomic bombing of Hiroshima and Nagasaki, the Empire of Japan unconditionally surrendered, and the war ended. Karafuto (Sakhalin), Taiwan and Korea were severed from Japanese territory, and the non-Japanese 'Japanese' who lived in those areas ceased to be 'Japanese.' However, even in the postwar, some people situated on the boundaries of 'the Japanese' did exist, namely Koreans resident in Japan, Ainu, and Okinawans.

From here on, I will examine the historical path which Okinawa followed during that period. This is because although the question of Koreans resident in Japan and Ainu is not insignificant, either, as an issue of the boundaries of 'the Japanese' accompanying territorial amendment – the subject of this book – it is still Okinawa that constitutes the biggest target, it having undertaken a transition entailing segmentation from and reversion to Japan. Moreover, it encompassed numerous problems around 'the Japanese' in the postwar.

Okinawans as an 'racial minority'

Immediately after the defeat, Koreans, Taiwanese and Ainu who were living in Japan, as well as Okinawans, were each placed in a different legal situation. Here, firstly, I will give only a brief explanation of the first two, then launch into a discussion of the situation in Okinawa.

The first postwar step that the Japanese government took towards Koreans, Taiwanese and the like who had been living in mainland Japan (*naichi*) was to 'terminate' the voting rights of 'people to whom the Family Registration Law does not apply,' in December 1945. These people had had suffrage in mainland Japan, where the Lower House Members Electoral Law, which was a territorial law, was in force, but such a measure was possible because those people were demarcated by means of the legal structure of the Family Registration Law. Yet, even after that, the Japanese government did not immediately revoke their nationality, and did such things as to intervene in Korean ethnic schools under the rationale that it was natural for it to control the education of 'Japanese' who had Japanese nationality. On the other hand, in the Foreign Registration Order, which was the last imperial edict issued in 1947, they were made the object of registration by their curious positioning as 'deemed foreigners.' As such, after their positioning as both 'Japanese' and not 'Japanese' had been sustained from 1945 to 1951, after the San Francisco Peace Treaty came into effect in 1952, they were unconditionally and simultaneously divested of their Japanese nationality. Since then, while still receiving treatment such as special permanent residence, which is not extended to other foreigners, it means that basically they are treated as 'foreigners.'[1]

Meanwhile, in the case of the Hokkaido Ainu, who were not demarcated by the Family Registration Law, unlike Koreans resident in Japan, in legal terms they consistently continued to be 'Japanese' in the postwar, as well. In the spring of 1947, however, Major General J.M. Swing, who had GHQ jurisdiction over Hokkaido and Northern Tohoku, had invited leaders of the Hokkaido Ainu Association and asked them whether they had the will to become independent from Japan. At that time, the invited Ainu declared: 'We are Japanese. We are not a special race. We have not the slightest idea of doing such a thing (= of independence)' (see Masuko 1989). It is unclear as to what intention the GHQ side had, but even if the Ainu had become independent with the assistance of the U.S. military at that time, surmising from the example of Okinawa which I will later describe, it can be considered that there would have been a high likelihood of it having been turned into a puppet regime as an anti-Soviet military base. Whatever the case, the opportunity for the Ainu to separate from 'the Japanese' vanished at this point, and it is common knowledge that even while remaining 'Japanese,' they continued to be made the object of the Hokkaido Former Natives Protection Act until 1997.

As I have explained, even while involving numerous issues, within several years postwar, Koreans resident in Japan were legally positioned as 'foreigners,' and Ainu as 'Japanese,' respectively. By contrast, it is Okinawa that continued to be placed in a boundary area for twenty-seven years after the war.

So, under what kind of circumstances was the non-Japanisation of Okinawa conducted? This chapter will explain the sequence of events and legal situation, but first let us begin with an examination of America's wartime view of Okinawa.

It is said to have been from around the summer of 1942 that the U.S. government held repeated discussions about the postwar disposition of Okinawa.[3] At this time, the State Department's political subcommittee in charge of diplomacy held the view that it would be all right to allow Japan possession of the islands south of thirty degrees north, starting with Okinawa, on condition of prohibition of turning them into military bases. However, the security subcommittee which placed more emphasis on military strategy did not yield, saying that these islands should be placed under sole U.S. control.

Later, the purport of the government of the Republic of China's demands for reversion of Manchuria, Taiwan and Okinawa was conveyed, but a tripartite conference of American, British and Chinese was held in Cairo in November 1943, with China advocating the joint occupation of Okinawa by the U.S. and China, and its trusteeship by international organisations. Further, in the Cairo Declaration, along with insistence upon Korean independence and reversion to the Republic of China of Taiwan and Manchuria, it was recorded that 'Japan will be expelled from all other territories which she (*sic*) has taken by violence and greed.' It was taken as being almost self-evident to those involved that Okinawa was included in these territories which Japan had 'taken by violence and greed,' but as it was not made explicit, the historical interpretation as to whether Japan had 'taken' Okinawa by 'violence' came to be debated in the later reversion movement.

Whatever the case, within the U.S. government it was the military, which placed importance upon national defence, that strongly advocated the sole occupation of Okinawa. What should be noted, moreover, is that the U.S. side deemed Okinawans to be a racial minority different from 'the Japanese.' In autumn 1944, which was immediately prior to the invasion of Okinawa, several Okinawan survey reports were prepared by anthropologists and others, so let us examine their views of Okinawa.

Out of this type of report, those compiled by groups led by the anthropologist Alfred Tozzer and yet another anthropologist, George Murdock, are well-known. Murdock, in particular, is a scholar also known for his creation of the concept of the nuclear family; and, playing a central role in groups surveying not only Okinawa but also the South Sea Islands, which were territories under Japanese mandate from 1922 to 1945, he was treated as a naval commander.

Naturally, under the circumstances at that time, researchers were unlikely to have been able to conduct fieldwork or anything in Okinawa while it was under Japanese military control, but they used Okinawan Studies documents by Ifa Fuyū and others, of course, as well as Japanese government statistics; and Okinawan history, its residents' ethnicity, religion, customs, kinship groups, its administrative mechanism, economic situation and so forth were reported upon in detail.

As previously mentioned, these survey documents took the view that Okinawans were a different people (*minzoku*) from 'the Japanese.' Despite having used Japanese Okinawan Studies by Ifa and his ilk as reference materials, they came up with a totally opposite point of view, but Tozzer's report states as follows about Japanese Okinawan Studies.[4]

> All books relating to the cultural background of the Japanese and Okinawans are classified into one or the other of two categories. The first category emphasises the commonalities between these two peoples, and hardly touches upon their points of difference. Works by local Okinawans, almost without exception, belong to this type. In most cases, they quite unconsciously consider the cultural level of the mainland Japan to be the higher, and feel an obligation to raise

their own people up to the same level in cultural terms. Authors of the second type of works are mostly not Japanese, and clearly differentiate the cultures of these two peopless. As will be pointed out later, it is extremely natural for a southern people ... to have quite different characteristics from the Japanese in the north (Tozzer 1944).

Having situated Japanese Okinawan Studies in this way, Tozzer and Murdock's groups spoke as follows about the situation in Okinawa, based on work in anthropology and linguistics by such scholars as Torii Ryūzō and Basil Hall Chamberlain, In other words, Japanese ethnicity is a mixture of Ainu, Mongol and Malay types. Okinawans also are a mixed race with almost the same composition elements, but generally they are hirsute, 'containing many more Ainu elements than the mainland Japanese.' And in linguistic terms, 'Modern Japanese and Ryukyuan have similar differences to those seen between French and Italian, and are not mutually intelligible.' In terms of such physical features as head hair, height and body hair, and language, customs, religion and so on, they say that Okinawans 'have a different racial structure from the Japanese' (Okinawa Kenritsu Toshokan Shiryō Henshūshitsu 1995, pp. 75, 76; Okinawa Kenritsu Toshokan Shiryō Henshūshitsu 1996a, p. 111).

In relation to history, the legend of Tametomo's visit is also mentioned, but what is emphasised is that until Meiji, Okinawa had formed a separate state from Japan, as the Ryukyu Kingdom; and that the Ryukyu Disposition had been forced through, overcoming opposition from China and local inhabitants. Moreover, it was pointed out that, after incorporation into Japan, 'the Japanese had contempt for Okinawans, exploited their islands, and did hardly anything for the welfare of the people,' 'the prefectural governor is always [mainland] Japanese, and is appointed by the central government in Tokyo,' and 'islanders are not regarded by the Japanese as being equal in racial terms.' Under the heading of 'Colonial policy,' Murdock et al. comment as follows, under the title of 'Assimilation of island residents' (Okinawa Kenritsu Toshokan Shiryō Henshūshitsu 1996a, pp. 41, 47, 193; Okinawa Kenritsu Toshokan Shiryō Henshūshitsu 1995, pp. 75, 150).

> ... The aim of the Japanese government was to consolidate the [Ryukyuan] islands completely into the Japanese political, economic and cultural mechanism ... Due to the racial and linguistic points of

similarity between these two peoples (Japan and Ryukyu), and the support of scientists who never tired of pointing out other cultural likenesses, Japanese regard Okinawans as Japanese (albeit Japanese of somewhat uncouth and of low social status). More importantly, the assimilation policy had succeeded to the point where almost all Ryukyuans thought of themselves as being Japanese.

Murdock et al. further report on such affairs as visiting Shinto shrines, the distribution of Imperial Portraits, the Imperial Rescript on Education and Standard Japanese (*hyōjungo*) education – 'the sole aim of Japan's entire education system being to create loyal nationals' (Okinawa Kenritsu Toshokan Shiryō Henshūshitsu 1995, pp. 211–213).

In addition, Tozzer carried out a survey report on Okinawan migrants in Hawai'i. In it are cited such examples as that 'Okinawans almost never 'pass' as Japanese,' 'intermarriage between the two groups ('Japanese' and Okinawans) is very rare, not reaching even one percent of the total,' and that there were cases of Okinawan migrants in Hawai'i having stressed that the attack on Pearl Harbour was a war that Japan started, and was something unconnected with themselves (Okinawa Kenritsu Toshokan Shiryō Henshūshitsu 1996a, pp. 105, 106, 111).

Of course, the aim of these reports was not to criticise Japan in ethical terms, but to gain an understanding of such actual circumstances and put them to use for governance. Tozzer remarked: 'I wonder if we can utilise the fissure between the Okinawans and the Japanese in the current war,' and has asserted that 'a promotional campaign oriented towards inflating the idea that Okinawans have been downtrodden, and, by making them compare themselves to the Japanese as a whole, encouraging their self-awareness as Okinawans – in other words, a softly-softly approach, is likely to bear fruit.' As a result of such surveys, in the Battle of Okinawa, fliers targeting residents were dispersed, saying: 'This war is not your war. All of you are simply being used as pawns of the mainland Japanese' (Okinawa Kenritsu Toshokan Shiryō Henshūshitsu 1996a, pp. 112, 113; 1996b, p. 262).

However, such propaganda measures did not have a very conspicuous effect. In a local report addressed to Tozzer, dated December 1946, which was after the occupation of Okinawa, it says: 'I regret that there is no information I can send you about the fissure between the Okinawans and the Japanese' (Okinawa Kenritsu Toshokan Shiryō Henshūshitsu 1996b, p. 185). In reality, there were examples of confrontation arising in internment camps and the like between Okinawan residents and Japanese soldiers, as well, and the fissure did latently exist in its own way, but not to the extent to which the U.S. side had hoped

Such a view of Okinawa persisted among U.S. administrators until later years, however. In 1966, Lieutenant General F.T. Unger, who assumed the post of fifth High Commissioner – as I shall later explain, this was a status corresponding to the 'Governor-General of the Ryukyus,' as it were – said: 'In racial terms, Okinawans are not Japanese,' 'Politically, they formed a kingdom and have lived in it,' and 'They have not even achieved much economic and social advancement under Japanese governance, and that has been unceasingly recalled in the Ryukyu archipelago.' In the same vein, Lieutenant General J.B. Lampert, who became the sixth High Commissioner, also was of the opinion that 'Okinawans are usually looked down upon by the Japanese. It is probably not correct to compare this to the status of Black people in American society, but it is something fairly similar' (double-quoted from Kano 1987, pp. 26, 28).[5]

Nonetheless, one must bear in mind that America's pointing the finger at Japanese discrimination against Okinawa was tied to its own self-justification and narcissism. In 1949, a reporter from *Time* magazine, while saying 'Okinawans were exploited for the long period of over sixty years by the Japanese military and Japanese merchants who disparaged them as rustics,' also proposed such things as 'when the U.S. military landed and gave the Okinawans food and temporary huts, [the Okinawans] were surprised and delighted,' and 'They liked Americans, and plainly hope that Okinawa will become an American territory.' Moreover, in 1952, certain U.S. military authorities, assessing the state of affairs in which most of the children born between U.S. military personnel and Okinawan women were being raised only by their mothers, made the exaggerated claim that 'they are used to this kind of thing, because before the Americans came, Japanese government officials would often leave their wives in mainland Japan and make resident women their lovers' (Nakano 1969, pp. 59, 63).

In many cases, a ruling side's emphasis on the vices of rulers that preceded them includes the motivation of relatively glorifying their own actions. When Japan controlled Korea and Taiwan, too, it used deliberately to stress their exploitation by the Joseon and Qing dynasties. Even if the U.S. had guessed the truth in one aspect, whether it was going to carry out more praiseworthy governance than the previous rulers was an entirely different matter. Even in the case of the view that Okinawans were a different people from 'the Japanese,' it goes without saying that it had circulated the idea because it was convenient to itself, just as the Empire of Japan's discourses of consanguinity between Japan and Ryukyu, and between Japan and Korea had been. Furthermore, contrary to U.S. criticism of its administration by Japan, the reality of U.S. rule of Okinawa was so harsh that it made the Okinawan people turn towards reversion to Japan.

The birth of the Government-General of the Ryukyu Islands

As previously discussed, Okinawa had been treated by the U.S. government as a different target from the Japanese mainland from the very beginning. Moreover, in contrast to the fact that postwar policy towards mainland Japan had been drafted through repeated research in collaboration with departments and agencies within the U.S. government, with the State Department taking a central role, Okinawan occupation and military government documents were compiled by Military Government Section and operational units under the direction of the Department of the Navy's Office of Strategic Services.[6]

In this manner, not only had there been a dense military air in regard to Okinawan administration from the start, but the chaos of the fierce fighting had spurred it on. In the circumstances where a quarter of the resident population had died, there was not even any prospect of producing food on the devastated land, the currency from Japanese times ceased to 'pass,' and the economy was being run on rationing and barter, military government was progressively laid down by means of operational units. After seesawing back and forth over whether the Army or Navy would have jurisdiction over Okinawa's military government, from July 1946 the Army took charge of the military government, and as for currency, a system of military scrip called 'B Yen' was imposed. The fact that rule began from military government came to determine the later destiny of Okinawa, as also been the case with Japan's possession of Taiwan, as I will discuss in Volume 2 of this book.

After that, in 1950, the establishment of the 'civil administration' upon which I will later elaborate (a virtual 'Government-General of the Ryukyus') came to be ordered, but what must be mentioned here is that the quality of those sent to Okinawa to take charge of the military government was low. In the extremely early stage, the anthropologist Murdock and political scientists who conducted the aforementioned surveys worked under the assigned status of military personnel, but they were soon replaced by real military personnel. A report from the U.S. side at the time says: 'If someone were deployed to the Far East, if they were a little better kind of person, then they would go to Tokyo. The next best thing would be to go to the Eighth Army in Yokohama. Next, they would be sent off to The Philippines to work at the Philippines-Ryukyus Command (PHIL-RYCOM). And if they did not make the grade there, they would probably be made to go to RYCOM (Ryukyus Command). If they further did not pass muster even at RYCOM, then they would be exiled to the United States Military Government of the Ryukyu Islands.' 'No matter whether they were military or civilian personnel, their main interest was deemed to be the date when they themselves would be leaving Japan' (double-quoted from Kano 1987, pp. 97, 95).

For such reasons, the morale of the Americans undertaking Okinawan governance could not have been called high. A commercial attaché who worked in Okinawa from 1949 through into 1950 has said: 'Most of the people sent there (= Okinawa) seemed to feel that their career advancement, too, would end at that point,' and censured the commanding officers who came by turns as being 'men who had no ability, understanding or desire whatsoever to continue doing the job of governing the Ryukyus.' In prewar Japan, Okinawa Prefecture was called 'the dumping-ground for regional administrators,' but news reports from the American side at the time also appraised Okinawa as having become 'a well-deserved garbage dump for those without talent and outcasts from the American army.' Naturally, 'military discipline was worse than at any other American military post in the world,' and there were also many crimes committed by American military personnel. That situation is said to have been somewhat ameliorated from around 1950, but it turns out that the model for the system which continued until later was almost completed in the few years of the initial period of rule (Kano 1987, pp. 97; Nakano 1969, p. 59).

While such martial rule was being implemented, the separation of Okinawa from Japan steadily became conclusive. In 1944, the U.S. had already removed the return of Okinawa to China from its options and begun to cement a policy aiming at sole occupation or trusteeship by the U.S. Moreover, in January 1946, General MacArthur issued a memorandum to make a small number of peripheral areas politically and administratively separate from Japan, making clear the separation of Okinawa. In 1947, MacArthur stated that as Okinawans were not Japanese, they seemed not to be opposed to the U.S. occupation of Okinawa, and this implies that the recognition that Okinawans were not 'Japanese' existed in the background (Nakano 1969, p. 4).

What especially strengthened the intention to hold onto Okinawa was the intensification of the Cold War and the establishment of the People's Republic of China. According to the words of one commanding officer in the American Air Force, 'the operational range of B-29 [bombers] dispatched from Okinawa extends to the Kamchatka Peninsula in the north, and from there it crosses Siberia, spans the Baikal Lake area and the whole of mainland China, and in India, it reaches Calcutta,' and Okinawa came to be called the 'keystone of the Pacific.'[7]

In 1951, on the occasion of Japan's becoming independent of American military occupation, Article Three of the San Francisco Peace Treaty was concluded, acknowledging that the American military would control Okinawa and the Ogasawara (Bonin) Islands:

> Japan will concur in any proposal of the United States to the United Nations to place under its trusteeship system, with the United States as the sole administering authority, Nansei Shoto south of 29° north latitude (including the Ryukyu Islands and the Daito Islands), Nanpo Shoto south of Sofu Gan (including the Bonin Islands, Rosario Island and the Volcano Islands) and Parece Vela and Marcus Island. Pending the making of such a proposal and affirmative action thereon, the United States will have the right to exercise all and any powers of administration, legislation and jurisdiction over the territory and inhabitants of these islands, including their territorial waters.

The article is one expressing the expectation that U.S. trusteeship of Okinawa and the Bonin Islands would be carried out, but until it actually eventuated, the U.S. would exercise the three powers of government (administrative, legislative and judicial) in the interim.

This trusteeship system, in a fairly similar manner to the mandate by which prewar Japan controlled the South Sea Islands, is one in which the ruling nation carries out overall administration, though the territory in question is not its own. The great difference between the two, however, is that while mandatory rule forbade military use by the ruling nation, under a trusteeship, in some cases it was deemed possible. As the U.S. had placed the South Sea Islands which it had already seized from Japan under its own trusteeship, if it established trusteeship over Okinawa, then it would have been possible to extend its military bases from the Pacific as far as the Far East.[8]

Even after that, though, the U.S. did not carry out the proposal to assume the trusteeship of Okinawa, and it continued the monopoly situation of administrative right that had been specified as an interim measure. This was because, according to authorities in the U.S. State Department, if it were to implement the proposal to transition to trusteeship, then it would have to discuss it at the United Nations Security Council, and in that event, 'it would mean giving the Soviet Union the opportunity to drive a wedge between Japan and the United States.' In 1957, Australia and others advised the U.S. that it should unequivocally annex Okinawa; but there was fear that this would contravene the Atlantic Charter, which insisted upon no territorial expansion. What is more, under Cold War circumstances, if the U.S. went ahead with annexation, then it was certain to become the target of criticism from the Soviet Union and China (Nakano 1969, p. 165).

In almost the same way as the prewar mandate, the trusteeship system decreed as its aim that the trustee nation would 'encourage inhabitants' political, economic, livelihood and educational advancement,' and 'encourage inhabitants' progressive development towards autonomy or independence.' Nevertheless, in a reply to the Diet on 5 November 1951, Nishimura Kumao, Director-General of the Japanese Foreign Ministry's Treaties Bureau, stated that despite the argument that there was a necessity for the United States to control those islands (= Okinawa) for the time being for the maintenance of peace and security, he had never heard that there was a need to raise the political, economic or cultural standard of compatriots living on those islands and bring them to self-government or independence

(Takano 1962, Appendix, p. 368). In short, it was a 'provisional' occupation for entirely military purposes.

For the U.S. military, if they annexed Okinawa and made it a U.S. territory, then they would have to grant Okinawan residents human rights as 'Americans.' Not only was trusteeship difficult to implement due to opposition from China and the Soviet Union, but it would also mean being bound by United Nations provisions. If Okinawa reverted to Japan, of course marshal rule by the U.S. military could not be carried out. This was because it was precisely through continuing martial rule in the form of a temporary measure and making Okinawa 'a land that was [both] America, and not America' that the U.S. could have free hand.

So, in the thick of these circumstances, what kind of system of governance did the United States establish in Okinawa?

In December 1950, when moves towards conclusion of the Peace Treaty had grown energetic, the U.S. Army Forces – Far East (USAFFE) issued an order abolishing the military government and setting up the 'United States Civil Administration of the Ryukyu Islands (USCAR)' – in other words, a virtual 'Ryukyu Government-General.' This 'Civil Administration' was one in which the Supreme Commander of USAFFE held the concurrent post of Civil Administrator, and the Commanding General of the U.S. Army, Ryukyu Islands, that of Deputy Civil Administrator, so it was a 'civil' administration in name only.

Moreover, the various clauses specified in that order could not on the whole have been said to aim for the protection of human rights. Firstly, U.S. government policy on the administration of the Ryukyu Islands was stipulated as being to strive for the enhancement of residents' economic and social welfare to the extent allowed by military necessity, with the rights of Ryukyuan inhabitants being guaranteed as long as this did cause any impediment to the military occupation. The Deputy Civil Administrator (the Commanding General of the U.S. Army, Ryukyu Islands) was able to order the publication of ordinances at his own discretion, and the Civil Administrator (the Supreme Commander of USAFFE), had the power to order the amendment or revocation of judicial rulings. In other words, the Civil Administrator and Deputy Civil Administrator, who were military personnel, effectively monopolised the three powers of government – administrative, legislative and judicial.

In 1957, this institution of 'Deputy Civil Administrators' was altered to 'High Commissioners,' but its substance did not change. Control of Okinawa by the American government came under the Department of Defense, and the Army took charge under that. It was stipulated that serving military personnel would be appointed by the Secretary of Defense as High Commissioners, who were the heads of the Civil Administration of the Ryukyu Islands, and they could issue orders (called 'proclamations') which had the same potency as laws.

Looking at these, it can be seen that the power and status of Deputy Civil Administrators and High Commissioners bore a close resemblance to the Governors-General of Korea and Taiwan in the days of the Japanese Empire. That being said, the way such High Commissioners were deployed cannot be considered to have drawn upon the Japanese system. Along with its announcement of the institution of High Commissioners, the U.S. Department of Defense had also come up with a policy of compiling a law for the organisation of administration of the Ryukyu Islands, emulating the administrative organisational laws pertaining to Guam, Puerto Rico, the Virgin Islands, Samoa, and so on, which shows where the U.S. sought precedents for its administration of Okinawa (Nakano 1969, p. 161).[9] That said, as there is commonality in that both prewar Korea and Taiwan, and postwar Okinawa were forms of administration where, out of martial necessity, military personnel monopolised the three powers of government under the appellation of 'provisional measures,' it could be argued that it was natural for them to come to resemble one another.

This does not mean that such a method of governance met with no objections within America. In 1949, a proposal was made – as the opinion of Lieutenant Commander Willard A. Hanna from the U.S. military authorities – that if the U.S. were to return Okinawa to Japan and manage it through the GHQ (General Headquarters) in Tokyo, then not only would America's noble purpose be elevated, but it would be able to foist the economic burden of Okinawan reconstruction onto Japan. As the next best plan, Hanna further advocated that the U.S. cease its rule by the military, and switch jurisdiction from the Department of Defense to the Department of the Interior, but ultimately a mood forbidding the relinquishing of Okinawa, which it had 'purchased with American blood,' apparently comprised the general trend in the military (Kano 1987, pp. 91–92; Nakano 1969, p. 48). The recognition that the Okinawan administration would be a deficit operation was shared by the American side, and the view that the burden would be more greatly reduced by reversion to Japan was tabled in the U.S. Congress and so on, as I will later mention, but the mood of the military overcame it. Furthermore, the U.S. military went on to invest an enormous amount of its budget and maintained bases, ports, roads and suchlike in Okinawa, and in 1958, it switched the Okinawan currency to U.S. dollars.

On the other hand, the U.S. repeatedly emphasised that it was not maintaining Okinawa for the benefit of its own country. In 1952, the then Deputy Military Governor Robert Beightler, who was equivalent to the Governor-General of Ryukyu, stated: The United States has no ambitions of any kind towards territorial expansion. We have no colonial aspirations whatsoever. We are only here in order to maintain a Pacific outpost in response to the demands of an unstable world situation,' and asserted: 'The stationing of U.S. troops does not indicate the colonisation, enslavement or permanent occupation [of the Ryukyus], but rather is for the sake of mutual defence against communist invasion'(Nakano 1969, p. 93). He means that the administration of Okinawa was no more than something 'provisional' for the sake of 'peace in the East,' and not for territorial ambitions or colonial rule.

Behind such a speech lay not only narcissism on the American side, but also pragmatic issues to do with the Cold War. The (Melvin) Price Report, which came up with a policy of expropriation of land for bases by means of lump-sum payments, and met with violent opposition, expresses the recognition that '[t]he eyes of the world, and particularly the hooded eyes of the Communist world, are fixed attentively on our actions in Okinawa, the latter in concentrated study to discover what can be used as propaganda against us.' Amid Soviet criticism of 'U.S. imperialism,' it would not do for the U.S. to be implementing 'colonial rule' (Nakano 1969, p. 177).

In order to counteract the Soviet Union, the U.S. military was proposing to make Okinawa a 'show-window of democracy.' However, not only was the reality of their administration far from 'democratic,' in regard to the time limit for ending U.S. military rule, which in the first place was supposed to be 'provisional,' as Major General David A.D. Ogden, Deputy Civil Administrator (= Deputy Governor of the Ryukyu Islands) stated in 1954, the only answer to emerge was to the effect that the U.S. would remain in the Ryukyus until peace and order were established in the Far East. According to Lieutenant General James E. Moore, who became the first High Commissioner in 1957, it was not possible to answer as to whether the U.S. would remain in Okinawa indefinitely, or stay until a fixed time in the future, because the cause of tension lay in communism' (Nakano 1969, pp. 94, 165). Morton H. Halperin, the Deputy Assistant Secretary of Defense in the 1960s, has testified that as Okinawa, where the U.S. military held full authority, was absolutely ideal from a military viewpoint, even if there were to be reversion to Japan, it was considered to be something that would eventuate in the twenty-first or twenty-second century (NHK Shuzai Han 1996, p. 49).

In regard to Okinawan residents who opposed the forcible seizure of land, Lieutenant General Moore further said that it was necessary for the U.S. to maintain military bases for the protection of free nations in the Far East, and that the U.S. was investing its own wealth and making all-out efforts for that purpose; and he emphasised the point that the U.S. was making selfless sacrifices for the sake of peace in the Orient. According to current reports, not only Moore, but other Americans living in Okinawa, also, apparently were mystified as to why most Okinawans disliked Americans, even though the U.S. was pouring several hundreds of millions of dollars in order to assist Okinawa (Nakano 1969, p. 189; Fonaker 1958). As had been the case with the Japanese administration in Korea and Taiwan, as discussed in Volume 2 of this book, loss-making operations motivated by national defence had transformed into narcissism on the part of the rulers.

Exclusion from being 'American'

Nevertheless, the U.S. administration of Okinawa did also differ greatly from the domination of Korea and Taiwan by the Japanese Empire, in that while the Empire of Japan had the intention of assimilating the native people into 'the Japanese,' America did not.

The United States – which had overwhelming military power from the start, and had no rivals, either, in maintaining Okinawa in its sphere of influence – had scarce necessity to implement policies of territorial annexation or education for the fostering of loyalty and so on, such as the Japanese Empire had put into practice. As previously noted, incorporation of territory was not merely difficult because of Atlantic Charter constraints and the gaze from the communist sphere, but it was also a nuisance for the U.S. military for Okinawans to receive human rights protection as 'Americans.' In May 1952, immediately after the Peace Treaty came into effect, the reply to Japan by a legal consultant from the U.S. State Department stated that Okinawan residents had not acquired American nationality, and further, in 1954, Okinawans living in Hawai'i, which was U.S. territory, received a guilty verdict because they had not carried out the necessary reporting procedures as foreigners. As I will later elaborate, in 1962 the then Assistant Secretary of State said in a reply in Congress that the U.S. did not intend to incorporate the Ryukyus permanently into America.

This not only simplified rule on-site in Okinawa, but was also useful in the utilisation of Okinawans as a migrant labour force. A certain U.S. military authority is purported to have remarked that the merit of using Okinawan instead of Filipino workers was that by using Okinawans in Guam, they could do away with the problem of Filipino workers intruding upon them by marrying women from Guam and going on to acquire American citizenship. In 1948, the U.S. military government in Okinawa issued an ordinance prohibiting marriage between local inhabitants and U.S. military personnel. This was later repealed, but an intention not to allow Okinawans to intrude onto American nationality can probably be read into this (double-quoted from Kano 1987, p. 110; Nakano 1969, p. 10).

For the U.S., it was necessary to curtail Ryukyuan residents' sense of belonging towards Japan, but due to policies like those above, policies such as would have assimilated Ryukyuan residents into 'Americans' were not adopted. In education, the eradication of traditional education emphasising cultivation of loyalty to the emperor was thoroughly carried out, but there were no moves to make English the 'national language (*kokugo*),' for example, nor was a ban placed on the Japanese language. Overall, zeal was lacking in primary education policy, and though English classes were initially made compulsory from primary school onwards, they were scrapped in 1957, and even at middle schools, the number of required units in English was reduced. In addition, English centres were established and a system of dispatched volunteer English teachers attached to the U.S. military was created, but these were far from being called mandatory.

Rather, it was into higher education to foster local elites who would become U.S. collaborators that America applied efforts. While on the one hand rebuilding the primary education, which had been devastated by the war, as early as 1947 a policy of university establishment was hatched. A military government statement at the time said that General MacArthur was not happy about Okinawans going to mainland Japan to study; and that as Okinawa was in a special position which differed from Japan, Okinawan education should be conducted at an Okinawan university (Nakano 1969, p. 30). In 1951, the University of the Ryukyus was established in accordance with this direction, and a system of sending students to the U.S. to study was also adopted.[10]

What was carried out concurrently was the encouragement of Ryukyuan culture. Under U.S. occupation, traditional performing arts which had been banned during the period of Japanese rule were revived. It is well-known that in the early stages of the administration, there was an attempt at creating textbooks written in Okinawan, though it eventually failed. In reverse of during Japanese rule, the name 'Ryukyu,' not 'Okinawa,' was used by formal institutions, and in 1950 the creation was recommended of a 'flag of the Ryukyus,' featuring the three colours of blue, white and red, with a star.

In the political mechanism, also, Okinawan autonomy was preferred over assimilation into the American nation. From immediately after the defeat, an Okinawa Advisory Council was convened and a governor appointed, and direct elections for city, town and village mayors were also held. Moreover, in 1951, a provisional central government took shape, integrating the various 'island-group governments (*guntō seifu*)' from the main island of Okinawa, Miyako and Yaeyama, respectively which had had their own governments under the 1950 system. The new government was launched as the 'Government of the Ryukyu Islands' – not to be confused with the U.S. military's 'Civil Administration of the Ryukyu Islands (USCAR)' which corresponded to a Ryukyu Government-General – and was tentatively an autonomous government by Okinawan residents, equipped with a Chief Executive corresponding to a Prime Minister and a legislature equivalent to an assembly.

However, after the pro-American faction's candidate lost on the occasion of the *guntō seifu* election on Okinawa's main island in 1950, the U.S. military halted the public election of the Chief Executive, and adopted a system of appointment by the High

Commissioner. What is more, the High Commissioner held not only *de facto* legislative power by means of proclamations, but also the right of veto over bills that the Okinawan legislature had passed, and the power to invalidate laws that had temporarily been enacted, and, further, the authority to dismiss civil servants of the Ryukyuan government, and so self-government by residents was something that was extremely limited.

Numerous speeches showing what the American side thought of such a relationship emanated from the U.S. military authorities. In 1946, at a meeting of the Okinawa Advisory Council, words spoken by Naval Lieutenant Commander James T. Watkins to the effect that the military government was a cat and Okinawa a mouse, the mouse being free to play only as much as the cat allowed; and USCAR High Commissioner Lieutenant-General Paul W. Caraway's 1962 utterance: 'Autonomy at the present time is a myth; it does not exist,' are well-known examples. Generally, the U.S. side did not trust Okinawan residents' political capability, and when candidates who did not comply with their ideas won in an election, it expressed its 'disappointment' towards the residents who had let a 'Communist' win, and so on. In 1950, an American reporter wrote that Okinawan residents mostly could not even tell the difference between Communists and extreme conservatives; and that at any rate, Japan had dominated Okinawa over many years, and so the ordinary people were bewildered by the strange term 'residents' democracy,' and even if they had shaken their heads, it would not have been enough to make them at all suspicious. This may well have been the average understanding. In fact, it was the American side that indiscriminately deemed people who did not comply with its wishes to be 'Communists' (Nakano 1969, pp. 23, 389, 61).

Japanese historical scholar Kano Masanao cites the below-mentioned episode which the U.S. Vice-Consul reported in 1949 as an example of how the first Governor on the Okinawan side was treated by the U.S. military (Kano 1987, p. 81).[11] Incidentally, in official documents at the time, the U.S. military did not refer to the governor of Okinawa by the English title of 'Governor,' but used the Romanised form of the Japanese term '*chiji*,' meaning 'governor.'

> When I told a military government officer that I wanted to visit the governor (they call him 'Chiji,' but without understanding that it means 'Governor' – they think it means 'administrative assistant' or

something), he called the lieutenant who was the liaison officer with the civil government. Along the way, riding in a jeep, he told me how well he got on with the *chiji*, and how well they understood each other. 'Oh, so the *chiji* speaks English, then?' I said. 'No, he doesn't speak a word of it, but he understands well.' 'So does that mean you speak Japanese?' 'No, but the *chiji* already understands what I say in English before the interpreter converts it into Japanese.' We arrived at the governor's office and were introduced. When we sat down around the table, that lieutenant, speaking just like an Indian in a western, first indicated the governor, then pointed to himself, and said: 'You, me, friends.' The governor nodded with a smile. 'See? He understands perfectly,' said the lieutenant. Then I asked the governor in Japanese: 'Did you understand what he just said?' The governor replied: 'No. I don't understand English, but I have learned to nod and smile when I am spoken to. That way, we can get along fine.'

It is hard to imagine that the governor could only understand this level of English, but this is probably an episode which primarily indicates the attitude of the U.S. military and the eye of observers from the American side.

Later, along with the swell of the reversion movement, certain administrative reforms were instituted under President Kennedy in 1962, and a Civil Administrator, a civilian, was formally placed under the High Commissioner, who was a member of the military. The reform plan discussed by the U.S. Senate Committee on Foreign Relations also included making the High Commissioner a civilian, and transferring jurisdiction to the Department of the Interior or the State Department. However, the Pentagon would not relinquish the post of High Commissioner, and, moreover, it was decided that the Secretary of Defense would also appoint the Civil Administrator. The then High Commissioner, Lieutenant General Paul W. Caraway declared in a reply to Congress (double-quoted from Takano 1962, p. 159) that the qualifications required of a Civil Administrator were to be a good person, and secondly, to recognise that to the last, the Civil Administrator was nothing more than an assistant to the High Commissioner (Kano 1987, p. 92).

Under such a system, even though the laws issued by the Okinawan autonomous government were insisting upon the protection of human rights, the proclamations issued by the High Commissioner were given priority. In 1953, the autonomous government's legislature enacted a labour relations law with the same content as that of mainland Japan, which had been democratised by reforms following the Pacific War, but the working conditions of workers hired by the U.S. military were kept low by proclamation, and they had no collective bargaining rights, either. The expropriation of land for bases, which often became the cause of conflict with the U.S. military, did not comply with the stipulations of the autonomous government's land expropriation law, and was implemented by means of proclamation.

Moreover, proclamations were often issued on a whim, and on each occasion they influenced the destiny of Okinawa. In 1957, after a candidate from the People's Party – a left-wing political party which promoted reversion to Japan – was elected Mayor of Naha City, the local government and regional electoral laws were amended by proclamation, the quorum for no-confidence motions in municipal chiefs and their eligibility for election were changed, and the mayor in question ended up being forced from office. Again in 1958, the High Commissioner rejected the commodity tax act reform bill which the autonomous government legislature had passed, and a different taxation rate was fixed by proclamation, though this arguably was the result of some members of the business community who would be disadvantaged by the reform having appealed to the High Commissioner.[12]

Of course, a series of public order laws was established by proclamation. The first proclamation, which was issued immediately after occupation in 1945, determined that those who took up arms against America, those who raped female U.S. military personnel or their family members, those who were employed by an enemy nation or conducted spying activities and suchlike would be put to death, while imprisonment or fines would be imposed upon those who participated, or allowed others to participate, in demonstrations or assemblies not permitted by the military government, or those who made harmful or unjust speeches ridiculing the U.S. government. Proclamation No. 23 issued in 1959, which invited fierce opposition, stipulated the prohibition of political activities except by registered political parties and a system of registration of the publishing industry, in addition to imprisonment and fines for those who participated in any public demonstrations that were hostile, harmful or insolent towards the U.S. government or the United States.

What further drew attention at the time was that in the clause in this proclamation that specified the ability to execute spies who acted for the benefit of a 'foreign country,' 'foreign countries' were defined as 'all countries apart from the United States and the Ryukyu Islands.' This was criticised as having defined Japan as a 'foreign country,' and was said to imply the likelihood that the reversion movement would be seen as espionage.

An existence that is 'Japanese' and not 'Japanese'

As such, in the eyes of the Japanese government, what kind of situation did Okinawa occupy? Speaking from the conclusion, it was land that was both 'Japan' and not 'Japan.'

What must first be confirmed is that from the defeat until Okinawa's reversion in 1972, the administrative unit called 'Okinawa Prefecture' did not exist. The prefectural office organisation was almost completely annihilated by the Battle of Okinawa, but the U.S. military naturally did not rebuild Okinawa Prefecture, which was an administrative unit of an enemy nation. On the other hand, in 1947, in postwar reforms instituted by GHQ, the Japanese Interior Ministry which had taken charge of regional administration in the prewar was dismantled, and that provided the opportunity for control of most affairs pertaining to Okinawa to be transferred to the Foreign Ministry. This was an event that took place seventy-three years after control of the Ryukyuan Affairs Bureau had been transferred from the Foreign Ministry to the Interior Ministry in early Meiji. In this manner, prior to the conclusion of the 1951 Peace Treaty, Okinawa had become the object not of domestic but of foreign affairs within the mechanism of Japanese government. Japanese research into U.S. government declassified documents in 1979 uncovered the fact that Emperor Hirohito had sent a message to the U.S. side in 1947, asking it to rule Okinawa on a semi-permanent basis for the sake of 'peace in the Far East.' This had been kept secret at the time, it being something which could have caused a scandal if it had been made public in 1947. Even today, this is only common knowledge among Japanese historians of Okinawa.

As previously stated, at the 1951 San Francisco Peace Talks, Okinawa came under U.S. administrative jurisdiction, but the then Japanese Prime Minister Yoshida Shigeru declared that Japan held 'latent sovereignty' vis-à-vis Okinawa. At that time, however, this expression, 'latent sovereignty,' was utterly novel.

In reply to a question in the Diet as to whatever it meant to say that Japan had sovereignty despite the fact that the U.S. held the three powers of government (administrative, legislative and judicial), the then Director-General of the Foreign Ministry Treaties Bureau, Nishimura Kumao, gave the following response on 6 November 1951:

> As it is by no means a rare notion, when I entered Tokyo University in 1920, I had already heard it in Professor Minobe [Tatsukichi]'s constitutional lecture ... On that occasion, what I heard explained had to do with leasehold land. In the case of leasehold land, Chinese sovereignty in regard to Kwantung Province [leased territory on the Liaotung Peninsula] still remains, and none of the Chinese who were living on this land have ever acquired Japanese nationality (Takano 1962, p. 376).[13]

Certainly, unlike the Koreans and Taiwanese after annexation to Japan, it was true that the Chinese of the Liaotung Peninsula, which was territory leased to Japan, did retain their Chinese nationality. Moreover, according to the reply from Director-General Nishimura, in terms of nationality, 'all [Okinawan] residents [were] still Japanese.'

If that be the case, though, then the question was whether Okinawans would be guaranteed their rights as 'Japanese' that were specified in the Japanese national constitution. In response to this question, Nishimura said: 'There is no change to their being Japanese, but ... it is the United States that exercises authority,' and replied: 'The constitution applies within parameters not contradictory to the stipulations in Article Three of the Peace Treaty, but is excluded where there is contradiction.' According to Nishimura, in Japan since the prewar 'all stipulations in the constitution were not of a nature to be wholly applied equally to every sphere of the state,' and forms of enforcement where there was sovereignty, but no protection of human rights, were not rare (Takano 1962, pp. 375, 377, 371). Through Nishimura, a disciple of Minobe's, the form of constitutional enforcement from Korea and Taiwan ended up dragging on to postwar Okinawa. After their annexation, Korea and Taiwan became Japanese territory, and Japanese nationality was forcibly

Islands on the Boundary

assigned to their inhabitants, but the human-rights stipulations guaranteed by Japan's Imperial Constitution were not applied. As I will mention in Volume 2 of this book, Minobe was a scholar who refused the application of the Constitution to Taiwan. In this way, while being 'Japan,' Okinawa was excluded from 'Japan,' and Diet members ceased to be elected from Okinawa.

In the midst of this, however, there was one part which the Japanese government continued to apprehend as a domestic affair – family registers (*koseki*).[14] Family registers compiled by the Japanese government were documents in which the administration recorded such personal information as details of birth, marriage, death, place of origin, current address, kinship, and so on, and were used for such purposes as taxation, conscription and local government. As discussed in Volume 2, after the forced assignment of Japanese nationality to Koreans and Taiwanese in the prewar, the government differentiated its application of law by means of the family registers, and implemented restrictions on travel to *naichi* and control of intermarriage.

Starting with their loss by fire in the great U.S. military air-raid of October 1944, almost all Okinawan family registers were scattered in the war on the main island of Okinawa. For a while in the postwar, these were substituted by the ration register and the like, but later, out of local necessity, provisional family registers were created from 1947. Due to the postwar confusion, surveys were insufficient, and because of a concurrent boom in altering surnames, many notifications were made of amendment to a Yamato-style surname, or, in some cases, a converse change back to Ryukyu-style.

However, in addition to this, the Japanese Ministry of Justice made Okinawans individually create an interim family register at the Okinawa-related family registry office it set up in 1948 in Fukuoka Prefecture in Kyushu, the southernmost part of mainland Japan. At the time, there were many Okinawan inhabitants who had sought refuge in Kyushu, having fled from Okinawa, which had been the site of fierce fighting in the final stages of the war; and Fukuoka was the prefecture where Kyushu's central city was located. As it could not carry out surveys in Okinawa, which was then under U.S. military occupation, those that were registered were mostly Okinawans living in mainland Japan, but the Japanese government deemed this interim family register alone to be accredited, and took a position of not recognising family registers created locally in Okinawa.

In 1953, along with the heightening of the Cold War, amid the U.S. military's feeling the necessity to gain a strict grasp of the residents, the Law for Reconstruction of Family Registers was enacted, and recompilation of registers was begun. The Japanese Ministry of Justice, which took the position that laws relating to family registers were the jurisdiction of the Japanese government, initially reacted sharply to this, but later changed tack, using this as an opportunity to apprehend family registers within Okinawa. The Ministry of Justice entered this scheme in the form of cooperative guidance in family register technique: advocating the thorough preclusion of false declarations, it instructed the Ryukyu Government Legal Affairs Bureau to aim for the complete recompilation of prewar family registers. To that end, while on the one hand having people provide Okinawa-related written notifications, copies and executive summaries of registers and so on held overseas and in other prefectures, it had overseas Okinawan Associations of migrants in Hawai'i and South and North America make statutory declarations, and in 1954 family registers within Okinawa also came within the grasp of the Ministry of Justice.

As previously mentioned, control of the major part of matters to do with Former Okinawa had been transferred to the Foreign Ministry. In such circumstances, almost the only thing to have been inherited as a domestic affair was family registers over which the Ministry of Justice had jurisdiction. Moreover, the name 'Okinawa Prefecture' continued to be employed as the registered domicile and current address in the Ministry of Justice's family registers relating to Okinawa. At that time, when the administrative unit called Okinawa Prefecture had disappeared, it may be said that officially, 'Okinawa Prefecture' existed solely in family registers.

However, family registers created in this way also came to be utilised by the U.S. military. The U.S. military's civil administration had already recorded in the 1952 Government of the Ryukyu Islands (GRI) Bill of Rights that a 'Ryukyu resident' meant 'a natural person whose birth and name were inscribed in the Ryukyu archive of family registers,' and being recorded in a family register was a characteristic of residents, but immediately after the 1954 upgrade of family registers, it issued a directive saying it would restrict the transfer of registration from the Japanese mainland to the Ryukyu Islands which hitherto had been free. Furthermore, at the end of 1956, the permission of the Deputy Civil Administrator (later, High

Commissioner) also became necessary for entry into Ryukyu family registers due to marriage, adoption and the like.[15]

The reason for this restriction on changes to the registry was not officially revealed. In this period, however, there was a crackdown in 1954 on the left-wing People's Party, and in 1956, there was violent turmoil in the administration, including the escalation of 'island-wide conflict' opposing the seizure of land for U.S. military bases, and the United States itself, too, was in the thick of commotion that arose over McCarthy's hunt for Communists. Originally, in the Ryukyu Government Bill of Rights, eligibility to take office as Chief Executive or Deputy Chief Executive of the Government of the Ryukyu Islands, and eligibility for election as a member of the legislature, as well, was limited to 'Ryukyu residents' in terms of their family register, and it was obvious that the intention of the U.S. military was to forestall a state of affairs in which 'Communists' from the Japanese mainland would transfer their registration and assume public office.

In 1951, almost simultaneously to this limitation on transfer of registration, a proclamation entitled 'Control of Ryukyu residents' travel' was issued, in the form of an improvement to the previous travel restriction stipulations, and a travel certificate issued by the Deputy Civil Administrator (later the High Commissioner) became necessary even for passage to and from the Japanese mainland. When they were to travel, people for whom it was seen by the U.S. military to be necessary had to submit a supplementary application in which was recorded the past and present organisations to which they belonged, their association with Communist Party members or extra-government organisations, the names of the individuals and groups they would visit during their stay, and so on, and it was not rare for them to be further required to submit to questioning, either.

As such, amid a series of measures comparable to limitations on the acquisition of nationality and immigration, 'Japanese' from mainland Japan were treated as 'foreigners' according to the necessity of the U.S. military. In 1958, after a string of incidents in which the aforementioned People's Party candidate was forced out of the mayoralty of Naha City, when a lawyer from the Civil Liberties Union in mainland Japan who was asked to defend him tried to travel there, he was rejected by the U.S. military authorities under the pretext that the 'entry of a foreign lawyer to the islands' was unnecessary.[16]

On the other hand, Okinawa residents had Japanese nationality, and the U.S. military's legal control was a local one. Accordingly, in cases where Okinawan residents, too, were living in mainland Japan, it was also possible for them to obtain the same legal status as ordinary 'Japanese,' and exercise voting rights and eligibility for election. However, this only applied within the sphere of Japan's administrative rights, and was unconnected with residents living in Okinawa.

In this way, while fixed in an ambiguous position by the U.S. military and the Japanese government, outside the country Okinawans were not made the object of diplomatic protection by either regime. The Japanese government took the view that because Okinawa's administrative rights were under American jurisdiction, diplomatic protection would constitute interference in its domestic affairs. On the other hand, the U.S. government assumed that as Okinawans did not have American nationality, they would not be the target of its diplomatic protection. However, the U.S. did not attempt to relinquish Okinawa because of its military value, and the Japanese government continued to assert its territorial rights as far as this did not cause friction with America.

In territorial terms, Okinawa was part of 'Japan,' and in terms of nationality, too, Okinawans were 'Japanese,' but the constitution was not enforced, nor did they have suffrage; transfer of their family registers and travel were restricted, and they were governed by a military Governor-General who monopolised the three powers. To the Japanese, such a simultaneously 'Japanese' and not 'Japanese' presence was Okinawa. To the United States, too, Okinawans were not 'American,' and had neither citizenship nor legal protection.

In 1962, the then Assistant Secretary of State, Lyndon B. Johnson, standing in reply at the U.S. Congress, spoke as follows.

> They [=Okinawans] are not considered to be Americans, nor are they treated as Americans. We do not intend to incorporate the Ryukyuans into America permanently. Accordingly, they have no prospect of getting closer to America in the future. In addition, the Ryukyus are too small, and consequently, when we determine that there is no longer any necessity to remain there, they have none of the resources needed for surviving as an independent state ...
>
> Accordingly, the psychological question could be said to lie in that they themselves are neither Americans nor Japanese, and yet they

do not think of themselves as Ryukyuans from the independent state of the Ryukyu Islands, either. When they travel abroad, the High Commissioner hands them travel documents, but these are not passports, and this means that overseas Customs and Immigration officers look at them and ask curiously: 'Are you Japanese or American or what?' ... When they have faced troublesome situations, we do not know whether they went to an American consulate or to a Japanese one. We are cooperating with the Japanese side, but at any rate, this kind of problem arises from their ambivalent position (double-quoted from Takano 1962, p. 157).

It is not certain whether the 'cooperation' with the Japanese side was something for ameliorating this situation, or to entrench it. The Okinawan poet Yamanokuchi Baku published the following poem in 1958:

The words we use
They are Japanese
The money we use
It is dollars
It's like Japan
But not so much like it
It's like America
But not so much like it
[These] are elusive islands (Yamanokuchi 1960, pp. 22–23)

An existence without protection or identity from the state, which is used by the state. What kind of course did the people of Okinawa aim for? That is what I wish to elucidate by my examination in the following chapters.

6 From Pro-independence to Pro-reversion Discources

Between the end of the war in 1945 and the conclusion of the San Francisco Peace Treaty in 1951, the question of where Okinawa belonged remained unclear amid the implementation of American martial rule. The expected options in the near term, apart from possession by China, which scarcely even merited discussion, were the three comprising reversion to Japan, trusteeship by America, or independence. In reality, none of those three materialised in 1951, it being decided that martial rule would be continued as a 'provisional measure,' and debate over the question of belonging at that point in time was not, as in later years, consolidated into one of reversion to Japan.

In this chapter, I will examine the controversy over identity as far as 1951. In that debate, respective Okinawan views on Japan and America naturally became vital components in determining whether the Okinawans themselves were 'Japanese.'

The independence debate and perspectives on America

In November 1945, the 'Okinawa-jin renmei (League of Okinawans)' was formed by Okinawans resident in mainland Japan, with Ifa Fuyū as its president. Its main objective was to attempt mutual assistance for Okinawans amid the chaos and starvation due to Japan's defeat, but numerous studies on the question of territoriality, also, were published in their bulletin, *Jiyū Okinawa* (Free Okinawa).

The earliest example of these was a contribution by Nagaoka Tomotarō printed in the second issue published in January 1946. Nagaoka was a journalist who had worked in the prewar as a reporter for the magazine *Kaizō* (Reconstruction) and its Moscow correspondent, among other things, and a character who later also served as Chair of the Okinawa Association (Okinawa Kyōkai). Here, he states:

... According to news reports, the inhabitants of the main island of Okinawa have petitioned for Okinawa never to be returned to Japan. This is all too likely to be true. The Japanese government has hitherto never established a single national policy in Okinawa. Moreover, the Okinawan populace was indiscriminately forced into completely meaningless mortal combat in the latest war; they were recruited for construction work for quartering troops and had labour imposed upon them with whips; and what little food they did have was plundered; and so their resentment towards the Japanese military clique was enormous. For that reason, wanting not to invite rule by Japan until it is thoroughly democratised seems to me to be extremely natural (Nagaoka 1946a).

Nagaoka composed a pamphlet entitled *Okinawa minzoku dokuhon: Okinawa minzokusei no keisei katei* (Reader [on the] Okinawan nation: the formation process of Okinawan national characteristics)[2] at the end of 1946. In this, he expressed a keen awareness of the 'sorrow of a minor people' in that he himself is 'racially Okinawan,' stating: 'Because I love Ryukyu, I could not become a narrow-minded pro-Japanist.' Furthermore, based on Ifa's Japan–Ryukyu common-ancestry theory, he claimed that while Okinawans were 'racially a collateral line of the Japanese people,' they had 'historically achieved their own development' and made 'ethnically-specific progress,' and though 'a series of assimilation policies' had been implemented since Meiji, 'we Okinawans have become "non-Japanese" because of losing the war' (Nagaoka 1947, pp. 2, 26, 30, 94; 1946c).[3] As I will later elaborate, such a historical perspective and view of the 'Okinawan people' could be said to be one that was shared by most on the Okinawan side at that time.

Nagaoka's conjecture was that after Okinawa had temporarily become a U.S. trust territory, it would follow 'a course from autonomy to independence.' The assumption behind this argument was a confidence in the U.S. that seemed to be in inverse proportion to its wariness towards Japan, namely: 'Seeing that [America] is the home of democracy, the popular will of ethnic Okinawans is likely to be greatly respected.' Predicting a future for Okinawa as flourishing under U.S. economic assistance and cultural benefit, Nagaoka cited Panama as an example of American governance, though this was probably naïve:

The Panamanians left everything up to the Americans: using banknotes, having had the U.S. print them; drinking water, having had the U.S. provide the water supply; sleeping peacefully, having had the U.S. kill their mosquitoes; driving cars, having had the U.S. build them; wearing clothes, having had the U.S. sew them; living in houses, having had the U.S. build them; and eating food, having had the U.S. transport it; and yet they are cheerful and have not a bit of servility ... I have the feeling that gaining knowledge of the above outline of the Panamanian Republic will give us some insight into the shape of Okinawa to come' (Nagaoka 1947, pp. 115, 118–119).

Indeed, discussion on belonging did not develop in much depth even at the League of Okinawans, whose hands were full at that time with Okinawans' mutual aid. Its president, Ifa, took the stance that 'for the time being, the urgent problem is the relief of Okinawans living on the mainland. The question of where Okinawa belongs is one that the Allies will decide, and though in future it might be put to a referendum of Okinawans living in their native place, this is not a current issue for us, the people who are here.' Even Nagaoka, who was passionate about the question of belonging, remarked: 'As a league, it has not developed to a stage of handling such an issue' (*Jiyū Okinawa* 1946a, Nagaoka 1946b).

Nonetheless, there was heavy criticism of Japan and awareness of an 'Okinawan *minzoku* (people)' in the media of Okinawans residing on the mainland after the defeat. Among this, though opinions emerged such as that of Nakahara Zenchū, who became the second president at the League of Okinawans headquarters in place of Ifa, namely: 'There is nothing constituting an Okinawan people (*minzoku*) that warrants distinction from the Japanese *minzoku*,' or 'I would like even those who believe themselves to belong to the Okinawan *minzoku*, and to be of non-Japanese ethnicity, to try somehow not to impose their sentiments upon others,' but the words 'reconstruction of Okinawa, our ancestral land (*sokoku*),' and 'saving the nation (*minzoku*)' were often seen in the newspapers (Nakahara 1947).[4] In almost all cases, what was called '*sokoku*' and '*minzoku*' was something that referred not to Japan, but to Okinawa.

Even on the ground in Okinawa, voices calling for reversion to Japan could not at first have been called plentiful. In 1947, on Miyako Island, a group of reporters made a plea to an American military administrator, saying: 'Ryukyans hope to live in an independent country called Ryukyu, under American protection,' while the Miyako Socialist Party, which was formed in the same year, touted a mission statement saying: 'Our party has the belief that the happiness of the Ryukyuan people lies in belonging to the U.S., and anticipate the materialisation of the State of Okinawa in future.' On Yonaguni Island, the arguments on where to belong espoused by three candidates running in the 1949 election for town mayor were split into reversion to Japanese, Ryukyuan independence, and belonging to Taiwan.[5]

On the main island of Okinawa, it is known that the Okinawa Democratic League, which was formed in 1947, adopted the principle of 'establishing an independent republic.' Moreover, according to Yoshida Shien, when he travelled to Okinawa in the summer of 1946, 'Messrs Kaneshi Saichi and Senaga Kamejirō presented the idea of Okinawa as an American protectorate. In reply to my question as to specifically what it would be, they said they were thinking of a configuration like that of the Republic of Panama, for instance.'[6] As I will later elaborate, Kaneshi and Senaga were characters who would later become the nucleus of the anti-U.S.-base struggle and the reversion movement, but if we suppose Yoshida's words to be true, then it means that at that time they, too, were advocating a plan for a Panama-type protectorate based upon reliance on the United States.

As of 1946, a worldview consisting of lack of faith in Japan and trust in America had widely permeated. In April of that year, when the U.S. military appointed an Okinawan as Governor, an Okinawan local newspaper, *Uruma shinpō* (Uruma news) – 'Uruma' being an ancient word meaning 'coral islands,' which refers to Okinawa – welcomed this, saying: 'The U.S. military government, which was unstinting in its devoted efforts for Okinawan reconstruction and its residents' protection, liberated our native land of Okinawa this year under a peaceable morality' (*Uruma shinpō* 1946b [1978], p. 14). The newspaper's president, Shima Kiyoshi, also published the following message of congratulation.

> Though the Kingdom of Ryukyu was renamed Okinawa Prefecture, the Okinawan world was replaced by the world of Yamato, and feudalism transformed into the enforcement of autonomy, these were in name only. The true situation of the political administration is that it is still a colonial bureaucratic administration, and for many years

we Uruma residents have groaned under heavy colonial pressure, and met with today's ill fortune as defeated nationals ...

When they attempt to scrutinise the content of the Japanese government's policy of assistance for Okinawan industry, many people will probably realise that the aim of that assistance placed emphasis on industries that could be transferred out to the Japanese mainland ...
Not only the American side not viewing us as people of an enemy nation, despite our having been in the position of enemies until seeing the conclusion of the Peace Treaty, but also the recent appointment from among us Uruma islanders of a governor and vice-governor in the capacity of general managers of the political administration, constitute the greatest delights ever to have been seen in Uruma island history in modern times, even excepting our present status, and historians in future ages will forever acclaim the present splendid day (Shima 1946 [1978], p. 14).

It goes without saying that this congratulatory message is premised upon the fact that not once in the prewar had an Okinawan native been appointed by the Japanese Home Affairs Ministry as the senior bureaucrat, and therefore the appointment of a local as the governor (*chiji*) by the U.S. military seemed epoch-making. Of course, how this 'governor' was treated by the U.S. military is as described in the previous chapter, but such a state of affairs had not been predicted at the above point in time.

At a press conference with a group of American reporters in August 1947, Shikiya Kōshin, who had thus become the inaugural governor, was asked: 'Do Okinawan residents want to belong to Japan, or do they want to become independent in future, under U.S. protection?' In reply, he said: 'There also seems to be a minority with hopes of belonging to Japan, but I think that most want to build a peaceful country under American protection.' In addition, at a conference with the U.S. military High Commissioner in November that year, he declared: 'Seeing Americans before our very eyes, we have become able to trust the United States from the bottom of our hearts.' In 1948, the following year, as well, he expressed a hope for Okinawan independence (*Uruma shinpō* 1947 [1978], p. 88; Nakano 1969, pp. 14, 16).

This kind of independence discourse was not advocated merely within Okinawa. In February 1946, at the party congress of the

Japanese Communist Party, a 'message celebrating the independence of the Okinawan people' like the following was sent by unanimous vote to the national convention of the League of Okinawans.

> For all of you Okinawans who were made to suffer through exploitation and oppression from Japanese imperialism since Meiji, having been enslaved under Japanese feudal rule over several centuries, to have at last been able to reach the path to securing the independence and freedom for which you longed for many years, in the midst of the current worldwide expansion of the democratic revolution, surely must be something over which you are feeling enormous joy. Up till now, Japanese imperialists have claimed that domestically, the emperor and members of the nation have family-like ties of blood, and, externally, that Koreans are of the same lineage as Japanese, and Asian peoples (*minzoku*) are the same Asians as the Japanese; and they have brazenly declared that the Japanese emperor is Asia's leader. Onto you Okinawans, too, they foisted the idea of being the same race. I think that you were able quickly to discern the true nature of this imperialistic evil design.
>
> Even though the Okinawans had diverged from the same ancestors as the Japanese in ancient times, in history since modern times Japan has clearly dominated Okinawa. In other words, Okinawans are a people who have been oppressed as an ethnic minority (Nakano 1969, p. 6).

This message, which criticises the Japan–Korea common-ancestry theory and Japan–Ryukyu common-ancestry theory in parallel, implies the recognition that Okinawa was an area under domination, similar to Korea.

The personal experience of Tokuda Kyūichi, who at that time was the Communist Party Committee Chair, also lay behind the issuance of this message. At a symposium organised in 1947 by the Okinawa Youth League (*Okinawa seinen dōmei*, formed in 1923 as the Okinawan branch of the All-Japan Proletarian Youth League), the Okinawan-born Tokuda recalled: 'My grandfather was a native of Kagoshima, but conversely, I have the experience of bearing a deep grudge for that reason. Even though I was living together with Satsuma relatives, uncles, and so on, just because I had grown up in Okinawa I was not even allowed to use the same bathroom.' He remarked: 'From both a political and an economic aspect, Ryukyu was completely exploited as a colony,' and asserted that Okinawa had to 'become an ethnic, self-governing republic' which respected 'ethnic (*minzoku*) autonomy' (Nakano 1969, pp. 7–8).

Such an assertion was not only one belonging to the Communist Party. Again at a symposium organised by the Okinawa Youth League, a Socialist Party representative said: 'In future, we must naturally consider the significance of the Okinawan people's self-determination,' and 'I think that it is absolutely necessary for Okinawa to advance as an autonomous state.' The representative of the Association of Japan-residing Korean Democratic Youth (*Zainichi Chōsen minshu seinen dōmei*, a Communist-aligned youth organisation) also deemed the 'happiness of the Okinawan people' to lie in 'Okinawans freely creating their own country of Okinawa' (Senaga 1949 [1978], p. 189). Advocacy of independence for 'the Okinawan people' could be said rather to have been a general thing among mainland leftists at that time.

However, such an independence discourse was qualified by two assumptions. One was the ethnic perspective that Okinawans were an 'ethnic minority' that differed from ethnic Japanese, and the other the historical perspective that saw the Ryukyu Disposition as a Japanese invasion. Support for the Okinawan independence discourse had the potential to be influenced, depending upon the ethnic and historical perspectives, as also can be inferred from the fact that at the abovementioned symposium, a representative from the Democratic Youth League of Korea said: 'If we assume that Japan and Okinawa historically were essentially the same, then [Okinawa] must return to Japan, but if not, then it must independently build a republic.'

Another assumption was, as we have already seen, a confidence in the U.S. that was akin to a negative image of a lack of faith in Japan. On Miyako Island, where a discourse of belonging to the U.S. was advocated, there were reportedly even leaders who decided to decorate the town with arches and to mobilise all of the inhabitants to welcome U.S. troops, and who preached the Americanisation of lifestyles and the everyday use of English. The Japan Communist Party's message about Okinawan independence was also something that was inseparable from the definition of the U.S. military as a liberating army by party leaders released from Japanese imperial prisons. Senaga Kamejirō, who as the Committee Chair of the Okinawan People's Party, later came to wage all-out confrontation with the U.S. military, also had declared in August 1949 that he would 'cooperate with the U.S. military as a liberation army' and 'devote himself body and soul to the formation of a Ryukyuan national front, and work in order to establish a solid livelihood for our people' (Senaga 1949 [1978], p. 189). However, it could be predicted that if such a view on America crumbled, then the debate on belonging would have to alter greatly.

The Okinawan independence discourse immediately after the defeat was one that stood upon such views on Japan and America, as well as the perspective of an 'Okinawan nation.' Gradually, however, as disillusionment with rule by the United States spread, change began to grow in this kind of worldview.

Reversion as a conservative movement

In the midst of such circumstances, what is known as the earliest example of the reversion movement is a petition by Nakayoshi Ryōkō, a former mayor of Shuri City.

Nakayoshi's impetus for beginning a reversion movement is said to have been an American magazine that he saw at an Okinawan prison when working as a prisoner-of-war. There, his eye alighted upon an article to the effect that 'the current emperor is a war criminal, and is likely to be forced to abdicate, but the crown prince would succeed to the throne after him, and so ultimately the emperor system would be preserved.' He said: 'I felt a warm upwelling of courage in my flesh.' On that impetus, after having consulted with friends, he submitted a petition for reversion to the Okinawan Occupation Forces on 4 August 1945, prior to Japan's defeat.[8]

According to Nakayoshi's summary, its drift was apparently something like: 'There is neither theory nor reason to this. It stems from natural human sentiment, because Okinawans are Japanese, just as a child wants to return to its parental home.' However, the Okinawa Advisory Council, a collection of influential Okinawans which the U.S. military launched, replied: 'This is not necessarily the view of the majority of residents,' and the U.S. military also shelved it. Nakayoshi was not daunted by this, however, and submitted a reversion petition to General MacArthur in October 1946. This petition argued as follows:

> ... As [Okinawans] have the same blood as their mainland Japanese compatriots, just as in the prewar, they are burning with the sheer

desire to return to Japanese government administration. Just as blood is said to be thicker than water, all Okinawan residents have a powerful self-awareness of being ethnically Japanese, and no matter whatever circumstances befall them, their earnest desire to share a destiny with their mainland compatriots prevails.

In parts of the West, there are also some who argue that Japanese nationals despised Okinawan people as poor cousins, and treated them coldly, but this is a fallacy; there is absolutely no truth to the Japanese government and Japanese people having meted out discriminatory treatment to Okinawans. Okinawan people have always received equal treatment to residents of each mainland prefecture (Okinawa-ken Sokoku Fukki Tōsō Shi Hensan Iinkai (1982), pp. 6–8).

This petition further insisted: 'Okinawans are of the Japanese race, and their language, manners, customs and faith are also the same,' called Minamoto-no-Tametomo the father of the 'first Ryukyu Kingdom,' and described the Ryukyu Disposition as having 'happened most naturally, just as a child returns to its father's house, and not being a change by such means as armed action.'

At that time, however, it seems that there was no air of support for a reversion argument such as Nakayoshi's among the majority of Okinawans. In 1946, Nagaoka Tomotarō, touching upon the reversion petition, criticised it severely, saying that it would probably only be supported by people who, 'having been placed under the influence of the education they received from Japanese militarists or imperialists, still have been unable to convert their thinking' (Nagaoka 1946c). Furthermore, as previously mentioned, Governor Shikiya also remarked at the 1947 press conference that there also seemed to be a minority that held hopes of belonging to Japan; but that he thought most wished to build a peaceful country under American protection.

Perhaps for that reason, also, Nakayoshi's petition to MacArthur was submitted in the form of joint names of Okinawan sympathisers, starting with Nakayoshi, without any sort of organisational name, either. Signatories included Baron Ie Tomoo, who championed the enforcement of Standard Japanese during the Okinawan language debate, as well as Kamiyama Seiryō, who became President of the Okinawan Association, and the Okinawan historian Higaonna Kanjun. The Japan–Ryukyu common-ancestry theory seems to have been one which Higaonna taught to Nakayoshi. Moving to Tokyo, Nakayoshi later rallied these members to form the Okinawa Guntō

Nihon Fukki Kiseikai (Council for the Return of the Okinawan Islands to Japan).

If we assume that the movement launched by Nakayoshi and his supporters was the pioneer among unofficial reversion movements, then one which took a form that adhered more closely to the Japanese government was the activities of Yoshida Shien, who fought with Yanagi Sōetsu in the Okinawan language debate.

Conscripted into the military after the debate and repatriated from the battlefield on Bougainville Island, Yoshida had been appointed Head of the Okinawa Prefecture Tokyo Office as a surviving public official from the old prefectural office. This Tokyo Office was a vestige of the administrative unit called 'Okinawa Prefecture' on the Japanese end, in the days when the Okinawa Prefectural Office was in ruins. A government official, Yoshida engaged in the relief of Okinawans living on the mainland, but he concluded that the mainland League of Okinawans was something that imitated the 'Association of Korean Residents, which was in an advantageous position in terms of livelihood, craftily utilising third-worlder privilege,' and he 'staunchly opposed' it as 'something in which they (= the Okinawans) themselves renounce their Japanese identity.' Such a stance of Yoshida's naturally invited repercussions, even reportedly to the extent that a written resolution was composed by Okinawan groups and sent to the GHQ and Prime Minister, saying: 'Yoshida Shien always gathers conservative reactionary elements around him, and is an ultra-nationalist who advocated Okinawan reversion to Japan' (Yoshida 1976, p. 24).

In Tokyo, Yoshida ran the office while also maintaining contact with Nakayoshi's Fukki Kiseikai; but in 1947, the Interior Ministry was dissolved and 'Okinawa Prefecture' vanished, as well, so he was appointed Chief of the Okinawa Section at the Foreign Office. While conducting 'diplomatic' business on the one hand, he became Director-General of the 'Nanpō Dōhō Engokai (Southern compatriots' protection association)' in 1956, and came to be engaged in the reversion movement. This Southern Compatriots Protection Association had Shibusawa Keizō as its president, and the former prefectural governor from 1940, Fuchigami Fusatarō, against whom Yanagi Sōetsu had argued, as its vice-president. It had a strong connection with the Liberal-Democratic Party, and also advocated the reversion of the Ogasawara Group (Bonin Islands) and Northern Territories at the same time as Okinawan reversion.

As Nakayoshi and Yoshida's orientations also imply, Okinawa's Japanese reversion movement at first could be said to have been regarded rather as a conservative one. In July 1947, there was an incident in which a Socialist Party parliamentarian demanded an explanation in the Diet, claiming that the then Foreign Minister Ashida Hitoshi's mention of the reversion of the Kuril Islands (Chishima) and Okinawa at a press conference with a group of foreign reporters constituted a demand for territorial acquisition in contravention of the Potsdam Declaration. Ashida, while describing the Kuriles and Okinawa as 'islands that are both racially and historically one with our mainland, maintained from days of old as secure homes for the Japanese people,' fought hard to shake off the question, saying: 'I have never yet dreamt of anything such as using force to acquire territory' (Nakano 1969, p. 7). Demands for Okinawan reversion were regarded on the mainland at that time as equating to an imperialist invasion.

The sudden rise of the identity debate

Another ground for the weakness of the reversion discourse was the international situation in the late 1940s. America had already announced that it intended to occupy Okinawa long-term out of military necessity. The Republic of China was demanding its reversion to China, and the British Labour Party and the Shanghai City Council had expressed their opposition, saying that it would be dangerous for Japan to have possession of Okinawa. The Philippines, in turn, was wary of Chinese possession of Okinawa, and advocated trusteeship.[9] Whatever the case, there were but scant international moves supporting Japanese reversion.

Yet another reason that could be cited as to why the argument for reversion was weak in Okinawa was that news from the mainland was not reaching it. In March 1948, an article in an Okinawan local newspaper cited an article in which a mainland news agency introduced 'the solitary islands of Okinawa, cut off from the world' in their blockaded situation, but it was one that described Okinawa as 'a different world, like a paradise seen from Japan's perspective,' overflowing with food provided by the U.S. military, and where residents were enjoying music concerts and films (*Uruma shinpō* 1948 [1978], p. 129). This article can be considered to be one that probably relied upon an American military press release, but at that time newspapers on the Okinawan end also were in a situation where they gleaned their external news from listening to the radio, and actual comparison with the mainland was not possible. As described below, the reversion movement gained strength as information about the mainland's recovery and economic growth was conveyed; at the time when the only information obtainable was such that Okinawa was enjoying a better lifestyle than the mainland, the desire for reversion was accordingly weak.

Moreover, seen solely from the mass media, in 1940s Okinawa, interest in the question of where to belong did not seem to be high. The pages of *Uruma shinpō* (Uruma news), an Okinawan newspaper of the day, show that until 1950 there was only a smattering of articles on the reversion issue, and even those were mostly ones that merely communicated the international situation, as previously mentioned. The majority of articles conveyed information on improvements in everyday life and specific policies of the U.S. military. Even given that an independence discourse did exist, the inhabitants arguably had their hands full with daily living and postwar recovery in Okinawa's circumstances at the time, when the entire land was laid waste and a quarter of the population had been lost.

It was reportedly from around the time of the election for Governor of the Ryukyus held in September 1950 that such circumstances began to change. Only the previous year, the People's Republic of China had been established, the U.S. military was intensifying its policy towards the militarisation of Okinawa in readiness for the Cold War system, and Okinawans were starting little by little to awaken from their illusions about America.

There were three candidates standing for election as governor of the Ryukyu Islands: Matsuoka Seiho, who had returned from studying in America and was supported by the U.S. military; Senaga Kamejirō, the Committee Chair of the Okinawan People's Party; and Taira Tatsuo. Of these, Taira was someone who had been in the upper echelon of the Okinawa Prefecture branch of the Imperial Rule Assistance Association (*Taisei yokusankai*) in the prewar, and, for a time immediately following the defeat, had been close to being purged. In 1940, almost all existing political parties were dissolved, and the Imperial Rule Assistance Association was formed with the aim of having one party for the one country, modelled on the Nazis. In mainland Japan, those connected with it were purged from public office in the postwar by the U.S. Occupation Forces.

Though admittedly the purging of prewar leadership had generally been weaker in Okinawa than on the mainland, Taira also had been able to make a comeback by this time. The election campaign was described as a one-on-one contest between Matsuoka, effectively representing an emergent force under American governance, and Taira, representing an established force from the days of Japanese rule, but it turned into a crushing victory for Taira. Following this, the U.S. military put an end to the system of popular election of the Governor and Chief Executive, and switched to a system of appointment.

In this election campaign, none of the three candidates had yet raised the question of reversion or possession as his policy pledge, Taira's victory merely being said to be something which indicated residents' pro-Japanese orientation. After the election, however, the news that peace talks were going to be held the next year was circulated, and from around early 1951, discussion over where to belong abruptly began to heighten.

In the possession debate which rapidly swelled in 1951, the advocates for Japanese reversion were the People's Party, with Senaga as Committee Chair, and the Socialist Masses Party, which was formed as Taira's ruling party. The Socialist Party advocated trusteeship, while the Republican Party argued for independence. Of these, because the Republican Party's independence discourse was one which purported to aim for independence while implementing trusteeship in the interim, in substantive terms it could be called a contest between the two alternatives of reversion and opposition to reversion (trusteeship and independence). Here, let us first look at the claims of trusteeship advocate Ikemiyagushiku (in Okinawan pronunciation, more like Ikemiyagusuku) Shūi, who at that time was editor-in-chief of *Uruma shinpō*.

The reasons Ikemiyagushiku raised for opposing reversion were roughly as follows. Firstly, the Japanese economy was only just managing to be maintained by means of American aid, and even if Okinawa were to revert, 'we could not expect a large share from the Japanese economy.' Rather, if reversion occurred, the aid directed at Okinawa from America would probably be curtailed. Moreover, it was 'all too obvious that if war were to break out between the U.S. and the U.S.S.R, Japan would be America's front line of defence,' and so 'if Okinawa belonged to Japan, Okinawan youth would also be recruited again.' Moreover, as long as tension in the Far East remained unmitigated, the U.S. would absolutely not relinquish its Okinawan bases, and so even if Okinawa were to revert to Japan, land for bases would probably end up being leased (Ikemiyagushiku 1996, pp. 17, 24).

Ikemiyagushiku was arguing for trusteeship on the rationale that there was little feasibility of Okinawan independence, but the demerits of Japanese reversion were ones that Republican Party assembly members who extolled independence were also asserting, and may be deemed to be ones shared by the opponents of reversion. That opposing faction vigorously emphasised the discrimination Okinawa had received from Japan in the prewar, further arguing that post-reversion lease payments for bases would be seized by the Japanese government, and that the Japanese government would probably not forward most of the aid it received from America to Okinawa. Ikemiyagushiku (1996, pp. 23–24) also pointed out the 'reality that in the days of Japanese administration, Okinawans had colonial treatment from Japan,' and at the GRI assembly on 19 March 1951, Republican Party member Shinzato Ginzō even expressed the wish to 'reconstruct the independent nation of Ryukyu from the old days' with U.S. backing (Okinawa Kengikai Jimusho 1995, p. 349). All in all, what the opponents of reversion asserted was that if Okinawa reverted, then the benefits it received from the U.S. would be snatched by Japan, and it would be burdened with the obligations of conscription and the payment of taxes.

What is important here is the anti-reversion discourse's perspective on Japan–U.S. relations. The opposition discourse, as described above, was grounded upon the recognition that Japan was poorer than America, its degree of democratisation was also inferior, and that Okinawa had nothing to gain from reversion, either economically or politically. In this assumption there was the observation that Japan–U.S. relations under the Cold War situation were immutable. For example, Ikemiyagushiku remarked: 'It is an established fact that as long as Japan does not turn into a satellite nation of the Soviet Union, Japan will move with America's guidance. Consequently, it would not be unreasonable to consider that America will be able to grant Okinawa even more freedom than Japan could give, both politically and economically.' In addition, a Republican Party assembly member asserted: 'Okinawa is America's first line of defence, and as long as America has predominance over Japan, the bases in Okinawa will be more and more fortified, and there will be commensurate assistance' (Ikemiyagushiku 1996, p. 23; Okinawa Kengikai Jimusho 1995 p. 349). In other words, its having been premised upon a dependent relationship vis-à-vis the U.S. under the Cold War system is what characterises the anti-reversion discourse of this period, and on this point it differs greatly from the anti-reversion discourse of later years which touted an anti-war, anti-base discourse.

On the other hand, the primary argument of the reversionists was that Japan and Okinawa were inseparable. A statement by the Socialist Masses Party in March 1951 insisted: 'Nobody disputes that Japan and Ryukyu are the same people (*minzoku*), and it is extremely natural that the same people be placed under the same political stance (*sic*),' while a statement from the People's Party also asserted: 'The Ryukyuan people are part of the Japanese race, and in all respects, Ryukyuans' happiness cannot exist without their joining the Japanese people.' According to the Secretary-General of the Socialist Masses Party, Kaneshi Saichi, who became President of the Nihon Fukki Sokushin Kiseikai (Council for promotion of return to Japan), 'When all is said and done, it is most ideal in terms of the composition of a country for its members to be of the same race, to possess the same culture and the same manners and customs, to use the same language and script, and to be under the same living and economic conditions.' The reversion faction, in turn, emphasised the economic inseparability of Japan and Okinawa, saying, for instance: 'There can be no Okinawan economy separate from the Japanese economy,' and: 'Joining the Japanese nation is the only path to liberation from poverty for the Okinawan people' (*Uruma shinpō* 1951d [1978], p. 415; Kaneshi 1951, pp. 38, 40; Senaga 1951, p. 34) .

Furthermore, in contrast to the anti-reversion discourse, the reversionist camp declared its confidence in Japan. What was stressed there was the difference between the prewar Empire of Japan and Japan the postwar democratic state, and the difference between the rulers of Japan and its people. Kaneshi, from the Socialist Masses Party, emphasised that postwar Japan 'had made a 180-degree about-face from a sovereign emperor to sovereignty residing in the people, from imperialism to democracy, and from a war-loving state to a peaceful state,' while Senaga, from the People's Party, declared that in the prewar, 'it was the Japanese capitalists, large landowners, bankers and the vicious bureaucrats and military clique who colluded with them that exploited the Okinawan populace,' and that people such as Japanese workers and 'farmers from the mainland's north-east (Tohoku)' were victims in the same way as Okinawans (Kaneshi 1951, p. 39; Senaga 1951, p. 15).

Furthermore, again in contrast to the anti-reversion discourse, the reversionist side gave a low assessment of the Ryukyu Kingdom. Senaga claimed that the important confrontation was not 'Japan versus Okinawa' but 'rulers versus people,' and warned against forgetting that both the 'King of Ryukyu' and the 'big shots of Okinawa' had 'exploited [Okinawa's] farmers.' Moreover, Nishime Junji – who in later years became a claimant that reversion was premature – also criticised the Ryukyu Kingdom at this point in time, proposing that 'if one comes to realise that it was something built upon the blood and sweat of the commoner class, and that its prosperity was nothing more than the prosperity of the privileged class, then the Ryukyu of the past will become the very object of hatred, and unable to be the target of glorification' (Senaga 1951, p. 15; Nishime 1951, p. 54). By pointing out the class divisions within Okinawa, this could be said to have countered the anti-reversion discourse which touted Okinawan nationalism, regarding Okinawa as a single entity.

This does not mean, though, that the People's Party and Socialist Masses Party were making exactly the same claims. In comparison to the People's Party, which emphasised the class-related component, the Socialist Masses Party had a stronger tendency to assert ethnic identity with Japan. Kaneshi, in turn, declared: 'We are greatly optimistic about the future of Japan's financial circles,' and a point such as this differed both from the anti-reversion discourse, which viewed the Japanese economy with pessimism, and again from the People's Party, which criticised Japan's financial clique. In contrast to the People's Party side's assertion that 'Japanese reversion links with the protection of peace,' the Socialist Masses Party's Governor Taira declared: 'I want to get rid of anti-Americanism. However, I do not consider the issue of Japanese reversion to be anti-Americanism, because Japan has assumed a stance of full cooperation with the U.S.' (Kaneshi 1951, p. 40; Senaga 1951, p. 12. *Uruma shinpō* 1951b [1978], p. 395). This said, in sum, the contrast was almost clear-cut between the anti-reversion discourse, which advocated mistrust of Japan and trust in America, and the reversion discourse, which asserted identity with Japan.

The vacillating discourse of belonging

Apart from the tenor of argument employed by politicians and journalists, what might general public opinion have been? News coverage of several voices from the streets appeared in newspapers of the day.

Here were found expressions from supporters of reversion of a sense of familiarity towards Japan, including: '[We are] also ethnically the same as Japan,' and 'It is human nature to return to one's parents' care,' and of caution towards the U.S., namely: '[We can] also be reconciled with the Japanese people because they are the same ethnic group, but in the case of Americans, perhaps because their language, customs and so on are different, after all, [we] will somehow not get along well,' or, '[We] always feel oppressed, with a perception of racial discrimination that was not seen in the days of Japan.' In counter to this, opponents of reversion asserted such things as: 'There is talk of racial discrimination and so forth as the voice of opposition to belonging to America, but on that point, I suspect that we would experience an even worse dose of it if we attached to Japan,' or, 'If we attached to America, we would be able to make our way as fine world citizens, receiving economic assistance and being able to improve our future livelihood and standards, too, with Christian-like and democratic ideas being disseminated, as well' (*Uruma shinpō* 1951a [1978], pp. 435–437). In other words, even in terms of public opinion, it could be argued that supporters and opponents of reversion were divided by their respective combinations of views on Japan and views on America.

Yet even in the assembly or in popular opinion, opponents to reversion remained a minority. An opinion poll of the younger generation was conducted by the Okinawa Seinen Rengōkai (Federation of Okinawan Youth, a different organisation from the Communist-affiliated Okinawa Youth League) from March into April 1951, the results being that out of a total of approximately 12,000 responses, reversion was chosen by eighty-six percent, trusteeship by seven percent, independence by two percent, and 'other' by four percent (Okinawa-ken Sokoku Fukki Tōsō Shi Hensan Iinkai 1982, p. 50). Moreover, by August, signatures numbering more than seventy percent of eligible voters were collected on a reversion petition which was sent to the United Nations and the

Supreme Commander of the Allied Powers (SCAP) immediately prior to the Peace Treaty being concluded in August.

Even so, why might the discourse of Japanese reversion, which had been weak in the initial period after the defeat, have garnered so much support?

To be sure, superficially the drift of argument was often that Okinawans were 'essentially Japanese, and from its historical and political relationship, and economic and cultural relationship, as well, [Okinawa] naturally should revert to Japan' (*Uruma shinpō* 1951a [1978], p. 435) or, as reflects Senaga's criticism of the frequent occurrence of such a drift, that it was 'just the emotion of a child yearning for its parent, an irrepressible feeling that defies explanation' (Senaga 1951, p. 22). However, it is uncertain as to how far this was true, because once the peace treaty was imminent, there were many who switched to arguing for reversion.

Nagaoka Tomotarō, for one, who in 1946 had spoken of independence of the 'Okinawan people,' citing the example of Panama, also posed the question in February 1951: 'Are there any among the heirs to even a little Okinawan blood who would now gladly offer their native soil to be an American military colony, I wonder?' He then asserted: 'I want to remain part of Japan, as of old.' Furthermore, five years after that, he had begun to state: 'It is said that "blood is thicker than water." Okinawans are Japanese; furthermore, the Okinawan language has a close association with Japanese, it being a dialect.' Moreover, Kaneshi Saichi, too – who in 1951 was to become President of the Nihon Fukki Sokushin Kiseikai, which advocated the 'same ethnicity' discourse – had declared in a 1947 speech that 'we were nothing but slaves of Japan under the name of Japanese ethnicity,' and said: 'I ended up holding an extreme grudge against Japan for causing several tens of thousands of our compatriots to die in battle, turning Okinawa into scorched earth, and ignoring and not considering the most pitiful sight [of Okinawans] without homes in which to live' ((Nagaoka 1951; Yohena (= Nagaoka) 1956, p. 199).[10] Both Kaneshi and Senaga seem to have supported the idea of a Panama-type of protectorate in 1946, as previously mentioned.

Ikemiyagushiku, an advocate of trusteeship, remarked: 'There are probably few Okinawans who are not surprised when they look back and wonder whenever it was that they came to have a consciousness of being Japanese,' but without even tracing as far back into the past as early Meiji, people who had spoken in 1946 of the independence of the 'Okinawan nation' had come to call themselves 'Japanese' in 1951. Moreover, there was the view that this was not a situation that had slowly evolved within a five-year period, but one that had become established in a few months in 1951. Neither the Republican Party, People's Party or Socialist Masses Party had solidified its attitude about the question of belonging as of the end of January 1951, but after these parties had come up with policies one after another once February had begun, a declaration of intent regarding belonging to Japan was resolved by a Socialist Masses Party and People's Party majority at the Government of the Ryukyu Islands (GRI) assembly in March (Ikemiyagushiku 1996, p. 18).[11]

If one assumes that the logic of reverting because Okinawans were 'Japanese' was a superficial one, then one wonders what the motivation behind the reversion discourse was. Of course, it is also true that disillusionment towards America was spreading, but in this period confrontation over confiscation of land for military bases and so on was not as intense as in later years. Something like the following sentiment, seen in a Socialist Masses Party declaration, is thought probably to be close to the reversion side's actual feeling.

> Now, when Japan and Ryukyu have equal rights and have entirely amalgamated into the same manners and customs due to efforts during the past century, to tear them apart would make the past century's achievements come to nothing (*Uruma shinpō* 1951d [1978], p. 415).

Rather than saying that they wish to revert because they are 'Japanese,' they are loath to waste the efforts expended in 'the past century' in order to become 'Japanese.' A Socialist Masses Party member expressed this sentiment more tangibly in the following way in a GRI assembly debate on 19 March 1951: 'In the days when we were integrated with Japan, there was some divergence in language, manners and customs, but later, along with the progress of education, we advanced to the point where there was no difference whatever in those quarters, either, and even considered from the political aspect, we have been granted the same right to vote as other prefectures in Japan.' '[Our] having attained so much is the result of efforts by all residents over almost a century, and for that reason, too, we hope to attach to Japan' (Okinawa Kengikai Jimusho 1995, p. 338). It could be argued that it was a reversion discourse not because they were oblivious of the memory of not having been treated as 'Japanese,' but conversely, for the very reason that they remembered it to a painful degree.

What is important here is that unlike Korea and Taiwan, in the prewar institutional equality had been tentatively achieved as 'Japanese' in the case of Okinawa. Even in the above declaration, their having acquired 'equal rights,' including suffrage, is taken to be a major premise for going back to being 'Japanese' once more. Even in response to the anti-reversion argument that Okinawans would be conscripted if they were to revert, the reversionists counter-argued that they, too, could 'put up ... parliamentary candidates from the main island of Okinawa and establish a movement in utter opposition to this' (Okinawa Kengikai Jimusho 1995, p. 343). If merely a system similar to that in Korea or Taiwan had been applied in prewar Okinawa, such a reversion discourse would have been unlikely to arise. In prewar Korea and Taiwan, assimilation policies had been implemented in which local inhabitants were forcibly incorporated into the Japanese family register system and were taught Japanese language and patriotism; and in the final stage of the Pacific War, they were conscripted. Nevertheless, to the last, no Diet members were elected from Korea or Taiwan.

In this respect, it was the same in the case of the aforementioned Nakayoshi Ryōkō, who was treated as a vestige of education for imperialisation. In his reversion petition submitted to the mainland Democratic Party in June 1947, he spoke of reversion saying: 'Up till mid-wartime, five members from Okinawa were elected to the House of Representatives,' and in his petition submitted in 1951 to the Committee for the Far East, also, he complained: 'Okinawan residents have lost Japanese political suffrage and all other rights ... they enjoyed equally with their compatriots on the mainland until the war's end, as well, and have to live lives devoid of vitality.' There is no glorification of the emperor or the like to be seen in his petitions, even those addressed to mainland conservative politicians (Nakayoshi 1947).[12] He spoke of wanting to have Okinawa revert to 'the same as the prewar,' but this did not mean reversion to such things as conscription, Japanisation, the sago-palm hell or discrimination.

This could also be said of the economic aspect. The Socialist Masses Party declared in its statement that 'Ryukyu was within the Japanese economic sphere, and it was almost impossible to separate from it,' but even as a general view, there were voices saying, for example: 'In order to develop the market in a rational manner, we simply must implement the kind of free shipping we had in the prewar by means of a connection with Japan,' or 'Even if we were in a merchant's position, free business dealings would be demanded in domestic transactions, and business simply could not be done in foreign trade mode if we attached to America' (*Uruma shinpō* 1951d [1978], p. 415; *Uruma shinpō* 1951a [1978], p. 437). In addition, as I will discuss in the next chapter, prewar postal savings, pensions, superannuation and the like were still deposited with the Japanese government side, and the question of whether these would be accessed had become the target of concern. For Okinawa, some economic vested rights already existed in Japan.

Moreover, in economic terms, the expectation of Okinawa's ability to receive assistance from the Japanese government if it reverted was also an indispensable viewpoint. Governor Taira stated, for example, that 'as the Government (of the Ryukyu Islands), [we] have also made requests as to guarantees for war damages, and if we revert to Japan I think that this will be further accelerated' (*Uruma shinpō* 1951b [1978], pp. 417); and Socialist Masses Party assembly member Nakazato Seikichi further remarked at the assembly on 28 August 1951: 'If we belonged to Japan, we could receive large sums in aid from the Japanese government' (Okinawa Kengikai Jimusho 1995, p. 244). An Okinawan business expert of the day, Takane Meitatsu, deemed it 'a mistake to argue for belonging to Japan simply on the rationale that Okinawans are Japanese and that blood is thicker than water. I myself advocate it with the idea that by reverting to Japan, Okinawan reconstruction will be expedited' (double quoted from Ikemiyagushiku 1996, p. 22). Already in 1951, news of the mainland's economic revival was gradually being communicated, and a gap was beginning to be perceived between this and Okinawa's reconstruction, which was proceeding at a snail's pace.

Moreover, when compared to reversion, trusteeship under the U.S. had too many unknown anxieties. According to a letter to the editor in *Okinawa no tomo*, regardless whether it were reversion or trusteeship, 'absolute opposition to colonial possession' was probably a shared sentiment among Okinawans; but in contrast to reversion, in which case institutional equality as 'Japanese' seemed somehow or other possible to secure, trusteeship constituted throwing in their lot at America's discretion, and there was already a prediction that 'trusteeship would be nothing but being used by a specific country, having been turned into a military base' (*Okinawa no tomo* 1951f; 1951g).

Furthermore, in the sense of cultural assimilation, as well, it was impossible to ignore the fruits of 'the past century.' As also evidenced by voices from the anti-reversion camp which emphasised discrimination from Japan: 'Our reward for having evacuated to Kyushu during the war, with pride and a sense of responsibility in being of the Yamato race, was being treated as an alien people by the local people, and being treated with contempt,' there were many people who criticised 'this treatment as an alien people.' Lurking there was a fear of being excluded as an 'alien people,' and though it took the form of an objection to discrimination, it actually was of the same nature as the mentality which had supported a pro-assimilation orientation. From the perspective of such a mentality, comparing the degree of difficulty of assimilation to Japan, which had a record from 'the past century,' with assimilation to America, which would require starting efforts from scratch, it was natural that the argument of reversion supporters would be in the ascendant, saying: 'We fear that in the case of U.S. trusteeship, we would perhaps be subjected to extreme treatment as an alien people.' Among anti-reversion advocates, there were also some who, while criticising past 'treatment as an alien people' by Japan, claimed that under American rule, they would be forced to become 'English-speaking nationals,' but it was clear to all that this was unrealistic (*Uruma shinpō* 1951a [1978], p. 437; Higa 1951 [1978]).

Voices in support of reversion arose from the parents of the generation that had expended enormous effort and mastered Japan's standard language, expressing their uneasiness that if trusteeship eventuated, then the likely result would be that their children would 'be able to become neither Japanese nor American.' In the aspect of their children's education, as well, they spoke from the position that they themselves had received Japanese education, and so it was natural for them to welcome Japanese education. Arguments against reversion also included the view that Okinawa should decide whether to revert to Japan at an advantageous time, having temporarily come under trusteeship and having cultivated its competence. In regard to this, Kaneshi remarked that he had 'fear' that 'if Okinawa faced the kind of situation where it were isolated from Japan, the Japanese would then come to regard Okinawans as foreigners, and would eventually end up viewing them as an alien people' (*Uruma shinpō*

1951a [1978], p. 437; Kaneshi 1951, p. 37). There was the risk that if Okinawa were temporarily severed from Japan, then even if it were to revert in later years, it would have to make endless efforts to assimilate all over again.

The common feature in these arguments was the unwitting assumption that acceptance or rejection of reversion was, in short, a choice between assimilating to Japan and assimilating to America. Due to the tragedy of the Battle of Okinawa, loyalty towards the Japanese state had reached a point of being relativised, as would be expected, and support for reversion was not advocated from that kind of motivation. However, the fear of being seen by its rulers as an 'alien people' and the consciousness that assimilation constituted a way of evading this was stamped upon the reversion discourse in critical circles, just like a conditioned reflex. When the future happiness of Okinawa was considered from such a worldview, Japanese reversion appeared more advantageous in terms of being an accumulation of efforts towards assimilation.

The reversion discourse which emerged from Okinawans' fear of being 'viewed as an alien people' also happened to become integrated with the exclusion of people who deserved to be seen as even more of an 'alien people' than themselves. In the eyes of some pro-reversionists, trusteeship was something to be applied to 'savages' who lacked the ability to self-govern or to form a nation, a successor to the mandate implemented in the South Sea Islands under Japanese rule in the prewar – in other words, demoting Okinawans to a status equivalent to 'South Sea Islanders' or 'Kanakas.' Conservatives like Nakayoshi and Yoshida argued that 'coming under the same trusteeship as places like Saipan or Tinian would be "doing wrong" by the ancestors,' meaning that Okinawans would themselves negate the education and level of civilisation achieved in Okinawa. 'Becoming like Kanakas' would be 'inevitable once Okinawa, too, was placed under U.S. trusteeship,' but Senaga from the People's Party, who should have been leftist, also asserted that 'advocates of trusteeship ... are a bunch of people who reject our ability to self-govern of their own volition.' One opponent of reversion suggested that 'their real motive was the single point that they "would not like [Okinawa] to descend into a colonial nation under United Nations entrustment, nor would they want to be placed in the position of an international orphan,"' and this probably hit the mark to a certain degree (*Okinawa no tomo* 1951c; Yoshida 1976, p. 49. Senaga 1951, p. 11; Higa 1951 [1978], p. 435).[13]

Though admittedly arising from such a worldview, the reversion discourse from the Okinawan side may be seen by no means as unconditional allegiance to Japan, but as having been proposed through the judgement that it was perhaps an advantageous choice for Okinawa. In an editorial foreword to Nagaoka (1951), a newspaper published by Okinawans residing in Kumamoto on the mainland warned against overlooking the fact that even when it came to the same expression, '*Nihon kizoku* (belonging to Japan),' there was an essential difference between what mainland 'Japanese' and Okinawans respectively advocated. That being the case, though the pro-reversion discourse might have been superficially dominant, it was something that ought to have enabled the advent of rapid change in accordance with the circumstances, just as in the five years postwar many advocates had changed their position, and most political parties had decided upon their policy within a space of a few months. More than anything, every person wavered internally: 'Each individual, while desiring on the one hand to belong to Japan, desires trusteeship in the back of her or his mind' (Higa n.d).

The controversy over belonging was a wavering of Okinawan identity, caught between two others, namely Japan and America, and a vacillation over whether to continue a 'century's worth' of Okinawan efforts to secure rights as 'Japanese.' This kind of wavering, moreover, came to increase its swing ever more widely amid the situational changes which were to follow.

7 The Significance of 'Japan, the Ancestral Land'

In the Peace Treaty which came into effect in April 1952, it was decided that Okinawa would be severed from Japan, and 'provisional' martial rule by the United States would be continued. Moreover, as the American military's base-expansion policy and its human rights violations were uncovered, animosity towards the U.S. heightened; and, as if in parallel, so did a direction towards reversion to Japan.

Yet the reversion movement in the 1950s had a somewhat different character from that of the 1960s, which was called 'anti-war reversion.' Here, I will investigate how the reversion movement discourse up to the mid-1950s unfolded, as it will afford glimpses as to what the Okinawan side endeavoured to express by the word 'Japanese.'

'Japanese' as a euphemism for human rights

Construction of U.S. military bases on Okinawa, which attracted full-scale budget funding from the 1950–51 Fiscal Year, increased its momentum after the conclusion of the Peace Treaty. At that very time, the Korean War began, and American strategic bombers set out from Okinawan bases on sorties to the Korean peninsula almost daily. According to one American newspaper editorial, the U.S. strike force in the Far East was confined to Okinawa, and if the Japanese government had not allowed this in a time of war, then the U.S. would have been unable to conduct its military operations. Thus Okinawa was not only an ideal base for the U.S. military in geographical terms, but it was also a valuable presence in the sense of being a place with which the military could do as it wished. In 1953, the Commander of the Ryukyus Command said: 'Pulling out of Okinawa would be equivalent to announcing that the United States was going to withdraw from the Far East as a whole,' and President Eisenhower's State of the Union address the following year stated: 'We shall maintain bases in Okinawa indefinitely' (Sulzberger 1958, p. 49; Nakano 1969, p. 78).[1]

In response to this, in October 1951, immediately after it became clear through the Peace Treaty that rule by the U.S. military would be continued, an extraordinary meeting of Directors on the Okinawan side compiled a list of requirements spanning fifteen items vis-à-vis the U.S. military.[2] The first item spelled out the wish for 'nationality to be Japanese, and for the raising of the Japanese national flag to be permitted.' At the time, the raising of the *Hi-no-maru* was also forbidden, as an anti-U.S. act.

The hope of the Okinawan side was not for mere assimilation into 'the Japanese.' From the second item in this schedule of requirements onwards, there were listed such demands as: 'to adopt Japanese laws to the maximum extent;' 'to treat all trade with Japan as domestic, and establish no restrictions whatsoever;' and 'to carry out the swift payment of [prewar] pensions, annuities, savings, insurance, and bonds such as government bonds.' In other words, here 'the Japanese' arguably refers to the protection of human rights by Japanese law and trade with Japan, or the payment of pensions by the Japanese government, and the like. Moreover, there were also many items mentioned in the petition which, though logically distinct from Japanese reversion, were of importance to the Okinawan side, including: 'to establish an autonomous government in the Ryukyus, and institute the public election of local chief executives and members of parliament;' and 'to sustain U.S. economic assistance in future, also, and for Japan to assist in a positive manner, as well.'

What became a particularly important issue in this petition was an item saying: 'to pay the rent for land for military use, and also to pay compensation for land ruined for cultivation by military facilities, as matters of urgency.' After this, the land which the U.S. military used until 1954 increased to fourteen percent of Okinawa's total area, and forty-one percent of its cultivated land, but this problem actually comprised a huge factor in the rise of intentions towards reversion. This was because on the mainland, whenever the U.S. military expropriated land, it had to follow the procedures which the Japanese government had stipulated in the Special Measures Law for Land Used by the American Forces (Special Measures Law), and the rental value of the expropriated sites was also set; but in Okinawa, where this was not applied, both expropriation and compensation were left at the whim of the U.S. military.

In 1953, a member of the Okinawan Legislature stated: 'As to why the village council decided upon Japanese reversion, it is because [the U.S. military's expropriation of land] is just too horrendous, and if we decide to revert to Japan, as there will be but one law in Japan, it will mean we will be able to obtain [compensation payments] on that basis' (Ryūkyū Seifu Bunkyō Kyoku Kenkyū Chōsa Ka 1956, p. 124). This Special Measures Law was one which the Japanese government enacted for the U.S. military immediately following the establishment of the Treaty of Mutual Cooperation and Security between the United States and Japan (AMPO), because the postwar Land Expropriation Law did not recognise the expropriation of land for military purposes; and yet, as was seen in the struggle against the expansion of the Tachikawa Air Base in the 1950s, and in Okinawa in the 1990s, it was something which gave local government chief executives in those places the leeway to resist in such ways as rejecting the procedures of public notice and inspection of land records. In pre-reversion Okinawa, however, no such law even existed.

In addition, this 1951 petition also contained an item saying: 'to raise Ryukyuans' wages for labour appropriately,' but this, too, was inseparable from the issue of reversion. There were increasing cases of farmers whose land had been seized becoming workers for the military, but when hired by the U.S. military, the minimum hourly wage by comparison with Okinawans was: Americans, fourteen times as much; Filipinos, five times as much; and 'Japanese' 2.6 times as much. Moreover, in the Okinawans' case, they had nothing like the collective bargaining rights set down in Japanese labour legislation. Needless to say, this meant that if they became 'Japanese' through reversion, then they could obtain the protection of Japanese labour laws, and their wages would more than double. A certain 1952 labour-dispute petition from the Okinawan side remonstrated against the U.S. military, citing the prewar Factory Law from 'Japan, the ancestral land' and saying: 'We Ryukyuans have reached today without enjoying the benefits of our Japanese ancestral land's various democratic laws' (Nakano 1969, pp. 146, 129).

However, just because the expression 'Japan, the ancestral land' was employed, the question of whether this signified unconditional affection for Japan was a different matter. Labour disputes in this period were often ones mounted against mainland business people contracted to construct U.S. military bases. Mainland builders and contractors, having used Okinawans whom they could hire for lower wages and inferior working conditions than

Japanese workers protected by Japanese labour laws, fired them for reasons such as that notice of termination was not obligated in U.S. military proclamations. In June 1952, an appeal issued in such a dispute against a mainland firm criticised 'the Japanese' by saying: 'Compared with the treatment of Japanese workers, it is as different as heaven and hell,' and: 'No matter where Ryukyuan labourers go, exploitation from Japanese business people and others awaits them.' At the same time, however, it called for 'ancestral land reversion,' saying: 'This is the shape of us workers and all Ryukyuans, severed from Japan by Article Three of the Peace Treaty.' The first Okinawan May Day, held in that year, also decided upon 'immediate Japanese reversion,' along with the 'immediate establishment of laws to protect workers' (Nakano 1969, pp. 129, 128, 131). It goes without saying that in such a form, even though members of the Okinawan side asserted that they were 'Japanese,' this could not be said to be a simple preference for assimilation.

The response from the U.S. military, however, was a totally rigid one. The Ryukyuan Legislature on the Okinawan side attempted to enact a similar labour-related law to the postwar mainland, but the U.S. side pressured it not to approve the extension of mainland laws such as this on the rationale that Okinawa was 'different' from the mainland, arguing: 'The Japanese Basic Law ... is a complete and complex, all-embracing law for application solely in Japan, which has been industrialised to a high degree, and not at all suited to the Ryukyuan economy, which is mainly an agrarian economy.' In 1953, when the Legislature defied that objection and approved labour legislation, this time the U.S. military issued a proclamation making military-related workers exempt from its application, and in 1955, it made the formation of all labour unions subject to approval (Nakano 1969, p. 132).[3]

In the land issue, also, the U.S. military carried out unilateral land expropriation by means of proclamation, and the rent paid to farmers was said to amount to as little as one fiftieth of the annual yield. From the start, the rent paid to the owners of land used for U.S. military bases on the Japanese mainland was something which the Japanese government, not the U.S., had borne. In April 1955, one mainland newspaper carried the following critique: 'The U.S. military's fundamental plan of action seems to be to want the country in question to bear the expense of land rent and acquisition as far as possible, and though Japan can pay because it has the economic leeway, Okinawa cannot pay, and so the U.S. military itself is reluctantly footing the bill. At a press conference on the thirteenth, too, U.S. government authorities let slip the words: "Wherever else is there a victorious nation that pays rent for land?" but these probably represent their underlying true feelings, which take too much for granted' (Nakano 1969, p. 154). Naturally, protests were mounted by residents in each locale, but the U.S. military often sent out armed troops, forcing through the expropriation and arresting the protesters as 'communists.'

As economic recovery advanced on the mainland, this kind of disparity with Okinawa became all the more pronounced. A resolution issued at the March 1956 '*Okinawa henkan yōsei kokumin taikai* (Nationals' rally to appeal for return of Okinawa)' describes the reasons for reversion as follows, namely: 'Compensation for land for military use in Okinawa is far lower than on the mainland, not even amounting to a tenth of its fair price,' 'the collection and remittance of savings and other bonds located on the mainland are hindered, and hundreds of millions of yen have been lying idle since the end of the war without earning any interest,' 'conditions for Okinawan public servants and teachers, which once matched that of other prefectures, have now dropped to an extremely inferior level,' and, 'the conditions for military workers are also much worse than on the mainland ... they receiving treatment tantamount to racial discrimination.' Furthermore, as a situation that was unpredictable at the time of the Peace Treaty, an item was also present that said: 'On the Japanese mainland, assistance from the public purse towards local administration amounts to one third of the regional budget ... and because of administrative separation, this means that Okinawa suffers losses several times greater than the amount of assistance it receives from the U.S.' A preliminary calculation was recorded as predicting that if Okinawa were to revert, it would be able to receive subsidies from the Japanese government that would be at least 3.5 times the sum of U.S. aid. Of course, the words: 'The spiritual agony of Okinawan compatriots due to their separation [from Japan] cannot be overlooked, either,' were also added, which implies it was something redolent of the tangible human rights and economic demands made by the reversion movement of the day (Nakano 1969, p. 145).

While it was some years later, Nakayoshi Ryōkō spoke as follows in 1961:

If Okinawa returns to Japan, it will bear the burden of national taxation along with the people of the whole country, and as one Japanese family, just as in prefectures nationwide, financial aid will be paid to it from the government. Nearly ten billion yen will be provided annually in compulsory education costs and local finance subsidies, budget allocations for public works, outlays for promotion of various kinds of industries, social welfare costs, social security, public health subsidies, and so on. We have the right to receive these, not as handouts, but as 'Okinawa Prefecture.' In accordance with the Constitution, which says: 'All people shall have the right to maintain the minimum standards of wholesome and cultured living,' the state will forever guarantee the residents of Okinawa Prefecture, as Japanese nationals, a minimum standard of living. This is unlike America, which, if Okinawa ceases to be of use as a military base, will abandon it to become a wilderness of plains and mountains (Nakayoshi 1947a).

The anticipation that if Okinawans became 'Japanese' through reversion, an affluent and peaceful life would await them inflated with the passing years. In 1958, a local newspaper, *Okinawa taimusu*, ran a thirty-nine-part series of articles entitled; 'A blueprint for Okinawa Prefecture: if mainland reversion materialises,' depicting the image of a future in which, thanks to reversion, taxes would be cut, public finances would be enhanced by subsidies, the economy, too, would develop, and the governor would be chosen by public election, as well. Of course, as no administrative unit called 'Okinawa Prefecture' existed at that time, both the title of this newspaper series, 'A blueprint for Okinawa Prefecture,' and Nakayoshi's words referring to 'the right to receive ... as "Okinawa Prefecture"' were ones which intentionally employed the term 'prefecture.' Furthermore, the 1954 bulletin of the Okinawa Shotō Sokoku Fukki Sokushin Kiseikai (Okinawan Islands preparatory council for return to the ancestral land) carried out preliminary calculations which indicated that if reversion took place, then not only would a rise in all kinds of social security payments and public servants' salaries be implemented, but large amounts of aid would be obtained for agriculture, transport, construction and the like; and the bulletin maintained: 'If reversion is fulfilled, because the above projections will become reality, we can expect Okinawa to become the most affluent prefecture in Japan' (Uechi and Kinjō 1960; *Okinawa fukki kaihō* 1954). The more severe the oppression from the U.S. side became, the more such hopeful observations gripped people's hearts like the mirage of an oasis.

On the other hand, in the face of successive U.S. military policies, the view of America held by the Okinawan side grew decisively worse. In the words of Ahagon Shōkō, a farmer from Iejima whose land had been expropriated: 'During the war the Japanese army gave us a terrible time. Partly for that reason, at first we trusted America, thinking it was the land of democracy, the land that spawned Lincoln.' He went on to say, however, that this transformed into a view of America as a 'brute (*kichiku*), after all, though in a different sense from what the Japanese government meant during the war.' From 1955 to 1956, there was a string of criminal incidents, including the rape and murder of a young girl and the fatal shooting of a resident by American soldiers, but as the U.S. side held jurisdiction, the Okinawans were unable to try the offenders, and a resolution was made by the Legislature, stating: 'Even in the age when Japanese militarism was at its zenith, we had never heard of an example of a soldier firing a gun at a civilian.' One newspaper in 1956, predicting the future of Okinawa under U.S. military domination, wrote, for example: 'Okinawans are total Yankees whose hair and eyes are both black, and they are already total slaves,' and 'this is plausible if we think of the lives of the Blacks in the U.S.A. and the way of life in The Philippines over this half-century' (Ahagon 1973, pp. 40–41; Nakano 1969, pp. 126–127; Ishikawa 1956).

Expectations towards the mainland side could not help but heighten not only in terms of hopes for the future, but also in terms of resisting immediate oppression from the U.S. military. In November 1953, the Zen-Okinawa Rōdōsha Taikai (All-Okinawa workers' rally) issued a declaration saying that the workers of the whole of Okinawa anticipated 'enormous support from the eight million organised workers in the ancestral land' in order to rectify the situation under U.S. military control. In addition, when it became impossible for farmers who had had their land expropriated, including Ahagon, to resolve the problem even after exhausting every avenue, such as negotiation with the U.S. military, non-violent resistance, petitioning the Ryukyu government, and so forth, they sent a petition to various mainland groups, entitled: 'To all in *naichi*, our motherland,' stating: 'All of you in the ancestral land are the last resort for us now' (Nakano 1969, p. 130; Ahagon 1973, p. 108).

The mainland 'Japanese' did not necessarily live up to what the Okinawans expressed with the words 'ancestral land' and 'the Japanese,' however. In November 1953, for example, at a meeting on the occasion of a visit to Okinawa by members of the mainland's Lower House, the Okinawan side, including Kaneshi Saichi, issued requests for such things as the guarantee of land rent and pensions from the Japanese government, and assistance towards school construction, pleading that 'the desire of the Ryukyus as a whole is for Japanese reversion.' By contrast, Hirai Giichi, a mainland Liberal Party Member, while stating: 'Not for a single day have we forgotten you all, either, as always being our fellow Japanese,' he merely mouthed such platitudes as: '[We] must wholly fight to defend Japan's beautiful history and culture,' and: 'The true form of the Japanese race lies where spirit touches spirit, and sincerity touches sincerity.' His response to the various requests from the Okinawan side was: 'As there is also the problem of public finance, as a representative of the government, it is hard for me to say' (Ryūkyū Seifu Bunkyō Kyoku Kenkyū Chōsa Ka 1956, pp. 123, 126). Even while using the same word, 'Japanese,' the expectations of each side were at cross purposes.

The pro-American anti-communist reversion movement

After the conclusion of the Peace Treaty, the Republican Party and Socialist Party, which had advocated Ryukyuan independence or trusteeship, headed little by little towards dissolution. The U.S. side appointed a Chief Executive with a cooperative attitude to the U.S., and the pro-American conservative Democratic Party was formed as his ruling party. In this way, the three major parties, namely the Democratic Party, Socialist Masses Party, and People's Party, came to exist in Okinawa.

In that environment, it was the People's Party that became the target of the most pressure from America. In August 1952, Major General Robert S. Beightler, the then Deputy Governor of Okinawa (Deputy Governor of the Ryukyus Command) sent a message to the Legislature saying that it was 'no exaggeration' to suggest that the aim of the People's Party in the Ryukyus was totally identical to that of Comintern (Communist International), and that it was not going too far to say that they were one and the same. An anti-communist pamphlet bearing a portrait of Senaga Kamejirō, Committee Chair of the People's Party, was attached (Nakano 1969, pp. 92, 93).

That being said, while in later years the People's Party did strengthen its relationship with the Japanese Communist Party, it is doubtful whether it had been the kind of presence that the U.S. military claimed from the beginning. When Senaga stood as a candidate in the 1950 election for Guntō Governor, supporters of the pro-U.S. candidate voiced the criticism that 'the People's Party is the Communist Party,' but the People's Party side rebutted by saying: 'This goes against the facts.' In official documents, the People's Party in 1950 declared: 'We thank the U.S. military who smashed the Japanese military clique and liberated the Okinawans,' and, as I have previously mentioned, Senaga had called the U.S. military a liberating army (Naha-shi Kikakubu Shishi Henshū Shitsu 1978, p. 312, cited in Jinmin Tō Seinen Bu 1950; Nakano 1969, p. 64). It was only later that the People's Party employed such a descriptor as 'American imperialism' and progressed to total confrontation, and a tendency for this to evolve rapidly along with U.S. military suppression can be perceived.

The U.S. military's high-pressure stance and the fact that a pro-American party became the ruling party also made the Socialist Masses Party, which had been seen as more moderate, more of a hard-liner. In March 1953, when a Socialist Masses Party candidate won a by-election in central Okinawa, the U.S. side ordered the withholding of the electoral victory for the reason that the winning candidate had a minor criminal record. The Socialist Masses Party formed a '*Shokuminchi-ka hantai kyōdō tōsō iinkai* (Joint struggle committee against colonisation)' along with the People's Party in order to protest at that time, but the U.S. military ordered its dissolution as 'something which, from the committee's very name, heaps insult upon the United States' (Nakano 1969, p. 120). For the U.S., Okinawa was not a 'colony' or the like, but an area which was retained for the purposes of national defence and 'peace in the Orient.'

Nonetheless, it would not be correct to say that the reversion movement in this period was entirely advocating an anti-U.S., anti-war line. Rather, on paper, there were many examples touting cooperation with the U.S. military and anti-communism. A letter addressed to Deputy Governor David A.D. Ogden in February 1954, Yara Chōbyō, the then president of the Okinawa Shotō Sokoku

Fukki Sokushin Kiseikai (hereafter referred to as the Kiseikai), for example, stated as follows:

> Residents, too, well understand that Okinawa is strategically vital as a defence base for the free nations against the invasion of world communism, and to that end, residents have contributed precious land and effort to the construction work for American bases, and cooperated with it. In addition, we also acknowledge that the existence of the bases has become one of the things supporting residents' livelihoods in the current international situation. Accordingly, we are not in a position either ideologically or economically to oppose the maintenance of U.S. bases in Okinawa. However, it is unimaginable to us that enjoyment by the residents of the Okinawan Archipelago of life as Japanese would cause even the slightest interference to the maintenance of U.S. bases. Our ancestral land, Japan, has a close, cooperative relationship with the United States, and through AMPO, the U.S. maintains numerous large bases on the Japanese mainland, as well. We think that if Okinawa reverts to Japan, Okinawa's bases will naturally be able to be retained in accordance with the Treaty. Some inflow of anti-U.S. activity can be expected at the time of reversion, but the residents of Okinawa are neither as stupid nor as unrealistic as to be taken advantage of by this type of activity (Yara 1954, in Okinawa-ken Sokoku Fukki Tōsō Shi Hensan Iinkai 1982, p. 36).

In a letter to the *Mainichi shinbun* in January 1954, also, Yara wrote: 'I have promoted the reversion movement under the firm belief not only that restoration of sovereignty to the ancestral land will not contradict America's Far-East defence structure in any way, but that it is something conducive to even more cooperation between America and Okinawa than ever before,' and this arguably was the official view of the Kiseikai in those days. Moreover, Kyan Shin'ei, who, along with Yara, headed the Okinawa Teachers' Association and led the reversion movement, also stated in a newspaper in April 1954: 'Even the reversion movement we extol says, if bases are necessary to Okinawa in order to defend the camp of the free nations, including Japan and America, then we will provide them, too, and also cooperate in military tasks' (Okinawa-ken Sokoku Fukki Tōsōshi Hensan Iinkai 1982, p. 34; Kyan 1954).

Such a tone was one that had existed since the very beginning of the reversion movement. As I mentioned in the previous chapter, in 1950 Governor Taira announced: 'I do not consider the issue of Japanese reversion to be anti-Americanism, because Japan has assumed a stance of full cooperation with the United States,' and Kaneshi Saichi, in turn, wrote in 1951: 'Our Japanese reversion movement is by no means an anti-U.S. movement. It is rather one which, following a line of the co-existence and co-prosperity of both countries, Japan and the U.S., endeavours to equip ourselves against external enemies who threaten democracy, and is a legitimate movement based on a grand vision which means to cooperate with the U.S. even more than at present.' Moreover, a petition submitted in January 1954 by Nakayoshi Ryōkō and others to the U.S. Secretary of State, John F. Dulles, stated: 'Even if the total restoration to Japan of administrative rights is permitted, U.S. military bases will be maintained in the Okinawan Islands by means of AMPO, there will be not the slightest inconvenience to U.S. Pacific defence; rather, the people of Japan will be thankful for American goodwill, and the bond between Japan and the U.S. will be strengthened even more,' while in an open letter to Deputy Governor Ogden of the Civilian Government in March the same year, also, he asserted that if reversion were delayed, then 'we fear that it will give our common enemies the Communists the opportunity to take advantage of it and extend their influence' (Kaneshi 1951, cited in Naha-shi Kikaku Bu Shishi Henshū Shitsu 1978, p. 456; Okinawa-ken Sokoku Fukki Tōsō Shi Hensan Iinkai 1982, pp. 15, 39).

The worldview adopted here was one which, unlike the reversion trend which depicted Japan and America in a diametrical manner, emphasised the oneness of Japan and America by establishing a common enemy, namely communism, as a target of exclusion. By deeming Japan and the U.S. to be one entity, it tried to spell out that reversion to Japan as not anti-American.

The tone of the mainland's principal media also had a similar tendency. At this time, mainland newspapers hardly ever focused upon Okinawan issues, but of the few related articles there were, a *Tōkyō shinbun* editorial of December 1952 saw 'no reason why our country, which actually is providing bases in every corner of the mainland ... should refuse to offer both areas [Okinawa and the Ogasawara Islands] as military bases, and to cooperate,' while a *Mainichi shinbun* editorial in January 1953 also asserted: 'Reversion will probably not be something that weakens the U.S. military's defence plans. Moreover, U.S. claims which criticise the Soviet

Union's unlawful occupation of Japan's northern areas will also go even further because of this' (Nakano 1969, pp. 143, 144). From an extension of the 1940s pattern in which the progressive camp advocated an argument for Okinawan independence, it was natural for the reversion discourse to become what the conservative side advocated.

In the Okinawans' case, however, there is a necessity to take into consideration the fact that these sentences were written in a period when people could be regarded as 'communists' and arrested, simply for conducting a reversion campaign. A February 1955 letter from farmers on Iejima, appealing to the mainland's *Asahi shinbun* (Asahi newspaper) for assistance, for example, speaks as follows:

> We are not anti-American, nor are we communists ... But there is no assistance apart from compensation for eviction, and we simply cannot agree with terms in which the alternative sites are rock-strewn, dreadful land, and rent amounts to about one fiftieth of the annual harvest ... If we are going to die anyway, we are resolved to do it on our own land, and sent a telegram to the Internal Bureau on the 26th last in the name of the village mayor, rejecting expropriation. Our first request was called insurrection, and because we were interrogated by the military, we are in the midst of composing prudent rules for petitions, such as: to smile when we encounter the military; not to carry farming implements at interviews (because we will be mistakenly regarded as rebellious); and, when we part, to bow our heads and say: 'Please.' We want you please to help the residents of Okinawa (Nakano 1969, pp. 123–124).

In these circumstances, they need not be blamed for being unable to help including cooperation towards the U.S. military on their list, and for having expected the support of 'Japan, the ancestral land' even if it meant overlooking its prewar discrimination. Even if that were the case, though, excluding the People's Party and the like, listing the abolition of the AMPO Treaty and the elimination of bases head-on could not have been called the mainstream in the reversion movement at that time. On the contrary, it would probably be more accurate to say they did not have the leeway vis-à-vis the situation confronting them.

What many of the 1950s reversion campaigns advocated was to return only civilian government administrative rights to Japan, leaving the U.S. military bases as they were. In particular, due also to the fact that President Eisenhower's January 1954 State of the Union address had declared the indefinite maintenance of bases in Okinawa, the removal of bases was thought to be impossible. For that reason, Yara Chōbyō said: 'The "indefinite retention of Okinawan bases" was an utterly different issue from that of "ruling Okinawa," and that is from where the potential for the restoration of Okinawa's sovereignty to the ancestral land strongly emerges.' Alternatively, the logic of separating military affairs and civil government was often adopted, as the petition from Nakayoshi and his supporters asserted: 'We think that if America were to concentrate upon military affairs and leave civil administration to Japan, they could gain the heartfelt cooperation of the local inhabitants along with assistance from Japan, and it would also be rather convenient for American military activities.' If the aim of reversion were the improvement of Okinawan people's welfare, then even if anti-war and anti-base campaigns were shelved, it would still represent tentative progress if reversion were achieved, and as the U.S. mainland held the view that it would mean a spending cut if Okinawan civilian government were restored to Japan, this course appeared realistic (Nakano 1969, p. 79; Nakayoshi 1954b).[4]

For this reason, reversion movement petitions in those days did not raise specific ideologies such as anti-war, many of them conversely emphasising their lack of ideology, saying, for example: 'Our movement promoting reversion to the ancestral land has no deep theory or logic of any kind. It springs from the natural expression of human feeling of wanting to return to Japan because we are Japanese.' It not being proper to cite advantage to the Okinawan side squarely as a reason for reversion, or if it were a matter of being suppressed if they extolled an anti-American and anti-war message, then it was natural for them to have no recourse but to reiterate: 'We want to return to Japan because we are Japanese.' Even in that case, though, the word 'Japanese' was inseparable from the protection of human rights by the constitution. Yara Chōbyō, for instance, asserted in 1954: 'The reversion movement is based on the extremely natural and fundamental principle of wanting to live as Japanese under the Japanese Constitution, because we are Japanese.' Similarly, Kyan Shin'ei also stated: 'We residents, too, want to have our basic human rights and lives and property protected under the

Japanese Constitution as true Japanese as soon as possible, and want to cooperate wholeheartedly [with the U.S. military]' (Nakayoshi 1954a, p. 33; Yara 1954, p. 35; Kyan 1954).

However, apart from a portion of the U.S. mainland, diplomats and military personnel who stressed national defence amid Cold-War ideology opposed even this kind of reversion movement. This was even more the case when it came down to the U.S. military in Okinawa, who did not want to relinquish their vested rights. In 1954, Deputy Governor Ogden declared: 'Military bases in the Ryukyus have a special character, and for defence purposes, it is not possible to separate the Civilian Administration and the military.' Secretary of State Dulles showed concern that if the U.S. returned educational rights to Japan, the Japan Teachers' Union (*Nikkyōso*) would become involved and education would become anti-American. According to a 1952 report in the *Tōkyō shinbun*, a certain 'high-ranking U.S. government official' apparently commented: 'If an anti-U.S. regime materialised [in Japan], we would have to pull the U.S. military out of Japan ... We must have bases in an area close to Japan which is not influenced by the Japanese government.' A 1953 article in an American newspaper reported: 'US authorities in Okinawa generally believe that even if Japan sought the return of Okinawa, there is absolutely no hope of that happening. These military and government authorities cannot understand why Japan, which is not finding it easy even merely to attempt to stabilise its own country's economy, should want to take on Okinawa, which cannot support itself economically,' and something like this was what the majority on the American side recognised (Nakano 1969, pp. 143, 78).[5]

The reply to Yara's letter advocating cooperation towards the U.S. military was a curt one, saying: 'Your continuing to incite reversion in Okinawa merely arouses confusion among Ryukyuans, as well as delighting the communists.' Furthermore, Deputy Governor David Ogden published the following opinion in May 1954:

Communism has anti-Japanese intentions, the same as anti-American ones. Nobody can be a communist at the same time as being a loyal Japanese citizen ...

If Okinawan residents were to think they wanted to make Okinawa into part of Japan through reversion, then we would announce to the entire world that we would completely withdraw our troops from the Far East, and leave it to communist rampancy ... and this would result in the overthrow of the Japanese government. Would there be anybody who hoped for reversion from the standpoint of a loyal Japanese citizen, in spite of the suggestion that reversion would bring about the overthrow of the Japanese government? (Bramley 1982, p. 38; Nakano 1969, p. 94).

He says that the reversion movement is anti-American, anti-Japanese, and un-'Japanese.' A similar logic was seen also in the 1954 court case over the People's Party Incident. A prosecutor on the U.S. side at that time stated: 'Senaga says that he is Japanese, and is serving the people, but ... though the Japanese are cooperating with the United States and other countries, Senaga is opposed to the United States' (Nakano 1969, p. 121).

Ogden also urged Okinawan farmers to surrender their land, saying: 'A communist regime would spell the end of land ownership. Landowners should always be anti-communist,' but it would be no mean feat if such an extreme reversal of logic were to arise (Nakano 1969, p. 95). For Ogden, 'the Japanese' merely meant people who submitted to U.S. rule.

The terminology of Japanese nationalism

Under such circumstances, what was the reaction of the Japanese government? At the Peace Talks, Prime Minister Yoshida Shigeru claimed that Japan had residual sovereignty over Okinawa, and Prime Minister Hatoyama Ichirō, also, stated in Diet Question Time that while Japan did not have administrative rights, sovereignty, legislative powers, executive powers, or suchlike, it did have territorial rights, after all (Nakano 1969, p. 82). Given the conclusion, the government's efforts towards Okinawa completely lacked zeal.

To cite one example, consider the response to the signatures collected towards the Peace Talks in 1951, as described in the previous chapter. According to the memoirs of Yoshida Shien, a petition with 230,000 signatures addressed to the Prime Minister which was sent by airmail from Okinawa went missing at its point of arrival in Tokyo, and after a worried Yoshida had looked all over the place for it, he apparently found it abandoned in the corner of a storeroom at the prime minister's official residence. The Japanese

Foreign Ministry's Director of the Treaties Bureau and Foreign Minister replied in the Diet that Okinawa would eventually be returned if they believed in the good intentions of the United States, but as to the question of specifically when it would be returned, they simply admitted to 'gradual progress,' saying, for instance, that it was 'still too soon,' or that they had to 'disentangle the issues one by one' (Yoshida 1976, p. 51; Nakano 1969, pp. 81, 82).

The Okinawan side, however, had no resort but to petition this government and the conservative ruling party. This was because, for many reversion campaigns, priority was given to improvement in their situation by means of reversion, rather than to left or right in ideological terms. The logic of a reversion movement such as that described above, which was cooperative towards the United States, also had a tendency to be aligned with the pro-U.S. line of mainland conservative parties. One mainland Diet member who visited Okinawa in 1953, for example, warned the Okinawan side not to expand their activities to the point of intensifying anti-American campaigns in emulation of the Japanese mainland (*naichi*) (Ryūkyū Seifu Bunkyō Kyoku Kenkyū Chōsa Ka 1956, p. 129).

In fact, the Japanese government had no inclination to take the risk of provoking the U.S. for the sake of Okinawa. In 1949, a newspaper editorial on the Okinawan side probably hit the nail on the head when it stated: 'Nowadays, when Okinawa's significance as an advance position for Japanese imperialism has ceased to exist, the Japanese government's asking that Okinawa be returned is a mere humanistic gesture on its part, meaning it has to display sympathy for Okinawa which was victimised by Japan; and emphasising this is a sort of misapprehension, is it not?' According to a statement by U.S. government authorities in January 1955, the Japanese government had 'never formally requested the return of the Bonin (Ogasawara) Islands or Okinawa' (*Uruma shinpō* 1949, in Naha-shi 1970, p. 213; Nakano 1969, p. 80).

In May 1955, a Leftist Socialist Party Member, Fukuda Masako, conducted the following dialogue in the Lower House with the Foreign Minister, Shigemitsu Mamoru:

> Fukuda: 'Are the residents of Okinawa Japanese? Whatever is their nationality?'
> Foreign Minister: 'Their residual sovereignty is recognised. As such, we regard Okinawan residents as being Japanese.'

Fukuda: 'So does that mean those Okinawans in other countries are protected by Japanese diplomatic missions abroad?'
Foreign Minister: 'That is correct' (Nakano 1969, p. 110).

This reply from Shigemitsu was not a unified opinion from the government. In fact, as discussed earlier in Chapter Five, the Japanese government took the position that the people of Okinawa had no right to its diplomatic protection, on the rationale that it was the U.S. that held administrative rights in Okinawa. Moreover, it was at the time of the 'island-wide struggle' which erupted in 1956 that the issue of whether Okinawans were legally 'Japanese' was greatly exposed.

The 'island-wide struggle (*shimagurumi tōsō*)' was a non-partisan struggle in Okinawa which occurred in the wake of a report by a special subcommittee of the U.S. House Armed Services Committee (the so-called Price Report) published in June 1956. As mentioned earlier, only meagre rent had been paid for expropriated land in Okinawa, but as this was a measure determined exclusively by the U.S. military in Okinawa and the Pentagon, the Okinawan side had high expectations towards this investigation by the U.S. House of Representatives. The content of the Price Report highlighted the importance of military bases in Okinawa, however, and stated that the lump-sum payment of land rent would be carried out. The whole of Okinawa was enraged at this report which, far from recommending the return of land, set forth lump-sum payments equivalent to its *de facto* purchase, and rallies advocating the so-called four principles (opposition to lump-sum payments; reasonable compensation; damages; and opposition to new expropriation) were held throughout Okinawa.

The reaction of the U.S. military to this was as rigid as ever. Deputy Governor James E. Moore said, for example: 'Though the military and the residents are working together, there are agitators among them. These are persons who have contact with the Communist Party of Japan,' and he threatened that if resistance were going to continue, then the U.S. would abolish the autonomous government and return Okinawa to the direct rule of the U.S. military. The U.S. reaction ended up pouring oil on the fire, and a series of opinions voiced from the Okinawa side declared: 'It gave us the impression that our decade of cooperating with the U.S. military means that the U.S. can do what it likes with Okinawa,' or 'We have had faith in

American democracy, but our hopes have been totally betrayed.' Even the pro-U.S. Democratic Party commented: 'Okinawa is called a showcase of democracy, but if you enforce those recommendations, it will surely become a showcase for anti-Americanism' (Nakano 1969, pp. 190, 193). Through these recommendations, it was confirmed that the movement hitherto which had championed pro-American anti-communism had had no effect but to inflate the U.S. military's arrogance.

Of course, in such circumstances, the kind of pro-U.S. terminology previously used was abandoned in the expansion of the campaign. However, the terms employed in the 'island-wide struggle' differed again from those in the late 1960s which had advocated anti-war peace. The words used in this struggle were those of nationalism as 'Japanese,' namely that the struggle to protect Okinawan land was one in which 'Japanese people' defended 'Japanese territory.'

One of the reasons why the movement was implemented using these words was that it had to request support from the mainland conservative regime. For example, a resolution sent by the Legislature in June 1956 to the Japanese Foreign Minister and Prime Minister emphasised that the U.S. government's 'acquisition of ownership of land in Okinawa, or its effectively indefinite lease' was something which would 'affect the territorial sovereignty of Japan.' Furthermore, the 'four-party coalition formed for the purpose of the struggle (consisting of the Legislature, the Municipal Mayors' Association, the Okinawan Federation of Landowners of Land Used for Military Purposes, and the Administration)' appealed to the Japanese government, saying: 'Bearing in mind that the protection of Japanese residents who have banded together with desperate resolve to defend their country's soil is the responsibility of the Japanese government, we desire strong negotiation vis-à-vis America.' In addition, the Municipal Mayors' Association also sent a telegram saying: 'Awaiting assistance from 80 million compatriots,' while the Teachers' Association resolved that it wanted the Japanese government to 'take measures so that not even an inch of our country's land is taken from us.' Furthermore, following the release and popularity of the motion picture called 'Himeyuri-no-tō (Star lily monument),' the sacrifices made for 'ancestral land defence' due to the Battle of Okinawa were also stressed, with Yara Chōbyō, for one, making a speech saying: 'The heroic spirits of 160,000 compatriots fought for the defence of their ancestral land's soil, and for peace, and died glorious deaths in vain. In recompense for this, too, we cannot sell even a sliver of land to another country.' All in all, this implies that the Okinawan side tried to mobilise the conservative government and mainland public opinion by advocating that Okinawan land was 'Japanese' territory, and that its residents were 'Japanese' (Nakano 1969, pp. 179, 188, 189, 192).

In this struggle, a similar tone was adopted in statements other than those directed at the mainland, also, and little clear-cut differentiation can be seen, however. One more probable reason for such a tone having been adopted is thought to be that the type of language for expressing political will was limited for the people of Okinawa in those days. At that time, when the terminology of the later anti-war reversion discourse was still not in general circulation, the main expressive means they used when talking about politics were likely to have been the language of Japanese nationalism which had been implanted since the prewar, and the language of democracy and anti-communism which had flowed in via the U.S. in the postwar. In those circumstances, after campaigns couched in the anticommunist, pro-U.S. terminology which had entered via the U.S. faced their limits, it is no wonder that the language which Okinawans subsequently employed half-unconsciously as a medium to express their intention to fight the U.S. military was that of Japanese nationalism. The idea that this incorporated an element of requesting the mainland conservative government for assistance is considered to be close to the truth.

Even though superficially the language of Japanese nationalism was used, it was imbued with different meanings, in a similar way to how the minorities in the Empire of Japan had expressed their desire to resist in the language of their rulers. In fact, while it was emphasised on the one hand that Okinawans were 'Japanese,' such expressions as: '[They] have driven our race (*minzoku*) into catastrophic danger,' 'the ultimate means for the race to live,' and 'the cherished wish for racial survival' were often seen in statements issued from within Okinawa during the struggle. While these admittedly were not the words 'Okinawan race (*minzoku*)' or 'Ryukyuan race' used in the immediate postwar, they still imply there was a residual consciousness which described Okinawa as an individual 'race' in this period. The delegation which set off at the end of June for the Japanese mainland did, however, offer a statement for negotiation with the Japanese government, claiming to the bitter end that 'the land which we are about to lose [is] Japanese territory,' and 'this struggle is not only a struggle of 800 thousand Okinawans, but one of 80 million Japanese' (Nakano 1969, pp. 191, 187, 189, 193).

The Japanese government, fearing provocation of the U.S., took a 'wait-and-see' attitude. The question which arose at this time was whether Okinawans were legally 'Japanese.' In other words, while the Ministry of Justice displayed the view that 'given that Okinawan residents are obviously Japanese, the Japanese government naturally can request protection for the residents from the United States,' the Foreign Ministry and Cabinet Legislation Bureau opposed this, saying that 'because the nationality of Okinawan residents is interpreted as perhaps being dual American and Japanese nationality ... it would constitute interference in U.S. internal affairs for the Japanese government to negotiate with the U.S. government.' According to Yokota Kizaburō, a professor at the University of Tokyo whose pronouncements echoed the Foreign Ministry's assertions, as Okinawans had 'a status similar to that of U.S. citizens, ... Japan could not exercise its right of diplomatic protection in terms of international law,' and 'at best, it would only conduct mediation in a moral sense, or from a political standpoint, for instance' (*Asahi shinbun* 1956b; Yokota 1956).[6]

Several years prior to this, Yokota had already published his own views in a collection of essays on the legal status of Okinawa edited by the Japanese Society of International Law. Incidentally, the then president of the Japanese Society of International Law was Yamada Saburō, who had once released an opinion paper on the issue of Koreans' nationality, as mentioned in Volume 2 of this book. Here, too, there appeared a legal interpretation which did not let them escape when they were needed by deeming them to be 'Japanese,' but avoided trouble by saying they were not 'Japanese' when they became unnecessary. In reality, as I previously stated in Chapter Six, this controversy over nationality was a tilt at windmills on Japan's part, as the United States had no such inclination to transfer its own citizenship to Okinawan residents, but the extent to which the Japanese government handled the Okinawa problem can be imagined from the fact that there was no unified opinion within that government even on nationality.

As I have already stated, when the Home Ministry was dissolved and the administrative unit called 'Okinawa Prefecture' disappeared, it was the Ministry of Justice which held onto *koseki* (family registers), which had become almost its sole domestic administrative job. Though it may have been natural for the Justice Ministry to assert that Okinawans were 'Japanese,' emphasis on Japan–U.S. relations took priority for the government as a whole. After Cabinet meetings had been held about this issue, the Minister for Justice also overturned his previous statement, saying: 'The Justice Ministry's view announced yesterday merely said that Okinawans were Japanese. Foreign Minister Shigemitsu should mediate,' and it was ironically reported in newspapers that 'he was probably warned not to talk too much at Cabinet meetings' (*Asahi shinbun* 1956c), For the Japanese government, the question of whether the residents of Okinawa were 'Japanese' or not was, as always, nothing but a diplomatic pawn.

The essence of the 'mediation' which the government mentioned was also apt to be something with no palpable sincerity. The then Prime Minister, Hatoyama Yukio, said: 'I want to intercede so that the United States will provide an alternative site [for them to live],' but when he was told of the comment by an Okinawan representative who had travelled to mainland Japan that 'the current government cannot be counted upon,' he remarked: 'That is probably true. The alternative site which I suggest does not mean that there is already a concrete plan such as choosing the South Sea Islands (Uchi Nanyō=Japanese Micronesia)' (*Asahi shinbun* 1956g). Even at this time, more than a decade after the end of the Pacific War, they did not recognise the problem in any way except by a feeling involving a suggestion of having the people of Okinawa relocate to the 'South Sea Islands.'

On the other hand, public opinion on the Japanese mainland showed sympathy towards appeals from Okinawa which emphasised 'the Japanese,' 'the ancestral land,' and 'compatriots,' and criticised the government for being 'weak-kneed.' The truth, however, was not necessarily something that Okinawan residents had anticipated. The Okinawan side expressed its sentiments in the language of Japanese nationalism, and tried to extract *naichi* support, but in *naichi* public opinion there was seen a tendency to advocate simple nationalism and territorial expansion in literal terms. The *Asahi shinbun* of the day commented as follows on readers' letters regarding the Okinawa issue.

> ... A point common to almost all the letters ... [was] that, along with hoping that the government would engage with a forceful attitude in

negotiations with the U.S., many hoped that all Japanese nationals would support the residents of Okinawa and launch a campaign of 'anti-U.S. resistance.' ... Unsophisticated opinions demanding Okinawa's return out of mistrust of the U.S. and sympathy for the residents of Okinawa were also strong; and the view appeared in some letters – from a technician in Tokyo, for one – proposing that if return were said to be impossible, then the 'next best plan' would be to 'request the U.S. to lease part of Alaska, or to open its doors to immigration.' Moreover, such a way of thinking vis-à-vis the Okinawa issue also was seen as if it were linked with a hard line towards Japanese–Soviet negotiations, that is, to the view that Japan must not abandon the South Kuriles (Minami-chishima). A certain student from Tokyo argued: '[Japan] should request the South Kuriles in the same way as it requests Okinawa, and if that is said to be difficult, then Japan should have 'dormant sovereignty' over the South Kuriles, too, just as it has residual sovereignty over Okinawa.' In this manner, there was an aspect to the Okinawa problem which came to heighten Japanese people's concern for territorial issues even further (*Asahi shinbun* 1956d).

Not only were large numbers of such letters received, but it was also not regarded as strange at the time that they were introduced without any particular criticism.

I will elaborate in the following chapter how leftists also shared anti-U.S. nationalism in those days, as well, there even being a tendency to hammer out nationalism strongly in order to criticise the conservative regime's reliance on the U.S. It was the very time of the House of Councillors election, and the opposition parties simultaneously censured the government's 'weak-kneed' stance on this issue. The Committee Chair of the Leftist Socialist Party commented on the expropriation of Okinawan as being a 'grave problem connected with the destiny of the *minzoku*,' and, criticising the government's slant towards the Northern Territories issue, said his party 'wholly supported the Okinawan Islanders' campaign, and would hereafter fight with the aims of revising the Treaty of San Francisco and the scrapping of AMPO.' Moreover, the Socialist Party requested the LDP to hold a non-partisan 'all-out people's rise-to-action rally for resolution of the Okinawa issue (Okinawa mondai kaiketsu kokumin sōkekki taikai),' but the LDP refused to participate, claiming that 'there is fear that it will turn into an anti-

U.S. movement because the Communist Party and left-wing groups including the General Council of Trade Unions of Japan (Sōhyō) would take part (*Asahi shinbun* 1956e; 1956a).

It is hard to say, however, that the direction of such Japanese mainland progressive camps was consistent with that of the Okinawan side. As we have already seen, assertions tying the Okinawan issue with the abolition of AMPO were not the mainstream in the reversion movement at the time. For the Okinawan side, waging an 'island-wide struggle' in which even pro-U.S. parties joined, it was not a situation where they would directly link the conflict over land with anti-war peace, either. The majority of statements issued in the thick of the 'island-wide struggle' called for the assistance of '80 million compatriots in mainland Japan,' but those which brought reversion to the fore were surprisingly few. When a roundtable conference involving students at the University of the Ryukyus and Okinawan students at Japanese mainland universities who were home on holidays was held in the summer of that year, the question was raised as to whether there was 'some reason for the appearance of a tendency for the local Okinawan side's reluctance to tie peace – which was their ultimate aim – to Japanese reversion, even though [Japanese mainland progressive forces] conducted their campaign [on the land issue] in conjunction with opposition to bases, restoration of Okinawa and the peace issue,' but students from the University of the Ryukyus replied that it was a 'complex issue' (Nakano 1969, p. 197).

Little antagonism between left and right could be seen, as voices from the Okinawan side published in the newspapers of the day included: 'By no means are we shouting for the withdrawal of the U.S. military. We are opposed to the semi-permanent confiscation of land,' and 'Shouldn't both the conservatives and progressives band together and embark on a solution from a national position?' From the Okinawan end, the mainland trend was something which prompted the emergence of the view that said: 'Looking at the Japanese response, though the progressive camp is supportive, the attitude of the conservative camp is cold. It is the exact opposite of its demands to the Soviet Union over Chishima (the Kuriles)' (*Asahi shinbun* 1956f).

At a press conference held in July with an Okinawan delegation, representatives appealing for assistance were showered with questions from the mainland press, such as: 'Prime Minister Hatoyama Yukio suggests that, for example, you be allowed to emigrate to other islands,' and: 'Ashida Hitoshi says that life in Okinawa has improved due to the presence of the U.S. military, [doesn't he?]' While offering such responses as: 'We are desperately fighting to defend Japan's territory,' and 'Why is the government so weak-kneed?' the representatives said:

> Our resistance is neither pro- nor anti-U.S. If the kind of policy is going to be adopted which places more marked emphasis upon military advantage than upon residents' advantage, then we intend to fight resolutely, no matter which country may govern Okinawa (Nakano 1969, p. 194).

This was probably their true cry, as these words were ones suggesting the possibility of 'fighting resolutely' should any country – whether it be America or Japan – adopt a policy which would place 'more marked emphasis' upon military rather than residents' advantage; and, in actual fact, that became a reality after reversion.

For the Okinawan side, the improvement of people's welfare was primary, and the categorising of their own movement as rightist or leftist was not a priority issue. For the various right and left political forces on the mainland, however, the classification of Okinawan campaigns as right or left was of greater import. Moreover, as long as the Okinawan side needed to gain the support of one or another of the mainland forces, it, too, had to tout its claims in a form which fitted that classification. In those circumstances, with the mainland conservative regime not being dependable, those upon whom hopes could be pinned tended to be the progressive forces; and it was already obvious that in order to extract assistance from those progressive forces, the Okinawan side would need to switch from a tone which had extolled a pro-U.S., anti-communist line. In addition, it was both a tactical changeover which matched the situation wherein the reversion movement which had upheld cooperation with the U.S. had been rejected by the U.S. side, and one which conformed to the anti-war sentiment which the Okinawans had cultivated throughout wartime and in the postwar.

In this manner, from the mid-1950s onwards, the tone of the reversion movement gradually changed. There was progressive disappearance of the kind of petitions which hitherto had extolled such things as pro-American anti-communism or humanity and nature as 'Japanese,' and ones which touted anti-war peace grew more numerous. On the mainland, as well, in contrast to immediately following the defeat, Okinawan reversion gradually began to look as if it had switched from conservative to progressive claims. In that atmosphere, the locating of Okinawans as 'Japanese' also went on to be discussed in a different context.

8 The Idea of Progressive Nationalism

As noted in Chapter Six, in 1946 the Japanese Communist Party issued a 'message to celebrate the independence of the Okinawan people.' While criticising the Japan–Korea common-ancestry theory, it was worded: '[Japanese imperialists] also imposed the idea upon you Okinawans that they were of the same race (*minzoku*) as you,' and: 'Okinawans are a people (*minzoku*) who have been oppressed as a minority.'

In February 1956, however, the Japanese Communist Party's organ, *Zen'ei* (Vanguard), carried the following essay announcing its renunciation of this view.[1]

> From the beginning of the Occupation, the American invaders implemented propaganda saying that Ryukyuans were non-Japanese, and in order to substantiate this, they gathered all kinds of documents relating to Ryukyu not only from Okinawa and Amami-Ōshima, naturally, but also widely within Japan, and studied these. The more their research progressed, however, the clearer it became that Ryukyans were Japanese, so they have abandoned their governing policy of rule through a puppet regime of the independent country of Ryukyu, and firmed their resolve to cling tenaciously to Article Three of the San Francisco Treaty and enforce the permanent preservation of Okinawan bases.
>
> ... The view that they constitute a minority race has become an enormous obstacle to the fight for restoration of Okinawa and the Ogasawara (Bonin) Islands. This view must be thoroughly overcome, and the expansion of struggle will pulverise it completely (Nakano 1969, p. 6).

This change in the Communist Party's line, which could also be described as a 180-degree about-face, exerted a huge impact upon the Japanese side's perspective on Okinawa. What was especially influential was the positioning of Okinawa in Japanese history. This was because the basis of the argument that Okinawans were 'Japanese' and that it was correct movement policy for Okinawa to revert to the mainland was being sought from a historical perspective.

In this chapter, I will examine leftist historians' tenor of argument from the 1950s to the early 1960s relating to 'the Japanese,' and will subsequently track how this influenced views on Okinawa. Changes in positioning in relation to Okinawa were not things that happened in isolation, either, but ones that occurred amid changes in the historical view of 'the Japanese' at that time. Responses to the other 'other,' that is, America, cast a shadow over these, as well.

'Japan as an Asian colony'

The greatest misunderstanding relating to Japan in the 1950s, especially vis-à-vis the drift of argument of leftist intellectuals generically termed the 'progressive faction,' was the view that it was 'an age when nationalist sentiment was clearly unpopular' (Koschmann 1994, p. 105). When people ignorant of the then-current ideological situation read works by progressive intellectuals of that decade, they are sometimes surprised at the advocacy of nationalism appearing there. This is because they have the preconceived notion that in this period, immediately following liberation from the chauvinism of the Empire of Japan, progressive intellectuals were unlikely to tout the very nationalism they had opposed as being a reactionary influence.

In this period, though, progressive intellectuals including Maruyama Masao, Nanbara Shigeru, Ōtsuka Hisao and Yanaihara Tadao were actively promoting 'nationalism (*kokumin shugi* or *minzoku shugi*).' Moreover, of all political parties from the 1950s onwards, it was the Japanese Communist Party which most emphasised nationalism. Of course, there were ideological differences between the liberals Nanbara and Maruyama and the Communist Party, but in this book I will refer to the latter system of nationalism, in particular, by the term 'progressive nationalism.'[2] In postwar Japan, the Socialist Party and Communist Party, which were in opposition to the pro-U.S. conservative regime, were called 'progressive forces.' Even if non-Marxists, those people oriented towards democratisation who disliked the conservative parties which had aspirations of a return to the prewar supported these 'progressive forces.'

Even so, why did moves to promote nationalism appear from amongst the progressive intellectuals of that age? I need not explain to people who are familiar with those years, but here I will begin from confirmation of the political situation of the times.

Japan in the late 1950s was neither the military power of the past, nor the economic power of the 1980s. Its military force was dismantled, its trade balance was always in deficit, and the overcoming of starvation and economic recovery were imminent challenges. Moreover, until the conclusion of the San Francisco Peace Treaty, it had been placed under the governance of U.S. Occupation Forces, and its independence as a Japanese state had been lost. That peace treaty, too, was a so-called one-sided reconciliation which lacked the recognition of the Soviet Union and the like, while at the same time the U.S.–Japan Security Treaty (AMPO) that acknowledged the continuation of an American military presence was entered into. For that reason, leftist forces, including the Communist Party, ranked this peace treaty as something that merely deepened Japan's dependency upon the U.S., and claimed that Japan had not achieved true independence.

Around this time, via the escalation of the Cold War, the outbreak of the Korean War, and the Red Purge by U.S. Occupation Forces, the Communist Party renounced its immediate post-defeat definition of the U.S. military as a liberation army, and in its place, the term 'American imperialism' became fixed. Furthermore, influenced by the 1949 establishment of the People's Republic of China, the Communist Party endeavoured to adopt a similar revolutionary line in Japan, as well. In other words, the Communist Party defined the Japanese situation as a semi-colonial one controlled by U.S. imperialism, and extolled a policy of forming a 'democratic national (*minzoku*) front' for disrupting this state of affairs.

At that point, the opposition struggle against the expansion of U.S. military bases and the Japan–U.S. Security Treaty was being situated both as a peace movement and, at the same time, as a 'patriotic' struggle for saving their home country from colonial rule and winning true national (*minzoku*) independence. It is well known that the slogan 'anti-U.S. patriotism' was often employed right up till the 1960 AMPO conflict somewhat later.

Nowadays, we often feel antagonism towards the word 'nationalism.' On the other hand, when nationalism has been undertaken by the weak, we do not necessarily regard it as something which should be condemned. Few people would probably condemn the nationalism of Korea which won independence from the Empire of Japan, the nationalism of Vietnam which fought with America, or the nationalism of Poland which resisted the Soviet Union, simply for the reason that it was nationalism. This is because the nationalism which the strong uphold for the sake of exclusion and aggression is implicitly distinguished from the nationalism which the weak uphold for independence and liberation. Furthermore, the Japanese Communist Party positioned 1950s Japan, weakened by its defeat in war, as a member country of Asia which was exposed to the colonial rule of Western imperialism in a similar manner to Korea, China, India and Vietnam.

When Japanese solidarity towards colonial independence movements in Asian and African countries was discussed among progressive intellectuals in the period from the 1950s through to the early 1960s, it was often conducted from the perspective of questioning whether the Japanese situation had 'commonality with the case of Asian and African countries, in regard to their political dependency [on the U.S.]' rather than from a self-critical context from a standpoint as a military ruler formerly, or as an economic ruler later. In these cases, nationalism advocating 'anti-U.S. patriotism' was integrated with the slogans of 'anti-war peace' and 'solidarity towards Asia,' and students who died because of police violence at the 1952 May Day were described by the Association of Democratic Scientists, a body of progressive historians, as having 'fallen in the battle for liberation of the nation (*minzoku*)' and as 'heroes of the nation.'[3]

A debate as to whether Japan was 'an American colony,' which stemmed from such a situational definition by the Communist Party, was carried on in the critical arena in the early 1950s. The following is a simple marshalling of each political faction's view in this regard.[4]

Firstly, the Communist Party stated that Japan was in a semi-colonial situation controlled politically and economically by U.S. imperialism, and that Japan's conservative government and major firms were a comprador force and anti-national force dependent upon America, and that the Communist Party was the true patriotic party. In order to break free from this situation, it was deemed imperative to prioritise national (*minzoku*) independence over class struggle, and to form a national unification front comprising workers, farmers and native capital, centred upon the Communist Party, and also involving native (*minzoku*) Japanese capitalists who were not dependent upon U.S. capital.

In response to this, a politician from the Liberal Party, the party in power, counter-argued: 'Japan is definitely not a colony.' The entry of U.S. troops and capital into Japan was natural in an age of mutual exchange and internationalisation, and any 'sense of servility' which exaggerated the influence of a foreign country was an obstacle to international cordial relations. He further asserted that a claim such as that Japan was a colony was nothing more than agitation for the sake of the left-wing; that Japan had already restored its independence by means of the Peace Treaty; and in order also to make a clean sweep of such servile feelings, it should aim for economic reconstruction in cooperation with the U.S.

In addition, the Leftist Socialist Party, advocating emphasis upon class struggle with the claim that Japan was a dependent country but not a colony, opposed the Communist Party's national unification front line. Furthermore, the Rightist Socialist Party asserted that Japan was an independent country, but that it should implement social democracy through the Diet. Moreover, the Labour–Farmer Party clearly situated Japan as a colony. Broadly speaking, leftist parties took a line of struggle for national liberation which emulated that of Asian countries, while conservative parties chose collaboration with the U.S., and circumstances arose in which the further left the faction, the more it advocated anti-U.S. nationalism.

In this situation, a book entitled *Rekishi to minzoku no hakken* (The discovery of history and the nation) by Ishimoda Shō, known as a progressive historian, became a best-seller in 1952. Ishimoda's thought gives an insight into the sentiments of such progressive nationalism.

In his Preface to *Rekishi to minzoku no hakken*, Ishimoda wrote that egoism and nihilism were rife in postwar 'Japanese.' Having lost confidence and pride due to defeat in war, all had become 'grasping people' because of livelihood hardship, and he said that among 'the young,' a situation was widespread in which 'only the feeling of wanting to climb to even a slightly better social position [wa]s strong, the desire to listen to serious talk ha[d] vanished, and no longer [we]re there any workers reading documents or the like issued by union headquarters' (Ishimoda 1952, Intro. pp. 7–8).

A strong indication of the rampancy of such egoism is political indifference. Ishimoda cites an anecdote about fishermen from

Uchinada in Ishikawa Prefecture, a symbolic presence in the anti-U.S. base struggle at the time. Even though they went to a nearby town in order to plead their wretched condition, the town was bustling uneventfully, and the fishermen were not even afforded an ear. In a later year, the political scientist Sakamoto Yoshikazu, also, cites the words of an observer who said he wondered whether those who were indifferent to the circumstances at Uchinada were 'members of the same nation (*kokumin*), even so,' but the egoism that was rife among people had destroyed the solidarity and empathy among fellow 'members of the same nation.'

Ishimoda uses the expression 'national (*minzoku*) crisis' to describe the situation in which his home country becomes a semi-colony, its territory is seized for foreign bases, and its people are buried amid egoism and indifference in spite of their 'Japanese' compatriots being in dire straits. Ishimoda himself, being a historian, says that he will research history in order that 'fellow Japanese' will awaken to the crisis of being a 'single (*tan'itsu*) [people]' and restore their sense of solidarity, and wants to ponder how to have as many Japanese people as possible aware of the pride and traditions of the nation (*minzoku*).' And, according to Ishimoda, the mission for historians was precisely to 'prove that the Japanese nation (*minzoku*) had a proud history which could not be resigned to subordination towards America, having a tradition of transformation fit for fighting a great battle to the bitter end in order to bring peace, independence and democracy to their ancestral land, and, in that age of transformation, striving to show from within the history of the Japanese a demonstration of enormous cultural creativity – in other words, to create a 'history of members of the Japanese nation (*kokumin*)' in order to form the identity of a revolutionary subject, that is, 'this is Japan' (Ishimoda 1954, p. 63).[5] By appealing to the awakening of nationalism, Ishimoda attempted the breeding of a sense of solidarity and political mobilisation.

What should be borne in mind here is that just as even now the term '*kokumin* (members of the nation/nationals)' is used in Japan in the sense of 'the populace' or 'the masses' (*minshū*), as in 'nationals are the protagonists in politics,' and so on, there was a tendency at the time for the word '*minzoku*,' also, to be frequently used as a synonym for 'the people (*jinmin*)' or 'the masses.' For example, immediately after Japan's defeat in the Pacific War, the Japan Historical Association (Nihon Rekishi Gakkai) stated in its opening remarks that history from then on 'had to be "the people's (*jinmin*)" history – the history of the Japanese people (*Nihon minzoku*),' not the history of the state and emperors (Nihon Rekishi Gakkai 1946).

Such a 'people (*minzoku*)' was situated as something in a competitive relationship with imperial and state power. According to Uehara Senroku, a scholar of German history known as one of the progressive intellectuals, what constituted 'so-called national consciousness (*minzoku ishiki*)' prior to the defeat was actually nothing more than a 'projection of state consciousness (*kokka ishiki*).' Moreover, he stated that 'recognising the nation (*minzoku*) as something in opposition to the state, or which rebels against it, or transcends it, was not the major trend, at least until the Pacific War,' and asserted that 'on the whole, national consciousness – that being something which should be distinguished from state consciousness and government-initiated patriotism – ha[d] been sparse in the Japanese up till now' (Uehara and Munakata 1952, p. 150–151; Uehara 1992, pp. 37, 10).

Uehara further criticised the fact that due to the rampancy of egoism and nihilism, 'young people, especially, had no awareness of being members of a nation (*minzoku*) who shared a common destiny,' saying:

> In other words, in order to make young people have consciousness of a national (*minzoku*) community, firstly it is necessary to wash away the confusion between the national community and the state that has been present hitherto. Accordingly, one has them consider that it is not that a state exists first, and then a national community is created, but that a state can simply be thought of as a political expression of a national community. At the same time, I think that perhaps one ought to make them consider that as a state is nothing more than the political form of a national community, it does not matter what form it takes (Uehara and Munakata 1952, pp. 145, 147).

Uehara says that the backlash in the younger generation against the word '*minzoku*' is something that arose because of prewar patriotic education which made the nation (the populace) subordinate to the state, and he suggests that if they overcome that, it should be easy to implant a national consciousness of taking action in the struggle for anti-U.S. independence. If a state is nothing more than the 'political form' of a nation (*minzoku*), then, having shaped the nation as the subject, one should simply create a democratic state. Preferably, a nation will be created in order to become a subject that will transform the state, as it is considered that a *minzoku* is consciously created by means of historical education and class consciousness. As I will discuss in the next chapter, based on this kind of thinking, Uehara advocated 'educating each individual Japanese to the point of membership of the nation (*minzoku*)' so as to respond to the challenge of 'how to overcome the atomisation of each group and each individual in the land, and to form a unified national (*kokumin*) front there,' and, along with the Japan Teachers' Union (Nikkyōso), he started to propose a 'national education movement (*kokumin kyōiku undō*)' (Uehara1989, p. 79; Uehara and Munakata 1952, p. 136).

Uehara's claim that it is the nation which exists as an entity, while the state is nothing more than its political expression, is a reversal of the argument stated in the imperialisation policy that the nation (*minzoku*) is merely something created by the state, as discussed in Volume 2 of this book. In the '*kōminka* (turning people into Imperial subjects)' policy, '*minzoku*' were created by the state (*kokka*), and therefore such things as 'Korean popular rights' did not exist, as Koreans were deemed to be part of 'the Japanese.' While the discourse of the imperialisation policy was one that aimed to deny national self-determination, this arguably also was natural, as progressive nationalism was something which brought national self-determination to the forefront.

In the same way as Uehara, Ishimoda stood on the premise that the cultivation of 'national consciousness' in 'the Japanese' was insufficient, and mentioned the existence of two things which were antagonistic to the growth of wholesome nationalism (*minzoku shugi*). One was exclusionist, feudal reactionism, while the other was 'modernism [and] cosmopolitanism.'

Firstly, in regard to the former, according to Ishimoda, 'exclusionism itself [was] something different from wholesome national (*minzoku*) consciousness,' and something that would not grow among the masses unless the rulers systematically educated them. For him, such confidence in the masses was absolute. Fujitani Toshio, also known as a progressive historian, went so far as to state that as the emperor system was already something which could not continue to exist without the aid of American imperialism, it would be possible to counter the emperor system by raising the national (*minzoku*)

The Idea of Progressive Nationalism 221

consciousness of the Japanese populace. Even if not as optimistic as this, the assertion was not rare among progressive intellectuals of the time that nationalism itself was neither good nor evil, but would become either progressive or reactionary according to how it was organised. Moreover, in opposition to moves by the conservative regime for revival of prewar-style nationalism, it was a perception in accordance with such a line to say that conflict was necessary over 'who would get the nation (*minzoku*)' (Ishimoda 1952, Intro. p. 15; Fujitani 1953, p. 66; Tōyama 1976; *Chūō kōron* 1948).

What, then, was the latter cosmopolitanism? According to Ishimoda, that very thing was the main cause of prewar Japanese intellectuals' inability to mount effective resistance against fascism. He cites Nagai Kafū and Kōtoku Shūsui as typical examples. In Ishimoda's opinion, Nagai finished up as a transcendent critic who lamented the backwardness of Japan and its populace in comparison with the West. Kōtoku, who was preoccupied with anarchy which repudiated the state, confused a true affection for the homeland which was striving to reform Japan with the exclusionism which the rulers had built up, and he slid into terrorism which was detached from the populace. Furthermore, he was unable to face Korean nationalism, which sought independence for its homeland, except with an attitude of repudiation of the notion of the state.[6] Standing on the recognition that, due to the attitude of such intellectuals, the patriotism of the populace had not been led in a revolutionary direction in the prewar, but had been structured in the direction of aggression by the rulers, Ishimoda criticised the prewar intellectuals, arguing:

> ... Seeing that energy – which was hard to defy – with which the members of the nation were mobilised by aggression and nationalism (*minzoku shugi*), and thinking that they [=the intellectuals] alone were not jingoists, they were ready to frown upon the patriotism of the masses as being something unconnected with themselves. Setting themselves alone on a pedestal, they were unable to grasp the contradiction that existed between [their] nationalism as organisers, and the naïve, intense patriotism of the masses. As such, they were isolated from the masses, and were unable even to find a way to enter into their midst and fight. The good intentions and enthusiasm of intellectuals who were trying to modernise their native land, also, were always accompanied by a violent animosity towards the word

and idea of a '*minzoku*,' and if they attempted to resist it, they had no choice but to become cosmopolitans; and if they tried to put down roots in their native land, they tended to be dragged in a direction of nationalism and imperialism (Ishimoda 1953c, p. 416).

The cosmopolitans which Ishimoda mentions are egoists and nihilists who isolate themselves from the populace (*minshū*) (= *minzoku*), and choose not to get their own hands dirty rather than help solve a crisis in their home country. These are people like those who are more interested in new books from Paris and New York than the fact that student demonstrators were killed in Tokyo. Ishimoda pointed out that this cosmopolitanism turned into an egotistical concern for social advancement which was oblivious to other people's misfortune, and that as the sentiment of government officials and industrialists, it became a supporting pillar for the Empire of Japan. In addition, he said: 'Cosmopolitans are playing the role of props for the global empire of American monopolistic capital' (Ishimoda 1953c, p. 59) as can be seen in the present day in the comprador forces who, calling themselves internationalists, exploit Japan's dependent position vis-à-vis the U.S.

Furthermore, the evil 'modernism' to which Ishimoda refers was something that again was not rooted in the populace, but which followed foreign countries in the name of modernisation. As an example, he cited the attitude of Japanese intellectuals who, when the Chinese conducted a boycott campaign against Japanese products in the prewar, retorted that they should buy cheap, superior-quality goods regardless of where they were manufactured. In addition, in prewar Japan, there were also some who agreed with the amalgamation of Japan and Korea from the perspective that if Japan annexed Korea, Korean modernisation would be accelerated (Ishimoda 1953c, pp. 330–331).[7]

This means fighting the dual aspects of communal reactionism and atomic cosmopolitanism, and building a higher level of solidarity. This could have been called an application to nationalism of Marxist class-struggle theory of the time, which promoted dialectics. As previously mentioned, there were differences among those people who were collectively dubbed progressive intellectuals. For example, there were dissimilarities in assertions between those who deemed the establishment of the modern ego as being essential to democracy, and those who considered the modern ego to be akin to egoism.

However, there was no dearth of intellectuals in the critical arena at that time who, while criticising both reactionism and excessive individualism, touted '*minzoku shugi* (nationalism)' and '*kokumin shugi* (nationalism),' which were distinguished from '*kokka shugi* (statism/ nationalism)' or '*chō-kokka shugi* (ultra-nationalism) – in other words, 'wholesome nationalism' from below, in opposition to 'evil nationalism' from above. Accordingly, history was situated as something which took as its mission the creation of 'history of members of the nation' in order to mould 'Japanese nationals.' In his 1953 work, *Zoku rekishi to minzoku no hakken* (Sequel to the discovery of history and the nation), Ishimoda commended Amino Yoshihiko, a young scholar of history at the time who was engaged in educational activities at a labour school, as a practical example of 'national history,' but the cultivation of what Ishimoda termed 'wholesome national consciousness' was deemed necessary in order to raise workers into revolutionary subjects in the state (*kokka*), as well.[8]

Such ideas could be called true nationalism. Above all, the criticism that 'it is only the Japanese who are uselessly wallowing in despair, saying that Japan is an American colony' had existed since those days (Sone 1953, p. 120). However, Ishimoda asserted that it was obvious that 'Japan had switched from being an imperialistic, dominant nation to a dependent country or oppressed nation,' and that 'without seizing authority from foreign imperialistic rulers and establishing independent sovereignty – in other words, without forming a "nation-state (*minzoku kokka*)" – not only national liberation, but also domestic progress and revolution, would not be able to exist' (Ishimoda 1953c, pp. 420, 329).[9] It was not only philosophers that criticised the prewar Korean independence movement as an anachronistic illusion of a nation-state, as mentioned in Volume 2 of this book, but what exactly was this supposed to mean?

The progressive nationalism espoused by Ishimoda and his ilk was underpinned by this sort of logic. However, this thought, which defined Japan as an Asian colony and aimed to foster nationalism, would come to run up against many limitations.

The criticality of 'wholesome nationalism'

At the time, what had become a point of contention within the progressive nationalism debate was the boundary between 'wholesome patriotism' and 'exclusionism.' This question often surfaced as a dispute among historians, too.

An example I could cite is one regarding an article entitled 'Minzoku no sakebi (The cry of the nation),' published in 1952 in the Association of Democratic Scientists' journal, *Rekishi hyōron* (Historical Review).' This 'Cry of the nation' was something abstracted from a pamphlet which a young worker at the Yūbari coalmine in Hokkaido had composed on the subject of the end of the Tokugawa Period (–1868). Its contents stated that the shogunate, which had exploited the people of Japan, had concluded treasonous unequal treaties with the American black ships which had come to colonise Japan 'in exactly the same way as [the then Prime Minister] Yoshida [Shigeru]'s government,' but the people and those samurai who advocated loyalty to the emperor and expulsion of foreigners had risen up and toppled the shogunate, creating an independent country by means of the Meiji Restoration (Sakamoto 1952).

Esteem for the Meiji Restoration, which had protected Japan's independence and achieved its modernisation, was high among progressive historians, as well. It was also their hope that moves would emerge from workers to uphold such a 'national tradition.'

Nevertheless, this text by a coalminer was quite a simplistic and vehement one. The titles of each of its chapters were in the style of: 'The people arose, angered at the muddy boots of foreign lands that sully Japan,' 'These abominable, hairy foreigners,' and 'The patriots of Satsuma fought to protect Japan's independence.' Moreover, in the conclusion, 'drumming out the black-clawed, hairy foreign devils that cover the ground of Japan' was advocated (Sakamoto 1952, pp. 68, 71–73, 77).

Nezu Masashi, a scholar of ancient history, criticised this. According to Nezu, those members of the Satsuma and Chōshū domains who expounded loyalty to the emperor and expulsion of foreigners were merely feudal exclusionists, while Yoshida Shōin was an invasionist who championed rule over Korea and China. In essence, Nezu concluded that this author 'had an idea that confused loyalty to the emperor and expulsion of foreigners, which constituted a return to feudalism, with present-day national independence, and this was not even the slightest bit different from the idea of 'American devils and British devils' held by the military during the Pacific War (Nezu 1953, p. 74).

On the other hand, the side which had lavishly praised 'The cry of the nation' as being 'an impassioned cry in opposition to foreign pressure and the oppression of a treacherous government,' argued that while there were indeed many errors of historical fact, this only held true in the case where it was seen as a historical treatise. As it was an anti-U.S. inflammatory speech in the guise of history, 'if there were any historians who would strike down the value of this work and slice it in two in the manner of a samurai exercising his right to kill, for the sake of the few misapprehensions of historical fact or mistakes in historical analogy in the work, then would not that already tentatively [mean] there was need for reconsideration?' (Ōtani 1953, p. 45).

In fact, even among the progressive historians of the time, the question of how to evaluate the Meiji government and the expulsion of foreigners was a subject of controversy. In the opinion of Inoue Kiyoshi and others, a national consciousness throughout Japan which transcended clan boundaries developed from expelling foreigners and led to the Meiji Restoration; Japan 'saved itself from semi-colonisation' and was positioned as 'spearheading Asian progress at that time and for a while afterwards, being able to carry the honour of becoming the hope of Asian people' (Inoue 1951, p. 15). This was accompanied, however, by the limitation that the expulsion of foreigners itself was mere conservative exclusionism, and following that 'while afterwards,' the Meiji government, too, switched to a principle of aggression.[10]

Even if one were to attempt to tout national tradition and make it into the energy-source for a movement, trying to purge expulsion and invasion from nationalism in history would become an inarticulate form of agitation, with multiple annotations attached. For that reason, there were also some who, like Hirano Yoshitarō, claimed that 'even if it were promoted by means of the feudal way and idea called exclusionism, its character would be an expression of national resistance' (Hirano 1952, p. 13), but this was haunted by the dilemma that if this occurred, it would mean affirming the evil parts of nationalism, as well.

A similar problem also appeared in the dispute over national heroes and national culture in history. The 1951 annual meeting of the Historical Science Society of Japan was held under the theme of 'Issues of the nation (*minzoku*) in history.' There, Tōma Seita, as well-known as Ishimoda as a historian tackling questions of the nation, presented a report entitled 'National issues in ancient times.' Tōma is also said to have been impressed with the aforementioned 'Cry of the nation,' but his report was a controversial one in many senses.

Prior to his report, Tōma wrote a short article explaining its aim. According to him, in regard to the then-current crisis of 'colonisation,' it was necessary to have 'national unity for making workers into leaders,' but 'culturism, which was imbued with cosmopolitanism and modernism, gave the entire populace an unnecessarily strong sense of inferiority vis-à-vis foreigners, and also hindered national unity.' Moreover, 'in order to resist such a national crisis, it was imperative to inform the entire populace of their national pride; for our nation to have confidence; and to make it into a lesson in order to achieve the unity of our current nation' (Tōma 1951a, p. 167).

According to Tōma's report at the meeting, a Japanese nation with a common race, language, territory, culture and so on had already been formed in ancient times. Its national consciousness was symbolised in the eighth-century *Kojiki* (Record of Ancient Matters) and *Nihonshoki* (Chronicles of Japan) mythology in the shape of national (*minzoku*) heroes such as King Bu of Wa (ancient Japan) and Yamato Takeru. Later, in spite of the strengthening of rule by the nobility, which had been infected by imported culture from China and lost its national consciousness, a culture unique to the nation was progressively formed amid conflict between those rulers and the nation (the general populace) by mobilising the power of that nation. This native culture included the construction of the eighth-century Tōdaiji Temple, the invention of Japan's own *kana* syllabaries, and the *honji-suijaku* theory, which argued that Shintō gods were manifestations of Buddhist deities.[11]

Debate erupted at the meeting over this report. Why was Yamato Takeru, who conquered all the land on the orders of the Emperor, a hero of the nation? Was it not simply a revival of the prewar, badged with the Order of the Golden Kite for military valour, in the guise of Emperor Jimmu's eastern expedition? Had those things such as the tea ceremony, *ikebana*, Tōdaiji and the *honji-suijaku* theory not been taken up without regard to principles? If it had been the folk art (*minzoku geijutsu*) movement, which delved into folk tales and mass culture, this might have been understandable, but why did Tōdaiji, which rulers had built by the forced labour of the common people, constitute national culture?

Tōma responded to this criticism by saying that Yamato Takeru appeared to be an agent of the imperial family because the rulers had recorded in a distorted manner those myths which had originally been wholesome expressions of national spirit. Tōdaiji had been built on the orders of the nobility, but its completion would have been impossible without the people's cooperation. There was significance in citing the example of a personage familiar to every member of the masses such as Yamato Takeru, and this would enable the patriotic education with which the rulers had inculcated the populace to be turned to the latter's advantage. Tōma said that most arguments against him were intellectual, not 'grounded among the people,' and would only lead to the national consciousness of the general populace being snatched away by their rulers (Tōma 1951c; Tōma 1951d, pp. 290–291).

Debate at the Historical Science Society meeting ended without compromise on either side, but support for Tōma continued to be voiced within historians' circles. According to these supporters, a national hero was any person – even someone from the ruling echelon – who had performed the 'role of a progressive hero, condensing in one flesh the fighting power which welled up from below, and overcoming the old classes of the entire nation'; and 'cultural heritage was entirely something based upon the productivity of the masses, and also none other than a product of the development of the nation, even if it were something created through the desires of the rulers' (Minka Kyōto Shibu Rekishi Bukai 1951, p. 24). If products of the ruling class were not national culture, then 'the only future national treasures [would be] records of peasant uprisings or thereabouts.' Supporters further argued that 'if [we] said: "The Daibutsu (Great Buddha statue at Tōdaiji) is a work of the ruling class," they would probably reply: "That is correct. You people, if you are vexed, then try making something like it yourselves!"' Yet there was the risk that any action would be justified by such reasoning if it were something in which the masses participated (Naramoto 1951, p. 41; Fujitani 1953, p. 65).

Against this backdrop, Maruyama Masao wrote a paper called 'Nationalism in Japan' in 1951. According to Maruyama, Japan was 'the only country' in Asia which had experienced the transformation of nationalism into aggression, and which had 'already (*sic*) lost its virginity in regard to nationalism.' Moreover, he argued, it was not that the traditional nationalism of the prewar had perished, but that it had been molecularised by the underclass, as symbolised by the masses frenziedly hurling abuse at the U.S. team at Japan–U.S. baseball matches; and he offered the criticism that 'even if the progressive camp happened to be dazzled by that fragmentary form of expression and mistakenly viewed it as the germination of future national consciousness, or, while aware of its preliminary nature, still succumbed to the temptation to mobilise it for immediate political ends, this would eventually rebound upon that camp in the form of a serious backlash' (Maruyama 1964, pp. 154, 168).[12] It was not that Maruyama was rejecting nationalism *per se*, but he could not agree with any argument that emphasised 'national culture' and 'national heroes' as his ideal nationalism was one which spontaneously congealed once each individual's independent ego had been established. To Tōma and others like him, however, such a cold analysis must have seemed to be something not 'grounded amid the people.'

While nationalism is necessary in order to build unity, it not infrequently leads to the concealment of internal conflict within the 'nation (*minzoku*),' and to the glorification of the ruling class. Historians of the day were confronted with the same kind of difficulty that Ifa Fuyū faced when he created Okinawan nationalism, as discussed in Chapter Three. Nevertheless, there were other problems involved which existed in a form that did not even arise in discussion.

The rise of the historical view of a single people

There was, for example, an issue which the idea of progressive nationalism unintentionally contained, this being that it depicted 'the Japanese' as a single people (*minzoku*). However, for the very reason that this idea championed independence through national (*minzoku*) self-determination, it was a phenomenon which emerged half-inevitably. The principle of national self-determination tacitly presupposes that what germinates as the result of independence is a state comprising a single people. If multiple peoples exist within a state, this will be due to a situation where thoroughgoing national self-determination has not existed.

Furthermore, progressive nationalism was something which defined the Japanese race as an oppressed race, and told 'American imperialism' to get out of Japanese territory. For that purpose, it was necessary for the Japanese race to have been the inhabitants of the archipelago from ancient times. In prewar archaeology and ancient history, the dominant theory was that the Ainu were the indigenous race of the entire archipelago; they had established the Jōmon period (about 10,000 to 300 BCE) culture, but the imperial family and its people (*minzoku*) who had arrived from the Korean peninsula along with Yayoi period (from 300 BCE to 300 CE) culture had conquered them (Kudō 1979).[13] However, if the Japanese race had conquered the indigenous race and occupied the archipelago, then the justice in telling the U.S. military to get out would greatly diminish. Moreover, if Japanese culture were not something unique to the Japanese people, and if external influences, including that of people from overseas, were large, then the significance of touting national (*minzoku*) culture would also be lost.

Aside from the question of to what extent people were aware of such things, postwar historical studies continued to depict the Japanese race and Japanese culture as single entities. A marked example of this can be seen in Tōma Seita.

The aforementioned report by Tōma at the Historical Science Society meeting was delivered along with a declaration saying: 'Our ancestors have made their living in this Japanese archipelago since far-off old times. And now, as the result of archaeological studies, it has gradually come to light that there were no indigenous people (*minzoku*) here.' Moreover, the first page of his 1951 book, *Nihon minzoku no keisei* (Formation of the Japanese nation), which became a best-seller alongside Ishimoda's *Rekishi to minzoku no hakken* (Discovery of history and peoples), began with the words: 'The Japanese people were the original inhabitants of this Japanese archipelago' (Tōma 1951c, p. 2; Tōma 1951d, p. 1). These words were probably aimed to inspire the hearts of people who were about to have their land seized for U.S. military bases.

According to Tōma, a Japanese nation which shared such elements as language, territory, and culture had already been established in ancient times because 'the people who lived in the Japanese archipelago were racially identical.' Moreover, while sub-communities throughout the archipelago had been forcibly unified by the Yamato regime, as expressed in the myth of Yamato Takeru, this was not a 'global empire = multi-racial (*i-minzoku*) state' similar to the Roman empire which militarily dominated diverse peoples, but a merging of members of the same race, albeit a unification by the emperor; and was 'one vital milestone for the formation of a nation' (Tōma 1951c, pp. 3, 5, 52).

On the other hand, Tōma declared: 'When a state is formed by means of the conquest of other races, no nation whatever can be created. Rather, this method hinders nation-formation.' This, too, was probably an expression of his will to resist occupation by the U.S. He strongly opposed the theory of migration of a horse-riding people (*kiba minzoku torai setsu*) that was gaining repute at the time, which argued that the imperial family had crossed from continental Asia and conquered the indigenous inhabitants of the archipelago (Tōma 1951b, pp. 174–175).[14]

In Tōma's view, the change from Jōmon to Yayoi was nothing akin to a racial replacement which came about through the arrival of a conquering people, but one due to productivity development, namely a shift from hunting-and-gathering to agriculture. Tōma praised the ancient Japanese nation, saying: 'Even uncivilised peoples know two ways of endeavouring to develop their own livelihoods, just as in present-day hierarchical society. One way is that in which they take the line of productivity development, and the other is exploitation by means of conquest.' Tōma stressed that of these two alternatives, 'the Japanese people of those days truly adopted the former way, and did not follow the latter course' (Tōma 151d, p. 35).'

At the time, the Korean War had broken out, and the National Police Reserve, the forerunner of the Self-Defense Forces, had been established by order of the U.S. Occupation forces. In concert with this, there was spreading apprehension that Japan would perhaps become a vanguard of U.S. imperialism and try to shake off its economic woes through military intervention. By bringing up the idea that the Japanese nation had chosen the development of productivity, not conquest, Tōma was attempting to signal the direction in which Japan should advance.

Further, Tōma claimed that even if rice cultivation were something taught by instruction from continental Asia, 'this fact is not one that harms the subjectivity of the Japanese people of those times in the least.' Even if seeds and techniques had been conveyed from the continent, what had caused its development was the fact that the

Japanese people were already equipped with the intrinsic conditions for it. For Tōma, the theory that rice cultivation had diffused through the group migration of outsiders was a biased view which ignored the subjectivity and cultural competence of the Japanese nation (Tōma 1951d, 38–46).

For Tōma, who lamented that cosmopolitanism 'gave the entire populace an unnecessarily strong sense of inferiority vis-à-vis foreign countries,' and wished to 'apprise the entire nation of its national pride,' so that 'our nation would have confidence,' such a point of view was inevitable. Moreover, at the time, a call for development by means of a spontaneous self-reliance that broke away from cultural and technical dependency upon the West was lauded as part of national independence movements in Asia and Africa.

In Tōma's view, the national consciousness of the Japanese nation had achieved robust development in ancient times, but later on, members of the central nobility had 'adopted foreign-style culture' from the Chinese empire and lost their national consciousness; and, borrowing the authority of imported culture beyond the reach of the general populace, exploited the people (the masses) (Tōma 1951c). It is not hard to imagine that in Tōma's mind this was superimposed by Japanese comprador forces which were imbued with American culture and served the U.S.

From such a historical perspective, Tōma's book, *Nihon minzoku no keisei* (Formation of the Japanese nation), published in the very midst of the Korean War, dealt with the history of East Asia, including Japan, from the Jōmon Period to the early seventh century. To summarise its content somewhat rudely, it argued that though a single Japanese race which developed spontaneously committed the error of invading the Korean Peninsula, thereby repeating the mistake of the Chinese Empire (*Chūka teikoku*) which had been attempting to dominate it, it was defeated by counterattack from the Korean nation.

Tōma stated in this book that King Bu of Wa, whom he had described as a hero of the nation, had asserted the dignity of the Japanese nation in resolute words directed at China, in contrast to the way the nobility in later generations had been subordinate to Chinese culture. I hardly need to point out that there was probably an awareness here of comparison with the conservative regime dependent upon the U.S. Moreover, in his Introduction, Tōma says: 'The things written about in this book happened a very long time ago. However, from an isolated position, there is something striking in the actions of our own ancestors and the ancestors of Koreans, who entered into the world politics of that age and continued to follow their own paths amid the maelstroms arising both internally and externally ... I think that to describe these unstinting trends in East Asia is something that can have a particular significance in today's Japan, which prefers to tread the easy path and is willing to conclude peace treaties and the U.S.–Japan Security Treaty' (Tōma 1951d, p. 209; Intro. p. 2).

Such a tendency was not restricted to Tōma alone. Fujitani Toshio, for one, advocated a 'historical union of a pre-feudal Japanese people (*minzoku*) who had lived an independent life over several millennia in Japan, a narrow island country, united from early on by a common language; and who, having undergone roughly equal economic development, and without having been dominated by another people during that period, had carved out a common historical development by their own individual effort, and so richly moulded a shared psychological character.' According to Fujitani, 'When seen in racial terms, the Japanese race (*minzoku*) has the proto-Japanese of the New Stone Age as its ancestors, and since then no marked change can be seen.' This view was shared even by Inoue Kiyoshi, who stood at the forefront of criticism of Tōma at the Historical Science Society of Japan meeting, in that he asserted: 'We the Japanese people (*minzoku*) are composed mostly of a single race ... [and] this same Japanese race has cohabited in the same area for 2000 years, and grown into a nation (*minzoku*).' Ishimoda, too, stated that the Japanese language had been a native tongue since the Jōmon period, and that the subjectivity of the Japanese race had been a major factor in the establishment of rice cultivation, as well, rather than the influence of migrants from continental Asia (Fujitani 1953, p. 64; 1952, p. 41; Inoue 1976, p. 171; Ishimoda 1990, pp. 260–261).

The opening address at the 1952 Historical Science Society of Japan meeting stated: 'Through its present descent into a U.S. colony, the once-brilliant history of the nation is about to be trampled under American military boots ... Its culture, superior from time immemorial, has ceaselessly been born from amid the awareness of the nation, and its tradition has always been something that has saved us from the brink of despair.' Culture which was not rooted in national (*minzoku-teki*) tradition was even described as 'colonial culture' by those historians who took the position that 'a subject of cultural formation separate from the nation would be unthinkable.' As for the Great Buddha (Daibutsu) at Tōdaiji, which Tōma had cited as an example of national culture, there was even the argument that 'a certain person has denigrated the Daibutsu, going so far as to say it is a bad imitation of continental culture, and a "monument of humiliation"' (Naramoto 1952, p. 1; *Nihonshi kenkyū* 1951b; Fujitani 1952, p. 33).

Furthermore, the expression '*ta-minzoku kokka* ("multi-ethnic," "multi-national," or "multi-racial" state)' was one which did not carry a positive image. The model answer to the question of *minzoku* at the time was not multi-*minzoku* coexistence, but *minzoku* self-determination. Tōma used the expression '*ta-minzoku kokka*' as a homonym for a 'global empire' in which a conquering *minzoku* ruled other *minzoku*. Fujitani Toshio, describing the race to acquire colonies in modern times, stated: 'Countries like Britain, France and Italy, which first formed mono-*minzoku* states, became multi-*minzoku* states, that is, states with colonial possessions, through having obtained the territory of other *minzoku*, and no longer were [mono-]*minzoku* states ... By Japanese rulers holding Taiwan and Korea and gaining leased territory in China, Japan came to form a multi-*minzoku* state and, having become a state with colonial possessions, it finally blocked its own path to becoming a democratic nation-state (*minzoku-kokka*).' Here, the very Empire of Japan was a 'multi-*minzoku* state,' but the goal to which Japan was urged to aspire was a 'mono-*minzoku* state' (Tōma 1951c; Fujitani 1952, pp. 37, 39).

The point to note here is that just as '*minzoku*' was more or less a homonym for '*minshū* (the masses/the general populace),' the word '*tan'itsu* (single/mono-)' was frequently used as a homonym for 'solidarity' or 'unification.' In *Kōjien*, a leading Japanese-language dictionary, the example cited to illustrate the usage of '*tan'itsu*' up till its Third Edition in 1983 was '*tani'itsu kumiai* (unified labour union),' and this was a term which positively appraised workers' organisation and solidarity. That is to say, the word '*tan'itsu*' was not necessarily one with a negative connotation, and if we were to translate the nuance of '*tan'itsu minzoku*' as used by Tōma, Fujitani and the like, it might have meant something like 'unified masses.' In this connection, it was from *Kōjien*'s Fourth Edition published in 1991 that the expression '*tani'itsu minzoku ron* (the theory of a single *minzoku*)' made its appearance as an example of the usage of '*tan'itsu*,' and this was explained as an exclusionist political ideology originating in the 1986 pronouncements of Prime Minister Nakasone Yasuhiro. This signifies that perceptions vis-à-vis the word '*tan'itsu*,' or 'everyone unites into one,' underwent a change between the 1970s and the 1980s.

Moreover, the country which has often been cited in Japan both now and long ago as an example of a multi-*minzoku* state has been the United States. At the time, however, America was the symbol of racial discrimination and imperialism for advocates for progressive nationalism, and the issue of Black people in America was frequently discussed in a form which emphasised the misery to which minorities in a multi-*minzoku* state were subjected under majority rule.[15] It was in the late 1970s that the expression '*ta-minzoku kokka* (multi-*minzoku* state)' began to be employed in a positive sense, when, through the civil rights movement, minorities in the United States had, after a fashion, gained their rights as 'Americans,' and also when the Vietnam War had ended and the struggle opposing U.S. bases had more or less come to an end.

In a 1977 collection of talks, the Japan-residing Korean novelist Kim Tal-su criticised the way in which the existence of migrants from continental Asia had been neglected in Japanese historical studies. According to Kim, when the influence of those migrants was mentioned, many historians 'thought as if their subjectivity as Japanese might be diminished.' 'Even in the case of Ienaga[16] [Saburō]'s textbooks, this part is totally dreadful, and could be called the epitome of the Emperor-centred view of history' (Kim 1977, pp. 278, 114).[17] Ironically, the historical view which attempted to promote solidarity among the people by depicting 'the Japanese' as a single *minzoku* drew closer to the 'Emperor-centred view of history' which was deemed to be an evil form of nationalism.

Of course, the so-called myth of a single *minzoku* has diverse aspects, and such a progressive nationalistic aspect was nothing more than one manifestation among many. In addition, even if it did cite 'the Japanese' as a single *minzoku*, in the question of if that really did constitute the 'epitome of the Emperor-centred view of history,' there is a serious dividing line between whether it affirmed aggression and oppression, or not. In this period, the issue of domestic minorities, which later appeared as a criticism of the myth of a single *minzoku*, hardly drew any attention. Koreans residing in Japan were understood as a problem of the postwar disposal of colonial rule rather than as an issue of minorities within Japan, and it was considered more desirable for them to return to their ancestral land rather than to coexist with the Japanese within Japan.[18] The

Japanese economy was still in the recovery stage, and an influx of foreign workers was absolutely unforeseen. The existence of Ainu, whose being an indigenous *minzoku* of the archipelago had been denied, was something which could have become a grave Achilles heel for progressive nationalism, but it was left almost untouched, being regarded as a problem affecting all too few people.

Nevertheless, among the people who fell within the border regions of 'the Japanese' there was one group whose presence became a huge point of contention: Okinawa.

From 'colonial rule' to '*minzoku* unification'

In attempting to make the residents of Japan have a consciousness of being a 'single *minzoku*' and trying to unify them, the issue of how far to extend the parameters for considering people as 'Japanese' was a huge problem. Firstly, even if Koreans and Taiwanese were not seen as 'Japanese,' and Ainu were almost ignored, there was a major shift in regard to whether Okinawa would be the target of unification as a part of 'the Japanese' who were a 'single *minzoku*.'

To reiterate, as of 1946, the Japanese Communist Party had defined Okinawans as a 'minority *minzoku*' which had been ruled as a 'colony' by the Empire of Japan. As we have seen at the beginning of this chapter, however, these provisions came to be abandoned along with the rise of the reversion movement, and regarding Okinawans as 'non-Japanese' was deemed to be propaganda by the 'American invaders,' and it started to be emphasised that Okinawans were 'Japanese.'

There were a number of factors behind this shift. As far as domestic politics was concerned, as we have already seen, because the conservative regime gave weight to relations with the U.S. and their demands for return of Okinawa – which, if anything, had been advocated by the conservative side in the immediate postwar – grew half-hearted, those demands were gradually switching to being those of the progressive side. Moreover, in international terms, Okinawa had become the base for U.S. forces' sorties in the Korean War, and after that, also, for the additional reason that it had become the largest military stronghold from which to keep a stern eye upon East Asia, including China, the Soviet Union and the People's Republic of China supported the return of Okinawa to Japan, and criticised American rule of Okinawa.

In this way, though there were both domestic and international factors involved in this shift, the major one was nonetheless that Okinawan public opinion had rapidly inclined towards reversion to Japan. Admittedly, in the 1950s, when the Okinawan reversion movement had no alternative but to advocate a pro-U.S., anti-communist line, the Communist Party's anti-U.S. line was not always consistent with mainstream public opinion in Okinawa. In those circumstances, however, in the process of seeking the support of the Japanese mainland, the Okinawa People's Party, which had been the most suppressed by the U.S. military as 'communists,' gradually deepened its relationship with the Japanese Communist Party.

When the Left came to shoulder the reversion movement in this way, the ideology of progressive nationalism was applied there, as well. In other words, the return of Okinawa was regarded as the integration, through *minzoku* unification, of 'the Japanese' who had been divided by the U.S. military into Okinawa and mainland Japan.

The ideology of progressive nationalism, which positioned Japan as part of Asian-African countries, and advocated struggle for colonial independence and *minzoku* liberation, likened the division of Okinawa and mainland Japan to the divisions in Korea and China. At that time, Korea and China had already been respectively divided into the Democratic People's Republic of Korea (North Korea) and the People's Republic of China, which adopted socialism, and the Republic of Korea (South Korea) and Taiwan (seat of the Republic of China, which encompassed Mainland China as well), which received assistance from the United States. In regard to this situation, the Japanese Communist Party positioned South Korea and Taiwan as puppet regimes of U.S. imperialism, and argued that until the people of South Korea and Taiwan were liberated by North Korea and the People's Republic of China and national unification achieved, the national independence of Korea and China would not be complete. In the subsequent Vietnam War, as well, this way of thinking was extended in the form of support for the liberation and national unification of South Vietnam by North Vietnam, and this logic was also applied to Okinawa. In other words, as seen in the essay at the beginning of this chapter, 'the American invaders' attempted 'rule through a puppet regime of the independent country of Ryukyu' in Okinawa, too, but crushing this with the help of the forces of democracy in mainland Japan and making Okinawa revert was taken to be the liberation of Okinawan populace, and, by those means, the true unification and independence of the Japanese *minzoku* was deemed achievable.

One of the favourite metaphors in the 'reversion movement' or 'return movement' was that, in contrast to the thirty-eighth parallel which divided the Korean *minzoku*, and the seventeenth parallel which divided the Vietnamese *minzoku*, the Japanese *minzoku* was split into mainland Japan and Okinawa along the 'twenty-seventh parallel.' On 28 April, when the Treaty of San Francisco came into effect (called 'Okinawa Day'), as well as on 15 August, rallies were held on the sea on this 'twenty-seventh parallel' to advocate *minzoku* unification, boats having set sail from both the mainland Japan side and Okinawan side.

The 1964 maritime rallies ended up being held separately by those aligned with the Socialist Party and Communist Party, respectively, because of the importation of conflict between the Mainland parties, but a pamphlet recording the rally connected with the Communist Party was entitled: 'The Cry of the Nation (*minzoku*),' and was published by the Committee for Asian-African Solidarity in Tokyo. The positioning of the return of Okinawa as part of the struggle for *minzoku* liberation in Asia and Africa had come to prominence through the carrying out of a resolution criticising U.S. military rule vis-à-vis 'Okinawa, an integral part of Japanese territory' at the First Afro-Asian-Latin American Peoples' Solidarity Conference held in Tanzania in 1963. Moreover, the figure of Senaga Kamejirō, Chair of the Okinawa People's Party, wearing a headband saying 'Liberation of Okinawa Prefecture' and calling for the 'overthrow of American imperialism, which has severed Okinawa from its homeland and crushed Japanese independence underfoot' and urging the 'winning the liberation of Okinawa and the independence of Japan' is shown in this pamphlet. 'Okinawa Prefecture' was an administrative unity which did not exist at the time, but this rally, too, was named '*Okinawa-ken kaihō kokumin daishinkō* (Great march of nationals [for] liberation of Okinawa Prefecture),' and the pamphlet's postscript also pleaded for the 'driving out of the U.S. military' from 'Okinawa Prefecture which had been militarily colonised through American imperialism and made into an Asian ammunition store,' and 'the winning of *minzoku* independence' (Okinawa Henkan Kokumin Undō Tokyo Jikkō Iinkai 1965).[19]

Of course, the 'Cry of the nation' and '*minzoku* independence' mentioned here not only meant independence of the 'Okinawan *minzoku*,' but the 'independence of the Japanese *minzoku*' which was to be achieved by the return of Okinawa. In these circumstances, naturally, the expression 'Okinawan *minzoku*' which had been faintly visible up till the time of the 'island-wide struggle for land' began to disappear, and the word '*minzoku*' in the reversion movement came to be one that indicated the Japanese *minzoku*, which included Okinawa. The song '*Okinawa o kaese* (Give Okinawa back!)' is a good illustration of the way this '*minzoku*' was used.

> Oh, Okinawa, islands that break the hard earth, and burn in the anger of a people (*minzoku*),
> Oh, Okinawa, that we and our ancestors guarded and nurtured with blood and sweat,
> We cry: Oh, Okinawa; Okinawa – it is ours,
> Give Okinawa back, give Okinawa back!
> (Zen Shihō Fukuoka Shibu and Araki 1956)

Naturally, both the '*minzoku*' and the 'ancestors' are terms referring to 'the Japanese' as a whole, including Okinawans, and were ones which demanded the return of Okinawa to 'the Japanese.' Moreover, in contrast to the way Okinawa and Japan began to be deemed the 'same *minzoku*,' 'rule by a different nation (*i-minzoku*)' became fixed as the denomination for rule by the United States.

In this context, the view that Okinawa was part of the Japanese *minzoku* became established even among historians. As early as 1952, Fujitani Toshio had asserted that Okinawa had belonged since days of old to a 'single (*tan'itsu*) Japanese *minzoku*,' saying: '[From ancient times], a common language has been used from Tōhoku to Kyūshū and further to Amami Ōshima in the south, and now as far as Okinawa, which is about to be separated from Japan, and therefore they have been bound together by a common sentiment and psyche.' Though his political lineage was different, the lecture entitled '*Kaijō no michi* (The maritime road)' given by Yanagita Kunio in the month following the enforcement of the San Francisco Peace Treaty was also one which emphasised that Okinawa was part of Japan. In 1953, the next year, a special feature on Okinawa was incorporated in the journal *Rekishi hyōron* (Historical review),' but it was basically one which asserted that Okinawans had been a branch of the Japanese *minzoku* since ancient times, in line with the prewar framework of the Japan–Ryukyu common-ancestry theory, and that the view of Okinawa as being a different *minzoku* was nothing more than a bias originating from the Satsuma policy forbidding assimilation, which aimed to widen the gap between Japan and Ryukyu, and from prewar discrimination against Okinawa. The essay from *Zen'ei* cited at the beginning of this chapter also insisted that since ancient times Okinawans had 'developed a similar culture as part of the Jōmon-type cultural sphere in the Japanese archipelago,' and claimed that 'discrimination against minority *minzoku*' was something which Japanese imperialism had fostered (Fujitani 1952, p. 42; Kinjō 1953; Nakano 1969, p. 6).

From then on, repudiation of the view of Okinawa as a minority *minzoku* became the established stream in history, as well. The historian Inoue Kiyoshi, while stating that 'we the Japanese *minzoku* are almost a single race,' discussed the issue as follows:

> Japanese policy towards the Okinawa issue can become decisively different things according to the answer to the question of whether Okinawans are a part of a single, inalienable Japanese *minzoku*, or a minority *minzoku* that held Japanese nationality within the Empire of Japan until [Japan's] defeat, and not a part of the Japanese *minzoku*. In concert with Japan's modern development since Meiji, though their local tongue strongly remains, Okinawans have basically come to speak Japanese in common with Japanese people in general, and to share a livelihood area with Japanese in general; their economic life has also become an indivisible part of the Japanese economy; and they have a shared character with ordinary Japanese – in other words, they are members of the Japanese *minzoku*, and are by no means a minority *minzoku* which differs from it. As such, Okinawa's present placement under American governance means that the Japanese *minzoku*, which ought to be a single (*tan'itsu*) individual entity, is being forcibly divided; and, speaking from the viewpoint of the *minzoku* issue, Okinawa's being placed under American rule is no different from Shikoku or Kyushu being torn away from Japan and placed under American governance (Inoue 1976, pp. 175–177).

Ironically, the likening of the target area for integration to 'Shikoku or Kyushu' was similar in tone to that often used in the prewar theory of assimilation of Korea and Taiwan. Moreover, Inoue criticised a message for Okinawan independence which the Communist Party issued in the days when Tokuda Kyūichi was Chair, saying it had 'completely mistaken Marxist theory on *minzoku*,' and spoke as follows:

> There are some historical reasons for this kind of mistake having arisen. It is still less than a century since Okinawans were amalgamated into the Japanese *minzoku*, and, moreover, that amalgamation was not one which arose effortlessly as the natural result of Okinawan and mainland Japanese economic and cultural development, but which began from aggressive unification by the power of the emperor system against the Ryukyu Kingdom; and for a while after that, as well, Okinawa was made the object of semi-colonial exploitation and oppression. This is probably one of the reasons that made Okinawans with class-consciousness fall into a misconception like Mr Tokuda's. Even so, what a tragic error this is! (Inoue 1976, pp. 175–177)

Even while being exposed to 'semi-colonial exploitation and oppression' through 'aggressive unification' by the 'power of the emperor system,' if they came to speak Japanese and were economically integrated as a result, would they be 'part of a single, individual Japanese *minzoku*?'

Such positions were also related to then-current Marxist understanding, including that of Inoue. Marx regarded the French revolutionary government's stifling of minority languages such as Occitan in southern France as the unavoidable price of historical progress. Lenin argued that as economic consolidation was strengthened, minority *minzoku* inside the Soviet Union would gradually have no choice but to learn the Russian language. Being an assimilated Georgian who spoke Russian himself, Stalin made linguistic, regional, economic and cultural commonality a condition of the *minzoku*, and did not give weight to past history or the like.[20]

Even if iron-fisted rule were carried out temporarily, such a Marxist understanding invited an outcome which tended to position it as a necessary evil in the progress of history if a unified *minzoku* were formed as a result. Ishimoda highly praised Bismarck as having fulfilled the role of inducing unification of the German *minzoku* and modernisation, even if it 'were iron-fisted' (Ishimoda 1953c, pp. 342–346). Tōma's assessment of Yamato Takeru, whom he called a hero of national (*minzoku*) unification though he had been a member of the imperial family, was one made in light of such circumstances.

While on the one hand discrimination against Okinawa in the prewar was criticised in the context that it was something which viewed Okinawans as a 'different *minzoku*,' criticism of assimilation policies was weak. In the special feature on Okinawan history in *Rekishi hyōron* in 1953, in relation to 'assimilation policies vis-à-vis Ryukyu,' there were 'such things as the system of punishment placards in the ban on use of local dialects, which could be seen as going a bit too far, but, in combination with the compulsory propagation of Standard Japanese (*hyōjungo*) (called *futsūgo* in Okinawa), these rapidly achieved results, and Okinawans who had formerly been regarded by mainland Japanese as being a different *minzoku*, or who had special treatment forced upon them, also … [had integrated] almost to the extent that they were no different from Mainlanders in terms of their lifestyles and ways of thinking,' and this was credited as having played a definite role in *minzoku* unification, albeit under coercion (Kinjō 1953, p. 27).

Of course, this does not mean that such a shift was not also accompanied by any distortion. In his discussion of Okinawa in 1960, Ishimoda criticised the extent to which prewar Japan had discriminated against Okinawa, saying: 'It would be no surprise if prefectural residents were to say they never again wanted to be Japanese.' At the same time, though, he asserted: 'The reason why the residents of Okinawa Prefecture are shouting for return to their homeland in spite of that, without giving in to [U.S.] military repression, is that they have confidence that their own national consciousness is a new national consciousness tied to democratic demands, unlike in the past when it was exploited by nationalism.' Moreover, though Japan was a divided state like Germany, he criticised the Mainland side's indifference to Okinawa, writing that 'while the word Ryukyu is representative of an Okinawa in a feudal, semi-independent past, Okinawa represents a modern Okinawa as part of Japan' (Ishimoda 2001, pp. 203, 205–206, 207)

The assimilation policy created by the Imperial Japanese in Okinawa was described by Ishimoda as follows:

> From a friend hailing from Okinawa, I have heard tell of memories of being punished by having a placard hung on his chest every time he used Okinawan dialect instead of Standard Japanese in the classroom when he was a student at Naha Middle School. While recalling the situation at Polish schools under the Russian Empire which appears

in the biography of Madame Curie that I read long ago, I was made to ponder anew how Standard Japanese, which constitutes one aspect of the history by which [our] modern people is formed, becomes something belonging to the members of the nation.

The modern French, too, who make liberty, equality and fraternity their motto, are a people (*minzoku*) established by unifying the Provençal of Southern France through a similar process, and modern peoples are not created in any other way (Ishimoda 2001).

Ishimoda says that the Empire of Japan's assimilation policy was a necessary evil for *minzoku* unification. What constituted the prototype for this discussion on Okinawa was a paper in which he discussed the connection between the Tohoku region and Standard Japanese. Areas in northern Japan, excluding Hokkaido, were called Tohoku ('north-east') as they lay to the north-east from Tokyo's perspective; and, along with Okinawa, they are known as areas with strong local dialects. In addition, in the Meiji Restoration (*Meiji ishin*), whose occurrence was driven by clans from Western Japan, Tohoku waged war against the Meiji Government's troops and was occupied because it had sided with the shogunate. The Meiji Government was dominated by men hailing from Western Japan, and no-one from Tohoku was chosen. There, he says: 'I think that the process in which the Tokyo dialect destroyed the dialect of the Tohoku region was something similarly terrible to the people of Tohoku, who loved the language of their native region which they were accustomed to using, as oppression and exploitation from the central government,' and describes Tohoku as having been 'a colony of the Emperor system and monopoly capital' (Ishimoda 1953c, pp. 303, 307–310). In fact, Tohoku was his home region.

Why does Ishimoda, who himself hailed from a 'colony' and knew the pain of cultural deprivation, affirm a policy of assimilation in Okinawa? Quoting the words of Engels, who talked about the 'iron fist of the [National] Convention that first turned the inhabitants of Southern France into *Frenchmen* and, as compensation for their nationality, gave them democracy' (1848 [1994]), Ishimoda advanced his own argument in the form of a counterargument to Kinoshita Junji, who defended regional languages.

Just as Southern France was the conservative part of France, Tohoku, too, was a backward area in which 'the oldest type of feudalism' held sway, according to Ishimoda. In the Meiji Restoration, it was the centre of supporters of the shōgun, and in the prewar, being 'loyal,' it was a source of supply of 'robust infantry,' and in the postwar, too, it produced the largest number of conservative politicians. It was a 'bastion of reaction and counter-revolution.' Ishimoda said that for that reason he felt very ashamed, and could not help envying his classmates from Tosa in Shikoku, who loudly chanted the well-known counting song whose lyrics alluded to 'the place where revolution and freedom were born.'

Ishimoda argued that in modern Japan, Tohoku was the place which most experienced modernisation by iron-fisted rule – just as Engels described historical development as having been 'inexorable' (1848 [1994]). Ishimoda further stated that 'however brutal the conquest and domination of feudal Tohoku by emperor-system absolutism had been, ... after the Meiji Restoration, Tohoku's having cast off its feudal isolation, and its being caught up in a huge progressive movement, namely the formation of unified Japanese nationals, were – it goes without saying – a great historical advance, even in terms of having created and encouraged the conditions for liberating Tohoku.' Moreover, he asserted that 'the Tokyo dialect's becoming the standard language for the entire country ... is a necessary condition for moulding feudal Japan into a nation (*kokumin*).' The opinion he presented towards Okinawa was no more than an extension of this.

Seeking independence and liberation from 'American imperialism,' they advocated a 'Japanese people' who had a single culture and language. If it were not possible, though, to create this except by an assimilation policy imposed by force, and if the domination of surrounding areas were affirmed for that reason, then what exactly would the independence of the *minzoku* and liberation from domination which they advocated be? Ultimately, no answer to this emerged.

The Ryukyu Disposition as *minzoku* unification

Among such historical scholars, there was one thing which became the focus of debates on Okinawa. This was the positioning of the Ryukyu Disposition.

As we have already seen, the assumption in the discourse of Okinawan independence in the immediate postwar was the historical view that Okinawans were a minority *minzoku* which differed from 'the Japanese,' and that Okinawa, once an independent country, had been invaded by the Empire of Japan after the beginning of the Meiji era. In other words, this meant that the historical view that the Ryukyu Disposition had been an invasion was the premise of the independence discourse, but this was something which did not harmonise with the return movement as national (*minzoku*) unification.

Towards the rest of the world, as well, it was not possible for the return movement to hold that the Ryukyu Disposition was an invasion. This was because, as we saw in Chapter Five, while the independence of Korea and return to Chinese sovereignty of Manchuria and Taiwan were advocated in the Cairo Declaration of 1943 on the one hand, it was stated that Japan would be expelled from 'all other areas which Japan had pillaged through its violence and greed.' As there were no explicit place-names in these 'all areas,' the question of whether Okinawa was one of them depended upon the interpretation of whether the Ryukyu Disposition constituted an invasion. In other words, if it were assumed that the Ryukyu Disposition was an invasion, this would mean that Japan would lose its international grounds for seeking the return of Okinawa, and this was a matter of life and death for the return movement. Speaking from the conclusion, the historical view came to be established that even if the Ryukyu Disposition had been heavy-handed in the same way as the assimilation policy, it constituted 'national (*minzoku*) unification from above' which contributed to the progress of history, and was not an invasion.

In this case, too, the prewar theory that Japan and Ryukyu had the same ancestry underlay such a historical perspective. In a special edition on Okinawan history in *Rekishi hyōron* in 1953, the Okinawan historian Kinjō Chōei, quoting Ifa Fuyū, claimed that the abolition of domains and establishment of prefectures was 'a kind of liberation from slavery,' and asserted that 'those who opposed the new system of abolition of domains and establishment of prefectures mainly belonged to the ruling class from the upper echelons of the Royal Government' (Kinjō 1953, p. 27). Such a historical view was one that had already existed among advocates for return on the Okinawan side, such as the People's Party, but it began to be granted historical authority.

In 1957, a special project on Okinawan history also published in *Rekishi hyōron* was one which later became the prototype for the historical view held by the reversion movement until the 1960s. This special issue, whose compilation was led by Shinzato Keiji, an Okinawan-born historian, made such claims as that 'in anthropological terms, Okinawans are a branch of the Japanese, and linguistically, their language is a dialect of Japanese'; Satsuma had forbidden their assimilation to the language and culture of Japan, thus 'greatly hampering the normal growth of national consciousness'; it was the conservative samurai class of the Ryukyuan Royal Government that opposed the abolition of clans and establishment of prefectures, while 'enlightened members of the samurai class welcomed "amalgamation"; and when it came to the peasants, it was they, rather than others, who pinned their hopes on the Meiji government's new system, and longed for it.' Esteem for the Ryukyuan samurai class was extremely low, and there was criticism that 'even after the measures for establishment of prefectures, there were many conservative, backward-looking foot-soldiers among the upper echelons of the previous generation which had the backing of the old Royal Government, and among the privileged ruling class; anticipating the cooperation of Qing China, they caused friction towards government policy in every matter' (Shinzato et al. 1957, pp. 4, 9, 13, 17).

Of course, this does not imply that Meiji government policy was all positive in the view of history held by Shinzato and his colleagues, as well. The target of censure there was primarily the way Mainlanders regarded Okinawans as a 'different *minzoku*,' in addition to 'discriminatory treatment' and 'being treated like outsiders' in comparison to other prefectures, and the policy of preserving old customs which favoured the samurai class from the Ryukyuan Royal Government. Such things as economic woes as a result of the policies and a personnel administration in which the Okinawan-born were given the cold shoulder were strongly criticised. On the other hand, the position was taken that 'the most successful of policies towards Okinawa since the establishment of prefectures was education,' and high praise was given to the fact that 'there was a growing number of people among the younger generation who regarded themselves as Japanese, and had no qualms about it.' According to Shinzato, the process of 'assimilating' to 'the Japanese' was one which simultaneously brought together the people of Japan who had been oppressed and dispersed; it eliminated *minzoku* bigotry; and a consciousness which endeavoured to do away with old things, together with the people of Okinawa as compatriots, began to grow steadily (Shinzato et al. 1957, p. 25).

In such a historical perspective, the existing view on the Japanese Mainland side of Okinawans as a 'different *minzoku*' was presumed to be a bias which had been indoctrinated into the people by the Satsuma policy forbidding assimilation – Satsuma having striven to maintain the framework of the Ryukyu Kingdom and make a profit – and through the ulterior motives of the ruling side, including the policy of preserving old customs by which the Meiji government tried to win over the former samurai class. Among prewar movements on the Okinawan side, the Ryukyuan samurai class's *Ryūkyū kyūkoku undō* (Movement for salvation of Ryukyu), and the Kōdōkai incident which aimed for special autonomy, were positioned as reactionary behaviour by conservative former samurai. What was lauded, by contrast, was the fact that Jahana Noboru, who hailed from a peasant background, had petitioned for Okinawans' suffrage as 'Japanese.' This movement of Jahana's received high praise as a pioneering effort promoting the national integration of Okinawa from the aspect of rights, and, due to the existence of the theory that Jahana had had exchange with Nakae Chōmin and Kōtoku Shūsui, it was dubbed 'Okinawa's Freedom and Popular Rights Movement.' The Freedom and Popular Rights Movement was a Meiji-era democratisation movement in which numerous Tohoku intellectuals and youths who had been criticised by the Meiji Government participated. It was Hara Takashi who, through the influence of such a movement, organised a political party in the Imperial Diet which was formed, and became Japan's first Prime Minister of commoner descent.

The theory about interchange between the Mainland's Freedom and Popular Rights Movement and Jahana was asserted in Ōzato Kōei's *Gijin Jahana Noboru den* (Biography of a selfless man, Jahana Noboru), self-published in the prewar. Ōzato was a settlement activist, but the place where he was active was Fukagawa, an area where Korean and Okinawan workers had been exposed to discrimination and poverty. Amid such circumstances, he wrote a book which described Jahana, who had aimed for institutional equality with mainland Japan, as a 'selfless man.'

In actuality, as hardly any original materials penned by Jahana about the issue of voting rights now remain, it is unclear as to what kind of ideological basis Jahana used in conducting his campaign of petitioning the Diet. In Ōzato's book, however, there are many expressions such as: 'Gaining suffrage for Okinawa was not the mere acquisition of voting rights, but meant expelling "Governor-General" Narahara, who had been appointed by the *han* government, and abolishing governor-general-style rule,' and in this book, whose first edition was published in 1935, Ōzato is thought to have had a gaze which superimposed Jahana over movements for acquisition of suffrage from Korea and Taiwan (Ōzato 1969, p. 181).

Jahana's campaign rapidly attracted attention amid the reversion movement, and Ōzato's book, too, which had been self-published in the prewar, came to be reissued in the 1960s. As I will later elaborate in Chapter Nine, as doubts began to germinate towards the reversion movement, the evaluation vis-à-vis Jahana's campaign was questioned anew, and doubts came to be harboured as to the authenticity of Ōzato's claim about his exchange with mainland Japan's Freedom and Popular Rights movement. If we consider that the movement to petition for establishment of a parliament in Taiwan, which I will mention in Volume 2 of this book, was discussed on the Japanese side as an analogous to the Freedom and Popular Rights movement, Ōzato's tying of Jahana's campaign to that movement also might have been due to the influence of the times.

This does not mean that there were no counterarguments from that time to such a history of Okinawa and especially to its position vis-à-vis the Ryukyu Disposition. Within Japanese history, the dispute between Inoue Kiyoshi and Shinzato is well-known. As previously stated, Inoue criticised the view that deemed Okinawans to be a minority *minzoku*, but, in regard to the Ryukyu Disposition, based on the premise that 'Ryukyu, though admittedly small, was an independent country from old times,' he asserted that the way the Meiji government had annexed it had to be called an invasion (Inoue 1955, pp. 26, 30).

Shinzato had argued against this view of Inoue's since 1957, but even more thoroughgoing rebuttal was added in the Iwanami Shinsho publication, *Okinawa*, which he co-authored in 1963 with Higa Shunchō and Shimota Seiji. Here, too, it was emphasised that Okinawans were anthropologically, linguistically and archeologically part of the Japanese *minzoku*, and viewing them as a different *minzoku* was a bias that had circulated from the Satsuma prohibition on assimilation, and along with this, it was advocated that 'it could not be said that the people opposed it, and objectively speaking, it rather meant a kind of liberation.' Vis-à-vis Inoue's opinion, the Ryukyu Kingdom was no longer an independent country after invasion by Satsuma, and, 'in regard to the unification of the modern state of Japan,' it was taken that 'incorporating this into its territory as Okinawa Prefecture in equal manner to other domains likewise could not be called "aggressive annexation"' (Higa et al. 1963, pp. 124, 127).[21]

This Iwanami Shinsho publication, *Okinawa*, was one which richly reflected the progressive nationalism of that age. In other words, 'Okinawa's reversion to the homeland' was a 'matter for the entire nation (*minzoku*),' and though 'the sacrifices which Okinawan prefectural residents made for the defence of the homeland were not inferior to those of any other Japanese,' it attributed the reason for the weakness of a 'national (*kokumin-teki*) sense of solidarity towards Okinawa' to the 'weakness of Japanese nationalism=national sense of solidarity.' Within such logic, viewing Okinawa as a 'different *minzoku*' was taken to be discrimination arising from the immaturity of Japan's national consciousness and its rulers' policies; the denomination '*Ryūkyūjin* (Ryukyuans)' was a discriminatory term, 'Okinawa *kenmin* (prefectural residents)' being correct; and the word 'Ryūkyū' was deemed 'not to have been the original name for Okinawa from the start, but one which the Chinese gave it' (Shinzato 1972, pp. 12, 4, 14, 21). It goes without saying that Jahana Noboru's suffrage campaign was lauded while the prewar policy of preserving old customs was criticised.

Behind Shinzato and his colleagues having stressed to this extreme that Okinawa was part of Japan lay not only the sort of political situation mentioned above, but also bias and lack of understanding on the part of Japanese society towards Okinawa. In their book, *Okinawa*, they cite a comment by the leader of a Japanese Socialist Party delegation to the Soviet Union which called at Okinawa in 1954, who said: 'So there are Japanese-language newspapers in Okinawa?' and one by the former prime minister, Ashida Hitoshi, who stated: 'Before the war, the natives of Okinawa used to eat palm fruit and walk barefoot, but now, thanks to America, they are leading good lives, aren't they?' Remarks illustrating general bias, such as: 'Are Okinawa and Ryukyu the same thing?' 'Is it near the Philippines?' 'Are the textbooks in English?' 'For [someone from] Okinawa, your Japanese is excellent,' were lined up alongside the additional question: 'Are the people of Okinawa racially really Japanese?' Shinzato records his experience of 'expounding the theory that Okinawans=Japanese' when he was attending an old-system high school in mainland Japan immediately after the end of the war. Asked by a classmate: 'What kind of lives do indigenous Okinawans lead?' he replied: 'I am an indigenous Okinawan. Do you think I am different from a Japanese person, or something?' but the circumstances necessary for a Japan–Ryukyu common-ancestry theory in order to resist bias against Okinawa did not change much after the war, either (Shinzato 1972, pp. 3, 7–8, 12; Shinzato et al. 1957, p. 3).

The degree of general understanding of and interest in Okinawa on the part of Japanese Mainlanders at the time could be said to have been at the same level as that vis-à-vis a far distant country. No matter what kind of human-rights violations occurred in Okinawa, these only attracted about the same amount of concern as human-rights violations in South Korea or Taiwan. For champions of the reversion movement, raising such Mainland interest from 'the level of international news' to 'the level of domestic news' was a momentous task. For that purpose, it had to be emphasised that Okinawa was part of 'Japan,' and were 'the same Japanese.' The expression 'a pain in the little finger is a pain for the entire body' was frequently employed from the Okinawan side, too, but this analogy, imbued with the idea of the state as an organism, was also a last resort for exciting the concern of the mainland Japanese side.

Okinawa, the book by Shinzato and colleagues, was widely accepted at the time as a valuable introductory volume on Okinawan issues. Inoue Kiyoshi, too, subsequently amended his opinion, and the historical perspective in the reversion movement after that became one which hardly diverged from that described here. This tendency continued until the end of the 1960s, when questions began to arise about the reversion movement.

In this period, moreover, while on the one hand the implementation of 'Japanisation' in prewar Korea and Taiwan was deemed to be discrimination, in the case of Okinawa, exclusion from 'the Japanese' having been carried out was taken to be discrimination.

In a book entitled *Gendai Nihon no sabetsu* (Discrimination in contemporary Japan), published in 1966, there was condemnation of prewar 'policies to erase Koreans' awareness of being Korean,' and 'policies to make them think they were Japanese.' In the same book, though, there were such statements as: 'The ruling side covertly and overtly carried out thought control, and still do so now, saying that Okinawans are not Japanese: people of Okinawa Prefecture are "Japanese nationals," but a little bit different to people from other prefectures.' 'They deliberately call Okinawa Prefecture "Ryukyu," for example, and call residents of Okinawa Prefecture "Okinawan residents" or "Ryukyuans." By having people indicate mainland Japan and deliberately call it "Japan" or "*naichi*" (literally, "internal territory"), they put effort into the pretence that Okinawa is an individual independent country separate from Japan or something (*gaichi*=external territory, that is a colony, in contrast to *naichi*).' What is more, here, too, it is emphasised that 'for the Okinawan people, who are Japanese, to return to Japan, and for Okinawa Prefecture, which is proper Japanese territory, to be restored to Japan, mean the recovery of its original form,' and unless Okinawa returned, 'Japan's true independence would not be achieved' (Tokyo Buraku Mondai Kenkyūkai 1966, pp. 128, 85, 111, 112–113). In this manner, the reversion movement, naturally, and the Ryukyu Disposition, also, began to be deemed not to be aggression, but to be Japan's restoration, 'recovering its original shape.'

The worsening image of Ryukyuan independence debates

Among such multitudes, a rare example of counterargument against the historical perspective of Shinzato and his colleagues was the journalist Mori Hideto. In 1963, Mori took up the book *Okinawa* by Shinzato et al. in a book review, harshly criticising it by saying Mori himself was until his dying day unlikely to have any connection with a strange nationalistic view of history purporting to rejoice from the people's position at the annexation of Okinawa, which had materialised for the first time through the mobilisation of Japanese troops. Mori also asserted that to say that Jōmon pottery was present in Okinawa was propaganda from 'nationalist historians,' that it was no more than a theory from 'extremely political nationalists who aspire artificially to prove that Okinawans had belonged to the Japanese race since ancient times,' and that Ryukyu had been an independent country until invasion by the Meiji government (Mori 1963a; 1963c; 1963d).

Behind Mori's claims lay the issue of the presence of the Communist Party in the leftist movement at the time. As previously mentioned, the Communist Party line of a *minzoku* unification front was one which positioned Japan as a vassal state of the U.S., firstly giving priority to the anti-U.S. struggle and national independence, and allying itself for the time being with indigenous capitalists inside Japan. However, Japanese capital, already revived by rapid economic growth, began to advance into Asia, and its positioning of Japan as a vassal state in the same way as Asia and Africa was losing its persuasiveness. In a related development, student organisations, including radical ones, had begun to break away from the Communist Party since the late 1950s out of dissatisfaction, later forming a trend which led to the later New Left, and it was a period when a shadow was cast also over the leadership of the Communist Party in the leftist movement in Japan. Moreover, Mori had previously surveyed the actual situation with sugar-cane cultivation in Okinawa, and complained that mainland Japanese capital was exploiting Okinawan workers, he being more opposed to a policy of prioritising anti-U.S. struggle than fighting against capitalism.

According to Mori, the *minzoku* unification line which the Japanese Communist Party and the Okinawan People's Party which collaborated with it took was full of 'racial bias and nationalistic inclinations'; 'the fact that the Okinawan people were placed in an inhumane environment as a result of violation by Japanese monopoly capital was suppressed' and was something which 'focused' the rage of the Okinawan populace 'solely upon the anti-U.S. struggle,' becoming merely something which 'depicted Japan as a democratic utopia and publicises that in order to rationalise the reversion movement.' He further pointed out the fact that the Japanese Communist Party and Okinawan People's Party had not advocated the reversion-movement line in the immediate postwar, and said that what was vital for Okinawan liberation was not the question of whether Okinawans were 'Japanese,' but 'to create a true internationalism which denies all states and denies all class domination' (Mori 1963b).[22]

Shinzato's reaction against these opinions of Mori's was severe. According to Shinzato, the idea that Jōmon pottery had been discovered in Okinawa was an established theory in the academic community; saying that the Kingdom of Ryukyu was an independent country was 'just as nonsensical as advocating the existence of the "independent Kingdom of Manchuria,"' and he ends by saying: 'When I ponder that even one proper scholar of Okinawa might try to conduct academic debate against Mori, I wonder if they seriously believe him. His pretentiousness is also extreme.' Furthermore, he criticised Mori's ideology, saying:

> In 'On the National Pride of the Great Russians,' Lenin once preached that Bismarck's unification of the Germanic peoples was something that 'promoted economic development by bringing together the disunited Germans,' saying that he had 'accomplished a progressive historical task.' Marx, too, has expounded that one ought not to call oppression by the north of France of the south of France at the end of the Middle Ages a 'shameful injustice.'
>
> As far as one can see from an overall look at history, the correctness of a position which, while severely criticising the Meiji government's policy towards Okinawa, simultaneously acknowledges the ruling on establishment of prefectures as a historical necessity, is almost self-evident to those who comment upon the Japanese revolution (Shinzato 1963d; 1963b).

Shinzato further asserted: 'Mori is intoning nonsensical revolutionary theory, saying such things as a "true internationalism which denies all states and denies all class domination," but to us what is necessary is to commandeer the state power of a specific nation-state called Japan into the hands of the people.'

The titles of Shinzato's written rebuttals to Mori include such ones as 'An extremely irresponsible accusation: Is Mr Mori Hideto an advocate of Ryukyuan independence?' and 'The "fallacy" of an advocate of Ryukyuan independence: a criticism of Mori Hideto, a provocateur of ignorance and hyperbole,' and it can be seen that 'advocate of Ryukyuan independence' was a descriptor of reproach. Already, through Communist Party policy reversal and expansion of the reversion movement, the expression 'advocate of Ryukyuan independence' had come to be used as a homonym for an 'advocate of discrimination' who regarded Okinawa as a 'different *minzoku*,' or for a 'traitor' who followed America, fragmenting the front line for national unification (*minzoku tōitsu*) and trying to defend a 'puppet state.'

Kokuba Kōtarō, a former Central Committee member in the Okinawan People's Party, joined this dispute between Shinzato and Mori, and it developed into a debate which questioned the very line of the reversion movement. Kokuba had only just left the People's Party, having clashed with mainstream members of the People's Party such as Senaga Kamejirō over the movement's line.

Unlike Mori, Kokuba's way of regarding Okinawa as a minority *minzoku* emphasised the sequence of events in which it was used by America, and also acknowledged the value of the past *minzoku* unification front line in its own way. Even so, according to Kokuba, mainland Japan of course 'must not shut its eyes to the very situation of the non-existence of the form of such "nationalist" movements, even in Okinawa under the rule of the U.S. military occupation,' and there was a necessity 'at present, [to] break free from an idealistic "nationalism" and take on a class-like character and international character.' That, he argued, would 'not be considered achievable simply by mechanically transplanting Japanese progressive parties' platforms to Okinawa, or by fitting themselves into any of the moulds of Japanese progressive parties.' While Shinzato (Keiji) and the like, stressing that Okinawans were 'Japanese,' were trying to advance the reversion movement by means of nationalism, Kokuba asserted that 'this was a sentimental nationalist tendency born from the result of laying stress on the bourgeois nationalistic challenge of *minzoku* unification and considering the Okinawa issue in a reactionary manner, and was lagging far behind the practical matters at hand.'[23]

Shinzato harshly criticised such an opinion of Kokuba's, too, saying: 'Your theoretical acts are politically barren and harmful, and also scientifically wrong.' According to Shinzato, the idea that Okinawa was not an American colony was consequently nothing but a '"justification" for U.S. imperialism' which underestimated the seizure of Okinawa by America (Shinzato 1963c; 1963a). Shinzato, too, was captive to the worldview that those who disrupted the solidarity of a movement were, in short, betrayers to the enemy.

If we look at Shinzato's counterargument against Mori and Kokuba, it reveals that what irritated him most was that though Mori and Kokuba criticised the *minzoku* unification front line, 'they consistently did not show any sort of practical conclusion.' Shinzato probably meant to say that if they had criticisms towards the reversion movement, were they suggesting Okinawa be left under U.S. military domination? At the time, it was a period of stagnation for the movement, so to speak, after the air of excitement in the 'island-wide struggle for land' and the AMPO struggle of the 1960s had cooled, and even in a new book, *Okinawa*, it is recorded that only fewer than 500 people had gathered at the Tokyo 'National rally for demanding return of Okinawa' held in April 1962 (Shinzato 1963a; Higa et al. 1963, p. 13). In such a situation, being censured without indication of any concrete alternative must have been hard to bear for Shinzato, who had made efforts to heighten the concern of the general public even a little by emphasising that Okinawans were 'Japanese' and to advance the resolution of discrimination and the reversion movement. His description of Mori's assertion as 'nonsensical revolutionary theory' might have been a manifestation of such a sense of impatience.

From the 1950s into the 1960s, the view which saw Okinawa as part of 'the Japanese,' and the reversion movement as racial unification, took firm root along with a corresponding historical perspective. Under such circumstances, the pointing-out of conflict with mainland Japan and the invasive quality of the Ryukyu Disposition began to be taken as discrimination which regarded Okinawa as an 'alien race,' and any 'argument for Ryukyuan independence' as colluding with American imperialism. Moreover, this tone of argument later went on also to impact upon attitudes and awareness within Okinawa.

9 The Dialect Placards of the 1960s

Mention of the Okinawa Teachers' Association is indispensable when discussing Okinawa's reversion movement. The Teachers' Association not only produced such core figures in the movement as Yara Chōbyō and Kyan Shin'ei, but as an organisation, it was also the pillar of the reversion movement from the 1950s through the 1960s, as well.

In this chapter, I take up the topic of the 'national education' movement which this Okinawa Teachers' Association implemented. As I will elaborate in the chapter, this movement originally was one that the mainland Japan Teachers' Union (Nihon kyōshokuin kumiai, or Nikkyōso) had begun from the 1960s as something to foster a self-awareness of 'being Japanese,' based on the ideas of progressive nationalism discussed in the previous chapter. However, when this entered Okinawa, which traditionally had had a delicate consciousness towards 'the Japanese,' it came to present a complex modality. Moreover, this movement developed into something that highlighted the question of what the word 'Japanese' meant within the reversion movement.

Reversion as a reconstruction effort

Postwar education in Okinawa began from the extremes of devastation. Eighty percent of school buildings had been lost in the Battle of Okinawa, and few of the remaining classrooms were fit for use, too. There were no textbooks, exercise books or writing implements, and even today, how those textbooks which had survived the flames were read in turn by multiple students, and how classes were conducted by writing characters with a finger on the sandy beach, still form topics of conversation.

The facilities aspect aside, there was also an enormous loss of teachers. In the Battle of Okinawa, about a third of teachers perished, and damage to the rising and mid-career cohorts was particularly serious. In addition, for teachers – who were public servants – the demise of 'Okinawa Prefecture' as an administrative unit of Japan meant that the supplier of their salaries disappeared. Though salaries were later paid under the American military government, the amount was only about half that of a worker for the military. As their livelihood security had vanished and they were exposed to intense postwar hardships in their lives, in the eight years postwar, the proportion of teachers on the main island of Okinawa who changed jobs or resigned reportedly reached as high as fifty-seven percent. As teachers' colleges ('normal schools') were annihilated and would-be teachers could not go to mainland Japan to study, either, vacancies were filled by graduates of temporary, short-term training institutions.[1]

Despite such circumstances, the American military's stance vis-à-vis education was completely cold-hearted. Requests for increases in teachers' remuneration and reconstruction of school buildings were repeatedly issued, but apart from allowing a miniscule increase in pay, the U.S. military refused on the grounds that it would constitute an 'unreasonable increase in the budget.' Improvements to school buildings were carried out through donations from residents, but as of 1951, permanent school buildings amounted to only a quarter of the total, and temporary school buildings such as tents supplied by the American military accounted for nearly seventy percent, and seven percent of children were attending classes in the open air (Ryūkyū Seifu Bunkyō Kyoku Kenkyū Chōsa Ka 1956, pp. 33, 189).

In the first place, the American military did not trust the teachers. In a survey prior to the Occupation, it was explained how nationalistic education in Okinawa had been, and, according to a member of the initial military government authorities, '[teachers] were forced to convert by enthusiastic exponents of the destiny of the Empire of Japan. Accordingly, the military government authorities hesitated to permit the restoration of schools, regardless of their type.' In the meantime, the U.S. military allowed the recommencement of education after having emphasised the strict prohibition of 'martial drill and education extolling Japan,' but, according to one of the authorities at that time, 'though restrictions were made, it was almost impossible for them to find out what sort of things teachers were saying of their own volition [in the classroom], due to the difficulty of the language' (Kano 1987, pp. 61, 62). For the U.S. military, something such as cutting into its budget for the sake of school buildings and teachers who might implement anti-U.S. education was no target for enthusiasm.

While Japanese-style teaching materials were banned, education that emphasised Ryukyuan identity and expounded international goodwill with America was deemed desirable, and the compilation of textbooks in Okinawan was also considered, but the American military's zeal for primary education was scant to begin with, and such an education policy only materialised in an unsatisfactory form. In the early postwar period it forbade the importation of textbooks from Japan in primary and secondary education, but the U.S. military had neither the ability nor the enthusiasm to produce texts to replace them, and so textbooks started to be imported from the Japanese mainland from 1948. The thing that could be done at the lowest cost for America was to construct a higher-education institution to cultivate a pro-U.S. local elite, and while on the one hand primary education was left to decay, the University of the Ryukyus was opened in 1951.

The fact that postwar education in Okinawa was in such a state is vital to finding out why the Okinawa Teachers' Association became the core of the reversion movement. Efforts by local residents had already reached their limit, and in terms of school buildings and equipment, and teachers' pay and treatment, as well, the disparity with mainland Japan, which continued to achieve economic growth, only became ever more conspicuous. Amid such circumstances, the teachers' reversion movement began firstly as a movement for improvement of the educational environment.

When speaking of the reversion movement by the Okinawa Teachers' Association, it would not do to omit mention of Yara Chōbyō, its inaugural president and also the president of the Okinawa Shotō Nihon Fukki Kiseikai (Council for the return of the Okinawan Islands to Japan). Yara was born in 1902, and after becoming a teacher in Okinawa, he was transferred to appointments at Tainan Number Two Middle School and Taipei Teachers' College in Taiwan, where he passed the end of the war. There was no small number of Okinawa-born teachers assigned to Taiwan, and these became the supporting pillars for the acculturation (*kyōka*) of Taiwan, Yara being among them.

A science teacher, Yara showed no trace of devotion to education for fostering imperial subjects, as far as his memoirs and suchlike reveal. Rather, what was impressed upon him in Taiwan seems to have been the sight of his pupils cowering and falling into despair, their path to further education and promotion being barred amid Japanese rule.[2] In postwar Okinawa, too, the situation continued where even if students graduated from school, they had no way of advancing to higher education on the Japanese mainland, and had no future except to become workers for the military. In the subsequent reversion movement, Yara expressed his misgivings towards the way Okinawan youth lost hope 'amid the colonial circumstances' and fell into a 'decadent life' (Yara 1968a, p. 119), and this is thought likely to be something which reflects his experiences in Taiwan.

Having returned home from Taiwan, Yara was shocked at Okinawa's devastation and the state of affairs in which middle-ranking teachers of his age had died, and he started to rebuild Okinawan education as the principal of a high school. In 1950, under Taira Tatsuo, a reversionist who had won the post of Chief Executive in the Government of the Ryukyu Islands (GRI) elections, Yara was especially selected and appointed to the position of Director of Education.

It goes without saying that the tasks given top priority by Yara as Director of Education were the reconstruction of school buildings and the improvement of teachers' treatment. His impetus on that occasion was his inspection of the Japanese mainland in 1950 on a training course for educational leaders. At a roundtable discussion held in the summer of the same year, following their return home, Okinawans connected with education – shocked that postwar recovery on the mainland had advanced beyond estimation – made such remarks as: 'Okinawa suffers by comparison with the way [teachers on the mainland] are granted a basic salary sufficient to make ends meet easily even if, for instance, they devoted themselves entirely to teaching.' Yara, too, recalls that he was 'astonished at the huge disparity, and it was deplorable to think of the present situation in Okinawa' (Ryūkyū Seifu Bunkyō Kyoku Kenkyū Chōsa Ka 1956, p. 73; Yara 1977, p. 7). Their shock that the gap between Okinawa and the mainland, which had begun to shrink as a result of efforts in the prewar, had again widened beyond conjecture became one factor spurring them towards a movement for improvement of the educational environment 'to equal the mainland.'

However, as previously mentioned, the reaction of the U.S. military was one of complete indifference. According to Yara's memoirs, when he requested school buildings be brought up to the standard of the mainland, the American military officer in charge apparently replied: 'It is not democratic to imitate other people, saying such things as: "On the mainland, there are school buildings like this. American ones are like this. In comparison with these, ours are such-and-such." Democracy means getting along according to one's own means' (Yara 1977, pp. 8, 16). What is more, the American military asserted that if it were a matter of democratic education, it would be better for Okinawans to learn directly from America rather than via Japan, and that it would put an end to the system of study tours to the mainland.

In a situation where nothing could be expected from the U.S. military, in February 1951, Yara attempted to petition the Japanese Minister for Education through the Parliamentary Vice-Minister for Education, who had come to Okinawa upon invitation to the opening ceremony for the University of the Ryukyus. The substance of the petition asked for assistance towards the reconstruction of school buildings and the continuation of the training system, but another thing which was of great concern for teachers who had accumulated years of prewar service was the payment of pensions. At the aforementioned post-return roundtable discussion by the study-tour group from the educational leaders' training course, also, attention was drawn to the issue that it would be difficult to receive a pension unless Okinawa reverted to being under the executive power of the Japanese government (Ryūkyū Seifu Bunkyō Kyoku Kenkyū Chōsa Ka 1956, p. 75).

In such circumstances, in January 1952, at a meeting of the All-island Association of School Principals, it was resolved to demand reversion to Japan. Furthermore, after a pro-American Chief Executive had succeeded Taira, Yara quit the post of Director of Education and became President of the Okinawa Teachers' Association, which was launched in the spring of 1952. He reorganised the Okinawa Shotō Nihon Fukki Kiseikai, which had been in a state of dissolution since the Peace Talks, and began a movement to tour mainland Japan collecting monetary donations for the reconstruction of school buildings.

After this, Yara went on to spearhead the Teachers' Association and become the leader of the reversion movement, but in his case, it seems that his feelings towards his 'ancestral land' could not have been described as simplistic, either. At the GRI Assembly in March 1951, during his period as Director of Education, Yara had said: 'In historical terms, too, [Okinawa] was in a pitiable state, said to have been independent at times, but subordinate to China according to some, while subordinate to Japan according to others.' On the other hand, two months later, in the petition he submitted to the Japanese government's Parliamentary Vice-Minister for Education, he requested support for Okinawa 'equal to the mainland,' writing: 'The children and students of Okinawa ... are missing their mother tongue' (Ryūkyū Seifu Bunkyō Kyoku Kenkyū Chōsa Ka 1956, pp. 92, 108). His stance of telling the mainland politicians about children 'missing their mother tongue,' while privately describing the history of 'subordination to Japan' as 'pitiable' when he was in Okinawan company, arguably included elements that could not be neatly fitted into a simple pro-reversion orientation.

In a 1968 interview, Yara spoke as follows about the sequence of events in the formation of the Kiseikai:

> During my time as Director of Education, I thought that education in Okinawa was something that should be Japan's obligation and responsibility to implement. In Okinawa, there were absolutely no prospects for the reconstruction of school buildings ... While the improvement of teachers' livelihoods was also important, because their pay was low, ... I made preparations to start a huge movement to bring Okinawan conditions to the attention of the entire mainland, publishing several tens of thousands of copies of the education newspaper. If I were going to engage in such action, though, it would not do to have a movement only for restoration of school buildings. I had to start a reversion movement. If I were going to run a reversion movement, I had to have an organisation, so in great haste I set up the Okinawa Shotō Nihon Fukki Kiseikai ... The Kiseikai at that time was a combination of four private democratic groups: the Teachers' Association at the core, along with the Council of Youth Organisations, PTA Federation, and Women's Federation. We did not include any political parties (Yara 1968a, p. 121).

This reveals the circumstances in which there was no alternative but to rely upon mainland assistance for the reconstruction of school buildings and amelioration of the treatment of teachers, and the necessity to engage in a reversion movement for that reason. The question of whether the reversion movement was perceived as a means of upgrading the educational environment aside, at least it could be said with certainty that a naïve yearning for Japan was not the sole motivation.

Apparently, the Kiseikai thus launched also received requests from political parties to be allowed to participate, but Yara reportedly tried to refuse on the rationale that 'difficulties should not be permitted to arise from differences in thinking.' In those days, it was the People's Party that touted reversion most prominently, but, as I said in Chapter Seven, Yara at that time was upholding the idea of cooperation with the U.S. military, and in 1952, also, he said that he would 'cooperate with America and firmly maintain a liberalist ideology' (Yara 1968a, p. 122; Ryūkyū Seifu Bunkyō Kyoku Kenkyū Chōsa Ka 1956, p. 121). It was probably a matter of course that if the reversion movement were one from a standpoint affording greatest weight to reform of the educational environment, then it would attempt to avoid unnecessary ideological confrontation.

Moreover, the reversion movement's demand in the 1950s was one saying that if total restoration of administrative rights were impossible, then it would be acceptable to limit it to partial restoration of executive power of the civil government sector, and especially the restoration of educational rights. In the demand which an interim council of directors on the Okinawa side submitted to the U.S. military in October 1951, when Yara was serving as Director of Education, though restoration of other administrative rights was not touched upon, an item was raised asking that 'in regard to education and culture, the Japanese government supervise, guide and assist in all aspects, in the same manner as in other prefectures.' The U.S. military's response to this was a curt one, saying that it was 'impossible to place Okinawa's Department of Education under the direct jurisdiction of the Japanese Ministry of Education, and that there was no necessity for discussion at that late stage,' but this implies that even within the reversion movement, the restoration of educational rights was emphasised from the beginning (Nakano 1969, pp. 73, 74). I reiterate that though it took the form of nostalgic yearning for the culture of the 'ancestral land,' it was something closely tied to issues such as the reconstruction of school buildings and the reform of teachers' conditions.

On the other hand, in 1954, when rebellion escalated all over Okinawa due to the land issue, the U.S. military at last embarked upon the reconstruction of school buildings. However, the disparity with the mainland, which was achieving high economic growth, did not shrink in the least. On the mainland, a principle had been established by which the salary of teachers in compulsory education was half borne by the public purse, and in the 1960s, the free distribution of textbooks and the complete implementation of school lunches was also realised. The Okinawa Teachers' Association complained that even in 1965, the rate of adequacy of school equipment was only about twenty percent of the standard set by the Japanese Ministry of Education, and teachers' actual pay was only about two-thirds of that in similar prefectures on the mainland (Fukuchi 1965, pp. 3, 25). In such circumstances, though Yara came to resign from the presidency of the Fukki Kiseikai in 1954 due to pressure from the U.S. Civil Administration, in 1960 he became the president of the newly-formed Okinawa Ken Sokoku Fukki Kyōgikai (Council for the reversion of Okinawa Prefecture to the ancestral land, or Fukkikyō), and additionally, he repeatedly petitioned the Japanese government as president of the Kyōikuhi Kakutoku Kiseikai, an association for the acquisition of educational expenses.

What is known to be a vital result of the reversion movement on the education front is the so-called Four Laws on Education which the GRI promulgated in 1958. This act, though passed by the legislature in 1956, was one that was rejected at the inclination of the U.S. Civil Administration and later only managed to reach promulgation upon its third adoption. Its major point was the insertion of the phrase 'as members of the Japanese nation' in the preamble to the Basic Law of Education. This was the only act which explicitly stated that Okinawans were 'Japanese,' both in Okinawa at that time, of course, but also on the mainland, where the administrative unit called 'Okinawa Prefecture' had ceased to exist.

It is hard to judge, however, whether this stipulation of being 'members of the Japanese nation' was fervently desired from the immediate postwar. In the Okinawa Basic Education Ordinance which was implemented prior to the Four Laws on Education, the residents who were its target were specified not as 'members of the Japanese nation,' but as 'Okinawans.' Moreover, when this ordinance was debated at the March 1951 session of the Government of the Ryukyu Islands (GRI), Yara, who was Director of Education, said in his explanation of the provisions that he had 'simply amended' the Japanese Basic Law of Education's 'members of the nation' to 'Okinawans.' Neither Yara nor any of the participants attached any comment or question to this (Ryūkyū Seifu Bunkyō Kyoku Kenkyū

Chōsa Ka 1956, pp. 92). In this GRI arena, no particular problems were seemingly perceived in adopting the stipulation of 'Okinawans.'

By the late 1950s, as the reason for seeking a definition as 'members of the Japanese nation,' there was emphasis on the spiritual significance of making explicit an awareness of being 'Japanese' in counter to U.S. military pressure. Naturally, this was probably also important, but at the same time, Kyan Shin'ei, who led the Teachers' Association and reversion movement along with Yara, stated: 'Until then, the GRI made all kinds of petitions to the Japanese government, but these were always tossed back at us. [The Japanese government] could escape on the rationale that these constituted interference in U.S. internal affairs, or that there were no laws to substantiate that Okinawa was a member of the Japanese nation.' The GRI's Basic Law came to be used as a pretext when the Japanese government gave assistance.

This stipulation appears to have been useful also in negotiations with conservative politicians from the mainland. Yara himself, for example, also succeeded in gaining public funding in 1958 negotiations for extracting aid in order to build the Teachers' Association's *Kyōsai Kaikan* (Mutual-aid meeting hall). He moved the Liberal-Democratic Party's Minister for Education by showing him the provision that extolled 'members of the Japanese nation,' and overcame the opposition of Finance Ministry bureaucrats through the influence of the Liberal-Democratic Party. Publications by the Teachers' Association in 1965 also demanded that 'the mainland government should bear even only the education supplement for those same Japanese teachers who were educating 'members of the Japanese nation' (Ōta et al. 1968, p. 65; Yara 1977, p. 61; Fukuchi 1965, p. 3). This Basic Law of Education was one in which Okinawan residents themselves – fixed by both Japan and America in a position of being 'Japanese' and not 'Japanese' – had, within the scope of their own authority, made the legal provision that they were 'Japanese,' but this was not a question merely of identity.

In this way, the Teachers' Association had consistently borne central responsibility for the reversion movement ever since its formation, but criticism towards it also lurked within Okinawan society. At the 1966 Teachers' Association educational research rally (*Kyōken*), it was reported that there was public opinion to the effect that 'the teachers' movement to do with reversion is something for the sake of getting a pension.' Furthermore, at a roundtable discussion in 1968, Ōta Masahide commented: 'As a criticism of the Teachers' Association, I often hear it said that when restoration of administrative rights has materialised, the Teachers' Association will not suffer whichever way things turn out, but there are many people in small and medium-sized businesses and so forth who are worried about various things because the economic benefit from bases will completely disappear' ('Dai 12-ji Kyōken Shūkai Shūroku' 1966, p. 11; Ōta et al. 1968, p. 69). However, such voices did not officially surface much at the time when the reversion movement was gathering steam, and the Teachers' Association side did not make a definite response to it, either.

Moreover, as a tendency of the reversion movement that was hard to eradicate, it was also a fact that the Teachers' Association often idealised the mainland. In 1967, according to an official from the mainland JTU who had visited Okinawa to have interchange with the Okinawa Teachers' Association said that a certain leader in the Teachers' Association had remarked: 'On the mainland, eighty percent of prefectural budgets constitute financial aid from government coffers, right? So if we revert, we will be able to have them give us assistance from the public purse.' This JTU official criticised this, saying: 'Certainly, it is true that in terms of wages and the like, there is a compelling battle to have these "at least equal the mainland," but there are many other aspects on the mainland, also, in which [Okinawa] must not "equal the mainland." The point that "if they reverted, things would become equal to the mainland, and all would be resolved" is given so much emphasis that I sense a danger that the mainland will give the illusion of being a rosy reality' (Kikuchi 1968, p. 26). It is unclear as to how the Okinawa Teachers' Association responded to such an opinion.

It is necessary to bear in mind, though, that such an idealisation of the mainland differed from that of the prewar. As for the Teachers' Association having become the core of the reversion movement, from the context of reflecting upon the role teachers played in turning prewar Okinawans into imperial subjects, the criticism already existed at the end of the 1960s that 'even within the reversion movement ... at the initial stage, it quite often happened that we began at the point where we said: "We want to return to Japan where His Majesty the Emperor is; we want to become able to sing the Japanese national anthem; and we want to become able to fly the *Hi-no-maru* (rising sun) flag."' As I will later discuss, it is true that due to such issues as displaying the '*Hi-no-maru*' flag, there existed some aspects which could not help being interpreted in such a way. However, in response to the question about whether there had been deep affection for the emperor in the reversion movement, Kyan Shin'ei, who led the Teachers' Association, stated: 'There was no such thing. What do you say the emperor or the crown prince did for Okinawa?' (Kinoshita et al. 1968, p. 103; Seki 1968, p. 96). As this was in an interview in 1968, when the image of the reversion movement had solidified into one of an anti-war peace movement, there may be a need to take this somewhat with a grain of salt. For a fact, however, from after the defeat through into the 1950s, no such mention of deep affection towards the emperor can be seen in reversion-movement texts written by Yara or Kyan. What they had consistently advocated was the upgrading of the educational environment through reversion.

The words: 'What do you say the emperor or the crown prince did for Okinawa?' are considered likely to have been their true sentiments from the beginning of the reversion movement. For Yara and his ilk, 'becoming Japanese' meant nothing like allegiance to the emperor, but rather their own happiness, comprising such things as the restoration of school buildings or improvement in teachers' conditions through Japanese governmental support. In the process of trying to inspire the reversion movement, however, 'becoming Japanese' began gradually to show an autotelic dimension.

The resurrection of dialect placards

There were some differences in character between the way the Teachers' Association ran the reversion movement and that of other groups. In short, this means they exerted influence upon children by means of their educational activities. In concrete terms, this was manifest in the form of fostering in children a consciousness of being 'Japanese,' and the rigorous enforcement of Standard Japanese (*hyōjungo*).

In present-day Japan, when criticism of prewar education for becoming imperial subjects has become established, it is not well known that a movement to promote Standard Japanese (*kyōtsūgo*, or 'common language') was implemented in Okinawa from the 1950s to the 1960s. It is not thought to have been carried out in postwar Okinawa because dissemination of *hyōjungo* (another term for Standard Japanese) was something had taken place in Empire of Japan times. As previously noted, the Teachers' Association's reversion movement was one that arose inseparably from the upgrading of the educational environment, and not something that aspired to a return to prewar Japan or suchlike. However, in an atmosphere where a sense of competitiveness towards America strengthened, and 'Reversion to the ancestral land' and the fostering of 'members of the Japanese nation' later became slogans, things which teachers who had been involved in education since the prewar could do were limited.

Immediately after Japan's defeat, there was also a U.S. military policy for encouragement of Okinawan language and Okinawan culture, and the use of Okinawan language was more or less free. It is not clear when this started to change into reviving the promotion of Standard Japanese. However, in the educational situation which was in a state of extreme devastation and turmoil, the tendency for teachers to find a means of escape in promoting Standard Japanese seems to have existed since immediately after the defeat. A report from a certain district states:

> Having lost the battle, having been occupied by the U.S. military and being under the U.S. military's command, supervision and protection, those whose belief in certain victory for the Japanese Army was more unshakeable fall into a worse spiritual state of bewilderment and confusion. They sometimes come to reject the path they followed in the past. From the first step of their life of confinement, they entered a world of English, and at that time of confusion when they were made to experience its necessity day after day, there was indeed both a discourse of distrust and perturbation towards the national language (*kokugo*). Actually, I have also heard voices oriented towards questioning what direction school education is heading.
>
> At that time, a directive came to Ishikawa City from high-ranking teachers ... who were worried about education, ordering us to carry out language education persistently in *hyōjungo* (meaning Japanese), and not to waver. I cannot forget how the school affairs division employees and school staff were struck by the joy of welcoming clear skies and a sense of stability.[3]

One cannot deny that amid the disturbance of values due to the defeat, a state of mind of wanting to attain 'joy and a sense of stability' at the affirmation of 'the path they followed in the past' was probably one of the factors that prompted the recommencement of encouragement of Standard Japanese. As well, in Okinawa, where the pursuit of war responsibility and the purging of public officials had been weak from the start, aided by a severe shortage of teachers, prewar teachers went on engaging in the teaching profession without any particular problems.

In some localities, it appears that 'dialect placards' the same as the prewar had already been revived at primary schools from around 1947 or 1948, but it seems to have been around 1950 that this spread to the whole of Okinawa. Moreover, in April 1951, at the second all-islands principals' meeting held in the thick of the signature-collecting campaign for reversion in advance of the Peace Talks, the 'consistently rigorous enforcement of Standard Japanese' was already listed as one of the 'priority aims for this fiscal year.'[4]

That said, at the Teachers' Association's First All-Okinawa Educational Research (*Kyōken*) Rally held in January 1955, the major topics of discussion were still such things as teachers' livelihoods, the issue of school buildings, and students' economic and academic environment. At the second Kyōken rally the following year, however, the Director of Education, Kyan Shin'ei, announced: 'The children that we are educating are by rights Japanese, and are unmistakeably young people of Japan,' and the 'ongoing daily nurturing of children who have consciousness as proper members of the Japanese nation' was touted (Kyan 1956). At the third Kyōken rally in 1957, which had come through the '*shimagurumi tōsō* (island-wide struggle [for land]),' along with an address by the President of Tokyo University, Yanaihara Tadao, who had been invited from the mainland, the issue of the promotion of Standard Japanese was much discussed.

A middle-school teacher from the Naha District, who took up this issue in a report, writes:

> It is of course necessary to remedy incorrect language or give instruction on how to speak, and schools everywhere are putting this into practice, but firstly, when all is said and done, [we need to] foster in students themselves an attitude to living of speaking in Standard Japanese anyhow, without using dialect, if it is something that they are able to say in Standard Japanese ...

> It will have no effect, though, if we simply force and urge them. However much a teacher on weekly duty tries shouting at them, it will

be only temporary, and when that teacher leaves, [the students] might be using dialect in the same way as before. The kind of instruction which makes [students] realise from the bottom of their hearts the beauty of the Japanese language, the soul that the language has, and the indescribable atmosphere that Japanese exudes, and makes them feel the joy of speaking Standard Japanese, is extremely important ('Dai 3-ji Kyōken Chūō Shūkai Kenkyū Shūroku' 1957, p. 40).

At this Kyōken rally, reports were made on a detailed fact-finding survey on the language situation in each district. According to this, even in the Naha District, where Standard Japanese would be expected to have diffused to the largest extent, middle-school students using Standard Japanese in their entire lifestyle was no greater than thirteen percent, and in the Nago District report, families within the school catchment area living their lives solely in Standard Japanese were 0.3 percent, rising to ten percent even with the addition of families which frequently used Standard Japanese. 'Because I can't speak it fluently,' 'Because most of my friends use dialect,' and 'I take care, but dialect slips out unintentionally' were often given as the 'reason for inability to enforce Standard Japanese rigorously,' and others listed include: 'Because my friends laugh,' 'Because I don't want to use Standard Japanese,' and so on ('Dai 3-ji Kyōken Chūō Shūkai Kenkyū Shūroku' 1957, pp. 39, 15, 40).

Teachers' attention was directed not only at Okinawan, but also towards the remediation of 'incorrect language' in which Standard Japanese vocabulary was wrongly used. Examples cited as being incorrect language included ones like: 'Sharpen a pencil = *Enpitsu o togu* (~*kezuru* in Standard Japanese),' 'Put up an umbrella = *Kasa o kaburu* (~*sasu*),' but there were also numerous subtle inclusions whose 'wrongful usage' was in doubt, such as 'Get out of the way = *Dokinasai* (*Yokenasai*),' or 'Play a record = *Chikuonki narasu* ('Cause the gramophone to make sound') (Standard Japanese: *Rekōdo o kakeru*).' In regard to methods of instruction, as well as making effort charts and charts for correcting pronunciation, such examples were reported as, for example, making students resolve at class meetings to 'warn each other in cases where they have used incorrect language, and correct each other on the spot,' 'In the homeroom period, daily monitors announce those people who used incorrect language and those who corrected it,' 'At daily review sessions, committee members gather [examples] and make charts,' as 'I make printed handouts as occasion calls and notify families, seeking cooperation regarding elimination of incorrect language' ('Dai 3-ji Kyōken Chūō Shūkai Kenkyū Shūroku' 1957, pp. 26, 28, 49).

The promotion was not only done in schools, but was also undertaken by teachers towards the local community. In Kyōken rally reports can be seen such expressions as: 'The reason that many students have given for not being able to enforce Standard Japanese rigorously is that the people with whom they talk use dialect, but to remove this obstacle, we teachers must plan and give guidance so as to create a mood of Standard Japanese usage among everyone in their group or living environment,' or 'In the countryside, where use of dialect is frequent, those who stand on the front line of language instruction are the teachers.' Furthermore, such views from parents and guardians as: 'Even at home, everyone has come to speak Standard Japanese, and I feel so happy that light has shone into the house,' and 'Recently, I have decided not to sell things to people who come shopping in dialect, and when they use incorrect words, I make them wait until they say them correctly' were introduced ('Dai 3-ji Kyōken Chūō Shūkai Kenkyū Shūroku' 1957, pp. 40, 15; 'Dai 4-kai Kyōiku Kenkyū Taikai Kenkyū Shūroku' 1958b, pp. 60, 61).

The use of 'dialect placards,' also, was reported at Kyōken rallies. Cases were introduced in which this was abandoned, however, when 'the class [developed] a gloomy feeling,' and there were many that were ranked as 'not good methods' because 'there emerged some dual-personality-like, two-faced children such as would check the whereabouts of dialect placards, and, when there was no risk of being handed one, use dialect.' In a report on a questionnaire on instruction methods targeting students, among examples of methods which had a bad reputation, dialect placards were listed alongside such ones as: 'making people who used dialect do cleaning,' or 'making those who used dialect come to the front and face everyone' ('Dai 4-kai Kyōiku Kenkyū Taikai Kenkyū Shūroku' 1958a, p. 19; 1958b, p. 36; 'Dai 3-ji Kyōken Chūō Shūkai Kenkyū Shūroku' 1957, p. 30). That said, even though it was not recognised as a reputable system, it still can be inferred that dialect placards were used for the encouragement of Standard Japanese.

According to Arasaki Moriteru, 'dialect placards existed in all localities until about the mid-1960s, in other words, until 1965, when the Japanese government adopted a reversion policy.' Arasaki further states: 'I have the feeling that the [1940] dialect debate was accepted as having a connection with education for becoming imperial subjects because reversion to Japan had drawn near' (Tsuitō Bunshū Kankō Iinkai 1990, p. 339). As I will later elaborate, when reversion became a reality and people awoke from their overblown dreams, exorbitant aspirations towards assimilation to the Japanese mainland also cooled. In this period, the Okinawan language debate which I mentioned in Chapter Four came to attract attention as something which symbolised the repression of Okinawan languages by the Empire of Japan. As reports related to the rigorous enforcement of Standard Japanese were made at Kyōken rallies of the Okinawa Teachers' Association until 1966, they could be said to conform more or less to Arasaki's testimony.

Even so, how did the atmosphere of postwar democratic education attune with the promotion of Standard Japanese, which was reminiscent of the prewar? In a Kyōken rally report, there was the view that the encouragement of Standard Japanese 'was effective in making [students] do things autonomously, in partnership with the student association,' and it can be appreciated that such 'democratic' methods were being explored for. In addition, something that sheds light on how Standard Japanese and 'democracy' were tied together among teachers is the following text recorded by a middle-school teacher at the 1957 Kyōken rally:

> For human beings to have the power to express their own thoughts and opinions freely, and to live in a society where that is actually carried out is a great happiness; and by doing so, democratic societies come into existence.
>
> More than that, when we look at the linguistic life of the students in our charge, it is in a state where they have not firmly equipped themselves even with Standard Japanese, which should perhaps be called its basis, and the errors in Standard Japanese which come from a double life with the dialect are enormous. Besides, honing it into beautiful language is the emphasis of our instruction from now on ...
>
> I set up this topic [=the rigorous enforcement of Standard Japanese] as it is thought that being able freely and spontaneously to listen to and speak what [one] thinks also forms the basis for the smooth expansion of learning in all subjects, and it is the urgent business of school education in respect to adaptability after they emerge into society, as well ('Dai 3-ji Kyōken Chūō Shūkai Kenkyū Shūroku' 1957, pp. 40, 39).

'Being able freely and spontaneously to listen to and speak what [one] thinks' is the foundation of democracy, and they promote Standard Japanese for that reason. Such a view also arose from other teachers. A certain primary-school teacher from Nago District, for one, explained the necessity for Standard Japanese, saying: 'If their spoken language is impaired, then they cannot declare their own intentions, either, and cannot make an active human being. That is why I want to create the kind of children who can light-heartedly address anybody, anytime, anywhere, and to raise them to be cheerful children.' A report from Hentona District also cited encouragement of Standard Japanese, expressing a wish to 'create enjoyable classes where [students] can say anything they have thought.' On the other hand, in reports from each locality, issue was made of a situation having developed where students 'avoid being spoken to,' 'their speech is unintelligible,' 'they do talk, but are faint-hearted and lack self-confidence,' and so on ('Dai 3-ji Kyōken Chūō Shūkai Kenkyū Shūroku' 1957, pp. 27, 22, 21; 'Dai 4-kai Kyōiku Kenkyū Taikai Kenkyū Shūroku' 1958a, p. 18). However, there were no opinions that deemed these to be an adverse effect of the thorough enforcement of Standard Japanese, and on the contrary, they were seen as problems that would be resolved if students mastered Standard Japanese.

It is not that teachers were implementing such a campaign with the intention of mistreating students. Far from it – it can be inferred that this campaign was thought to be an expression of affection towards students. In rally reports, there could be seen many such voices as: 'It is necessary for teachers to catch even slightly incorrect language and irregular language with loving ears, not failing to hear it, and giving guidance and compliments filled with warm kindness,' and 'I want to set my eyes upon each child individually, and raise them splendidly, equipping them adequately for the future.' Of course, at Kyōken rallies, too, there were some minority opinions such as: 'In our excessive haste to teach Standard Japanese, we must not make children's attitude to speech wither,' but more frequent views were such things as: 'There are people who worry that when we rigorously enforce Standard Japanese, we perhaps impose a feeling of inferiority upon students, or become servile, but students do not think so,' 'Rather, it is conjectured that a feeling of inferiority will arise due to their being unable to use Standard Japanese adequately after they go out into society, and that is precisely what is a big problem' ('Dai 4-kai Kyōiku Kenkyū Taikai Kenkyū Shūroku' 1958b, p. 36; 'Dai 3-ji Kyōken Chūō Shūkai Kenkyū Shūroku' 1957, pp. 22, 12, 40).

It is obvious that the phrase 'children who can light-heartedly address anybody,' which teachers are stating here as an ideal, is premised on their being able to speak in Standard Japanese. In their local area, Standard Japanese was almost never used, and the teachers also must have been well aware that there was nobody whom students could 'address' in Standard Japanese. Nonetheless, an imagined 'ancestral land' and 'mainland' solemnly existed as a goal at which to aim in teachers' minds.

For Teachers' Association officials, including Yara, the repeated chants of 'ancestral land' and 'members of the Japanese nation' in the reversion movement did not necessarily mean cultural assimilation, and it was probably perceived to a certain extent that these were also a strategy for the upgrading of the educational environment. For teachers at the chalk-face, however, aiming for an educational environment 'to equal the mainland' for which they yearned was linked to aiming 'to equal the mainland' in terms of language and awareness, as well.

The promotion of the '*Hi-no-maru*' and '*Kimi-ga-yo*'

Through this kind of encouragement campaign for Standard Japanese, the Okinawa Teachers' Association set up a new 'national education branch' from the ninth Kyōken rally in 1963, and launched a 'national education campaign.' It is necessary first to make some mention of the mainland Nikkyōso's attitude in relation to this.

It was in 1961 that the mainland Nikkyōso newly established a branch for 'national education (*kokumin kyōiku*)' at its own Kyōken rally. This movement was one which succeeded the 1960 heightening of conflict over the U.S.–Japan Mutual Security Treaty (AMPO) in the previous year, and was launched in order to raise children's consciousness of being 'members of the Japanese nation,' in line with the ideas of progressive nationalism. It was the historian Uehara Senroku that delivered a speech on the notion of a national education campaign at this Nikkyōso Kyōken rally.

As stated in the previous chapter, based on the premise that 'the Japanese' had had sparse 'national consciousness' since the beginning of the 1950s, Uehara advocated smashing the pervasive egoism of the younger generation, making them have an awareness of being a 'national community,' and making them rise to struggle against the United States. An enthusiastic educator, Uehara made speeches at Kyōken rallies in each location from the 19050s into the early 1960s, and according to him, education by means of 'democracy in an American-style form' which had been adopted in the postwar accelerated the rampancy of egoism and atomisation due to its emphasis solely upon individual freedom, and he argued that the 'issues of formation of national consciousness and the cultivation of patriotism had been almost forgotten in "new education" (free democratic-type education introduced under the U.S. military Occupation).' Standing upon such an acknowledgement, he declared: '"National education" takes as its general objective the creation of "nationals" as the subjects of action and responsibility who can elevate contemporary Japan into a tightly-knit nation (*minzoku*) with independence and autonomy vis-à-vis all the worlds apart from itself, and makes the realisation of that objective its general agenda' (Uehara 1987–97, vol. 7, p. 47; vol. 14, p. 17).

In discussion on nationalism in recent years, so-called 'postwar democracy' is sometimes said to have solely stressed modern individual liberation and despised the creation of 'the Japanese' as subjects of action and responsibility towards the international and domestic situations. That is a misapprehension, however, and postwar leftists enthused over the topic of 'national independence (*minzoku no dokuritsu*).' Nikkyōso's national education movement had expanded this to the classroom.

As was usual in progressive nationalism, though, Uehara lays emphasis upon the differences between the national education movement and prewar education. As previously mentioned in Chapter Eight, according to Uehara, in prewar Japanese education, not only was there 'replacement of what constituted national (*minzoku*) consciousness with state (*kokka*) consciousness,' but it descended into a narrow-minded national particularism which lacked international solidarity. The new national education movement had to be one that deepened solidarity with Asian and African nations which were fighting Western imperialism, including that of America, and with the democratic force of the world. To that end, he said, education had to be implemented that differentiated between the prewar, emperor-centric 'state-manufactured patriotism' and genuine national consciousness, and emphasised Japan's independence and peace (Uehara and Munakata 1952, p. 135; Uehara 1987–97: vol. 7, p. 10).

The model for Uehara's 'national education' was the nationalism of Germany's classical period and dawn of the nineteenth century, which was his speciality. While commending the way Johann Gottlieb Fichte and Heinrich Von Kleist had faced the people and expounded patriotism for rebuilding the fatherland in Germany at the beginning of the nineteenth century, which was a land defeated in the Napoleonic Wars, Uehara criticised postwar Japan's 'sò-called "new education"' for 'lacking Fichte's preparedness which aimed to raise children into members of the nation (*minzoku*).'[5] In his well-known speeches entitled: 'Addresses to the German Nation,' Fichte spoke of the conception of national education (*Nationalerziehung*), and it is surmised that Uehara was influenced by this. In Japan at that time, not only Uehara, but people like Nanbara Shigeru also displayed a strong sympathy with Fichte, and among the general education they had acquired, Fichte's ideas looked to be the most compatible with Japan immediately after its defeat. Moreover, both Uehara and Nanbara were trying to inspire patriotism in the 'nationals' of Japan, a defeated country, while stressing the difference between Nazi racism and Fichte's love for his fatherland.

In line with such ideas, the mainland Nikkyōso launched its national education movement, and, as stated above, it was from the 1963 Kyōken rally that the Okinawa Teachers' Association established its national education branch, so this was clearly something inspired by the mainland Nikkyōso. Laid out in the branch report of this rally, also, is the wording: '[On the mainland,] democratic education has come to be called national education' (Okinawa Kyōshokuinkai 1963, p. 35). However, the fear that confusion would arise in the national education movement between the 'state-manufactured patriotism' which Uehara criticised and national consciousness did exist as a problematic issue shared with progressive nationalism. Speaking in terms of the outcome, that problem ended up actualising on a larger scale in Okinawa, a typical example being its response to the '*Hi-no-maru*' flag and '*Kimi-ga-yo*' anthem.

The '*Hi-no-maru*,' a red circle on a white background, became Japan's national flag from Meiji onwards, but until 1999 it had no legal endorsement. '*Kimi-ga-yo*,' in turn, means 'His Majesty's era,' and was composed in the Meiji era as an anthem praising the imperial house; but it, too, was not designated by law as the national anthem until 1999. The circumstances were that under 1930s military domination, every household was requested to purchase and display a '*Hi-no-maru*,' and whenever there was occasion for it, '*Kimi-ga-yo*' was required to be sung. For that reason, the flag and anthem tended to be shunned in the postwar by intellectuals, labour unions, teachers and the like. The mainland Nikkyōso, in particular, carried out a campaign in opposition to the Ministry of Education having compelled the use of the '*Hi-no-maru*' and '*Kimi-ga-yo*' at schools.

In actuality, behind the mainland Nikkyōso having started a national education movement there lay a backlash against the Ministry of Education having made the '*Kimi-ga-yo*' into compulsory teaching material from primary school in its government-approved curriculum. In other words, Nikkyōso's national education movement involved a context of organising the people's nationalism in line with the progressive side, in opposition to the Ministry of Education. In the case of the Okinawa Teachers' Association, however, there were circumstances in which it was difficult to assume a totally oppositional stance, as it had undertaken all kinds of petitions to the mainland's Ministry of Education and conservative politicians. For that reason, as well, the Ministry of Education's policy of making the '*Hi-no-maru*' and '*Kimi-ga-yo*' compulsory came to be mixed together with Nikkyōso's progressive nationalism under the term 'national education.'

In addition, there was also the question of the delicate position of the '*Hi-no-maru*' in postwar Okinawa. Since the defeat, the raising of any national flag except that of the United States was forbidden all over Okinawa, and though the raising of another flag was partially allowed along with Peace Treaty coming into effect in April 1952, it was still banned at public institutions or assemblies. Naturally, this was an act of suppression against the reversion movement's sudden surge in popularity. Ironically, the '*Hi-no-maru*' became established as a symbol of the reversion movement and of anti-Americanism for that reason. In fact, photographs from those days show that the '*Hi-no-maru*' was almost unfailingly flown at anti-base campaign and reversion movement rallies from the 1950s to the early 1960s.

On New Year's Day, 1953, the displaying of the Japanese flag was permitted at private homes and private gatherings alone, within the bounds of non-involvement of any political implication. One teacher recalls the scene at that time, saying: 'The hoisting of the *Hi-no-*

maru was permitted only on 1 January. It was pleasant, so pleasant, that nobody took it down.' Kyan Shin'ei, in turn, remarked: 'The Civil Administration building had the Stars and Stripes, while our [=the Teachers' Association] meeting hall had the *Hi-no-maru*. It was truly a pleasant sight' (Seki 1968, pp. 99, 100). The Teachers' Association implemented the flying of the '*Hi-no-maru*' at schools, purchasing a large quantity of the flags from the mainland and distributing to every home and school. There was a succession of warnings from the U.S. military about schools displaying the flag, but as a result of talks in 1961 between Prime Minister Ikeda Hayato and President Kennedy, it was decided that the hoisting of the '*Hi-no-maru*' would be permitted even at public institutions such as schools only on Japanese and 'Ryukyu' public holidays and the first three days of January.

A report by a newspaper reporter who visited from the mainland in 1961 introduced Okinawa's 'treatment of the "*Hi-no-maru*" which would have been somewhat unimagined on the mainland.' It conveyed such news as the Teachers' Association having sold every last one of 10,000 '*Hi-no-maru*' flags, the walls of the headquarters of the supposedly ultra-left-wing People's Party being 'plastered with *Hi-no-maru*,' and the red flag and *Hi-no-maru* having been 'companionably displayed on the same pole at a certain bus workers' union office.' When Yara Chōbyō attended Kyōken rallies held by the mainland Nikkyōso, which showed opposition to the '*Hi-no-maru*,' he reportedly asserted that the campaign for the flying of the *Hi-no-maru* was 'the cry of those who, placed under the domination of a different people, desire to break away' (*Asahi jānaru* 1961, p. 6, 7; Yara 1977, p. 48).

As the U.S. military regarded the reversion movement as a campaign solely run by Communists, it would be no mystery for a custom to arise among members of the Okinawan side who opposed the U.S. military to see the '*Hi-no-maru*' and red flag as similar things in the space that such a gaze created. The problem was, however, that like the word 'Japanese,' '*Hi-no-maru*' also had a different sense in the mainland camp, and through the medium that comprised the national flag, it was difficult for a meaning that differed from resistance to the U.S. American military to flow into the Teachers' Association, as well. Those circumstances can be inferred from Kyōken rally reports from about 1963 to 1966, which could be called the heyday of Okinawa's national education campaign.

One thing that was widely implemented in Okinawa's national education movement was children's awareness surveys. The list of items included: 'Is there a national flag (*Hi-no-maru*) in your house?' 'Do you fly the national flag at your house on national holidays?' and 'Do you like the *Kimi-ga-yo* song?' and basically, a policy was stated saying that 'a plan of instruction should be set up to nurture national sentiment from the early years of primary school through the familiar '*Hi-no-maru*' and '*Kimi-ga-yo*.' A survey in the Koza district criticised the fact that homes possessing a '*Hi-no-maru*' remained at around sixty percent, saying: 'Instruction should be given that every home should purchase one without fail,' and the Yomitan–Kadena branch, too, assessed the fact that ninety percent of children harboured deep emotion towards the '*Hi-no-maru*' as being 'a problem in which the national consciousness of the remaining ten percent should be a concern.' In other cases, in Yaeyama district, the survey made an issue of 'a total of fifty-two percent of children not knowing [*Kimi-ga-yo*] to be the Japanese national anthem,' and concluded that: 'huge effort and many days will probably be needed in order to make all students, young and old, aware that it is something to be sung from an upwelling of national consciousness and state sentiment.' Further, 'educational *tonarigumi* (neighbourhood associations)' were created in every district for guidance, and were utilised for the promotion of the flying of the '*Hi-no-maru*' (Okinawa Kyōshokuinkai 1965, pp. 27, 63, 81, 33, 100, 37, 38). *Tonarigumi* had been the smallest organisational units when nationals were organised in wartime Japan, and were utilised for such purposes as rationing, mobilisation, and so on.

In the abovementioned survey, items which were always present alongside those about the flag and anthem were the questions: 'What nationality are you?' and 'What country does Okinawa belong to?' In most districts, over ninety percent of respondents answered that they were 'Japanese,' and responses saying that Okinawa was Japanese territory were in the eightieth percentile (respondents answering that it was American territory being around ten percent) but efforts towards a 100-percent response were demanded. In Yaeyama district, in particular, where answers saying they were 'Japanese' stopped at sixty-seven percent, criticism of this 'truly sad response' said that 'in the former colony of Taiwan, its residents, both adults and children, apparently thought of themselves first as Taiwanese and then as members of the Japanese nation, and, though it could perhaps not be said to be completely the same, it is alarming that at both primary schools and middle schools, nearly thirty percent of students still cannot definitely reply that they are members of the Japanese nation' (Okinawa Kyōshokuinkai 1965, pp. 27, 36).

In addition to the encouragement of the '*Hi-no-maru*' and '*Kimiga-yo*,' modification of historical perspective was also carried out for cultivation of 'Japanese' consciousness. In Koza district, the report cited the 'idea that the Ryukyuans of eighty years ago did not think of themselves as Japanese' as being one of the 'things hindering reversion to Japan,' and the Yaeyama district's report placed emphasis on teaching children that 'Okinawan prefectural residents are Japanese, and the dialect which they use is a regional dialect of Japanese.' In addition, it encouraged the use of 'ancestral land (*sokoku*)' rather than 'Japan,' and 'prefectural residents' rather than 'Okinawans' as everyday terms; a campaign to have Okinawa inserted into the maps of Japan issued by mainland publishing houses was implemented; and it was insisted that the words 'Okinawa Prefecture' be inscribed in correspondence with the mainland. Of course, at that time, 'Okinawa Prefecture' did not exist as an administrative unit, but in order to make children aware of the 'prefecture,' making them check in their *koseki shōhon* (abstract of the family register) – the sole official document in which the word 'prefecture' was inscribed – was encouraged. In the cultural aspect, also, such objectives as the cultivation of an 'attitude of protecting and nurturing Japan's beautiful traditions and culture,' the 'promotion of Standard Japanese' and the 'reform of manners and customs' were listed (Okinawa Kyōshokuinkai 1965, pp. 66, 48, 43; 'Dai 13-ji Kyōken Shūkai Shūroku' 1967, p. 39). Even at that juncture, twenty-five years after Yanagi Sōetsu's assertions, Okinawan language and 'manners and customs' were not regarded as part of 'Japan's beautiful traditions and culture.'

Naturally, this does not mean that there were no expressions of doubt as to a national education campaign of this kind. In particular, there was also some confusion about the way to advance a movement that differed from the mainland Nikkyōso, and in reports on Kyōken rallies, too, such views emerged as: 'The unification of ideological trends with a central focus on the national flag must not be attempted, nor must its being used as a slogan for unification such as the Japanese spirit.' On the other hand, however, in reports from other districts on the result of a questionnaire that was implemented, asking: 'If the Emperor or Crown Prince were to come to Okinawa, what would you think?' the fact that respondents who replied: 'I would be delighted' was limited to eighty percent at primary schools and sixty-six percent at middle schools was taken to be 'a problematic issue that required attention.' Determination of what constituted the patriotism that should be aimed for in the movement was wavering, and even in the summing-up of the plenary session at the eleventh Kyōken rally held in January 1965, it was said that 'we have not reached the point of working out a unified, fixed policy' (Okinawa Kyōshokuinkai 1965, pp. 13, 77, 80, 1; 'Dai 12-ji Kyōken Shūkai Shūroku' 1966, p. 18).

There does not seem to have been any opposition expressed in any of the districts to promoting the display of the '*Hi-no-maru*,' but given that it involved the emperor, it does appear that debate wavered about '*Kimi-ga-yo*.' In material which the Teachers' Association published in 1962, arguments that had emerged from the Association for and against the handling of '*Kimi-ga-yo*' were introduced. Opinions opposed to its promotion included: 'it is glorification of the emperor,' 'a supporting pillar for militarism,' and 'there should be a public appeal for a new national anthem,' but opinions in favour constituted the following five:

1. It can raise consciousness as members of the Japanese nation, and foster an earnest desire for reversion.
2. We are placed in a position where we have to teach it because it also appears in textbooks.
3. Freely hoisting the *Hi-no-maru* is our cry; and singing the national anthem is also for the same reason.
4. '*Kimi-ga-yo*' has been sung for a long time as the national anthem, and in all foreign countries it is played as the national anthem at the Olympic Games and when entertaining dignitaries from Japan.
5. It would be extremely shameful if it seemed that [we] could not sing the *Kimi-ga-yo* at various events on the mainland (*Okinawa kyōiku* 1962, p. 20).

This implies a situation in which a desire for reversion, resistance to the U.S. military, obedience to the Ministry of Education, a warped orientation towards 'the mainland,' and so on, are intertwined.

At Kyōken rallies, as well, there was internal criticism of the 'uncritical importation of the mainland's reactionary education policy, with the idea that everything should be equivalent to the mainland.' In this 1962 material, however, even while laying out the pros and cons of '*Kimi-ga-yo*' side by side in this manner, it concluded: 'Given the real situation in which Okinawa is placed, it is considered that we should teach and have [students] sing it.' Here, though, there were conditions attached, namely: 'It would be troublesome if it were taught using the kind of ultra-nationalist way of thinking we were taught in the prewar,' and 'the teachers themselves who teach must give correct instruction from the standpoint of a new national consciousness.' There were no clear-cut indications as to what sort of thing that 'new national consciousness' might be, however (Okinawa Kyōshokuinkai 1963, p. 40; *Okinawa kyōiku* 1962, p. 20).

At the January 1966 Kyōken rally, there was debate on the '*Kimi-ga-yo*' issue. In the debate, such opinions emerged as: 'On the mainland, it is being used as a symbol of right-wing power,' and 'Doesn't a new democratic state need a suitable national anthem?' but in the end, the only conclusion to be presented was that '[we want teachers] to leave the *Kimi-ga-yo* as it is in the interim, and to go back to their schools and do more research on the matter' ('Dai 12-ji Kyōken Shūkai Shūroku' 1966, pp. 20, 21).

In this atmosphere, reports from each locality showed disjointed reactions. One participating teacher said: '[I] run a campaign to popularise a national song (*kokumin no uta*) in place of the state anthem, *Kimi-ga-yo*,' while another claimed to be 'teaching from a qualitatively different position from that of the mainland's *Kimi-ga-yo* debate,' and yet another requested a 'more clear-cut conclusion.' Some changes of interpretation which were being implemented in multiple districts included: 'I think it is all right not to force a link between the '*kimi* (you/lord/prince)' in '*Kimi-ga-yo*' with 'the Emperor,' but rather to understand it as meaning that 'nations should mutually accept their respective sovereignty' or 'I want to interpret it as a just and upright reign that is good' ('Dai 12-ji Kyōken Shūkai Shūroku' 1966, pp. 57, 21; Okinawa Kyōshokuinkai 1965, p. 73). This was a measure of last resort for satisfying the contradictory demands of saying that a national anthem was necessary while being conscious of the criticism that it was glorification of the emperor.

At this 1966 Kyōken rally, while on the one hand awareness surveys asking students: 'Are you Japanese?' were conducted as usual, one district reported on an awareness survey of teachers. According to this, eighty-eight percent of teachers in the district responded that the fostering of patriotism was necessary, while ten percent replied that they 'somehow or other felt resistance.' Similarly, eighty-six percent answered 'Yes' to the question of whether they could 'sing "*Kimi-ga-yo*" with pride as their national anthem,' and twelve percent said they 'somehow or other felt resistance.' On the other hand, though, only fifty-eight percent of teachers replied that they actively taught children '*Kimi-ga-yo*' as the national anthem, which implied that teachers were at a loss ('Dai 12-ji Kyōken Shūkai Shūroku' 1966, p. 71).

In some localities, however, the diffusion of the '*Hi-no-maru*' and '*Kimi-ga-yo*' was absolute. In a newspaper report of January 1966, at a Teachers' Association branch meeting in a certain district, when one teacher announced that he or she was not teaching '*Kimi-ga-yo*' as the national anthem because it was a song of emperor-worship, criticism reportedly 'emerged from many participants,' to the tune that it was a 'grave problem for a teacher to bring in her or his personal biased way of thinking and not teach [the song] in the educational arena, arguing that it is not the national anthem.' At Kyōken rallies, an atmosphere redolent of the prewar was fomented in some parts, reports being made that included: 'Posture, especially, must be kept in mind when singing '*Kimi-ga-yo*,' and I make [students] stand to attention while singing it,' and 'I take special care in the handling of miniature (paper) '*Hi-no-maru*' flags, and I give detailed instruction even as far as how to treat them before and after' (*Okinawa taimusu* 1966; 'Dai 12-ji Kyōken Shūkai Shūroku' 1966, pp. 57, 56).

The coexistence of yearning and rejection

Nevertheless, even given its grounds in the reversion movement, why did a national education movement like this gather momentum?

In Kyōken rally reports there could be seen such language as: 'For us Okinawan prefectural residents, the '*Hi-no-maru*' is a symbol of education, a symbol of freedom, a symbol of reversion, and a symbol of resistance,' or 'The idea of peace must not be cosmopolitanism without a nation (*minzoku*), but must to the bitter end be an international spirit based upon an ancestral land,' which suggests that progressive nationalist thought from the mainland was clearly tied to Okinawan conditions. At the same time, reports that made Ministry of Education guidance into grounds for the promotion of the '*Hi-no-maru*' were also seen, and this, too, seems to have been one of the factors ('Dai 12-ji Kyōken Shūkai Shūroku' 1966, p. 56; Okinawa Kyōshokuinkai 1965, pp. 68, 71). How might teachers' feelings have been, though, apart from such superficial factors?

Firstly, the thing that was consistently present in teachers was an awareness of disparity with the mainland. At Kyōken rallies, such views as: 'We call for substantial assistance from the mainland government in order urgently to consolidate the upgrading of all educational conditions to equal the mainland' were presented from every district, and the president's address to the rally also spoke of 'impatiently crying out for a standard to match the mainland, but in the meantime, mainland education is steadily continuing to advance with a speed greater than Okinawa's. In this way, the gap will only widen further' (cited in Kaminuma 1966, p. 60). The orientation towards assimilation to 'the Japanese' spawned from impatience for equality was one that had seized teachers throughout both the pre- and postwar (Okinawa Kyōshokuinkai 1963, p. 83).

The inferior feeling that the upkeep of the educational environment was lagging behind the mainland was also linked to a feeling of inferiority in academic terms, namely that 'the children of Okinawa have extremely low scholastic ability. They are by far the worst, still lower than the worst of Japan's prefectures.' At the 1963 Kyōken rally, following after words to the effect that due to the disparity in academic ability, Okinawan students had 'ended up being naturally implanted with an extremely great feeling of inferiority in comparison with people from the mainland,' it was said that 'all the same, it is necessary to make them conscious of being Japanese' (Okinawa Kyōshokuinkai 1963, pp. 43, 44). Teachers harboured a sense of responsibility, wanting to resolve that situation by means of a national education campaign to nurture 'Japanese' to 'mainland standard,' based on the recognition that the reason for Okinawan scholastic achievement not reaching 'mainland level' was that they could not develop the educational environment to 'mainland standard' for students' sake.

Certainly, at that time, the average score in Okinawan students' scholastic achievement tests was lower than that of the mainland. However, although the inferiority of the educational environment was also to blame, it had already been pointed out in some quarters that the burden of education in two languages, Okinawan and Standard Japanese, was the cause. In one particular survey, the result was shown that the measured intelligence of Okinawan children was high in non-verbal tests, but low in verbal tests compiled on the mainland. However, there were no reports at Kyōken rallies that were aware of such a thing, and it was regarded rather that 'academic ability would naturally improve when [children] became able to speak Standard Japanese' (Kaminuma 1966, p. 112; 'Dai 4-kai Kyōiku Kenkyū Taikai Kenkyū Shūroku' 1958b, p. 40).

The logic seen in the abovementioned utterances, namely, overcoming children's 'sense of inferiority' by making them 'conscious of being Japanese,' was of the same mould as the logic that they would be children who could talk in a bright, lively manner if they learned Standard Japanese. At the 1963 Kyōken rally, it was declared that 'when cultivating members of the Japanese nation in Okinawa, it is especially important that they have the self-confidence befitting Japanese nationals. Speaking from a reverse perspective, this means doing away with their feeling of inferiority' (Okinawa Kyōshokuinkai 1963, p. 18).

Yet, as seen in Chapter Five, Okinawan residents could not legally be called 'Japanese.' They neither had the right to vote in Japanese national politics, nor the human rights which ought to have been guaranteed by the Japanese constitution. The national education campaign could be called a movement for the acquisition of rights as 'Japanese' by making becoming 'Japanese' in cultural and identity aspects take the lead, so to speak, but even if they were to gain an awareness of being 'Japanese,' there was no assurance at all that the Japanese government would bestow any rights. As teachers, they did perceive the contradiction in making children who could not be called 'Japanese' in terms of rights have consciousness of being 'Japanese,' but the campaign was advanced even while allowing such anxiety to lie dormant.

At the 1965 Kyōken rally, a report from the Yaeyama district said:

> ... It is natural that people in their right mind should feel anger at how prefectural residents who are not protected by the Japanese Constitution could state definitively that they are true members of the Japanese nation ... And yet, undeniably we are each absolutely a member of the Japanese nation. Based on this thought, unless we adults implement national education as proper Japanese in this generation, in the next generation they will have to continue the same doubts and worries as we have. Moreover, in the event that administrative rights are restored, which is the dearest wish of the

people (*minzoku*), if there should happen to be a large gap between prefectural residents' national consciousness as true Japanese, or misalignment in national culture, or suchlike, then the suspicious eye of mainland compatriots and discriminatory treatment will probably be unavoidable (Okinawa Kyōshokuinkai 1963, p. 44).

Teachers were placed in a position where, even if they had some anxiety about acquiring rights as 'Japanese,' or, rather, precisely because they *did* have some, they had to say they were 'undeniably ... a member of the Japanese nation.'

That described here as 'the dearest wish of the people (*minzoku*)' no longer referred to 'the Okinawan people (*minzoku*),' but had come to mean what was termed in progressive nationalism as 'the Japanese people (*minzoku*),' which included Okinawa. Of course, in the national education movement for fostering self-awareness as 'Japanese,' an expression such as 'the Okinawan people (*minzoku*)' was taboo. When discussing the relationship between Okinawa and the mainland, too, in a Kyōken rally report, it had come to be expressed in terms of: 'We unfortunately have created a consciousness of inferiority towards our own group [=Okinawa] as opposed to our nation (*minzoku*) [= Japanese], but we do not want our children, least of all, to be the victims of a consciousness of inferiority' (Okinawa Kyōshokuinkai 1963, p. 63).

However, the mainland was not the only opposite number towards which they had to overcome a 'consciousness of inferiority.' Rather, what was even larger than that was America, their direct ruler. In 1961 the following text, entitled: 'Are we Japanese, regardless of this?' was carried in the class newspaper of a primary school on Iriomote Island.

> Lately, America has come to Iriomote for jungle warfare exercises ... This means that the children who gather there ... follow after the American troops, and when [the Americans] toss them bread or chocolate they gleefully eat it like hungry, skinny dogs. This being the case, it cannot be helped if they are mocked as being not human beings, but the offspring of dogs. Without enough courage to kick it away, saying that this kind of thing is not what Japanese that are human beings eat, we will not be able to shoulder responsibility for Japan from here forward. We are fine members of the Japanese nation. We do not want to be mocked ... We are children of Japan who will make

a peaceful Japan. Not forgetting that we have been mocked as being 'dogs,' let us apply the spurs to our hearts and advance straight ahead, as honourable members of the Japanese nation (Nihon Kyōshokuin Kumiai and Okinawa Kyōshokuinkai 1970, p. 135).

The state of mind in which people who were pushed to the brink by U.S. military pressure had no choice but to rely upon an identity that comprised being 'Japanese' is revealed here. The teacher who introduced this class newspaper said: 'Their Japaneseness will progressively be lost if things go on this way. In education for being Japanese (*Nihonjin kyōiku*), thinking that we had to protect and nurture the children's spirits, at no time did we forget the word 'Japanese (*Nihonjin*),'' and added that from the motivation that 'mothers are the maternal bodies that bear and raise the members of the nation who form the state,' he or she boosted the national education campaign while enlightening local women (Nihon Kyōshokuin Kumiai and Okinawa Kyōshokuinkai 1970, pp. 133, 135).

Amid such American oppression, the 'Kanakas,' who had once been the target of discrimination, were similarly sketched as being victims of the U.S. Around 1960, a certain Okinawan university student demanded: 'Who can guarantee that Okinawan prefectural residents will not pursue a similar sad fate as the Hawai'ian Kanakas who died out under American rule?' and claimed 'to give children self-awareness and pride as Japanese' was 'the most important thing' (Kaminuma 1966, p. 3). Here can be seen a variation of the prewar ranking schema of Japan > Okinawa > Kanaka.

In the abovementioned Iriomote Island class newspaper, the 'Japan' as a basis for standing up to the U.S. military was taken to be the postwar, 'peaceful Japan,' but for the generation that had received prewar education, that was not necessarily so. Again around 1960, one member of the prewar generation said:

Sometimes, more than anyone, when I hear martial songs, the *Kimi-ga-yo*, and the like, I feel something nostalgic. Even now there are occasions when I think it regrettable that we lost the war to America. Of course, in its age of being a military nation, Japan cold-bloodedly killed many innocent people in other countries. As the thing which supported that was education, and the *Kimi-ga-yo* and other martial songs, I believe I have rejected them, but, regrettably, they sometimes pop out. When the weak felt resistance to a colossal power, what they sought was not postwar democratic education, but militaristic education from the prewar – and that is how I am (Kaminuma 1966, p. 4).

This person is by no means the possessor of a reactionary political perspective, and owns up to having had 'enormous sympathy' towards the anti-AMPO treaty conflict on the mainland. The situation in Okinawa at the time, where the '*Hi-no-maru*' coexisted with the red flag, can be said to have been underpinned also by such a state of mind.

Miyata Setsuko, a researcher into Korean history, has depicted Korean friends permanently resident in Japan from the generation that received education for becoming imperial subjects as 'While arguing for "the [Korean] people (*minzoku*)'s independence" by day, once they get some drink into them, they can only sing "martial songs."' Even in the case of those resident Koreans who were antagonistic towards the Japanese government, the stamp of prewar education was such a deep one. More than that, Okinawan teachers were adopting education 'as members of the Japanese nation' as their policy, even while being in opposition to America, which was a 'colossal power,' on a daily basis. In 1967, one teacher wrote: 'For those who had lived for thirty or more years in Okinawa, the words '*Hi-no-maru*' and '*Kimi-ga-yo*' are liable subconsciously to evoke a powerful nostalgia.' Moreover, at Kyōken rallies, it was reported, for example, that 'young people are not participating' in the national education campaign, and that even in regard to the '*Hi-no-maru*,' also, feelings were 'obviously out of synch' between the younger generation and people in their thirties and above, and so it appears that the sensitivity of teachers from the prewar generation was a hidden backdrop to the national education movement (Miyata 1985, p. 2; Gima 1967, p. 117).

Moreover, examples were cited among teachers of the existence of disorder in students' public morals, as well as caution towards postwar changes in values, as psychological grounds for the national education movement. At Kyōken rallies, along with warnings about public morals in the vicinity of U.S. military bases, much discussion was made of such topics as a disarray in students' etiquette, a decline in public morals and a degeneration in the language usage and *keigo* (honorific expressions); and these were juxtaposed with the assessment that 'the concept of state (*kokka*) is weak, and national (*minzoku*) consciousness has also diminished.' In reports relating to the national education movement, there could be seen such utterances as: 'In postwar democracy, with emphasis being placed upon freedom and liberation, [children] lost their sociality, and this created a selfish, egocentric social tendency,' and 'the teaching of manners at home, at school and in society has no strictness, and [children] want to copy the bad aspects of Americans,' and 'the kind of education that will foster national consciousness' was worked out as the countermeasure. In the promotion of Standard Japanese, too, there were reports saying, for instance: 'There are many voices demanding instruction for young people in the local tongue, which has fallen into disorder,' and 'There is no everyday usage of honorific language towards people of higher status,' which implies that an awareness of the need to tighten discipline was in the background ('Dai 12-ji Kyōken Shūkai Shūroku' 1966, pp. 64, 66, 63; 'Dai 3-ji Kyōken Chūō Shūkai Kenkyū Shūroku' 1957, pp. 21, 22).

Such a tightening of discipline was something that reflected Okinawan circumstances in which the island as a whole was covered in bases and the disorder of public morals had long been pointed out. As previously mentioned, even while lamenting that his former students fell into a 'decadent lifestyle' and 'colonial character' amid the situation where they had no future except to become base workers, Yara Chōbyō, too, upheld the upgrading of the educational environment to 'mainland standard,' and the cultivation of 'members of the Japanese nation.' At Kyōken rallies, however, there were also reports made that said, for example: 'Isn't it partly due to a misapprehension of democracy that even such beautiful Eastern customs as parent–child relationships and the order of seniority are being lost?' and 'Adults often cry that children now are not at all properly behaved, and that this is because there is no moral training (*shūshin* – a school subject in the days of Imperial Japan),' so there appeared perhaps to be a tendency for it to have combined with elder teachers' prewar nostalgia, as well. In addition, reports contained such remarks as: 'The status and honour which we built up by cumulative efforts in the prewar all fell to the ground along with the end of the war, and I think that there are things which arose, along with the advent of a new generation, from a misunderstood sense of freedom and misunderstanding of democracy.' It appears that there were some teachers who, having had pride in themselves as regional leaders from the prewar, were bewildered at their postwar decline in status ('Dai 12-ji Kyōken Shūkai Shūroku' 1966, pp. 65, 50).

The psychological factors in the national education movement which I have listed thus far – in other words, an awareness of disparity vis-à-vis the mainland, pressure from the U.S. military, the residue of prewar education, and a consciousness of the need for tightening of discipline – are not things that can be distinctly separated, and appear to have been mixed. A report at the 1966 Kyōken rally, for example, described incessantly telling students heading to the mainland for group employment (a scheme in which schools cooperated with mainland Japanese firms to introduce jobs to students who were then sent to Tokyo and Osaka to work) about 'past examples of Okinawans' language-related failures and experiences on the mainland, and, while stressing the necessity of Standard Japanese, urging them at school to become able to speak it sufficiently.' As for the teaching of manners, the students were said to be 'deficient in their ways of greeting and expressing thanks,' the report saying that teachers gave those students guidance by 'taking up the material integration of textbooks, the *Hi-no-maru*, language, manners and customs, everyday life, and so forth (the language and etiquette in group employment),' all of which implies that an orientation towards assimilating to the mainland and the tightening of discipline were blended together ('Dai 12-ji Kyōken Shūkai Shūroku' 1966, p. 60).

In teachers' eyes there was reflected a situation of overwhelming oppression by the American military, an inferior educational environment, and students who, in that midst, were being encroached upon by a 'decadent lifestyle.' Moreover, when they fretted in the face of that situation, the only things they could put forward as goals towards which to aim were the development of an educational environment to 'mainland-standard,' the cultivation of 'mainland-standard' academic ability, the promotion of 'mainland-standard' Standard Japanese,' and the nurturing of a 'mainland-standard' awareness of 'being Japanese.' The national education movement was a phenomenon which erupted, so to speak, when such diverse sentiments as a sense of responsibility and affection for students, an impatience towards the state of affairs which had no outlet, and a desire for their own happiness were given the form of 'becoming Japanese.'

Nonetheless, even in the Okinawa of those days, which superficially was blanketed with the '*Hi-no-maru*' flag, there was unceasing discord. One teacher from the central district cites the following episode, which occurred in '1954 or 55.'

> Recently, my singing circle had occasion to tour the southern battle sites. I don't know who brought it along, but a *Hi-no-maru* was fluttering somewhere at the head of the line as we headed towards the Kenji-no-tō (a memorial to fallen high-school boys and teachers) from the Himeyuri-no-tō ('Star lily monument,' a memorial to female students who lost their lives as war nurses, the name deriving from a blending of the titles of school magazines from the Okinawa Number One Higher Girls' School and the Female Division of the Higher Normal School). As it was a time when scars from the war were still smarting, the ranks threading their way through the millet fields and the *Hi-no-maru* flapping in the breeze made an uncanny scene almost like a hallucination. When we arrived at the Kenji-no-tō, the aforesaid *Hi-no-maru* had been set up at the side of the monument. Suddenly, an angry voice flew out from behind: 'Get rid of that *Hi-no-maru* immediately! They died because of it.'
> It was a voice trembling with emotion. Then, without a moment's pause, there came a voice from a different side: 'It's the symbol of our ancestral land.'
> That was all. Silence reigned (Nihon Kyōshokuin Kumiai and Okinawa Kyōshokuinkai 1970, p. 242).

This teacher writes that 'around the time of the movement for raising the *Hi-no-maru*, people were vying with each other to buy the flags. That smelled of a nostalgic ancestral land. I suspect, though, that a yearning for and rejection of an ancestral land co-existed at the bottom of their hearts.' The campaign for national education continued to be implemented in an environment where such 'yearning and rejection' were allowed to co-exist 'at the bottom of their hearts.'

'Is our ancestral land Japan?'

What might the reactions of students have been to such a campaign for national education? In the 1960s, as part of the reversion movement, there was prolific implementation of correspondence between Okinawan and mainland children, and reciprocal invitations to schools. Given that it was also at a time of travel restrictions, the latter appears often to have taken the form of exchange observation tours by student representatives chosen by a tie-up between schools. After that, it became usual in such a campaign to publish collections of written impressions which allowed students' voices to be heard.

It was most common for students' essays, too, to echo the ideas of the teachers' national education movement exactly. The following essay by a first-year middle-school student, entitled 'Japan, our mother,' was published in 1966 in an anthology called *The children of Okinawa*, jointly edited by the mainland JTU and the Okinawa Teachers' Association.

> The *Hi-no-maru* – that is the mark of our country. It is the symbol. The members of our Japanese nation have a splendid national flag called the *Hi-no-maru*. The red circle in the centre of the flag has no corners, and is said to be a symbol of peace ... Why can't we stand majestically, without chattering to each other, when raising and lowering the national flag? [Why] can't we take an honourable attitude to the country's symbol? That is what I feel questionable (Nihon Kyōshokuin Kumiai and Okinawa Kyōshokuinkai 1966, p. 104).

Whichever of the anthologies published at that time one reads, they brim with essays telling of Okinawan students' consciousness of being 'Japanese.' Students who crossed to the mainland on exchange field trips wrote about being moved to see Mt Fuji, or described how they themselves faced 'the ancestral land' and cheered from the port. They spelled out such words as: 'When I stepped onto the soil of my ancestral land, I was touched almost to tears, and the feeling welled up that I had come to my ancestral land,' 'I could not help thinking that Okinawa and the mainland were one, after all, and we were the members of the same Japanese nation in whom blood mutually flows,' and 'Our teacher said: "Even though militarily Okinawa is on the American side, the blood that flows through our bodies is Japanese." Every time I recall these words, the joy to think: "That's right. I am Japanese," bubbles up from the bottom of my heart.' One girl had written: 'When I stepped down from the wharf at Kagoshima, I suddenly felt my breast grow hot, and I thought: "I have come to my ancestral land." ... Treading the earth of my ancestral land, I raced around with all my might.' Thus, even Kagoshima (= Satsuma), which once ruled the Ryukyus, was also taken to be the 'ancestral land' (Yamamoto 1966, pp. 286, 91; Nihon Ajia Afurika Rentai Iinkai, Hondo to Okinawa no Kodomo no Sakubun Kōryū Jikkō Iinkai 1971, p. 226; Shimoji 1967, p. 136).

That said, it is unclear to what extent such 'school essays' expressed their true feelings. One cannot deny that there was probably a tendency for essays by so-called 'model students' which were selected by teachers to attempt faithfully to reflect the values taught in schools as ideals. In fact, while in the minority, there were also some students who openly expressed doubts about the national education movement. At the Okinawa Teachers' Association's Kyōken rally in January 1965, the existence of an essay such as that below was reported (Okinawa Kyōshokuinkai 1965, p. 88).

> Adults who received education from the Empire of Japan nonchalantly call Japan their ancestral land. And they hope that [Okinawa] will again become Japanese territory. And they believe it will happen. They are trying to hammer that idea even into us who were born after the defeat ...
>
> It was when the Minister for Education came to Okinawa in 1963. As one teacher who had received Japanese imperial education said: 'Everyone must wave a miniature *Hi-no-maru* flag, without fail,' when Master A asked: 'Even people who do not have the will to wave one?' the teacher replied: 'Of course!' So, the opinion emerged that we should put it to the homeroom. We lost no time in debating it. Firstly, there was a comment by Master A, saying: 'A welcome is something that should be done on one's own conviction, not something forced by somebody else.' Seventy-five percent of students agreed with this view of Master A's. However, the teacher ordered us to go and wave a flag, even those unwilling to do so, saying it was because it was the decision of the Teachers' Association ...
>
> In newspaper reports, it was written just as if students had waved flags in all sincerity. Why do we not acknowledge the Japan-the-ancestral-land discourse? Have we perhaps received any benefit from Japan, economically or spiritually, until reaching our present stage of growth? People talk about national (*minzoku*) solidarity, but that idea is too narrow for us who have a future. They say that Japan is our ancestral land. It has neither the qualifications nor the obligation [to be so]. When we become adults, we will probably not hear anything like the Japan-the-ancestral-land discourse. We will probably get a bigger idea.

At that time, a considerable amount of courage must have been needed for this student to write such an essay. From the 1950s into the 1960s, almost every time a mainland politician came to the islands, a welcome was held by children waving '*Hi-no-maru*' flags, winning the favour of conservative cabinet ministers, but behind this, such discord lay.

However, the Teachers' Association of the day was not in a mood to acknowledge the voices of such students. The reason for the introduction of this essay at the Kyōken rally was to report on the particulars of having made district middle-school students read it and write rebuttals. These rebuttal arguments were, of course, ones including: 'Even if I receive no benefit from Japan, I believe that Japan is my ancestral land,' 'I will become a person who can have pride as a Japanese,' and, 'I wonder if people like this felt nothing even when they saw the "*Hi-no-maru*" rise or heard the "*Kimi-ga-yo*" anthem at the recent [Tokyo] Olympics [in 1964]' (Okinawa Kyōshokuinkai 1965, pp. 89, 90).

That being said, the voices of such students were a shock to teachers. Even while attaching such headlines as: 'We Japanese,' or 'Blood Cries out,' newspaper reports which conveyed the scene at the Kyōken rally wrote that 'the naïve question of "Is our ancestral land Japan?" gave quite a shock not only to teachers but even to parents and guardians.' The policy which the Teachers' Association showed in response, however, was an even stronger promotion of the national education campaign (*Ryūkyū shinpō* 1966a).

The repercussions spread even as far as the press because of a letter to the editor about this newspaper reportage from a seventeen-year-old high-school girl. Entitled 'Japan is not [my] ancestral land,' this letter, while listing the history of conquest by Satsuma and the Ryukyu Disposition, was one which argued that 'those people with the disease of Japan-worship might fanatically believe that if only we revert, then everything will be resolved, but Japan is nothing more than a simple ruling country for Okinawa, and is neither its ancestral land nor anything.' Counter-counter-arguments were received in response to this, again from high-school students, including: 'Even in terms of folkloristics, both the people of the mainland and people of Okinawa are the same Japanese nation (*minzoku*),' and 'What I fear most is becoming something like a rootless wanderer, opposing reversion even while belonging to the same nation (*minzoku*), personally discarding my pride as a Japanese' (*Ryūkyū shinpō* 1966b; 1966c).

At a glance, such a dispute by students appears to comprise a definite confrontation, but many student essays from this period give the sense of being underpinned by a subtle vacillation even in cases where the writers declare themselves to be 'Japanese.' It is unthinkable that without inner conflict there could have been such wording as: 'I really want to make the *Hi-no-maru* my own. Even if they fly the *Hi-no-maru* on holidays, it is still a formality to the people of Okinawa, and I cannot consider that they have really made it their own,' or, 'I am sure that feelings towards the mainland such as mine formed naturally. There is nothing unusual in that.' In her record of a visit to Okinawa, one mainland writer noted the words of a high-school student who said: 'In emotional terms, we do not have a sense of being Japanese. We merely think we are Japanese by means of reason and education,' and this was probably a sentiment shared by both sides of the dispute (Ōhama 1967, p. 128; Yamamoto 1966, p. 42; Kaminuma 1966, p. 69).

Amid such wavering, for students who endeavoured to be 'Japanese,' the most hurtful thing was the mainlanders' attitude. In contrast to the emotion that Okinawa directed at the mainland, the mainlanders' level of understanding towards the Okinawa of those days was extremely low. In 1967, as a result of a questionnaire survey of more than a hundred mainland high schools, a reported forty-three percent of respondents said that the country to which Okinawa belonged was 'America,' while thirty-one percent replied that its newspapers were published in English. In a collection of exchange essays it is recorded that the students who had made the crossing from Okinawa were almost without exception asked such questions by mainlanders as: 'Okinawans can speak Japanese, too, can't they?' 'Is the language English?' 'Are books written in the same Japanese?' (Shimoji 1967, p. 138; Yamamoto 1966, pp. 67, 65).

The more they were exposed to such lack of understanding, the more students also tended deliberately to emphasise that they themselves were 'Japanese' in order to counter this. In a roundtable discussion held by a mainland magazine in 1968, Okinawan high-school students remarked: 'People who came from the mainland said one thing and another, asking such things as whether we were really Japanese,' and 'Foreigners suggested that prior to Meiji, Okinawans had perhaps belonged to China,' to which they replied: 'We asserted that we were Japanese' (*Sekai* 1968, pp. 149, 164). The more they perceived the gaze and discrimination of Orientalism, the more a structure that made them fall for being 'Japanese' existed there.

However, it was not rare for their very intention to become 'Japanese' to be viewed as bizarre in mainland eyes, either. A certain female student wrote that when she unwittingly cried out 'It's the *Hi-no-maru*!' at the sight of the flag from the window of a train on the mainland, the people around looked mystified. In 1967, also, at a teachers' roundtable discussion planned by a mainland magazine, entitled 'The difficulty of teaching the Japanese (= Yamato) spirit in Okinawa,' when the mainland moderator stated that 'it is no big thing even if the Japanese in *naichi* proper do not particularly think that they are Japanese on a daily basis,' an Okinawan teacher responded by saying: 'That would be untrue unless one went so far as to behave so naturally as to forget that one were Japanese, after all.' Here lay the ironical situation of making 'forgetting that one is Japanese [in] the mainland way' into one's objective in order to become 'Japanese.'

Nevertheless, the greatest motivation for students still to continue aiming at being 'Japanese,' in a similar manner to teachers, in one sense, could be said to have been a desire to rid themselves of the circumstances binding them. In concrete terms, the path of advancement for capable young people in Okinawa in those days was to become a public servant in the Ryukyu government, to become a teacher, or to go to the mainland. There were restrictions on travel to the mainland, teachers' pay was low, and local industry was unstable, so no small number became military workers. One high-school student whose elder brother was a teacher and whose mother was a day-labourer at a base complained in 1967, saying: 'There would be barely enough to feed ourselves on my brother's pay alone,' and 'There is no hope whatsoever in working at a base. There is no reason for living.' This was followed by the words: 'In both name and substance, becoming a Japanese national is the very way to having a real livelihood.' Yet another high-school student, while declaring that the sorrow of having had friends and relatives die in accidents caused by the American military 'would remain always, as long as we live,' added: 'I would like to live my life with pride as a Japanese' (*Gekkan jiji* 1967b, pp. 166, 167). Here, the word 'Japanese' was a homonym for human dignity and hope for the future.

One female student remarked: 'There are also people who say "Japan is not our ancestral land." ... I want to have those people, too, tread the soil of our ancestral land, for if they did, they would probably not say such things, either.' She then continued:

> I am often shown too much of a lack of understanding from people of our ancestral land. There appear even to be some who think we use English and live life in bare feet. People who do nothing but quibble over theory can also be found. But it is reality for us. The suffering that is visible on the surface is only the tip of the iceberg ...
>
> We who are called such things as an oppressed people (*minzoku*) do not want to be called that any more. We are already sick of having sacrifice thrust upon us under all kinds of beautiful names. Even an instant sooner, we want to embrace true happiness in these arms. I want to make my beloved Okinawa into a beautiful, affluent prefecture of the south, as one prefecture of Japan. As a member of the Japanese nation (*minzoku*), I want to savour the joys and the sorrows of the nation (*minzoku*), together (Yamamoto 1966, pp. 99, 100).

It is obvious that the wording 'an oppressed people (*minzoku*)' seen here means 'the Okinawan people.' However, for the time being, the only method she could find for escaping the situation was becoming 'one prefecture of Japan' 'as a member of the Japanese nation (*minzoku*).'

In 1967, in the homeroom class at a certain high school in Okinawa, which a mainland magazine published as 'We Japanese,' opinions were 'divided three ways,' comprising 'those who agreed with immediate, complete reversion, those who opposed it, and those who could not say either way, with about the same number in each.'

There were also those who extolled independence as 'the Okinawan people (*minzoku*),' and wanted to know why everyone was 'forever fixated on being Japanese nationals.' In reply, students who advocated reversion responded by saying: 'If we decided that from now on we would cease to be members of the Japanese nation, then they would become more autocratic towards us, and would stop giving us any rights whatsoever, as if we were slaves. Okinawa, it's a total colony.' 'That is why we tentatively make being members of the Japanese nation our prerequisite.' It is not clear whether the 'they' mentioned here as the counterpart that would 'become more autocratic' indicates the American military, or the mainland. Alternatively, it might have referred not to a specific government or country, but to somebody that triggered the vague fear and sense of entrapment which the students felt. In either case, the argument of the students on the reversion side was: 'We think that if we are Japanese we have the right to be treated equally. Absolutely' (*Gekkan jiji* 1967b, pp. 166, 168).

At these roundtable discussions, when students began debating whether or not they were 'Japanese,' there were occasions seen of teachers bringing it to an end by saying: 'From the aspects of archaeology, ethnology, linguistics and anthropology ... it has already been proven that the people of Okinawa are Japanese' (*Sekai* 1968, p. 149). In questionnaires and suchlike from Kyōken rallies, it was reported that students who were conscious of being 'Japanese' and desired reversion accounted for about ninety percent of respondents. Even given that there was economic benefit from the bases, respondents who agreed with the situation of U.S. military rule as was were in the minority, and as independence was regarded as being impossible, the view that the remaining realistic option was reversion was probably shared for the most part.

If we borrow an expression from a certain 1967 letter to the editor, however, 'it was too complicated to grasp the sentiment of the people living in Okinawa numerically and accurately.' This contribution uses the expression 'duality of spirit' to describe the 'mental state of residents who, even while desiring reversion to their ancestral land from the bottom of their hearts, still continue to question in part of their minds what "*sokoku*" means' (Shimoji 1967, p. 138). In the case of both teachers and students, the aspiration to be 'Japanese' existed atop such a perilous balance of duality to the bitter end.

Political change and transition

It was from around 1966 that changes began gradually to emerge in such a national education movement. Political change both within and outside of Okinawa was connected with this.

The first impetus was the so-called 'Two Laws on Education (*Kyōkō 2-hō*)' issue around the enactment of the 'Special Act for Education Personnel (*Kyōiku kōmuin tokurei hō*)' and 'Act for Personnel in Regional Education Districts (*Chihō kyōiku-ku kōmuin hō*),' which were based on mainland laws. On the mainland in the 1950s, the conservative governing party forced through a bill which incorporated such items as the scrapping of public elections and the adoption of a system of appointment for Boards of Education; the limitation of political activity and prohibition of strikes by teachers; and the strengthening of the Minister for Education's right to command and supervise. Furthermore, in advance of the implementation of assumption of the burden of educational expenses by the national treasury, it was attempted to extend these laws from *naichi* to Okinawa.

Restriction of political activity was something that was perfect for the suppression of the reversion movement, so naturally the Okinawa Teachers' Association vehemently opposed it. The opposition movement especially intensified from 1966, but Okinawa's pro-U.S. ruling party, the Democratic Party, which had cordial relations with the mainland's Liberal-Democratic Party, reportedly denounced it, saying: 'Why does the Teachers' Association, which up until now has advocated doing everything to mainland standard, oppose the two bills on education, which are the same as mainland laws?' (Yara 1977, p. 81). In February 1967, more than 20,000 people, including teachers, staged a sit-in in front of the legislature, and it escalated even into clashes with police armed to the teeth, and so the bill was finally rejected. Through this process of struggle, however, a definite rift developed between the Teachers' Association and conservative Okinawan political parties, while conversely a coalition framework with progressive opposition parties, including the People's Party, came into being. And more than anything else, here the Teachers' Association became painfully aware that being 'mainland standard' was not necessarily rosy, and in the process of conflict, it came to hammer out 'Okinawa's special circumstances.'

Furthermore, from around this time, relations between the mainland Nikkyōso and the Teachers' Association grew even deeper. From the 1950s into the early 1960s, Yara and others maintained contact with Nikkyōso, as well, but they also exacted assistance through their connection with the mainland's Liberal-Democratic Party, to the extent of winning praise from Araki Masuo, the LDP's Minister for Education who visited Okinawa in 1963. Gratified at his welcome by children waving *Hi-no-maru* flags, Araki said: 'Okinawa also has a teachers' union, but it does not have a single member who is considering anything as stupid as Nikkyōso's code of ethics. This, too, can be thought to be something where the specification of "as Japanese" in the Basic Law of Education is coming into play in large measure.' By contrast, around 1960, even though the Okinawa Teachers' Association requested a mainland progressive group to send some '*Hi-no-maru*,' the response was apparently cold (Araki 1963, p. 18; *Asahi jānaru* 1961, p. 7). Until the early 1960s, the Okinawa Teachers' Association could even be said to have enjoyed a better reputation on the mainland from the conservatives than from the progressives.

The Okinawa Teachers' Association was originally not a workers' union like the mainland Nikkyōso, but an employees' group which included managerial positions such as principals, as is indicated by the fact that Yara, who had served as a principal and the Director of Education for the Ryukyu government, had taken the post of its inaugural president. This was also an inevitable choice given the then climate of extreme vigilance by the U.S. military regarding the intrusion of the mainland Nikkyōso's anti-U.S. line, but in the organisational aspect, as well, there was the reason that the Ministry of Education's educational line was more readily reflected there than was Nikkyōso's. On the mainland, moreover, Nikkyōso and the Ministry of Education held separate Kyōken rallies, but in Okinawa, it also cooperated with the Ryukyu government's Education Bureau for the sake of the reversion movement. In 1961, led by the Youth Division, moves arose to reorganise the Teachers' Association into a teachers' union, but circumstances dictated that this ended up being indefinitely postponed, but there was a tendency to suppress factional activity for the sake of 'national (*minzoku*) solidarity.' However, antagonism deepened between the conservative ruling party and the Education Bureau over the 'Two Laws on Education' issue, and as the relationship with the relatively progressive side grew, criticism began to appear from the mainland Nikkyōso vis-à-vis the national education movement in Okinawa.

One example of this was a report published in Nikkyōso's official organ by its leading figures that had been sent to Okinawa as an exchange delegation in 1967. Criticising the Teachers' Association's running of Kyōken rallies on advice from the Ryukyu Government's Education Bureau which in turn received guidance from the mainland's Ministry of Education, the report was one that argued there was 'necessity for more essential unity of thought, as the *Hi-no-maru*' problem would not be solved by insisting it should be understood merely in a tactical manner.' The report further said that in order for the Okinawa Teachers' Association to come under the umbrella of Nikkyōso after reversion, it would be necessary to 'press children to change their values; and, above all, for Okinawan teachers themselves to undertake a huge switch in their own values,' and that there was 'a need for discussion in the course of interaction about the way to prompt Okinawan teachers' self-metamorphosis' (Kikuchi 1968, p. 27).

A further motivation was the visit to Okinawa by the then Prime Minister, Satō Eisaku, in August 1965. Reactions within Okinawa were divided in regard to the visit of a prime minister who took a conciliatory line towards the U.S. and did not specify the prospect of Okinawan reversion. Just then, it was the very midst of an escalation in the Vietnam War and the further heightening of anti-U.S., anti-base sentiment. Okinawan bases were being used as bases for bombing missions, and more and more U.S. troops were being stationed there, so the burden of bases increased. While on the one hand the Ryukyu Government and conservative ruling party indicated that they welcomed Prime Minister Satō's visit to Okinawa, progressive forces centring on the People's Party initiated a policy of obstruction, with the rationale that the visit would lead to entrenchment of the current situation. At this time, the Teachers' Association, which was beginning to enter a state of confrontation due to the Two Laws on Education issue, rejected a directive from the Ryukyu Government's Education Bureau to mobilise children holding '*Hi-no-maru*' flags, as had been conventional practice.

Prime Minister Satō made a speech saying that the postwar would not end until Okinawa reverted, but violent anti-Satō demonstrations were held, and '*Hi-no-maru*' were abandoned by the wayside. One teacher described the state of affairs at this time thus: 'The *Hi-no-maru* and red flag, which until then had coexisted amicably, parted company according to their separate roles. Hearts that sentimentally yearned for the ancestral land and hoped it would embrace them as soon as possible waved the *Hi-no-maru*. Hearts that could not forgive the acceptance of nuclear bases and sorties to Vietnam even now, twenty years postwar, spouted their burning desire for immediate total reversion and raised the red flag (Gima 1969, p. 71).

On the other hand, however, Yara Chōbyō gained a vital result from this prime ministerial visit to Okinawa. At this time, Yara petitioned Satō, and made him promise to bear Okinawa's educational expenses from the public purse to the same extent as other prefectures, which had been a pending question. As Yara recalls in his memoirs, this was the result of his having carried out ample preliminary behind-the-scenes negotiations through the personal connections he had nurtured hitherto, and of 'the preamble in the Basic Law of Education, which proclaimed "members of the Japanese nation," having come to be of enormous force here, too' (Yara 1977, p. 77; Kaminuma 1966, p. 82). As promised, the Liberal-Democratic regime doubled its aid to Okinawa in its budget for the 1966–67 fiscal year, and education spending, especially, was increased approximately sevenfold, teachers' pay approached mainland level, and the free distribution of textbooks was also implemented. With this, the agenda which the Teachers' Association had tried for long years to extract from the mainland Ministry of Education and Liberal-Democratic Party saw a certain measure of resolution, and the way was opened for devoting itself to opposition to the Two Laws on Education and the anti-war pro-peace reversion movement.

In the late 1960s, even on the mainland, interest in Okinawa had risen in concert with the upsurge of a movement against the Vietnam War. Unlike the conservatives' interest in the 1950s, this was one that arose from an anti-war, pro-peace standpoint. From this time, the '*Hi-no-maru*' gradually disappeared in the Okinawan side's reversion campaign, as well. Moreover, in a public election held in 1968 for the long-desired position of Chief Executive, Yara Chōbyō ended up beating the conservative candidate and winning as a progressive joint-campaign unification candidate, touting 'Anti-U.S.–Japan Security Treaty,' 'anti-base,' 'immediate, unconditional reversion,' and so forth.

This kind of a political trend also triggered change in the Teachers' Association's national education movement. The aforementioned debate over the '*Kimi-ga-yo*,' as well as reflection on the national education movement up till then, were carried out at the Kyōken rally in January 1966, five months after the Satō visit to Okinawa. There emerged such internal criticism as: 'Can we enhance national consciousness merely by the formalistic aspect of simply hoisting the *Hi-no-maru*?' and 'Mainland teachers' strength lies in their contemplation of responsibility for the war. There was none in Okinawa, was there?' and in terms of Teachers' Association policy, as well, there were proposals for strengthening of peace movement, such as a 'campaign to support the Ienaga lawsuit' (see Chapter 8, note 16) and a 'movement to refuse cooperation in Self-Defense Forces recruitment.' Even while Standard Japanese was still deemed necessary, 'not making [students] have a feeling of inferiority about their dialect more than necessary,' and a 'movement to deepen understanding of local culture' also started to be cited ('Dai 12-ji Kyōken Shūkai Shūroku' 1966, pp. 4, 12, 5).

However, as symbolised by the fact that no conclusion to the '*Kimi-ga-yo*' debate had emerged, no clear-cut change of policy had yet been made at this rally. Rather, there was emphasis on a sense of crisis that 'among pupils, some harbouring such doubts as "Is Japan our ancestral land?" or "Are we Japanese?"' have appeared,' and district reports premised on the conventional encouragement of the '*Hi-no-maru*' and '*Kimi-ga-yo*' were numerous ('Dai 12-ji Kyōken Shūkai Shūroku' 1966, p. 69).

It was from the Kyōken rally in January 1967, in the following year, that a definite shift began to occur. This time, it was a rally held in the midst of a situation where leading officials from the Teachers' Association were maintaining a hunger strike over the Two Laws on Education in front of the Legislature. The opinion was stated that 'much criticism has already arisen everywhere about fostering and enhancing consciousness as members of the Japanese nation through the *Hi-no-maru* and *Kimi-ga-yo*.' There was also the reflection that teachers felt as if they had judged students to have national consciousness, or that such consciousness was high, if students replied that traditionally there had been a national flag in the house, or if they displayed the national flag on holidays, or said such things as: 'I am Japanese' 'Okinawa belongs to Japan,' or 'I like the *Kimi-ga-yo* because it is the Japanese national anthem.'

Reports that praised the promotion of Standard Japanese vanished from Kyōken rallies. What came to the forefront instead was a policy that was a simplified form of progressive nationalism, that is: 'When we say "national consciousness," [we mean] not merely an awareness of being Japanese ... but the determination and desire to live seeking peace, with pride and responsibility as sovereign members, fairly and squarely asserting the rights of nationals determined in the constitution' ('Dai 13-ji Kyōken Shūkai Kenkyū Shūroku' 1967, pp. 32, 29, 30).

The Constitution of Japan promulgated in 1946 after the Pacific War, containing such elements as Article Nine renouncing the state's right to wage war, as well as stipulating the sovereignty of the people and equality of the sexes, was a more democratic one than the prewar Imperial Japanese Constitution had been. The mainland Japanese conservative regime endeavoured to amend the new constitution and bring it closer to the Imperial Constitution, but was blocked by 'progressive forces' and did not succeed. Moreover, the mainland's Nikkyōso implemented a national (*kokumin*) education campaign situating respect for the Constitution of Japan as national consciousness (*kokumin ishiki*) which differed from prewar patriotism.

In Okinawa, though a tone of argument expressing the wish to obtain the human rights that were extolled in the constitution had existed since around 1950, it was rare for the peacefulness of the Japanese constitution to enter the picture in the 1950s reversion movement, which had no alternative but to tout cooperation with the U.S. military. In the mainland Nikkyōso, it was advocated that the Peace Clause in the Japanese constitution be made a focal point in national education, as the pride of Japan. However, even in the case of the Teachers' Association, a response to the view from the 1966 Kyōken rally that importance should be placed upon the constitution in national education can be seen, namely: 'We did not think about it until the Japanese constitution was brought out. We would like this to be discussed as a problem for the future' ('Dai 12-ji Kyōken Shūkai Shūroku' 1966, p. 5). Be that as it may, this means that though a shift occurred in the national education movement, consisting of upholding the peace constitution instead of the '*Hi-no-maru*' and '*Kimi-ga-yo*' as the symbol of 'Japan' and 'the Japanese,' such a tenor was circulated widely in the reversion movement of the late 1960s, which is taken to have written off '*Hi-no-maru* reversion.' Those in the field were not necessarily completely able to support such a policy shift, and reports which took the stand of promoting the '*Hi-no-maru*' continued to be submitted until the Kyōken rally in 1968.

However, when Yara Chōbyō was later elected as Chief Executive by a progressive united front, and, furthermore, when a policy was officially announced by means of a joint statement made in November 1969 by Prime Minister Satō and President Nixon that administrative rights over Okinawa would revert to Japan in 1972, albeit with retention of U.S. military bases, that air of indecisiveness also disappeared. This so-called 'with-bases, mainland-standard' reversion policy received vehement censure from the mainland critical arena, as well, and in Okinawa, too, the anti-reversion discourse which will be later discussed in the next chapter rapidly came to prominence. Along with 'mainland reversion' changing from a distant dream to reality, fantasies vis-à-vis the mainland, which hitherto had been glamourised, began to turn to disillusionment. In this manner, a stand began to be taken at the Kyōken rally in December 1969 which said: 'It has become obvious that most schools display the "*Hi-no-maru*" at events, and play the *Kimi-ga-yo* tune on sports day. This should be emphasised in relation to the mainland's reactionary turn,' and: 'The fact that [Okinawans] regard their local tongue with shame and cannot speak Standard Japanese well in other prefectures is the fault of the prewar policy on the local language which has made those dialect placards, with the School Affairs Division as the central player' (Okinawa Kyōshokuinkai Kyōiku Bunka Bu 1970, pp. 1, 3).

Of course, perplexed voices arose from every district at such a shift. One district's report, fearing 'predicted student confusion in the case of a sudden 180-degree about-face on the display of the *Hi-no-maru*," which for twenty-four years postwar had been positively encouraged by schools and democratic groups as a symbol of reversion to the ancestral land and resistance to colonialism,' stated that 'at the present point in time, the question has emerged as to how to guide and convince the 75.6 percent of students who associate the "*Hi-no-maru*" with Japan, the ancestral land, if we were to abolish the "*Hi-no-maru*." Ultimately, even at that year's Kyōken rally, the conclusion reached in regard to the promotion of the '*Hi-no-maru*' was that 'it should be decided after thorough debate at branch meetings, because problems would arise if it came to immediate cessation,' but there were reports from districts which had held debate that 'arguments both for and against emerged, and in the end things remained as they were, without any uniformity of intent.' At the 1971 Kyōken rally, as well, there was a district report that said 'the *Hi-no-maru* and *Kimi-ga-yo* ... issue is still unresolved,' which implies that the problem was still dragging on at ground level (Okinawa Kyōshokuinkai Kyōiku Bunka Bu 1970, pp. 51, 3, 47; 1971, p. 33).

That said, the national education movement itself was continued along the lines of progressive nationalism, and even around 1970, collections of essays in which teachers and students extolled the 'ancestral land' kept on being issued. When this time arrived, however, even in such anthologies, essays that expressed a warped sentiment towards the 'ancestral land' could be seen. Here, I cite two passages by Okinawan teachers, both of which were published in 1970.

> What do you demand that Okinawan teachers – who have taught, being moved to tears simply at the free distribution of textbooks in schools at all levels of compulsory education which the mainland government implemented for the first time more than twenty years after the end of the war – do about this anguish? I do not want to give vent to resentment and bitterness, but it is enough that adults alone bear the sadness of being under alien rule, not even being allowed self-government under a policy of prioritising military affairs, being forced to cohabit with nuclear weapons, and having been denied even the merest sliver of constitutional guarantees. [We are] sick of the suffering of a people without an ancestral land. As those who stand at the chalk-face, we at least want to let these children live their lives unconditionally as Japanese, under a peace constitution.
>
> There is a necessity to question whether an element of voluntary assimilation in order to break loose from discrimination might not still remain within the reversion movement.
> ... Oh, to what a sorry extent did the Koreans (who received prewar education for being imperial subjects) resemble the people of Okinawa! I saw the figures of wartime Okinawans in those Koreans resident in Japan who, 'aspiring to become *Yokaren* (Naval Preparatory Flight Trainees) or applying to join *Tokkōtai* (*kamikaze* attack units), tried to gain influence [as Japanese] in return for their lives.'
> '*Han-Nihonjin* (halfway Japanese)' is what is used to call Koreans who, assuming Japanese names and using the Japanese language skilfully, tried to break away from being Korean and become completely like Japanese. Yet even in return for their own lives, they could not become wholly Japanese. Apparently, *Panchoppari* is the hate-infused pejorative spat out when Koreans are hurt at their being that way, have self-contempt and condemn themselves. In that sense, the people of Okinawa, too, were similarly 'Half-way Japanese' (Nihon Kyōshokuin Kumiai and Okinawa Kyōshokuinkai 1970, pp. 198, 245–246).

In his memoirs, Yara Chōbyō writes about the occasion when he has told by a mainland bureaucrat to write a 'tear-jerking petition' as follows: 'I finished composing the petition in one night. Tear-jerkers are my forte. In any case, ever since the movement for reconstruction of school buildings, that is all I have been doing' (Yara 1977, p. 60). If ordinary teachers and students in Okinawa had also been equipped with the same toughness as Yara, the movement which touted the nurture of 'Japanese' would not have needed to leave so many conflict-ridden words. Okinawa's national education campaign led in the elicitation of aid from the mainland and the acquisition of an upgrade in the educational environment and an improvement in teachers' conditions. Only those directly involved, however, could judge whether the price paid to that end was ultimately one that measured up to its result.

After Okinawa's reversion to the mainland, the Okinawa Teachers' Association was incorporated under the umbrella of Nikkyōso, reorganised as the Okinawa Teachers' Union, and intensified its movement against the Ministry of Education's policy of displaying the '*Hi-no-maru.*' In 1978, the Okinawa Teachers' Union abolished its national education branch, and newly established a peace education branch in its place. It was after the 1980s that Okinawa came to draw attention as a place of strong resistance to the '*Hi-no-maru*' and '*Kimi-ga-yo*,' even compared with the rest of Japan.

10 Anti-Reversion

Arakawa Akira, the best-known of the 'anti-reversionists,' said:[1]

> The issue of what constituted Okinawa's 'reversion to Japan' is an excellent ideological question involving what Japan was, is and will be to Okinawa in future, and what Okinawa was, is and will be to Japan. While this is so, there is tragedy and comedy in present-day Okinawan thought and movements because postwar Okinawa's 'ancestral-land reversion' movement (whether '*Hi-no-maru* reversion' or 'anti-war reversion') has been established upon the lack of ideological positioning vis-à-vis this question.
>
> Moreover, this is not something significant merely in postwar Okinawan thought and movements, but something both tragic and comic which has fundamentally determined all political theory, behavioural indicators and scholarly moment up till so-called 'Okinawan Studies' established by Ifa Fuyū, starting with the 'Japan–Ryukyu common-ancestry theory' of Hanji Chōshū and Shō Shōken back in old times, and including Jahana Noboru's People's Rights Movement during Meiji.

'Anti-reversion' ideology rapidly gained currency from around 1969, when the policy of 1972 reversion, which I will later explain, was decided between the Japanese and U.S. governments. Until then, mainland political parties, movements, intellectuals, and the like, who based themselves on the recognition that the people of Okinawa overwhelmingly supported reversion, were bewildered at the emergence of this ideology, or were sympathetic, or had vehement objections to it.

This ideology, which readdressed the existing reversion movement, was something of a somewhat different nature from the conventional Ryukyuan independence discourse which had existed since the 1940s. It was an ideology that not only criticised assimilation to 'the Japanese,' but extolled rejection of the very logic of the nation-state which hitherto had been supported without regard to left or right.

The emergence of this ideology became something that questioned the very nature of the nation-state which for a century had continued uninterruptedly to implement inclusion into and exclusion from 'the Japanese' (Arakawa 1971, pp. 64–65).

The genealogy of the Ryukyuan independence discourse

Before examining the anti-reversion discourse, let me give an overview of the Ryukyuan independence discourses which had existed from around the time of the Peace Treaty. This is because the anti-reversion discourse was often regarded by those on the reversion movement side as identical to these independence discourses, but its character was actually considerably different.

Known politicians who ascribed to the independence discourses in postwar Okinawa include Nakasone Genwa, who set up the Okinawa Democratic League, and Ōgimi Chōtoku, who became the leader of the Ryukyu Nationalist Party. Firstly, Nakasone's perception of Japan at the beginning of the 1950s was something like the following:

> If Japan is calling for the return of Okinawa, it is because it wants Okinawa's land. Japan, with its overpopulation, wants not the people of Okinawa, but its land ... If one suggests that the Japanese government and Japanese political parties wish for the return of Okinawa, it is only because they want the votes at election time along with Okinawa's land, and not because they are truly worried about the happiness of all the residents of Okinawa.
>
> This is due to a reduction in the size of their territory. Both the Japanese government and Japanese political parties do not know what to do with their excess of population, not being able even to make the current Japanese populace fully happy, and so if Okinawa is further carried in, it would be extremely annoying. This is unlikely to delight Japanese workers, as it would mean that large numbers of workers content with low wages would muscle into their midst; and their conditions of livelihood hardship would only worsen. If there were people in Japan who would be delighted, it would be the Japanese capitalists who wanted to hire workers content with low wages. If people and capital could enter or leave Okinawa from Japan freely without any restriction or conditions, then large numbers of the Japanese unemployed would flow in and Okinawan workers would

finally be placed in a difficult position. If Okinawan workers had no choice but to flow in the reverse direction to Japan, they would have no alternative but to dive down lower than the lowest in Japan. It would probably not take much time for the capital strength that would flow in from Japan to overwhelm Okinawa's feeble capital completely. Okinawan politicians who ought to know this well-understood logic loudly clamour for reversion to Japan simply in order to conceal the responsibility for their incompetence in real politics, and to gain 'popularity' (Nakasone 1955 [1973], p. 230).

In part, such perceptions by Nakasone also correctly predicted later reality. However, his projections that the Japanese government wanted Okinawan land as an outlet for its excess population and that reversion would cause a huge influx of mainland unemployed into Okinawa were totally off the mark. His expectation that Okinawans would become the lower stratum of workers on the mainland proved correct, but this was a situation that had arisen prior to reversion. Moreover, the economic disparity between the mainland and Okinawa, which had become ossified due to their division, had facilitated migrant labour, and as mainland capital had supported the argument that reversion was premature in order to take advantage of this, the issue tended rather to become grounds for promoting the reversion movement from the 1960s onwards. Just as most of his arguments against reversion at the beginning of the 1950s had been, it was against Nakasone's expectations that it would be the mainland which would achieve economic growth, rather than Okinawa under American occupation.

In addition, the independence discourse of the day also generally had a strongly pro-U.S. hue, as the anti-reversion argument and trusteeship discourse of the 1950s had been. Nakasone had publicly declared: 'I am opposed both to being exclusively pro-American and being exclusively pro-Japanese,' but while on the one hand his distrust towards Japan was marked, he regarded control of Okinawa by the U.S. as an immutable international environment, and called for cooperation with the U.S. In his resistance to the Okinawa People's Party, he deepened his anti-Communist hue, starting to shout: 'The People's Party argument for Japanese reversion is an argument for Russian possession wearing a mask of Japanese reversion,' 'I will fight the Communist Party in order to protect my beloved Ryukyuan people,' and so on; and making statements immediately prior to reversion that could be called praise for American rule, such as: 'Several decades of rule by an alien people (*minzoku*) achieved far more astounding progress than several centuries of rule (since the Keichō era) by the same people (*minzoku*)' (Nakasone 1955 [1973], pp. 316, 232, 242).

In the case of Ōgimi, who founded the Ryukyu Nationalist Party, a stronger pro-American, anti-Communist hue came to the fore. The Socialist Party, a short-lived Okinawan political party formed in 1947 with Ōgimi as its central figure, touted a policy which said: 'Our party firmly believes that the happiness of the Ryukyuan people (*minzoku*) lies in belonging to the U.S., and we hope for the Americanisation of industry, education and culture,' and in the 1951 possession debate, it advocated trusteeship, urging 'support for U.S. world policy,' 'strengthening of anti-Communist spirit,' and the like. Later, after the Socialist Party had ceased to exist, Ōgimi formed the Ryukyu Nationalist Party in 1958, promoting 'anti-Communist self-government for Ryukyu,' 'making English-language education a formal subject from primary school,' and so on. After the mainland's economic growth, as well, it emphasised the brittleness of the Japanese economy, and advocated becoming independent as an anti-Communist bastion in Asia with American aid, along with such places as Taiwan and South Korea. Naturally, it was Ōgimi's cherished opinion that 'Ryukyu had improved since Japanese days,' and though he ran for election to the legislature and the mayoralty of Naha City in the 1960s, he garnered very few votes as a fly-by-night candidate, even being described as a 'circus clown' (Shimabukuro 1982, pp. 658, 60, 63, 64).

In such a manner, most of the Okinawan independence arguments in the initial stage of the postwar seem to have been ones more or less based on a pro-U.S. anti-Communist line. A pamphlet issued in 1957 by the Ryūkyū Dokuritsu Kyōkai (Ryukyu independence association) said: 'However much the Communists criticise the U.S., they probably cannot get away with denying the magnificent results of the civil economy which the U.S. has implemented in Ryukyu.' A text published in the name of the Okinawa Kirisutokyō Dōshikai (Association of Christian kindred spirits), in turn, advocated Okinawan independence by means of 'the spreading of the gospel and the power of the United States,' saying that 'America itself flourished due to Christianity, and is like a senior and big brother to us who are guided by Christianity' (Sai 1957, p. 41; Takemoto n.d., pp. 16, 17). As such independence discourses were grounded on the premise that it was more advantageous to depend on America rather than Japan in economic terms, they could not help losing support when, for example, Japanese economic growth exceeded expectations, and conflict with the U.S. military over the issue of land intensified.

There was another characteristic to these independence arguments apart from their pro-U.S. anti-Communist line, however. It goes without saying that this was an even severer degree of distrust of Japan. The aforementioned pamphlet from the Okinawa Kirisutokyō Dōshikai (Association of Christian kindred spirits) said that 'in the more than 300 years from the tyranny of Satsuma to Japanese politics, Okinawa's economy of exploitation squeezed out islanders' flesh and blood to the very last, and made them wither.' The Ryūkyū Dokuritsu Kyōkai (Ryukyu independence association), citing the words of American scholars who claimed that the Japanese government used Ryukyu in every way, but was averse to making sacrifices for the good of Ryukyu, described the reversion discourse as a 'discourse of subordination to Japan' and a 'fragile, anti-people (*minzoku*) sense of slavery.' Ōgimi, too, in turn, warned against forgetting that the eighty years of Ryukyuan history in the age of Japanese possession were 'times of suffering for the people (*minzoku*), of astounding, undemocratic ordeals of poverty, ill-treatment and subordination caused by its authoritarian economic domination,' and declared that 'young people now do not know this fact, but it was something totally cruel' (Takemoto n.d., p. 14; Sai 1957, pp. 15, 16).

In a 1955 discussion, Nakasone Genwa stated:

> I doubt that the sentiments of those who stress 'Japanese reversion' are really superior to those pro-American or America-reliant people whom they regard with a critical eye. While they censure reliance upon the U.S., aren't they, too, inclined to rely on Japan? ... By contrast, ordinary residents are neither exclusively pro-American nor, at the same time, exclusively pro-Japanese. The first aim of the general public is for their lives to become comfortable, and next, their greatest wish is to improve them ...

> In present-day Okinawa there are no proponents of fanatical reliance upon the U.S., but there are many who advocate fanatical reliance on Japan. The reason for this is that there is discontent and dissatisfaction

with reality to a greater or lesser degree due to the close politico-economic connections that actually exist with the U.S., but because Okinawa has been torn away from Japan, everything [about the latter] is idealised, feelings of yearning and longing become stronger, and every single thing is romanticised (Nakasone 1955 [1973], pp. 314–315).

Next, while emphasising the history of domination by Satsuma and the Meiji government, Nakasone warned that 'the very idea that dissatisfaction with reality would ideally be completely resolved if only the ardent wish for Japanese reversion were fulfilled would be a ridiculous mistake' (Nakasone 1955 [1973], p. 316).

The current of postwar independence discourses, including Nakasone's, was one germinated in the soil of distrust towards the Japanese mainland which lurked in Okinawa. Regardless of its content and reality in its own terms, it had elements of requestioning the image of Japan which advocates of reversion had moulded amid opposition to America. However, these barely attracted interest in an age when reversion was still a dream and an ideal. At the end of the 1960s, though, when Okinawan reversion started to take on a realistic form, anti-reversion thought began to erupt.

The realisation of reversion

As a precursor to an examination of the anti-reversion discourse, first let me roughly explain its temporal background.

What is known to be the change in Okinawa's reversion movement is what is called the switch from '*Hi-no-maru* reversion' to 'anti-war reversion,' as discussed in the previous chapter. The visit to Okinawa in August 1965 by Prime Minister Satō Eisaku is what is often indicated as its turning point, with the intensification of the Vietnam War as its backdrop. Okinawa's value to the U.S. both as a refuelling base and an air force base was again heightened by the Vietnam War, but, combined with increasing crime by U.S. military personnel and the like, the anti-war, anti-base sentiment which had been latent in Okinawa from the start began to gather strength.

This Okinawan visit by Prime Minister Satō also marked a turning point in the trilateral U.S.–Japan–Okinawa relationship. From around this period, in concert with holding proactive negotiations with the U.S. government over reversion, the LDP regime doubled its aid to Okinawa from the 1966–67 fiscal year, again as mentioned in the previous chapter, making it almost twice the amount of aid from the U.S. government in one stroke. This trend continued year by year, and by 1972 aid to Okinawa from mainland Japan had been increased to more than six times the 1966 figure, but this drove the ratio of American aid down in inverse proportion (Yara 1977, p. 192). For the U.S., it was necessary to appease Okinawan internal discontent through economic assistance in order to run its bases, but its burden was great even from execution of the war alone, and it was necessary to have the Japanese government shoulder the governing expenses for Okinawa, which had been a heavy burden of long standing.

While economic assistance was increased on the one hand, the question of the reduction of bases and the U.S. military's administrative rights, which were the main cause for suppression of human rights, was shelved for the time being. In formal terms, such a line was called, among other things, a 'step-up approach (*tsumikasane hōshiki*)' or 'integration-oriented policy (*ittaika seisaku*),' and it was assumed that rather than abandoning Okinawan reversion, it would first raise Okinawan standards to 'match the mainland' through economic aid and the like, and the issue of administrative rights would be solved 'incrementally.' Mainland progressive forces criticised the LDP's gradualist line as an ossification of the current situation, and advocated 'unconditional, immediate, and complete reversion' which stressed 'elimination of U.S. military bases.'

From the late 1960s onwards, along with the rise of a movement opposing the Vietnam War, the Okinawan issue also began to draw interest in general, though it was impossible to erase the impression that the mainland's concern was something that suddenly swelled when it came to this point. As previously mentioned, after a period of 'island-wide struggle,' general public opinion and the interest of the mass media were in low gear, and the issuing of publications relating to the Okinawa problem was almost entirely concentrated into the late 1960s. Most of these publications were ones from a progressive, anti-war reversion standpoint, and it can be argued that the image existing in Japan until today of the reversion movement was more or less shaped in this period.

What must be pointed out in relation to this is that the mainland peace movement until the early 1960s was one that was prone to ignore Okinawa. On the occasion of the 1960 amendment to the AMPO treaty, it had been questioned whether the area of joint defence, namely, what was called 'Japan' in the treaty, encompassed Okinawa. Nakayoshi Ryōkō and others had petitioned the LDP regime to include Okinawa in the amended treaty as a matter of course, but some progressive forces and LDP members opposed this. The opposing argument's rationale was that Okinawa had already become an important military base in the American Asia-Pacific region, and including Okinawa in 'Japan' would mean that the mainland would be completely caught up in the Cold-War military order. The inclusion of Okinawa in AMPO was called 'gathering chestnuts from the fire,' and ultimately the area of joint defence in the treaty was restricted to 'territory under the administration of the Japanese government.'[2]

This provoked the result that the mainland peace movement unintentionally spurred the further development of Okinawa as a military base. In 1957, Prime Minister Kishi Nobusuke and President Eisenhower held talks, and the American side promised to withdraw its ground combat forces from the Japanese mainland where anti-U.S.-base struggle was strong, but these troops converged on Okinawa, which had no treaty or legal constraints. From the 1950s to the beginning of the 1960s, the construction of bases continued one after another in Okinawa, and in contrast to the shrinkage of the mainland's U.S. military bases to about one quarter, Okinawan bases increased to about double their number, but there was no conspicuous movement opposing this from the mainland.[3] In circumstances where demonstrators encircled the Diet Building on the occasion of the 1960 anti-AMPO campaign, President Eisenhower, who was scheduled to visit Tokyo, had no choice but to head to Okinawa, but the leaders of the demonstrators reported at this time: 'Eisenhower's Japanese visit has been blocked. We have won. The cowardly Eisenhower has run away to Okinawa,' and demonstrators apparently broke into cheers (Nakasone 1969, p. 59). Okinawa was not included in the 'Japan' whose peace they endeavoured to preserve.

As might be expected, such a mentality in the mainland peace movement had almost disappeared in the late 1960s, but still it could not be said that every last remnant had vanished. For example, in the 1960s the expression 'the Okinawaisation (*Okinawa-ka*) of the mainland' was often employed. This meant that if nuclear weapons and U.S. military bases were going to remain even if Okinawa were returned, then this conversely would mean bringing nuclear weapons and U.S. troops into Japan; and dragging the mainland's peace situation down to 'Okinawa level' instead of pulling Okinawa up to 'mainland level.' This was something advocated with the intention of accomplishing anti-war reversion, but on the Okinawan end there were some who were repelled by this as constituting mainland egoism.[4]

As a whole, mainland concern towards the Okinawan problem in the late 1960s was something that emerged against the background of the Vietnam War. On the assumption that the conservative government began aid to Okinawa as part of international relations with the U.S. in concert with the Vietnam War, the progressive side directed attention at the Okinawan issue within the anti-Vietnam-War movement. Speaking in terms of the outcome, Okinawa, which had been integrated into Japan on the grounds of the first Sino-Japanese War, was separated from Japan by the Pacific War, and, after having been stuck in a situation of being 'Japan' and not 'Japan' along with the Korean War, came to 'return' to Japan again amid the changes in international relations that accompanied the Vietnam War.

The changes which occurred along with the Vietnam War manifested themselves in aspects of Okinawan domestic policy, as well. In 1968, as the Vietnam War reached its climax, when Okinawan residents' anti-base sentiments were rising, the public election of the Chief Executive, who had for a long time been appointed, became a reality. In this election, while what was the *de facto* Okinawan branch of the mainland LDP (having had a change of nomenclature from the Democratic Party, a local Okinawan party), extolling a line of gradual progress and arguing that reversion was 'premature,' attacked the progressive camp, saying that if the latter were to win, then Okinawa would economically become an island of 'sweet potatoes and bare feet.' Yara Chōbyō was elected with the support of the progressive joint campaign which publicly pledged such issues as 'immediate, unconditional reversion' and 'opposition to bases.' Here, in company with the reversion movement's transition from '*Hi-no-maru* reversion' to 'anti-war reversion,' there were indications of an escalation of expectations towards a 'peaceful ancestral land' rather than economic interests such as in the 1950s reversion movement among Okinawan residents who had been threatened by the intensification of war. Through support for this election, mainland progressive political parties also deepened their relationship with the Okinawan side, and, along with the People's Party which became the ruling party as a progressive joint campaign, they towed the reversion movement towards more of an anti-war, pro-peace line.

Though according to a description by Nishime Junji, a rival candidate, Yara himself was 'a nationalist and a humanist, but not someone to recite progressive ideology,' Yara maintained cordial relations with the mainland LDP, also (Yara 1977, p. 97). Immediately after his win, a B-52 strategic bomber crashed, and in February 1969, moves to press for the removal of B-52s by means of a general strike escalated, but Yara took the path of negotiation with the U.S. military and LDP, and made them avoid a general strike. In February 1971, again, members of Zengunrō (a union of Okinawan base workers), fired in large numbers due to U.S. military 'lean and mean' cost-cutting measures, went on strike, but Yara took a stance of avoidance to this, as well.

One of the methods which Yara adopted in mitigating confrontation in such peace issues and strikes was to exercise his natural negotiating ability and his ties with the LDP, and extract economic assistance from the mainland government. In the Zengunrō strike, he tried to circumvent the strike by having the mainland government give those who had been retrenched a lump-sum payment; and in the issue of removal of gas which occurred due to an accidental poison gas leak at a U.S. military base in July 1969, because there was strong opposition from residents of the area constituting the transport route, settlement was again made by having the mainland government pay the expense and build a new transport road.[5]

In such an environment, through talks between the then U.S. President Richard Nixon and Japanese Prime Minister Satō Eisaku in November 1969, a plan to return Okinawan administrative rights to the Japanese government in 1972 was announced. This plan, which in vulgar terms is dubbed 'nuclear-free, mainland-standard' or 'with bases, mainland-standard,' was one which spelt out that U.S. military bases would remain 'to mainland level,' and that 'prior consultation' would be conducted with the Japanese government as to the importation of nuclear weapons. Four months earlier than this, the U.S. government had announced its plan to withdraw troops from Vietnam, and the U.S. side, troubled by the financial burden, inclined towards the pre-existing view that it would cut costs if it returned administrative rights to Japan once it had secured its bases, and it convinced its military, which adhered to its vested interests.

At that very time, in 1970, the deadline for revision of the U.S.–Japan Security Treaty was approaching; and for America, which wanted to secure Japan as an anti-Communist ally, and, of course, for the Japanese government and the LDP, a revival of the situation in 1960 when the Japanese government was exposed to crisis by the opposition movement was a state of affairs which had to be avoided at all costs. Even if it meant abandoning U.S. military vested interests in Okinawa, it was considered a wiser plan to stabilise the conservative government by seizing the moot point of the anti-war movement by restoring Okinawan administrative rights, and satisfying the nationalism of the Japanese side. Moreover, at the time of reversion, the U.S. side made Japan accept such conditions as that the Japanese government would bear the rental costs of land for U.S. military use post-reversion, and that the Japanese government would buy up the facilities which the U.S. military had constructed outside the bases.[6]

Critical voices arose from both conservative and progressive camps about this way of reversion. Originally, as Ashida Hitoshi had once said, a strongly-rooted feeling remained in the conservative regime that Okinawa was 'not of much importance to the Japanese economy' (Ōe 1970, p. 124). In 1969, Kon Tōkō, an LDP member of the House of Councillors, courted a backlash when he remarked: 'Frankly speaking, we do not want islands that can produce only sweet potatoes and brown sugar,' but in the mainland business world, also, there lurked a view that Okinawan reversion would do nothing but increase the financial burden. As previously mentioned, due also to the fact that retaining the current state of separation and disparity was more convenient for having low-paid workers migrate to the mainland for jobs, no small number of financiers espoused the idea that reversion was premature. As Okinawa's value to Japan as a bastion of national defence, as it had been in the prewar, had disappeared, in the eyes of such politicians and financiers, it constituted nothing more than having taken on a burden from the connection with America. For that reason, when complaints about this reversion arose from the Okinawan end, these were countered with cries of 'Don't indulge Okinawa.'

For the progressives, as well, reversion with retention of U.S. military bases was intolerable from an anti-war standpoint. In the progressives' view, when all was said and done, this reversion consisted of none other than assumption by the Japanese government of the expense of administration while the U.S. side secured the *de facto* free right of use of bases. In 1960s Japan, rather than orthodox progressive parties such as the Socialist Party and Communist Party, it was the radical New Left movement that came to prominence and became a huge presence in the student movement and anti-AMPO movement of the late 1960s. Moreover, both the New Left and progressive parties were opposed to such a LDP reversion plan, and talks between Satō and Nixon provoked violent demonstrations and strikes both on the mainland and in Okinawa.

Yara, however, did not reject this reversion. Being a realist, Yara thought that this form of reversion, though admittedly not quite ideal, still represented progress, and it was one that was close to the reversion idea which Yara and his ilk had originally advocated in the 1950s. Moreover, upon negotiation with the LDP, Yara succeeded in having the Japanese government take on the burden of half the amount of the Ryukyu government's accumulated deficit, which had climbed to 18.53 million dollars, consolidating the outcome of reversion (Yara 1997, p. 193).

Though there was latent dissatisfaction as to this stance of Yara's among mainland and Okinawan progressive political parties, they could not help supporting him in light of the sequence of events that had him elected by means of a progressive joint campaign. In the autumn of 1970, in advance of reversion, 'national political participation' in which members of both houses of the Japanese Diet were elected from Okinawa – Yara claims that from a standpoint of the strengthening of integration into Japan, he had originally been thinking that he wanted 'national political participation, national rather than the public election of the Okinawan Chief Executive, to materialise first' (Yara 1997, p. 188), but for progressive parties on the mainland side, division in the progressive force had to be avoided in that sense, as well. To this end, mainland and Okinawan progressive parties touted 'anti-war reversion' to the LDP and its vision of reversion, and while strengthening their position, decided to take the irresolute attitude of continuing to support Yara, who maintained cordial relations with the LDP.

Nonetheless, even though the LDP's reversion vision was criticised, the progressives did not reject reversion *per se*. The progressive camp's emphasis was on overcoming '*Hi-no-maru* reversion' and making 'anti-war reversion' unequivocal, and raising the mainland's peace constitution into the symbol of 'Japan' in place of the '*Hi-no-maru.*' As this was implemented based on the view of excluding such foreign elements as the '*Hi-no-maru*' and '*Kimi-ga-yo*' with confirmation of the orthodox progressive nationalism, rather than being a change of line, the Okinawan People's Party and mainland Communist Party did not alter their attitude that reversion equated to the unification of the Japanese people (*minzoku*).

When this period arrived, a tendency to reappraise Okinawan traditional culture arose in both the People's Party and the Communist Party, but this was in the shape of a variation on the 'national (*minzoku*) performing arts movement' which applauded grassroots 'Japanese popular (*minzoku*) culture' or 'Japanese regional culture' in contrast to top-down culture from the rulers. In 1971, for instance, a mainland progressive theatre group which presented folk entertainment visited Okinawa, and performed Ryukyuan dances under the title of 'An evening of popular arts.' The Okinawa People's Party organ, *Jinmin* (The people), reviewed it, saying: 'Let us fight against the colonial, degenerate invaders' "culture" which America pours in' and 'win national unification from below by firmly joining Okinawa and the mainland with national (*minzoku*) performing arts, in order to protect and foster national culture.' Along with this, there was criticism pointing out the 'magnificence of the creative work of mainland cultural groups and the backwardness of Okinawa's' (Janamoto 1971; Kawamura 1971).

In such an environment, it was natural for persons who were not only disillusioned with the reality of reversion, but who also harboured discontent with Yara's administration and with progressive parties to have appeared. Though their ways of expressing dissatisfaction were diverse, roughly two types were present.

One, it goes without saying, was that the reversion ideal had been smashed, and it criticised the selfishness of the Japanese side. Ōta Masahide, a historian who became Governor of Okinawa Prefecture from 1990 to 1998, studied the Japanese treatment of Okinawa since the Ryukyu Disposition, and wrote a critique entitled *The ugly Japanese*. Ōshiro Tatsuhiro, a writer who came to notice as the first Okinawan winner of Japan's most prestigious literary award, the Akutagawa Prize, also criticised the reversion movement in Japan and inside Okinawa (Ōta 1969).[7]

In addition, in concert with the extension to Okinawa of the confrontational relationship between the Communist Party and New Left on the mainland, the People's Party and Communist Party, which supported Yara and touted reversion by means of national (*minzoku*) unification, went up against student organisations from the University of the Ryukyus and suchlike.

The other type was a conservative or pro-American one which derived from the existing Ryukyuan independence discourse. The LDP's championing of the argument that reversion was premature was as previously described, but the Democratic Party, the forerunner of the Okinawan LDP, was a pro-American party, and had garnered the support of financiers and business people who had gained vested interests under U.S. military rule. As previously noted, economic interests had been the reversion movement's logic in the 1950s, but in the 1968 election for Chief Executive, the side that stressed economic interests was the one with LDP connections which argued the prematurity of reversion; and in this period, the Okinawan conservative camp, which attached importance to economic vested interests, asserted the prematurity of reversion, or opposed it altogether. Its designated head, Matsuoka Seiho, the appointed Chief Executive Officer from 1964 to 1968, for one, was known originally as an advocate of Ryukyuan independence, and people such as Matsukawa Kunio, Director of the Ryukyu Chamber of Commerce and Industry, criticised the Teachers' Association's reversion campaign as being something aimed at the 'empty slogan of "*Nihonjin kyōiku* (education for becoming Japanese)"' and school teachers' pensions and severance pay. As reversion became tangible, opposition to reversion, or the argument that it was premature, also raised its head from business operators around the bases, and a 'Ryukyuan parliament' movement and 'Okinawa-jin no Okinawa o tsukuru kai' (a group to make an Okinawa for Okinawans), which emphasised praise for the Ryukyu Kingdom and the aggressiveness of the Ryukyu Disposition, made their appearance.[8]

The latter's conservative anti-reversion or prematurity arguments also subtly intersected with the anti-reversion discourse based on cost and discriminatory feelings present in mainland conservative forces. In April 1969, a letter from a certain doctor in Tochigi Prefecture sent to the *Ryukyu shinpō* was worded:

> Oh, people of Ryukyu! You originally must have been an independent country ... Caught up in the turmoil of the Meiji Restoration, you were made into residents of Japan's Okinawa Prefecture, and occupied. And you were governed by functionaries relegated from the bureaucracy in

Japan proper (*naichi*), and made into a Japanese deficit prefecture ... Most fortunately, thanks to the Pacific War, you have separated from Japan and have come under U.S. military administration, and because of that, apart from the military facilities, you have a freedom that is completely unimaginable in mainland Japan. Even though it was similarly a territory, Korea has become independent. Taiwan also has achieved independence. Why doesn't Ryukyu become independent? ... There would be no worries about financial affairs. You could fund these by tourism and gambling ... You should make [Ryukyu] into a land of entertainment. You should hurry up and forget such things as war damage. You should merely think of it as having met with a big typhoon or the like ... Stop yearning for petty reversion to the mainland! It is the finest opportunity you have been given (Ōe 1970, pp. 78–79).

Furthermore, in regard to the election of members from Okinawa to the Diet in Tokyo, this doctor remarked: 'Why interfere in the politics of a foreign country? At the present point in time, Okinawa is a foreign land, and Japan, too, is a foreign country, is it not?' Naturally, there was criticism in response to this from the Okinawan side, saying: '[This person] seems to understand Okinawa only to be something alien, to look down upon it, and to be unable to bear that alien thing entering Japan' (Ōe 1970, p. 79; Gima 1969, p. 74).

In other words, at this time, the reversion plan which the LDP and the U.S. proposed, the progressives' anti-war reversion and national reunification line, the Ryukyuan independence discourse, and so forth, all intersected in a complex manner. For that reason, even if there were objections to reversion, a structure took shape in which it was hard to support anti-reversion if they wanted to keep a distance from the conservative independence discourse. This was all the more the case even if it were not the ideal form of reversion, if it came down to being able to anticipate improvement in the human rights situation, and so on. For that reason, even Ōta and Ōshiro, or Nakano Yoshio and Ōe Kenzaburō, who were known as conscientious mainland intellectuals of the day, did not go so far as to work out a definite opposition to reversion, in spite of their criticism of the mainland's prejudiced sentiments or history of domination. In that atmosphere, Arakawa Akira, who advocated 'anti-reversion' while distancing himself from the conservative independence discourse, came to attract notice.

Aversion to the 'mask'

The Arakawa who became an anti-reversion discourse polemicist had been known earlier as a poet. There are several points that must be touched upon in discussing him.

The first is that Arakawa, born in 1931, had been a student at the University of the Ryukyus in its foundation days. As previously mentioned, the University of the Ryukyus was originally a university set up for the training of pro-American elites, and was also one of the few sites in postwar Okinawa where students could receive a modern higher education. The phenomenon of resistance to governance which emerges from opportunities for higher education created by a ruling side is something often seen in cases of colonial rule in the world, such as the movement petitioning for establishment of a parliament in Taiwan, as discussed in this book's second volume. People who harboured doubts about U.S. military rule also grew from among students at the University of the Ryukyus.

Arakawa, once a 'boy of the martial nation,' met with Japan's defeat on Yaeyama, and, hearing that Japan had lost, apparently was so vexed that he resolved to 'take revenge' when he grew up. He seems to have been an English major when he entered the University of the Ryukyus, but later switched to the Department of Japanese Literature. At the time of his enrolment, the university had poor facilities, and many students aspired to go abroad to America or to the Japanese mainland to study. Though most of the 'bunch aspiring to study in the States' was attached to the English Literature Department, Arakawa reportedly felt repelled by 'their kind of smartness, which could perhaps be described as America-crazy' (Arakawa and Arasaki 1985, pp. 40, 50). After that, though Arakawa attempted to go to mainland Japan, this did not eventuate, and he went on to become a founding member of the journal *Ryūdai bungaku* (University of the Ryukyus literature), and to immerse himself in literature.[9]

In 1956, the year of 'island-wide struggle,' this *Ryūdai bungaku* journal was banned, its club activities were suspended for half a year, and the editors responsible were punished. This was partly due to Arakawa's poetry anthology, 'The Coloured Race.' I cite an excerpt below:

> Even within the yellow race
> There are all kinds of races.

There are people who
Defend pure blood
Believe in pure blood
Encourage, firmly join
And advance in step with each other

There are those with worldly wisdom who
Devoting all their coquetry
Betray their blood
Sell over their blood
Hiding a monkey-like, hideous countenance
Beneath a clever mask

We will strip off the mask
We keep our eyes open
In order to drag it out into the light of day
We keep our eyes open 24 hours a day
In order to expose the snare set
To sully our blood

We the yellow race
Have pride in being the yellow race
We walk in order to rip apart
The paunchy fat bellies
Of the monkeys within the yellow race and
The white wolves that threaten our blood
Snapping our eyes wide open
We walk (Arakawa 1956, pp. 41–42).

Priding themselves in belonging to the derided 'yellow race,' they fight against the 'white wolves' they disdain, and, above all, the 'monkeys within the yellow race' that betray their 'blood.' Even in Okinawa at that time, there were people who aimed for upward social mobility by equipping themselves with the culture of the American side, and at the University of the Ryukyus, as well, there were some whom Arakawa describes as being 'America-crazy.' Revolt against the gaze of the 'wolves' who were the rulers, and disgust at the 'monkeys' who aligned themselves with them, were shared sentiments arising in intellectuals who lived in colonial circumstances. The stance that Arakawa took in his later anti-reversion discourse could be described as one of substituting the 'yellow race' in this poem with 'Okinawans,' and 'wolves' with 'Japan,' endeavouring to 'strip off the mask' of the reversionists whom he regarded as the 'monkeys' within Okinawa.

However, Arakawa himself, who extols 'blood' here, was actually not the possessor of 'pure blood' as an 'Okinawan.' He was the son of an Okinawan-born father and mainland-born mother, and he could not speak Okinawan very well until he grew up. After dropping out of university, Arakawa joined a newspaper company and worked in Osaka; and there, too, he had a colleague with a mainland-born mother and an Okinawan father. At this colleague's constant emphasis on his mother's origins, and his attempts to demonstrate that he himself was 'Japanese,' Arakawa reportedly 'felt a violent inward repulsion and contempt,' and continuously murmured to himself: 'I, too, have one *Yamatonchu* (Yamato-born) parent, the same as you, but I am definitely an Okinawan.' Moreover, while he was working in Osaka, he tried to master Okinawan with his wife as a sounding-board, and 'though mistakes in accent and paucity of vocabulary could not be helped,' he 'somehow managed to get [his] tongue around it.' After Arakawa began to criticise 'Japan' in his anti-reversion discourse, he went so far as to say: 'It was an almost unbearable humiliation for me even to be conscious of the fact that the country where my own mother was born was Japan, and that Japanese blood was flowing within my own blood,' but it can be argued that he harboured the same kind of anguish as the so-called 'mixed-blood' intellectuals in colonies (Arakawa 1971, pp. 76–92).

In addition, what is indispensable to a discussion of Arakawa's thought is that the place where he spent a little of his infancy, and, again where he worked after returning to Okinawa from Osaka, was Yaeyama, which had been exploited by the Ryukyu Kingdom as a frontier region of Okinawa. There, he discovered that 'just as *Yamatu* (Yamato) and *Uchinaa* (Okinawa) were contraposed and engaged with each other in the form of "centre" and "periphery," an equivalent relationship also exists between *Uchinaa* and *Eema* (Yaeyama).' In cultural terms, as well, 'just as the people of *Uchinaa* since modern times, by deeming their own culture to be of the same nature and same origin as *Yamatu*, seek to raise themselves from a frontier and secure an equal status, the people of *Eema* similarly hope to outgrow their own feeling of being a frontier by making their own cultural heritage comparable to that of *Uchinaa*, and making it the same quality.' In other words, a relationship between 'wolves' and 'monkeys' was present here, too (Arakawa 1971, pp. 35, 37).

Awareness of this kind of regional disparity within Okinawa made Arakawa adopt a complicated stance towards Okinawan nationalism, in the same way as Ifa. He championed Okinawa as against 'Japan,' but, as I will later elaborate, around 1970 he kept a certain distance from the Ryukyuan independence discourse. This was not only because he resisted the conservative Ryukyuan independence discourse, but also because he was conscious that 'when there is talk of Okinawan self-reliance or independence, there will be a real backlash from the people of Yaeyama and Miyako, demanding: "What about us? Will only [the main island of] Okinawa become independent?"' (Arakawa and Ikezawa 1996, p. 30).

In a controlling relationship, and especially amid a sense of cultural inferiority where they admire the 'wolves,' they make themselves decline into 'hideous monkeys' – this arguably was what Arakawa consistently hated and made his enemy, and even in his later anti-reversion discourse, his concern was focused more upon issues of cultural or spiritual self-respect, rather than economic or political inequalities. Furthermore, the awareness that he himself had inherited the 'blood' of 'wolves' and his interest in the controlling relationship within Okinawa came to bring a peripherality which transcended mere glorification of Okinawa and Okinawan nationalism.

That said, it was only from the late 1960s that Arakawa made his anti-reversion stance explicit in his works, he having been a reversionist prior to that. In Arakawa's words, 'in the midst of getting through the confusion of defeat, Japan was a kind of utopia for Okinawa,' and, 'of course,' for Arakawa, too; and for him, personally, Japan was the country of his mother's birth. However, his feelings towards reversion, unlike the pragmatic ones that existed in the leaders' cohort in the 1950s reversion movement, were ones imbued with an extremely existential expectation, namely: 'for me, previously, "reversion" meant a "battle" which would allow no avoidance for the sake of the full liberation of Okinawa(ns), including myself' (Arakawa 1971, pp. 66, 68).

Arakawa's internal disappointment towards such expectations had already arisen from the beginning of the 1960s, however. 'I can see Japan,' a poem contained in an anthology published in 1960, and especially well-known among his poetry, declares:

Anti-Reversion

Oh Japan
Oh ancestral land
The Japan that has approached so near
Turns its rascally face away
The Okinawan Sea
The Sea of Japan
The 27 degrees north latitude line dividing them
Dissolves in the waves
Like a jack-knife
It slashes at our hearts (Arakawa 1971, pp. 72–73).

This poem was one that Arakawa penned in the period when he was working in Osaka, and he said: 'By then, Japan as a utopia had already vanished from inside me, based on my experience of having set foot in its reality,' Nonetheless, this does not mean that reversion itself had already been rejected within him, and Arakawa goes no further than to express his 'distrust of Japan' in the part of the poem worded: 'turn its rascally face away' (Arakawa 1971, p. 73).

Yet this poem was often cited within the reversion movement as one which expressed Okinawan poets' deep affection towards Japan. Not only was it used in the report of a 'national unification' event held on the sea on the 27 degrees north latitude line, but when it was employed for the ending of a particular film, it was apparently cited with omission of the 'rascally' bit in order to project the Okinawa side's 'pure sentiments.' As already mentioned, in the reversion movement up to the early 1960s, in order to summon mainland interest and to mask the lack of theory, descriptions such as 'the blood of a people (*minzoku*) is thicker than water' and 'the pure feeling of a child yearning for its mother' were recklessly fired off, enabling the avoidance of accusations of discrimination and the voicing of distrust towards Japan.

It was natural that Arakawa, on his part, 'felt irritation at not succeeding in having people interpret the perverse sentiments' with which he had intended to imbue this poem (Arakawa 1971, p. 75). And at the end of the 1960s, when the reality of reversion began to become definite, such irritation had already become hard to bear, and to manifest itself by turning into the anti-reversion discourse.

Arakawa's anti-reversion argument, which was advanced from such a position, made reversion an issue more of identity than a politico-economic phenomenon. What he criticised most in his anti-reversion discourse was the idea of 'making Okinawans into "complete, fine Japanese"' in the name of reversion and 'national unification' (Arakawa 1971, p. 96). He elucidates his own idea of 'anti-reversion' as follows:

> ... The 'reversion' I mean when I say 'anti-reversion' does not indicate an external phenomenon consisting of territorially and institutionally reintegrating divided Japan and Okinawa, but the business of spontaneous thought in which Okinawans voluntarily absorb themselves in 'the state (*kokka*),' so to speak. In that sense, it would not matter if we re-phrased 'anti-reversion' as a spiritual preference that continues to reject unification into 'the state' in an individual phase to the bitter end. In other terms again, anti-reversion is anti-state and an anti-national (anti-*kokumin*) orientation (Arakawa 1971, p. 304).

The 'state' that Arakawa mentioned was also a nation-state which demanded the allegiance and assimilation of its constituents and involved even as far as individual identity, rather than a sovereign state as a political notion. Moreover, his 'anti-reversion' could be called an ideology that consistently rejected identification with the state from an 'individual phase.' For that reason, he placed importance upon 'this consciousness structure, which realises that [one] is persistently Okinawan before being Japanese,' as constituting Okinawa's 'alien-ness,' and he advocated making this 'feeling of being different arise spontaneously as an ideology of rejection of the state, and making this an ideological strongpoint in the fight against state power' (Arakawa 1971, pp. 8, 97). This might also have been influenced by Yoshimoto Takaaki's collective illusion theory, which had gained a good reputation among the then Japanese mainland's New Left, but it was an idea substantially derived from Arakawa's experience.

Here, identification with and integration into the Japanese state themselves were rejected, and whether the form of integration was equal or unequal was not the question. Rather, according to Arakawa, as long as Okinawans continued to seek 'equality as members of the nation' in order to escape from discrimination, 'movements for the elimination of discrimination, too, would be subsumed on an even larger scale into the state and nationalism ... and would be unable to develop into struggles for fundamental reform of the national polity.' In this kind of structure, 'including even movements which at a glance are seen as being anti-regime ... make people strongly demand "departure from discrimination" from within Okinawa in response to the scale of discriminatory measures, and function so as to draw out the energy vis-à-vis positive Japanese assimilation from inside Okinawa.' Moreover, he defined 'reversion' as being rooted in the intention to assimilate to Japan, and to fuse Japan and Okinawa as a homogeneous nation, and being 'a feeling in which we of Okinawa beg to be granted equal eligibility to be members of the nation as Japanese people, without an iota of discrimination' (Arakawa 1971, pp. 122, 119, 66).

According to Arakawa, the process by which Okinawa intensified its intentions towards assimilating with Japan in order to escape from discrimination 'closely resembled the correspondence relation between emperor-system ideology and popular consciousness in modern-day Japan, and its reception and continuation.' The more miserable real discrimination and their lives were, the more people would fantasise about the emperor as a symbol of 'universal benevolence' and salvation, and intensify their worship of him. Efforts to escape from such discrimination 'betrayed their own intentions by continuing to function as something that made them relentlessly surround themselves in *Yamatu* (= Japan), which continued to exist in actuality as a concrete entity; and, conversely, by means of those efforts which they themselves had made, they repeated the foolish and wretched cycle of solidifying the existence of a state that continued to strangle the people of Japan and Asia, including themselves' (Arakawa 1971, pp. 27, 31).

In Arakawa's opinion, the historical precursors of this kind of movement which sought equality as 'Japanese' were precisely the suffrage petition movement of Jahana Noboru, who had been viewed as a hero in the progressive reversion movement, and Ifa Fuyū's Japan–Ryukyu common-ancestry theory. Jahana's movement, in particular, was both 'the most prominent anti-regime movement in modern Okinawa,' but also 'one that took on an extremely important and pioneering role in integrating the Okinawan populace into Japanese nationalism.' Arakawa offered his doubts about the hypothesis then in circulation that there was exchange between Jahana and the radical thinkers Nakae Chōmin and Kōtoku Shūsui, saying: '[Jahana's] ideas did not take the direction of rejecting the emperor system and state power as the source which compelled authoritarian oppression and exploitation, as did those of Nakae and Kōtoku, ... but extended no further than to a desire to gain complete rights as Japanese imperial subjects,' and suggested that the facts of Jahana's thought 'rather fell within the range of so-called popular rights rightists such as Itagaki Taisuke' (Arakawa 1971, pp. 121, 123–124, 168–169). If Arakawa had known that Itagaki was the person who had organised the 'Taiwan Assimilation Society,' then this, too, might have been emphasised (see Oguma 1998).

In fact, as Arakawa himself had also pointed out, it was around the autumn 1970 election for membership of the Japanese Diet that Jahana Noboru's suffrage petition movement attracted attention. In other words, it was something called up from history as a prior example of an attempt by Okinawans to gain suffrage as 'Japanese.' In this election, Kyan Shin'ei, who had been leading the Okinawa Teachers' Association in place of Yara, and Senaga, Committee Chair of the People's Party, were elected with the support of mainland progressive forces, but Arakawa called for a boycott on voting. According to him, this was because it was only to make the Japanese and U.S. governments' 1972 reversion a *fait accompli*, a measure to swell the number of parliamentarians from mainland progressive forces, and to further Okinawa's integration into 'Japan' through the form of suffrage.

Moreover, once having rejected integration into the state itself, it was not an issue of whether the state into which it would be integrated was a 'good state' or a 'bad state,' either.

In Arakawa's view, 'what we essentially have to keep on fighting is state power itself, which tirelessly oppresses the people;' 'as such, neither does it matter in the slightest whether the one we fight against is the same people (*minzoku*) or an alien people;' and, 'whether a capitalist state or a socialist state, ... state "power" still functions similarly as a compelling force which demands obedience from the masses as the ruled.' In his words, right-wing nationalism 'extolled "anti-Communist nationalism" on the one hand,' while the Communist Party's national unification front, in response, 'merely waved the banner of "anti-U.S. nationalism" on the other' (Arakawa 1971, pp. 184, 215, 218–219).

Whether in terms of the circumstances at the time, or the 'mask'-hating Arakawa's orientation, even stronger criticism was directed at the People's Party and Communist Party's reversion movement, which he regarded as something that 'continued to impose a nationalistic bias which spread and dissolved Okinawa's struggle into Japan as a state' than at the U.S. military with its blatant discrimination, or at conservative advocates. Arakawa criticised Yara's administration, and also commented on the anti-war reversion touted by progressive forces as 'remaining within the firing range of Japanese nationalism, as a mutation of so-called "reversion" ideology,' and he described what was disputed as being 'simply a rivalry between nationalisms which compete over a "better reversion," reducing the Okinawa issue to one solely of "keeping bases, or getting rid of bases"' (Arakawa 1971, pp. 11, 66, 84).

Rather than being a simple argument against reversion, Arakawa's 'anti-reversionism' was one that endeavoured to oppose the very logic of the nation-state by means of Okinawa's 'alien'-ness, and those who most fiercely resisted Arakawa were the mainland's Communist Party and Okinawan People's Party, who advocated an ideology of national (*minzoku*) unification and progressive nationalism.

The distance from the independence discourse

It was not merely for ideological reasons that the Okinawa People's Party and Japanese Communist Party opposed Arakawa. The People's Party of the day, unlike in the 1950s, had already integrated with the Japanese Communist Party, but, as previously mentioned, the New Left movement which emerged from the 1960s not only threatened the leadership in the Communist Party's progressive forces on the mainland, but criticised the People's Party and Communist Party in Okinawa, as well. Even if Arakawa personally was nothing more than a newspaper reporter to the Communist Party and People's Party, it was necessary for them openly to substantiate the correctness of the national unification line by censuring Arakawa, whom they regarded as a representative of critics of reversion.

Firstly, the Okinawa People's Party organ, *Jinmin* (The people), published several anonymous articles criticising Arakawa. According to these, Arakawa's claims were 'unforgivable acts that spat upon the democratic forces of reversion to the ancestral land,' and it was 'an objective fact that his position and outlook took on multiple roles amid the "*hidari*" *migi* (a unique term employed by the Japanese Communist Party at the time to mean 'apparently leftist, but in effect rightist') tide of the "anti-Communist, anti-People's Party,"' and the anti-reversion discourse was a 'losers' ideology' considered only to be 'urging the continuation of occupation rule by American imperialism.' It argued that it was precisely 'bottom-up national unification' comprising reversion that was 'the 'road to conquering discrimination,' and it would be the 'ruling class in Japan and America and their state power that would be the first to welcome' the anti-reversion discourse (Sashida 1970; Ōmichi 1971; Asato 1971; Nankai 1971). In the People's Party organ of the day, articles criticising the emergence of the New Left appeared in succession, and it was obvious that criticism of Arakawa formed part of these.

The Japanese Communist Party's organ, *Zen'ei* (Vanguard), also took up the anti-reversion discourse in a big way in a special feature on the Okinawa question, and sternly criticised Arakawa's debate as 'having the role of destroying or obstructing the Okinawa–mainland unification front.' In this special feature, Ueda Kōichirō assessed Arakawa's way of understanding the Okinawan problem as an issue of the national sovereignty of the Japanese people as being 'fundamentally mistaken,' and described this as 'potentially leading to the acceptance, in both ideological and practical terms, of America's having seized administrative rights.' In addition, Arakawa's having criticised Yara was taken to be tinged with 'anti-popular criminality,' and there were repeated assertions that the reversion movement was 'an important part of the Japanese people's struggle for true independence, and peace and democracy' (Senaga et al. 1971, pp. 62, 79, 63, 75).

A particular trigger for backlash was Arakawa's having described Okinawa as an 'alien people.' In the words of the Communist Party side: 'Our having demanded political participation, and prefectural residents, in turn, having demanded it ... sprang from the very principle that [Okinawans] are Japanese nationals,' and Arakawa's assertion was taken to be 'one which rejected the proposition in "Okinawan Studies" ever since Ifa Fuyū.' In other words, 'when one takes indicators relating to ethnicity (*minzoku*) into account,' given that 'linguistically the ancient language of Man'yō times is also alive in Okinawa, and the Okinawan dialect is unmistakeably Japanese; and regionally, historically, and in economic life, as well, there are commonalities,' 'Mr Arakawa's particular "alien people" is an "alien people" as a sensation,' and his 'way of thinking vis-à-vis nations or peoples (*minzoku*) is not at all scientific' (Senaga et al. 1971, pp. 79, 77, 59, 76).

Naturally, Arakawa's view of history was also exposed to criticism. Arakawa's perspective on the Ryukyu Disposition was deemed to be 'on the same line as arguments such as that the Meiji government annexed the "independent country of Ryukyu," as a certain historian (referring to Inoue Kiyoshi) claimed at one time,' and what Ifa and Jahana had aimed for was 'true national (*minzoku*) unification,' and 'it goes without saying that this was not the kind of national unification directed at contributing to the "establishment of the emperor system and state power" [such as described by] the reporter Arakawa.' According to the Communist Party and People's Party, Arakawa's idea was 'one that totally ignored the results of conventional research, and one-sidedly distorted historical fact,' and was a 'jumble of miscellaneous knowledge aimed at attacking the democratic forces of reversion to the ancestral land and the People's Party and making them confused' (Senaga et al. 1971, pp. 59, 78; Sashida 1970).

Arakawa was also made the brunt of critical accusations of being an 'epigone of an "independence discourse" dressed up as "left"-wing,' in the same way as Mori Hideto and his ilk once had been. According to the People's Party organ, it was an 'awkward "sense of being a victim of discrimination" that was the very thing which became the "theoretical foundation" for advocates of Okinawan independence at the beginning of the 1950s,' and the anti-reversion discourse was a 'sterile flower blooming wildly in a period of historical transition, as had the anti-reversion discourse, equating to an independence discourse, hitherto in Okinawan history.' The fact that the early postwar Communist Party had issued a 'message celebrating the independence of the Okinawan people (*minzoku*)' was deleted by the party from chronological tables attached to pamphlets it published on the Okinawa issue in later years, and the Ryukyuan independence discourse established its position as an act of betrayal towards national unification by conservative reactionary forces colluding with U.S. imperialism (Haebaru 1970; Nankai 1970).[10]

Arakawa also refuted such criticism. In his opinion, an 'alien people' meant an individual orientation which refused to identify with the state, and was 'unconnected (on a different dimension) with the kind of debate as to whether Okinawans were undisputed members of the Japanese people (*minzoku*) in an academic sense.' Moreover, the anti-war reversion referred to by the Communist Party and People's Party was 'nothing more than a neutralising and dissolving of such potential as Okinawa possessed into Japanese nationalism, touting the just cause of "building a peaceful Japan" by means of the "complete reversion of Okinawa with neither nuclear [arms] nor bases," and was simply using Okinawa as a tool for the Japanese anti-war peace movement, or else for the sake of national reform, namely, for 'Japanese independence' or 'Japanese democratisation' (Arakawa 1971, pp. 11, 137).

Arakawa made the following comment about the Communist Party's anti-war reversion argument:

> Slogans such as 'construction of a democratic, peaceful, neutral Japan,' which even pass wholesale as billboards for current members of the regime as is, would have been better fed to the dog or something in the first place. We could not care less about any peaceful, beautiful, independent country of 'Japan,' and having the peaceful existence of the Japanese nation made into the target of struggle in Okinawa is something we must refuse by all means. This is because it is nothing more than winning by making the trivial logic of the past Battle of Okinawa – in which [we] took upon ourselves the calamity of modern warfare by 'sacrificing ourselves for the country' – cloak itself in 'democrat'-isation ('*minshu*'-*ka*) [*sic*].
>
> What Okinawa historically possessed and decisively learned amid the calamity of the past Battle of Okinawa should have been none other than a rejection of that kind of logic; and Okinawa's struggle which derived from it was, I dare say, what ought to have been something which rejected the very existence of the state when ultimately in the grasp of any kind of political authority (Arakawa 1971, p. 101).

From Arakawa's perspective, when the anti-war reversion discourse emphasised the peace constitution instead of the '*Hi-no-maru*' as the symbol of 'Japan,' it was nothing less than an extension of the logic of drawing forth a desire to assimilate by depicting Japan as a utopia.

The people of Okinawa created an image of Japan as a dream-space where they could escape from postwar poverty and the cruel human-rights situation, and as an affluent and peaceful country where human rights were protected. According to Arakawa, though, just as in the case of all utopias, 'it should be understood in the sense of a faraway paradise for which the people never stop hoping, imagined only inside Okinawans' minds; and that by no means indicates the real Japan itself, either.' In spite of this, he asserted, 'the movement for "reversion to the ancestral land" in postwar Okinawa truly set out from the point of imagining that delusion; and, moreover, in combination with the fierce agitation of sentimental nationalism on the part of those who organised the movement, in the form of "blood is thicker than water," it focused the sentiments of the populace – who in one aspect were simple nationalists, while being egotistical utilitarians in another – through depicting a rose-coloured dream by the supra-logical theory of a Japanese (mainland) utopia, consisting of the idea that "at any rate, if Okinawa reverts to Japan, its human rights will be protected by the constitution; and everything will be better."' Furthermore, the harder the real circumstances, the more that illusion 'ceaselessly impelled people, ignited their passion to leap away from the reality before their very eyes, and spurred people on to that "open world,"' but 'needless to say, Japan had never been a utopia, even within the bounds described in the wording of this constitution, neither has it striven to be so, and the fact that it was something fantasised by people merely as a delusion of so-called postwar democracy in Japan has already become clear in the present day' (Arakawa 1971, pp. 26, 67, 31).

The Communist Party and People's Party criticised Arakawa as espousing an 'independence discourse,' but Arakawa clearly stated the difference between his own assertions and the conventional independence discourse. He described the Ryukyuan independence discourse in the following terms:

> Incidentally, as regards my repeated mention of overcoming a preference for assimilation to Japan = 'reversion' ideology, and my emphasis on the heterogeneity of Japan and Okinawa = 'alien'-ness for the sake of Japanese relativisation, there is considered to be a danger of these being seen as identical to the train of thought comprising the Ryukyuan independence discourse, once it has been reduced to Okinawan nationalism as the flip-side of Japanese nationalism. It goes without saying that this ties with the Ryukyuan independence discourse as a manifestation of so-called Ryukyuan nationalism when the idea conservatively blossoms of relativising to Japan by means of the heterogeneity and 'alien'-ness which Okinawa historically and geographically possessed in relation to Japan, ... and this is what developed the practice of dreaming of a revival of the former Ryukyu Kingdom by advocating an 'Okinawa for Okinawans' (Arakawa 1971, p. 133).

There were two reasons for Arakawa's emphasis on the difference between the independence discourse and his own assertions. One was that he regarded the traditional independence discourse and the then 'Okinawa-jin no Okinawa o tsukuru kai' movement as nothing more than 'movements principally aiming for the preservation of the interests they had secured under the rule of the U.S. Occupation.' The other was that due to his idea that 'anti-reversion was, in short, an anti-state and anti-national orientation,' he did not hold 'Okinawan restoration nationalism' in high esteem (Arakawa 1971, pp. 21, 178).

At the time, Arakawa declared: 'Independence parties contain themselves by calling for "Okinawan independence." This means "independence" based upon the recognition of the current global situation of state groupings which encircle every bit of the earth's surface with national boundaries, and, moreover, contain themselves upon doing so.' In later years, also, he remarked: 'Whether it is a matter of decentralisation or of independence, if we imagine an insular living space or social space like Okinawan nationalism in an extremely narrow sense, I think this would be meaningless. It would be exactly as if we had simply minimised the current Japanese *jus sanguinis*, and the country imagined at that point would just be a mini Japan' (Arakawa et al. 1972, p 82; Arakawa and Ikezawa 1996, p. 35).

The reversion movement ideology which Arakawa tried to oppose was one which, upholding the unification of the 'Japanese people (*Nihon minzoku*),' strove to integrate (in Arakawa's parlance, to 'assimilate') Okinawa into 'the Japanese' in order to make 'Japan' independent as a nation-state. And, if it were going to make Okinawa 'independent' as a nation-state, as well, then it would have to confront the question of where to set the boundaries of a single 'Okinawan people (*minzoku*)' – would it include or exclude the people of Miyako and Yaeyama in 'Okinawans,' for example? If it were to exclude them, then this would be regarding them as 'aliens,' and if it were to include them, then this might affirm assimilation, as when Ifa created Okinawan nationalism. Even if Okinawa achieved 'independence,' if it were according to existing principles of nationalism and the nation-state, then it could reproduce a relationship of exclusion and assimilation on a diminishing scale, and there would likely be no place for people of 'mixed blood' like Arakawa to belong.

In contrast to Arakawa, the People's Party and Communist Party made the 'reversion' movement their absolute precondition for the people's liberation struggle in Okinawa, and censured those who interjected even the slightest whiff of criticism towards this, saying that they 'could only exercise their own thinking within the parameters of being separatists who promptly played a part in the Japanese and American ruling cohort, or else as advocates of Ryukyuan independence who similarly conspired with it (Arakawa 1971, pp. 183). Here, the target of Arakawa's criticism was the very form of thinking which was unable to grasp the state of affairs except in terms of the dichotomy of 'reversion' or 'independence,' as it were, or, in other words, the dichotomy of inclusion or exclusion.

The ideology of 'refusal'

The greatest criticism from the Communist Party and People's Party towards Arakawa's thought, however, was that 'even though, in short, it was to "refuse,"' it was 'something totally devoid of realism' with 'no prospect of "what to do."' In the journal *Zen'ei*, Ueda Kōichirō ranked Arakawa as 'ideologically, someone falling within the current of *petit-bourgeois* radicalism,' and summed up by saying: 'What we now have to set at the centre of our question is what kind of joint action we can take in the political challenge of total Okinawan reversion, not a dispute over philosophical positions' (Senaga et al. 1971, pp. 61, 65, 66; Nankai 1970).

Shinzato Keiji, who had once debated with people like Mori Hideto over assessment of the Ryukyu Disposition, also asserted: 'As the people, led by the proletariat, seize state power though class struggle within the nation-state and win liberation, even if I were to pretend gallantry by paying lip-service to rejecting state power, this would not mean that the state as a mechanism of violence would vanish.' The writer Tōma Tsugunao, in turn, expressed the criticism that 'Arakawa and others probably have no alternative but to uphold their mission statement and policies with boldness, make personal efforts and organise the masses with their own thought, and conduct their campaign. In sum, the logic of the Communist Party and People's Party side was that 'in a word, Mr Arakawa's debate should be called an ideology which rationalises losers' thinking and the abandonment of struggle' (Senaga et al. 1971, pp. 76, 75; Tōma 1971).

Arakawa's response to this was, in a sense, one that was completely off topic. Originally, his anti-reversion discourse had been an ideological undertaking over identity rather than a political movement.

In reply to such criticism as the above, he asserted that 'thought was something whose life was conceived in the individual, and became independent in its individuality,' asking in return: 'Why are mission statements or policies necessary for a single individual who wants to live by one idea?' According to Arakawa, the thesis of anti-reversion = anti-state as an ideological undertaking to eliminate the curse of such things as mission statements and policies had already been presented (Arakawa 1971, p. 325).

As Ueda Kōichirō had written in *Zen'ei*, this kind of 'philosophical' discussion probably appeared meaningless from the standpoint that politics consisted of organising mass movements and political parties. Arakawa himself claimed that 'such a thing as expressive action fixated upon a single person's denouncing and condemning the state and state authority is unlikely to exist' (Arakawa 1971, p. 55). In this atmosphere, both debates could not help running a parallel course from the start.

Even without the Communist Party as his opponent, there was no small amount of criticism of Arakawa's ideas as being unrealistic. In 1971, in a roundtable discussion published in the magazine *Sekai* (The world), Arakawa engaged in the following exchange with Hokama Yoneko, an Okinawan housewife, and Asato Yoshio, Managing Director of the Ryukyu Chamber of Commerce and Industry (though mention of the 'Okinawan independence discourse' was a misunderstanding vis-à-vis the anti-reversion discourse).[11]

> Hokama: I would like to ask Mr Arakawa what is happening with the connection between the Okinawan independence discourse and the ideology of the 'Ryukyu Assembly,' the 'Society of Okinawans for Making Okinawa,' and so on, which existed prior to the joint statement on reversion, for example.
>
> Arakawa: In short, in the case of '[the Society of] Okinawans for [Making] Okinawa' or the 'Ryukyu Assembly,' a perspective towards U.S. military domination is completely absent, is it not? Ultimately, it was nothing more than the sort of awareness that constituted a resolve to preserve the privileged interests that they themselves had cultivated amid the bitter circumstances of these twenty-five years.

Hokama: Another thing is that, for example, Britain has some autonomous territories, but is the Ryukyuan independence discourse a plan such as to make the entire nation an autonomous territory?

Arakawa: As a way of thinking, wouldn't it be desirable after all for Japan as a whole to have something like a federation of local government bodies in each separate block, such as [the whole of] Kyushu in the case of Kyushu?

Hokama: So this would lead in the end to demands for expansion and establishment of the right of regional autonomy, do you mean?

Arakawa: But I think that it would end up being a denial of the state itself, as our ultimate ideal. Regardless of whether the country is capitalist or socialist, we have to push forward our aim as far as rejection of state power itself … If not, then ultimately we will have no choice but to take on the role of supplementing systemic nationalism from below.

Asato: Where in the world are there places that have no power? That is what I want to know. Every country is likely to have power.

Arakawa: So unless we establish a situation where there is no power as our ultimate aim while we live our lives or engage in behaviour, this will be inevitable, won't it? (Shiomi et al. 1971, pp. 112, 113)

This conversation well exhibits part of how Arakawa's ideas were received. People tried to classify his anti-reversion discourse using existing political terminology such as 'independence,' 'autonomous territory,' and 'regional autonomy,' and when they saw that this was impossible, they cut it down, saying: 'Where in the world are there places that have no power?'

Even Arakawa, in a real situation, acknowledged that it was natural for reversion to be a step forward, and was not an issue he would particularly dispute, saying: 'As it is a situation stipulated by presidential executive order in which human rights and so on have been completely ignored, it goes without saying that the application of the constitution [by means of reversion] would be a step forward.' Certainly, being formally classified as 'Japanese' would have been still better than the situation with no rights in which Okinawa continued to be placed as 'Japanese' and not 'Japanese,' and as 'people without an ancestral land.' To Arakawa, however, 'though the principal factor binding us and pushing us into an oppressed condition while in a state of "uncertain nationality" was the "state (*kokka*)" itself,' it was precisely the postwar reversion movement which, 'rather than going in the direction of repudiating the "state" that constituted the main culprit, propelled mass movements which desired to be even more strongly restrained by the "state"' (Shiomi et al. 1971, p. 111; Arakawa 1971, pp. 216–217).

Nonetheless, moves for reversion were resolutely advancing, and Arakawa himself also acknowledged: 'It is clear that we are only an extremely small number of "dissenters,"' and he merely commented: 'In short, I feel truly gloomy at the mention of 1972.' Still, the reason he expressed for advocating anti-reversion was that he had 'continued stubbornly to say "no" as an initial means of ideologically striking a hard blow to Okinawa's (and Okinawans') stupid and cruel internal passion, consisting of ceaselessly continuing to support the fortification of a system of control by devoting themselves unquestioningly to the state (= Japan)' (Arakawa 1971, p. 47; Shiomi et al. 1971, p. 116). For Arakawa, anti-reversion meant above all the idea of 'refusal.'

Is there no way to be liberated except by being classified and subsumed as constituents of a nation-state called 'Japan,' 'America' or 'Okinawa' by means of the function of power? Can there be no means of opposition bar through the acquisition of rights by being classified more deeply as 'Japanese,' or by becoming 'independent' and forming a new nation-state, or by gaining 'autonomy' within a state? These points were truly those to which Arakawa at the time slammed down his 'no,' not only to Japanese reversion and U.S. military domination, of course, but also to all existing arguments right up to Okinawan independence, and came to interrogate with the word 'anti-reversion.' This, moreover, was a clear-cut 'anti-state' ideology which appeared at the end of the century-long history of the modern nation-state called Japan, which had implemented control by ceaselessly redrawing the boundaries of 'the Japanese.' It was not enough, however, to stem the tide of reversion.

On 15 May 1972, Okinawa 'reverted' to Japan.

Conclusion

The status of Okinawa

The status of Okinawa has been determined by various political expectations relating mainly to the economy and military affairs. As I also mentioned in the Introduction, these two have moulded the vectors of inclusion and exclusion. The same applied to the 1972 restitution of administrative rights.

Something also discussed in Chapter Nine was that the United States military initially insisted upon its vested right to rule Okinawa with a free hand, and opposed the restoration of administrative rights. In spite of this, the American government decided upon restoration for the economic reason that the cost burden of the Vietnam War had become too heavy, and the military reason that Okinawa's value had fallen amid U.S. withdrawal from Vietnam and advancing U.S.–China rapprochement.

1950s Okinawa was a base from which to keep an eye on North Korea and Beijing. 1960s Okinawa was a relay station for supplies in the Vietnam War, and a base for strategic bombers taking off on bombing missions to North Vietnam. Okinawa has little value as an anti-Soviet military base. When U.S.–China rapprochement progressed and the Vietnam War headed towards its end, Okinawa's worth for the U.S. military declined.

Okinawa's military value also changed due to the technological standard of weapons. One of the reasons for the U.S. military having expanded its air force bases in Okinawa in the 1950s was a shift in strategy by the U.S. military which accompanied the development of nuclear weapons. After the Korean War ended in 1953, President Eisenhower announced a 'new look' in strategic affairs, of strengthening nuclear armaments and air power while drastically curtailing the army's conventional armaments. In line with this strategy, Okinawa's air force bases were expanded and nuclear bombs stored.

Later, medium-range nuclear missiles were deployed in Okinawa. It was in 1967 that the U.S. military deployed nuclear weapons in East Asia in the largest quantities, but of its total number of approximately 3200 missiles, some 1300 were placed in Okinawa, far exceeding the approximately 900 in Korea, which took second place.[1] Moreover, this period was when the Vietnam War was intensifying, and in that sense, as well, it was the time when the military value of Okinawa grew to its greatest heights.

Such a concentration of nuclear weapons was simultaneously due to Okinawa's geographical advantage and its political advantage of being under U.S. military governance. The deployment of nuclear weapons in Japan was something that was impossible, to maintain the stability of the Japanese conservative regime. If the U.S. were to deploy nuclear weaponry on the Japanese mainland, there would be the risk that this would court a backlash from Japanese public opinion, the support of Japanese nationals for the pro-U.S. conservative regime would be lost, and a Socialist Party regime would take its place. On the other hand, nuclear weapons were deployed even among newly anti-Communist countries in Asia where the level of democratisation was low, that is, Korea, Taiwan and The Philippines. The number of deployed nuclear weapons was in inverse proportion to their level of democratisation, so to speak. In that sense, it was natural, as it were, for the number deployed in Okinawa, which was under military administration, to have been the largest of all.

In parallel with this, from the late 1950s into the early 1960s, withdrawal of the U.S. Army from the Korean Peninsula and the Japanese mainland took place. As I stated in Chapter Nine, while on the one hand U.S. military bases in mainland Japan reduced to one quarter, bases on Okinawa expanded almost twofold, and half of U.S. military bases were focused in Okinawa, which has only about 0.6 percent of Japan's land area. This was because the peace movement in mainland Japan was strong, and also the result of the actual relocation of bases to Okinawa under U.S. military rule, but it also coincided with a strategic shift by the U.S. military.

At the end of the 1960s, however, along with the Apollo Project, inter-continental ballistic missiles (ICBMs) were put to practical use, as were submarine-launched ballistic missiles (SLBMs) and nuclear-powered submarines. Further, if these were used in combination with missiles deployed in Korea and those with which the Seventh Fleet were equipped, it would now be sufficient even if nuclear weapons were removed from Okinawa. The Pentagon, which took the stability of Japan's conservative regime seriously, and the Secretary and Assistant Secretary of Defense, who attached importance to long-term strategy, used these as their rationale for advocating the nuclear disarmament of Okinawa and the restoration of administrative rights, in spite of the opposition of the Joint Chiefs of Staff (Gabe 2000, p. 81).

In negotiations for the return of Okinawa, the Japanese government of the day proposed the removal of nuclear weapons. This was an outcome that gave consideration to Japanese public opinion, with its strong feelings of rejection towards nuclear weapons. In Diet deliberations relating to Okinawan restoration in 1968, the then Prime Minister, Satō Eisaku, extolled the 'three non-nuclear principles' of 'non-possession, non-production, and non-introduction' of nuclear weapons.

This also fitted with American government interests. This was because not only had the necessity for nuclear weapons in Okinawa declined, but, at the time, the U.S. and Soviet Union had initiated their Nuclear Non-Proliferation Treaty (NPT), and were pressing Japan and West Germany to sign it.

Kishi Nobusuke, Ikeda Hayato and Satō Eisaku, who became prime ministers in Japan's conservative regimes from the late 1950s into the 1960s, each were secretly desirous of nuclear arms. Especially after China's nuclear testing in 1964, Satō began to mention nuclear arms at talks between Japan and the U.S., out of a sense of rivalry with China (Matsuoka et al. 2003, pp. 194–195).

Ultimately, the Satō government bowed to U.S. persuasion and signed the NPT in 1970, though its ratification in the Diet was delayed until 1976 due to rightist opposition within the LDP. Furthermore, a 1969 Foreign Ministry document advocated signing, but with retention of the technical and economic capability for nuclear armament (Gaikō Seisaku Kikaku Iinkai 1969).[2]

While the development of a nuclear fuel reprocessing facility to extract plutonium was pushed forward in accordance with such a line, the first commercial nuclear power plant went into operation in 1970. The U.S. continued to provide nuclear power generation technology to Japan, which had complied with its urging to sign the NPT. It was in 1971 that the Fukushima No. 1 Nuclear Power Plant, later damaged in the 2011 earthquake and tsunami, was completed with the technical cooperation of the American General Electric Company, and started operation.³

While promoting nuclear power generation, Prime Minister Satō Eisaku also proclaimed the 'three non-nuclear principles.' Taking advantage of this, Satō won the Nobel Peace Prize in 1974, though the Satō regime was censured by rightists for signing the NPT. Among their number was the renowned writer Mishima Yukio, who committed suicide, leaving a note calling for the Self Defense Forces to overthrow the Satō government and criticising the signing of the NPT.⁴

1970 was also the year when the U.S.–Japan Security Treaty (AMPO) expired. AMPO, which was concluded in 1951, could be called a treaty for providing bases to the U.S. military even after Japanese independence, and no expiry date was established for it. In 1960, it was revised, being recast into a form requiring renewal every ten years by the mutual agreement of both countries. In the late 1960s, even in Japan, the student movement and anti-Vietnam War movement came to prominence, and the campaign to abolish AMPO, which had become the basis for U.S. military provision of bases for sorties to Vietnam, intensified. Students from the New Left shared anti-U.S. sentiment which criticised the placing of Okinawa under U.S. military occupation, and some of them also showed sympathy with Mishima on an emotional level.

If one considers such criticism from left and right, it was important for Satō to advocate the reclaim of Okinawa under Japanese administrative rights, and to extol the three non-nuclear principles at the same time. It also dovetailed with the interests of the American government, which hoped for the stability of the Japanese conservative regime, and feared nuclear proliferation.

In the negotiation process, the Japanese government exchanged a secret treaty with U.S. government, recognising the continuing right of free use of bases, and tacitly approving the entry into port of ships carrying nuclear weapons. Knowledge of this secret treaty, which contradicted the 'three non-nuclear principles,' was kept from the people of Japan, and it only came to light in 1994 in statements by parties on the Japanese side who had been involved in the negotiations. At this, the U.S. military's Joint Chiefs of Staff, who had initially voiced disapproval, assented to the restoration of administrative rights.

Upon this restoration, the Japanese government purchased facilities such as roads and communications lines which the U.S. military had maintained, as assets, and it also bore the costs of nuclear disarmament. For this reason, the amount which the Japanese government paid to the U.S. government at the time of Okinawan reversion was explained to a Japanese domestic audience as being 320 million U.S. dollars, but this was the product of deft manipulation of the explanation, a sum of 395 million dollars actually having been paid.

Furthermore, after the restoration of administrative rights, the Japanese government governed Okinawa, paid the land rental for U.S. military bases to landowners, and bore the cost of the wages of U.S. military base workers. For that reason, for the American government, adding up the approximately twenty million dollars per annum it paid in aid to Okinawa, and about ten million dollars annually in land rent, much of its financial burden vanished.

If one totals these, the American government gained 645 million dollars between the return of administrative rights in 1972 and 1977. This amounts to the entire gross expenditure which the U.S. government invested in Okinawa from 1945 to 1972.[5] Apart from that, the American government also had the Japanese government promise voluntarily to curtail its export of textile products.

From 1978 onwards, land rent and the costs borne by the Japanese government for employees of the U.S. military were systematised and dubbed the 'sympathy budget (*omoiyari yosan*).' This was something which gained currency due to a high-ranking official in the Japanese government at the time having announced to the Japanese domestic audience that it was a budget which showed 'sympathy' for the U.S. which was suffering under its trade deficit with Japan. Deception which conceals the real circumstances of the unequal relationship between Japan and the U.S. by means of a warped expression of national pride is something often observed in Japanese conservative politicians.

Furthermore, in the process of Japan–U.S. negotiations accompanying Okinawan return, the Japanese government was forced to agree to the voluntary restraint of textile exports to the U.S. The Japanese government also promised to make efforts for the liberalisation of trade and capital; and, in addition, to increase its volume of aid to anti-Communist countries in South-East Asia on behalf of the U.S. Moreover, the U.S.–Japan Status of Forces Agreement (SOFA), which said that even if U.S. military personnel committed crimes, Japan had no jurisdiction over them, was left as it was. This Status of Forces Agreement was one which determined the status of forces from U.S. military bases in Japanese domestic law after Japan had achieved independence by the 1951 San Francisco Peace Treaty. The shouldering of the burden of land rent for U.S. military bases and their employees' wages was also implemented through a broad interpretation of this Status of Forces Agreement.

While concealing such a reality, the Satō government, which achieved success in arranging the return of Okinawa, won the support of public opinion, and in the December 1969 election the LDP enjoyed a huge victory. The regime was stabilised, and AMPO was extended without mishap. From 1968 to 1973, moreover, it succeeded in making the U.S. reduce its mainland bases to about half, and this caused the mainland peace movement to lose its point of contention. By contrast, bases on Okinawa hardly reduced. In this manner, a situation eventuated where seventy-four percent of U.S. military bases in Japan are concentrated in Okinawa.

Thanks to this restoration, the Okinawan side became able to send Members to the Japanese Diet, though with only five Members in the House of Representatives and two in the House of Councillors, it could not have much clout. Disappointment grew in Okinawa, and support for 'return' in a public-opinion poll in Okinawa, which had been ninety percent in 1965, plunged to fifty-one percent in 1972, and thirty-eight percent in 1973 (Arasaki 1996, p. 54).

Post-return Okinawa

What Okinawa gained was subsidies from the Japanese government rather than political rights. The Japanese government raised the rental for military areas to approximately six times the sum in the days of U.S. military rule as compensation for the entrenchment of bases (Arasaki 1996, p. 34). Many subsidies, including the Government Financial Contribution to the Management of Compulsory Education, were poured out from the Japanese government. These were nominally for Okinawan development, but in fact they were paid in order to pacify Okinawan dissatisfaction, and to smooth Japan–U.S. relations.

In one aspect, such subsidies benefited the Okinawan economy, but they bred dependence upon the Japanese government, and brought about all kinds of distortions.

Though rental for military areas was raised, this was in exchange for the limitation that, regardless of the wishes of landowners, the land would be for 'public use' for five years, in accordance with 1971 special legislation called 'The act concerning the temporary use of public land in Okinawa' (Arasaki 1996, p. 38). After that, various kinds of political pressure were exerted upon land-owners who refused to renew their contract.

Sugar-cane cultivation, which had been one of pre-reversion Okinawa's main industries, was exposed to the risk of decline along with 'return' to Japan and the Japanese government's market liberalisation policy. The Japanese government bought Okinawan sugar cane at a fixed price, but that purchase price was low, amounting to about six-tenths of the rental for leasing farmland in the same area for use of the U.S. military (Arasaki 1996, p. 37). The proportion of landowners choosing contracts for military sites over cultivation increased, but there was also an emergence of people who, having lost the will to work, became dissolute.

After the 1972 'return,' many subsidies were poured into Okinawa, but the majority of these were public-works projects for infrastructure maintenance, such as roads, and industrial development barely progressed. In present-day Okinawa, tertiary industry accounts for ninety percent of the working population, with tourism, food-and-beverage, and construction being the main players.

Revenue such as land rent and employment from bases in 2012 amounted to 5.3 percent of Okinawa's Gross Regional Product, which is not very large, being about half of the 10.9 percent from tourism revenue. Bases make up about twenty percent of the area of Okinawa's main island, but if this is translated in terms of average land productivity, it would equate to an annual increase of 160,000,000,000 yen if bases were completely restored (Maedomari 2012, p. 124).[6]

It is Japanese government subsidies that are soothing the discontent which arises from that situation, and are substantially ossifying that state of affairs. The people of Okinawa, too, know that subsidies and public works come to them precisely because there are bases there. For that reason, Okinawa is nicknamed the 'island that lives by the three Ks (*kankō* = tourism, *kichi* = bases, and *kōkyō jigyō* = public works).' Anti-base sentiment is strong, but so is the fear of losing the subsidies.

Why does the Japanese government continue to dish out subsidies? Kubo Takuya, who was involved in the 'return' as Director-General of the Bureau of Defence Policy in the Defence Agency, remarked: 'As Japan has gained an enormous trade surplus vis-à-vis the United States, thanks to AMPO, if it sets aside part of that, then it will be able to offset the sacrifices of the Okinawan people' (Fujii 1995, p. 7). Kubo is known as a pacifist among Japanese connected with defence, so this is likely to be how he expressed an idea shared by the Japanese government in a somewhat conscientious form.

The Okinawan unemployment rate is the highest in the land, its per capita income is about seventy percent of the national average, and its university entrance ratio, also, is about twenty points lower than the mainland average. If one compiles an income graph classified by age and industry, while the national average 'employment peak' is in the manufacturing industry, with annual earnings of three to four million yen, Okinawa's is taken to be the food-and-beverage and hotel industry, with annual earnings of 550,000 to 990,000 yen (Maedomari 2012, p. 122).

At present, most roads have been upgraded in Okinawa by means of subsidies, and at a glance, the streets seem in good order. However, even if major arteries and community centres are constructed by public works, and shopping malls erected by mainland capital along major routes, the existing commercial districts have been left to rust. This tendency is prominent even in Naha, the central metropolis. As many tourists visit Okinawa at package rates offered by mainland tourism operators in league with airline companies, the amount of money which reaches local hotels is only a portion of that paid by the tourists.

While the manufacturing industry and finance business are not growing, and the service industry has also plateaued, the place where employment has been increasing in recent years is call centres which take advantage of the cheapness of Okinawan wages. Complaints from purchasers of all kinds of manufactured goods which various companies on the mainland have made are routed to Okinawan call centres, and young Okinawan women receive them. Okinawa is the place with the lowest wages which has people who can speak Japanese.

According to public-opinion polls, affirmative views of the 'return' in Okinawa have been stable at almost eighty percent since the 1980s. This is because the Okinawan economy has improved in accordance with its superficial activation through Japanese government subsidies. There is arguably general agreement that Japanese 'reversion' has been better than U.S. military rule, apart from the period of disappointment immediately following reversion.

Future shifts are undetermined, however. Changes in Okinawan society due to post-'return' economic growth and modernisation have been marked. These have brought about an affluence which can be measured by market trading volume, but on the other hand, it has caused the dismantling of traditional society. This is a phenomenon which occurred on the mainland due to rapid economic growth in the 1960s, but in Okinawa a similar phenomenon arose in the 1980s. Since the 1990s, moreover, the economic growth effect from subsidies has declined, and since the 2000s, subsidies have also dwindled. For that reason, while the dismantling of traditional society has accelerated on the one hand, sufficiently stable employment to compensate for that is not being maintained.

In the 2000s, views advocating 'Okinawan independence' increased even more than in the 1980s. One factor in this is a rise in 'Okinawan consciousness' or 'Okinawan nationalism' which transcends settlements or kindred due to the demise of traditional society, just as in all cases of modern nationalism. As can be seen in the example of Ifa Fuyū in Chapter Three of this volume, regional consciousness within Okinawa blocks the establishment of nationalism based on Okinawa as its unit. The advance of modernisation brought about the decline and transfiguration of existing Okinawan culture on the one hand, but on the other, it facilitated the formation of a unitary Okinawan nationalism.

Even within Okinawa, the areas which are directly adversely affected by noise from bases and crimes by U.S. military personnel are limited. Due to the emergence of an Okinawan nationalism that exceeds the village level, however, the issue of bases had not been confined to just one area. It has become the symbol of the 'unjust treatment of Okinawans as a whole.' Even the young generation who have no direct knowledge of prewar days and during the war, or the period of U.S. military rule, have a tendency to discuss 'Okinawan independence' symbolically. This is probably not unconnected to the fact that Okinawa's youth unemployment rate is the highest in Japan, and there are no jobs except in the low-paid service industry.

In 1985, when the Japanese government supported the flying of the *Hi-no-maru* flag at public schools all over the country, Okinawa stood out as the place with the strongest resistance. Moreover, in September 1995, in Naha City on the main island of Okinawa, there was an incident in which a twelve-year-old girl was gang-raped by three U.S. Marine Corps personnel. This incident inflamed Okinawan people's discontent, and the month after the incident, a prefectural residents' general protest rally was held. The progressive-affiliated governor, who was also a scholar of Okinawan history, also participated in this rally which was attended by 85,000 people – seven percent of the Okinawan population – which would equate to 800,000 if it were Tokyo.

For the U.S. military, this situation gave cause for anxiety. In November 1995, the Special Action Committee on Okinawa (SACO) was set up by Japanese and U.S. authorities. At the Japan–U.S. summit meeting held in February 1996, the issue of the relocation of the Futenma base in central Okinawa Island was raised, and in combination with the April visit to Japan of President Clinton, the SACO interim report proposed the return of the Futenma Air Station within five to seven years. Futenma Air Station is a Marine Corps base constructed under the U.S. military occupation, it is surrounded by a densely-populated urban area, and is said to be the base with the highest risk of serious accident in the world.

The Marine Corps, however, demanded an alternative base, and plans for relocation changed repeatedly. Consideration was given, for example, to relocation to Guam or Australia, or amalgamation with Okinawa's Kadena Air Base, the U.S. Air Force's largest in the Far East. Ultimately, though, it was decided during negotiations to move the facility to Henoko, on the central coast of Okinawa's main island. The plan to build a base by filling in the coral reef on the Henoko coastline was one that had existed since the Vietnam War period. The facilities at Futenma Base had already deteriorated, and in exchange for returning it, a plan to construct a state-of-the-art base with Japanese government funding was agreed upon.

After this, the Japanese government poured subsidies intensively into Nago City, and obtained the agreement of the local municipalities and city council. Even though public facilities and roads were built with the subsidies showered upon the area, industry was not promoted at all, and the city's business district continued to decay. Eventually, subsidies to Okinawa – a combination, after budget amendments, of Cabinet Office Okinawa General Bureau (*Naikakufu Okinawa Tantō Bukyoku*) and Okinawa Development and Promotion Bureau (*Okinawa Kaihatsu Jigyō*) budgets – began to decrease along with Japan's recession and fiscal difficulties; and these had declined to about half in 2009 compared with their peak in 1998 (Shimabukuro 2012, p. 51). A mayor who was opposed to the relocation of the base to Henoko was elected, and opponents of the base came to account for the majority in the city council, as well.

While relocation had hit a setback, there was a rising possibility that the Futenma base would become entrenched. In 2012, Ospreys – the Marine Corps' newest transport aircraft which have a record of frequent crashes – were deployed to Futenma. In protest, approximately 100,000 attended the Okinawan Residents' Rally in September, outstripping the 1995 figure. The Japanese government took the attitude that the deployment of Ospreys was a matter of the U.S. military's exclusive right, so the Japanese government could not become involved; it then temporarily increased its subsidy. While the situation remained in deadlock, discontent rose higher and higher in Okinawa.

On the other hand, the military position of Okinawa changed again. As previously mentioned, one of the factors in Okinawa's situation having changed in 1972 was a shift in U.S. military strategy, namely, the ending of the Vietnam War and the development of nuclear weapons. In 2012, the U.S. military withdrew from Iraq and was doing so from Afghanistan, and a transformation in the U.S. military had taken place through advances in information and transport technology. As these advances have enabled the deployment of troops on demand if a state of emergency arises, reorganisation in the U.S. military and the dismantling of its overseas bases has progressed.

Since 1990, the number of U.S. military personnel stationed in Europe has already fallen to about half, and that in Korea, also, to about two-thirds. The abovementioned advances in military technology, the ending of the Cold War, and U.S. fiscal difficulties are among the causes for this.

A 2011 paper published in the journal *Foreign Affairs* by U.S. experts on AMPO warns against clinging to 'faith in forward defences,' which it describes as a 'holdover from the Cold War.' It insists that the money would be better spent on reviving the U.S. domestic economy, saying:

> [P]reventing Chinese and North Korean adventurism demands rapid-response forces with strong reserves, not the 30,000 soldiers currently stationed in each country [=Japan and South Korea]. Phasing out 20 percent of those forces while repositioning others to Guam or Hawaii would achieve the same results more efficiently ... The demobilisation of 50,000 active-duty soldiers in Europe and Asia alone could save as much as $12 billion a year (Parent and Macdonald 2011).

While the above paper does not touch upon the issue, rather than being anti-Chinese or anti-North Korean bases, the current bases in Okinawa are relay stations for when and if the U.S. military advances into the Middle East or Western Asia. That character intensified after Okinawa became the largest U.S. military base remaining in the Far East, especially following the 1991 withdrawal of the Subic Bay U.S. Naval Base and the Clark Air Base in The Philippines immediately after the end of the Cold War.

The people of Okinawa have doubts, however, about the continuing presence of huge U.S. military bases which are not directed at Chinese or North Korea, even after the U.S. military withdrawal from Iraq and Afghanistan. As I noted in the Introduction, in February 2012, the United Nations Committee on the Elimination of Racial Discrimination (CERD) submitted a questionnaire to the Japanese government based on the 2010 International Convention on the Elimination of All Forms of Racial Discrimination, problematising the construction of a base at Henoko, and calling the disproportionately high concentration of U.S. military bases in Okinawa a 'modern form of discrimination' (CERD 2012).

In fact, the greater part of the financial burden for U.S. military bases in Japan, such as rent for base land, base employees' pay, their housing, and so on, has been borne by the Japanese government since Okinawa's 'return.' According to a 2003 Pentagon report, the host nation support paid by the Japanese government was deemed to be about 120,000 dollars per U.S. soldier stationed in Japan, which amounts to twelve times that in Germany, and six times that in South Korea (Hisae 2005, p. 21). For this reason, regardless of decreases in U.S. military personnel stationed in Germany and Korea, U.S. military numbers in Japan have hardly declined at all.

The presence of bases in Okinawa is becoming the now-meaningless, vested right of the U.S. armed services. Present-day Japan is no major economic power, unlike in the 1980s when it had an enormous trade surplus vis-à-vis the U.S., and the government had fiscal leeway. Not only in Okinawa, but all over Japan, the unemployment rate has risen, and even more than that, low-paid, short-term employment has increased, and in 2012, the average annual income for employed persons was approximately fourteen percent lower than in 1997. The overall poverty ratio, also, reached sixteen percent in 2009, and among OECD countries this was second only to the United States. Claims justifying subsidies to Okinawa on the rationale of a trade surplus vis-à-vis the U.S. are losing their influence.

Japanese taxpayers, too, are beginning to have doubts about this state of affairs, because the Japanese and American governments cannot give definite answers to the question of why they pay enormous amounts in costs for the stationing of U.S. troops, and pour subsidies with limited economic effectiveness into Okinawa, in spite of the fact that U.S. military bases do not exist for the sake of Japanese defence. It could be argued that if both governments let this issue lie, then anti-U.S. sentiment in Okinawa and Japan would be ignited, and it would also have the potential to damage international relations.

A trilateral relationship in construction of 'the Japanese'

In this book, I have depicted the conflict over how 'the boundaries of "the Japanese"' have been established since the introduction to East Asia of the principle of the modern nation-state.

I anticipate that I have gained your understanding as to the dynamics of inclusion and exclusion which I described in the Introduction, and the dilemmas of the people caught up in them. This is the history of the relationship between Japan and Okinawa, but the form of discord which appears there is probably one that is omnipresent in the world. Here, based on an investigation of this historical sequence of events, I wish to present a point of view for analysing such a ubiquitous problem.

Usually, the relationship between a majority and a minority is often discussed on the assumption that the majority and minority in question substantively exist, and that their boundary is clear-cut. Speaking in terms of the example of this book, this would mean that

'Japanese' and 'Okinawans' existed in advance, and their history is depicted as antagonism. The final answer would be something like either separating, becoming independent and creating a discrete state; or assimilating into the majority; or else being subsumed into a state which recognised multiple cultures.

'Majorities' and 'minorities' cannot, however, be said to be things that exist in a substantive manner beforehand. As will be understood from the investigation in this book, it is not true that 'Okinawans' and 'Japanese' existed from the very beginning. 'The Japanese' are constructed in concert with the construction of 'the Okinawans' and the setting of boundaries between them.

This construction process, however – at least in the case of the relationship between Japan and Okinawa – progressed not by excluding 'the Okinawans' from 'the Japanese,' but amid their inclusion into 'the Japanese.' This point differs from the way many theories based on constructionism consider that a majority is built by setting up a minority as a target of exclusion. Why did such a relationship come into being? Elucidation of this point can constitute this book's theoretical contribution.

The cause was not that the establishment of boundaries was conducted amid the bilateral relationship consisting of 'the Japanese' and 'the Okinawans,' but that there were third connections, such as Qing China and the West. For the Japanese government, the expansion of 'the Japanese' within its relationship with Qing and the West was prioritised over the exclusion of Okinawa, and for that reason, the vector of inclusion worked strongly. After the Pacific War, when such dynamics ceased to work, the Japanese government was either indifferent to Okinawa, or, rather, exclusionary. It is not possible to explain these moves unless we think of it not as a bilateral relationship between a 'majority' and a 'minority,' but as a trilateral one in which another external to it is present.

This was also why an assimilation policy was later pursued vis-à-vis Taiwan and Korea. On the occasion of Japan's possession of Taiwan after the First Sino-Japanese War, a British foreign advisor proposed not adopting an assimilation policy, because an assimilation policy would mean costs for education and the like would be high, and it would also easily provoke a local backlash. Within the Japanese government, also, there were many similar opinions.

Even so, it was out of the necessity to expand 'the Japanese' to resist China and the West that Japan enforced an assimilation policy and adopted a policy of teaching Japanese language and allegiance to the emperor in Korea and Taiwan. I described this sequence of events in detail in Volume 2 of this book.

Underpinning this was the fact that Japan was militarily inferior to Western countries. The U.S., which occupied and governed Okinawa after the Pacific War, adopted a policy of severing Okinawa from Japan by stressing Okinawa's uniqueness, and it did not conduct an assimilation policy in Okinawa, simply establishing a university to foster cooperative local elites and setting up a route for them to study in America.

The assumption here was that the U.S. was superior to Japan in terms of both military and economic power, and there was no possibility that Okinawa would be seized even if the U.S. did not implement an assimilation policy or suchlike. In the case of British rule in India, which tends to be made a typical example of colonial rule, no assimilation policy was carried out, either, but the dark backdrop to that was Britain's military strength in those days, which was superior to that of other countries. By contrast, the Japanese government feared that unless it subsumed Okinawa and Korea into 'the Japanese' by means of assimilation policies, it would have them taken from it by Western countries.

The second underlying factor was that in the process of border-demarcation in neighbouring areas, the establishment of the boundaries of 'the Japanese' was carried out. Though it was not obvious at the time of the possession of Okinawa, at the time of the possession of Taiwan, conflict erupted within the Japanese government as to whether to include Taiwan in Japan, or to exclude it from Japan. As previously mentioned, British advisors suggested a form of rule in which Taiwan was separated from Japan proper, after the model of British rule in India.

Within the Japanese government, however, the view that Taiwan should be secured as part of Japan was strong. Hara Takashi, the then Vice Foreign Minister, later to become Prime Minister, referring to the German rule of Alsace-Lorraine, proposed the inclusion of Taiwan. In this manner, it came to be debated whether Taiwan was a Japanese colony, or part of the Japanese state.

In consequence, it was decided to adopt the position that like Okinawa, Taiwan and Korea had been officially subsumed as part of

Japan, and were not colonies. Similarly, it was deemed that officially, Japan had not implemented colonial control like the West's, or had been racially prejudicial.

This recognition was further strengthened by the Japanese government's submission of a racial equality proposal to the United Nations in 1919, in the face of U.S. ostracism of immigrants of Japanese descent (Oguma 2005). This kind of recognition was also repeated when Japan advanced into Manchuria and South-East Asia, and even today, it survives at the root of rightist historical revisionism in Japan.[7] The fact that a large-scale independence movement arose in March 1919, the very time when Japan was conducting its racial equality proposal, symbolised the contradictions in such recognition.

On the occasion of such subsumption, the linguistic and cultural or anthropological commonality with the indigenous people of Korea and Taiwan were emphasised (Oguma 2002a). As was seen from the times of Okinawan possession, however, it is closer to the truth to say that linguistic and cultural similarity was constructed because there was a necessity to include Okinawa in Japan, rather than saying that it was included in Japan because its language and culture were close. Such a disparity was something that was constructed rather than being tangible.

Unofficially, though, prejudice against Okinawa, Taiwan and Korea continued to remain. 'The Japanese' whom the Japanese government had defined in the first place were people who spoke Japanese and devoted their allegiance to the emperor. Things such as political rights and equality as 'Japanese' were ones added as benefits once such cultural assimilation and allegiance had been completely achieved. In Okinawa's case, suffrage was granted on the main island in 1912, and in other islands in 1920, lagging far behind other prefectures, whereas in the case of Korea and Taiwan, no suffrage was ever granted.

As there were misgivings about Okinawans' spirit of allegiance, there was hesitation about incorporating them into the Japanese Army, as well. Even earlier than the granting of suffrage in Okinawa, conscription was imposed on the main island in 1898 and in 1902 in other areas, but the conscripted soldiers were dispersed into separate Kyushu units. In the last stages of the Pacific War, conscription was implemented in Korea and Taiwan, as well, due to a lack of military capability, but again the soldiers were incorporated separately into various units from the Japanese mainland, the army having issued a directive forbidding the proportion of such soldiers within a unit not to exceed a fixed level. This contrasted with the way Britain established local military units in its colonies, and the U.S. segregated Black soldiers into separate units.

By contrast, the side that was subsumed into 'the Japanese' responded in several ways. The first response was to aim for the acquisition of rights through assimilation into 'the Japanese.' The second was to separate from 'the Japanese,' establish an identity of their own, and ultimately to become independent.

These responses were accompanied by many difficulties, however. Firstly, as for assimilation, as long as the Japanese government had hold of the definition of 'the Japanese,' it was unclear as to how far people had to assimilate in order to become 'Japanese.' Still more, the ones in control did not present a clear-cut definition, and it often happened that they altered it at their convenience.

Especially in Okinawa's case, the construction of its own identity also involved many problems. What Ifa Fuyū tried to do was to enlist the help of modern linguistics to construct an 'Okinawan' identity. He learned that method in the Department of Philology at Tokyo Imperial University. His teachers were ones who endeavoured to construct a grammar of nationalism which European countries first established – in other words, to construct 'Japanese,' 'Okinawans' and 'Koreans' as groups which had uniqueness in linguistic, cultural, racial and historical terms, just as all modern nationalism did. Ifa tried to use this as a tool for constructing Okinawa's unique identity.

However, if Ifa were to emphasise Okinawa's uniqueness, this could have attracted exclusion and discrimination from 'the Japanese' as an inevitable outcome of the methods he adopted. For that reason, Ifa made a convoluted utterance saying that, in line with established theory of the day, 'Okinawans' had the same ancestry as 'the Japanese' in linguistic terms, as well, yet they were a group which had uniqueness. This was a strategy forced upon them as a group in an overwhelmingly inferior position.

Even more problematic was the fact that if he were to construct a unit comprising 'Okinawans,' this would mean concealing its internal disparity and discrimination. Specifically, the problem would arise of whether to acknowledge the Ryukyu Kingdom and affirm the status discrimination and sexual prejudice that had existed in conventional society as 'racial traditions.' This problem was one that emerged even in Japan amid post-war Japanese progressive nationalism.

Ifa himself, too, was not of the Shuri samurai class, and he also pondered the improvement of the status of Okinawan women. For that reason, being unable to acknowledge the Ryukyu Kingdom, he had no choice but to declare that the Ryukyu Disposition had been slave liberation. In other words, here, too, when the construction of the bilateral relation of 'Japan' and 'Okinawa' is being conducted, a third relationship was having an influence.

Moreover, in the circumstances of the dialect debate in 1940, people who were in a low position in Okinawa society – natives of the northern part of the main island who could not speak the language of the Shuri samurai class, and women, for example – asserted that opposition to the dissemination of the Japanese language was something which preserved the discrimination within Okinawan society. In Korea, also, examples can be seen of activists in the women's movement having positively participated in assimilation campaigns by the Japanese government during the Pacific War. In the anti-Japanese resistance movement by Han Chinese in Taiwan there were some who blatantly showed a prejudiced consciousness vis-à-vis indigenous Taiwanese, as reportedly inscribed in the Taiwanese Constitution.[8] Such an issue is one which the Third-World feminist movement is confronting even today.

A departure from boundary-setting

Both assimilation (inclusion) into 'the Japanese' and separation (exclusion) from 'the Japanese' are tasks which decide the boundaries of 'the Japanese' and 'the Okinawans.' Both assume that boundaries exist, and the boundaries have merely shifted. This necessarily involves some difficulties. As to the question of whether a 'universality' which transcends such boundaries exists, the majority of Okinawan people would probably answer that it does not, at least in American culture.

The reason for this volume's discussion of Arakawa Akira's anti-return discourse as one to which attention should be paid is because it contains parts which transcend such limits. Arakawa, who had mixed 'Japanese' and 'Okinawan' blood, and who could not speak the existing Okinawan language, could not define the boundaries within his own self. What he adopted was a rejection of the very dynamics of inclusion and exclusion. In other words, he endeavoured to depart from the act of setting boundaries itself.

Arakawa himself also spent his infant years on Ishigaki Island, and many Okinawan intellectuals who have studied the relationship with Japan were born outside the main island of Okinawa. Ifa did not hail from the Shuri samurai class, either. The fact that people native to Okinawa's periphery have to conceive of a multi-layered structure is considered to be one factor.

One of the strategies employed when rejecting the dynamics of exclusion and inclusion is the seizure of the right to interpret what is meant by 'Japanese' and 'Okinawans.' This does not constitute shifting the boundaries of 'the Japanese,' nor seeking a 'universality' which transcends boundaries, but altering the frame from within. In 1970, when 'return' was imminent, Gima Susumu, an Okinawan high-school teacher, stated:

> ... If it is a Japan which does not allow Okinawans to become Japanese while remaining Okinawans, then I do not want it. I do not want to become such a Japanese ... The people of Okinawa are Japanese, and so it could be said not that they are returning to Japan, but that they are choosing to be Japanese. For that reason, conversely, I think it would be permissible to attach the question of what kind of Japanese they want to become (Gima 1970 , p. 245).

The claim here is neither an assertion of the mere 'uniqueness' of 'Okinawans,' nor an all-out affirmation of their becoming 'Japanese.' It is an assertion of the right of 'Japanese,' and, in turn, of 'Okinawans,' to the autonomy and self-determination to determine the content. Autonomy here does not necessarily mean fixing the boundaries of 'the Okinawans.'

Naturally, it is autonomy over 'Okinawan traditions,' and also the right to interpret these. For example, in the 'Cornerstone of Peace,' which was built to mark the fiftieth anniversary of the Battle of Okinawa on the initiative of the Okinawa Prefectural Office, not only Japanese troops and Okinawan residents, but also American and British troops who lost their lives in the fighting, and Koreans and so on who died after having been incorporated into the Japanese army, are commemorated on an equal footing as 'victims of the Battle of Okinawa.'

In recent years, many Okinawans of the younger generation have already made Standard Japanese (*hyōjungo*) their mother tongue, and yet, they continue to construct an '*Uchinaanchu* (Okinawan)' identity. The medium they employ on that occasion is no longer the Okinawan language of the past, replete with its conventional honorific expressions employed between males and females, and between people of different status. Even while the language is still Japanese, they speak it with an accent that diverges from Tokyo speech; and they use it to recount the history of their grandparents who were massacred by the Japanese and U.S. militaries.

Okinawa is an archipelago in the ocean, and all kinds of cultures flow into it. The musical instrument called the '*sanshin* (three strings)' which crossed over from China, and was made from raw materials that Okinawa was able to import, spread in the post-war period of economic growth period, rather than before. The start of its post-war popularity was the '*kankara sanshin*' which Okinawan residents detained in U.S. military camps after the Battle of Okinawa made, using empty cans (*kankara*) discarded by the U.S. military for the body of the instruments. The *kankara sanshin*, with its unique sound, is still sold in musical instrument stores in Okinawa. It is an example of blended culture formed by an inflow of culture from China and America.

Nowadays, third- and fourth-generation migrants from Okinawa who live in South America or Hawai'i are working in Tokyo and Naha as foreign labour. They can speak neither Okinawan nor Japanese, but they brought in Latin guitars and tacos. At Okinawan mass eateries, they cook *gōya* (a bitter gourd grown in Okinawa), pork and tacos that the U.S. military brought over, and rice and tofu produced in Japan, all together. Okinawan rock culture began from performances for U.S. troops during the Vietnam War, and it now features a combination of *sanshin* and electric guitar, with the addition of Latin rhythms.

In Okinawa in recent years, people call such a mixed culture '*chanpuru* (mixed) culture.' Traditional dance from the age of the Ryukyu Kingdom is being passed on at the Prefectural University of Arts, but at the same time, '*chanpuru* culture' has also achieved legitimacy in Okinawan culture. This is the autonomous manner in which 'Okinawan culture' exists.

This is not an issue only for 'Japanese' or 'Okinawans,' but one shared by 'Americans,' 'Australians,' 'Chinese,' 'Indians,' 'Thais,' 'Palestinians,' or any 'XX-ese' or 'YY-ians' in the world. The history of Japan and Okinawa suggests a clue for considering this problem.

Notes

Chapter 1

1 On the Ryukyu Disposition, in addition to a special feature put together in 1978 in *Shin Okinawa bungaku* (New Okinawa literature), No. 38, studies prior to 1979 have been listed in Yokoyama (1980). Works on the Disposition and the tone of argument of the day include Kinjō (1978); Gabe (1979; 1981); Hiyane (1982); Hentona (1982); Yasuoka (1983); Yamashita (1990), though their discussions are not conducted from the perspective of setting the boundaries of 'the Japanese' in the negotiations. The Chamber of the Left's 'internal humanity' reply and Matsuda's historical treatise are introduced, for example, in Ōta (1976), but the debate on the maintenance of the Ryukyu Kingdom and its relationship with views on Europe and America are not discussed, and there is no reference to issues such the historical discussion in negotiations between Japan and Qing, and their intermediary. Moreover, in this chapter, I excluded from consideration the movement for national salvation by Ryukyuan nobility, and suchlike. Furthermore, all of the original texts of the historical materials cited in this chapter were written in *kanji* (Chinese characters) and the *katakana* syllabary.

2 On the connection between Yamagata Aritomo and the Ryukyu Disposition, see Yasuoka (1992).

3 Negotiations held in Peking in June 1873. Speaker for the Japanese side was Yanagihara Sakimitsu, who accompanied Ambassador Fukushima. Recent studies on the Taiwan Incident include Kobayashi (1994).

4 'Futsujin Boasonādo no iken (The opinions of the Frenchman, Boissonard),' dated 17 March 1875, in Hiratsuka (1982, p. 32). Hereafter, citations from this text are from pp. 32–35 in the same book. On Boissonard, see Ōkubo (1977).

5 Sino-Japanese negotiations are in Gaimushō (1950b, p. 288). The latter is a dialogue from 20 April 1885 between the Minister to Qing, Enomoto, and Lǐ Hóngzhāng. Punctuation added to both.

6 There are various theories as to whether the early years of Okinawan rule were operating at a deficit, but here I affirm simply the point that the government side had the argument that a deficit was inevitable.

7 'Ryūkyū no kokugo shūkyō shuzoku kanshū (The national language, religions, tribes [and] customs of Ryukyu),' in Kokuritsu Kokkai Toshokan Kensei Shiryōshitsu (n.d.), *Itō Hirobumi kankei bunsho* (Papers relating to Itō Hirobumi), Itō family papers No. 356: an in-house publication of the Interior Ministry, with no page numbers or signatures. Mention is made of the philologist Aston and so on, and is thought to be the response of a foreign advisor.

8 On deployment of Japanese troops, see Hara (1992).
9 On the usage of *'minzoku'* and *'minshu,'* and the connection between the democratisation movement in Japan and nationalism, see Oguma Eiji (2002), *'Minshu' to 'aikoku'* ('Democracy' and patriotism'), Shin'yōsha.

Chapter 2

1 On the trends in Uesugi's prefectural ordinances in this period, see Ryūkyū Seifu (1965b). Works on Okinawan education in the early period include Ahagon (1966), Yoshihara (1968), Asano and Sakugawa (1976), Satake (1974; 1978), Nishihira and Ginoza (1983), Shimabukuro (1987), Asano (1991), Tanaka 1984), as well as the series of studies by Kondō (1993a; 1994b; 1995a; 1993b; 1996). In this book, I have placed special emphasis upon contradictions between 'civilisation' and 'Japanisation' in the formation of consciousness of being 'Japanese,' and, further, a comprehensive structural analysis of the worldview taught by education, incorporating reconfiguration of historical perspective.
2 Matsuda advocates selective 'reform of old regulations' in taxation and so on, but his opinion was not always reflected without modification. Nishizato (1981) details the so-called policy of preservation of old customs.
3 Satake (1974) mentions this study. Moreover, Tsuji (1890, No. 177, p. 7) asserts that such education in borderlands for the purpose of national defence 'of course requiring an even greater amount of expense, things like this should all only be paid for from government coffers.' This point is of deep interest as one which suggests the contradiction between the notion of assimilation and the financial burden in later educational policies in Korea and Taiwan. Citations of the petition to the prefectural office are in Ryūkyū Seifu (1965c, p. 410).
4 From here until the tenth item, reform of manners, prohibition of tattooing, and so on, continue. The text has added content for attention, but here I have cited only the main wording in each item. Cited from *Ryūkyū kyōiku* (1896 [1980], p. 115).

For instruction on hygiene, see *Ryūkyū kyōiku* (1901). On the concept of labour, see Taira (1901). Citations from Naha Shiyakusho (1970, p. 101).
5 Here, I ventured to depict 'civilisation' and 'Japanisation' as conflicting, but in many cases 'civilisation' in Western countries was also something carried out along with the homogenisation of language and culture in the states in question. For that reason, I have doubts as to whether there can be a universal kind of 'civilisation' or 'modernisation' which is not confined within the limits of a specific nation-state. Accordingly, one could also argue that, to be exact, what should be contraposed here to 'Japanisation' (that is, the thing of which scholars of the times were conscious), was 'Westernisation.' 'Japanisation' was rather what was left over after those parts perceived as comprising 'Westernisation' had been removed from the reform of manners and modernisation policies. My design in establishing the dichotomy here between 'civilisation' and 'Japanisation' was to try to distil out the contradictions between modernisation policies and national (*minzoku*) unification, which frequently are carried out in parallel to a certain extent.

6 After Vol. 1 was published in 1897, this was completed with Vol. 8 in 1899. In the reprint, a commentary was added by Asano Makoto, and mention of Tametomo was made in Vol. 4, pp. 21–24. Description of Tametomo's son 'Sonton' having become King Shunten, the first monarch of the Ryukyu Dynasty, is in Vol. 7, pp. 5–7.
7 This study by Nitta is often mentioned as an example of the theory of assimilation education, but its historical perspective has not been examined. The hypothesis that the 'Liuqiu' in Sui Dynasty writings means Taiwan is what Nitta himself asserts was his own discovery, but it is unclear as its veracity. In later years, Ifa Fuyū and Higaonna Kanjun came to dispute in later years over whether this 'Liuqiu' was Taiwan or Okinawa, but I would like to discuss that in a separate work.

In postwar Taiwan, as evidence that Taiwan had appeared since ancient times in Chinese dynastic historical documents, this hypothesis was deemed to be historical grounds for the argument that China and Taiwan were indivisible, and was reportedly circulated under the Nationalist Party regime. The hypothesis which excluded Taiwan in order to make Okinawa belong to 'Japan' turned into historical grounds for Taiwan belonging to China.

Chapter 3

1 'Ifa' apparently more closely approximates the Okinawan pronunciation of the name Japanised to Iha. The people of Ryukyu assigned Chinese characters to their names, but from Meiji onwards these were given Standard Japanese readings, meaning that the original pronunciation was not reflected in many cases.
2 See Hattori et al. (1974b, p. 417). Studies on Ifa include Kinjō and Takara (1972), Hokama (1979 [1993]), Hokama and Fujimoto (1978), Hiyane (1981), Kano (1993), as well as Hokama (1976), and the series of studies included in *Shin Okinawa bungaku* (1976), No. 31; and, more recently, Murai (1993–94), Kawamura (1996) and Tomiyama (1997). Important studies which mention Ifa include Arakawa (1973) and Araki 1980. This book, too, relies much upon these studies, starting with the exclusion of Ainu and 'wild tribespeople (*seiban*)' and the changes occasioned by the 'sago-palm hell,' but all of the research hitherto has discussed Ifa as a person who sybolised the ambiguity of Okinawan assimilation and independence within the oppositional schema comprising 'Okinawa' versus 'Yamato.' In response to this, this book examines such issues as: 1) Ifa showing ambiguity in regard to the relationship between Shuri and the Ryukyu Kingdom; 2) Ambivalence in Ifa towards 'politics' and 'power'; 3) that the Japan–Ryukyu common-ancestry theory and emphasis on Okinawan 'uniqueness,' which at a glance appear to comprise the dual meanings of 'assimilation' and 'independence,' actually became one entity; and 4) Okinawan Studies as the creation of Okinawan nationalism and its limitations. In addition, using Ifa as a case study, this book has analysed the characteristics of modern nationalism such as the creation of a historical perspective and enlightenment activities and the problematic points in the formation of nationalism by minorities.

3 There was and is continuity and discontinuity in the nomenclature for Japan proper: even today, in Hokkaido the term for Japan's main island of Honshū is *naichi*, but in Okinawa after the separation of Korea and Taiwan from Japan, and especially in the midst of Okinawa's reversion movement, mainland Japan came to be called *hondo* (mainland).
4 On the description of Jahana as a 'rebel (*hangyakusha*),' see Ōzato (1969, pp. 53, 72). There are numerous studies on Jahana's campaign and the acquisition of suffrage in Okinawa, and Ōzato (1996) lists these, but as far as I am aware, no works are to be seen which have focused upon the parallels between Hara's administrative reforms in Taiwan and Korea, and the granting of suffrage to Okinawa. Matsuo (1983, p. 469) and Hiyane (1996, p. 140) have criticised Hara's view which makes Okinawa the model for Korean rule as one that 'treats Okinawa not as a region within the country of Japan, but ranks it ... as a colony' (Hiyane), but I think that the reverse might be true. This is because for Hara, the precedent for making Korea or Taiwan not into a 'colony' but into 'a region within Japan' was Okinawa; and, as I have discussed in this book, Hara promoted the incorporation of Okinawa legally into 'a region within Japan.'
5 Takaesu (1996) details the reforms to Okinawa's local government system. Moreover, on the occasion of presenting a rescript on the enforcement of the suffrage law in Okinawa to the Privy Council for deliberation on 28 March 1912, Hara was expected to include Okinawa in the parameters of implementation in the amendments to the Lower House Members' Law which he was advancing at the time, but he stated that he had switched to a policy of issuing a rescript 'in order to allow the election of members of parliament from Okinawa Prefecture under the current law, as it was not possible for the bill in question to gain the approval of the Imperial Diet,' from which his positivity towards this issue can be perceived (Kokuritsu Kōbunshokan 1985, p. 407).
6 Hara's aspiration to make Okinawa the model for the administration of Taiwan and Korea was not something which had only arisen in 1911, as evidenced by an article in the *Ōsaka mainichi shinbun* on 8 December 1897 in which he stated in relation to arguments against the enforcement of the amended treaty towards Taiwan that though 'there are many current laws and regulations, let alone the new legal code, which will not be permitted to be implemented in the Ryukyu Islands ... furthermore, in implementing the new treaty, it is [not] considered that there can be any kind of objections from the countries forming the alliance.' Moreover, as I discuss later in this chapter, Hara sent a letter of thanks to Sasaki Shōjurō, an *Ōsaka mainichi* newspaper reporter whose advance scoop of the Kōdōkai Incident – a campaign for Okinawan autonomy which occurred in 1897 – played a role in the failure of the campaign. This is thought to be because for Hara, it was clear that Okinawa's gaining special autonomy would not crush the transformation of the Taiwan Government-General into a kingdom.
7 On the Nan'yōdō establishment issue, see Hiyane and Isa (1995, pp. 296–302).
8 Studies on Ōta include the commentaries by Hiyane (1993; 1995), contained in Hiyane (1996a; 1996b). Hiyane's assessment of Ōta was one which reappraised the Ōta who had been depicted hitherto as an advocate

of 'Japanisation,' calling for assimilation even to the Japanese manner of 'sneezing,' but he has a perceptible tendency to overemphasise the aspect of '"civil"-isation ("*bunmei*"-*ka*)' in Ōta's assimilation discourse (Hiyane 1996a). I think that more weight should be given to the very process in which Ōta, who originally was oriented towards 'civilisation,' was absorbed into the 'Japanisation' discourse which the ruling side had established. Ishida (1997) pays attention to issue of the desire for modernisation in Ōta connected with the assimilation discourse.

Kano (1996) points out that a shift in emphasis can be seen in Ōta's view of civilisation from the 1890s to the 1910s, from an assimilation discourse to one of industrial development, and further to a discourse of political autonomy, but here I described only the period of the assimilation discourse. That said, the shift in Ōta's view of civilisation is considered to be more one that arose from a situational analysis of what would be prioritised in the development of Okinawan society, rather than a change in his spontaneous thought. In my mind, Ōta was the type of nationalist intellectual who consistently aimed for Okinawan development, and who regarded thought as a means to that end. In light of the fact that Ōta was a graduate of Keiō Gijuku (the present-day Keio University), and esteemed Fukuzawa Yukichi, I think that Ōta Yoshihiro's description of him as 'the Fukuzawa Yukichi of Okinawa' is apt (Ōta 1996). Fukuzawa, too, harboured mistrust and enmity towards Westerners, saying such things as 'The cunning and fierceness of today's foreigners are incomparably worse than those of the [Japanese] nobility and shogunate officials' (Hattori et al. 1974d, p. 200); and he was a person who, while expounding awakening and civilisation to members of the nation, asserted when he judged Japan to be inferior to the West: 'It is not [too] soon to put an end to the idea of alienating ourselves, making [our] cultural products [and] institutions resemble [the West], and making customs and religion also resemble it, making everything the same colour as the West and not allowing there to be any difference between them, and regarding them as having no mutual points of differentiation' (Hattori et al. 1975d, p. 531). If that last pronouncement alone had remained until later generations, Fukuzawa, too, would probably have been remembered as an exponent of an unconditional assimilation discourse, as Ōta was misunderstood to be. This can be argued also in the sense that, like Ōta, Fukuzawa not only was a nationalist intellectual who gave top priority to Japan's development and amended his thinking by means of situational analysis, but he shared the stance of being willing to advocate aggression and discrimination towards Asia when the occasion arose for the sake of 'Japan's development.'

9 The Kōdōkai campaign petition is contained in Hiyane and Isa (1995). Ifa's description is in Hattori et al. (1974b, p. 393).
10 On the education of migrant workers from Okinawa and emigrants, see Kondō 1995.
11 On the Jinruikan incident, see, for example, Kaiho (1992, Chapter 6); Maehira (1994); Matsudo (1996).
12 Kodama's remark is in Hattori et al. (1975b, p. 366). Ōta's description is in Hiyane and Isa (1993, p. 267).

Hiyane details the circumstances of this incident, but it is thought that Hiyane tends to give an excessively high estimation of the teacher

Shimoguni Ryōnosuke, who was fired from his job due to antagonism against Kodama. Shimoguni was a teacher who was at first adored by his students from the Okinawan side, including Ifa, but he was also a person who pressed them to cut off their topknots, using the metaphor of 'American Indians.' He was later appointed to a position in Korea, and published a study in 1922 on Korean education, but his view was a typical 'conscientious' assimilation discourse, being one which urged the cultivation of talented people who would 'contribute to and serve the state (*hōkoku*)' by means of the elimination of discrimination through the 'coeducation of Japanese and Koreans,' connection to higher education, and the like (Shimokuni 1922). Even if Shimokuni had conflicted with Kodama, this is considered to be something which did not overstep the boundaries of criticism of the '*isshi dōjin* (treating everyone equally)' model, just as in the case of the Chief Justice of the Taiwan Supreme Court.

13 Hekigotō (1910) is a published record of Ifa's conversation on 17 May by a reporter who visited Okinawa.

14 Considerable additions were made to these between newspaper serialisation and consolidation into the book, *Ko-ryūkyū* (Old-Ryūkyū) (Ifa 1911), and revisions were carried out three times before the final version published in 1942 which is included in Ifa's *Collected Works* (Hattori et al); but there were no major changes made by means of those revisions to the parts comprising historical discussion mentioned in this chapter. The first edition of *Ko-ryūkyū* is held in the collection of the National Diet Library.

In *Ko-ryūkyū*, moreover, Ifa spelled his own name alphabetically as 'Ifa' rather than as the Japanised 'Iha.' On this point, Kano (1993, p. 71) and others interpret this as Ifa having 'incorporated a self-recognition as a Ryukyuan' through Okinawan pronunciation, but Arakawa conversely argued: 'What made him call himself by the older 'Ifa' rather than 'Iha' was not in order self-consciously to adhere to and assert Okinawan indigeneity, but something which derived from the idea that [Old-Ryukyuish things] embodied something more 'Japanese-like,' something purer than Japan,' which 'most straightforwardly displayed his 'orientation towards mainland Japan (*hondo*)"' (Arakawa et al. 1972, pp. 88–89). In this book, I ranked Ifa's Japan–Ryukyu common-ancestry theory as being one which endeavoured to preserve Okinawan uniqueness and create Okinawan nationalism within the framework of a discourse structure set up by the Yamato side, but I hold a similar opinion in regard to the transcription of this name. This, in other words, is because the spelling 'Ifa' is considered to have been simultaneously something which indicated distinctiveness vis-à-vis Yamato, and, in the sense of being a purer form of Japanese orthography, something which occupied a superior position in the values hierarchy established by the Yamato side.

If one considers the act of formation of nationalism to be one configuration of social-order formation which diffused across the globe from Western Europe in modern times, then it will not be strange for the basic values of nationalism in each locality to imitate those belonging to the nationalism of developed countries, even while uniformly claiming uniqueness. When this happens, adjustments in claims of uniqueness and values coexist without contradiction. Such a drift as, for example, 'the mausoleum of the Japanese Emperor Nintoku is larger than the historic ruins of Rome' simultaneously asserts Japanese distinctiveness and exhibits a desire for upward mobility within the hierarchy established by Europe. In the first place, there is no dearth of cases in which the very formation of a logic that comprises emphasis upon the 'uniqueness' of 'tradition' and 'culture' as a 'nation (*minzoku*)' imitates developed countries' nationalism.

In a roundtable discussion with Gabe Masaaki and Hamashita Takeshi entitled 'An "Okinawa Renaissance": its possibility,' Takara Kurayoshi (1997, p. 268) stated: 'To Okinawa, Ifa Fuyū is the founder of *kokugaku* (Japanology = the study of (ancient) Japanese culture and literature)'; and 'refashions nationalistic issues within one prefecture into an Okinawan-style modern *kokugaku* ... When someone hailing from Okinawa enters into it, they become wholly entangled within *kokugaku*'s construct. His pointing out that as long as researchers followed the framework of 'Okinawan Studies' which Ifa had inaugurated, they would be led structurally in the direction of 'modern national studies' is considered valid, because above all, Ifa's early work is faithful to the nature of scholarly conduct for the formation of modern nationalism which he had learned in Tokyo.

The abovementioned conjecture about Ifa's representation of his name remains within the bounds of supposition, but, as I demonstrated in this book, the values in his Okinawan nationalism could be said to have introduced then-current values of Japanese nationalism such as governing capability or ambitious venturing abroad (*kaigai yūhi*). In other words, I reiterate that Ifa's nationalism of this period was both an assertion of Okinawa's uniqueness and, at the same time, an expression of a desire for upward mobility within the framework of values set down by Yamato. In that sense, it was arguably inevitable, as it were, that emphasising Okinawa's 'tradition' of 'venturing abroad' went on to be incorporated into a variation of Japanese nationalism in the form of the later discourses of promotion of migration and 'southerly advance.' These are difficulties with which minorities who have expression in the 'words' of their rulers imposed upon them are saddled, but what I would prefer to focus upon is rather the fact that Ifa could not full assimilate to the values of Okinawan nationalism (in other words, Japanese nationalism) which he himself had created, and continued to harbour ambivalence towards it.

15 See Oguma 1995a.
16 There is no guarantee that this conversation accurately records Ifa's pronouncements as far as quoting his actual words, but it is thought to be something which probably conveys to a certain extent Ifa's aspiration to avoid decisive conflict with Yamato.
17 In his 1915 work, 'Those who give us things [= rights] are our true masters,' he describes this expression – one likely to be much of a muchness with 'a principle of double-dealing (*futamata gōyaku shugi*)' – as 'the painful cries of Okinawans who want to live a better life' amid cruel circumstances (Hattori et al. 1976a, p. 74). Here could be said to be expressed the ambivalence of pain and self-loathing for being the weak.
18 Studies which focus upon Ifa's view of women include Kano (1993) and Wakao (1994), but these seem not to have grasped the dilemma in the

view Ifa held of women's 'equality' through modernisation and Okinawan identity.
19 See, for example, Hattori et al. (1975b, p. 53; 1975d, p. 365). On eugenics in Japan at that time, see Suzuki (1983).
20 See Kano (1993, p. 143). Cited in Hattori et al. 1974a, p. 66.
21 In this book, I focus upon Ifa prior to the time of the 'sago-palm hell' in order to discuss the problematic points in a minority's formation of nationalism, and would like to leave discussion of Ifa's research on the 'Nan'yōdō,' the evolution of his views of the Ainu, his connection with Yanagita Kunio, and so on, for a separate work.

Chapter 4

1 On Yanagi Sōetsu and the Okinawa language debate, apart from a special feature compiled in *Shin Okinawa bungaku* (1989), there are Kaminuma (1976); Naha Shiyakusho (1970) which anthologised studies relating to this language debate; and Ōshiro Tatsuhiro and Tanigawa Ken'ichi's commentaries in Tanigawa (1970). Studies which, as critical biographies of Yanagi, mention the language debate include Tsurumi (1976), Mizuo (1992) and Yatsuda (1985); and in Yanagi (1981a; 1981b), Tsurumi and Mizuo took charge of the commentaries in Vol. 6, on Korea, and Vol. 15, on Okinawa. An early example praising Yanagi's discourse on Korea is Ubukata (1961); while Takasaki (1979) is a work which empirically surveys the relationship between Yanagi and Korea, Takasaki having consolidated the main research relating to the discourse on Korea up to around 1980. Oyafuso (1986) and Ōta (1987, Chap. 4) give positive assessments of Yanagi's later Korean discourse in a form linking it with discourses on Okinawa. Furthermore, works which have studied the actual situation of the campaign to encourage the use of Standard Japanese in Okinawa include Kondō (1997).
2 As a whole, along with a standardised appraisal of Yanagi's Korean discourse, criticism towards its non-political nature and his argument that Korean art equated to the 'beauty of sorrow,' and a positive assessment of Yanagi relating to the Okinawan language debate, have become cemented. Commentary by the aforementioned Kondō does, however, point out Yanagi's limitations in considering language as being akin to a fixed object like folk craft. Hanada (1995), in turn, discusses the dilemma of development and cultural identity. Kano points out that a tendency can be seen in the Mingei Kyōkai's drift of argument for their 'hearts to lean more towards pure Japan the more they expound respect for Okinawa' (1993, p. 274); while Tomiyama says that Yanagi's discovery of 'Okinawan culture' was 'linked to the fresh discovery of a superior "Japanese culture,"' and that Yanagi emphasised the disparity between Okinawa and Taiwan or Korea (1995, p. 39). In this chapter, I have analysed such things as: 1) the point of contact between Yanagi's folk-craft ideology and Orientalism; 2) how a sense of antagonism vis-à-vis the language debate functioned as an investment in the assimilation discourse; and 3) how Okinawa's incorporation into 'Japan' advanced (rather than retreated) in the language debate. Takenaka (1995) praised Yanagi's folk-craft ideology, arguing

that it had been able to become anti-Orientalism, but this is hard for me to judge. Also see Nakami (2003)'s series of studies on Yanagi.

On Leach's interest in Korean art, see Tsurumi's commentary in Yanagi (1981a, p. 680). In 1914, Yanagi encountered Joseon Dynasty ceramics due to Asagawa Noritaka's visit. In his discussions of Korea, Yanagi stated: 'I always think missionaries' histories of sin have more pages than their histories of good deeds,' 'The quality of missionaries in Korea, especially, is extremely tawdry,' and, 'It is a fact which has appeared in many colonies that they have plotted political intrigue time and time again.' He then asserted: 'Nevertheless, I think it is a base attitude to hide our own sins by solely attributing the cause of the misfortune to Koreans and missionaries because of this,' and 'Many foreign missionaries are under the delusion that they are a superior people, but I cannot help feeling that the same ugliness is also in the attitude of us who believe that we are superior.' When criticising the discriminatory behaviour of colonists from *naichi* towards Koreans, he claimed: 'What hostility would arise in Japan if [the Japanese] found out that people from other countries took a similar attitude towards Japan!' (Yanagi 1981a, pp. 30, 49, 68). Such a view of missionaries which Yanagi held is very interesting in the aspect that his anti-Western-civilisation consciousness had superficially become something close to Asianists' assertions. Lafcadio Hearn, too, out of a fear that Japanese traditional culture would be violated by Western civilisation and Christianity, highly praised one Inoue Tetsujirō, who attacked Christian missionaries in a debate which spurred by an incident of disrespect towards the Christian thinker Uchimura Kanzō; and Hearn advocated educating the populace in 'old-time patriotism and love for the Emperor' (Ōta 1994, pp. 124–133). Yanagi did not advocate extreme nationalism (*kokusui shugi*) or Asianism, but even in the present day one occasionally encounters the phenomenon in which European intellectuals who maintain a stance of remonstrating against the destruction of non-Western culture through Western modern civilisation champion the emperor system, the whaling industry and suchlike, regarding these as 'Japanese traditional culture,' and superficially accord with Rightist assertions. In addition, this indicates one end of the reason why no small part of Japanese conservative thought since modern times has been shouldered by intellectuals who returned to Japan from studies in the West, having learned the then latest ideology.

4 As to be seen below, many of the letters counter-arguing against Yanagi were published in the *Okinawa nippō* and *Okinawa asahi* newspapers, but, according to Yoshida Shien, '*Okinawa asahi* and *Okinawa nippō* were resolutely antagonistic towards *Ryūkyū nippō*, and supported the enforcement of Standard Japanese (*hyōjungo*) in counter to *Ryūkyū nippō* having begun support for the Mingei Kyōkai' (Tsuitō Bunshū Kankō Iinkai 1990, p. 330). Accordingly, not only do certain difficulties accompany making conjectures about general Okinawan public opinion solely from letters to the editor in newspapers, but it also can be seen that oppositional relationships within Okinawa affected support for or rejection of the encouragement of Standard Japanese, though as far as can be seen from the list of these debates compiled by the Mingei Kyōkai (Naha Shiyakusho 1970, pp. 443–450), it could be said that in

the Okinawan critical arena, the majority was critical of Yanagi. This, however, is a different matter from any decision as to whether it could be argued that these letters really represented the feelings of the Okinawan populace in general.
5 Shimizu Ikutarō, Yanagita Kunio and others have mentioned discrimination and economic problems in Okinawa, and though not all mainland scholars focused their discussions solely upon cultural issues, it does seem certain that the focal point of issues was placed on these.

Chapter 5

1 For the chronology see, for example, Ōnuma (1993), Matsumoto (1988), Tanaka (1995), and Mizuno (1996).
2 For details, see Ōta (1996). In this chapter, I go on to describe the American perspective on Okinawa and worldview, the Japanese view on Okinawa, Okinawa's legal positioning, and so on, but each argument has been pointed out to a certain extent in the prior studies mentioned on each occasion. If we assume that this chapter has value as research, it will lie in its comprehensive analysis of these studies, and, by comparing them somewhat with the prewar rule of Korea and Taiwan, in its having sorted out Okinawa's postwar status of being both 'Japanese' and not 'Japanese,' as necessary to the context of this volume.
3 These are analysed in such works as Miyagi (1982), Ōta's studies, and Sakihara (1989), in addition to a commentary attached by Miyagi Etsujirō. There is, however, a perceptible tendency for these studies to rank the U.S. view which deems Okinawans not to be 'Japanese' as a 'mistake' stemming from prejudice. This is readily linked to the tacit regarding as 'truth' the positioning of Okinawans as linguistically and anthropologically part of 'the Japanese.' As can be seen in the main text, studies from the U.S. side based themselves on Chamberlain's theory that the relationship between 'Japanese' and 'Okinawan' was equivalent to that between 'French and Italian,' in the same way as Ifa, but Ifa understood this to be 'resemblance' while the U.S. side interpreted it as 'difference.' While it goes without saying that 'Okinawan' and Standard Japanese (*hyōjungo*) have a number of differences, whether to regard them as 'dialects' within the category of 'Japanese language' or as separate languages is a question of interpretation; and in my mind, it cannot be said which interpretation is 'true,' and which 'false.' In my previous work, Oguma (1995), I pointed out the arbitrariness of establishing the boundaries of 'the Japanese' in anthropological and linguistic research, but I would like to think that here, too, the very act of disputing the authenticity of anthropological studies and suchlike, and classifying Okinawans as 'Japanese' or non-'Japanese' is unproductive.
4 This chapter relies much on Kano (2008), Chapter 1, 'Caught between "Okinawa" and "Ryukyu."' In his examination of Okinawan identity, Kano is thought to have had little interest in the legal aspect, however.
5 See Ōta (1996).
6 For particulars of the separation of Okinawa, see Ōta (1996); for MacArthur's statement, see Nakano (1969, p. 58).
7 On the trusteeship system, see Takano (1962, pp. 100–102).

Notes

8 Ōta (1984 [1996]) details the Deputy Civil Administrator and High Commissioner systems. On the policies of the early-stage civil administration, see Nakano (1969, p. 55).
9 On English-language education, see Yamauchi (1995).
10 Kano did add that Governor Shikiya Kōshin, while understanding English, 'perhaps was hiding his true feelings inside a false bottom,' but I cited it as an episode indicating the attitude of the American side.
11 There are numerous studies on the points at issue in the official proclamations and composite penal code of the time, but first of all, Shiomi and Ōno (1959), Ōno (1959) and Shiomi (1959) convey the then-current response. On official proclamations relating to the expropriation of land, see Nakano (1969, pp. 105–106).
12 Kuwata (1959) and Miyazato (1975) have brought together the legal position of Okinawan residents.
13 See Nishihara (1975) on the process of family register maintenance and limitations on transfer of registration. Other Okinawa-related domestic affairs which the Japanese government held onto included pensions.
14 On the Ryūkyū government Bill of Rights, see Nakano (1969, p. 88).
15 On travel restrictions, see Nakano (1969, pp. 95–96). See Shiomi and Ōno (1959) for the travel ban on Freedom and Popular Rights Association lawyers. Examples of inquiries regarding travel and so on can be seen in Yokobori (1959).

Chapter 6

1 On the League of Okinawans, apart from a commentary written by Gabe (1969), its trends were studied in Arasaki (1982). In addition, works dealing with distortions of views on Japan within Okinawa at this time include Toriyama (1997); and it has been pointed out through the statements of Kaneshi Saichi and the like that in the initial stage of the reversion movement there existed a consciousness of not wanting to waste the 'effort' expended in the prewar to become 'Japanese.' Here, focus is aimed at three analyses: of American, Japanese, and Okinawan recognition, respectively, in territorial discussions at that time. Also see Tomiyama (1990), Chapter 4.
2 Here, the word *minzoku* implies that a 'people' or 'nation' is what creates an independent nation/state.
3 At the end of the main text in Nagaoka 1947, dated 7 December 1946, is written: 'This critique is one penned seven or eight months previously.'
4 Examples of such use of '*minzoku* (ethnic group/people/nation)' and '*sokoku* (ancestral land)' can be seen, for example, in Asato 1948, Nakada 1948.
5 For detail on trends in Miyako at this time, see Taira 1982; and Ōta 1982 on Yaeyama and Yonaguni.
6 In regard to the Okinawa Democratic Alliance (*minshu dōmei*), Nakasone Isamu (1982) emphasises the independence argument. Yoshida Shien's reminiscences are found in Yoshida (1976, p. 23). It is recorded on the same page where the then Committee Chair of the People's Party, Urasaki Kōka, also was talking of a Panama-type protectorate proposal.
7 Also included in Tokuda (1986), a magazine clipping in *Higa Shunchō*

bunko (Higa Shunchō library) (n.d.), held by Okinawa Prefectural Library, not included in the author's collected works.
8 For the circumstances of Nakayoshi's petition, see Okinawa-ken Sokoku Fukki Tōsō Shi Hensan Iinkai (1982, pp. 6–8).
9 On the international tenor of argument in this period, see Nakano (1969, pp. 4–5).
10 Kaneshi's remark is double quoted from Toriyama (1997, p. 53).
11 According to *Uruma shinpō* 1951e [1978], p. 392, none out of the Socialist Masses Party, People's Party and Republican Party had formally decided upon a policy relating to the attribution issue.
12 The petition was submitted with the names of Okinawan sympathisers resident in Tokyo, with joint signatures including those of Ie Chōjo, Kamiyama Seiryō, Higaonna Kanjun, and Nakahara (Nakabaru) Zenchū, in addition to Nakayoshi's (Okinawa-ken Sokoku Fukki Tōsō Shi Hensan Iinkai 1982, p. 8).
13 Nakayoshi also made a statement to the same effect as a witness at the House of Councillors Foreign Affairs Committee on 6 February 1951, saying: '[They] would lose their pride as Japanese' (Nakano 1969, p. 44).

Chapter 7

1 As described below, the reversion movement of Okinawa is often represented by the image of the *hansen fukki* (anti-war reversion) of the late 1960s and depicted as one continuous series of events starting from the petition drive of the 1950s towards the conclusion of the Peace Treaty, continuing on to the land disputes which peaked at the *shimagurumi tōsō* (island-wide struggle for land) and finally developing into the reversion movement of the 1960s. Although there are some studies which epitomise the shift from the so-called *Hi-no-maru fukki* (reversion to the Japanese flag) to the *hansen fukki* from the perspective of the progress and reflection of the movement, empirical studies which analyse the ideologies and worldviews which existed within the reversion movement are rarely found.
   Meanwhile, in his works including Arakawa and Arasaki (1985), Arasaki claims that there are three 'waves' in the reversion movement; namely, nationalism, democratisation, and anti-war and anti-base movements. According to his argument, the reversion movement of the period between the 1950s and the *shimagurumi tōsō* was mainly driven by nationalism – a call for unity with mainland Japan; then, around the 1960s, utilitarian demands started to be raised in political and economic aspects such as improvement of the human rights situation, as well as reduction of disparities; and then from the late 1960s, anti-war and anti-base voices became more prominent. Arasaki argues that 'those three constituent elements do not necessarily appear at the same time.' However, I believe that utilitarian ideas were the critical elements in the reversion movement from the very beginning, and that anti-war and anti-base sentiment was cultivated through the experience of the Battle of Okinawa and firmly established from immediately after Japan's defeat. I suspect that the term 'Japanese nationalism' came to be adopted in order to express these interests and sentiments in the context of the political activity called reversion.

Nonetheless, as discussed in this book, it is a fact that anti-war and anti-base views were not actively promoted during the reversion movement of the 1950s due to the political situation. As for utilitarian demands, these were present from the very beginning but grew larger as the gap between mainland Japan's and Okinawa's economic development became more prominent. The anti-war mindset was brought to the fore from the late 1960s as the Vietnam War intensified. This leads to the conclusion that while Arasaki's argument of the three 'waves' representing different periods of the reversion movement is valid in a way, it seems more accurate to say that a set of subconscious desires in Okinawans, such as peace and prospects which were manifested in the form of the reversion movement, varied from time to time depending on the circumstances, rather than that the reversion movements of different periods were caused by different constituent elements. Movements are not merely actions for achieving concrete political goals, but also media for expressing a range of abstract wills. The reversion movement tended more towards the latter. Without this interpretation, there is no way to comprehend the reason behind the emergence of anti-reversion sentiment in Okinawa shortly before 1972, when the political goals of the 1950s reversion movement had supposedly been fulfilled.
2 The citations from the following list of requirements are from Nakano (1969, p. 73).
3 On labour regulations, see Nakano (1969, pp. 132–141).
4 One example in support of the argument claiming that the U.S.'s reason for the Okinawa reversion was reduction of governance-related costs is a comment made by Senator Jackson at the Senate Committee on Armed Services meeting on 14 June 1962: 'If Okinawa is incorporated into the Japanese economy, then we will be able to avoid huge costs.' See Senate Committee on Military Affairs (1963, p. 124).
5 David A. D. Ogden's statement was made in January 1954, cited in Okinawa-ken Sokoku Fukki Tōsō Shi Hensan Iinkai (1982, p. 31). Dulles's statement is taken from Ōhama's comment in Yara et al. (1960, p. 26).
6 For the international legal perspective on Okinawa at the time, see Kokusai Hōgaku Kai (1955), which also contains Yokota (1955).

Chapter 8

1 Rekishi Kagaku Kyōgikai (Ed.) (1976), a collection of reprints of articles written by Matsubara Hiroshi, Hayakawa Jirō, Ishimoda Shō, Tōma Seita, Tōyama Shigeki, Inoue Kiyoshi, Eguchi Bokurō, Uehara Senroku and Ōta Hidemichi, provides major historians' views on nationality at the time. Bandō Hiroshi's commentary in the aforementioned book, 'Rekishi ni okeru minzoku no mondai (Concerning the nationality question in history)' (Bandō 1976), is one of the rare articles to discuss the nationality theories of the time from a comprehensive perspective. Furuya (1971) is an article more critical of the same era. Nevertheless, both perspectives are intrinsic. There have been only a limited number of studies which have set these thoughts as the subject of research, such as Isomae (1997), which analysed the discourse of Ishimoda Shō's 'Eiyū

jidai ron (Heroic age debate).' This topic has just recently started to gain attention from some scholars; for example, Yun (1997) made a reference to Ishimoda's nationalism theory and Kawamoto Takashi called attention to Ishimoda Shō and Uehara Senroku's views on nationalism in his article in Kawamoto et al. (1998). As far as my research is concerned, there are no studies that examine the relationship between the postwar nationalist ideologies and the historical viewpoint of the reversion movement. The content of the first half of this chapter was first published in Oguma (1995b).

2 As far as my research is concerned, Sakamoto (1960) was one of the earliest to use the term *kakushin nashonarizumu* (progressive nationalism). Takashima (1970, p. 38) and Furuya (1971) also use this term.

3 The 'Asian-African nations' comment is from Uehara (1987–97, vol. 14, p. 73); Minshushugi Kagakusha Kyōkai (1952, p. 38).

4 See Tsuboi and Wada (1954) and *Chūō kōron* (1953) for below. The latter special-edition journal includes 'Nihon wa danjite shokuminchi de nai (Japan is definitely not a colony)' from Aichi Kiichi of the Liberal Party, 'Mushiro shokuminchi teikokushugi no osore (Rather a threat of colonialist imperialism)' from Sone Eki of the Rightist Socialist Party of Japan, 'Amerika no jūzoku koku toshite no Nihon (Japan as a client state of America)' from Katsumata Seiichi of the Leftist Socialist Party of Japan and 'Nihon wa shokuminchi de aru (Japan is a colony),' from Hori Makoto of the Labour-Farmer Party.

5 For Sakamoto's reference to Uchinada, see Sakamoto (1960, p. 16); Ishimoda (1952, pp. 16–17; 1953, p. 3).

6 For opinions on Nagai and Kōtoku, see 'Kokumin shijin toshite no Ishikawa Takuboku (Ishikawa Takuboku as a national poet)' and 'Kōtoku Shūsui to Chūgoku (Kōtoku Shūsui and China)' in Ishimoda (1953c).

7 For the reaction of Japanese socialists towards Korea, see Ishizaka (1993).

8 Ishimoda's recognition of Amino Yoshihiko is from Ishimoda (1953c, pp. 151–155). It should be noted, however, that though Ishimoda recognised Amino, it cannot be directly generalised that they both held the same ideology. Amino's words at the time cited by Ishimoda show his focus on engaging workers, but no sign of emphasis on the nation.

It has been repeatedly pointed out that around the same time, Maruyama Masao and Ōtsuka Hisao advanced the idea of *kokumin shugi* (national consciousness) and *kokumin keizai* (national economy) respectively, representing the nationalism of postwar scholars. However, as described below, compared to other historians mentioned in this book, Maruyama is a relatively weaker advocate of nationalistic ideas in the world of nationalist debate of the time. Further discussions on the nationalism debate among postwar scholars which could not be covered to a satisfying extent in this book will be featured in a separate article, to keep the focus of this book upon the shift in historical perspectives related to the reversion of Okinawa.

Meanwhile, Katō (1959) points out that different terms are used in different contexts in the nationalist debate of the time; namely *minzoku shugi* (nationalism) for explaining positive aspects of nationalism such as independence movements of the Third World, and *kokka shugi* (statism) or *chō-kokka shugi* (extreme statism) when concerning negative aspects such as nationalism in prewar Japan. However, I found that such a distinction does not seem to have been strictly applied as I examined references.

9 In addition to the *Sekaishi no tetsugaku* (The philosophy of world history) discussion, *Ōsaka asahi shinbun* (1910) is another example of affirmation of the domination of Korea from the perspective of the denial of nationality, in which the following claim was made: 'From the point of view of socialism and anarchism, it should not matter at all if Korea were the Korean Empire, or Japan.'

10 For articles with a similar perspective, see Tōyama (1976) and Inoue (1950).

11 Tōma's reports and discussions below are from Tōma (1951c) and 'Kodai, chūsei no bu: tōron (Ancient times and medieval times section: discussion)' included in the same book. For national art movements, see Yamano (1952). It is also noteworthy that Tōma claimed the possibility of existence of nations in ancient times using the notion of *minzokutai* (folks) suggested by Stalin, while Marxism defined the formation of nations as occurring after the establishment of the modern unified market, resulting in much controversy.

12 Tōma explained the ancient Japanese nation he proposes refers to *Volk* and not to modern *nation* in the Rekishigaku Kenkyūkai annual report. It is well known that the terms *Volk* and *nation* are terms named by France's Ernest Renan after the Franco–Prussian War. He referred to the French nation as a *nation* formed by its citizens' voluntary intent whilst calling the German nation a *Volk* built on the ideology of blood and soil. Maruyama quoted Renan's 'A nation is a daily plebiscite' on page 161 of his article, affirming it as the ideal form of nationalism initiated by modern citizens, and held that the Japanese nationalism of the beginning of the Meiji era, which he praises highly, was similar to this. This illustrates not only that Maruyama's national consciousness argument which aspires to the unity of modern citizens differs from that of Tōma and other scholars; but also that Maruyama's criticism was not to deny nationalism, instead being an argument on the nature of nationalism. For recent criticisms of Renan, see Ukai (1992) and Renan et al. (1997).

13 Also see Oguma (1995b).

14 For Tōma's opinion towards the horse-rider invasion theory, see Egami et al. (1951) in which Tōma raises an objection to the theory, together with Hasebe who bases his argument on a purism-based discourse influenced by eugenics.

15 Kikuchi (1952) suggests that American imperialism is propagating a 'policy to exterminate Black people' and 'its dogmas and actions are already exercised upon Asian people of colour' through the Korean War, and highlights that 'America's Black issue is a direct issue for Japan too.'

16 Leftist historian Ienaga Saburō mounted a court battle against the Japanese government's vetting of school textbooks.

17 It is somewhat regrettable, but let me point out that Korean nationalism also used the term *tan'itsu minzoku* (a single people). Kim ([1986] 1991, p. 151), for instance, wrote: 'Koreans in Japan still cannot hold a single nationality representing one nation due to the division of their ancestral

land.' Even Ubukata Naokichi, the first to criticise the single-people theory in Ubukata (1979), highly valued Yanagi Muneyoshi and wrote that he 'discovered Korea as a nation with a single set of traditions through its folk art and artists' (Ubukata 1961, p. 74).

It is noteworthy that nationalism in Korea was a source of multiple positive effects from a political point of view, as it became not only a cornerstone for resistance against the Empire of Japan but also a foundation for the labour movement and democratic movement in South Korea, and, later, the drive for North–South dialogue. In my view, postmodern Korea has been a region suffering from disagreement over the boundaries of the state and the nation, due to Japan's annexation of the Korean Peninsula and the North–South division. Korean nationalism has always been 'nationalism as a vehicle to fight against the state; during the prewar era, it challenged a state called the Empire of Japan, and after the war, it questioned its own state as it had been divided into North and South. This time, in the name of democracy, it then drove another fight against the South Korean state which had been dependent on the United States. However, it is questionable whether Korean nationalism will continue to play only positive roles, now that South Korea has established itself as a legitimate state after having achieved a certain level of democratisation, or in the future when unification of the North and South will be realised.

This kind of remark could be slightly politically problematic in a context where some people with 'liberal' historical perspectives describe Asian nationalism such as that of South Korea as being 'immature.' Nonetheless, one thing that can be said is that, regardless of the future of South Korean and North Korean nationalism, the 'nationalism' (though whether this expression is a perfect fit is questionable) of Koreans in Japan will never be identified with a state and to them it will always be 'nationalism as a vehicle to fight against a state.'

18 Similar opinions are found in articles such as Fujishima et al. (1958). For the Japanese Communist Party's treatment of Koreans in Japan, see Chapter 5 in Tamaki (1967): 'Nihon kyōsantō no zainichi Kankokujin shidō (The Japanese Communist Party's guidance on Koreans in Japan.'
19 Analogies of the 27th parallel are often found in other literature, including Fujita (1967).
20 For views from historians of the time on national issues and standard language issues of Marx, Lenin and Stalin, see Ishimoda (1953b?), Tōma (1951d, pp. 286–287), and Inoue (1976); also http://www.marxists.org/archive/marx/works/1848/08/09.htm.
21 For the background of the Ryūkyū Disposition dispute and related articles, see Shinzato (1972).
22 For Mori's thoughts and examination of sugar-cane farming labour, see Mori (1963b).
23 Kokuba's discussions of the time are serialized in the 8 July, 19 August, 26 August, 2 September, 16 September and 4 November 1963 issues of *Nihon dokusho shinbun*. However, the citations here are from Kokuba (1963; 1962, pp. 90, 91).

Chapter 9

1 On the treatment and entitlements of teachers, see Ryūkyū Seifu Bunkyō Kyoku Kenkyū Chōsa Ka (1956, pp. 373, 398); Kaminuma (1966, pp. 54, 116); and Okinawa Kyōshokuinkai (1955, p. 1).

As far as my research is concerned, there are almost no summary documents or research papers regarding education in postwar Okinawa which mention the enforcement of the standard language or the national education movement; and there are hardly any thorough empirical studies conducted on these topics which are publicly available. Asano Makoto devotes one section of his book to a criticism of standard-language enforcement, remarking that the use of *hōgen fuda* (dialect placards) was 'implemented widely until the 1960s' (Asano 1983, p. 154). In another example from literature of the same era, Kaminuma (1966) also describes the development of the national education movement with a certain degree of criticism for its excessive promotion of the *Hi-no-maru* flag and *Kimi-ga-yo* anthem, despite being a supporter of the national education movement. Using relevant newspaper articles and other sources, Toriyama (1997) also depicts the unfolding of the beginning of the enforcement of the standard language. This chapter examines the tone of the discussion on these movements as reported mainly in materials prepared by the Okinawa Teachers' Association from the late 1950s onwards.

2 For Yara's experience in Taiwan, see Yara (1968b, pp. 35–42; 1984).
3 Recollections of the early postwar period are from Ryūkyū Seifu Bunkyō Kyoku Kenkyū Chōsa Ka (1956, pp. 7–8)
4 The description of the situation around 1950 and the citations are from Toriyama (1997, pp. 61–62)
5 Uehara's reference to Fichte is from Uehara (1987–97: vol. 7, p. 38). Fichte's *Reden an die deutsche Nation* (Addresses to the German nation) is included in Renan et al. (1997) *Kokumin to wa nani ka?* (What is a nation?), Trans. and Ed. by Ukai et al. For Fichte and Nanbara, see Ukai's 'Kokumin ningen shugi no rimitto (Limitations of national humanism)' included in the same book.

Chapter 10

1 The fact that this book focuses only on Arakawa Akira, with minimum reference to Nakano Yoshio, Ōe Kenzaburō, Ōta Masahide and Ōshiro Tatsuhiro, inevitably raises some criticisms that my argument is biased from the perspective of an attempt comprehensively to cover the reversion debate of the time, as Arakawa was not the only scholar between the late 1960s and 1972 who was skeptical about the reversion. I also admit that there are many issues that have not received adequate coverage, such as the Koza Riot and the rivalry between the Communist Party and the New Rightists. However, I reiterate that the main objective of this book is not to introduce the issue of colonial rule and Okinawa, but to examine debates on the boundaries of 'the Japanese.' I hope readers will understand that I

chose to place a strong focus on Arakawa at the expense of a number of other background events for this reason.

Meanwhile, I kept references to Arakawa's view on Okinawa's history as seen in his works such as Arakawa (1973) to a minimum in this book. Moreover, I avoided making reference to the influences of Yoshimoto Takaaki and Tanigawa Ken'ichi on Arakawa's ideology. I would like, however, to add the point that even if Yoshimoto's and Tanigawa's thoughts had triggered Arakawa's discussion of *i-zoku* (alien races/people), while Yoshimoto's and Tanigawa's argument saw Okinawa as consisting of a distinct people (*minzoku*) different from mainland Japan, based on anthropological and archaeological theories, Arakawa's claim of the time was that *i-zoku* refers to individuals who resisted assimilation into the Japanese state and the term 'has nothing to do with (or is of a totally different dimension from) discussions on whether the people of Okinawa are unambiguously Japanese in a theoretical sense.' This comment, made in the context of a counterargument to criticism based on the archaeological theory of the Japanese Communist Party, is a good representation of Arakawa's view and is of considerable interest.

Later, Arakawa started to view the independence of Okinawa as an ideological issue and most notably in recent years, he emphasised the ideological validity of the pro-independence argument in a discussion with Arasaki Moriteru. As can be seen in this chapter, Arakawa was critical of the pro-independence argument around the 1970s, but when asked about his position by Arasaki in 1985, he responded that he 'intentionally accentuated that point so as to avoid being put in the same category as the pro-independence argument (of the conservatives)' and commented that 'it is also a fact that if asked for a one-word explanation of anti-reversionism as a phenomenon, it can only be answered with secession or independence.' At the same time, though, he also added: 'It is not to be interpreted that Okinawa should just be a separate independent state, because if this is the case then the establishment of the state of Okinawa turns into an end in itself, which is quite simply the antithesis of the reversion movement' (Arakawa and Arasaki 1985, p. 58). While perceiving a gap between what he used to describe as 'anti-reversion' or as 'independence' in recent years, and another kind of 'independence' which referred to the formation of a nation-state in a political sense, Arakawa perhaps is continuing to use the term in an ambiguous manner just because he cannot find any alternatives.

The problem of how to convey concepts that are difficult to articulate in existing political terminology is one of the main themes of this book. Academics who attempt to express such notions often lack consistency in their arguments, and Arakawa is no exception. In specific terms, on the one hand, he conveniently adopts the idea of 'independence' when 'asked for a one-word explanation of anti-reversionism as a phenomenon' and continues to use the term. On the other hand, when he fears that his 'independence' is identified with 'independence' as the formation of a nation-state in a political sense, he tends to highlight the difference between the two. As described in the main text, it was always the case that Arakawa's claims were only recognised after having been mapped against predefined categories, and he invariably responded to such interpretations with denial. As a result, he appears to have returned inconsistent arguments depending on who the opposition was. However, above all else, the reason this chapter placed a focus on Arakawa around the 1970s was to discover the limits to the ability to express the various demarcation criteria of a nation-state (such as assimilation, independence, autonomy and pluralism).

Evaluating this kind of denial-oriented thinking is a challenging issue. There were, from back then, criticisms against Arakawa pointing out the lack of specific political direction in his argument; and, in fact, he never took political action except for demonstrating his 'denial' in the form of non-participation in national politics. It is an incontrovertible fact to everyone including Arakawa that the human rights and economic status of Okinawa improved to a certain extent. Therefore, the reversionists who endeavoured to achieve better reversion, and thus better national integration, were the ones who made the greatest contribution to improvement of the political status of Okinawa, and it could be a valid observation that Arakawa's ideology did not have political significance.

In the aforementioned dialogue of 1985, which created a foundation for later discussions reignited in 1997 between Arakawa and Arasaki, Arasaki made the following comment:

> I have no intention whatsoever of denying your approachl. I think it is necessary to map out all approaches in various forms, even only at the ideological level, in the present situation where we cannot see what lies ahead ... Suffice it to say, however, that I strongly believe that we must take realistic actions when dealing with real political situations.

In response to this, Arakawa said:

> In dealing with real political situations, such as the CTS (crude oil terminal station) issue, the Shiraho airport issue or the One-*tsubo* Anti-war Landowners protest, I suppose there are many concrete actions that could be taken but it would be a problem if those actions became ends in themselves. ... Indeed, the reversion movement failed because the reversion itself was turned into an end, and that is the lesson learned from the reversion movement (Arakawa and Arasaki 1985, p. 61).

I have repeatedly described thus far in this book the process where desires which we cannot articulate are reduced to self-fulfilling objects, losing their true meanings once they are expressed in existing language. The important issues seem to lie in how to speak of things that cannot be spoken, and how to recover unexpressed elements from obscurity when they are spoken.

2 A series of relevant petitions, including Nakayoshi's 'Nichibei anpo jōyaku kaitei ni Okinawa hōgan hō no ketsugi seigan (Petition for the inclusion of Okinawa in revision of the U.S.–Japan security treaty)' (n.d), are included in the aforecited unpublished documents: 'Nakayoshi Ryōkō fukki kankei shiryō,' Vol. 8, held at Ryūkyū Daigaku.
3 On military-base expansion, see Arasaki (1996, p. 14).
4 See, for example Ōshiro Tatsuhiro (1972: 244). I add that there were criticisms and afterthoughts directed at this comment from intellectuals in mainland Japan, as seen in Nakano (1970) and Ōe (1970, Chapter V).
5 Political analyses of the Okinawa reversion negotiation can be found in Nihon Kokusai Seiji Gakkai (1975) and Kōno (1994). For the process of

settlement of Japanese governmental funding, see Yara (1977, pp. 179, 181).

6 Details on Ōshiro are documented in Chapter 5: 'Ika, dōka, jiritsu: Ōshiro Tatsuhiro no bungaku to shisō (Alienation, assimilation and independence: literature and ideology of Ōshiro Tatsuhiro)' in Kano (1987).

7 For board members of Matsukawa's Ryūkyū Shōkō Kaigijo (Ryukyu Chamber of Commerce and Industry), see Kaminuma (1966, p. 157). For the Ryūkyū Gikai (Ryukyu Assembly) and Okinawajin no Okinawa o Tsukuru Kai (Society for the Creation of Okinawans' Okinawa), see Chapter 8 of Ōta (1984 [1996]). Yamazato Eikichi, a leading advocate of 'Okinawajin no Okinawa o Tsukuru Kai,' authored Yamazato (1969), a collection of contemporary opinions of the time, as well as Yamazato (1971), a commentary on the history of Okinawa. He argued: 'Our ancestral land is definitely not Japan. Our ancestral land is Okinawa' (Yamazato 1969, p. 25). Ōshiro Tatsuhiro, for example, while writing that he 'appreciated [Yamazato's] efforts in constructing an argument,' described Yamazato as 'never having criticised American control of Okinawa' (Ōshiro 1970). Similarly, Arakawa pointed out:

> Here and there in the magazine *Gekkan Ryūkyū* (Monthly Ryukyu) which [Yamazato] published as editor and publisher, one can see wording in which Yamazato seems to assert his worth as a loyal imperial subject, preaching respect for the national flag under this own byline and writing such things as: 'Anyone who does not understand what constitutes the Japanese spirit (*Yamato damashii*) is not a true Japanese.'

Arakawa positions Yamazato and other conservative pro-independence advocates of the time as opportunists, taking into account the fact that Yamazato was the head of the Ryūkyū Seifu Bunkazai Hogo Iinkai (Commission for Protection of Cultural Properties of the Government of the Ryukyu Islands) (Arakawa 1971, pp. 299, 135).

Yamazato, on the other hand, quoted Ifa Fuyū's statement praising the political ability of the Ryukyuans (Yamazato 1969, pp. 45–46), namely: 'Our ancestors ... had enough capabilities to form a state (*kokka*) society,' and used this as historical justification for the possibility of Okinawa's independence. By contrast, Arakawa categorised Ifa as an assimilationist, as discussed later. The fact that Yamazato saw Ifa as an Okinawan nationalist while Arakawa conversely regarded him as an assimilationist is a deeply interesting example of how Ifa's ambiguity could give different interpretations to different readers.

8 For Arakawa's biographical information and Ryūdai bungaku (The University of Ryukyus magazine on literature), see Chapter 2 '"Non" no bungaku: "Ryūkyū bungaku" no kōseki (Literature on "negation": in the wake of The University of Ryukyus magazine on literature)' in Kano Masanao (1987

9 The removal of the Okinawa independence commemoration message from the timeline can be seen in Nihon Kyōsantō Chūō Iinkai Shuppanbu (1966).

10 Arakawa says, on page 111 of this article: 'If someone asked me whether I were advocating independence from the ideological point of view, I would say "Yes,"' though at the same time he states: 'Then people would go and assume I am all pro-independence. If someone asked me if Okinawa could be independent in practical terms, I would say "No."' It can be observed

from this that he is in a situation where, despite feeling that the word 'independence' is somewhat unsuitable, he is unable to find an alternative way of expressing the concept.

Conclusion

1 On nuclear weapon deployment, see Gabe (2000, p. 79).
2 Gaikō Seisaku Kikaku Iinkai (1969), dated 25 September. This document became widely known due to NHK's reportage programme, '"Kaku" o motometa Nihon (The Japan that sought "nuclear"),' telecast in October 2010, and currently being published on the Ministry of Foreign Affairs home page due to lifting of its secrecy designation.
3 Chapter 4 of Yoshioka (2011) gives a detailed account of Japan's nuclear power generation policy in this period.
4 Mishima's posthumous work, 'Geki (Manifesto),' is contained in Mishima (1976). On p. 530, it says: 'Though there were people in the textile business who called the LDP "traitors" on the occasion of the textile negotiations, and though it is obvious the nuclear [test] ban treaty relating to the state's 100-year long-range plan is just like a reappearance of the former 5:5:3 unequal treaties, not a single general who protested and committed ritual suicide emerged from the Self Defense Forces.'
5 Chapter 6 in Gabe (2000) is well-informed on these quotes and the process of negotiating the payment amount.
6 Maedomari's article gives a detailed account of current economic conditions described in the song by the group Quikion, with vocals by Totoki Yukiko, featured in http://www.youtube.com/watch?v=wBZ-Tt-KmL0.
7 See Oguma and Ueno (2003).
8 See Oguma (1998), Chapters 15 and 16.

Bibliography

Ahagon Chokusei (1966), 'Shotō kyōiku (Elementary education),' in Ryūkyū Seifu, *Okinawa ken shi* (History of Okinawa prefecture), Vol. 4: Ryūkyū Seifu.
Ahagon Shōkō (1973), *Beigun to nōmin* (The U.S. forces and farmers): Iwanami Shoten.
Anderson, Benedict (1983), *Imagined Communities*, London: Verso Editions, and NLB; (Japanese edition), Shiraishi Takashi and Shiraishi Saya (Trans.) (1987), *Sōzō no kyōdōtai*: Riburopōto.
Andō Kiichirō (1897a [1970]), 'Hon ken ni okeru jofuku kairyō ni tsukite (About improving women's clothing in this prefecture),' in Naha Shiyakusho (Ed.), *Naha shishi: shiryō hen* (History of Naha city: reference materials edition), Vol. 2, 2–3: Naha Shiyakusho.
Andō Kiichirō (1897b), 'Kokutai ron ni tsuki zensetsu o fuen shi awasete honpō kyōiku no seishitsu o nobu (Discourse on the national polity in amplification of the previous argument together with the nature of education in this country),' *Ryūkyū kyōiku* (Ryukyu education), No. 22, reprinted edition Vol. 3.
Arakawa Akira (1956), '"Yūshoku jinshu" shō (sono 1): Ōshoku jinshu (II) ("Coloured races" abridged version (1): Yellow races (II),' *Ryūdai bungaku* (The University of Ryukyus magazine on literature), Vol. 2, No. 1, March.
Arakawa Akira (1971), *Hankokka no kyōku: Okinawa; jiritsu e no shiten* (Okinawa: antithesis to the evil Japanese nation-state): Gendai Hyōronsha.
Arakawa Akira (1973), *I-zoku to tennō no kokka* (Different peoples and the imperial state): Nigatsusha.
Arakawa Akira and Arasaki Moriteru (1985), 'Okinawa ni totte "fukki" to wa nan datta ka (What the 'reversion' meant to Okinawa),' *Sekai* (The world), June.
Arakawa Akira and Ikezawa Natsuki (1996), 'Okinawa dokuritsu no yume o katarō (Let's talk about the dream of independent Okinawa),' *Sekai* (The world), August.
Arakawa Akira, Okamoto Keitoku and Kawamitsu Shin'ichi (1972), 'Nihon kokka to naze dōka sienai ka (Why can't it assimilate with the Japanese state?),' *Chūō kōron* (Central review), June, pp. 88–89.
Araki Masuo (1963), 'Okinawa sunkan (A snapshot of Okinawa),' *Minami to kita* (South and north), No. 27, December.
Araki Moriaki (1980), *Shin Okinawa shi ron* (History of Okinawa: a new paradigm): Okinawa Taimususha.
Arasaki Moriteru (1996), *Okinawa gendai shi* (Modern history of Okinawa): Iwanami Shinsho.
Arazato Kinpuku and Ōshiro Tatsuhiro (1969), *Okinawa no hyakunen* (One hundred years of Okinawa), Vol. 1, *Jinbutsu hen* (People edition): Taihei Shuppansha.

Asahi jānaru (Asahi journal) (1961), 'Sōzō-gai no "Hi-no-maru būmu" (An unexpected "Japanese flag boom"),' 5 February.
Asahi shinbun (Asahi newspaper) (1956a), 'Asu gōdō kaigi (Joint council tomorrow),' 29 June.
Asahi shinbun (1956b), 'Jūmin no hogo o yōkyū (Resident protection requested),' 29 June.
Asahi shinbun (1956c), 'Kisha seki (Reporter's desk),' 30 June.
Asahi shinbun (1956d), 'Kono tsuki no seiji hyō (tōsho kara) (Political review for this month (from letters to the editor),' 30 June.
Asahi shinbun (1956e), 'Minzoku no kōhai ni kakawaru (Concerning the rise and fall of the nation),' 20 June.
Asahi shinbun (1956f), 'Nihon seifu wa yowagoshi (Week-kneed Japanese government),' 25 June.
Asahi shinbun (1956g), 'Okinawa wa tōzen kaerō (Okinawa would rightly revert),' 29 June.
Asano Makoto (1983), *Okinawa kyōiku no hansei to teian* (Reflections and proposals for education in Okinawa): Meiji Tosho Shuppan.
Asano Makoto (1991), *Okinawa ken no kyōiku shi* (History of education in Okinawa prefecture): Shibunkaku.
Asano Makoto and Sakugawa Norishige (1976), 'Okinawa ni okeru chiken chokugo no shōgakkō setsuritsu fukyū ni kansuru kenkyū (A study on diffusion of elementary schools in Okinawa soon after prefecture establishment),' *Ryūkyū Daigaku kyōiku gakubu kiyō* (Bulletin of the division of education of the Ryukyu University), Vol. 20, Part 1.
Asato Hikonori (1983), *Kindai Okinawa no kyōiku* (Education in modern Okinawa): San'ichi Shobō.
Asato Kazuo (1971), 'Shita kara no minzoku tōitsu (Racial integration from below),' *Jinmin* (People), No. 496, 4 September.
Asato Nobu (1948), 'Minzoku o sukuu mono wa idainaru hito dearu (One who saves a nation is a hero),' Kōsei Okinawa (Rehabilitating Okinawa), No. 4.
Bandō Hiroshi (1976), 'Rekishi ni okeru minzoku no mondai (Concerning the nationality question in history),' in Bandō Hiroshi (Ed.), *Rekishi kagaku taikei* (Anthology of historical sciences), Vol. 15, Azekura Shobō.
Bōkan Seitō (= Contribution by a bystander) (1899 [1965]), 'Hakitame (Rubbish heap),' *Ryūkyū shinpō* (Ryukyu newspaper), 1, 3 May, in Ryūkyū Seifu (Ed.), *Okinawa ken shi*, Vol. 19: Ryūkyū Seifu.
Bramley, Charles V. [spelling unconfirmed] (1982), 'Yara shokan ni taisuru kaitō (Response to Yara's letter),' *Okinawa-ken sokoku fukki tōsō shi shiryō hen* (History of Okinawa prefecture's reversion to the motherland, documents edition): Okinawa Jiji Shuppansha.
CERD (Committee on the Elimination of Racial Discrimination) (2012): http://www2.ohchr.org/english/bodies/cerd/docs/CERD_Japan.pdf
Chūō Kōron (1948), 'Dare ga minzoku o eru ka (Who will acquire a nation?),' *Chūō kōron*, January.
Chūō Kōron (1953), 'Tokushū Nihon wa Amerika no shokuminchi ka (Special edition: Is Japan an American colony?),' *Chūō kōron*, June.
Dai 12-kai Kokkai Sangiin (1951), 'Heiwa jōyaku oyobi Nichibei anzen hoshō jōyaku tokubetsu iinkai (The special committee for the peace treaty and the U.S.–Japan security treaty),' 6 November.
Dore, Ronald and Okuno Seisuke (1995), 'Watashi wa naze "fusen ketsugi"

ni hantaisuru noka (Why do I oppose the "resolution to renounce war"),' *Sekai* (The world), May.

Egami Namio, Hasebe Kotondo, Mikami Tsugio, Tōma Seita and Wajima Seiichi (1951), 'Nihon kodai kokka no keisei (The formation of the ancient Japanese state),' *Tōyō bunka* (Oriental culture), No. 6.

Fonaker, Peter J. (1958), 'Gaijin no mita Okinawa (Okinawa in the eyes of foreigners),' *Okinawa taimusu* (Okinawa times), 1 December.

Fujii Haruo (1995), 'Nichi-bei anpo: Okinawa to watashitachi (The US–Japan Security Treaty: Okinawa and us),' *Masukomi shimin* (Mass-communications citizens), November.

Fujioka Nobukatsu/Jiyū Shugi Shikan Kenkyūkai (1996), *Kyōkasho ga oshienai rekishi* (The history that textbooks don't teach): Sankei Shinbunsha.

Fujishima Udai, Maruyama Kunio and Murakami Hyōe (1958), 'Zainichi Chōsenjin rokujūman-nin no genjitsu (The realities of the 600,000 Koreans in Japan), *Chūō kōron* (Central review), December.

Fujita Hideo (1967), *Okinawa no sakebi* (A cry of Okinawa): Chōryū Shuppan.

Fujitani Toshio (1952), 'Minzoku, minzoku bunka to wa nani ka (What is a nation and national culture?),' *Nihon shi kenkyū* (Journal of Japanese history), No. 16.

Fujitani Toshio (1953), 'Minzoku, minzoku bunka o ika ni toraeru ka (Views of the nation and national culture),' *Nihon shi kenkyū* (Journal of Japanese history), No. 19.

Fukuchi Hiroaki (1965), *Sengo 20-nen, kyōiku no kūhaku – Hondo to Okinawa no hikaku* (Education vacuum in twenty years after the war – A comparison between mainland and Okinawa): Okinawa Kyōshokuinkai.

Fuller, John F. C. (1961), *The Conduct of War*, London: Eyre & Spottiswoode; (Japanese edition) Nakamura Yoshihisa (Tr.) (1975), *Seigen sensō shidō ron*: Hara Shobō.

Furuya Tetsuo (1971), 'Nashonarizumu hihan no genten (The origin of criticism of nationalism),' *Rekishi gaku kenkyū* (Journal of historical studies), No. 377.

Fusō shinbun (Fusang newspaper) (1899e), 'Taiwan kikyaku dan (Comments of tourists returning from Taiwan),' 10 September, reprinted in *Taiwan kyōkai zasshi* (Journal of the Taiwan institute), No. 12.

Gabe Masao (1979), *Meiji kokka to Okinawa* (The Meiji state and Okinawa): San'ichi Shobō.

Gabe Masao (1981), *Kindai Nihon to Okinawa* (Modern Japan and Okinawa): San'ichi Shobō.

Gaikō Seisaku Kikaku Iinkai (1969), *Waga kuni no gaikō seisaku no taikō* (Outline of our country's foreign policy),' dated 25 September: http://www.mofa.go.jp/mofaj/gaiko/kaku_hokoku/pdfs/kaku_hokoku03.pdf

Gaimushō (Ministry of Foreign Affairs) (Ed.) (1950a), *Nihon gaikō bunsho* (Documents on Japanese foreign policy), Vol. 8: Nihon Kokusai Rengō Kyōkai.

Gaimushō (Ministry of Foreign Affairs) (Ed.) (1950b), *Nihon gaikō bunsho* (Documents on Japanese foreign policy), Vol. 14: Nihon Kokusai Rengō Kyōkai.

Gekkan jiji (Monthly current affairs) (1967a), 'Okinawa de yamatodamashii o oshieru muzukashisa (The difficulty of teaching the Japanese spirit in Okinawa),' October.

Gekkan jiji (1967b), 'Warera Nihonjin (We Japanese),' October.
Gekkan mingei (Monthly folk arts) (1940a), 'Mondai no suii (How the issue is developing),' March.
Gekkan mingei (1940b), 'Sono go no Ryūkyū mondai (The aftermath of the Ryukyu issue),' May.
Gima Susumu (1967), '27-do sen inan kara no shuchō (Voices from the south of the 27th parallel),' *Sekai* (The world), August.
Gima Susumu (1969), 'Okinawa to hondo tono danzetsu kan (A sense of rupture between Okinawa and the mainland),' *Shin Okinawa bungaku* (New Okinawa literature), summer.
Gima Susumu (1970), 'Uchinaru Nihon to no taiketsu (Confrontation with the inner Japan),' in Nihon Kyōshokuin Kumiai and Okinawa Kyōshokuin Kai (Eds), *Okinawa no senseitachi: hondo to no shin no rentai o motomete* (The teachers in Okinawa: seeking true solidarity with the mainland): Papyrus Sōsho.
Gordon, Milton M. (1964), *Assimilation in American Life*, New York: Oxford University Press.
Haebaru Tōru (1970), 'Kokusei sanka kyohi o tonaeru torotsukisuto no ugoki (A Trotskyist movement advocating non-participation in government),' *Jinmin* (People), No. 450, 17 October.
Hagiwara Sakutarō (1940), 'Iseisha to bunka (Politicians and culture),' *Gekkan mingei* (Monthly mingei), March issue, in Naha Shiyakusho (Ed.), *Naha shishi: shiryō hen* (History of Naha city: reference materials edition), Vol. 2, 2–3: Naha Shiyakusho.
Hanada Toshinori (1995), 'Okinawa hōgen ronsō sankō (Three thoughts on the Okinawan dialect debate),' *Nihon kindai bungaku* (Modern Japanese literature), No. 52.
Hara Takashi (1911), *Hara Takashi nikki* (Diary of Hara Takashi), Vol. 3, April 24, 31 May.
Hara Takeshi (1992), 'Meiji shoki no Okinawa no heibi (Armaments in Okinawa in the early Meiji era),' *Seiji keizai shigaku* (Journal of the political and economic history), No. 317.
Hasegawa Nyozekan (1940), 'Nihongo no senrensei ni tsuite (On sophistication of the Japanese language),' *Gekkan mingei* (Monthly mingei), March.
Hattori Shirō et al. (Eds) (1974–76), *Iha Fuyū zenshū* (The complete works of Ifa Fuyū): Heibon Sha (Vol. 1 1974a; Vol. 2 1974b; Vol. 3 1974c; Vol. 4 1974d; Vol. 5 1974e; Vol. 6 1975a; Vol. 7 1975b; Vol. 8 1975c; Vol. 9 1975d; Vol. 10 1976a; Vol. 11 1976b)
Hekigotō (1910), 'Zoku ichinichi isshin (Second series of daily letters),' *Nihon oyobi Nihonjin* (Japan and Japanese), 15 July.
Hentona Chōyū (1982), 'Ryūkyū shobun (Ryukyu disposition)' in Kano Masanao & Yui Masaomi (Eds), *Kindai Nihon no tōgō to teikō* (Integration of modern Japan and resistance): Nihon Hyōron Sha.
Higa Junjō (1940 [1970]), 'Okinawa ganrō (Toying with Okinawa),' *Okinawa nippō* (Okinawa daily), 11 January, in Naha Shiyakusho (Ed.), *Naha shishi: shiryō hen* (History of Naha city: reference materials edition), Vol. 2, 2–3: Naha Shiyakusho.
Higa Kōichi (1951), 'Okinawa no kizoku mondai ni tsuite (5) (On the Okinawa sovereignty issue (5)),' *Uruma shinpō*, 21 April.
Higa Sei (1904 [1965]), 'Jisei shōkan (Observation of the times),' *Ryūkyū*

shinpō (Ryukyu newspaper), 11 June, in Ryūkyū Seifu (Ed.), *Okinawa ken shi*, Vol. 19: Ryūkyū Seifu.
Higa Shunchō (1970), *Shinkō Okinawa no rekishi* (New manuscript: History of Okinawa): San'ichi shobō.
Higa Shunchō (1971–73), *Higa Shunchō zenshū* (Complete works of Higa Shunchō): Okinawa taimususha.
Higa Shunchō (n.d.), 'Ryūkyū no higeki (Ryukyu's tragedy),' magazine clipping in *Higa Shunchō bunko* (Higa Shunchō collection), (noted as 'three years after the war's end'), held by Okinawa Kenritsu Toshokan.
Higa Shunchō, Shimota Seiji and Shinzato Keiji (1963), *Okinawa*: Iwanami Shinsho.
Hirano Yoshitarō (1952), 'Bakumatsu ni okeru han shokuminchi ka no kiki to jōyaku kaisei no futatsu no michi (The threat of semi-colonization and two ways to the revision of treaties),' *Rekishi hyōron* (History review), No. 35.
Hiratsuka Atsushi (Ed.) (1982), 'Futsujin Boasonādo no iken (The opinion of the Frenchman Boissonard),' dated 17 March 1875, in *Zoku Itō Hirobumi hiroku* (Confidential records of Ito Hirobumi, second series), reprinted edition: Hara Shobō.
Hisae Masahiko (2005), *Beigun saihen; Nichi-Bei 'himitsu kōshō' de nani ga atta ka* (US force realignment: what happened in the Japan–US 'secret negotiations'?): Kōdansha Gendai Shinsho.
Hiyane Teruo (1981), *Kindai Nihon to Iha Fuyū* (Modern Japan and Ifa Fuyū): San'ichi Shobō.
Hiyane Teruo (1982), *Jiyū minken shisō to Okinawa* (The idea of democratic rights and Okinawa): Kenbun Shuppan.
Hiyane Teruo (1996a), *Kindai Okinawa no seishin shi* (Spiritual history of modern Okinawa), Shakai Hyōronsha.
Hiyane Teruo (1996b), 'Okinawa: jiritsu, jichi e no kutō (Okinawa: the struggle for independence and autonomy),' *Sekai* (The world), August.
Hiyane Teruo and Isa Shin'ichi (Eds) (1993), Ōta Chōfu senshū (Selected works of Ōta Chōfu), Jō (Vol. 1): Ryūkyū Shinpōsha.
Hiyane Teruo and Isa Shin'ichi (Eds) (1995), Ōta Chōfu senshū (Selected works of Ōta Chōfu), Chū (Vol. 2): Ryūkyū Shinpōsha.
Hiyane Teruo and Isa Shin'ichi (Eds) (1996), Ōta Chōfu senshū (Selected works of Ōta Chōfu), Ge (Vol. 3): Ryūkyū Shinpōsha.
Hoashi Tōki (1903), 'Gengo ni tsuite (About language),' *Ryūkyū kyōiku* (Ryukyu education), No. 47.
Hokama Shuzen (1979), *Ifa Fuyū ron* (Essays on Ifa Fuyū): Okinawa Taimususha. A new enlarged edition was published from Heibonsha in 1993.
Hokama Shuzen (Ed.) (1976), *Iha Fuyū hito to shisō* (The person and thought of Iha Fuyu): Heibonsha.
Hokama Shuzen and Fujimoto Hideo (1978), *Iha Fuyū Kindaichi Kyōsuke (Nihon minzoku bunka taikei dai 12 kan)* (Ifa Fuyu Kindaichi Kyosuke (Anthology of Japanese folk cultures Vol. 12)): Kōdansha.
Honda Toyokichi (1898), 'Okinawa kyōiku no hōshin (Education policy for Okinawa),' *Ryūkyū kyōiku* (Ryukyu education), No. 32.
Huxley, Julian S., and A. C. Haddon (1935), *We Europeans: a Study of 'Racial' Problems*, London: Jonathan Cape.
Ifa Fuyū (1906 [1965]), 'Okinawajin no sosen ni tsuite (On the ancestors of

Bibliography

Okinawan people),' *Ryūkyū shinpō* (Ryukyu newspaper), 5– 9 December, in Ryūkyū Seifu (Ed.), *Okinawa ken shi*, Vol. 19: Ryūkyū Seifu.
Ifa Fuyū (1911), *Ko-Ryūkyū* (Old-Ryukyu): Okinawa Kōronsha.
Ikemiyagushiku Shūi (1996), 'Okinawa wa Kokuren shintaku tarubeshi (Okinawa should be entrusted to the U.N.),' 'Naze Kokuren shintaku o shuchō suru ka (Why do I insist on U.N. trusteeship?),' 'Nihon kizoku wa nani o imisuru ka? (What does the reversion to Japan mean?),' in *Ikemiyagushiku Shūi, Hankotsu no jānarisuto Ikemiyagushiku Shūi korekushon* (Uncompromising journalist: Ikemiyagushiku Shūi selection): Niraisha.
Inoue Kiyoshi (1950), 'Futatsu no aikoku shugi to kokusai shugi (Two kinds of nationalism and internationalism),' *Rekishigaku kenkyū* (Journal of historical studies), No. 137.
Inoue Kiyoshi (1951), 'Bakumatsu ni okeru han shokuminchi ka no kiki to tōsō (2) (The threat of semi-colonization and struggles at the end of the Edo period (2)),' *Rekishi hyōron* (History review), No. 33.
Inoue Kiyoshi (1955), *Jōyaku kaisei* (Treaty revision), Iwanami Shinsho.
Inoue Kiyoshi (1976), 'Marukusu shugi ni yoru minzoku riron (Marxist theory of a nation),' *Rekishi kagaku taikei* (Anthology of historical sciences), Vol. 15, *Minzoku no mondai* (Nationality issues): Azekura Shobō.
Ishida Masaharu (1997), 'Okinawa ni okeru kindaika no kikyū (A quest for modernization in Okinawa),' *Hōsei kenkyū* (Journal of law and politics, Institute for Law and Politics, Kyūshū University), Vol. 64, No. 1.
Ishiguro Osamu (1940), 'Hyōjun go no meishō to yōken (The name and criteria for standard language),' *Gekkan mingei* (Monthly mingei), May.
Ishikawa Ryuzō (1956), 'Bei ryōdo ni nattara Okinawa wa dō kawaru (How will Okinawa change if it is annexed to the U.S.),' *Kichi Okinawa* (Military base Okinawa), No. 6.
Ishimoda Shō (1960), 'Minzoku, rekishi, kyōiku (Nation, history, education),' *Ishimoda Shō chosaku shū* (Collected works of Ishimoda Shō), Vol. 16: Iwanami Shoten.
Ishimoda Shō (1952), *Rekishi to minzoku no hakken* (The discovery of history and the nation): Tokyo Daigaku Shuppankai.
Ishimoda Shō (1953a), 'Atarashii toshi o mukaete (On seeing in the new year),' *Rekishi hyōron* (History review), No. 41.
Ishimoda Shō (1953b), 'Kotoba no mondai ni tsuite no kansō (Thoughts on the question of language), *Zoku rekishi to minzoku no hakken* (Sequel to the discovery of history and the nation): Tokyo Daigaku Shuppankai.
Ishimoda Shō (1953c), *Zoku rekishi to minzoku no hakken* (Sequel to The discovery of history and the nation): Tokyo Daigaku Shuppankai.
Ishimoda Shō (1954), 'Yowasa o ika ni kokufuku suru ka (How to overcome weaknesses),' *Nihon shi kenkyū* (Journal of Japanese history), No. 20.
Ishimoda Shō (1988–90), *Ishimoda Shō chosaku shū* (Collected works of Ishimoda Shō): Iwanami Shoten.
Ishimoda Shō (1990), *Ishimoda Shō chosaku shū* (Collected works of Ishimoda Shō), Vol. 12: Iwanami Shoten.
Ishizaka Kōichi (1993), *Kindai Nihon no shakaishugi to Chōsen* (Modern Japanese socialism and Korea): Shakai Hyōronsha.
Isomae Jun'ichi (1997), 'Rekishiteki gensetsu no kūkan (Space for historical discourses),' *Gendai shisō* (Contemporary thought), Vol. 25, No. 10.

Iwasaki Isao (1921), 'Hokkaidō no dai naru mono (The largeness of Hokkaidō),' *Nihon oyobi Nihonjin* (Japan and the Japanese people), special November.
Janamoto Keifuku (1971), '"Minzoku geinō no yūbe" igi to seika (jō) ("An evening of folk arts": Its significance and outcome (1)),' *Jinmin* (People), No. 510, 11 December.
Jinmin Tō Seinen Bu (1950), '"Nakasone Genwa shi ni tou (jō) (Questions to Mr. Nakasone Genwa (1)),' *Uruma shinpō* (Uruma newspaper), 25 August.
Jiyū Okinawa (Free Okinawa) (1946a), 'Ifa kaichō to ichimon ittō (Questions and answers with Chairman Ifa),' No. 9.
Jugaku Bunshō (1940 [1970]), 'Hyōjun go to hōgen (Standard language and dialect),' *Gekkan mingei* (Monthly mingei), March issue, in in Naha Shiyakusho (Ed.), *Naha shishi: shiryō hen* (History of Naha city: reference materials edition), Vol. 2, 2–3: Naha Shiyakusho.
Kaigo Tokiomi & Naka Arata (Eds) (1979), *Nihon kyōkasho taikei* (Compendium of Japanese school textbooks), Vol. 17, *Chiri* (Geography) (III): Kōdansha, pp. 489, 579.
Kaiho Yōko (1992), *Hoppō kindai shi* (Modern history of the northern regions): San'ichi Shobō.
Kaminuma Hachirō (1966), *Okinawa kyōiku ron* (Essays on education in Okinawa): Nanpō Dōhō Engokai.
Kaminuma Hachirō (1976), 'Okinawa no "hōgen ronsō" ni tsuite (On the Okinawa "dialect debate"), *Chihō shi kenkysu* (Local history studies), No. 141.
Kaneshi Saichi (1951), 'Futatabi Nihon fukki teishō (7) (Another proposal for reversion to Japan (7)),' *Uruma shinpō* (Uruma newspaper), 29 May.
Kaneshi Saichi (1951), 'Nihon fukki no teishō ni tsuite (On the proposal to return to Japan),' *Seron shūhō* (Public opinion weekly), June.
Kaneshiro Shizuka (1940 [1970]), 'Hyōjungo no tachiba (The position of the standard language),' *Okinawa nippō* (Okinawa daily), 21 January, in Naha Shiyakusho (Ed.), *Naha shishi: shiryō hen* (History of Naha city: reference materials edition), Vol. 2, 2–3: Naha Shiyakusho.
Kano Masanao (1987), *Sengo Okinawa no shisō shi zō* (Images of the history of thought on postwar Okinawa): Asahi Shinbunsha.
Kano Masanao (1993), *Okinawa no fuchi* (Borders of Okinawa): Iwanami Shoten.
Kano Masanao (1996), 'Ōta Chōfu no bunmei kan (Ota Chofu's view of civilization),' *Ōta Chōfu senshū* (Selected works of Ōta Chōfu), *gekan geppō* (Vol. 3, monthly bulletin).
Kano Masanao (2008), *Kano Masanao shisō shi ronshū* (Collected essays on the history of Kano Masanao's thought), Vol. 3: Iwanami Shoten.
Katō Shūichi (1959), 'Minzoku shugi to kokka shugi (Nationalism and statism),' *Chūō kōron* (Central review), April.
Kawakami Toyozō (1896 [1978]), 'Honken jidō ni Nihon kokumin taru no seishin o hakki seshimu beshi (Teaching children of this prefecture to be members of the Japanese nation),' *Ryūkyū kyōiku* (Ryukyu education), No. 8, in Naha-shi Kikakubu Shishi Henshūshitsu (Ed.), *Naha shi shi: shiryō hen 3-kan 3* (History of Naha city: reference materials edition) Vol. 3-3: Naha-shi Kikakubu Shishi Henshūshitsu.
Kawamoto Takashi, Takahashi Tetsuya and Komori Yōichi (1998), 'Nashonaru hisutorī o koete (Beyond the national history),' *UP*, No. 307.

Kawamura Kaoru (1971), 'Subarashii geinō no yūbe (A wonderful evening of performing arts),' *Jinmin* (People), No. 508, 27 November.
Kawamura Nozomu (1996), *G. H. Mīdo to Iha Fuyū* (G. H. Mead and Iha Fuyū): Shinjusha.
Kawarada Moriharu (1875), 'Okinawa bibōroku (Records of Okinawa),' cited in Ryūkyū Seifu (Ed.) (1965-1977), *Okinawa ken shi*, Vol. 14: Ryūkyū Seifu.
Kikuchi Ken'ichi (1952), 'Minzoku mondai toshite no Amerika kokujin mondai (America's black issue as a nationality issue),' *Rekishi hyōron* (History review), No. 40.
Kikuchi Yoshitsugi (1968), 'Shiranasugita Okinawa no koto (Things we didn't know about Okinawa),' *Kyōiku hyōron* (Education review), No. 219.
Kim Tal-su (Ed.) (1977), *Nihon to Chōsen* (Japan and Korea): Kōdansha.
Kim Ilhwa ([1986] 1991), 'Zainichi Chōsenjin no hōteki chii (Legal status of Koreans in Japan),' in Yamada Terumi and Pak Chong-myong (Eds), *Zainichi Chōsenjin* (Koreans in Japan): Akashi Shoten.
Kinjō Chōei (1953), 'Ryūkyū no rekishi to bunka (History and culture of Ryukyu), *Rekishi hyōron* (History review), No. 48.
Kinjō Seitoku (1978), *Ryūkyū shobun ron* (Ryukyu disposition): Okinawa Taimususha.
Kinjō Seitoku and Takara Kurayoshi (1972), *Iha Fuyū*: Shimizu Shoin.
Kinoshita Junji, Hidaka Rokurō and Taminato Tomoaki (1968), *Shinpojiumu Okinawa* (Symposium Okinawa): Sanseidō.
Kobayashi Takao (1994), 'Taiwan jiken to Ryūkyū shobun (The Taiwan/ Mudan incident and Ryukyu disposition),' *Seiji keizai shigaku* (Journal of political and economic history), Nos. 340, 341.
Kokuba Kōtarō (1962), 'Okinawa no Nihon fukki undō to kakushin seitō (The Okinawa reversion movement and progressive political parties),' *Shisō* (Thought), February.
Kokuba Kōtarō (1963), 'Nihon dokusen shihon no kyōryoku no konkyo (Reasons for the cooperation of Japanese monopoly capital),' *Nihon dokusho shinbun* (Nihon dokusho newspaper), 16 September.
Kokuritsu Kōbunkan (1985), *Sūmitsuin kaigiroku* (Records of Privy Council meetings): Tokyo Daigaku Shuppankai.
Kokuritsu Kokkai Toshokan Kensei Shiryōshitsu (n.d.), 'Ryūkyū no kokugo shūkyō shuzoku kanshū (Language, religion, ethnicity and customs in Ryukyu),' in *Itō Hirobumi kankei bunsho* (Documents relating to Ito Hirobumi); *Itō-ke bunsho* (Documents of the Ito family), No. 356.
Kokusai Hōgaku Kai (Ed.) (1955), *Okinawa no chii* (The status of Okinawa): Nanpō Renraku Jimusho.
Kondō Ken'ichirō (1993a), 'Gakkō ga "yamato ya" to yobareta koro (A study on the schools in Okinawa immediately after the close of the Ryukyu Court),' *Hokkaidō Daigaku Kyōikubu kiyō* (Bulletin of the Faculty of Education, Hokkaido University), No. 61.
Kondō Ken'ichirō (1993b), 'Ryūkyū shobun chokugo no Okinawa kyōiku (Education in Okinawa immediately after the Ryukyu disposition)' in Kyōiku Shigaku Kai, *Nihon no kyōikushi gaku* (Studies in the history of education in Japan), Vol. 36.
Kondō Ken'ichirō (1994a), 'Nisshin sensō go no Okinawa ni okeru "fūzoku kairyō" undō no jittai (Movement to "improve social customs" in Okinawa

after the Sino-Japanese War),' *Nantō shigaku* (Studies of the history of the southern islands), No. 44.

Kondō Ken'ichirō (1994b), 'Okinawa ni okeru chōheirei shikō to kyōiku (The enforcement of conscription and education in Okinawa),' *Hokkaidō Daigaku Kyōikubu kiyō* (Bulletin of the Faculty of Education, Hokkaido University), No. 64.

Kondō Ken'ichirō (1995a), 'Kokutei kyōkasho no Okinawa zō (The image of Okinawa in government-approved schoolbooks),' *Hokkaidō Daigaku Kyōikubu kiyō* (Bulletin of the Faculty of Education, Hokkaido University), No. 68.

Kondō Ken'ichirō (1995b), 'Okinawa ni okeru imin/dekasegisha kyōiku (Education of migrants/migrant workers in Okinawa),' *Kyōikugaku kenkyū* (Japanese journal of educational research), Vol. 62, No. 2.

Kondō Ken'ichirō (1996), 'Nisshin sensō chokuzen no Okinawa kyōiku seisaku (Education policy in Okinawa immediately before the Sino-Japanese War),' *Nantō shigaku* (Studies of the history of southern islands), No. 48.

Kondō Ken'ichirō (1997), 'Kokka sōdōin taisei ka no Okinawa ni okeru hyōjun go reikō undō (The standard Japanese enforcement campaign in Okinawa under the national mobilization system),' *Nantō shigaku* (Studies of the history of southern islands), No. 49.

Kōno Yasuko (1994), *Okinawa henkan o meguru seiji to gaikō* (Politics and diplomacy surrounding the reversion of Okinawa): Tokyo Daigaku Shuppankai.

Koschmann, J. Victor (1994), 'Minshushugi kakumei to kokka (Democratic revolution and the state),' trans. Kasai Hirotaka, *Gendai shisō* (Contemporary thought), January.

Kudō Masaki (1979), *Kenkyū shi Nihon jinshu ron* (History of research: Theories of the Japanese race): Yoshikawa Kōbunkan.

Kuwata Saburō (1959), *Okinawa jūmin no kokusaihōteki chii* (The legal status of Okinawa residents under the international law): Nanpō Dōhō Engokai.

Kyan Shin'ei (1954), 'Okinawa no ryōshin (Okinawa's conscience),' *Okinawa taimusu* (Okinawa times), 5 April.

Kyan Shin'ei (1956), 'Dai 2-kai Kyōken taikai o kaerimite (Review of the 2nd Kyōken conference on education),' *Okinawa kyōiku* (Okinawa education), No. 4.

Kyō Shō-chū (Kang Sang-jung) (1996), *Orientarizumu no kanata e* (Beyond orientalism): Iwanami Shoten.

Mahira Fusaaki (1994), 'Jinrui kan jiken (Anthropological pavilion incident),' *Kokusai kōryū* (Journal of international exchange), No. 63.

Maruyama Masao (1964), 'Nihon no nashonarizumu (Nationalism in Japan),' *Gendai seiji no shisō to kōdō* (Modern political thought and action): Miraisha.

Mashiko Yoshihisa (1989), 'Maboroshi no Ainu dokuritsu ron o ou (Chasing the phantom argument for Ainu independence),' *Asahi jānaru* (Asahi journal), 3 March.

Matsuda Kyōko (1996), 'Pabirion gakujutsu jinrui kan (Anthropological pavilion),' *Nihongaku hō* (Journal of Japanese studies), No. 15.

Matsumoto Kunihiko (1988), 'Zainichi Chōsenjin no Nihon kokuseki

hakudatsu (The Japanese nationality divestment of Koreans in Japan),' *Hōgaku* (Tohoku University law review), Vol. 52, No. 4.
Matsuo Takayoshi (1983), 'Okinawa no inshō (Impressions of Okinawa),' *Motokura*, Misuzu Shobō.
Minka Kyoto Shibu Rekishi Bukai (1951), 'Minzoku mondai no rikai ni tsuite (On the understanding of the national question),' *Rekishi hyōron* (History review), No. 31.
Minshushugi Kagakusha Kyōkai (1952), 'Minzoku kaihō no tatakai ni taoretafu Hiroshi-kun e no tsuitō no kotoba (A eulogy to Mr. Kondō Hiroshi who was felled in a struggle for national liberation),' *Rekishi hyōron* (History review), No. 37.
Mishima Yukio (1976), 'Geki (Manifesto), in *Mishima Yukio zenshū* (Collected works of Yukio Mishima), Vol. 33: Shinchōsha.
Miyagi Etsujirō (1982), *Senryōsha no me* (In the eyes of the occupiers): Naha Shuppansha.
Miyata Setsuko (1985), *Chōsen minshū to "kōminka" seisaku* (Koreans and "kōminka" policies): Miraisha.
Miyata Setsuko, Kim Yongtal and Yang Teho (1992), *Sōshi kaimei* (The name change): Akashi Shoten.
Miyazato Seigen (Ed.) (1975), *Sengo Okinawa no seiji to hō 1945– 1972* (Politics and law in postwar Okinawa: 1945– 1972): Tokyo Daigaku Shuppankai.
Mizuno Naoki (1996), 'Zainichi Chōsenjin Taiwanjin sanseiken "teishi" jōkō no seiritsu (The origin of the clause suspending the electoral rights of Koreans and Formosans in Japan),' *Kenkyū kiyō* (Annals of the Center for the Study of World Human Rights Issues), No. 1.
Mizuo Hiroshi (1992), *Hyōden Yanagi Muneyoshi* (Critical biography of Yanagi Sōetsu): Chikuma Shobō.
Mori Hideto (1963a), 'Hikisakareta rekishi (Ripped-apart history),' *Nihon dokusho shinbun* (Japan reading newspaper), 11 February.
Mori Hideto (1963b), Kansho bassai ki no shisō (Thoughts in the sugar cane harvesting season): Gendai Shisōsha.
Mori Hideto (1963c), 'Okinawa kaihō sensen no kokuseki (The nationality of the Okinawa liberation front),' *Nihon dokusho shinbun* (Nihon dokusho newspaper), 15 April.
Mori Hideto (1963d), 'Sokoku fukki ron to Nihon dokusen shihon (Argument for Okinawa reversion and Japanese monopoly capital),' *Nihon dokusho shinbun* (Nihon dokusho newspaper), 10 June.
Morita Toshio (1970), *Anpo kyōiku taisei to Okinawa mondai* (The education system under the Japan-U.S. security treaty and the Okinawa issue): Meiji Tosho Shinsho.
Murai Osamu (1993–94), 'Kigen to seifuku (Origin and conquest),' *Hihyō kūkan* (Critical space), Nos. 11, 12 & Vol. 2, No. 1.
Nagaoka Tomotarō (1946a), 'Okinawa no kizoku mondai (The Okinawa sovereignty issue),' *Jiyū Okinawa* (Free Okinawa), No. 2, January.
Nagaoka Tomotarō (1946b), 'Okinawa no seijiteki dōkō (Political trends in Okinawa),' *Jiyū Okinawa* (Free Okinawa), No. 10.
Nagaoka Tomotarō (1946c), 'Okinawajin renmei no seikaku ni tsuite (On the nature of the Okinawans' Association),' *Jiyū Okinawa* (Free Okinawa), June.

Nagaoka Tomotarō (1947), *Okinawa minzoku dokuhon*: *Okinawa minzokusei no keisei katei* (Reader [on the] Okinawan nation: the formation process of Okinawan national haracteristics): Jiyū Okinawasha.

Nagaoka Tomotarō (1951), 'Okinawa no kizoku mondai ni tsuite (On the Okinawa sovereignty issue),' *Okinawa no tomo* (Friends of Okinawa), No. 11.

Naha Shiyakusho (1970), *Naha shishi: shiryō hen* (History of Naha city: reference materials edition), Vol. 2, 2–3: Naha Shiyakusho.

Naha-shi Kikakubu Shishi Henshūshitsu (Ed.) (1978), *Naha shishi: shiryō hen 3-kan 3* (History of Naha city: reference materials edition) Vol. 3-3: Naha-shi Kikakubu Shishi Henshūshitsu.

Nakahara (Nakabaru) Zenchū (1947), 'Okinawa-jin to wa (What is an Okinawan?),' *Jiyū Okinawa* (Free Okinawa), No. 13.

Nakami Mari (2003), *Yanagi Muneyoshi: jidai to shisō* (Yanagi Sōetsu: [his] times and thought), Tōkyō Daigaku Shuppankai.

Nakano Shigeharu (1970), '"Hondo no Okinawa ka" to iu kotoba no koto (About the expression "Okinawaization of mainland Japan"),' *Bungei* (Literature), February.

Nakano Yoshio (Ed.) (1969), *Sengo shiryō Okinawa* (Postwar documents on Okinawa): Nihon Hyōronsha.

Nakasone Genwa ([1955] 1973), *Ryūkyū kara Okinawa e* (From Ryukyu to Okinawa): Gekkan Okinawasha.

Nakasone Isamu (1969), 'Okinawa no nazo (The riddle of Okinawa),' *Shin Okinawa bungaku* (New Okinawa literature), summer.

Nakasone Isamu (1982), 'Okinawa minshu dōmei (Okinawa democratic alliance),' *Shin Okinawa bungaku* (New Okinawa literature), No. 53.

Nakata Chūichirō (1948), 'Kangei no ji (Welcoming address),' *Kōsei Okinawa* (Rehabilitating Okinawa), No. 4.

Nakayoshi Ryōkō (1947a), '"Okinawa-ken" fukkatsu ga mokuhyō (The goal is the "reinstatement" of Okinawa prefecture),'' in 'Nakayoshi Ryōkō fukki kankei shiryō (Reversion-related documents of Nakayoshi Ryōkō),' Vol. 1, unpublished documents, Ryūkyū Daigaku.

Nakayoshi Ryōkō (1947b), 'Okinawa no Nihon fukki nō chinjōsho (Petition for Okinawa's return to Japan),' in unpublished documents: 'Nakayoshi Ryōkō fukki kankei shiryō (Reversion-related documents of Nakayoshi Ryōkō),' Vol. 1, Ryūkyū Daigaku.

Nakayoshi Ryōkō (1954a), 'Fukki no rinen (The ideology of reversion),' *Okinawa-ken sokoku fukki tōsō shi shiryō hen* (History of Okinawa prefecture's reversion to the motherland, documents edition): Okinawa Jiji Shuppansha.

Nakayoshi Ryōkō (1954b), 'Okinawa no Nihon fukki gojinryoku onegai (Request for your effort for Okinawa's reversion to Japan),' in unpublished documents: 'Nakayoshi Ryōkō fukki kankei shiryō (Reversion-related documents of Nakayoshi Ryōkō),' Vol. 4, Ryūkyū Daigaku.

Nakayoshi Ryōkō (n.d.), 'Nichibei anpo jōyaku kaitei ni Okinawa hōgan hō no ketsugi seigan (Petition for the inclusion of Okinawa in revision of the U.S.–Japan security treaty)' in unpublished documents: 'Nakayoshi Ryōkō fukki kankei shiryō (Reversion-related documents of Nakayoshi Ryōkō),' Vol. 8, Ryūkyū Daigaku.

Nankai Kiyoshi (1970), 'Kindai Okinawa no rekishi kara nani o manabuka

(What can we learn from the history of modern Okinawa),' *Jinmin* (People), No. 441, 15 August.

Nankai Kiyoshi (1971), 'Arakawa Akira "Gensō toshite no Nihon" no gensōsei (ge) (The illusion of Arakawa Akira's "Japan as an illusion" (2)),' *Jinmin* (People), No. 499, 25 September.

Narahara Shigeru (1902), *Kagoshima jitsugyō shinbun* (Kagoshima business newspaper), 16 April, cited in Ōta (1995).

Naramoto Tatsuya (1951), 'Minzoku zakkan (Thoughts on the nation),' *Nihon shi kenkyū* (Journal of Japanese history), No. 14.

Naramoto Tatsuya (1952), 'Taikai aisatsu tōron o hajimeru ni saishite (Conference opening address before the start of discussion),' *Nihon shi kenkyū* (Journal of Japanese history), No. 20.

Nezu Masashi (1953), 'Sakamoto Toshio "Minzoku no sakebi" ni tsuite (On "A cry of a nation" by Sakamoto Toshio),' *Rekishi ryōron* (History review), No. 43.

NHK Shuzai Han (1996), *Okinawa henkan/rettō kaizō* (Okinawa reversion/ the rebuilding of the Japanese archipelago), *Sengo 50 nen sonotoki Nihon wa* (Japan's postwar 50 years), Vol. 4: Nihon Hōsō Shuppan Kyōkai.

Nihon Ajia Afurika Rentai Iinkai, Hondo to Okinawa no Kodomono Sakubun Kōryū Jikkō Iinkai (Ed.) (1971), *Okinawa no ko hondo no ko* (Okinawan children, mainland children): Yuri Shuppan.

Nihon Kokusai Seiji Gakkai (Ed.) (1975), 'Okinawa henkan kōshō no seiji katei (Political process of the Okinawa reversion negotiation),' *Kokusai seiji* (International relations), No. 52.

Nihon Kyōsantō Chūō Iinkai Shuppanbu (Ed.) (1966), *Okinawa Ogasawara mondai to Nihon Kyōsantō* (The Okinawa and Ogasawara issue and the Japanese Communist Party): Nihon Kyōsantō Chūō Iinkai Shuppanbu.

Nihon Kyōshokuin Kumiai and Okinawa Kyōshokuinkai (Eds) (1966), *Okinawa no kora* (Children of Okinawa): Gōdō Shuppan Kabushiki Gaisha.

Nihon Kyōshokuin Kumiai and Okinawa Kyōshokuinkai (Eds) (1970), *Okinawa no sensei tachi* (School teachers of Okinawa): Gōdō Shuppan Kabushiki Gaisha.

Nihon Mingei Kyōkai (1940 [1970]), 'Okinawa gengo mondai ni taisuru ikensho (Proposal regarding the Okinawa language debate),' *Gekkan mingei* (Monthly mingei), November/December issue, in Naha Shiyakusho (Ed.), *Naha shishi: shiryō hen* (History of Naha city: reference materials edition), Vol. 2, 2–3: Naha Shiyakusho.

Nihon Rekishi Gakkai (1946), 'Atarashii Nihon shigaku no tachiba (The perspective of new Japanese historiography),' *Nihon rekishi* (Japanese history), No. 1.

Nihon shi kenkyū (Journal of Japanese history) (1951b), 'Minzoku bunka o umu mono (The source of a national culture),' No. 14.

Niizaki Moriteru (1969), *Dokyumento Okinawa tōsō* (Documentary records of Okinawa's struggles): Aki Shobō.

Niizaki Moriteru (1982), 'Okinawajin renmei (The Okinawans association),' *Shin Okinawa bungaku* (New Okinawa literature), No. 53.

Nishihara Jun (1975), 'Koseki hōsei no hensen to mondai ten (Change in the family registration law and its problems),' in Miyazato Seigen (Ed.), *Sengo Okinawa no seiji to hō 1945–1972* (Politics and law in postwar Okinawa: 1945–1972): Tokyo Daigaku Shuppankai.

Nishihira Hideki and Ginoza Shigō (1982), *Kyōkasho to Okinawa kyōiku* (School textbooks and education in Okinawa): Okinawa Jiji Shuppan.
Nishikawa Nagao (1995), 'Nihon gata kokumin kokka no keisei (The formation of a Japanese-style nation-state),' in Nishikawa Nagao and Matsumiya Hideharu (Eds), Bakumatsu Meiji-ki no kokumin kokka keisei to bunka henyō (The formation of a nation-state and cultural transformation from the late Edo to Meiji period): Shin'yōsha.
Nishime Junji (1951), 'Dokuritsu ron o bakusu (Refuting the pro-independence argument),' *Seron shūhō* (Public opinion weekly), June.
Nishizato Kikō (1981), *Ronshū Okinawa kindai shi* (Collected essays on modern history of Okinawa): Okinawa Jiji Shuppan.
Nitta Yoshitaka (1895), 'Okinawa wa Okinawa nari Ryūkyū ni arazu (Okinawa is Okinawa, not Ryukyu),' *Ryūkyū kyōiku* (Ryukyu education), No. 2, reprinted edition, Vol. 1.
Nitta Yoshitaka (1896), *Ryūkyū kyōiku* (Ryukyu education), No. 10, reprinted edition, Vol. 1.
Nitta Yoshitaka (1897a), *Ryūkyū kyōiku* (Ryukyu education), No. 14, reprinted edition, Vol. 2.
Nitta Yoshitaka (1897b), *Ryūkyū kyōiku* (Ryukyu education), No. 14, reprinted edition, Vol. 2.
Ōe Kenzaburō (1970), *Okinawa nōto* (Okinawa notes): Iwanami Shinsho.
Ōgimi Umeko (1940 [1970]), 'Oerai katagata e (To the bigwigs),' *Okinawa nippō* (Okinawa daily), 13 January, in Naha Shiyakusho (Ed.), *Naha shishi: shiryō hen* (History of Naha city: reference materials edition), Vol. 2, 2–3: Naha Shiyakusho.
Oguma Eiji (1994), 'Shimin to busō (Citizen and armament),' *Sōkan shakaigaku* (Journal of interdisciplinary social sciences), No. 4.
Oguma Eiji (1995a), *Tan'itsu minzoku shinwa no kigen* (The origin of the myth of a single people): Shin'yōsha.
Oguma Eiji (1995b), 'Wasurerareta minzoku mondai: sengo Nihon no "kakushin nashonarizumu" (The forgotten nationality issue: the "progressive nationalism" of postwar Japan),' *Sōkan shakai kagaku* (Journal of interdisciplinary social sciences), No. 5.
Oguma Eiji (1998), 'Nihonjin' no kyōkai (The boundaries of the Japanese): Shin'yōsha.
Oguma Eiji (2002a), *A Genealogy of 'Japanese' Self-Images*, trans. David Askew: Trans Pacific Press, Melbourne.
Oguma Eiji (2002b), *'Minshu' to 'aikoku'* ('Democracy' and 'patriotism'), Shin'yōsha.
Oguma Eiji (2005), 'The Green of the Willow, the Flower's Scarlet: Debate on Japanese Emigrants and Korea under the Japanese Empire,' trans. Joseph Murphy, in Naoki Sakai, Brett de Bary, and Iyotani Toshio (eds), Deconstructing Nationality: East Asia Program Cornell University, New York.
Oguma Eiji and Ueno Yōko (2003), *'Iyashi' no nashonarizumu: kusa no ne hoshu undō no jisshō kenkyū* (The nationalism of 'healing': an empirical study of the grassroots conservative movement): Keiō Daigaku Shuppankai.
Ōhama Michiko (1967), 'Kyōin toshite no tachiba kara (From a viewpoint of a school teacher),' *Sekai* (The world), August.
Okabe Kazuaki (1991), *Nikkei Amerikajin kyōsei shūyō kara sengo hoshō e*

(Japanese-Americans: From compulsory internment to postwar compensation): Iwanami Bukkuretto.
Okinawa fukki kaihō (Okinawa reversion bulletin) (1954), 'Okinawa ga fukki shitara keizaimen wa dō naru? (What will happen to the economy after Okinawa's return?), inaugural issue.
Okinawa Gentarō (1901), 'Okinawa kyōiku shokan (Thoughts on education in Okinawa),' *Ryūkyū kyōiku* (Ryukyu education), No. 65.
Okinawa Henkan Kokumin Undō Tokyo Jikkō Iinkai (Ed.) (1965), *Minzoku no sakebi* (A cry of a nation): Tokyo-to Ajia Afurika Rentai Iinkai.
Okinawa ken shi (1965), 'Okinawa ken ni shūgiin senkyohō shikō no ken (Re implementation of Lower House Members' Electoral Law in Okinawa prefecture).'
Okinawa-ken Gakumu Bu (1940), 'Aete kenmin ni uttau mingei undō ni mayou na (An appeal to the residents of Okinawa prefecture not to be confused by the mingei movement),' *Ryūkyū shinpō*, *Okinawa mainichi* and *Okinawa nippō*, 8 January.
Okinawa-ken yō jinjō shōgakkō dokuhon (Elementary school readings for Okinawa prefecture) (1897–1899 [1982]): Bunka Hyōron Sha.
Okinawa Kenritsu Toshokan Shiryō Henshūshitsu (Ed.) (1996a), *Okinawa ken shi shiryō hen 1,* (History of Okinawa prefecture, resources edition 1, original materials): Okinawa-ken Kyōiku Iinkai.
Okinawa Kenritsu Toshokan Shiryō Henshūshitsu (Ed.) (1996b), *Okinawa ken shi shiryō hen 2, Wayaku hen* (History of Okinawa prefecture, resources edition 2, Japanese translations): Okinawa-ken Kyōiku Iinkai.
Okinawa kyōiku (1955), 'Kyōshi no mondai (The question of teachers),' No. 2: Okinawa Kyōshokuinkai.
Okinawa kyōiku (1957), 'Dai 3-ji Kyōken Chūō Shūkai Kenkyū Shūroku (Collected records of 3rd Kyōken central rally research),' Vol. 1, No. 5.
Okinawa kyōiku (1958a), 'Dai 4-kai Kyōiku Kenkyū Taikai Kenkyū Shūroku (Collected records of 4th Kyōken rally research),' Vol. 3, No. 7.
Okinawa kyōiku (1958b), 'Dai 4-kai Kyōiku Kenkyū Taikai Kenkyū Shūroku (Collected records of 4th Kyōken rally research): Kokugo (National language),' No. 6.
Okinawa kyōiku (1962), '61-nendo chiiki kondankai shuyō mondai kaisetsu (Explanatory notes on the main issues in regional discussion meetings for 1961),' No. 13.
Okinawa kyōiku (1966), 'Dai 12-ji Kyōken Shūkai Shūroku (Collected records of 12th Kyōken rally research): Kokumin kyōiku (national education)': Okinawa Kyōshokuinkai.
Okinawa kyōiku (1967), 'Dai 13-ji Kyōken Shūkai Kenkyū Shūroku (Collected records of 12th Kyōken rally research): Kokumin kyōiku (national education)': Okinawa Kyōshokuinkai.
Okinawa Kyōshokuinkai (1963), *Okinawa no kyōiku: Dai 9-ji kyōken chūō shūkai kokumin bunka no teian to tōgi shū* (Proposals and discussions at the national division of 9th kyōken central conference): Okinawa Kyōshokuinkai.
Okinawa Kyōshokuinkai (1965), *Okinawa kyōiku: Dai 11-ji kokumin kyōiku bunka* (11th national education division): Okinawa Kyōshokuinkai.
Okinawa Kyōshokuinkai Kyōiku Bunka Bu (Ed.) (1970), *Okinawa kyōiku: Dai 16-ji kyōken shūkai hōkokusho (kokumin kyōiku)* (Okinawa education: 16th kyōken conference report (national education)).

Okinawa Kyōshokuinkai Kyōiku Bunka Bu (Ed.) (1971), *Okinawa kyōiku – Dai 17-ji kyōken shūkai hōkokusho* (Okinawa education: 17th kyōken conference report).
Okinawa mainichi shinbun (1911 [1995]), 'Mitabi ōhaku o agu (Raising the large cup three times),' 29 June, in Ōta Masahide, *Okinawa no minshū ishiki* (Okinawa's popular consciousness), new edition, Shinsensha.
Okinawa nippō (Okinawa daily) (1940a [1970]), 'Hyōjun go mondō no Matsuo-shi kataru/ken shusshinsha kihei no omoide (Mr. Matsuo of the standard language debate talks about his memory of Okinawan cavalry soldiers),' 25 January, in Naha Shiyakusho (Ed.), *Naha shishi: shiryō hen* (History of Naha city: reference materials edition), Vol. 2, 2–3: Naha Shiyakusho.
Okinawa nippō (1940b [1970]), 'Kankō zadankai ronsen nigiwau (Heated debates at the tourism symposium),' 8 January, in Naha Shiyakusho (Ed.), *Naha shishi: shiryō hen* (History of Naha city: reference materials edition), Vol. 2, 2–3: Naha Shiyakusho.
Okinawa nippō (1940c [1970]), 'Kenmin yo Taiwan ni makeru na! (Okinawans, don't be beaten by Taiwan!),' 22 January, in Naha Shiyakusho (Ed.), *Naha shishi: shiryō hen* (History of Naha city: reference materials edition), Vol. 2, 2–3: Naha Shiyakusho.
Okinawa no tomo (Friends of Okinawa) (1951a), 'Nakayoshi Ryōkō no tegami (Nakayoshi Ryōkō's letters),' No. 10.
Okinawa no tomo (1951b), 'Suntetsu (Epigrams),' No. 10.
Okinawa no tomo (1951c), 'Wareware wa shuchō suru (We assert),' No. 11.
Okinawa taimusu (Okinawa times) (1966), 'Tarinai kokki no ninshiki (Inadequate recognition of the national flag),' 24 January.
Okinawa Taimususha (1978), *Shin Okinawa bungaku* (New Okinawa literature), No. 38.
Okinawa-ken Gikai Jimukyoku (Ed.) (1995), *Okinawa-ken gikai shi* (History of Okinawan prefectural assembly), Vol. 13: Okinawa-ken Gikai.
Okinawa-ken Sokoku Fukki Tōsō Shi Hensan Iinkai (Ed.) (1982), *Okinawa-ken sokoku fukki tōsō shi shiryō hen* (History of Okinawa prefecture's reversion to the motherland, documents edition): Okinawa Jiji Shuppansha.
Ōkubo Yasuo (1977), *Boasonādo* (Boissonard): Iwanami Shinsho.
Ōmichi Susumu (1971), 'Haiboku no shisō "han-fukki ron" ("Anti-reversionism": a defeatist idea),' *Jinmin* (People), Nos. 464, 465, 23 & 30 January.
Ōno Masao (1959), 'Odorokubeki senji keihō e no gyakkō (A surprising retrogression to the wartime criminal law),' *Sekai* (The world), September.
Ōnuma Yasuaki (1993), *Shinban tan'itsu minzoku shakai no shinwa o koete* (Moving beyond the myth of the homogeneous society, new edition): Tōshindō.
Osaka asahi shinbun (Osaka asahi newspaper) (1910), 'Tensei jingo (Vox populi, vox Dei),' 6 September.
Ōshiro Hikogorō (1896 [1978]), 'Honken shōgakkō ni oite chiri-ka o sazukuru ni tsukite omoiatarishi kotodomo (Some thoughts on teaching geography at elementary schools in this prefecture),' *Ryūkyū kyōiku* (Ryukyu education), No. 4, in Naha-shi Kikakubu Shishi Henshūshitsu (Ed.), *Naha shi shi: shiryō hen 3-kan 3* (History of Naha city: reference materials edition) Vol. 3-3: Naha-shi Kikakubu Shishi Henshūshitsu.
Ōshiro Hikogorō (1900 [1978]), 'Okinawa kyōiku ni kansuru shoken

(Comments on education in Okinawa),' *Ryūkyū kyōiku* (Ryukyu education), No. 53.
Ōshiro Tatsuhiro (1970), 'Bunka shi no atarashii jidai (A new age in cultural history)': *Okinawa taimusu* (Okinawa times), 28 May, subsequently reprinted in Ōshiro (1977), *Okinawa, aru hareta hi ni* (Okinawa, one sunny day): Ienohikari Kyōkai.
Ōshiro Tatsuhiro (1972), *Uchinaru Okinawa* (Inner Okinawa): Yomiuri Shinbunsha.
Ōta Masahide (1984 [1996]), 'Okinawa bunri no haikei ni tsuite no ichi kōsatsu (A study of the background of Okinawa secession),' *Okinawa no teiō kōtō benmukan* (The kings of Okinawa: The high commissioners): Asahi Bunko.
Ōta Masahide (1969), *Minikui Nihonjin* (The ugly Japanese): Saimaru Shuppankai.
Ōta Masahide (1976), 'Iha Fuyū no shisō to sono jidai (The thought and times of Ifa Fuyū),' in Hokama Shuzen (Ed.), *Iha Fuyū hito to shisō* (The person and thought of Ifa Fuyū): Heibonsha.
Ōta Masahide (1995), *Okinawa no minshū ishiki* (Okinawa's popular consciousness), new edition, Shinsensha.
Ōta Masahide, Uema Seiyu, Nagamine Ichirō, Higa Mikio, Kyan Shin'ei, Sunagawa Keishin and Hokama Yoneko (1968), 'Tettei tōron Okinawa no shisei ken henkan to kichi mondai (Thorough debate: Return of Okinawa's administrative power and the military base issue),' *Sekai* (The world), October.
Ōta Shizuo (1982), 'Fuhatsu no dokuritsu ron (Misfired arguments for independence),' *Shin Okinawa bungaku* (New Okinawa literature), No. 53.
Ōta Tetsuo (1987), *Taishō demokurashī no shisō suimyaku* (An approach to the thoughts of the Taishō democracy): Dōjidaisha.
Ōta Yūzō (1994), *Rafukadio Hān* (Lafcadio Hearn): Iwanami Shinsho.
Ōtani Takeo (1953), 'Rekishi bungaku shokan (Thoughts on historical literature),' *Rekishi hyōron* (History review), No. 41.
Oyafuso Keiko (1986), 'Yanagi Muneyoshi no Chōsen-kan to Okinawa-kan (Yanagi Sōetsu's views of Korea and Okinawa), *Kokusai kankeigaku kenkyū* (Journal of international relations), No. 12.
Ōzato Kōei (1969), *Okinawa no jiyū minken undo: senkusha Jahana Noboru no shisō to kōdō* (Okinawa's freedom and popular rights movement: the thought and action of pioneer Jahana Noboru): Taihei Shuppansha.
Ōzato Tomoko (1996), '"Jahana minken" ron ni tsuite no ichi kōsatsu (One study about the discourse on "Jahana popular rights"), *Okinawa bunka kenkyū* (Okinawan culture studies), No. 2.
Parent, Joseph M., and Paul K. Macdonald (2011), 'The Wisdom of Retrenchment,' *Foreign Affairs*, No. 12.
Peattie, Mark R. (1996), *Shokuminchi* (The Japanese colonial empire), translated by Asano Toyomi: Yomiuri Shinbunsha.
Rekishi Kagaku Kyōgikai (Ed.) (1976), Rekishi kagaku taikei (Anthology of historical sciences), Vol. 15, *Minzoku no mondai* (Nationality issue): Azekura Shobō.
Renan, Ernest, Johann Gottlieb Fichte, Joel Roman and Etienne Balibar (1997), *Kokumin to wa nani ka* (What is a nation?), Trans. and Ed. by Ukai Satoshi, Ōnishi Masaichirō, Hosomi Kazuyuki and Ueno Naritoshi: Insukuriputo.

Robinson, Ronald (1972), 'Non-European foundations of European imperialism: Sketch for a theory of collaboration,' in Roger Owen and Bob Sutcliffe (Eds), *Studies in the Theory of Imperialism*, London: Longman.
Rothschild, Joseph (1981), *Ethnopolitics*, New York: Columbia University Press; (Japanese edition), Uchiyama Hideo (Tr.) (1989), *Esunoporitikusu*: Sanseidō.
Ryūkyū kyōiku (Ryukyu education) (1896 [1980]), No. 3, in reprinted edition, Vol. 1: Honpō Shoseki.
Ryūkyū kyōiku (Ryukyū education) (1899a), 'Honken shihan gakkō joshi kōshū ka no fukusei (Dress code for female students at teacher's training school in this prefecture),' No. 44.
Ryūkyū kyōiku (1899b), 'Okinawa ken shiritsu kyōiku kai jōshū kai (Ordinary meeting of the Okinawa prefecture private education association),' No. 44.
Ryūkyū kyōiku (1899c), 'Shuri jinjō kōtō shōgakkō jokyōshi Kuba Tsuruko joshi (Shuri upper elementary school teacher Miss Kuba Tsuruko),' No. 44.
Ryūkyū kyōiku (1899d), 'Shuri shōgakkō joseito no futsū fuku (Standard clothing of female children at Shuri elementary schools),' No. 47.
Ryūkyū kyōiku (1901), 'Fukusō ni kansuru kokoroe (Guidelines for dress standards),' No. 64.
Ryūkyū kyōiku (1904), 'Gunshi gakkai (County school supervisors' association),' No. 95.
Ryūkyū kyōiku (1980), reprinted edition, Vol. 1: Honpō Shoseki.
Ryūkyū Seifu (Ed.) (1965a), *Okinawa ken shi*, Vol. 4: Ryūkyū Seifu.
Ryūkyū Seifu (Ed.) (1965b), *Okinawa ken shi*, Vol. 11: Ryūkyū Seifu.
Ryūkyū Seifu (Ed.) (1965c), *Okinawa ken shi*, Vol. 12: Ryūkyū Seifu.
Ryūkyū Seifu (Ed.) (1965d), *Okinawa ken shi*, Vol. 13: Ryūkyū Seifu.
Ryūkyū Seifu (Ed.) (1965e), *Okinawa ken shi*, Vol. 14: Ryūkyū Seifu.
Ryūkyū Seifu (Ed.) (1965f), *Okinawa ken shi*, Vol. 19: Ryūkyū Seifu.
Ryūkyū Seifu Bunkyō Kyoku Kenkyū Chōsa Ka (Ed.) (1956), *Ryūkyū shiryō* (Historical records of Ryukyu), Vol. 2: Ryūkyū Seifu Bunkyō Kyoku.
Ryūkyū shinpō (Ryukyu newspaper) (1898a [1965]), 'Kunigami tayori (News from Kunigami),' 7 October, in Ryūkyū Seifu (Ed.), *Okinawa ken shi*, Vol. 19: Ryūkyū Seifu.
Ryūkyū shinpō (1898b [1965]), 'Naha yūbin denshin kyoku no shukkin no honken-jin (Local people working at Naha postal and telegraph office),' 13 September, in Ryūkyū Seifu (Ed.), *Okinawa ken shi*, Vol. 19: Ryūkyū Seifu.
Ryūkyū shinpō (Ryukyu newspaper) (1900 [1965]), 'Okinawa saijiki (Okinawa chronicles) (1),' 5 January, in Ryūkyū Seifu (Ed.), *Okinawa ken shi*, Vol. 19: Ryūkyū Seifu.
Ryūkyū shinpō (1906a [1965]), 'Okinawa kenmin ni ichigon su (A word to Okinawa prefectural residents),' 12–21 July, in Ryūkyū Seifu (Ed.), *Okinawa ken shi*, Vol. 19: Ryūkyū Seifu.
Ryūkyū shinpō (1906b [1965]), 'Tahō tamen (Many directions and aspects),' 27 October.
Ryūkyū shinpō (1907), 'Okinawa-ken Miyako, Yaeyama ryōgunmin senkyo ni kansuru seigansho (Petition relating to elections [by] residents of both counties of Miyako and Yaeyama, Okinawa Prefecture),' 17 February.
Ryūkyū shinpō (1911 [1965]), 'Ware ni sanseiken o ataeyo (Grant me suffrage),' 12–21 July, in Ryūkyū Seifu (Ed.), *Okinawa ken shi*, Vol. 19: Ryūkyū Seifu.
Ryūkyū shinpō (1916a [1965]), 'Fūzoku kaizen no hitsuyō (Need for improve-

ment in manners and customs),' 23 July, in Ryūkyū Seifu (Ed.), *Okinawa ken shi*, Vol. 19: Ryūkyū Seifu.
Ryūkyū shinpō (1916b [1965]), 'Irezumi onna (Tattooed women),' 22 July, in Ryūkyū Seifu (Ed.), *Okinawa ken shi*, Vol. 19: Ryūkyū Seifu.
Ryūkyū shinpō (1940 [1970]), 'Kinkō bokuzetsu (Social leaders),' 19 January, in Naha Shiyakusho (Ed.), *Naha shishi: shiryō hen* (History of Naha city: reference materials edition), Vol. 2, 2–3: Naha Shiyakusho.
Ryūkyū shinpō (1966a), 'Sokoku wa Nihon ka (Is our ancestral land Japan?),' 13 January.
Ryūkyū shinpō (1966b), 'Nihon wa sokoku de wa nai (Japan is not our ancestral land), 24 January.
Ryūkyū shinpō (1966c), '"Nihon wa sokoku de wa nai" e hanron (A counter-argument to "Japan is not our ancestral land"),' Ryūkyū shinpō (Ryukyu newspaper), 15 February.
Ryūkyū Shinpōsha (Ed.) (1980), *Higaonna Kanjun zenshū* (Complete works of Higaonna Kanjun), Vol. 8: Daiichi Shobō.
Sai Shō (1957), *Ryūkyū mondai kaiketsu no sai ginmi* (Reexamining the solution for the Ryukyu issue): Ryūkyū Dokuritsu Kyōkai.
Said, Edward W. (1978), *Orientalism*: Georges Borchardt Inc.
Said, Edward W. (1986), *Orientarizumu* (Orientalism), trans. Itagaki Yūzō et al.: Heibonsha.
Said, Edward W. (1993), *Culture and Imperialism*, New York: Alfred A. Knopf.
Sakamoto Toshio (1952), 'Minzoku no sakebi (A cry of a nation),' *Rekishi hyōron* (History review), No. 39.
Sakamoto Yoshikazu (1960), 'Kakushin nashonarizumu shiron (An essay on progressive nationalism),' *Chūō kōron* (Central review), October.
Sakihara Mitsugu (1989), 'Ryūkyū rettō no Okinawajin: Nihon no shōsū minzoku (Okinawans in the Ryūkyūs: A racial minority in Japan),' *Buraku kaihō shi Fukuoka* (The history of buraku liberation: Fukuoka), No. 55.
Sashida Tsutomu (1970), 'Rekishiteki jijitsu to seisan shugi (Historical facts and liquidationism),' *Jinmin* (People), No. 444, 5 September.
Satake Michimori (1974), 'Meiji ki no kensei to kyōiku (Prefectural government and education in the Meiji era),' *Okinawa bunka* (Okinawa culture), No. 42.
Satake Michimori (1978), 'Okinawa kindai kyōiku no tokushitsu (Characteristics of modern education in Okinawa), *Hokkaidō Kyōiku Daigaku kiyō* (Journal of Hokkaido University of Education), *Dai ichibu C kyōiku kagaku hen* (Part 1C education science edition), Vol. 29, No. 1.
Sekai (The world) (1968), 'Zadankai watashitachi no hatsugen (Symposium: Our opinions),' October.
Seki Hironobu (1968), *Okinawa kyōshokuinkai* (Okinawa teachers' association): San'ichi Shobō.
Senaga Kamejirō (1949), 'Taisha seimeisho (Statement of resignation),' *Uruma shinpō* (Uruma newspaper), 5 August.
Senaga Kamejirō (1951), 'Nihon jinmin to ketsugō seyo (Join the Japanese nation),' *Seron shūhō* (Public opinion weekly), June.
Senaga Kamejirō, Shinzato Keiji, Tsunami Kōshin, Yogi Hiroshi, Ueda Kōichirō, Niihara Shōji, Hirayama Moto'o and Sakaki Toshio (1971), 'Shinpojiumu Okinawa mondai to ideorogī tōsō (Symposium: Okinawa issue and ideological battle),' *Zen'ei* (Vanguard), July.

Senate Committee on Military Affairs (1963), 'Shingi roku (Minutes of the meeting on 14 June 1962)' appendix to *Minami to kita* (South and north), No. 13.
Shibahara Takuji, Ikai Takaaki and Ikeda Masahiro (1988), *Nihon kindai shisō taikei* (Modern Japanese thought systems), Vol. 12, *Taigai kan* (Views of foreign affairs): Iwanami Shoten.
Shikiba Ryūzaburō (1940 [1970]), 'Ryūkyū to hyōjun go (Ryukyu and standard Japanese),' *Tokyo nichinichi shinbun* (Tokyo nichinichi newspaper), 29 March, in Naha Shiyakusho (Ed.), *Naha shishi: shiryō hen* (History of Naha city: reference materials edition), Vol. 2, 2–3: Naha Shiyakusho.
Shima Kiyoshi (1946), 'Chiji shūnin o iwau (Celebrating the appointment of the governor),' *Uruma shinpō* (Uruma newspaper), 24 April.
Shimabukuro Kuni (1982), 'Ryūkyū kokumin tō (The Ryukyu nationalist party),' *Shin Okinawa bungaku* (New Okinawa literature), No. 53.
Shimabukuro Tsutomu (1987), 'Kindai Okinawa ni okeru dōka seisaku no tenkai (The evolution of assimilation policy in modern Okinawa),' *Kenkyū nenpō* (Annual journal of the Asia-Africa culture research institute, Tōyō University), No. 22.
Shimabukuro Zenpatsu (1911), 'Kyōdojin no asu (3) (The future of my countrymen (3)),' *Okinawa mainichi shinbun* (Okinawa mainichi newspaper), 24 August.
Shimaoka Ryōtarō (1897), 'Kunigami gun kaki kōshūkai nite Shimaoka kyōyu no enzetsu hikki (Notes of Mr. Shimaoka's lecture at a summer course in Kunigami county),' *Ryūkyū kyōiku* (Ryukyu education), No. 21, reprinted edition Vol. 3.
Shimizu Ikutarō (1940 [1970]), 'Chūō bunka to chihō (Central culture and provinces),' *Tokyo asahi shinbun* (Tokyo asahi newspaper), 26 March, in Naha Shiyakusho (Ed.), *Naha shishi: shiryō hen* (History of Naha city: reference materials edition), Vol. 2, 2–3: Naha Shiyakusho.
Shimoji Hironobu (1967), 'Sokoku to wa ittai nanda (What is a homeland?),' *Sekai* (The world), August.
Shimokuni Ryōnosuke (1922), 'Shisetsu no kanpeki ni chikazuku o yorokobitsu (Delighted at the facilities nearing perfection),' *Chōsen*, No. 85.
Shimomura Fujio (Ed.) (1972), *Meiji bunka shiryō sōsho* (Series on cultural materials of the Meiji era), Vol. 4, *Gaikō hen* (Diplomacy): Kazama Shobō.
Shinohara Kazuji (1904), 'Futsūgo no fukyū ni tsuite (On dissemination of the standard language),' *Ryūkyū kyōiku* (Ryukyu education), No. 100.
Shinzato Keiji (1963), 'Bei teikoku shugi no "menzai ron" ("Justification" for American imperialism),' *Nihon dokusho shinbun* (Nihon dokusho newspaper), 29 July.
Shinzato Keiji (1963), 'Musekinin kiwamaru iigakari (Extremely irresponsible false accusations),' *Nihon dokusho shinbun* (Nihon dokusho newspaper), 6 May.
Shinzato Keiji (1963), 'Narisokonai no kōzō kaikaku ron (Flawed arguments for structural reform),' *Nihon dokusho shinbun* (Nihon dokusho newspaper), 7 October.
Shinzato Keiji (1963), 'Ryūkyū dokuritsu ronsha no "meiron" ("Fallacies" of pro-Ryukyu independence advocates),' *Nihon dokusho shinbun* (Nihon dokusho newspaper), 24 June.

Shinzato Keiji (Ed.) (1972), *Okinawa bunka ronsō 1 rekishi hen* (Essays on Okinawan culture series 1: History): Heibonsha.
Shinzato Keiji, Kikuzato Mineo and Ishikawa Akira (1957), 'Gendai Okinawa no rekishi (History of modern Okinawa), *Rekishi hyōron* (History review), No. 83.
Shiomi Toshitaka (1959), *Hō no shinkū chitai 'Okinawa'* (Okinawa in a legal vacuum): Nanpō Dōhō Engokai.
Shiomi Toshitaka and Ōno Masao (1959), 'Okinawa – "hō no shihai" no shinkū chitai (Okinawa – land without "rule of law"),' *Sekai* (The world), May.
Shiomi Toshitaka, Sunagawa Keishin, Sakugawa Seiichi, Matsumoto Tami, Uchima Takeyoshi, Asato Yoshio, Nakasone Isamu, Arakawa Akira, Kinjō Kiyoko, Hokama Yoneko, Nagamine Ichirō and Miyazato Tatsuhiko (1971), 'Shijō kenpō kōchōkai Okinawa henkan to Nihonkoku kenpō (Magazine public forum on constitution: Okinawa reversion and the Japanese constitution),' *Sekai* (The world), June.
Shiroma Tokue (1940a), 'Kotoba no shakaisei (chū) (Sociality of language (2)),' *Okinawa nippō* (Okinawa daily), 18 January.
Shiroma Tokue (1940b), 'Ryūkyū go ronsō (jō) (The Ryukyu language debate (1)),' *Okinawa Nippō* (Okinawa daily), 17 January.
Sone Eki, 'Mushiro shokuminchi teikokushugi no osore (Rather a threat of colonialist- imperialism),' *Chūō kōron*, June.
Sugiyama Heisuke (1940a [1970]), 'Bungaku to hōgen ni tsuite (On literature and dialect),' *Kaizō* (Reform), August issue, in Naha Shiyakusho (Ed.), *Naha shishi: shiryō hen* (History of Naha city: reference materials edition), Vol. 2, 2–3: Naha Shiyakusho.
Sugiyama Heisuke (1940b [1970]), 'Ryūkyū no hōgen ni tsuite (On the Ryukyu dialect),' *Shinchō* (New current), July issue, in Naha Shiyakusho (Ed.), *Naha shishi: shiryō hen* (History of Naha city: reference materials edition), Vol. 2, 2–3: Naha Shiyakusho.
Sugiyama Heisuke (1940c [1970]), 'Ryūkyū no hyōjungo (Standard Japanese in Ryukyu),' *Tokyo asahi shinbun* (Tokyo asahi newspaper), 22 May, in Naha Shiyakusho (Ed.), *Naha shishi: shiryō hen* (History of Naha city: reference materials edition), Vol. 2, 2–3: Naha Shiyakusho.
Sulzberger, Cyrus Leo II (1958), 'Foreign Affairs: An American "Cyprus" in the Pacific?' *New York Times*, 18 January, p. 14.
Suzuki Zenji (1983), *Nihon no yūseigaku* (Eugenics in Japan): Sankyō Shuppan.
Taira Hōichi (1901), 'Jitsugyō kyōiku ni tsukite (On vocational training),' *Ryūkyū kyōiku* (Ryukyu education), No. 66.
Taira Kōji (1982), 'Miyako shakai tō (Miyako socialist party),' *Shin Okinawa bungaku* (New Okinawa literature), No. 53.
Takaesu Masaya (1996), 'Tōsho gyōsei kōzō no kiso kenkyū no zentei toshite (As a precursor to basic research on the administrative structure of the islands),' *Okinawa kankei gaku kenkyū ronshū* (Collected research essays in Okinawan studies), No. 3.
Takano Yūichi (1962), *Nihon no ryōdo* (Japan's territory): Tokyo Daigaku Shuppankai.
Takara Kurayoshi, Gabe Masaaki and Hamashita Takeshi (1997), '"Okinawa runessansu" sono kanōsei (An "Okinawan renaissance": its possibility),' *Sekai* (The world), September.

Takasaki Sōji (1979), 'Yanagi Muneyoshi to Chōsen (Yanagi Sōetsu and Korea),' *Chōsen shi sō* (Essays on the history of Korea), No. 1, subsequently published as part of Takasaki Sōji (1990), *Mōgen no genkei* (The origin of thoughtless remarks): Mokuseisha.
Takashima Zenya (1970), *Minzoku to kaikyū* (Nation and class): Gendai Hyōronsha.
Takemoto Asao (n.d.), *Okinawa no arikata ni taisuru shuchō* (An opinion about the status of Okinawa): Okinawa Kirisutokyō Dōshikai.
Takenaka Hitoshi (1995), 'Yanagi Muneyoshi no mingei riron to "jissenteki ishiki" (Yanagi Sōetsu's mingei theory and "practical consciousness"),' *Soshioloji* (Sociology), Vol. 39, No. 3.
Takenaka Yutaka (1994), 'Teisei ki ni okeru Roshia nashonarizumu to dōka seisaku (Nationalism and assimilation policies in imperial Russia),' *Nenpō seijigaku* (Annuals of the Japanese political science association).
Tamaki Motoi (1967), *Minzokuteki sekinin no shisō* (The idea of national responsibility): Ochanomizu Shobō.
Tana Munenori (1940 [1970]), 'Hyōjun go mondai to kenmin no shimei (jō) (The language issue and the duty of prefectural residents (1)),' *Okinawa nippō* (Okinawa daily), 27–28 January, in .
Tanaka Hiroshi (1995), *Shinban zainichi gaikokujin* (Foreign residents in Japan, new edition): Iwanami Shinsho.
Tanaka Migaku and Sahara Makoto (1993), *Kōkogaku no sanpo michi* (A footpath of archeology): Iwanami Shinsho.
Tanaka Nobuko (1984), 'Okinawa kyōiku to Taiwan kyōiku (Education in Okinawa and Taiwan),' *Shin Okinawa bungaku* (New Okinawa literature), No. 60.
Tanaka, Stefan (1993), *Japan's Orient*, Berkley: University of California Press.
Tanigawa Ken'ichi (Ed.) (1970), *Waga Okinawa* (Our Okinawa), Vol. 2, *Hōgen ronsō* (Dialect debate): Mokujisha.
Tokuda Kyūichi (1986), 'Shokuminchi atsukai sareta boku no furusato (My hometown which is treated as a colony),' *Tokuda Kyūichi zenshū* (Complete works of Tokuda Kyūichi), Vol. 6.
Tokyo Buraku Mondai Kenkyūkai (Ed.) (1966), *Gendai Nihon no sabetsu* (Discrimination in modern Japan): Chōbunsha.
Tōma Seita (1951a), '"Rekishi ni okeru minzoku no mondai" no atsukai kata (Treatment of "the nationality question in history,"' Rekishigaku Kenkyūkai (Ed.), *Rekishi ni okeru minzoku no mondai* (The nationality question in history): Iwanami Shoten.
Tōma Seita (1951b), 'Kodai ni okeru minzoku no keisei (The formation of a nation in ancient times),' Rekishigaku Kenkyūkai (Ed.), *Rekishi ni okeru minzoku no mondai* (The nationality question in history): Iwanami Shoten.
Tōma Seita (1951c), 'Kodai ni okeru minzoku no mondai (The nation in ancient times),' Rekishigaku Kenkyūkai (Ed.), *Rekishi ni okeru minzoku no mondai* (The nationality question in history): Iwanami Shoten.
Tōma Seita (1951d), *Nihon minzoku no keisei* (The formation of the Japanese nation): Iwanami Shoten.
Tōma Shikō (1971), 'Kisei zakkan (Miscellaneous thoughts on coming home),' *Okinawa taimusu* (Okinawa times), 25 July.
Tomiyama Ichirō (1995), *Senjō no kioku* (Memories of the battlefield): Nihon Keizai Hyōronsha.

Tomiyama Ichirō (1997), '"Ryūkyūjin" to iu shutai (The identity of "Ryukyuan"),' *Shisō* (Thought), No. 878.
Toriyama Atsushi (1997), 'Yuragu "Nihonjin" (Uncertain "Japanese"),' *Okinawa kankeigaku kenkyū ronshū* (Collected papers of Okinawa-related studies), No. 3.
Tōyama Shigeki (1976), 'Futatsu no nashonarizumu no taikō (Two competing kinds of nationalism),' Rekishi Kagaku Kyōgikai (Ed.), *Rekishi kagaku taikei* (Anthology of historical sciences), Vol. 15, *Minzoku no mondai* (Nationality issues): Azekura Shobō.
Tozzer, Alfred M. (1944), *The Okinawas* (sic) *of the Loo Choo islands; a minority group*, Honolulu: United States Office of Research and Strategic Services, Research and Analysis Branch.
Tsuboi Tadashi and Wada Hiroo (1954), 'Minzoku ka kaikyū ka (A nation or a class?),' *Chūō kōron* (Central review), January.
Tsuitō Bunshū Kankō Iinkai (Ed.) (1990), Kaisō Yoshida Shien (Memories of Yoshida Shien): Tsuitō Bunshū Kankō Iinkai.
Tsuji Keishi (1890), 'Kakuitsu kyōiku hō no rigai (Advantages and disadvantages of uniform education),' *Kyōiku jiron* (Education journal), Nos. 175–177.
Tsurumi Shunsuke (1976), *Yanagi Muneyoshi*: Heibonsha.
Ubukata Naokichi (1961), 'Nihonjin no Chōsen kan (The Japanese perception of Korea),' *Shisō* (Thought), No. 448.
Ubukata Naokichi (1979), 'Tan'itsu minzoku kokka no shisō to kinō (The ideology and function of a homogeneous nation-state),' *Shisō* (Thought), No. 656.
Uechi Kazubumi and Kinjō Hisae (1960), *Okinawa ken no aojashin* (A blueprint for Okinawa prefecture): Okinawa Taimususha.
Uehara Senroku (1987–97), *Uehara Senroku chosaku shū* (Collected works of Uehara Senroku): Hyōronsha.
Uehara Senroku and Munakata Seiya (1952), *Nihonjin no sōzō* (The creation of the Japanese): Tōyō Shokan.
Uemura Hideaki (1992), *Sekai to Nihon no senjū minzoku* (Indigenous peoples of Japan and the world): Iwanami Shoten.
Ukai Satoshi (1992), 'Furansu to sono bōrei tachi (France and its ghosts),' *Jōkyō* (Situation), December.
Uruma shinpō (Uruma newspaper) (1946b [1978]), 'Shuku Okinawa minseifu hossoku (Celebrating the birth of the Okinawan government),' 24 April.
Uruma shinpō (1947 [1978]), 'Beikoku hogo no moto ni (Under the guardianship of the U.S.),' 1 August, in Naha-shi Kikakubu Shishi Henshūshitsu (Ed.), *Naha shishi shiryō hen* 3-kan 3 (History of Naha city, reference materials edition, Vol. 3-3): Naha-shi Kikakubu Shishi Henshūshitsu.
Uruma shinpō (1948 [1978]), 'Nihon kara nozokareta Okinawa no sugata (How Okinawa looks from Japan),' 5 March, in Naha-shi Kikakubu Shishi Henshūshitsu (Ed.), *Naha shishi shiryō hen* 3-3: Naha-shi Kikakubu Shishi Henshūshitsu.
Uruma shinpō (1949), 'Kōwa to Okinawa (Peace and Okinawa),' 29 November.
Uruma shinpō (1951a [1978]), 'Kizoku mondai meguri machi no koe o kiku (Listening to voices from the streets around the sovereignty issue),' 23 April, in Naha-shi Kikakubu Shishi Henshūshitsu (Ed.), *Naha shishi shiryō hen* 3-3: Naha-shi Kikakubu Shishi Henshūshitsu.
Uruma shinpō (1951b [1978]), 'Kizoku mondai ni taisuru jūmin no ugoki (Residents' action regarding the sovereignty issue),' 27 March, in Naha-shi

Kikakubu Shishi Henshūshitsu (Ed.), *Naha shishi shiryō hen*, 3-3: Naha-shi Kikakubu Shishi Henshūshitsu.

Uruma shinpō (1951c [1978]), 'Ryūkyū jūmin wa dono michi o erabu ka (Which course will Ryukyuans take?),' 19 March, in Naha-shi Kikakubu Shishi Henshūshitsu (Ed.), *Naha shishi shiryō hen* 3-3: Naha-shi Kikakubu Shishi Henshūshitsu.

Uruma shinpō (1951d [1978]), 'Ryūkyū no kizoku mondai (Ryukyu sovereignty issue),' 30 January, in Naha-shi Kikakubu Shishi Henshūshitsu (Ed.), *Naha shishi shiryō hen* 3-3: Naha-shi Kikakubu Shishi Henshūshitsu.

Vagts, Alfred (1959), *A History of Militarism, Civilian and Military*, London: Macmillan Co. Ltd.; (Japanese edition) Mochida Yukio (Tr.) (1973), *Gunkoku shugi no rekishi*: Fukumura Shuppan.

Wakao Noriko (1994), 'Iha Fuyū "Okinawa josei shi" no gendaiteki igi (Contemporary significance of Iha Fuyu's "History of Okinawan women"),' *Rekishi hyōron* (History review), No. 529.

Yamada Masataka (Tōma Shigō) (1940 [1970]), 'Hyōjun go no mondai (The standard language issue),' *Okinawa asashi shinbun* (Okinawa asahi newspaper), 15 January, in Naha Shiyakusho (Ed.), *Naha shishi: shiryō hen* (History of Naha city: reference materials edition), Vol. 2, 2–3: Naha Shiyakusho.

Yamagata Aritomo (1886), 'Fukumei sho (Report),' dated May archived in Kokuritsu Kōbunsho Kan, *Meiji 19 nen* kōbun zatsusan 9 Naimushō 1 (Collection of miscellaneous official papers 9: Ministry of Home Affairs 1 for the 19th year of the Meiji era).

Yamamoto Kazuaki (Ed.) (1966), *Sokoku no tsuchi* (Homeland): Hondo Okinawa Mamekisha Kōkankai Jimukyoku.

Yamano Yōko (1952), 'Nōmin no seikatsu kanjō ni tokekonde – "Minzoku geijutsu o tsukuru kai" no shigoto (The joys and sorrows of everyday life of farmers – The activity of the national art creation society),' *Rekishi hyōron* (History review), No. 39.

Yamanokuchi Baku (1960), 'Shōgatsu to shima (The New Year and the islands),' *Okinawa to Ogasawara* (Okinawa and Ogasawara), No. 12.

Yamashita Shigekazu (1990), 'Ryūkyū shobun gaisetsu (Outline of Ryukyu disposition),' *Kokugakuin hōgaku* (Law bulletin of Kokugakuin University), Vol. 27, No. 4.

Yamauchi Susumu (1995), 'Sengo Okinawa ni okeru Amerika no gengo kyōiku seisaku (U.S. language policies in postwar Okinawa),' in Teruya Yoshihiko and Yamasato Katsumi (Eds), *Sengo Okinawa to Amerika* (Postwar Okinawa and the U.S.A): Okinawa Taimususha.

Yamazato Eikichi (1969), *Okinawajin no Okinawa – Nihon wa sokoku ni arazu* (Okinawans' Okinawa – Japan is not our homeland): Okinawa Jihōsha.

Yamazato Eikichi (1971), *Okinawajin no Okinawa* (Okinawans' Okinawa): Daiichi Hōki.

Yanagi Muneyoshi (1940 [1970]), 'Okinawa go no mondai (The Okinawa language issue),' *Tokyo asahi shinbun* (Tokyo asahi newspaper), 1 June, in in Naha Shiyakusho (Ed.), *Naha shishi: shiryō hen* (History of Naha city: reference materials edition), Vol. 2, 2–3: Naha Shiyakusho.

Yanagi Muneyoshi (= Sōetsu) (1981a), *Yanagi Sōetsu zenshū* (Complete works of Yanagi Sōetsu), Vol. 6: Chikuma Shobō.

Yanagi Muneyoshi (= Sōetsu) (1981b), *Yanagi Sōetsu zenshū* (Complete works of Yanagi Sōetsu). Vol. 15: Chikuma Shobō.

Yanagita Kunio, Shikiba Ryūzaburō, Yanagi Muneyoshi and Higa Shunchō (1940 [1970]), 'Zadankai Okinawa no hyōjun go mondai hihan (Symposium on the criticism of the Okinawa language issue),' *Gekkan mingei* (Monthly mingei), April issue, in Naha Shiyakusho (Ed.), *Naha shishi: shiryō hen* (History of Naha city: reference materials edition), Vol. 2, 2–3: Naha Shiyakusho.

Yara Chōbyō (1954), 'Oguden fuku chōkan e no shokan (A letter to Deputy Governor Ogden),' 5 February, *Okinawa-ken sokoku fukki tōsō shi shiryō hen* (History of Okinawa prefecture's reversion to the motherland, documents edition): Okinawa Jiji Shuppansha.

Yara Chōbyō (1968), 'Sengo Okinawa no kyōiku (Education in postwar Okinawa),' *Sekai* (The world), June.

Yara Chōbyō (1968), *Watashi no ayunda michi* (The road I walked on): Yara-san o Hagemasu Kai.

Yara Chōbyō (1977), *Yara Chōbyō kaikoroku* (Memoirs of Yara Chōbyō): Asahi Shinbunsha.

Yara Chōbyō (1984), 'Watashi ga Taiwan kara mananda koto (What I have learned from Taiwan)': *Shin Okinawa bungaku* (New Okinawa literature), No. 60.

Yara Chōbyō, Shibusawa Keizō, Ōhama Nobumoto and Kaya Seiji (1960), 'Okinawa no kyōiku o kataru (Okinawa education debate),' *Okinawa to Ogasawara* (Okinawa and Ogasawara), No. 12.

Yasuoka Akio (1983), 'Meiji zenki kanpen no Okinawa ronsaku (Discussions on Okinawa in government circles during the early Meiji period),' *Okinawa bunka kenkyū* (Journal of Okinawan culture), No. 10.

Yasuoka Akio (1992), 'Yamagata Aritomo to Ryūkyū shobun (Yamagata Aritomo and Ryukyu disposition),' *Seiji keizai shigaku* (Journal of the political and economic history), No. 312.

Yatsuda Yoshiho (1985), 'Yanagi Muneyoshi no mingei ron (Yanagi Sōetsu's mingei theory),' *Tokuyama Daigaku ronsō* (The review of Tokuyama University), 23.

Yohena (Nagaoka's former family name) Tomotarō (1956), *Okinawa (genjō to rekishi)* (Okinawa: Current status and history): San'ichi Shobō.

Yokobori Yōichi (1959), 'Okinawa: Kono shirarezaru shinjitsu (Okinawa: this unknown truth),' *Sekai* (The world), December.

Yokota Kisaburō (1955), 'Okinawa to Nihon no shuken (Sovereignty of Okinawa and Japan),' Kokusai Hōgaku Kai (Ed.), *Okinawa no chii* (The status of Okinawa): Nanpō Renraku Jimusho.

Yokota Kisaburō (1956), 'Tōchi ken ni fukujū no gimu (Duty to submit to sovereign power),' *Asahi shinbun* (Asahi newspaper), 30 June.

Yokoyama Manabu (Ed.) (1980), *Ryūkyū shozoku mondai kankei shiryō* (Collection of documents relating to the Ryukyu sovereignty issue), Vols. 1–8: Honpō Shoseki.

Yoshida Shien (1940a [1970]), 'Aigan ken (Pet prefecture),' *Okinawa mainichi shinbun* (Okinawa mainichi newspaper), 10 January, in Naha Shiyakusho (Ed.), *Naha shishi: shiryō hen* (History of Naha city: reference materials edition), Vol. 2, 2–3: Naha Shiyakusho.

Yoshida Shien (1940b [1970]), 'Yanagi-shi ni atau (Presenting to Mr. Yanagi),' *Okinawa nippō* (Okinawa daily), 16 January, in Naha Shiyakusho (Ed.), *Naha shishi: shiryō hen* (History of Naha city: reference materials edition), Vol. 2, 2–3: Naha Shiyakusho.

Yoshida Shien (1976), *Chiisana tatakai no hibi* (Days of small struggles): Bunkyō Shōji.

Yoshida Shien Tsuitō Bunshū Kankō Iinkai (Ed.) (1990), *Kaisō Yoshida Shien* (Memories of Yoshida Shien): Tsuitō Bunshū Kankō Iinkai.

Yoshihara Kōichirō (1968), *Okinawa*: San'ichi Shobō.

Yoshihara Kōichirō (1970), 'Tennōsei kokka kakuritsu no tame no kyōiku (Education to support the establishment of the imperial state)' in Hashikawa Bunzō and Gotō Sōichirō (Eds), *Meiji no gunzō* (Collected papers on the Meiji era), Vol. 4: San'ichi Shobō.

Yun Koncha (1997), *Nihon kokumin ron* (Essays on the Japanese nation) V: Chikuma Shobō.

Zen Shihō Fukuoka Shibu (lyrics) and Araki Sakae (music) (n.d.), *Okinawa o kaese* (Return Okinawa).

Name Index

Arakawa, Akira 306–7, 320–38, 356–7, 361, 364, 370, 375–8
Asato, Yoshio 41, 56, 330, 336–7, 369
Ashida, Hitoshi 174, 211, 248, 316

Blake, Leach 109, 111

Caraway, Paul 154–5
Chamberlain, Basil Hall, 74, 77–80, 86, 141, 368

Dulles, John F. 198, 201, 371
Du Bois, William E. B. 101

Eisenhower, Dwight 188, 200, 313, 339
Engels, Friedrich 242–3

Fuchigami, Fusatarō 133, 135, 173
Fujitani, Toshio 220–1, 227, 232–3, 238–9

Garvey, Marcus 101
Gima, Susumu 286, 299, 320, 357
Grant, Ulysses S. 29–30, 32–3

Hani, Gorō 118
Hara, Takashi 58–61, 63, 246, 353, 360, 362
Hatoyama, Ichirō 202, 208, 210

Hearn, Lafcadio 111–12, 114, 367
Higa, Shunchō 60, 69, 86–7, 119, 185, 187, 247, 369
Higaonna, Kanjun 70, 130, 172, 361, 370
Hokama, Yoneko 336–7, 361

Ichiki, Kitokurō 41
Ie, Chōjo 370
Ie, Tomoo 172
Ienaga, Saburō 234, 300, 373
Ifa, Fuyū 54, 61, 63, 69–107, 120, 132, 140, 164–6, 228, 244, 306, 324, 327, 330–1, 334, 347, 355–7, 361, 363–6, 368, 378
Ikemiyagushiku, Shūi 176–8, 181–2, 184
Inoue, Kaoru 19, 21, 27
Inoue, Kiyoshi 225, 232, 239–40, 247–249, 331, 371, 373–4
Inoue, Tetsujirō 367
Ishimoda, Tadashi 217–18, 220–3, 226, 229, 232, 240–3, 371–2, 374
Itagaki, Taisuke 56, 328
Itō, Hirobumi 18, 29–30, 37, 39, 359
Iwakura, Tomomi 19

Jahana, Noboru 55–7, 63, 97, 246–8, 306, 327–8, 331, 362

Kawarada, Moriyoshi 17–18
Kennedy, John F. 155, 276
Kido, Takayoshi 18, 22
Kim, Talsu 234, 373
Kokuba, Kōtarō 252–3, 374
Kōyama, Masayoshi 29–32, 34, 359

Le Bon, Gustav 88, 101–2, 114
Lombroso, Cesare 101

MacArthur, Douglas 146, 153, 171–2, 368
Maruyama, Masao 214, 227–8, 372–3
Marx, Karl 214, 222, 240, 252, 373–4
Matsuda, Michiyuki 18, 26–9, 33–4, 37, 39, 359–60
Mori, Arinori 19, 29, 39, 96
Mori, Hideto 250–3, 331, 335, 374
Murdock, George 140–2, 145

Nagai, Kafū 221, 372
Nakae, Chōmin 246, 327
Nakahara, Zenchū 166, 370
Nakano, Seigō 83
Nakano, Shigeharu 377
Nakano, Yoshio 123, 145–154, 168–70, 174, 188, 190–2, 194, 196, 199–207, 210–11, 213, 239, 261, 320, 368–71, 355
Nakasone, Genwa 307–11, 313
Nakasone, Isamu 369
Nakasone, Yasuhiro 233
Nanbara, Shigeru 214, 274, 375
Nezu, Masashi 224
Nietzsche, Friedrich 101, 105

Nitta, Takayoshi 50–2, 361
Nixon, Richard 302, 315, 317

Ōe, Kenzaburō 316, 320, 375, 377
Ōta, Chōfu 61–8, 72, 96, 120
Ōta, Hidemichi 371
Ōta, Masahide 263–4, 318, 320, 359, 362–3, 368–9, 375, 378
Ōta, Shizuo 369
Ōta, Tetsuo 366
Ōta, Yūzō 367

Saionji, Kinmochi 58
Satō, Eisaku 299–300, 302, 311, 315, 317, 341–2, 344
Satō, Nobue 123
Senaga, Kamejirō 167, 170–1, 175–6, 178–9, 181, 186–7, 196, 202, 237, 253, 328, 330–1, 335
Shikiba, Ryūzaburō 128
Shikiya, Takanobu 168, 172, 369
Shimizu, Ikutarō 118, 123, 368
Shinzato, Keiji 177, 245–54, 335, 374
Shō, Shin 85, 105–6
Shō, Sōken 86–7, 95, 103, 306
Shō, Tai 75, 90–1, 93
Soejima, Taneomi 21
Stalin, I. V. 240, 373–4
Sugiyama, Heisuke 125–6, 13–2

Taira, Tatsuo 175–6, 179, 184, 198, 258–9, 360, 369
Tokuda, Kyūichi 169, 240, 369
Tōma, Seita 225–33, 235, 371, 373–4

Torii, Ryūzō 78–80, 88, 141
Tozzer, Alfred 140–2

Ueda, Kōichirō 78, 330, 335–6
Uehara, Senroku 13, 219–20, 272–4, 371–2, 375
Unger, Ferdinand T. 143

Washington, Booker T. 100–1, 103

Yanagi, Muneyoshi (Sōetsu) 13, 105–6, 108–36, 173, 238, 278, 359, 366–8, 374
Yanagita, Kunio 13, 105–6, 112–13, 117, 123, 238, 366, 368
Yanaihara, Tadao 214, 267
Yara, Chōbyō 196–7, 200–1, 205, 255, 257–63, 265, 272, 276–7, 297–300, 302, 304–5, 312, 314–15, 317–19, 328–30, 371, 375, 378
Yokota, Kisaburō 207, 371
Yoshida, Shien 117–18, 121, 124, 167, 173, 186–7, 202–3, 367, 369
Yoshida, Shigeru 157, 202, 224
Yoshida, Shōin 224

Subject Index

abolition of domains 16, 18, 29, 33, 37, 40, 60–1, 244–5

administrative rights xii, 2, 147, 162, 198–9, 202, 204, 261, 264, 283, 302, 312, 315–16, 330, 339, 341–3

Ainu 58, 67–8, 79–80, 87–9, 91–2, 98, 106, 113–14, 117, 127, 132, 137–9, 141, 229, 235, 361, 366

AMPO (United States–Japan Security Treaty) xii, 190, 197–9, 209–10, 215, 232, 253, 272, 286, 300, 313, 316–17, 342, 344, 346, 349, 377

ancestral land (*sokoku*) xii, 57–8, 166, 172, 180, 188, 190–1, 193–95, 197, 199–200, 205, 208, 218, 234, 259–62, 266, 272, 278, 281, 289–92, 295–6, 299, 301, 303–4, 306, 314, 325, 329, 331, 333, 338, 369, 378

anti-base movement xii, 167, 178, 200, 275, 300, 311, 313–4, 346, 370–1

anti-communist 195–6, 202, 205–6, 211, 236, 308–10, 316, 328–9, 340, 343

anti-reversion xii, 177–9, 183, 185, 302, 306–8, 311, 319–21, 322–6, 329–31, 334–8, 371, 376

anti-U.S. sentiment 197–203, 205, 209, 211, 215–9, 225, 236, 251, 257, 275, 298–9, 328, 342, 351

anti-war peace 205, 210–11, 216, 265, 300, 315, 332

anti-war movement 178, 196, 200, 300, 311, 370–1

anti-war reversion 188, 200, 206, 300, 312, 314, 316–7, 320, 331–2, 370

assimilation 6–7, 15–16, 34–5, 41–2, 46, 48–9, 59–62, 64–8, 70–2, 78, 80–3, 87, 89–94, 96, 98, 102, 110, 122, 132–3, 136, 141–2, 151–3, 165, 183, 185–6, 189, 191, 239, 240–6, 248, 270, 272, 282, 288, 304, 306, 326–8, 332–4, 352–6, 360–1, 363–4, 366, 376–8

awareness campaigns 95–6, 99, 104–5, 107

Battle of Okinawa xi, 3, 5, 137, 142, 157, 186, 205, 255, 332, 357–8, 370

Chief Executive xii, 153, 161, 176, 189–90, 195, 258–300, 302, 314, 317, 319

chiji see Governor

China 1–2, 6, 8, 13–16, 19–21, 23, 27–9, 30–3, 39, 48,

50–2, 66, 73–4, 84, 87, 90, 130–1, 133–4, 139, 141, 146–8, 164, 174–5, 215–16, 218, 224, 226, 231, 233, 235–6, 245, 260, 294, 323, 339, 341, 352, 357–8, 361, 372; *see also* Qing
Civil Administrator 148–50, 155, 160–1, 369
civilisation 26, 33, 41, 44–8, 58, 60, 64–6, 68, 71–2, 74, 84, 87, 90, 96, 98, 102, 104, 109–14, 122–4, 128–9, 186, 230, 360, 363, 367
clothing 45–6, 67–8, 70, 120–1, 129, 166
Cold War 146–7, 150, 160, 175, 177–8, 215, 349–50
common-ancestry theories 73, 75, 77, 80–4, 86, 89, 95, 102, 104, 106, 169, 172, 213, 239, 306, 327, 361, 364; *see also* Japan–Korea common-ancestry theory; Japan–Ryukyu common-ancestry theory
Communist Party xi, 9, 11, 13, 161, 169–70, 196, 204, 210, 213–17, 235–7, 251–2, 308, 317–18, 328–36, 374–6
Conscription Law xi, 47, 55, 57
conscription 38, 47, 54–5, 57, 159, 177, 183, 354
conservative regime 205, 209, 211, 214, 221, 231, 235, 302, 316, 340–2
Council for Promotion of Return to Japan (Nihon Fukki Sokushin Kiseikai) 178, 181

Council for the Return of the Okinawan Islands to Japan (Okinawa Guntō Nihon Fukki Kiseikai) 172–3
Council for the Reversion of Okinawa Prefecture to the Ancestral Land (Fukkikyō) xii, 262
'Cry of the Nation' 224–6, 237

Democratic Party 183, 195, 205, 297, 314, 319
dialect debate (language debate) xi, 103, 108, 115, 118, 121, 124, 127, 129, 132, 135, 172–3, 270, 356, 366
dialect placards 108, 241, 255, 265, 267, 269, 303, 375
discrimination 1, 4, 13, 18, 34–5, 52, 54, 56, 58, 61, 64, 67, 76–7, 80, 82–3, 88–90, 93–5, 101, 116, 118, 121–2, 124–6, 132–3, 135, 143, 172, 177, 180, 183, 185, 192, 199, 234, 239, 241, 245, 247–8, 250, 253–4, 284–5, 294, 304, 319, 325–7, 329–31, 350, 355–6, 363–4, 367–8
dual subordination (subjection) 16–18, 20, 23, 27–8, 38, 40, 50

education 1, 5, 8, 17, 26, 33, 36–54, 57–9, 62, 64, 66, 68, 71–2, 74, 96–100, 110, 137–8, 142, 147, 151–3, 172, 182–3, 185–6, 193, 201, 219–20, 223, 227, 245, 255–63, 265–7, 270, 272–9, 281–93, 296–305, 309, 319,

321, 344, 352, 360, 361, 363–4, 369, 375
elections xii, 55, 58, 95, 153–4, 156, 161–2, 167, 175–6, 189, 193, 196, 209, 258, 297, 300, 307, 309, 314, 317, 319–20, 328, 344, 362

family registers (*koseki*) 55, 138, 159–62, 183, 207–8, 278, 369
Futenma 348–9
futsūgo 14, 45–6, 53, 72, 102, 241; *see also* Standard Japanese

Give Okinawa back (*Okinawa o kaese*) 238
Government of the Ryukyu Islands (GRI) xii, 153, 160–1, 177, 182, 184, 258–9, 262–3, 378
Governor (*chiji*) xi–xii, 36, 49, 55–6, 61, 63, 133–5, 141, 153–5, 167–8, 172–3, 175–6, 179, 184, 193, 196, 198, 318, 348, 369
GRI *see* Government of the Ryukyu Islands
guntō seifu (island-group governments) xii, 153
Gwanghwamun xi, 109–10, 136

Hall of Mankind (*Jinruikan*) Incident xi, 68, 121, 363
High Commissioner xii, 143, 149, 151, 154–6, 161, 163, 168
Himeyuri (Star Lily) 205, 289

Hi-no-maru (flag) 189, 264–5, 272, 274–9, 281, 286, 288–94, 297–303, 305–6, 311, 314, 317–18, 332, 348, 370, 375
hōgen fuda 108, 375; *see also* dialect placards
hyōjungo 6, 14, 108, 142, 241, 265, 357, 367–8; *see also* standard Japanese

identity 12, 54, 65, 73, 89, 99, 113, 124–5, 163–4, 173–4, 179, 187, 218, 257, 263, 283, 285, 325–6, 335, 355, 358, 366, 368
Imperial Constitution 159, 302; *see also* Constitution
imperial subjects 63, 108, 131, 183, 220, 257, 264–5, 270, 286, 304, 328
imperialism 94, 114, 150, 169, 172, 174, 178, 196, 203, 213, 215–6, 220, 222–3, 229–30, 234, 236–7, 239, 243, 253–4, 273, 330–1, 372–3
island-wide struggle [for land] xii, 204–5, 210, 238, 254, 267, 312, 321, 370

Japanese Constitution 10, 55, 57, 65, 158–9, 162, 193, 200–1, 283, 301–2, 304, 317, 332–3, 337
Japanese language 6, 38, 41–2, 46–7, 50, 79, 102, 108, 115–6, 118, 120–2, 126–35, 142, 152, 172, 183, 232,

241–2, 265–72, 278, 282–3, 287–8, 301, 303–4, 353, 356–7, 361, 366–8; see also *futsūgo, hyōjungo*, Standard Japanese
Japanisation 5, 7, 36–9, 41, 43–5, 48, 52–3, 64–5, 71, 81, 95, 122, 135, 139, 183, 250, 360, 363
Japan–Korea common-ancestry theory 80–1, 106, 129, 169, 213
Japan proper *see* mainland Japan
Japan–Ryukyu common-ancestry theory 73, 75, 77, 80–1, 86, 95, 102, 104, 106, 129, 132, 165, 169, 172, 238–9, 249, 306, 327, 361, 364
Japan Teachers' Union *see* Nikkyōso
jinmin (people) 11, 218–19
Jinruikan *see* Hall of Mankind Incident

Kanakas 116, 118, 186, 285
katakashira see topknots
Kimi-ga-yo 272, 274–5, 277, 279–81, 285–6, 300–3, 305, 375
kokugo 14, 46, 72, 108, 128, 134, 152, 266, 359; *see also* Japanese language; national language
kokumin 14, 36, 82, 91, 107, 192, 209, 214, 218, 220, 223, 237, 243, 248, 272, 280, 302, 326, 372, 375

kokumin kyōiku 36, 220, 272; *see also* national education
Korea 2, 4–5, 7, 14–15, 21–2, 26, 29–31, 35, 39, 41, 52–6, 58–61, 65, 67–8, 78–83, 91, 93, 102, 106–14, 117, 122, 126–30, 134, 136–9, 143–4, 149, 151, 158–9, 169–70, 173, 183, 188, 207, 213, 215–16, 220–4, 229–37, 239, 244, 247, 249–50, 286, 304, 309, 314, 320, 339–40, 349–50, 352–7, 360, 362, 364, 366–8, 372–4
Korean War 5, 136, 188, 215, 230–1, 235, 314, 339, 373
Ko-ryūkyū see Old-Ryukyu
koseki 159, 207, 278; *see also* family registers
Kyōken rallies 263, 267–74, 276, 278–88, 291–2, 296, 298, 300–3

land for military use 189, 192, 316
League of Okinawans 164, 166, 169, 173, 369
Liberal-Democratic Party (LDP) 173, 209, 263, 297, 300, 311–7, 319–20, 341, 344, 379
Lower House Members' Electoral Law xi–xii, 56–9, 95, 138, 362
lump-sum payments 150, 204, 315

mainland Japan (*naichi*) 4, 9, 16, 19, 21, 27, 33–4, 36,

40–2, 45–48, 50, 52, 54–6, 58–60, 63, 65–8, 71, 73, 83, 93, 103, 105, 111–13, 117–8, 123, 126–7, 131, 138, 140–4, 153, 156, 159, 161–2, 164, 171, 175, 194, 203, 208, 210, 236, 237, 240–1, 247, 249–51, 253, 254–7, 259, 288, 294, 297, 302, 312, 320–1, 340, 353, 362, 364, 367, 370–1, 376–7
Meiji government 2, 5, 10, 15–18, 23–4, 28, 36, 81, 157, 225, 242, 245–7, 251–2, 311, 331
Meiji Restoration xi, 2, 10, 16, 224–5, 242–3, 319
Message celebrating the independence of the Okinawan people xi, 169–70, 213, 239, 331, 378
migrant workers 116, 119, 134, 152, 308, 316, 358, 363
military bases xii, 1–5, 7–8, 20, 39, 71, 139, 147, 150–1, 156, 161, 167, 177–8, 182, 185, 188, 190–1, 193, 197–201, 204, 210, 213, 215, 218, 229, 234–5, 264, 275, 286–7, 294, 296, 299–300, 302, 312–17, 319, 329, 332, 339–340, 342–51
Minamoto-no-Tametomo 30–1, 34, 47–8, 68, 141, 172, 361
minzoku 9–11, 13, 209, 213–26, 228–48, 251–4
  as race 18, 22, 27–8, 30–1, 34, 48–52, 68, 77, 79–81, 83–91, 98–9, 101–2, 104–7, 130, 138, 141, 169, 172, 178, 185, 195, 206, 213, 226, 229–33, 239, 251, 254, 376
  as people xi, 58, 140, 166, 169, 178, 181, 213, 228–30, 232, 242, 284, 295, 309–10, 318, 325, 328, 330–1, 334, 373, 376
  as ethnic (group) 9, 11, 14, 85, 98, 166, 233, 369
  as ethnically (Japanese) 51, 112
  as ethnicity 87, 94, 140, 141, 166, 330
  as folk 226
  as nation 90, 93, 165–6, 216–25, 228, 231–2, 237, 248, 273–4, 281, 292–3, 295, 365
  as national 98, 215–6, 218–20, 226, 228–9, 232, 240, 244, 253, 273, 284, 286, 291, 298, 318–9, 329, 331, 360
  as nationality 371
  as native 217
  as populace 222
  as popular 318
  as national consciousness (*minzoku ishiki*) 219–20, 273, 286
minzoku ishiki 219; *see* national consciousness
Miyako Island 21, 33, 47, 57, 60, 84, 89, 98, 104, 120, 153, 166, 170, 324, 334, 369
moashibi 65, 68

Naha 3, 29, 41, 64, 69, 70, 72, 74, 76, 92, 93, 97, 115, 123, 126, 135, 156, 161, 196, 198,

Subject Index

203, 241, 267–8, 309, 346, 348, 358, 360, 366–7
naichi see mainland Japan
national anthem 264, 274–5, 277, 279–81, 292, 301, 375; *see also Kimi-ga-yo*
national consciousness 43, 48, 219–20, 223, 225–8, 231, 241, 245, 248, 272–4, 277, 280, 284, 287, 300–2, 372–3; *see also minzoku ishiki*
national education 36, 44, 54, 58, 220, 255, 272–8, 281–92, 296, 298, 300, 302–3, 305, 375
national language 14, 46–7, 72, 80, 108, 128, 131, 134, 152, 266, 359; *see also kokugo*
Nikkyōso 201, 220, 255, 272–6, 278, 297–9, 302, 305
normal school *see* teacher training

occupation (by U.S.) xii, 4–5, 11, 13, 31, 139–40, 142, 144, 146, 148, 150, 153, 156, 159, 171, 175, 213, 215, 230, 253, 256, 273, 308, 330, 334, 342, 348
Okinawa o kaese (Give Okinawa back!) 238
Okinawa Ken Sokoku Fukki Kyōgikai (Fukkikyō) 262
Okinawa Shotō Sokoku Fukki Sokushin Kiseikai 193
Okinawa Shotō Nihon Fukki Kiseikai 257
Okinawa Teachers' Association *see* Teachers' Association

Okinawan nationalism 72, 77, 85–7, 89, 91–2, 94–5, 103, 106, 179, 228, 324, 333–4, 347, 361, 364–5
Okinawan Studies 54, 69, 106, 140–1, 306, 330, 361, 365
Old-Ryukyu 79, 84, 95, 101, 119, 131, 364

Peace Treaty xii, 4, 138, 146, 148, 152, 157–8, 164, 168, 181, 188–9, 191–2, 195, 209, 213, 215, 217, 237–8, 275, 307, 344, 370
people of other prefectures 48, 64–8, 83, 101, 134–5, 250
People's Party 156, 161, 170, 175–6, 178–9, 182, 186, 195–6, 199, 202, 236–7, 244, 251, 253, 261, 276, 297, 299, 308, 315, 318, 328–31, 333–5, 369–70
peripherality 324
petitions 28–9, 36, 40, 57, 61, 63, 165, 171–2, 180, 183, 189–90, 194, 198–200, 211, 262–3, 275, 299, 304–5, 313, 321, 327–8, 360, 363, 370, 377
Price Report 150, 204
pro-American *see* pro-U.S.
progressive forces 9, 210–11, 214, 299, 302, 313, 328–9
progressive nationalism 213–14, 217, 220, 223, 228–9, 234–6, 248, 255, 272–5, 284, 301, 303, 318, 329, 355, 372
pro-U.S. 153, 196–6, 203, 205–6, 210–11, 214, 236,

257, 259, 297, 308–10, 319, 321, 340

Qing 2, 6, 8, 17–18, 20–33, 37, 39, 41, 61, 63, 68, 71, 74, 144, 245, 352, 359; *see also* China

reversion movement 8–9, 117, 140, 155, 157, 167, 171, 173–5, 188, 192, 195–203, 210–11, 235–8, 245, 247, 249–55, 257–66, 272, 275–6, 281, 289, 297–8, 300, 302, 304, 306–8, 311–12, 314–15, 318–19, 324–5, 327–8, 330, 334, 338, 362, 369–72, 376–7
royal government 24, 26–32, 69, 90, 244–5
Ryukyu Kingdom xi, 2, 4, 15–19, 21, 23, 29, 36–7, 63, 74–6, 84, 90–1, 120, 141, 143, 167, 172, 179, 240, 246, 248, 252, 319, 323, 333, 355–6, 358–9, 361
Ryukyus Command (RYCOM) 145
Ryukyu Disposition (*Ryūkyū shobun*) xi, 15, 18–20, 24, 26, 29, 31, 33–4, 36–7, 47, 63, 69, 75, 78, 80–81, 84–5, 92, 97, 100, 105, 134, 141, 170, 172, 243–4, 247, 250, 254, 292, 318–19, 331, 335, 355–6, 359, 374

sago-palm hell xi, 103–4, 116–7, 120, 183, 361, 366

samurai class 6, 9–10, 13, 17, 34, 37–8, 41–2, 52, 55–6, 63–4, 69–70, 76–77, 97, 99, 224–5, 245–6, 356–7
San Francisco Treaty *see* Peace Treaty
Satsuma 15–17, 22, 27–8, 31–2, 54–5, 76, 84, 91–2, 94–5, 119, 169, 224, 239, 245–6, 248, 290, 292, 310–11
seiban (wild tribespeople) 21–2, 51, 68, 79, 87-9, 92, 361
shimagurumi tōsō see island-wide struggle
Shuri 69–70, 72, 74, 76–7, 84, 90–4, 97, 115, 117, 120, 171, 356–7, 361
Sino-Japanese War 6, 47, 51, 61, 63, 71–2, 75, 81, 108, 133–5, 314, 352
Socialist Party 9, 167, 170, 174, 176, 195, 203, 209, 214, 217, 237, 248, 309, 317, 340, 372
Socialist Masses Party 176, 178–9, 182–4, 195–6, 370
SOFA 344
sokoku see ancestral land
South Sea Islands 113, 116, 134, 140, 147, 186, 208
South Seas 5, 60
Standard Japanese 6, 42, 50, 79, 102, 108, 115–16, 118, 120–2, 126, 128–35, 142, 172, 241–2, 265–72, 278, 282–3, 287–8, 301, 303, 357, 361, 366–8
State of the Union address 188, 200

Subject Index

Status of Forces Agreement *see* SOFA
suffrage 6–7, 55–61, 63, 95, 103–4, 138, 162, 183, 246–8, 327–8, 354, 362

Taiwan 1, 4, 7, 15, 19, 21–5, 29, 33, 35, 41, 43, 51–5, 58–61, 65, 67–8, 72, 79, 87, 91, 93, 107–8, 113–4, 117, 122, 126–8, 130–1, 134, 136–9, 143–4, 149, 151, 158–9, 167, 183, 233, 235–6, 239, 244, 247, 249–50, 257–8, 277, 309, 320–1, 328, 340, 352–4, 356, 359–62, 364, 366, 368, 375
tattooing 44, 66, 71, 360
Teachers' Association xii, 197, 205, 255, 257, 259–60, 262–7, 270, 272, 274–6, 279, 281, 290–2, 297–302, 305, 319, 328, 375
teacher training 37, 39–40, 44, 50, 69, 77, 256, 259, 289
textbooks 1, 47, 153, 234, 249, 255, 257, 262, 279, 288, 300, 304, 373
three non-nuclear principles 341–2
topknots 62, 70, 99, 364
travel restrictions 159, 161–2, 290, 294, 307, 369
Treaty of San Francisco *see* Peace Treaty
Two Laws on Education 296, 298–301

Uchinaa (Okinawa) 323, 357

United States Civil Administration of the Ryukyu Islands *see* USCAR
United States–Japan Security Treaty *see* AMPO
University of the Ryukyus 153, 210, 257, 259, 319, 321–2
USCAR (United States Civil Administration of the Ryukyu Islands) 148–9, 153–4

vassal (relationship) 15, 18, 20–2, 25, 29, 73, 251
Vietnam War xii, 3–5, 216, 234, 236, 299–300, 311–2, 314–5, 339–40, 342, 348–9, 358, 371

wild tribespeople *see seiban*
women 13, 39, 44–6, 53, 64–8, 71, 90, 96–101, 120–1, 128, 143, 152, 260, 285, 346, 356, 365–6

Yaeyama (Island) 33, 47, 57, 60, 79, 84, 89, 98, 104, 120, 153, 277–8, 283, 321, 323–4, 334, 369
Yamato 40–1, 55, 62–3, 66, 68–71, 76–7, 81, 86, 91, 93, 97, 129, 132–3, 159, 167, 185, 226–7, 230, 240, 294, 323, 361, 364–5, 378
Yamato-ya (Japanese-style schools) 40, 55
Yamato-yū (Japanese age) 93
Yamatu 323, 327

www.ingramcontent.com/pod-product-compliance
Lightning Source LLC
Chambersburg PA
CBHW070007010526
44117CB00011B/1452